1983 YEARBOOK
EVENTS OF 1982

This gold-and-glass-plated Sun-sphere, 226 ft. high, rises above the Knoxville (Tenn.) International Energy Exposition. It was the first world's fair since 1975 and the first ever in the South.

FUNK & WAGNALLS NEW ENCYCLOPEDIA 1983 YEARBOOK

LEON L. BRAM
Vice-President and
Editorial Director

NORMA H. DICKEY
Editor in Chief
Yearbooks and
Special Projects

ROBERT HALASZ
Editor

Funk & Wagnalls

a company of
The Dun & Bradstreet Corporation

CONTENTS

MEMBERS OF THE STAFF

EDITOR   Robert Halasz

MANAGING EDITOR   Irna Gadd

SUPERVISING EDITORS   Charlotte R. Gross
                                  Geoffrey M. Horn
                                  Pamela Jones
                                  Steven Moll
                                  Donald Paneth
                                  Theodore Stavrou

PRODUCTION CHIEF   Frank A. Petruzalek

PICTURE EDITOR   John Schultz

DESIGNER   Angela Perretta

COPY EDITORS   Judith K. Johnson
                                  Stephan Owen Parnes
                                  Eleanor F. Wedge

INDEXERS   Charles Paul May
                                  Gerard Wallace

EDITORIAL ASSISTANT   Derek Giles

PRODUCTION EXECUTIVE   Edward Haas

FOREWORD TO THE EVENTS OF 1982 YEARBOOK

Like its predecessors, 1982 was a year of fast-moving events, and of both new and long-standing conflicts. Few would have forecast the war for possession of the bleak Falkland Islands in which Great Britain defeated Argentina. All too predictable, however, was the outbreak of another Middle East war—this time in Lebanon, where Israeli forces succeeded in forcing the ouster of Palestinian fighters. The United States assumed a high profile in the area, with Americans helping to patrol Beirut and the Sinai Peninsula, and President Ronald Reagan seeking a comprehensive settlement of the Arab-Israeli struggle.

A major event later in the year, with consequences difficult to foresee, was the assumption of power in the Soviet Union by Yuri V. Andropov, following the death of Leonid I. Brezhnev. New leaders also came to power in several other countries, including West Germany, Japan, and Spain.

The world economy suffered through another year of slow growth or actual recession. The growing level of debt accumulated by many developing countries, especially in Latin America, alarmed world bankers.

The U.S. economy was also mired in recession. Unemployment passed the 10 percent mark, and the automobile, steel, construction, housing, and mining industries operated far below productive capacity. Many voters held the Reagan administration responsible, and in November elections Democratic Party candidates made significant gains.

The space shuttle *Columbia* completed three more missions in earth orbit. Summer entertainment included the blockbuster film *E.T.—the Extra-Terrestrial,* but the perennial feature of fall Sundays—professional football—was abbreviated by a players' strike.

Eclipsed by the gloomy headlines, industrious and talented people continued in 1982 to improve the quality of life. Our feature articles deal with such efforts in three fields: fighting heart disease, creating a better environment for animals in captivity, and bringing live theater to audiences throughout America.

THE EDITORS

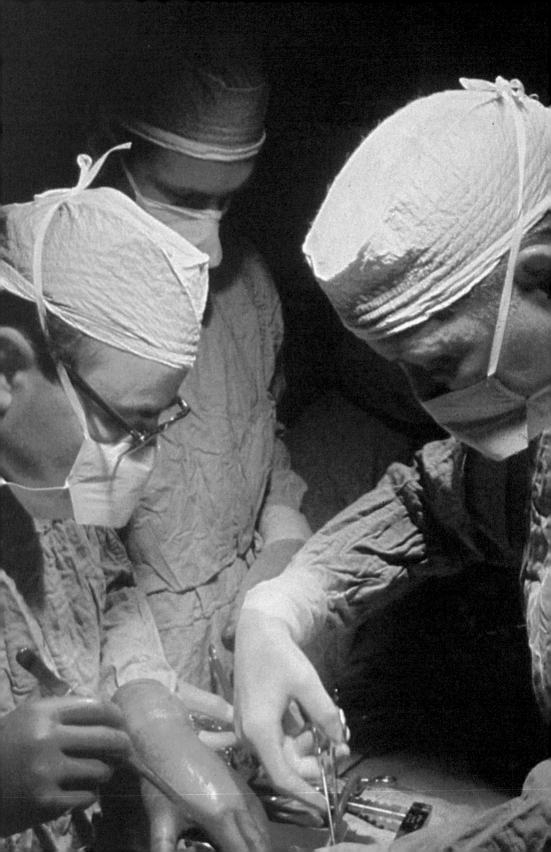

A STEADY BEAT
Treating Heart Disease
by JAY STULLER

Cardiovascular disease is the cause of death for about half of those who die in the United States each year. Some 30,000,000 Americans suffer from some form of heart disease. This illness is responsible for an economic toll of more than $50 billion in the cost of treatment and lost productivity.

Heart disease is, as it was 25 years ago, the leading killer in our society. The struggle against it often seems to make little headway. In this technological age, why is progress so seemingly slow? "It's *not* slow," says John Norman of Denton Cooley's Texas Heart Institute in Houston. "It might seem to be, since major advances aren't getting public recognition every week. But in nearly every city, nearly every major hospital center in the country, right next door to any American, there is work going on in cardiovascular research."

"Many of these are small developments," says Norman. "Variations on current knowledge. But if you look at where we were five or ten years ago, and at all the things we can do today, it's apparent that the advances in the *next* five years will be tremendous."

What the Heart Does

For all the things that can go wrong with a human heart, it is really a quite simple organ that pumps blood to other parts of the body. Fist-sized, the heart pumps a minimum of 4 to 6 liters of blood per minute, and it beats roughly 100,000 times per day. Although the actual heart is not terribly complex, the connecting systems and control mechanisms of the body make its workings complicated—and vulnerable to diseases not intrinsic to the heart itself.

Jay Stuller is a free-lance writer.

Opposite page: Denton A. Cooley (right) and Domingo Liotta are shown performing the world's first artificial heart implant on a human being in 1969. Although still in the experimental stage, artificial hearts may be prolonging hundreds of lives by 1990.

During the heart's diastole phase (1), oxygen-spent blood flows into the right atrium of the heart and oxygen-rich blood into the left atrium. (2): The sinoatrial node (A) then fires an electrical impulse that causes the atria to contract, opening valves that allow blood to fill the ventricles. During the heart's systole phase (3), the atrioventricular node (B) fires an impulse that causes the ventricles to contract, sending oxygen-poor blood from the right ventricle to the lungs and oxygen-rich blood from the left ventricle to the body.

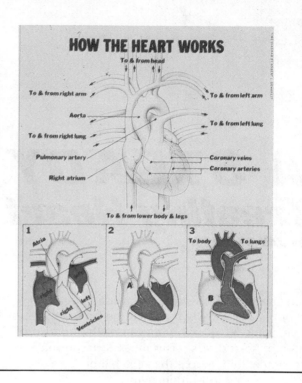

Heart function is inextricably entwined with the lungs because oxygen-rich blood is carried from the lungs to the heart and oxygen-depleted blood is transported from the heart to the lungs. The kidneys are essential in regulating blood volume and pressure. Diseases of these organs invariably lead to heart problems, too. In addition, there are thousands of enzyme, metabolic, and hormone systems that affect the strength of the heartbeat, the load under which it must work, and the types of nutrients the heart tissue is receiving. The liver, for example, must be in working order to govern the proper composition of the blood.

The heart is made up of four chambers: In the upper section are two atria, and below, two ventricles. During the heart's diastole, or relaxation, phase, oxygen-spent blood (which has already "fed" the body's tissues) from two main veins flows into the right atrium; simultaneously, oxygen-rich blood from the lungs flows from the pulmonary veins into the left atrium. Valves leading into the ventricles then open, and the blood flows into these chambers. During the heart's systole, or contraction, phase, blood from the right ventricle is ejected into the pulmonary arteries, which lead to the lungs. Blood from the left ventricle flows into the body's major artery, the aorta.

Heart Attacks

Heart attacks account for more than half the death toll from heart disease. A heart attack—more accurately known as a myocardial infarction—occurs when a coronary artery, which supplies blood and nutrients to the heart muscle itself, becomes obstructed, often due to deposits of fat-based plaque that form on the inner linings of the arterial walls. Without that supply of blood, the section of heart muscle fed by the particular artery begins to die. For most heart attack victims, there is the feeling of a crushing weight upon their chests.

If the damage is great enough, the heart stops

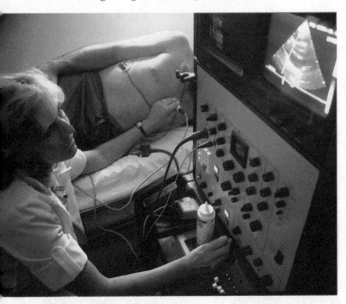

The echocardiogram is a useful diagnostic tool. Pulses of sound are bounced off the heart to provide a scan of its chambers and valves.

pumping. An infarction can also short-circuit the electrical impulses that govern the heartbeat, with the same result—cardiac arrest. More than half of all heart attack victims who die from the attack succumb before they reach the hospital. Some 85 percent of heart attack victims who reach hospital facilities alive subsequently live to tell about it.

Diagnosis

Early diagnosis of heart disease is essential to cutting the mortality rate—or prolonging life. Says Don Hill of the Pacific Medical Center in San Francisco: "Forty to 50 percent of those who die suddenly of heart disease have no previous knowledge of their condition. Widespread screening could prevent an awful lot of that."

In addition to the venerable stethoscope, chest X rays, and electrocardiograms, the chief method of heart disease diagnosis is angiography. With this procedure, a catheter, or thin tube, is inserted into the body and a dye is injected directly into coronary arteries and major veins. A special X-ray machine gives a fairly accurate depiction of blood flow and shows where valves and arteries may not be in proper working order.

Angiography is, however, expensive, costing as much as $2000. It is also an *invasive* technique, and one in 1000 patients dies during the procedure.

A safer, noninvasive, and increasingly useful procedure is echocardiography, in which pulses of sound are bounced off the heart to provide a picture of its chambers and valves. Although not quite as accurate as angiography, new echo developments have given this technique great promise.

Another diagnostic tool is the nuclear scan. Here the imaging device above the patient's heart records radiation emitted by a radioactive substance that has been injected into the bloodstream. The doctor in the background reviews data that a computer has translated into pictures of the heart. Left: An example of the pictures provided by the nuclear scan technique.

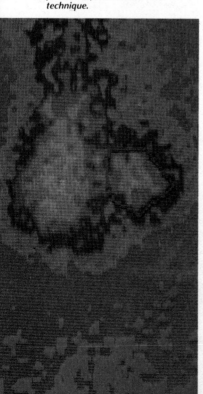

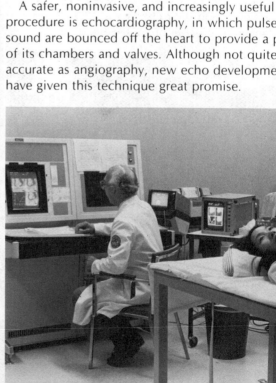

Another important noninvasive tool is the nuclear scan. With the scan, a radioactive substance is injected into the bloodstream. Special imaging devices pick up radiation emitted from the substance, and a computer translates the information into pictures, allowing the doctor a three-dimensional view of the heart with stunning clarity. A patient can even exercise in front of the nuclear camera, letting physicians see the effects of work or stress upon the heart.

Drugs

One of the most exciting fields of heart research and cardiovascular therapy relates to the development of drugs for the treatment of heart failure. New pharmacological agents are perhaps the easiest and most cost-efficient means of helping, and in some cases even "repairing," poorly functioning hearts. Many centers in the U.S. and around the world are testing a variety of heart drugs.

At the University of Pennsylvania School of Medicine, for example, several hundred patients have gone through controlled trials with four major drugs. According to Karl Weber, several have increased his patients' performance, as measured by their ability to exercise on a treadmill.

Two of these drugs are called cardiotonics. They are used for patients with low cardiac output, a condition where the heart, struggling to do its work, is enlarged to perhaps two or three times the normal size from the effort. Cardiotonics strengthen heart contractions and, as a result, can even lead to the heart's "shrinking" closer to normal size. "For some people this represents a major advancement in the treatment of their heart failure," says Weber. "For others, this could be used as a tune-up before surgery, so they go into the operating room in much better shape."

The other two drugs under study at Pennsylvania dilate blood vessels, relax blood vessels, and allow the blood to flow more freely from the overburdened and failing heart. They may be used to improve the heart's pumping ability and to relieve the congested lungs.

A group of drugs with great promise for the treatment of coronary artery disease and its effects on the heart muscle, which receives its nutrient blood flow from these vessels, are called beta blockers. These drugs work in conjunction with the body's sympathetic nervous system, limiting the output of nerve impulses in order to avoid overstimulation of the heart. Several beta blockers are available for use in

Administering drugs is an important way of treating heart disease. Here a heart patient in Finland has an electrocardiogram taken during a study of the effectiveness of a new drug intended to reduce the level of fatty proteins that carry cholesterol in the blood.

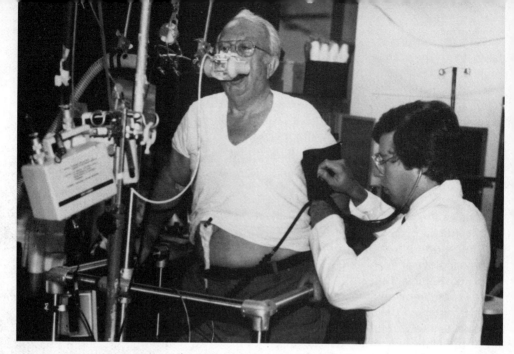

the U.S.; many others are under study. They are often prescribed to lower blood pressure, to relieve the pain of angina pectoris (chest pain that results from insufficient blood supply to the heart muscle), and at times to alleviate irregular heart rhythms.

Another promising class of drugs are the calcium channel blockers, which have been used to a great extent in Europe and Japan. These inhibit the flow of calcium ions in the muscle cells that help govern the electrical stimulation and contraction of the heart muscle. They seem to be effective in treating an array of heart maladies.

Still generally in the testing phase is the drug streptokinase, a protein enzyme that is used on patients early in the course of a heart attack caused by a blood clot. When a heart attack is apparent, and the tissue on a segment of the heart is dying from a blocked artery, a narrow tube is inserted into that artery. Streptokinase is then injected. Within an hour this drug may dissolve the clot, limiting the damage to the tissue, and perhaps "saving" even more heart muscle. Streptokinase was approved by the U.S. Food and Drug Administration in 1982 for use in treating heart attacks.

Researchers have also developed novel ways of delivering reliable remedies to trouble spots. For more than a century, nitroglycerin tablets have been used to treat angina. They are generally held under the tongue and offer relief for only about 12 min. With this

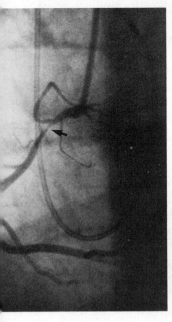
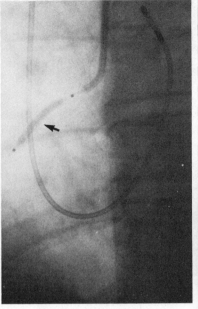
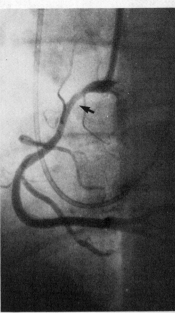

method, the nitroglycerin must pass through the liver, where it is detoxified and diluted before it reaches the heart. Increasing the dosage can harm the liver. A newer, more efficient method is the use of a nitroglycerin-laden patch, which is placed directly on the skin near the heart. With this patch, the drug enters the bloodstream through the skin and goes directly to the heart.

Surgery

"Surgery is in a constant state of flux," says John Norman. "If you compare surgery today with that of 1960, it's like looking at a Model T and a Porsche 928. And anything we can do today, we can still do better."

It was only a decade ago that surgeons began wearing jewelers' loupes on glasses during surgery, adds Norman. "And now we've reached the point where we're doing more microsurgery, repairing increasingly smaller blood vessels. Standardization of techniques has made us faster and more extensive in surgery; and during open-heart surgery, we have patients on the heart-lung machines a shorter time. Sure, technology evolves slowly, if you consider major advancements strung out over five years as slow."

Surgery, of course, is a drastic treatment. But it is also common and effective. Coronary arterial bypasses, first performed on patients with blocked arteries in 1967, are done by the hundreds every day. In this procedure, a vein is taken from the patient's leg and

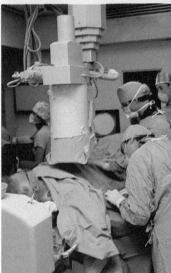

One method of unclogging coronary arteries is called percutaneous transluminal coronary angioplasty. A doctor is shown inserting a probe, with a balloon at the tip, into a narrowed portion (arrow) of a coronary artery. The balloon is then inflated, clearing the artery of plaque, which is composed mainly of cholesterol and other fats that might otherwise totally halt blood flow.

grafted to the aorta, or some healthy segment of coronary artery. The other end of the graft is then placed past the obstructed point in the artery, restoring circulation. This procedure is often done to relieve angina, or as a preventive measure, as partially occluded arteries are prone to clogging completely, causing a possibly fatal infarction.

Another method of coping with clogged arteries employs a catheter probe and a balloonlike device. Called percutaneous transluminal coronary angioplasty (PTCA), this procedure consists of working the probe into a narrowed segment of a coronary artery and inflating the balloon at the tip of the probe, thus dilating the narrowed artery from within. The PTCA has limitations, but it is much cheaper than a coronary bypass operation.

Devices to Aid Abnormal Heartbeat

As dangerous as an infarction is the irregularity of the heartbeat, resulting from the disruption of the heart's electrical impulses. Within minutes, abnormal heart rhythms, perhaps resulting from a heart attack, can lead to uncontrollable and fatal twitching of the heart muscle. Chest massage, drugs, or electrical stimulation is applied in an emergency in an attempt to get the heart's electrical impulses back in rhythm.

Irregular heartbeat, or arrhythmia, can be a chronic problem. To correct this, nearly 1,000,000 people have been fitted with pacemakers, devices implanted to regulate the heart through means of electrical impulses.

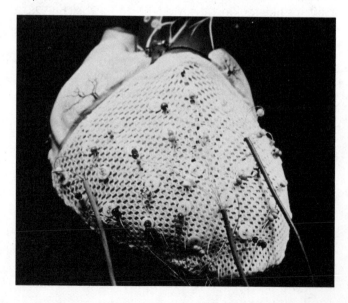

Similar, but for more severe cases, is a small device called an automatic defibrillator. Placed in the abdomen and powered by batteries, it discharges a relatively strong electrical shock to electrodes attached to the heart, whenever severe rhythm disruption occurs.

. These electrical irregularities may also be helped surgically, with an experimental method called "cardiac mapping." With this, patients are placed on a heart-lung machine—which can take over the work of the heart and lungs for several hours—while electrodes are attached to the inner and outer surfaces of the heart muscle. Doctors then painstakingly trace the path of the impulses, noting areas where these pulses are "short-circuited." These regions of muscle are then carefully excised in a thin slice, leaving the functioning electrical routes intact. In one group of 33 patients operated on at the Stanford University Medical Center, cardiac mapping stopped recurrent arrhythmias in 70 percent.

Transplants

First performed in 1967, the heart transplant appeared to offer a respite from certain death. However, due to high costs, the inability to match appropriate donors with recipients, and a rather high rate of failure, the procedure was nearly dropped in the mid-1970's. But there are today hints of a revival, spurred by the cautious-but-encouraging results at Stanford, where transplant patients now have a 70 percent one-year survival rate and a 50 percent five-year survival rate.

Heart-transplant patients at the Stanford University Medical Center have a 70 percent chance of surviving at least a year. Here (left), in a Stanford operating room, the nurse at left reads blood pressure while in the background a technician monitors the heart-lung machine, which performs the functions of the patient's heart and lungs during the operation. After the recipient's heart is removed (top), a healthy donor heart (bottom) is implanted.

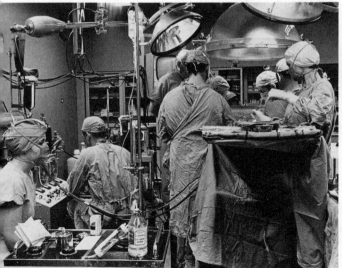

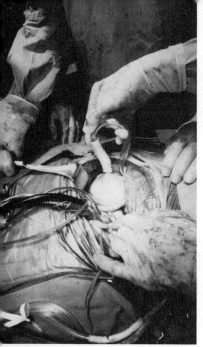

Stanford performs about 20 to 25 heart transplants a year, along with four or five much more difficult heart *and lung* transplants. Only a few other medical centers are considering this procedure on a regular basis.

Cost is a big problem, as a transplant can run nearly $100,000. It also requires an extraordinary amount of hospital resources. And although it produces some research benefits, the procedure is unlikely, for at least the next few years, to have a significant impact on public health.

Stanford has forged its success rate through careful patient and donor selection. Most transplant patients must be under 50 and be otherwise healthy. They must not have a history of psychological problems, since they must endure high doses of steroids and other drugs that promote psychological difficulties. These patients must also be blessed with strong and supportive families.

Donors must be brain dead but have no damage done to their hearts. The heart must be the approximate size of the recipient's own heart, the blood type must be identical, and the cells of donor and recipient must be compatible. Should the recipient's blood serum contain antibodies that would work against the cells of the donor's heart, a rejection of that heart would be almost certain.

Bruce Reitz of Stanford sees the possibility of a transplant as therapy for his terminal patients, more than enough reason to justify the procedure. "And 20 to 25 patients per year doesn't cost that much when you consider our total national health budget," he insists. "Maybe if there were more centers doing the procedure, and there were *20,000* of them in a year, it would be expensive. But I seriously doubt you could find any more than 100 suitable transplant candidates in the U.S.—much less the right donors—at any given time."

The future of heart transplants is a societal decision because of the critical need for federal funding. Many question whether the government should spend a lot of money to help a few. But the kidney dialysis program, for example, was originally intended to benefit some 8000 patients; thanks to dialysis, more than 46,000 individuals are alive today.

Artificial Hearts

In 1969 Denton Cooley implanted the first artificial heart in a human, in a man waiting for a transplant when none was available. But despite hopes that

Top: Artificial hearts designed at the University of Utah have been implanted in calves, one of which lived for nine months. A newer model, designed by Utah Professor Robert K. Jarvik (bottom), was approved in 1982 by the U.S. Food and Drug Administration for implantation in a human patient. Such an implant was performed on Dec. 2.

artificial hearts would be in widespread use by the end of the 1970's, not until 1981, the year Cooley again used an artificial heart as a "bridge" to a transplant, was the procedure tried again.

Although studies have shown that from 16,000 to 66,000 people in the U.S. could benefit from some kind of artificial heart, the problems of developing a workable device have proved difficult to master. One major hurdle is power.

Pneumatic (air-driven) mechanical hearts are the easiest to build, but pneumatic tubes would have to run through the skin, leaving the patient prone to infection. Moreover, an air compressor would have to sit at the patient's side at all times. Even most battery-powered hearts would require wires penetrating the skin, again posing the threat of infection.

The actual blood pump must not harm the blood, with inner surfaces so smooth and intricately designed that no clots of blood will form on these surfaces. Should a clot form and break loose, it could kill the patient, even if the heart functions quite well. A leak-proof pump also is a must, for even a drop of blood a day leaking into the body could eventually kill.

Although Cooley implanted a total artificial heart in both patients, and there are total artificial hearts that have kept calves alive for nearly a year, the National Institutes of Health has given priority in research funding to the development of a partial artificial heart, called the Left Ventricular Assist Device (LVAD). Since most heart disease tends to concentrate in the left ventricle, a sophisticated LVAD may be *the* artificial heart of the future. And it's a future much closer than any total heart implant.

Indeed, some LVADs have already been used in humans, a temporary postsurgical measure when patients are having trouble being weaned from a heart-lung machine. This machine takes over the function of the heart and lungs during surgery so the surgeons can work on a still and "dry" heart. But time on the machine is limited to four or five hours, before tissues and blood are seriously damaged. And some hearts will not respond after being taken off the machine.

An LVAD, which does not bypass the lungs and does not damage the blood, but merely gives the left ventricle a "boost," can allow an unresponsive heart to "rest" or "heal" after surgery. It can assist the patient for a few hours, or several days.

Most LVAD use today is as a temporary, postsurgical

On the way to a staff meeting at the Texas Heart Institute, director Denton Cooley (right), head of research O. H. Frazier (center), and Michael Duncan discuss medical problems in their continuing effort to develop more effective artificial heart devices.

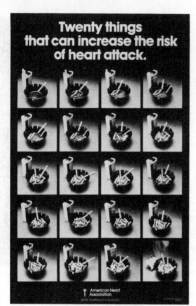

Twenty things that can increase the risk of heart attack.

American Heart Association

Cigarette smoking speeds the heartbeat, raises blood pressure, and constricts blood vessels. This American Heart Association poster urges Americans to quit the habit.

measure. And it's still experimental. Most are pneumatically powered, which is not practical for long-term use.

Within five to ten years, however, researchers expect that LVADs will have long-term uses. One LVAD model and power pack employs a pair of electromagnetic plates, one left outside the body and worn on a belt, the other implanted inside the stomach. A battery pack would transmit power from the external to the internal plate, in turn running the LVAD, which would be attached directly to the patient's left ventricle.

Any electrical system would require batteries, but the best possible LVAD would run on nuclear elements. "Everything else is merely progress," says John Norman. "With a nuclear-powered LVAD, the patient would need to wear nothing outside his body; he wouldn't have to worry about his batteries running low. It would be the definitive device."

There are, however, problems with nuclear power. "It would have to withstand great shock should the patient be in a bad auto accident," says Don Hill of the Pacific Medical Center. "It has to withstand great heat, should the patient perish in a fire. The plutonium-238 used in the device could be a threat to others should something serious happen to the patient."

Aside from the practical aspect of finding a ready supply of plutonium-238, a strong ethical question is involved. "It might sound farfetched," says Hill, "but there's nevertheless the chance of terrorists kidnapping patients for the plutonium supply."

Staying Healthy

For the past 20 years, "risk factor reduction" has been a key phrase among cardiologists. Cutting cigarette smoking, reducing the levels of cholesterol in the diet, reducing stress, exercising more, living a clean life—it's a familiar litany. Reducing one's salt intake sometimes lowers blood pressure; high blood pressure can damage coronary arteries and cause a number of other ills. Cutting excess weight tends to decrease the amount of work a heart must perform. Fortuitously, a little alcohol each day may actually reduce the chances of atherosclerosis, the accumulation of fatty deposits or fibrous tissue in the lining of the arteries.

Smoking is clearly a risk factor because nicotine speeds the heart rate, raises blood pressure, and constricts blood vessels. Since blood serum cholesterol is the prime ingredient in the buildup of atherosclerotic plaque, physicians advise against overindulgence in cholesterol-rich food. Even so, the benefits of low-cholesterol diets are disputed, since 60 to 80 percent of serum cholesterol does not come from diet but is manufactured by the body itself.

In a cynical moment, John Norman can question the benefits of "clean living." "We've cut open patients who are heavy smokers and those who have never touched a cigarette. We've had to operate on alcoholics and teetotalers. Fat patients, thin patients, and average patients. So who knows?" he says with a resigned shrug.

A few moments later, Norman reconsiders his words. "I should be more positive," he says. "We are seeing a profound change in national health habits. There's a preoccupation with health, and while it may almost go too far, this will obviously cut the instances of coronary disease. As people try to live more healthy lives, despite my clinical observations today, we surely will see a difference."

"On the other hand," Norman continues, "we're seeing more female heart patients than ever before. And I think this is due to the dual role many women have undertaken, caring for the home and holding a job. Stress is starting to bring them into the same risk category as men."

Stress is linked to a variety of ailments, including high blood pressure. And according to a growing body of evidence, stress can also lead to a high serum cholesterol level. An individual with an excitable sympathetic nervous system may produce more cholesterol from food than a calm individual. A person's heart may be stimulated to work harder, require more oxygen, and, combined with narrowed arteries, be prone to infarctions.

Regular exercise reduces stress and increases the efficiency of the heart and lungs.

Reducing risk is clearly the best way to fight heart disease and a lot less painful than treating disease once it has occurred. The new diagnostic techniques will catch heart disease earlier—if and when the unit cost of such procedures makes widespread screening possible. New drugs will do their part, and new surgical procedures will make repairs better and longer lasting. As a last resort, transplants and artificial hearts could be a solution for desperately ill patients.

Each small advance buys more time for a patient, staves off death a little longer, and may herald the day when heart disease is no longer the nation's leading killer.

by JOSEPH WALLACE

TODAY'S

Joseph Wallace is science editor for Museum *magazine.*

During the past decade a quiet revolution has been occurring in North American zoos. Until recently many zoos resembled 19th-century menageries: Tiny cages contained bored, unhealthy animals pacing back and forth across bare concrete. These decrepit animals often served as objects of derision to their human visitors. Elephants were pelted with peanuts, seals and alligators with coins and aluminum cans. Most denizens of these menageries did not live long.

The philosophy that produced those nightmarish carnivals has changed with startling rapidity, however. New zoos such as the Minnesota Zoological Garden and the Miami (Fla.) Metrozoo feature open-air, cageless exhibits that bear no resemblance to the concrete prisons of zoos past. Meanwhile, older zoos (such as the venerable Bronx Zoo) are instituting radical, large-scale alterations of their exhibits, with the ultimate goal of eliminating all the old-fashioned displays and replacing them with more colorful and interesting ones. The innovative new exhibits range from the Bronx Zoo's Sea Lion Pool to the Minnesota Zoo's huge Northern Trail, but they and dozens of other unusual displays share one important characteristic: The animals are kept in surroundings modeled on their natural homes. Animals that need room to thrive are given spacious enclosures; apes and monkeys, which languish without exercise, are provided with ropes and branches from which they can hang, swing, and jump. Visitors to these exhibits are rewarded by animals that are healthy and content and that show little neurotic or unnatural behavior.

The reasons behind this zoo renaissance are many and varied. In recent years increased scientific and technological knowledge has enabled zoo designers to create more complex and realistic exhibits. Improved control of artificial environments—of heat, moisture, and light—has led to larger and more ambitious displays. No longer must individual species be confined to small areas; now many species can

ZOO A Home Instead of a Jail

In this panel of the Renaissance artist Hieronymus Bosch's triptych painting, "The Garden of Earthly Delights," animals, including some exotic and some fantastical, are depicted before Adam and Eve's expulsion from Eden. In this age of exploration many artists used as models the strange creatures brought back to Europe from abroad for display in zoological gardens.

In 1907 the Bronx Zoo in New York City began a captive breeding program to rebuild the once-vast herd of American buffalo that had been decimated during the westward movement. Now many zoos have adopted captive breeding as a major reason for their existence.

coexist in environments precisely duplicating their natural ones.

Another, more basic reason for the new environments is growing concern for the animals themselves. In the past, when an elephant or gorilla died, it could easily be replaced from the wild. Now, for several reasons, this is often impossible. Collecting in the wild is carefully regulated; when zoos are forced to replace an animal that has died, they must usually buy it on the open market. Prices are exorbitant: A pair of gorillas might cost $60,000, as would a single Indian rhinoceros—if one could be found at all. Rarity, inflation, and transportation costs all contribute to the expense of buying new animals and make it crucial that zoos maintain their inhabitants in proper condition. Animals in naturalistic settings are often happier; they live longer and do not have to be replaced as frequently.

Perhaps the most important reason for the recent improvements in zoo design is the change in public expectations. In the past 15 years, hundreds of books and TV documentaries have shown millions of zoogoers the great African plains and tangled Amazon forests; animals sprawled in tiny cages no longer seem realistic or exciting enough. In an increasingly urban

American society within an increasingly overpopulated world, zoos serve to remind us of the natural beauty that still exists.

Outstanding Zoos and Zoo Exhibits

Many zoos have introduced unusual exhibits during the past few years; one of the most innovative is the Minnesota Zoo in Apple Valley, Minn. This six-year-old zoo is at present divided into four regions, representing the oceans, tropical Asia, the world's northlands, and Minnesota itself. Pathways through each region loop around large areas of the zoo's 480-acre expanse.

The Northern Trail is a large outdoor exhibit of northern animals. Siberian tigers occupy a wooded ravine about 5 acres in size, and although they are free to roam throughout their small patch of forest, clever design (a heated rock for basking, a flowing stream for cooling off) serves to lure them into view. Nearby, moose range across a 4-acre site, while Bactrian camels quickly grow and shed their thick coats, enabling them to adjust to Minnesota's—or their native Mongolia's—extremes of temperature. Eventually the Northern Trail will be expanded to include such mammals as wolves and polar bears.

In the zoo's indoor Tropics Trail, a multilevel pathway takes the visitors on a simulated journey through 3000 mi. of Asia, from arid Indian highlands to dripping Indonesian rain forests. More than 15,000 plants and trees are housed under the 75-ft.-high canopy of this exhibit, which also contains 650 animals. A fallen tree occasionally filled with

A monorail takes visitors through a portion of the San Diego Zoo's Wild Animal Park. In contrast to the concrete prisons of the past, zoo design now features cageless open-air exhibits in which many species coexist in environments duplicating their natural habitats.

honeycomb, for example, allows sloth bears to demonstrate their noisy "vacuum cleaner" eating technique. Other animals among the exhibit's 80 species are gibbons, leopards, pythons, and flamingos.

The two-year-old Miami Metrozoo is the newest major American zoo. It is not yet completed, but several large exhibits are open to the public. The 160-acre Eurasian Lobe features an exact replica of a 13th-century Buddhist shrine discovered in the Cambodian jungle; two resident Bengal tigers roam the grounds. Other animals on display in this outdoor cageless exhibit include camels, Siamese crocodiles, and

The Minnesota Zoo is one of the nation's most innovative ones. Bactrian camels (above, right) feel at home in the Northern Trail, an open-air exhibit, because Minnesota's climate is similar to that of their native Mongolia. By contrast, the enclosed Tropics Trail (above, left) is a multilevel pathway that takes visitors on a simulated journey through 3000 mi. of Asia, ranging from arid highlands to rain forests.

A Bengal tiger poses confidently in front of a replica of a Buddhist shrine in the 160-acre Eurasian Lobe of the Miami Metrozoo. The Florida climate is well suited for the animals displayed in this outdoor cageless exhibit.

Malayan sun bears, all living in careful representations of their homelands. The warm Florida climate is perfect for these animals, as it is for the plains animals that will live in the zoo's soon-to-open African section. This exhibit, and all those still being planned, will be cageless; the animals will reside on islands surrounded by moats.

Recently the British Broadcasting Co. produced a TV series on what it considered the world's seven most outstanding zoos. Two of these zoos are in the United States: the huge and pioneering San Diego Zoo; and the tiny, little-known but extraordinary Arizona-Sonora Desert Museum (ASDM), located outside Tucson in the Arizona desert. The ASDM's collection of 220 species—all native to Arizona and the neighboring Mexican State of Sonora—offers the largest North American fauna collection of any zoo in the U.S. The habitats found in the Arizona-Sonora area are among the most varied in the world: Desert, prairie, Alpine meadow, cold streams, and deciduous woodland are all present in this small section of the continent.

The ASDM, a stylistic innovator since its opening in 1952, displays animals from all these habitats in highly

The tiny but extraordinary Arizona-Sonora Desert Museum (top) offers the largest North American fauna collection of any zoo in the U.S.—all native to the area. When the museum first opened in 1952, it featured small exhibits of caged animals. Current exhibits include a glass-walled desert river (bottom) providing both overlooking and underwater views of mammals, fish, birds, and amphibians.

27

naturalistic settings. Three feline species—bobcats, ocelots, and margays—occupy rock grottoes shaped to mimic exactly these mammals' homes in the wild. A glass-walled desert river, complete with cottonwood-shaded pools, provides both overlooking and underwater views of river otters, beavers, and several species of birds and amphibians. At night, an occasional bobcat or coyote will forage through the grounds of the museum in an intermingling of wild and captive animals unthinkable at any of the large city zoos throughout the country.

While zoos such as the Minnesota, Miami, and Arizona-Sonora ones have featured creative exhibits since their inception, older zoos have had to undergo major renovations to accommodate the new philosophy. A striking example is the Woodland Park Zoo in Seattle. When David Hancocks was appointed director in 1976, the Seattle Zoo was a typical collection of unimaginative cages. Using his experience as an architect, Hancocks immediately began instituting changes. Many of the old-fashioned exhibits were dismantled and replaced with open-air naturalistic settings. This improvement program has already been so successful that the zoo's new African Savanna won the 1981 exhibit award from the American Association of Zoological Parks and Aquariums. The gorilla habitat is another impressive exhibit: ½ acre of dense thicket, it is among the largest and most realistic gorilla displays in any zoo.

One innovation that Hancocks brought to the Seattle Zoo particularly benefits the animals. The gorilla habitat and most sections of the African Savanna contain areas where the animals can retreat from the visiting crowds. Although this means that visitors occasionally cannot spot all the zoo denizens,

Seattle's Woodland Park Zoo features a multitude of school education programs and informative tours. At the prizewinning African Savanna exhibit, children and parents enjoy a close-up look at zebras from a covered pathway.

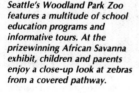

the benefits to the health and contentment of the animals are great, and most people do not seem to mind.

Many other zoos also feature exhibits that stand out for their creative quality. The Tulsa Zoo's Chimp Island allows chimpanzees to demonstrate their ability to fashion and use tools, a skill shared only by humans. In the wild, chimps carefully push thick grass stems or small sticks into termite mounds. After a few moments they pull out the stems, covered with termites, and eat the insects. Chimp Island re-creates this fascinating act by use of an artificial mound. Throughout the day mustard is released into a chamber in the mound. The chimps, attracted by the odor, retrieve the mustard using grass stems or twigs, thereby reproducing the actions of their wild relatives.

The MetroToronto Zoo is the most innovative zoo in Canada. Perhaps its most unusual exhibit is the polar bear habitat. Polar bears spend much time swimming, yet the MetroToronto Zoo may be the only zoo with large underwater viewing windows to give visitors a unique look at the world's only aquatic bear. The zoo also boasts an extensive Americas Pavilion, which presents in naturalistic settings animals ranging from the tamandua (a South American anteater) to the more familiar beaver.

Lincoln Park Zoo in Chicago recently unveiled an exhibit of penguins and other seabirds. A simulated glacial formation and glassed-in pool permit visitors to see penguins both swimming and on land. Another area contains a hidden wave machine, creating optimal conditions for the zoo's puffins and other seabirds.

The Milwaukee County Zoo's predator-prey exhibits are also cleverly designed. The zoo's pride of lions lives in an area that overlooks another exhibit—that of the lions' natural prey, including antelope and zebras. The two exhibits are separated by a large moat barely visible to the viewer. A similar design is employed for the South American display, with jaguars placed above and behind tapir and capybaras.

The zoo that presents the most fascinating contrast between old and new is the Bronx Zoo in New York City. One of the oldest zoos in the U.S., the Bronx Zoo features many brilliantly designed recent exhibits, as well as some that have not been renovated in many years. The big cat house, with its small grimy cages in contrast to its ornate stonework, recalls an era when the exterior of a building was more important than the

At the Tulsa Zoo's Chimp Island, curators have designed an artificial termite mound to display the ability of chimpanzees to fashion and use tools. The chimps use sticks, much as they would in the wild, as primitive tools to probe into holes in the mounds in search of food.

Part of the appeal of the Bronx Zoo is the accessibility of animals that, like the giraffes below, seem close enough to touch. Above: Elephants at the zoo are trained to respond to signals from their keepers, much like elephants in the circus.

condition of the captive animals. In the newer exhibits, the animals come first. One such exhibit is the crowd-pleasing Sea Lion Pool, which has been remodeled to resemble a West Coast rookery. The large pool contains an artificial coastal cliff, a pebbly beach, a tidal pool, and a large main pool—as well as several playful sea lions. The new De Jur Aviary is a 150-ft.-long free-flight aviary that resembles a rocky coastal island. This artificial seabird rookery, complete with sheer bluffs, reefs, and salty pools, houses penguins, guanay cormorants (famous for their role in the South American fertilizer industry), and other seabirds. The Carter Giraffe display, which opened in 1982, allows visitors and giraffes to inspect each other from only a few feet apart, separated by just three thin strands of wire.

Perhaps the most impressive display at the Bronx Zoo is also one of its original innovative exhibits: the World of Birds. Spiraling walkways within this cylindrical building carry visitors to the treetops of a South American rain forest. Lush vegetation hangs above the open pathways as brilliantly colored birds flit and call among the vines and flowers. As an act of simulation, the World of Birds is unsurpassed; the setting is so realistic that the birds are never tempted to escape, so no glass or bars are necessary.

Breeding Endangered Species

While zoos continue to redesign and rebuild in the unending competition to be the most innovative, they are also participating in a program that is cooperative: breeding endangered species in captivity.

As the world's human population continues to grow, more and more animals are becoming rare. The human population explosion means more land must be cultivated, more food grown, and less room left for the animals. The vast plains of Africa are being taken over for livestock grazing and food cultivation. The world's tropical rain forests—home to the majority of the earth's animal species—are being cleared at an alarming rate. At least 25 acres are cleared each minute, an area the size of West Virginia every year. Under such pressure, many species disappear; some scientists predict that 1,000,000 species of plants and animals may be extinct by the end of this century.

Many of the most endangered animals are those that are most popular at zoos. No more than 1000 mountain gorillas exist in the wild, and these few remaining great apes are threatened by destruction of their forest habitat and by poaching. Fewer than 400 Siberian tigers survive outside zoos. The elephant population in East Africa has been decimated by ivory hunters, and perhaps 90 percent of that continent's black rhinos have been killed by poachers in the past decade. Powdered rhino horn is much in demand as an aphrodisiac in the Far East, and Yemeni men use the horns as dagger handles to show their strength and masculinity. The elephant and the black rhino may not survive in the wild into the next century.

In the face of this flood of grim news, many zoos have adopted captive breeding as a major reason for their existence—some say *the* major reason. Whereas once a single gorilla sat alone in a cage for 20 years, zoos are now lending (and sometimes giving) these prime attractions to other zoos in an attempt to breed them. Extensive research programs have been established at most major zoos to discover the proper conditions for breeding rare species. Zoos are also

These African black rhinos, pictured in the wild, are endangered primarily because poachers want their horns. When ground into powder, rhino horns are believed to possess aphrodisiac properties; in Yemen, they are sought after as handles for ornamental daggers. The horns shown here have been confiscated from poachers.

A major accomplishment at the Miami Metrozoo was the hatching of five Orinoco crocodiles—the first in the U.S.—in 1980.

reducing the number of species they display (the Bronx Zoo now keeps little more than half the species it once did), while increasing the number of individuals of each species, in order to concentrate on breeding more effectively the species that remain.

Each zoo concentrates on breeding those animals for which it is best suited. The hatching of five Orinoco crocodiles at the Miami Metrozoo was the first in the U.S. The Metrozoo also hopes that its large outdoor gorilla enclosure will prove conducive to mating Ramar, a large male gorilla on loan from the North Carolina Zoo. The Seattle Zoo's densely wooded gorilla exhibit may also prove suitable for breeding this difficult species. The zoo also maintains a large collection of lion-tailed macaques, a monkey species that is extremely endangered in the wild.

The Minnesota Zoo's breeding program for clouded leopards, a species about which little is known, has been particularly successful. The Minnesota Zoo also hopes to establish a nursery herd of caribou, with the eventual goal of reintroducing the animals, which have been extinct in Minnesota for half a century, to wilderness areas within the state. In recent years the MetroToronto Zoo has had notable success breeding large African mammals such as the lowland gorilla, elephant, and giraffe. The ASDM is giving prime attention to breeding the San Esteban Island chuckwalla, an endangered lizard found only on a small island in the Gulf of California.

Hundreds of rare birds and animals are born each year in large zoos such as the San Diego and Bronx zoos and the National Zoo in Washington, D.C. These zoos have acquired vast areas, mostly barred to the public, that are reserved for the breeding of endangered species. The San Diego Zoo's Wild Animal Park covers 1800 acres, only a third of which is open to the public; the rest is reserved for breeding rare hoofed mammals. The National Zoo operates the 3000-acre Conservation and Research Center in Front Royal, Va. Among the rare species found there are European bison, Bactrian camels, and many types of birds. The Bronx Zoo's Rare Animal Survival Center occupies an entire 12-mi.-long island, St. Catherines, off the coast of Georgia. On this island are kept animals that require more room than is possible at the Bronx Zoo or that have problems breeding at the zoo. These include many species of gazelle and antelope, as well as kangaroos, zebras, and several rare birds. Many other zoos have sent animals to breed on St. Catherines.

The American Association of Zoological Parks and Aquariums has instituted a program to aid cooperative efforts among zoos. Called the Species Survival Plan, the program utilizes committees of experts and zoo representatives to provide centralized management of zoo collections. The committees use a computer, the International Species Inventory System (ISIS), which stores important information—such as age, sex, parentage, and present location—on 50,000 animals. By keeping these records, ISIS helps zoos maintain their breeding programs more efficiently.

There have been many successes in captive breeding. The world's entire population of Père David's deer—800—lives in zoos and is descended from a herd of 18. Ninety percent of the 750 Siberian tigers in captivity were bred in zoos. Lions breed so readily that the world's zoos are overstocked, and many lions are now routinely given birth control pills. Conversely, years of failure have marked the National Zoo's attempts to mate its giant pandas, and the Bronx Zoo is still trying to find the proper method of breeding South American giant anteaters.

Much time and effort are put into solving breeding problems, as zoos increasingly see themselves as "arks," refuges where animals can survive even if destroyed in the wild. A decade from now it may no longer be possible to see a Siberian tiger or a lion-tailed macaque in the wild, but at least these beautiful animals will live on in zoos. And sometimes it *is* possible to return a species extinct in nature to its original home, but only if viable zoo populations have been maintained. One example is the European bison, which is gradually resuming a natural existence after having been reintroduced to Soviet forests.

Meanwhile, the zoo renaissance continues. Almost every major zoo in the country is planning and

Among the most difficult animals to breed in captivity is the rare giant panda. Ling-Ling (top) and Hsing-Hsing (bottom) are popular attractions at the National Zoo in Washington, D.C. Ling-Ling was artificially inseminated in 1982 and began to exhibit nesting behavior, but in late August zoo curators announced that she was not pregnant and they would have to try again.

The Miami Metrozoo is still growing. This picture shows the site of construction of its new primate exhibit, scheduled to open in 1983.

Two thirds of the San Diego Zoo's Wild Animal Park is reserved for breeding endangered hoofed animals. Above: A zoo geneticist checks the sperm density of a sample taken from the black rhinoceros being examined in the background. Above, right: A topi antelope group at the park was not doing well, so each animal was captured, measured, tagged, and a blood sample taken prior to their being shipped in specially designed crates to another zoo. In the background, a curious giraffe monitors the veterinarian's job.

constructing new exhibits. The Minnesota Zoo hopes to create a large outdoor display for Asian mammals such as the Indian rhinoceros, Asian elephant, and orangutan. Other exhibits, featuring the animals of Australia and South America, are also in the works.

Much of the Miami Metrozoo remains to be completed. Its second phase of development includes the African Lobe, which will include an African veldt, desert, and jungle, housing species native to each habitat. A 1.2-acre free-flight aviary will include streams, bridges, "mountains," and lush plantings—and many species of Asian birds.

The Seattle Zoo is in the midst of an ambitious long-range plan to divide the zoo into ten different bioclimatic zones, including tundra, desert, chaparral, savanna, and tropical forest. Careful study of the park grounds has revealed enough variation in existing climate to permit this division. For example, evaluation of all conditions—site anatomy, slopes, drainage, tree types—helped zoo designers decide that a specific area in the zoo's northeast corner would be appropriate for the montane zone, which will now be built, planted with pines, juniper, and Alpine wild flowers, and stocked with mountain goats, bighorn sheep, and other mountain species.

While the massive renovation of the Bronx Zoo goes on in several areas, the most impressive exhibit, scheduled for completion in 1983, is the enormous indoor Jungle World. This exhibit will span 240 ft. under a glass roof—one of the largest enclosed habitat exhibits in the world. It will house real and artificial trees, streams, riverbanks, and waterfalls, as well as

Using a hand computer, behaviorist Don Lindberg studies lion-tailed macaques, extremely rare in the wild, at the San Diego Zoo.

Asian animals such as the Komodo dragon (the world's largest lizard), leopards, gibbons, and many other species of birds, reptiles, and small mammals.

Zoos in the U.S. are in a constant state of redesign, renovation, and improvement. Sometimes an exhibit is barely complete before a new technological or architectural advance renders it obsolete. More innovations will undoubtedly occur in the next few years; what splendors they may provide cannot be safely predicted. One fact, however, seems certain: We are in the midst of a new epoch in zoo design, an epoch that will not only increase our pleasure in visiting zoos, but should also guarantee that there will still be animals to visit.

One function of animal collections has always been to educate young people. Here, at Marine World Africa U.S.A., in Redwood City, Calif., a 2-year-old cheetah is brought out of its cage for close-up inspection, coupled with a lecture.

BEYOND

THE REGIONAL

by MEL GUSSOW

Mel Gussow is a theater critic for the New York Times.

For many years, Broadway was the traditional center of the American theater. Plays were tested out of town, came to Broadway, and then, if successful, were sent on tour. In the past 20 years, however, regional theater has become integral to the American landscape. Fully professional companies, presenting, in many cases, productions of the highest quality, crisscross America from Atlanta to San Diego, from Hartford to Honolulu and Anchorage, Alaska.

Today there are more than 50 major institutions and countless smaller companies bringing live theater to audiences outside New York City. Broadway is still the main marketplace, where playwrights, actors, and others can make their reputations and, possibly, even their fortunes, but in recent years theater has fragmented and diversified. Now there are many centers of the American theater. It is not unusual for theater professionals to decide to stay in a city or region other than the New York metropolitan area and devote themselves to working within a local company. The result is a revitalization of the American theater, with new stages, audiences, plays, playwrights, actors, designers, directors—and artistic visions.

The Rise of Regional Theater

As a movement, regionalism was more accidental than premeditated. No one sat down with a map of the United States and staked out cities that would benefit from theaters; the movement was organic. The label "regional theater" was generally accepted despite the fact that it is something of a misnomer, suggesting provincialism or small-minded localism. Admittedly, some of the theaters are in lightly populated areas, but, depending on their artistic

Opposite page: Adrian Hall, artistic director of the Trinity Square Repertory Company of Providence, poses with actors appearing in a stage version of John Steinbeck's novel Of Mice and Men. *One of the nation's leading regional theaters, Trinity Square has a company of resident actors, some of whom have been together for more than a decade.*

36

BROADWAY
THEATER MOVEMENT

BLUE JEANS

WRITTEN BY JOSEPH ARTHUR AUTHOR OF "THE STILL ALARM"

THE BIG 4 FAMOUS FEATURES OF THE PLAY THAT HAS MADE ALL AMERICA TALK

THE MIGHTY THRILLING THEATRICAL TRIUMPH —OF— 2 CONTINENTS

FEATURE Nº 1—THE BIG POLITICAL BARBECUE

FEATURE Nº 3—THE GREAT LYNCHING SCENE

FEATURE Nº 4—RISING SUN ROARERS

FEATURE Nº 2—THRILLING SAW MILL SCENE

Before the rise of regional theater, people outside New York City usually saw professional theater only when traveling companies came to town. This turn-of-the-century poster publicizes a coming attraction performed by a road company.

direction, they can be as sophisticated as any cosmopolitan institution. In addition, many of America's principal companies are located in urban centers: Los Angeles, Seattle, Houston, and Philadelphia. Almost every large city has one, and some cities, such as San Francisco, Chicago, and Washington, have an array of theaters of varying size and artistic perspective. Moreover, some theaters are regional in the best sense of the word: The Dallas Theater Center and the Actors Theatre of Louisville (Ky.) have been particularly effective in encouraging work by talented local writers.

Regional theaters are also sometimes referred to as repertory or resident theaters. The former label is imprecise. Few companies—San Francisco's American Conservatory Theatre is an outstanding exception—have permanent companies of actors performing plays in repertory. "Resident" is closer to an accurate description, but while the theaters themselves are resident, few employ a company of actors for any significant length of time. Moreover, many resident theaters send plays on tour through their state, to neighboring states, and in some cases (the Arena Stage in Washington, D.C.) to foreign countries. In most instances the character of the theater comes more from the artistic director and his or her artistic policy than it does from a geographical situation.

In common, regional theaters are not-for-profit, although they often produce work that eventually earns money in the commercial theater. In that sense, they are allied with many of New York's Off Broadway institutional theaters, such as the New York Shakespeare Festival, the Circle Repertory Company, the Manhattan Theatre Club, and the Negro Ensemble Company. These are New York's equivalent of regional theaters. In common with their out-of-town colleagues, they offer a full season of plays and often appeal to a subscription audience. In contrast, the average summer theater or music tent is strictly a booking operation, welcoming packaged shows in order to make a profit.

The concept of regional theater was born in 1915 with the founding of the Cleveland Play House (still in operation). The emergence of the movement as a national force, however, is attributable to a series of subsequent events, beginning with the establishment in 1947 of Margo Jones's Theater '47 in Dallas (no longer in operation). Jones became the first professional leader of regional theater, producing the earliest work of such playwrights as Tennessee Williams and William Inge, and in honor of her contribution the Margo Jones Award is given annually to a theater that best encourages new plays. Many of the most important regional theaters, as well as Off Broadway companies, have been grateful recipients of that prize.

The next major event in the life of regional theater was Zelda Fichandler's establishment of the Arena Stage in Washington, D.C., in 1950. The Arena Stage has since moved several times, expanded, and endured as an exemplary cultural institution. Significantly, when the first Tony Award was given for sustained achievement among regional theaters, the recipient was the Arena Stage. Equally consequential

Founded in 1965, San Francisco's American Conservatory Theatre (ACT) is the nation's largest and most active repertory company. Like other regional theaters, ACT depends on a subscription audience, as well as donations and grants, for survival.

Margo Jones, now deceased, is credited with launching the regional theater movement in establishing a company in Dallas in 1947. Here, in 1973, Jules Irving, former director of the Repertory Theatre of Lincoln Center, accepts the Margo Jones Award, given annually to a theater that best encourages new work.

in the history of regional theater has been the contribution of foundations, private and public, especially the Ford Foundation. With an arts and humanities program under the direction of W. McNeil Lowry, in the late 1950's the Ford Foundation began giving financial support to regional theaters.

The consolidation of the movement was symbolized by the creation of the Guthrie Theater in Minneapolis in 1963. Founded by the eminent British director Sir Tyrone Guthrie together with Peter Zeisler and Oliver Rea, this was the first major implantation of a theater in an area. Before, theater emerged from within a community. The founding triumvirate surveyed America, considered options, and chose Minnesota as a likely home for such a large-scale venture.

The Guthrie remains, through several changes of artistic leadership (from Sir Tyrone himself through Michael Langham and on to the present director, Liviu Ciulei), devoted to classics; it is a museum or library theater. Other groups, such as the Actors Theatre of Louisville, are principally concerned with new work. Most of them freely mix the two, furnishing an eclectic selection of classics, new plays, and guest engagements from experimental and/or foreign companies.

One of regional theater's chief influences has been in discovering and nurturing original plays. Regional theater exists for its own sake, as an alternative to Broadway and road companies, but it has also become a pipeline to commercial theater, films, and TV. In recent years, many of the most honored plays have begun their lives in the regions—a role that they share with Off Broadway, Off Off Broadway, and the London theater. With rare exceptions, and those mostly in the area of musicals and light comedies,

Donations by the Ford Foundation, under a program administered by W. McNeil Lowry (right), were instrumental in the spread of regional theater. Here Lowry appears with the late Nina Vance, founder and artistic director of Houston's Alley Theatre, in 1965.

Liviu Ciulei is artistic director of the Guthrie Theater in Minneapolis. This company, although dedicated to presenting classic plays in repertory, also presents new works under Ciulei's direction.

Broadway no longer begins new work. Among the plays that were first presented in the regions are Athol Fugard's *A Lesson from Aloes* and *"Master Harold"* . . . *and the Boys* (at the Yale Repertory Theatre in New Haven, Conn.); David Rabe's *Streamers* (the Long Wharf Theatre in New Haven); Beth Henley's *Crimes of the Heart* and D. L. Coburn's *The Gin Game* (the Actors Theatre of Louisville); Michael Cristofer's *The Shadow Box* and Mark Medoff's *Children of a Lesser God* (the Mark Taper Forum in Los Angeles); and Howard Sackler's *The Great White Hope* and Michael Weller's *Moonchildren* and *Loose Ends* (the Arena Stage). Several playwrights have had long-standing affiliations with regional theaters. Sam Shepard, for example, first presented *Buried Child, Curse of the Starving Class,* and other plays at the Magic Theatre in San Francisco, while *American Buffalo* and other plays by David Mamet premiered at the St. Nicholas Theater and the Goodman Theatre in his native Chicago.

Above, left: The Mark Taper Forum is located in the luxurious Los Angeles Music Center. Above: Phyllis Frelich and John Rubinstein are shown in a scene from Mark Medoff's Children of a Lesser God.

The Actors Theatre of Louisville is noted for presenting new plays, several of which have gone on to enjoy successful runs on Broadway. Left: A scene from Crimes of the Heart, *which was first presented in Louisville, moved to Broadway, and earned playwright Beth Henley a Pulitzer Prize in 1981.*

The Long Wharf Theatre of New Haven, Conn., presents both new plays and classics. Above: A scene from Arthur Miller's A View from the Bridge. *Above, right: The Arena Stage, founded in Washington, D.C., by Zelda Fichandler, was the first theater outside New York City to receive a Tony Award for theatrical excellence. The playhouse consists of two stages—an open arena and a smaller proscenium house—as well as a room for cabaret-style entertainments.*

Among them, these plays share five Pulitzer Prizes and innumerable Tony Awards and New York Drama Critics' Circle prizes.

With Broadway producers increasingly reluctant to attempt anything unusual, resident groups have become a chief testing ground for the commercial theater. This fact has led to certain abuses. One temptation is to think first about the marketplace, to choose work on the basis of a future life rather than on artistic grounds and to meet the needs of a company or a community. Nonprofit and profit theater remain somewhat suspicious of one another, circling warily as if afraid of being tainted. The best theaters have retained their independence and individuality and have also managed to survive economic recession. In common with all aspects of the arts, regional theater bears a heavy financial burden; it cannot be self-supporting even when it plays to capacity audiences.

To some degree, regional theaters remain competitive, in terms of seeking new plays and in acquiring grants, but there is more and more collaboration. A production may move, relatively intact, from theater to theater. In another development, two or more companies may schedule different productions of the same play, even simultaneously. Several seasons ago, Christopher Durang's *A History of the American Film* was staged in contrasting productions at the Hartford Stage Company, the Arena Stage, and the Mark Taper Forum before it opened on Broadway. This approach gives a play a longer life before it succeeds or fails in New York. Such compatible regionalism allows a playwright to remove himself from the Broadway hit-or-miss syndrome and also signifies that the various regional

The Alaska Repertory Theatre serves the entire state, which means a great deal of traveling. This picture shows the company taking a production of Fools *on the road.*

theaters have begun to accept the fact that they have something to learn from one another. An enormous help in communication is offered by the Theatre Communications Group (TCG), a central clearinghouse for all nonprofit professional theaters. Among its many activities TCG conducts group auditions of actors for resident companies and also furnishes these companies with new plays.

Regional theater standards vary as much as the size of the institutions and choice of material. Some fill up a season with boulevard comedies, mysteries, and familiar classics; others specialize in experimental work. Theaters can be as large as the Guthrie (with a budget of more than $5,000,000 and an annual attendance of 739,000) or as small as the People's Light and Theatre Company of Malvern, Pa. (a budget of less than $500,000 and annual attendance of 65,000).

Some Outstanding Companies

The following seven companies have all won Tony Awards for sustained achievement, as selected by members of the American Theater Critics Association:

• The Arena Stage has two stages—an open arena and a smaller proscenium house—in addition to a room for cabaret-style entertainments in a modern structure near the banks of the Potomac River. Led since its founding by Zelda Fichandler, with her husband, Tom Fichandler, as executive director, the Arena is the core of the burgeoning Washington theatrical community, which also includes the Folger Theatre Group, specializing in Shakespeare, and Roger Stevens's productions at the John F. Kennedy Center for the Performing Arts. Zelda Fichandler diversifies her seasons, with the emphasis on provocative classics and new plays. The Arena is very much an

international theater and often presents works by contemporary European writers in translation. Significantly, the Arena became the first American troupe to tour the Soviet Union under the auspices of the U.S. State Department. Fichandler has built a devoted audience and a nucleus of Washington-based actors (including Robert Prosky, Richard Bauer, and Stanley Anderson) who are among the finest in the country.

• The Mark Taper Forum was founded in 1967 by Gordon Davidson, who continues as artistic director. This is a forward-looking theater, responsive to the social concerns of its community, that has presented such controversial political works as *The Trial of the Catonsville Nine* and *In the Matter of J. Robert Oppenheimer,* both of which went on to engagements in New York. In addition to its main stage program (popular classics as well as new plays), the Mark Taper encourages nascent talent in its New

Theater for Now series. The theater is located in the luxurious Los Angeles Music Center.

• The Long Wharf Theatre in New Haven, founded in 1965, and led by Arvin Brown as artistic director and M. Edgar Rosenblum as executive director, is a firmly established, highly successful company that benefits from its proximity to New York. From there it draws actors as well as theatergoers and frequently moves productions from its small 484-seat theater to Broadway, or has them taped for public television. Over the years, the Long Wharf has achieved a reputation for presenting the U.S. premieres of new British plays, such as David Storey's *The Changing Room;* Peter Nichols's *Forget-Me-Not Lane* and *The National Health;* David Rudkin's *Afore Night Come;* and James Saunders's *Bodies.* At the same time, the Long Wharf has revived plays from the recent or more distant past (*American Buffalo, The Front Page*) and has also produced new American plays.

• The American Conservatory Theatre, founded in 1965 by William Ball, is one of America's largest regional theaters, with a budget of $7,000,000 and an annual attendance of 600,000 in the company's three stages in San Francisco. Ball offers true repertory, with the emphasis on highly theatricalized versions of standard classics.

• The Actors Theatre of Louisville has achieved an international reputation, especially for its annual Festival of New American Plays. Once a year, Jon Jory, the producing director (and one of the founders of the Long Wharf), presents a dozen or more plays in an intense weekend marathon attended by critics,

The Acadia Repertory Theatre of Bangor, Maine, has its winter home at the Unitarian Church Parish House. During the summer it stages classics in Bar Harbor.

Chicago's Goodman Theatre is one of the nation's oldest regional theaters, founded in 1925. Here playwright David Mamet (left) and artistic director Gregory Mosher take a break during a Goodman rehearsal of Mamet's play Lakeboat.

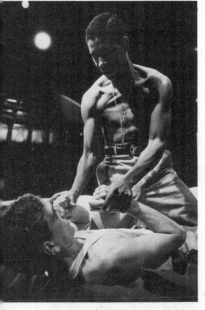

The Dallas Theater Center, founded in 1959, occupies a theater complex designed by Frank Lloyd Wright. Here is a scene from the company's 1981 production of a stage version of Lewis Carroll's Alice in Wonderland.

Members of the Theatre by the Sea in Portsmouth, N.H., are shown performing in a scene from David Rabe's drama Streamers.

producers, agents, and others. Besides *Crimes of the Heart* and *The Gin Game,* the Actors Theatre (founded in 1964) has been responsible for staging Marsha Norman's *Getting Out,* John Pielmeier's *Agnes of God,* James McLure's *Lone Star,* and Wendy Kesselman's *My Sister in This House,* all of which moved to New York. A number of talented Louisville playwrights have had work produced by the company, including Marsha Norman, the pseudonymous Jane Martin, and Ken Jenkins.

• The Trinity Square Repertory Company in Providence, founded in 1964 by its artistic director, Adrian Hall, works with a company of resident actors, some of whom have been together for more than a decade. Trinity operates on two stages in a converted movie theater in downtown Providence. Hall has stimulated his audience with work by such playwrights as Sam Shepard, Harold Pinter, and Samuel Beckett, while also finding time for entertainments such as a staged version of Charles Dickens's *A Christmas Carol.*

• The Guthrie Theater has furnished its subscribers with Shakespeare, Richard Brinsley Sheridan, Johann von Schiller, and George S. Kaufman and Moss Hart. Under its new director, Liviu Ciulei, it is moving into the area of lesser known and more difficult classics while also attempting new plays.

In addition to these seven, there are scores of other notable playhouses. Under the direction of Mark Lamos (succeeding Paul Weidner), the Hartford Stage Company has presented to its audience grand-scale performances of classics (such as Shakespeare's

Clockwise from top left: Playwright Sam Shepard; a scene from the English-language premiere of Europa; *American Repertory Theatre actors in* Lulu; Waiting for Godot *performed in a Maine bar by a traveling group of actors; a scene from the Yale Repertory Theatre's presentation of* A Lesson from Aloes; *Negro Ensemble Company actors in a scene from Charles Fuller's Pulitzer Prize-winning drama,* A Soldier's Play.

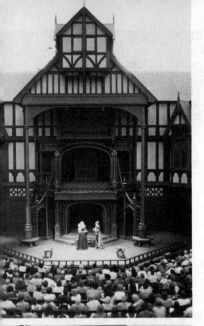

Shakespeare festivals dot North America in the summer. Top: The Oregon Shakespearean Festival in Ashland offers open-air summer performances in a replica of Shakespeare's Globe Theater. Bottom: The American Shakespeare Festival is an annual summer event in Stratford, Conn.

Cymbeline), as well as *Undiscovered Country, Kean,* and the marathon compilation *The Greeks.* At the Yale Repertory Theatre, Lloyd Richards has revived classics while also offering a stage to new American plays as well as works by the South African playwright Athol Fugard. Yale is a rare regional theater in that it has a fruitful connection with a university. The Yale School of Drama nurtures the repertory theater with actors, writers, directors, and playwrights, including, in past seasons, actors Meryl Streep and Henry Winkler, and playwrights Christopher Durang and Albert Innaurato. Gregory Mosher is guiding the Goodman Theatre in Chicago, one of the nation's oldest regional theaters (founded in 1925), into venturesome paths with new work by David Mamet, David Hare, Tennessee Williams, and others. Among the many other groups in Chicago is the enterprising Steppenwolf company, which in several seasons has earned a reputation as the Second City's most promising young theater.

Many regional theaters have begun as summer festivals and then expanded their operations. Shakespeare festivals circle North America, from the American Shakespeare Theatre in Stratford, Conn., to the Oregon Shakespearean Festival in Ashland. Canada's pride is the Stratford Festival, in Ontario. In Connecticut the Goodspeed Opera House specializes in revivals of antique musicals, with the occasional addition of a new show, such as *Annie.* The Williamstown Theatre Festival in Massachusetts welcomes distinguished actors to perform in brief engagements of world classics. The Acting Company, founded in 1972 by John Houseman and Margot Harley, is the nation's most peripatetic regional theater, touring with a rotating repertory of plays.

Almost every year new regional theaters are born. One of the more recent is the Denver Center Theatre Company, with a spectacularly modern structure facing the Rocky Mountains. At the same time, regional theaters regularly curtail their operation or change leadership. Companies are subject to economic stress and they may be second-guessed by ruling boards of directors. In the best situations, they remain independent and unencumbered. Today they are important community assets, along with dance companies, orchestras, art museums, and libraries. Fulfilling Margo Jones's prophetic vision, the regional movement has become the equivalent of an American national theater.

1983 YEARBOOK
EVENTS OF 1982

CHRONOLOGY FOR 1982

January

8 • The U.S. Department of Justice drops its antitrust suit against the American Telephone and Telegraph Co. (AT&T) in return for AT&T's agreement to divest itself of the 22 Bell System companies that provide most of the nation's local telephone service.

26 • In his State of the Union address, U.S. President Ronald Reagan proposes giving states and localities control over federal programs totaling $47 billion.

JAN. 8

February

6 • President Reagan releases a budget message for fiscal year 1983 that calls for a substantial increase in military spending and substantial cuts in such benefit programs as welfare, food stamps, Medicare and Medicaid, and subsidized housing. The projected deficit is $91.5 billion.

24 • President Reagan proposes an economic plan for the Caribbean area that includes trade and investment incentives.

28 • Union workers at the Ford Motor Co. approve a new contract that, for the first time in the history of the U.S. automobile industry, forgoes wage increases in return for profit sharing and greater job security.

March

1 • Members of the International Brotherhood of Teamsters ratify a pact freezing the basic wage levels of unionized truck drivers and warehouse workers for at least two years.

16 • Soviet President Leonid I. Brezhnev announces a freeze on the introduction of any new medium-range nuclear missiles west of the Ural Mountains.

20 • Members of the Organization of Petroleum Exporting Countries agree to cut oil production by about 700,000 bbl a day in order to bolster falling prices.

21 • Negotiators for the United Automobile Workers and General Motors Corp. reach agreement on a new contract under which workers are to give up annual raises and defer cost-of-living increases.

23 • Dissident army officers overthrow the government of Guatemala, denouncing

APRIL 2

the March 7 presidential election as fraudulent.

28 ● El Salvador's ruling Christian Democrats receive 41 percent of the vote and five right-wing parties 59 percent in elections boycotted by the country's left-wing insurgents.

30 ● The third and longest test flight of the space shuttle *Columbia* lands in the New Mexico desert after an eight-day mission.

April

2 ● Argentine troops seize the British-held Falkland Islands and the South Georgia and South Sandwich Islands in the South Atlantic.

17 ● Queen Elizabeth II formally transfers the power to amend Canada's constitution from Great Britain to Canada.

21 ● The U.S. Department of Commerce announces that the gross national product fell at an annual rate of 3.9 percent during the first quarter of 1982; the figure is later revised to 5.1 percent.

23 ● The U.S. Bureau of Labor Statistics reports that consumer prices declined in March for the first monthly decline in almost 17 years; consumer prices rose in the first quarter of 1982 by only 1 percent annually, the lowest quarterly rate since 1965.

25 ● Israel completes its withdrawal from the Sinai Peninsula, as provided by its peace treaty with Egypt.

May

9 ● President Reagan proposes a reduction of one third in the U.S. and Soviet arsenals of nuclear missile warheads.

51

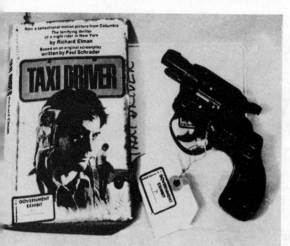

JUNE 21

24 • Iranian forces recapture the port city of Khorramshahr, virtually regaining all territory lost to Iraq in 1980.

30 • Spain becomes the 16th member of the North Atlantic Treaty Organization and the first new member since 1955.

June

2 • Pope John Paul II ends a six-day visit to Great Britain, the first ever by a Roman Catholic pontiff.

6 • Israeli forces invade Lebanon in an attack aimed at destroying the military bases of the Palestine Liberation Organization.

11 • President Reagan concludes a ten-day visit to Western Europe, his first overseas tour as President of the United States.

14 • Great Britain reestablishes its control over the Falkland Islands as almost 12,000 Argentine soldiers surrender.

18 • President Reagan widens an earlier ban on U.S. sales of oil and natural gas equipment to the Soviet Union by extending it to foreign subsidiaries and licensees of U.S. companies.

21 • A federal jury finds John W. Hinckley, Jr., not guilty by reason of insanity on all charges of shooting President Reagan and three other persons in 1981.

23 • Congress passes legislation extending for 25 years the Voting Rights Act of 1965, credited with barring discrimination against millions of blacks and Hispanics.

• Congress approves a budget resolution for fiscal year 1983 that calls for $20 billion in new taxes and $6 billion in spending cuts for such benefit programs as food stamps and Medicare and Medicaid, with a deficit of more than $100 billion.

25 • Alexander M. Haig, Jr., resigns as U.S. secretary of state; George P. Shultz, a former official in the administration of Richard M. Nixon, is appointed to replace him.

29 • The U.S. and U.S.S.R. begin talks in Geneva on reduction of strategic arms.

July

4 • The space shuttle *Columbia* successfully completes its fourth and final test flight in earth orbit.

14 • Iran takes its war against Iraq into the latter's territory in a drive on Basra, Iraq's second largest city.

21 • The Department of Commerce reports that the gross national product rose in the second quarter of 1982 at an annual rate of 1.7 percent after adjustment for inflation; the rate is later revised to 2.1 percent.

August

17 • The U.S. and China make public a communiqué whereby China pledges to seek reunification with Taiwan by peaceful means and the U.S. promises not to exceed current levels of arms sales to Taiwan and to reduce them gradually.

19 • Congress approves a three-year tax bill requested by President Reagan raising $98.3 billion in new federal revenues.

• Israel approves a plan to end its ten-week siege of west Beirut as agreement is reached on the withdrawal of up to 15,000 Palestinian and Syrian fighters from the Lebanese capital.

September

1 • The withdrawal of Palestinian fighters from west Beirut is completed, with the departure of about 12,000 from Lebanon.

• President Reagan endorses "full autonomy" under some form of Jordanian supervision for Palestinians living under Israeli occupation.

10 • Congress overrides President Reagan's veto of a $14.1 billion supplemental appropriations bill, handing him his first defeat on a major fiscal measure.

14 • President-elect Bashir Gemayel of Lebanon is killed by a bomb explosion in Beirut; the following day, Israeli forces enter west Beirut.

22 • Congress moves to end a four-day railroad strike by directing locomotive engineers to accept a new contract and return to work.

29 • U.S. Marines return to Beirut as part of the multinational force charged with restoring Lebanese governmental authority following a massacre of Palestinian civilians.

October

1 • West Germany's *Bundestag* (lower house of parliament) ousts Chancellor Helmut Schmidt and installs in his place Helmut Kohl, leader of the Christian Democratic Union.

8 • The U.S. Department of Labor reports that the national unemployment rate reached 10.1 percent in September, the highest monthly rate since 1940.

20 • The Department of Commerce reports that the U.S. economy expanded at an annual rate of 0.8 percent in the third quarter of 1982; the figure is later revised to zero growth.

28 • Spain's Socialist Workers' Party wins a landslide victory in parliamentary elections.

November

2 • Democrats gain 26 House of Representatives seats in U.S. congressional elections; Democrats also make a net gain of 7 governorships from Republicans.

SEPT. 22

NOV. 3

3 • The Dow Jones industrial average on the New York Stock Exchange closes at 1065.49, its highest closing level ever.

10 • Leonid Ilyich Brezhnev, president of the U.S.S.R. and general secretary of its Communist Party, dies at the age of 75. Two days later Yuri V. Andropov is chosen to succeed him as party chief.

13 • President Reagan announces that he is lifting sanctions earlier imposed against participation in the Soviet natural gas pipeline to Western Europe.

16 • The U.S. space shuttle *Columbia* successfully completes its first operational mission after deploying two communications satellites for the project's first paying customers.

December

2 • An artificial heart is implanted in a human patient in Salt Lake City, the first human to receive one as a permanent life-support aid rather than as a "bridge" to a heart transplant.

3 • The Department of Labor reports that the U.S. unemployment rate reached 10.8 percent of the labor force in November.

21 • Soviet Communist Party leader Yuri V. Andropov proposes reducing his country's medium-range nuclear missiles in Europe from more than 600 to about 162 if the U.S. and its allies abandon plans to deploy 572 new medium-range missiles.

23 • The 97th Congress comes to an end after approving, in its postelection session, a $379 billion stopgap money bill, a 5¢-per-gallon gasoline tax, and a system for burying radioactive nuclear wastes.

DEC. 2

A

ACCIDENTS AND DISASTERS. The following were among the notable accidents and disasters of 1982:

Jan. 3-6, Northern California: Mud slides following heavy rains kill at least 36 people and cause an estimated $111,000,000 in property damage.

Jan. 13, Washington, D.C.: An Air Florida jetliner taking off from National Airport hits the crowded 14th Street bridge and crashes into the Potomac River, causing the deaths of 74 people aboard the plane and 4 in vehicles on the bridge.

Jan. 23, Peru: At least 600 people are believed buried under mud and debris in Uchiza and 16 other towns and nearby farmlands after the area is flooded by the overflowing Chontaycu River.

• Soviet Union: About 150 people are unofficially reported killed in the crash of an Aeroflot jetliner as it attempts to land at the Siberian city of Krasnoyarsk.

Jan. 26, Algeria: At least 120 people are killed and more than 150 injured in the derailment of a passenger train on the Algiers–Oran line.

Feb. 6, South Korea: A military transport plane crashes on the island of Cheju, killing all 53 aboard.

Feb. 8, Japan: Fire in the top two floors of the ten-story luxury Hotel New Japan in Tokyo kills at least 30 people and injures 60.

Feb. 15, North Atlantic: All 84 men aboard the offshore oil drilling rig *Ocean Ranger* are lost when the rig sinks in a storm about 165 mi. east of Newfoundland.

Feb. 16, North Atlantic: More than 30 seamen are presumed drowned when the Soviet freighter *Mekhanik Tarasov* sinks in a storm off Newfoundland.

March 19, Illinois: All 27 aboard a National Guard jet tanker die in a crash 50 mi. northwest of Chicago.

March 29–April 7, Mexico: The eruption of El Chichón volcano causes what are reported to be about 100 deaths and much destruction in southern mountain communities; *see also* EARTH SCIENCES.

April 1-7, United States: At least 64 people die and hundreds are reported injured as heavy storms move across the country from California through the Rocky Mountains, the Southwest and Midwest, and into the Northeast, producing winds, tornadoes, hail, snow, and rain.

April 11, Burma: More than 160 people drown when a ferry hits a sandbar and capsizes in the Irrawaddy River near Rangoon; another ferry capsized on March 28, drowning nearly 130.

The tail section of an Air Florida Boeing 737 jet is lifted from the icy waters of the Potomac River at Washington, D.C., following the Jan. 13 crash that took 78 lives. Four were motorists killed when the airplane smashed into a bridge before plunging into the river.

Dazed survivors leave the site of a crash on Sept. 13 following the failure of a chartered DC-10 jet to clear the runway on takeoff from Málaga, Spain. Fifty of the 393 people on board were reported killed, most of them Americans who had been vacationing in Spain.

April 25, Italy: At least 34 people are killed and 60 injured by an explosion and fire during an antiques exhibit in a 15th-century building in Todi.

April 26, China: All 112 people aboard are killed in the crash of a Chinese jetliner 28 mi. southwest of its planned landing at Guilin.

May 12, China: Torrential rains and floods kill at least 430 people, destroy 46,000 houses and 40 bridges, and inundate 286,000 acres of farmland in Kwangtung (Guangdong) province.

• Yugoslavia: Gas explosions kill 39 miners in a coal mine in Zenica.

June 4, India: A hurricane kills about 200 people and leaves some 200,000 homeless on the Orissa coast.

June 8, Brazil: All 137 people aboard a Brazilian airliner are killed when the plane crashes in rain and fog in the Pocatuba Mountains 30 mi. south of Fortaleza.

June 24–29, Nicaragua and Honduras: At least 226 people are killed and 80,000 made homeless by tropical storm Aleta.

July 6, Soviet Union: An estimated 90 people are killed in an Aeroflot jetliner that crashes shortly after takeoff near Moscow.

July 9, Louisiana: All 145 people aboard a Boeing 727 jetliner and 8 people on the ground are killed when the plane, after takeoff from New Orleans International Airport during a rainstorm, crashes in nearby Kenner.

July 11, Mexico: At least 120 people are killed and 115 injured when the train known as *La Bala* ("the Bullet") runs off the track and crashes into a mountain ravine near Tepic.

July 23, Japan: At least 307 people are killed by monsoon rains, floods, and mud slides on the island of Kyushu.

July 31, France: The collision of three buses and seven automobiles on a rainswept road near Beaune in the Burgundy region kills 44 camp-bound children in one of the buses and 9 adults in that bus and the cars.

Sept. 4, California: Twenty-four people are killed and 38 injured by a fire in a downtown Los Angeles apartment house.

Sept. 11, West Germany: All 46 people aboard a U.S. Army helicopter, including a 38-member international parachuting team, are killed in a crash in Mannheim during an air show.

Sept. 12, Switzerland: Thirty-nine persons are killed when a locomotive strikes a bus at a railroad crossing about 12 mi. south of Zürich.

Sept. 13, Spain: A Spanish jetliner crashes on takeoff at Málaga, killing 50 persons.

Sept. 17–21, Central America: Five days of torrential rains set off floods and mud slides that kill at least 700 in El Salvador and 615 in Guatemala. El Salvador's crop loss is estimated at about $200,000,000.

Oct. 20, Soviet Union: More than 20 persons are trampled to death and dozens are injured in a crowd stampede at a soccer match in Moscow.

Nov. 8, Mississippi: Twenty-nine inmates die and 61 persons are injured in a fire at the county jail in Biloxi.

Nov. 18, Colombia: Twenty-two persons are killed and about 100 are injured as a result of a stampede of fans in a soccer stadium in Cali.

Nov. 23, Hawaii: Hurricane Iwa strikes the islands of Kauai, Niihau, and Oahu, killing a sailor and causing about $130,000,000 in property damage.

Dec. 2–9, U.S. Midwest: Torrential rains cause flooding in the Mississippi River valley that leaves 22 persons dead in Illinois, Missouri, and Arkansas. Property damage is estimated at more than $500,000,000.

Dec. 9, Nicaragua: Eighty-four persons, including 75 children, are killed in a helicopter crash 219 mi. north of Managua.

Dec. 13, North Yemen: An earthquake concentrated around Dhamar kills at least 2800 persons and leaves more than 700,000 homeless.

Dec. 19, Venezuela: Two oil and gas storage tanks explode near Caracas, killing at least 129 persons and injuring about 500.

Dec. 24, China: Twenty-three persons, including 3 American citizens, are killed in a fire aboard a Chinese airliner in Canton.

L.A.S.

ADVERTISING. As if advertising budget reductions in a recessionary environment did not present enough problems, the advertising industry was rocked by several unsettling incidents in 1982. Early in the year, J. Walter Thompson USA Inc., the nation's second-largest advertising agency, uncovered a scandal in its television syndication division. Under a practice called syndication bartering, the division bought television programs from independent producers and then bartered them to stations in return for free advertising air time, which was later to be charged to clients by the agency. The syndication division was found to have inflated its profits by listing nonexistent air time sold. Subsequently, the executive in charge of the operation was dismissed, the division was closed down, the agency's parent company, JWT Group Inc., had to write off $30,000,000 in earnings, a disgruntled shareholder filed a $10,000,000 suit, and the Securities and Exchange Commission began a lengthy probe of the whole affair.

Another dismaying event was the tainted-Tylenol panic that caused pharmaceutical maker Johnson & Johnson briefly to cancel advertising for the nation's largest-selling pain reliever. The annual advertising budget for Tylenol products had been more than $40,000,000. Many advertising executives doubted that the brand could fully return to favor with consumers in the future.

The television networks suffered an even more serious loss of business—perhaps $100,000,000 worth—in revenue from television commercials because of the autumn strike by professional football players. Cancellation of many National Football League televised contests also seemed likely to complicate the outcome of the three networks' race for supremacy in the ratings, since carefully hoarded movies and special programs had to be substituted.

Media. Going into the fall season, the networks had sold a record $1.7 billion worth of commercial time. Moreover, a potential threat to their stranglehold on the advertisers' dollars seemed to be weakening. CBS Cable, a $30,000,000 venture that had at-

E.T.—the Extra-Terrestrial, *the smash motion picture hit of 1982, also proved highly profitable for Hershey Foods Corp. In the film the extraterrestrial is lured out of hiding by a trail of Reese's Pieces, a Hershey candy product. Sales of the chocolate-covered peanut butter candies soared after the release of the movie.*

tracted support for its artistic programming from Kraft Inc. and other advertisers, went out of business. Its demise was called the beginning of a "shakeout" that would see other cable television services fail for lack of advertiser interest. One new rival, however, appeared on the print media scene in the fall when the Gannett Co. began to put out the initial copies of what was to become a national newspaper, *USA Today*. Among the advertisers in *USA Today*, which was initially distributed in Washington, Baltimore, and a few other cities, were Philip Morris, Oldsmobile, Kellogg, and Xerox.

Growth. As the sluggish economy affected spending late in the year, McCann Erickson Inc. executive Robert Coen lowered his earlier forecasts of 1982 advertising growth. He predicted an increase of 10.4 percent, to total expenditures of $68 billion, over 1981's $61.3 billion. Of the major media, network television would get the largest share, $6.2 billion.

Litigation. Three unusual court cases involved advertising. Operators of two fast-food chains, McDonald's Corp. and Wendy's International Inc., went to court after Burger King began running television commercials of a "taste test" that claimed consumers prefer Burger King's Whopper to a Big Mac or Wendy's single hamburger. Burger King agreed Oct. 29 to halt the campaign. Budget Rent A Car Corp. filed a $10,000,000 suit against Hertz Corp., charging that Hertz's actions had unfairly forced Budget to withdraw an advertising campaign comparing prices. The country's largest advertiser, Procter & Gamble Co., sued seven individuals who, it claimed, were responsible for circulating "false and malicious" rumors that tied Procter & Gamble products and commercials to a belief in Satanism.

Account Changes. Batten, Barton, Durstine & Osborn Inc., which handled Chrysler Corp.'s Dodge car and truck account for 38 years before losing it to Kenyon & Eckhart Inc. in 1979, welcomed the prodigal client home. At more than $100,000,000 in billings, Dodge was the largest account ever to come to the agency. In other changes, Continental Airlines moved its $16,000,000 account from Wells, Rich, Greene/West to a small Los Angeles agency, Keye, Donna, Pearlstein, and Dr. Pepper Co. moved its $8,000,000 Canada Dry account from Grey Advertising Inc. to Young & Rubicam Inc.   D.H.D.

AFGHANISTAN. For President Babrak Karmal, the Soviet-installed leader of Afghanistan, and his Moscow backers, 1982 was a difficult year. Infighting weakened the ruling Communist People's Democratic Party (PDP). Despite the presence of Soviet troops, Muslim guerrillas controlled most of the countryside and some important towns. The economy was scarcely functioning, and few foreign nations outside the Soviet bloc had any dealings with the Afghan regime.

Politics. The Afghan government claimed the loyalty of almost no one. There was continuing hostility between two wings of the PDP, Karmal's Parcham (Banner) faction and the Khalq (Masses) faction. Both groups carried out political assassinations, and diplomats stationed in Kabul reported that Khalq members often made common cause with the guerrillas.

In an effort to strengthen his control of the party, Karmal instituted a review of membership cards in January, in order to evaluate the records of party members and to purge those of dubious loyalty. Despite this action, however, the Khalq faction remained strong.

On March 14–15 the PDP held its first national conference since seizing power in 1978. Under strict security 841 delegates met at a Kabul school, where Karmal reiterated that cooperation with Moscow was the cornerstone of his policy. In an effort to gain public support, he proposed, and the PDP approved, a program that promised to respect Afghan cultural and religious traditions, permit private enterprise, and broaden a literacy campaign.

The Fighting. Muslim guerrilla activity remained widespread, despite the efforts of 100,000 Soviet troops and the 30,000-man Afghan army. During February and March official Afghan news sources admitted that guerrillas were active in 22 of the 28 provinces. Even Kabul was the scene of rebel attacks. In early March Soviet spokesmen reported a bomb explosion at the Ministry of Education. Guerrilla sabotage outside the capital caused a widespread power failure later that month.

Some of the year's fiercest fighting occurred in the 100-mi.-long Panjshir Valley, about 50 mi. north of Kabul, beginning in May. Major Soviet helicopter and jet strikes on this rebel stronghold were coordinated with 10,000 Soviet and Afghan ground troops. After a month of bitter fighting, the guerrillas withdrew. But by mid-August there were reports of renewed fighting and some guerrilla gains. As many as 300 to 400 Soviets and 500 to 800 Afghans may have died in late October or early November when a fuel tanker exploded as a convoy was moving through a tunnel 65 mi. north of Kabul.

In testimony before the U.S. Senate Foreign Relations Committee on March 8, Deputy Secretary of State Walter J. Stoessel, Jr., declared that, according to information in U.S. government hands, the Soviets were using chemical warfare in Afghanistan, in violation of a Geneva Convention. He said that more than 3000 deaths between the summers of 1979 and 1981 were attributable to such substances as "nerve agents, phosgene oxime and perhaps mycotoxins, mustard, lewisite and toxic smoke."

Earlier in the year, it was reported, Soviet bombardment and artillery fire killed hundreds of civilians in Kandahar, Afghanistan's second largest city and a center of resistance, in reprisal for the death of several Russians killed by rebels. Following guerrilla action in Herat, Soviet retaliation resulted in the forcible conscription of hundreds into the Afghan army.

Massive desertions by nearly two thirds of its strength had long weakened and demoralized the formerly 80,000-strong Afghan army. Such measures as higher pay, a lower entry age, and harsh punishment for evading military service failed to rebuild its ranks. The government, therefore, frequently resorted to seizing boys and middle-aged men in their homes during night curfew hours and sending them to army camps.

Increasing Soviet frustration with the war reportedly also led to the establishment of a secret police force, directed by Soviet and East German experts. In an effort to reduce the possibility of ambush, Soviet and Afghan

Rebels continued to defy the Soviet-installed government of Afghanistan, despite the presence of some 100,000 Soviet troops. Here insurgents repair old weapons and assemble new ones furnished by supporters abroad.

troops cleared broad tracts beside major highways. And as part of a long-term program, they improved existing airfields and constructed new ones.

The Economy. With more than 2,000,000 Afghan refugees, most of them farmers, camped in neighboring Pakistan, and because of the widespread civil war, the economy was at a virtual standstill. Despite heavy economic aid from the Soviet Union, Afghanistan's chief trade partner, shortages of basic commodities persisted.

Diplomacy. Non-Communist nations continued to demand Soviet withdrawal from Afghanistan, so that a popularly supported administration could be established. The U.S.S.R., however, indicated that it would permit no change in what it termed Kabul's "progressive, socialist" government. As part of intensified efforts to find a diplomatic solution, United Nations representative Diego Cordovez was taking soundings among members of the international community.

Afghanistan's diplomatic contact outside the Soviet bloc remained limited. President Karmal visited East Berlin in May and stopped in the U.S.S.R. for one month on his way home. In an August interview with the Press Trust of India, he blamed "U.S. imperialism" for "provoking a crisis in this region."

See STATISTICS OF THE WORLD.   F.W.

Africa

The African countries were deeply split in 1982 by territorial disputes and political rivalries. In addition, the worldwide economic recession threatened to deepen the continent's poverty.

The war in the Western Sahara and the policies of Libya's Col. Muammar el-Qaddafi threatened in 1982 to divide irrevocably Africa's main political and economic coordinating body, the Organization of African Unity (OAU). Founded in 1963, the OAU was intended to serve as an annual forum where the continent's leaders could meet to review and coordinate matters of common concern. By 1982, 50 states—all the continent's nations except South Africa—had become members. In addition to the summit conferences, the organization had also sponsored annual meetings of chief ministers and maintained standing committees on such matters as labor, tariffs, and trade. As a way of fostering and maintaining a sense of equality among the members, each annual meeting of OAU heads of state, held in summer, had been chaired by the leader of that year's scheduled host nation. The tradition worked better in theory than in practice, however, as sometimes the very question of who would, or should, act as host became a cause of dispute and discord.

Through the years the OAU succeeded in mediating many of the continent's territorial disputes and political rivalries. Some conflicts, however, defied a peaceful, negotiated solution. One such case certainly was the struggle between Morocco and the Polisario Front, a guerrilla movement, for control of the Western Sahara. After Spain abandoned the territory in 1976, Morocco laid claim to it and took control of its main towns and resources. In doing so, Morocco won the support of Africa's conservative governments and the United States, which provided the country with sizable amounts of military equipment. The Polisario sought independence for the Western Sahara; the guerrillas immediately found allies in Morocco's radi-

cal neighbors, Algeria and Libya, which supplied them with money, arms, and military bases. As fighting in the Western Sahara reached a bloody stalemate, the Polisario established its own government, the Saharan Arab Democratic Republic (SADR), and moved to gain international recognition.

The OAU proved unable to bring about a ceasefire or a negotiated solution. In 1980 it agreed to admit the Polisario government as a member. Morocco and its conservative allies threatened to withdraw from the organization if the SADR were seated; this threat effectively kept the Polisario out. But in February, 1982, at a meeting of OAU foreign ministers, the organization's general secretary took the initiative of seating the Polisario. Morocco and its allies, arguing that a two-thirds majority was required for such a move, walked out of the meeting. Subsequent consultative meetings were unable to resolve the issue, as host governments alternately blocked and supported Polisario delegations.

The diplomatic dispute promised little hope of solution as the annual meeting of OAU heads of state, scheduled for August, neared. If anything, the situation promised to become worse, since the scheduled chairman for the meeting, to be held in Tripoli, was Qaddafi. A supporter of radical groups, who did not hesitate, it seemed, to intervene in other countries' affairs, Qaddafi was regarded by many African leaders as unsuited to assume the chairmanship of the OAU. At the August meeting, therefore, only 28 delegations showed up, far short of the 34 states required for a quorum. With the OAU thus apparently in disarray, leaders of French-speaking African states met in October in Zaire to find a possible solution. A meeting in November in Tripoli was suggested; after

Pope John Paul II paid a visit to four West African countries in February. A crowd in Onitsha, Nigeria, with priests in the front ranks, awaits the pope's appearance at an open-air mass.

the Polisario agreed in late October to withdraw temporarily from the OAU, such a meeting seemed feasible. But Morocco insisted that the SADR withdraw permanently from the OAU, and on Nov. 5 Somalia, declaring that Qaddafi was an "international terrorist," announced that it would not attend the OAU meeting. A final attempt to convene the meeting collapsed on Nov. 25 after Libya refused to admit the delegation from Chad.

Other Strife and Instability. Africa continued in 1982 to be the scene of political dissension, often taking a violent turn, and military conflict. The civil war in Chad reached at least a temporary conclusion in June, when the government of President Goukouni Oueddei was overthrown by forces led by Hissène Habré. Habré quickly won diplomatic recognition from most African states, while Oueddei went into exile. Fighting in Ethiopia continued throughout the year, with the central government pushing rebels in its Eritrean province into outlying areas. In the Ogaden region the government succeeded in holding the guerrillas in check, and in late June the Ethiopians, along with a movement opposed to Somalia's President Muhammad

Siad Barre, launched an invasion of Somalia. Somalia, however, was able to contain the attack with U.S. arms. In another trouble spot, South-West Africa (Namibia), low-level fighting continued between the guerrilla forces of the South-West Africa People's Organization and South Africa for control of the territory. Diplomatic efforts engaged in by the U.S. to end South African rule appeared once more to be stalemated.

In Angola and Mozambique resistance to central authority continued, with South Africa reportedly providing arms and support for the anti-Marxist rebels in those black African countries. Similarly, in Uganda the central government was encountering opposition to its rule from disaffected elements. In Zimbabwe the escalating conflict between Prime Minister Robert G. Mugabe and his political rival Joshua Nkomo threatened to plunge the country into civil war. In the Sudan regional strife threatened to break out once more as the central government put forward development plans that to southern leaders appeared to favor the north.

Further evidence of political instability in much of Africa were coup attempts in Mauritania, Niger, and Nigeria in February; in the

Central African Republic and Guinea-Bissau in March; in Kenya and the Seychelles in August; and in Ghana in November. The government of Upper Volta was toppled on Nov. 7 by a military coup.

Economic problems increased throughout the continent in 1982. The worldwide economic recession dramatically reduced the demand for, and hence the price of, Africa's primary products, such as coffee, copper, and oil. At the same time, as a result of the renewed strength of the U.S. dollar, gasoline, machinery, and other imported items consumed a higher proportion of available foreign exchange. So did debt-service payments. In 1982 many African states found themselves unable to maintain scheduled foreign-debt repayments and under severe pressure from the International Monetary Fund and the world banking community to reduce imports and expenditures. These measures, in turn, threatened to deepen the continent's poverty and increase political instability.

Peaceful Transitions. The confederation of Senegambia, uniting Senegal and The Gambia, went into effect on Feb. 1. Abdou Diouf of Senegal was named president of the confederation and Dawda K. Jawara of The Gambia vice-president. In elections held in The Gambia in May, Jawara was reelected his country's president. Also in May, Sékou Touré was reelected president of Guinea for a seven-year term. Touré, president since 1958, was Africa's longest-serving chief executive. Ahmadou Ahidjo, the president of Cameroon, stepped down in November after serving since 1960. He was succeeded by Paul Biya, the prime minister. President Didier Ratsiraka of Madagascar was reelected in November.

In Algeria in March, in the second general elections since independence in 1962, more than 73 percent of the country's eligible voters went to the polls to elect a new National People's Assembly. In Djibouti elections for the legislative assembly were held in May. Voters in Mauritius swept out the ruling Labor Party in June, with Aneerood Jugnauth becoming prime minister. The citizens of Equatorial Guinea voted on a new constitution in a referendum held on Aug. 15. The constitution, one of the most democratic in Africa, appeared to pave the way for a return to civilian rule. Egypt and the Sudan agreed in mid-October to coordinate their political and economic policies through a joint parliament consisting of 60 representatives; the parliament was scheduled to convene twice a year.

See also individual articles on many of the countries mentioned. J.T.S.

AGRICULTURE. Agriculture in the United States in 1982 produced record or near-record crops, but low prices helped place the farm community near the top of the economic sick list.

Farmers saw their incomes drop. This decline hit hard at related industries supplying machinery and services. International Harvester Co., a major farm equipment manufacturer, was pushed to the brink of bankruptcy in 1982. The administration of U.S. President Ronald Reagan, in an attempt to bolster the sagging farm economy, retreated from its free-market policies and implemented programs designed to reduce farm production and prop up prices. In fiscal year 1982 the federal government spent $11.9 billion to aid farmers, more than twice as much as in fiscal 1981.

In January Agriculture Secretary John Block announced a set-aside program extending loans to farmers above the minimum amount required by the 1981 farm bill. In return, farmers would reduce their maximum planting by 10 percent for corn, barley, oats, and sorghum, and by 15 percent for cotton, wheat, and rice. However, only 40 percent of the nation's wheat farmers and 20 percent of the corn farmers signed on.

In August Block said that wheat farmers would have to idle 20 percent of their normal planting in 1983 in order to remain eligible for government aid programs. Corn farmers were told in September that they would receive direct payments for idling 10 percent of their acreage in 1983 but would have to idle an additional 10 percent without payment in order to remain eligible for commodity support programs.

The big winners in the oversupply situation were consumers. Retail food prices climbed at a pace near the overall rate of inflation. The Agriculture Department estimated in September that food prices would rise about 5 percent for 1982, compared with 7.9 percent in 1981.

U.S. Crop Production. The U.S. produced record wheat, corn, and soybean crops. Corn, the key grain used for animal feeding, reached about 8.3 billion bu. The soybean crop climbed 15 percent to more than 2.3 bil-

lion bu. The wheat crop was expected to reach 2.8 billion bu.

Farmers sold about $142 billion worth of crops and livestock during the year. But net farm income fell to $19 billion from $25 billion in 1981.

Livestock. Cattle raisers produced about 22 billion lb. of beef in 1982, the same as in 1981. Pork production fell to 14 billion lb. from the 15.7 billion lb. produced in 1981. Farm prices for both cattle and hogs increased during the year, helping to offset lower grain prices. Broiler chicken production reached 12.1 billion lb., up nearly 1 billion lb. over 1981. Wholesale prices declined slightly.

In the third quarter of 1982, cattlemen were receiving an average of $64.50 per hundredweight for choice steers, a slight increase over 1981. Hog prices were much stronger. Third-quarter prices averaged $62

A bumper grain harvest, including record yields of wheat, corn, and soybeans, drove farm prices and earnings down in 1982. So much grain, some of it from previous years, lay unsold in silos and elevators that more grain began piling up outside.

More farmers were reported to be selling food directly to the public in 1982. Here farmers from several states retail their crops in New York City's Union Square.

per hundredweight, compared with 1981 average prices of $44.45 per hundredweight.

Exports. The U.S. continued to be the world's leading food exporter in 1982. But large crop yields around the world, coupled with a strong U.S. dollar, caused a drop in the value of U.S. farm exports to about $40.5 billion. In 1981 the export value of agricultural products had reached $43.5 billion. Despite the drop in value, export tonnage actually increased to 165,000,000 tons.

The Medfly. In September federal and California officials declared victory in the fight against the Mediterranean fruit fly, a dangerous plant pest that threatened some $5.5 billion worth of California crops. The eradication effort involved thousands of people and required an expenditure of $96,000,000. At the height of the infestation in 1981, about 1400 sq.mi. in seven California counties were being sprayed weekly, and about 4000 sq.mi. were under quarantine regulations. Aerial spraying with the pesticide malathion was the major control method.

The Land. In 1982 farmland values dropped for the first time in several decades. The decline averaged 1 percent to $788 an acre,

compared with $795 an acre in 1981. The generally poor state of the farm economy, high interest rates, and negative conditions in the overall economy were blamed for the land value decline.

For a number of years, the value of farm acreage had been increasing at rates higher than the inflation rates. In 1979 acreage increased in value by 16 percent; similar increases had occurred throughout the 1970's.

The number of farms declined slightly in 1982 to 2,400,000, but the accuracy of these figures was debatable. Bruce Chapman, director of the U.S. Census Bureau, noted an increase in the number of small farms, particularly in the northeastern U.S. In most instances the operators of these farms relied on nonfarm jobs for a substantial part of their income and supplemented that income through the sale of farm commodities.

Studies showed that more farmers were bypassing traditional marketing channels and selling food directly to the public through farmers' markets, roadside stalls, or pick-your-own operations. More urban areas were making direct-sale facilities available for farmers.

Both public and private groups in 1982 began to devote more time to developing ways of preserving the nation's farmlands. These efforts came as the declining farm economy and falling land prices put new pressure on farmers to sell out to developers. The Farmers Home Administration and other agencies holding farm mortgages and extending credit to farmers reported a considerable increase in repayment delinquencies and loan foreclosures.

Sugar and Tobacco. On May 4 President Reagan approved the imposition of quotas on sugar imports for the first time since 1974 in order to prop up domestic prices. Total sugar imports to the U.S. were limited to 6,900,000 short tons for any fiscal year.

Legislation approved by Congress on July 15 obligated tobacco growers participating in the price-support program to contribute to a fund that would make payments when the price of tobacco fell below the support level. The federal government would pay only for administrative costs. The legislation also contained a provision requiring a few owners of tobacco allotments who do not actually grow the crop to give up their allotments rather than lease them to others.

World Food Production. The Soviet Union faced its fourth poor grain harvest in a row. Forecasts placed the 1982 harvest at 180,000,-000 metric tons for wheat and feed grains combined. Bad weather, along with structural difficulties in the Soviet agricultural system, accounted for the dim harvest prospects. The Soviets increased their imports of grain in order to keep up livestock, meat, and dairy production. On Oct. 13 Canada reported a record grain sale to Moscow.

China launched a program to increase the availability of food in urban areas. Wheat food products, primarily bread loaves, were to be made more available as a convenience to working people. A U.S. wheat group built a model bakery in Peking and an instant noodle plant in Shanghai.

The world's total production of grains fell slightly below 1981's record production. The total 1982 production was estimated at 1.6 trillion metric tons, down 1 percent. World wheat production was put at 448,000,000 metric tons, a small decline. World coarse grains, including corn, set a record, estimated at 782,000,000 metric tons, a 1 percent increase over 1981.

World rice production was expected to reach 404,000,000 metric tons, down 2 percent from the 1981 record crop. Dry weather reduced rice crops in India, South Korea, and Indonesia. World soybean production reached a record 99,000,000 metric tons, a 13 percent increase over 1981. Almost all the increase was attributed to the record crop in the U.S.

Cotton production reached 66,800,000 bales, down 4,400,000 bales from the 1981 crop. China, with a 14,500,000-bale crop in view, was expected to displace the U.S. as the world's leading cotton producer. Cotton production declined in the U.S., Mexico, Egypt, and Turkey. The Soviet Union stepped up cotton production with a crop of 13,800,-000 bales.   L.W.W.

ALABAMA. See STATISTICS OF THE WORLD.
ALASKA. See STATISTICS OF THE WORLD.

ALBANIA. On Jan. 14, 1982, Albania's parliament, acting on the recommendation of Enver Hoxha, the country's longtime dictator and Communist Party chief, chose Adil Çarçani, 60, as prime minister. Çarçani, a technocrat and economist, had been first deputy prime minister since 1974. He succeeded Mehmet Shehu, who died in December, 1981. The government announced that Shehu had committed suicide, and he was not accorded a state funeral. Rumors circulated abroad that Shehu had been killed in a shoot-out after a dispute with Hoxha over policy; according to these rumors, Shehu favored increased trade with the West.

Further indications of internal trouble came in late September, when the government declared that it had "liquidated" a group of armed émigrés who had landed on the Adriatic coast. No details were given, but foreign observers speculated that a power struggle might be under way in the wake of Shehu's mysterious death. In November Hoxha said that Shehu had been an agent for foreign powers, and a sweeping purge removed President Haxhi Lleshi and ten cabinet ministers from office.

Albania in 1982 continued to accuse Yugoslavia of mistreating ethnic Albanians in the southern Yugoslav province of Kosovo. Yugoslavia, in turn, repeated its charge that Albania was interfering in its affairs. Despite the dispute, however, the two nations reached new accords on commerce and agreed to begin building a railroad that would link the Albanian town of Shkodër with Yugoslavia's Titograd.

See STATISTICS OF THE WORLD. See also YUGOSLAVIA.   F.W.

ALBERTA. See STATISTICS OF THE WORLD.
ALGERIA. In 1982, as Algeria celebrated the 20th anniversary of its independence from France, President Chadli Benjedid remained in firm control of the country.

In December, 1981, the central committee of the National Liberation Front (FLN), the country's sole legal party, removed four of its members, among them Abdelaziz Bouteflika, a former rival of Chadli. A month later, in January, 1982, the government announced a cabinet reshuffle. Both moves were intended to strengthen Chadli's hand as he sought to guide Algeria away from a rigidly socialist program at home.

In March, for only the second time since 1962, elections were held for the 281-seat National People's Assembly. Nearly 73 percent of Algeria's eligible voters went to the polls to choose from a list of 843 candidates approved by the FLN. Only 68 of the 136 members seeking reelection were successful.

Algeria's economy suffered in 1982 because of a decline in foreign demand for oil and the resulting decline in world oil prices. A payments deficit of about $1 billion for 1982 was expected. Inflation continued to rise steeply, and a housing shortage remained the most pressing urban problem. A major economic gain, however, considering weak overseas energy demand, was the announcement by France on Feb. 3 that it would increase its purchases of Algerian natural gas from the current annual level of 140 billion cu.ft. to about 321 billion cu.ft. in 1983; the reported price would be about 5.2¢ per cubic foot, well above the 4.3¢ France paid in 1981. In return, Algeria agreed to place new orders worth about $2 billion for French industrial products.

In January, Libya's strongman, Muammar el-Qaddafi, visited Algeria to discuss a proposed merger between the two Arab countries, and in April Chadli chaired a joint ministerial meeting in Algiers intended to work out the details of such a union.

On May 3 Foreign Minister Muhammad Ben Yahia and 12 other Algerian officials were killed when their plane crashed in rugged mountains near Iran's border with Turkey and Iraq. Ben Yahia, who had played a key role in helping to win the release of the 52 American hostages in Tehran in January, 1981, had been on a secret mission to try to negotiate an end to the Iran-Iraq war. He was succeeded by Ahmed Taleb Ibrahimi.

See STATISTICS OF THE WORLD.   A.D.

AMERICAN SAMOA. *See* STATISTICS OF THE WORLD.

ANGOLA. The struggle to end colonial rule in neighboring South-West Africa (Namibia) continued to dominate Angolan affairs in 1982. At issue was the presence of some

15,000 Cuban soldiers in Angola. South Africa insisted that any negotiated settlement to end its rule over South-West Africa would have to be linked to a Cuban withdrawal from Angola. Angolan President José Eduardo dos Santos, however, rejected such linkage, contending that the Cubans were needed to help defend Angola against South African incursions and guerrilla attacks by internal dissident groups.

South Africa, for its part, continued to launch attacks on bases in Angola of the South-West Africa People's Organization (SWAPO). In March South African troops claimed to have killed about 200 SWAPO guerrillas in southwestern Angola. In April SWAPO retaliated with a raid of its own into South-West Africa, killing five South African soldiers.

Angola sought economic help from both the East and the West in 1982. In January Angola signed a long-term agreement with the Soviet Union providing for some $2 billion in aid, largely for the construction of several dams and an oil refinery. In April dos Santos held trade talks in Luanda with Portuguese President António Ramalho Eanes, the first Western head of state to visit Angola since its independence from Portugal in 1975. The government also began discussions with a consortium of Western banks, led by Chase Manhattan Corp., for a loan of about $100,000,000. The loan was needed to help offset a serious payments deficit caused by falling prices for Angola's chief exports—oil, diamonds, and coffee. In July Minister of Planning and Foreign Trade Lopo Ferreira do Nascimento unveiled an emergency economic plan that called for a radical improvement in agricultural production, which in 1981 had declined by more than 25 percent, and a curb on public spending.

Angola's economic difficulties apparently contributed to a government shake-up during the summer. Among those dismissed was Nascimento, who was once regarded as a hard-line Marxist but who lately had come to advocate closer economic links with the West.

See STATISTICS OF THE WORLD. *See also* SOUTH-WEST AFRICA.   J.T.S.

The oldest discovered fossil remains of a hominid (humanlike creature), estimated to be 4,000,000 years old, are displayed in the foreground. Fragments of a skull (left) and a thighbone (right) indicate, according to scientists, that the creature walked upright but had a brain no larger than a chimpanzee's. In the background, for comparison, are skulls of a modern human (left) and a chimpanzee.

ANTHROPOLOGY. Paleoanthropologists in 1982 reported new evidence of early human habitation in the Awash River Valley in Ethiopia, as debate over other Ethiopian fossils, especially the famous "Lucy" skeleton, continued. Newly found fossils from Pakistan raised questions about the date when humans began to diverge from apes. A reexamination of ancient tools found in Israel produced dates at least 1,000,000 years earlier than had been assumed, and new studies of African animal bones revealed evidence that they had been butchered by humans.

Filling the Pliocene Gap. The first evidence of human evolution during the Pliocene gap, the period from 10,000,000 to 4,000,000 years ago that probably spanned the transition from ape to walking hominid, was revealed by anthropologists John Desmond Clark and Tim D. White of the University of California at Berkeley. In the Awash River Valley in Ethiopia the Berkeley group found a thighbone and a frontal skull fragment, each about 4,000,000 years old. Together, these two fossils represented the earliest evidence thus far for human evolution. Experts believed that the development of the thighbone proved that the creature walked; the skull pieces indicated a brain the size of a chimpanzee's. Clark and his team planned to return to the Awash River Valley for more systematic reconnaissance.

The "Lucy" Debate. The 1974 discovery of "Lucy," a 3,500,000-year-old hominid fossil, by American anthropologist Donald C. Johanson, affiliated in 1982 with the Institute of Human Origins at Berkeley, Calif., continued to provoke debate. Johanson's view that Lucy belonged to a new species, *Australopithecus afarensis,* and constituted the earliest known walking hominid was questioned by anthropologist Randall L. Susman and anatomist Jack Stern of the State University of New York at Stony Brook. Another anthropologist, Russell Tuttle of the University of Chicago, also challenged Johanson's hypothesis after studying the Lucy bones and other fossils from the Hadar region of Ethiopia. These critics suggested that Lucy spent more time in the trees than on the ground, and had not yet fully adapted to walking upright. But C. Owen Lovejoy of Kent State University disagreed, citing Lucy's short fingers as a reason for rejecting the notion that *A. afarensis* lived in trees.

The question of early hominid terrestrial life is significant for the study of human evolution because anthropological theory states that abandonment of the trees represented a social adaptation necessary for the development of monogamy and the nuclear family. **Pakistani and Kenyan Fossils.** Analysis of 8,000,000-year-old fossils from Pakistan called into question the point at which humans and apes diverged. The skull and jawbone fragments indicated that *Ramapithecus,* usually classified as the earliest known hominid, was not related to the human family but instead represented an ancient ancestor of the orangutan. David Pilbeam of Harvard University's Peabody Museum of Archaeology and Ethnology concluded from the find that hominids diverged from apes about 7,000,000 to 9,000,000 years ago, and not as long as 14,000,000 years ago, as anthropologists had formerly believed.

Evidence uncovered in Kenya by Hidemi Ishida of Osaka University in Japan and Richard E. Leakey, director of the National Museum of Kenya, likewise filled the Pliocene gap. The jawbone fossil they found in the Samburu Hills of north-central Kenya was thought to be about 8,000,000 years old, but the date could not be confirmed without further testing. Initial reports indicated that the skull showed a mixture of humanoid and apelike characteristics.

Early Tools from Israel. Sophisticated tools from the Ubeidiya site near the Sea of Galilee were redated as being from 700,000 to between 1,900,000 and 2,600,000 years old. According to Charles A. Repenning of the U.S. Geological Survey, these tools were evidence of the existence of *Homo erectus,* the immediate ancestor of *Homo sapiens,* in the Jordan River Valley. Repenning and his colleague Oldrich Fejfar of Czechoslovakia's Geological Survey derived the new dating from the presence at the site of fossils of mammals believed to have been extinct 2,000,000 years ago, including a saber-toothed tiger. This finding was considered important because it was the first time that such early evidence for humans had been assigned to the Middle East.

New Evidence for Butchering. Glynn Isaac and Henry Bunn of the University of California at Berkeley and Richard Potts of Yale University reported that animal bones from Olduvai and Koobi Fora in East Africa bear fine nicks and grooves—evidence supporting the theory that ancient humans used a primitive type of cutlery to prepare their meat. Examined under a scanning electron microscope, these marks were distinguished from tooth marks and other impressions on the 2,500,-000-year-old fossils. Anthropologists viewed the discovery, together with previous finds of ancient stone tools, as an indication that primitive humans made choices about food and perhaps had assigned gender roles to the tasks of meat-gathering and butchering. While most anthropologists still believed that ancient humans subsisted primarily on vegetable matter, the new butchering data suggested that meat may have played a greater part in the diet at an earlier time than was previously supposed.   B.R.

ANTIGUA AND BARBUDA. *See* STATISTICS OF THE WORLD.

ARAB LEAGUE. At a 1982 summit meeting held Sept. 6–9 in Fez, Morocco, the Arab League adopted a unified Arab peace plan for the Middle East. The eight-point plan called for the creation of an independent Palestinian state "with Jerusalem as its capital" and reaffirmed the Palestine Liberation Organization (PLO) as the "sole and legitimate representative" of the Palestinian people. The program also called for the withdrawal of Israel from "all Arab territories" seized in the Six-Day War of 1967 and for the dismantling of all "settlements established by Israel" in those territories.

The West Bank and Gaza Strip, which had been under Israeli military occupation since

1967 (and which had been the subject of Palestinian autonomy talks under the Camp David agreements), would be placed under United Nations control "for a transitory period not exceeding a few months," according to the Arab League proposal. Although the document did not contain any specific reference to Israel's right to exist, it called upon the U.N. Security Council to guarantee the peace and security of "all states in the region," a clause that some Arab and Western diplomats interpreted as tacit recognition of Israel.

The Arab League plan, which was flatly rejected by Israel, took a considerably harder line on the Palestinian issue than did U.S. President Ronald Reagan's own Middle East peace initiative, announced the week before. But U.S. Secretary of State George P. Shultz said the Fez declaration signaled the possibility of a "genuine breakthrough," if Arab leaders had in fact decided to recognize Israel's right to exist. The Arab League proposal marked the first time the Arab world had agreed on a unified plan for resolving the Arab-Israeli conflict and was widely seen as a victory for such "moderate" Arab regimes as Saudi Arabia and Jordan. Only ten months earlier, a previous Arab League summit meeting at Fez had collapsed after four hours when radicals, led by Syria, rejected a remarkably similar peace plan that had been proposed by Saudi Arabia. The apparent willingness of the Arab states to reach a negotiated settlement with Israel reflected the dramatic change in the Middle East power balance as a result of the war in Lebanon, which had demonstrated Israel's overwhelming military superiority. The Arab League meeting was held only a few days after some 12,000 PLO fighters had been evacuated from Beirut for places of exile elsewhere in the Arab world.

The Arab League comprises 21 Arab states as well as the PLO. The total includes Egypt, which was suspended in 1979 for having signed a peace treaty with Israel. Libya boycotted the September summit in Fez.

See also MIDDLE EAST; PALESTINE LIBERATION ORGANIZATION; and articles on individual countries. A.D.

ARCHEOLOGY. Archeologists in 1982 salvaged a 16th-century British warship and discovered a wrecked 18th-century American freighter. Meanwhile, controversy surrounded the attempted excavation of a Caribbean shipwreck thought to be Columbus's *Pinta.* Other events were the discovery of the oldest building in North America and the announcement of a new archeological dating method.

Shipwrecks. A shipwreck found by treasure hunters in the Caribbean was tentatively identified as the *Pinta,* one of the three ships used by Christopher Columbus to sail to the New World in 1492. Even if this identification were not substantiated, the ship would still rank as one of the earliest European caravels (a type of small sailing vessel) ever found in the New World. The caravel immediately became part of a controversy centered on who would get the permit to raise it to the surface. Officials of the British-held Turks and Caicos Islands, southeast of the Bahamas, terminated a salvage contract with the treasure hunters who discovered it. The officials offered the site of the wreck for scientific exca-

In 1982 the American Museum of Natural History in New York City presented an exhibition of objects unearthed at the site of the Great Temple of the Aztecs in what is now the heart of Mexico City. The largest and most spectacular object on display was this cast of a circular carved stone, 11 ft. in diameter, excavated in 1978. The central image is the dismembered torso of Coyolxauhqui, evil sister of Huitzilopochtli, the Aztec war god.

vation to the Institute of Nautical Archaeology of Texas A & M University, an organization that not only trains nautical specialists but conducts underwater excavations worldwide. Observers reported, however, that unidentified armed divers had been seen at the wreck site, raising the possibility that the remains would be disturbed before archeologists ever reached them.

Climaxing the costliest archeological underwater salvage operation on record, the *Mary Rose,* a British man-of-war that sank off Portsmouth, England, in 1545, was brought to the surface in October. The wreck was first discovered in 1970 by Alexander McKee, a historian and an amateur diver, and it was identified as the *Mary Rose* a year later. During the next 11 years, 500 divers made some 35,000 dives into the murky waters around the sunken vessel, removing and indexing thousands of priceless Tudor artifacts. Funds for the entire 1982 salvage operation, which cost some $7,000,000, were raised by the Mary Rose Trust, whose president, Prince Charles, an accomplished diver, had inspected the vessel nearly a dozen times since 1975. Next on the agenda for this one-time pride of Henry VIII's fleet was a complex restoration process expected to take more than 20 years.

In early 1982 the remains of an 18th-century freighter turned up at a land site in New York City. Found in lower Manhattan, at 175 Water Street, the shipwreck was unique because it provided archeologists with the first opportunity to excavate scientifically an ordinary colonial American trading vessel. The site was full of colonial landfill and at first the old timbers that had been unearthed were diagnosed as discarded wood. But when the hull and bow appeared, New York City's Landmarks Preservation Commission stepped in to rescue this specimen of colonial shipbuilding. Excavations proceeded through March under nautical archeologists Sheli Smith and Warren Riess. Noting the gun ports on the hull and the evidence of warmwater shipworms in the hull's outer sheathing, the archeologists determined that the wreck had been a Caribbean merchantman.

Salvage excavations were completed at the Water Street site. Only a small 10-ft. portion of the bow was removed for preservation. The expense involved in attempting to preserve the old, waterlogged wood for museum display discouraged institutions from offering to take this piece of America's past.

Anasazi Solar Dispute. In 1979 three sandstone slabs and two spiral petroglyphs, all found on Fajada Butte in Chaco Canyon, N.Mex., were identified by artist Anna Sofaer as being part of an Anasazi Indian culture solar observatory. Her proposal that the stones were erected by humans was challenged in 1982 by Robert K. Mark and Evelyn B. Newman of the U.S. Geological Survey and by R. Gwinn Vivian of the Arizona State Museum. Writing in the Sept. 10 issue of *Science,* they maintained that the slabs were formed naturally as part of a large block that split because of a rockfall set in motion by the annual freeze-thaw cycle.

Anasazi culture experts agreed that the markers did not correspond with architectural styles in the Chaco Canyon during the 10th and 11th centuries, when the "observatory" was presumed to have been erected. Furthermore, megalithic construction was not known among these prehistoric people of the Southwest. It appeared likely that the spot actually was used for solar calendrical rituals and observation, but archeologists were certain that the Anasazi were merely taking advantage of a unique geological formation.

Oldest Building in North America. In April the National Trust for Historic Preservation announced the discovery of the oldest known building in North America, at Windy Gap, near Granby, Colo. The wattle-and-daub structure was dated by radiocarbon as being 4000 to 5000 years old; the oldest construction previously found in North America originated some 2500 years ago. Emergency excavations in August rescued the site, which was in the path of a water pipeline being dug by the Northern Colorado Water Conservancy District.

New Dating Method. Archeologists reported the development of a new technique called accelerator dating, over a thousand times

Completed in 1982, the tallest building in Miami is the 255-unit Helmsley Palace condominium adjoining Biscayne Bay. One part is stepped in order to provide terraces facing the bay.

more sensitive than standard radiocarbon dating. The new method, which requires a much smaller sample of a specimen to determine its age, may allow scientists to date artifacts that have so far not been tested because of the large pieces that would have to be destroyed in the radiocarbon dating process.

Accelerator dating involves chemically separating carbon from a small sample of an object, placing the carbon extract inside a nuclear accelerator, and bombarding it with highly charged ions. After the resulting atoms are sorted out and identified in the accelerator, the activity of the radiocarbon atoms (and therefore the estimated age of the artifact) can be determined.   B.R.

ARCHITECTURE AND CITY PLANNING.

Huge office towers continued to rise in many major U.S. cities during 1982 despite a softening of the office market. Commissioned during the office-building boom of the late 1970's, these new skyscrapers, with their unique forms and colorful facades, promised to change skylines throughout the United States, most notably in Houston, Chicago, and New York City. They also posed serious problems for many city dwellers; for example, New York's already congested midtown area would have to accommodate at least 150,000 more office workers in the 1980's.

A second building type, the art museum, also continued to proliferate. Several new structures or major expansions were under

A striking example of postmodernist architecture is the Public Service Building in Portland, Oreg., designed by architect Michael Graves and completed in 1982. The city office building aroused controversy, with one detractor comparing it to a "jukebox."

way or completed in 1982. They included Cesar Pelli's Museum of Modern Art Tower in New York City, Richard Meier's High Museum of Art addition in Atlanta, Edward Larrabee Barnes's Dallas Museum of Fine Arts, a new wing by Hardy Holzman Pfeiffer for the Virginia Museum of Fine Arts in Richmond, and an expansion designed by Henry J. Cobb of I. M. Pei & Partners for the Portland Museum of Art in Maine.

New U.S. Buildings and Commissions. In the spring I. M. Pei & Partners completed the tallest building in Houston, the Texas Commerce Tower. This five-sided glass and gray concrete structure boasts a five-story, glass-enclosed lobby that opens out to a 1-acre plaza embellished with patterned granite paving and lush landscaping.

At 75 stories high, Texas Commerce thus became the tallest structure outside Chicago and New York, but several taller ones were on the drawing board. In October, for example, Houston's Bank of the Southwest unveiled a model of its spectacular new building designed by Helmut Jahn of the Chicago

firm Murphy/Jahn. The 82-story structure, topped by a 150-ft. spire, would be 1400 ft. high, making it the world's second-tallest office building. (Chicago's Sears Tower is 1454 ft. high.) The cost was estimated at between $350,000,000 and $400,000,000. The lean granite tower would be supported by a steel brace in its center, allowing the base of the building to be nearly as slim as the rest of the tower. Located in the center of Houston's business district, the bank would face the street at a 45-degree angle, with four large entrances opening onto each of the four corners of the city block. Large interior public spaces, arcades, and other amenities would accommodate pedestrian traffic.

A young Miami firm, Arquitectonica International Corp., finished a 255-unit condominium project, called the Palace, for developer Harry Helmsley. This structure, the tallest in Miami, consists of three elements: a 2-story base, a 41-story rectangle on top of it, which is, in turn, intersected by a smaller-scale rectangle. The red-painted slab, clad in stucco, is stepped at one end, to provide terraces toward Biscayne Bay; the resulting angle makes the slab appear to be stabbing right through the slick, aluminum-framed glass wall of the taller section. The combination of contrasting materials and dramatic shapes is heightened by stair towers clad in glittering reflective glass. Also in the works at Arquitectonica was more than $400,000,000 in additional construction, including a $130,000,000 multiuse project for Helmsley and a large (approximately 1,000,000-sq.ft.) bank in Lima, Peru.

In Louisville, Ky., Humana, Inc., an international hospital management company, chose Michael Graves's colorful design for its new headquarters. This 27-story, $50,000,000 project, scheduled for completion by 1985, would be Graves's biggest commission to date, surpassing the controversial Public Service Building in Portland, Oreg., which was formally dedicated in October. The Humana design echoes the Portland tower's polychrome classical forms, covered arcades, and rows of small, square windows. Plans call for the entrance to be flanked by 60-ft.-high unbraced piers and backed by a curved wall of

The Lath House in Phoenix, designed by Robert R. Frankeberger, won a 1982 award from the American Institute of Architects. The handcrafted wooden lath umbrella shelters a building that contains meeting rooms.

cascading water (a reference to the nearby Ohio River). Graves was also designing a major addition to the Whitney Museum of American Art in New York City.

The Lath House, a small-scale, breezy pavilion in the center of Phoenix, has succeeded in drawing the community back to that part of the city. Designed by a local architect, Robert R. Frankeberger, this unique gathering place received a 1982 American Institute of Architects (AIA) Honor Award for "the great skill evidenced in this handcrafted pavilion's sizing, proportion, and sensitive interplay of wood textures, light, and shadow." The 22,800-sq.ft. see-through structure consists of 2×3-in. laths and is transparent enough to provide views of surrounding historic buildings. It can accommodate up to 1000 guests at seated dinners, fashion shows, and concerts.

Urban Development. In May New York City officials approved new zoning regulations, the first since 1961. These new laws, which would directly affect building design for the 1980's, were intended to prevent the worsening of such problems as diminished daylight, overcrowded sidewalks, and overtaxed streets and transportation systems that already afflict the east side of midtown Manhattan. Sunlight problems were to be solved through the use of a new, flexible formula for setting back the tops of buildings. The west side of midtown would be made more appealing to developers through generous allowances for bulk, some tax relief, and several "anchor" projects that should stabilize heretofore deteriorating west side areas.

One major "anchor" was to be the State Urban Development Corp.'s 42nd Street Plan, including a quartet of tall office towers on Times Square. The developer, George Klein of Park Tower Realty, chose Philip Johnson as master architect. The plan also calls for a 2,400,000-sq.ft. wholesale trade mart, a 500-room hotel, and the renovation of nine Broadway theaters. Another anchor project, the Portman Hotel, designed by John Portman of Atlanta, would be erected on nearby 46th Street. In late March, after a battle with preservationists the city authorized the demolition of two Broadway theaters to make way for the 54-story hotel.

Zoning requirements were announced in June by the city council of Houston, where uncontrolled building had caused extreme traffic problems and wind-tunnel effects on sidewalks in the downtown area. Many developers had built their office towers almost up to the edge of the pavement of major streets, so that the streets cannot be widened. Large commercial structures had been allowed to extend for several blocks, forcing cars to detour to already overtaxed side streets. The new code mandates that all residential and commercial development come before the planning commission for approval, that maximum block lengths be 1400 ft., and that the city's jurisdiction extend to 5 mi. beyond its borders, thus enabling officials to control development that is likely to be incorporated by the city in the future.

Awards and Prizes. In April the fourth annual Pritzker Architecture Prize, valued at $100,000, was awarded to Kevin Roche of Kevin Roche John Dinkeloo and Associates of Hamden, Conn. Roche, 60, had designed some 50 major projects over the past two decades, including, in New York alone, the Ford Foundation headquarters, five additions to the Metropolitan Museum of Art, and the highly visible One United Nations Plaza. He also designed the low-scale Oakland Museum in California, the Denver Center for the Performing Arts, and arts buildings in Massachusetts, Texas, and Connecticut. Corporate structures include new buildings for the Deere & Co. headquarters in Moline, Ill., the College Life Insurance Co. of America building in Indianapolis, and the Aetna Life & Casualty computer building in Hartford. Arthur Drexler of the Museum of Modern Art in New York described Roche, who excels in manipulating almost every kind of exterior material, from glass to masonry, as "an architect who makes technology serve his art. His quietly spectacular buildings reveal the fantastic in 20th-century urban life."

Gwathmey Siegel & Associates, a 12-year-old New York-based firm famous for its sleek, modernist designs, received the AIA 1982 Architectural Firm Award. The AIA cited four of Gwathmey Siegel's most outstanding projects: a residence in Purchase, N.Y. (1968); a dormitory, dining, and student union facility for the State University of New York at Purchase (1976); the Whig Hall renovation at Princeton University (1976); and the East Campus Complex at Columbia University in New York City (1981). Gwathmey Siegel won more than 45 design awards for the first three, which are low-scale projects. The Columbia complex includes the firm's first large-scale project, a 23-story building.

The AIA Gold Medal for 1982 went to Romaldo Giurgola, 61, a partner at Mitchell/ Giurgola Architects of Philadelphia and New York and a professor of architecture at Columbia University. Born in Rome, Giurgola came to the U.S. in the early 1950's and for many years taught with Louis Kahn at the University of Pennsylvania. Giurgola, who recently finished renovating the Wainwright Building (a Louis Sullivan skyscraper in St. Louis), was currently overseeing the major project of his career to date: the huge, 1,500,-000-sq.ft. Parliament House in Canberra, Australia, due for completion in early 1988.

See also CONSTRUCTION; HOUSING.   M.M.

ARGENTINA. A failed military invasion, together with skyrocketing inflation, high unemployment, and continued difficulty in repaying large foreign loans, caused Argentina to suffer severe political and economic setbacks in 1982. On June 17 President Leopoldo Galtieri was forced to resign. He was replaced that day as commander in chief of the army by military hard-liner Maj. Gen. Cristino Nicolaides and as president, on July 1, by retired Maj. Gen. Reynaldo Benito Antonio Bignone.

Falklands War and Aftermath. British ownership of the Falkland Islands, which lie 300 mi. east of the mainland and over which the Argentines claim sovereignty, calling them the Malvinas, had long been an irritant to Argentina, although most of the 1800 Falklanders are of British descent and prefer to remain under British control. Negotiations held sporadically between the two nations for 17 years, until early 1982, failed to settle the question of sovereignty.

In mid-March a civilian Argentine wrecking crew, under contract to dismantle an abandoned whaling station on the British-owned island of South Georgia, raised the Argentine flag. (South Georgia and the South Sandwich Islands, southeast of the Falklands, are also British possessions claimed by Argentina.) As a result, the crew was ordered off the island by scientists at the British Antarctic Survey Station. This action became the catalyst for President Galtieri to order the armed seizure of the Falklands, accomplished on April 2. Great Britain, calling the invasion "a wanton act," asked the United Nations Security Council to demand the immediate withdrawal of Argentine forces (*see* UNITED NATIONS), and the United States unsuccessfully tried to persuade Argentina to withdraw. Galtieri, however, backed by his people's fierce nationalism, remained determined to settle the question of sovereignty by force. Some observers believed Galtieri also sought to obscure serious domestic labor and social problems by what he hoped would be a swift victory.

Intense fighting developed between Argentine and British forces (*see* MILITARY AND NAVAL AFFAIRS) that resulted in Argentina's surrender on June 14. Three days later Galtieri was pressured to resign for his mishandling of the crisis.

Following the interim presidency of Maj. Gen. Alfredo Oscar St. Jean, President Bignone was sworn in on July 1, despite protests from the air force and navy, which wanted a civilian president. Bignone promised free elections by March, 1984, the end of his term. Nine of the ten cabinet ministers he named were civilians. On July 17 he signed a law lifting a six-year ban on political parties imposed after the 1976 military coup that ousted the government of President Isabel Martínez de Perón. In early September the air force and navy joined the government of President Bignone, reestablishing a three-man junta as the country's actual supreme power.

The Economy and Financial Crisis. Social unrest and strikes plagued Argentina much of the year. At the end of March more than 2000 demonstrators were arrested in what was considered to be the country's largest labor protest since military rule was imposed in 1976. Police killed two protesters and wounded five.

This picture, taken by a survivor from his lifeboat, shows the Argentine cruiser General Belgrano *sinking in the South Atlantic, victim of a British torpedo during the war for possession of the Falkland Islands. An estimated 368 of the reported 1048 aboard were killed.*

After the Falklands war, which cost the country an estimated $2 billion, Argentina suffered possibly the worst economic slump in its history. Fourteen percent of the labor force was unemployed or underemployed. Through August wholesale prices had risen by 248 percent over the previous 12 months. The gross national product dropped by 7 percent in the first half of the year. The country had nearly $40 billion in short-term foreign loans, was $2.3 billion behind in repayments, and had currency reserves estimated at less than $3.5 billion. Between January and September the currency plummeted in value from 10,000 pesos to 39,000 pesos per dollar.

In September Argentina requested a standby loan from the International Monetary Fund (IMF) to help meet Argentina's $12 billion in debt payments due by the end of the year. IMF loan negotiators sought the government's agreement to such belt-tightening measures as budget cuts to reduce the nation's deficit and high inflation, and further devaluation of the peso, in order to stimulate exports and to limit imports. The government announced on Oct. 27 that it had agreed to take these steps as a condition for an IMF loan of $2 billion.

On Sept. 14 Argentina and Great Britain agreed to lift the freeze on bank deposits that both countries had imposed on each other's funds at the start of the Falklands war. This freed $1.2 billion in cash to Argentina. The embargo on trade, however, remained fully in force between the two nations.

In trade with the Soviet Union, Argentina became first among developing countries in 1981, with the Soviets paying about $3.5 billion for nearly 77 percent of Argentina's grain exports. But this revenue appeared to be jeopardized when the U.S.S.R. postponed half its June purchase of Argentine grain. A reason given was that the Soviets feared they might have difficulty finding shipowners willing to enter Argentine waters in wartime. Argentina's trade options were already severely restricted by the European Community's boycott; see EUROPEAN COMMUNITIES.

See STATISTICS OF THE WORLD.   A.E.J.

ARIZONA. See STATISTICS OF THE WORLD.

ARKANSAS. See STATISTICS OF THE WORLD.

ART. After almost a decade of rising prices for artworks, the recession forced the art market to enter a period of reevaluation in 1982. The middle price range market for paintings, sculpture, prints, and other collectibles of secondary significance all but disappeared. This decline affected not only many commercial galleries, but also the world's two largest auction houses, Sotheby & Co. and Christie, Manson & Woods International, Inc. By midyear Christie's 1981–82 U.S. sales were down 15 percent and Sotheby's 1981–82 worldwide sales, 25 percent. These declines, together with recent overexpansion, forced Sotheby's to close its renowned Madison Avenue salesrooms in New York City as well as those in Los Angeles. It was announced that all future U.S. sales were to originate from Sotheby's York Avenue building in New York.

Auctions and Sales. Only art objects of the very best quality found a vital market, and several extraordinary prices were paid, especially for 20th-century art. Henry Moore's 6-ft. elmwood sculpture of a reclining figure, created in 1945–46, fetched $1,265,000 (including the 10 percent buyer's premium) at Sotheby's sale in May, the highest price ever paid for the work of a living artist. The same piece had been sold for $260,000 ten years earlier. The top attraction at Christie's May sale was Vasily Kandinsky's "Sketch for Composition II," a study for the right-hand side of what was to become a finished work. The oil sketch, dated 1910, was sold for $1,210,000, including the 10 percent buyer's premium. At Sotheby's in London, Piet Mondrian's "Composition in Gray-Blue" (1912–13) was bought by an unnamed European collector for $1,080,000, the highest price ever paid at auction for any abstract work. The most remarkable price for the work of a living American artist was the $462,000 paid at Christie's for Frank Stella's 1958 all-black painting "Reichstag."

"The Man With the Axe" (1891), from the postimpressionist Paul Gauguin's Tahitian period, was sold privately for what was reported to be about $6,000,000, which would make it probably the highest amount ever paid for a modern painting. The work was sold to an unnamed European collector by Alexander M. Lewyt, a New York investment executive, who had bought it 20 years earlier for a reputed price of more than $100,000. "The Gallery of the Louvre" (1832), by the 19th-century American artist Samuel F. B. Morse, inventor of the telegraph and the Morse code, was sold privately to the Terra Museum of American Art, Evanston, Ill., for $3,250,000, the highest price ever paid for an American work of art. The Kimbell Art Museum in Fort Worth, Texas, paid the second-highest price known to have been given for a work by Pablo Picasso, when the museum bought his 1906 "Nude Combing Her Hair" from the Norton S. Simon Foundation Inc., Pasadena, Calif., for $4,000,000.

International Exhibitions. In West Germany, the seventh in the series of Kassel's quadrennial art events, "Documenta," brought together 1000 works by 180 artists from 21 countries. The exhibition's organizer, Rudi Fuchs, director of the Abbemuseum in Eindhoven, the Netherlands, emphasized the wide diversity of world art. The massive and visually exciting display implied that dominance of the art world had shifted from New York artists to artists working in a new image, figurative expressionism, centered in Italy, Germany, and Holland.

Another important exhibition was the 40th showing of the "Venice Biennale." Although this venerable art event long ago yielded its place of preeminence to "Documenta," the "Venice Biennale" remained a prestigious attraction, largely because of Venice's popularity.

U.S. Museums and Exhibitions. Following a period of inactivity, 1982 was marked by a surge of museum construction and planned construction. Despite the recession, several corporations, foundations, and individuals financed both new structures and major additions to existing facilities. Important examples included the Dallas Museum of Fine Arts, designed by Edward Larrabee Barnes Associates to become the focal point of a downtown arts center. Major features of the Indiana limestone building are its several garden courts and patios. These allow natural light to flow through the galleries in order to

The largest loan exhibition of paintings by El Greco came to the U.S. in 1982. Among them was this 9-ft.-high painting entitled "Pentecost," thought to be one of six works in an enormous altar series.

highlight the museum's extensive collections, which range from pre-Columbian art to 20th-century masters. Richard Meier's design for the High Museum of Art in Atlanta, which primarily features collections of American paintings, also called for natural light to illuminate galleries clustered around a central atrium.

No fewer than five art building projects were being planned in Los Angeles, in preparation for a significant art and culture program to accompany the 1984 Summer Olympic Games in that city. Sculptor Robert Graham was commissioned to produce a monumental gateway entrance to the Olympics grounds.

"El Greco of Toledo" brought together 57 paintings, representing nearly one fourth of the Spanish master's authenticated works. After opening to an enthusiastic reception at the National Gallery of Art in Washington, D.C., this show, the first major international loan exhibition of El Grecos, was scheduled to appear at the Toledo Museum of Art, and the Dallas Museum of Fine Arts.

The Museum of Modern Art, New York City, opened some of its extensive new exhibition space to present the first large-scale exhibition of Italian surrealist master Giorgio de Chirico's early work. A total of 75 paintings and 20 drawings detailed de Chirico's output, mostly between 1909 and 1919. From New York the exhibition was to travel to London's Tate Gallery, the Haus der Kunst in Munich, and the Georges Pompidou Art and Cultural Center (Beaubourg) in Paris.

"Thomas Eakins: Artist of Philadelphia" set a new attendance record at the Philadelphia Museum of Art before it moved on to the Boston Museum of Fine Arts. The exhibition, divided into sections devoted to the various themes in Eakins's work, provided an opportunity for viewers to reappraise the artist's immense contribution to the history of American art between 1870 and 1910. Chosen specifically to help celebrate Philadelphia's 300th birthday, the exhibition vindicated Eakins, who remained unappreciated by his townspeople during his lifetime.

The Metropolitan Museum of Art, New York City, was given two major private art collections in 1982. The first, gathered by New Yorkers Belle and Jack Linsky, and valued at $60,000,000, consisted of one of the finest collections in the United States of European art dating from the Renaissance and later periods. The other, the so-called Dial Collection, was bequeathed to the Metropolitan by the late Scofield Thayer, formerly editor in chief of *The Dial,* an avant-garde literary magazine. Among the 450 works were paintings by such masters as Picasso, Henri Matisse, Marc Chagall, Pierre Bonnard, and Georges Braque.

In February the Metropolitan opened its new Michael C. Rockefeller Wing, in memory of the late Nelson A. Rockefeller's son, who died in Papua New Guinea, age 23, in 1961. Thousands of objects gathered by Nelson Rockefeller formed the nucleus of what was described by *Time* magazine as "the most spectacular permanent exhibition of 'primitive' art" in any museum in the world.

In St. Petersburg, Fla., a $2,000,000 museum opened in March, containing reportedly the world's largest collection of the works of Spanish surrealist painter Salvador Dali.

Controversy. Eliciting great interest in 1982 was the Vietnam War Memorial in Washington, D.C., designed by a 21-year-old Yale University architectural student, Maya Yang Lin. Her proposal consisted of two low 246-ft.-long black marble walls joining to form a "V" and embracing a gently sloping plot of ground between them. The names of all Americans killed in the war in Vietnam (about 58,000) were inscribed in the granite. The architectural press hailed the monument as "stunning" and "eminently right." The U.S. Commission of Fine Arts backed critics of the design, however, when it approved the addition to the memorial in 1983 of an American flag and a realistic sculpture of armed servicemen (designed by Frederick Hart), despite the contention of the art community that these insertions had changed the meaning of the monument. Dedication services took place in November. H.T.H.

The Metropolitan Museum of Art in New York City opened a new wing in 1982 devoted entirely to "primitive" art. Among the works displayed were these New Hebrides carved slitgongs.

A total lunar eclipse observed on the evening of July 5–6 was the longest since 1859. This eclipse was remarkable for the unusually deep red and purple hues of the shadow that the earth cast on the moon's northern hemisphere, a consequence of dust hurled into the earth's atmosphere by the eruption of the El Chichón volcano in Mexico. (Even during a total eclipse part of the moon can be seen because the sun's rays are bent by the earth's atmosphere so that some rays still reach the moon.)

ASTRONOMY. U.S. astronomers in 1982 faced the prospect of more modest budgets for scientific space research in the future. Although the Soviet Union set two spacecraft down on Venus, fewer launches and planetary landings took place worldwide than in recent years. A number of interesting discoveries were made, however, such as evidence for a magnetosphere around Uranus and rings around Neptune, a pulsating white dwarf star, and the fastest-spinning pulsar yet observed.

Space Policy and Programs. In a space-policy announcement released for the Fourth of July holiday, President Ronald Reagan asserted that the U.S. goal was to remain preeminent in space and to continue research into astrophysics and the nature of the solar system. Not included in this declaration, however, was a promise of increased funding for such activities, and his proposed budget for fiscal year 1983 indicated more of an interest in the military uses of space.

Scientific space programs were, in fact, falling on hard times. The Solar System Exploration Committee, formed to advise the National Aeronautics and Space Administration (NASA), therefore outlined a program of low- to medium-cost flights to keep planetary exploration alive. Use of existing spacecraft hardware and designs was emphasized, and top priority was given to a Venus Radar Mapper mission using leftover materials from the Voyager and Galileo spacecraft programs; it was to take the place of the canceled Venus Orbiting Imaging Radar program.

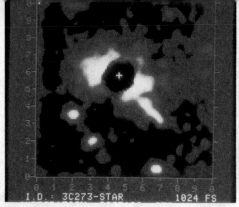

Quasar 3C273, the first quasistellar object to be identified, is so bright that the galaxy that apparently surrounds it was not observed until 1982. Astronomers at Lowell Observatory made it visible by blocking off the quasar image (cross) and using a Bell Laboratories device to record the light from this galaxy.

For its own part, the National Academy of Sciences advocated a $1.9 billion, ten-year space program in which top priorities would be given to the proposed Advanced X-ray Astrophysics Facility, a 1.2-m (3.9-ft.) orbiting X-ray reflector telescope, and to the enhancement of the Explorer series of small astronomy satellites. NASA, in turn, gave the go-ahead for development of the Cosmic Background Explorer, a polar-orbit satellite to be launched in the late 1980's to study cosmic radiation left over from the "big bang" that theoretically initiated the expansion of the universe. In addition, an International Halley Watch was established to coordinate observations, by amateur and professional astronomers, of the 1986 reappearance of Halley's comet.

Spacecraft and Telescopes. On Dec. 10 the Dutch-American Infrared Astronomy Satellite was launched on a one-year mission to conduct the first infrared survey of the entire sky. Also late in the year the European Space Agency orbited the Exosat X-ray astronomy satellite, which is similar to NASA's "Einstein" High Energy Astronomy Observatory (HEAO-2) that was retired, reentering the atmosphere and burning up on March 25. In conjunction with another European program, NASA signed an agreement to launch West Germany's Roentgensatellit in 1985 in exchange for half of the observing time it

would provide; this satellite also was to be similar to HEAO-2.

During the year Japan started to conduct studies in molecular astronomy with a new 45-m (148-ft.) dish antenna and a 5 × 10-m (16.4 × 32.8-ft.) interferometer. In Canada the National Research Council conducted a cost study on construction of a Long Baseline Array, using eight 32-m (105-ft.) interferometer antennas. NASA, on the other hand, planned to close its Infrared Telescope Facility (IRTF) in Hawaii because of budget cuts.
Solar System Research. The Soviet Union returned to Venus in 1982, landing Venera XIII and XIV on the planet on March 1 and March 5, respectively. Television images from the first craft showed a debris-strewn ground, but the second landing area exhibited basaltic lava flows. In May a team of researchers who had analyzed data received from the U.S. Pioneer Venus Orbiter concluded that the data indicated Venus had substantial water when it first formed but lost it as the planet grew increasingly hot.

Among the outer planets, further analysis of Voyager II data revealed four additional small moons of Saturn and the possibility of two others. The moons, which range from 10 to 20 km (6 to 12 mi.) in diameter, bring Saturn's current moon count to as high as 23. The moons of more distant Uranus, measured by the IRTF, were found to range from 1160 to 1690 km (719 to 1048 mi.) wide; unexpected evidence, based on radiation apparently coming from auroral activity at the sun-pointed pole of Uranus, indicated that the planet itself has a magnetosphere. Beyond Uranus, Neptune gave signs of being the fourth planet known to have a ring system. The data for this observation had been obtained in 1968 by a graduate student making occultation studies of Neptune from New Zealand. The rings appear to lie between 3600 and 7900 km (2230 and 4900 mi.) above the surface of Neptune.

At the center of the solar system, the sun was found to show variations as great as 0.23 percent in its total radiation output. The data came from the U.S. Solar Maximum Mission Satellite as it was observing the passage of large sunspot formations; one spiral-shaped

Doomsday Wasn't So Bad

March 10, 1982, touted as a day to remember, turned out to be a day to forget. On that date all nine planets, bunched on the same side of the sun, were closer together than at any time since 1803—a phenomenon two British writers had claimed would cause huge solar flares and catastrophic earthquakes. As "doomsday" neared, the Kitt Peak National Observatory in Arizona gave the reassuring word that planets are so small relative to the sun and so distant from it that their gravitational effect on the solar surface is negligible. The day passed unremarkably, except for mild tremors in Peru and the Aegean Sea.

sunspot noted on Feb. 19 was 80,000 km (50,000 mi.) wide, but it broke up into smaller spots two days later. During a 22-day period in June, astronomers observed a series of five white-light solar flares; such flares are seen only about 50 times in a century. Other unexpected observations included two sun-grazing comets, which passed so close that they either collided with the sun or were incinerated by its heat. Such comets had been expected to occur only every few hundred years, but another sun-grazer had already been spotted in 1981. These observations were made by an instrument aboard the U.S. P78-1 satellite.

Deep-Space and Cosmological Studies. Astronomers in 1982 made significant discoveries of pulsating stars, or stars that vary rapidly in the amount of electromagnetic radiation they emit. One discovery, made in May by scientists working in conjunction at the universities of Texas and Montréal, was of a pulsating white dwarf designated GD 358. It was of great interest because it was the first kind of variable star to be predicted before its observation. GD 358, like other white dwarfs, is a star in the late stages of its evolution, but unlike most known white dwarfs it has a surface of helium rather than hydrogen. The star has a diameter twice that of the earth but a mass three times that of the sun. Its six sets of oscillations, ranging from 125 to 950 sec.

long, may be caused by temperature changes and could make possible the study of the interiors of white dwarfs, just as seismic waves are used to study the earth's interior.

Extremely dense pulsating objects called pulsars, which are neutron stars, or "black holes," were also observed. Data from the HEAO-1 satellite revealed the fastest X-ray pulsar yet known. Labeled MXB 1728-34, it rotates 82 times a second. The 10-sec. bursts indicate that the source is a black hole with material spiraling inward. Also discovered, using data from HEAO-1 and HEAO-2, was the fastest known pulsar in a binary, or two-star, system. The pulsar is visible once every 16.6 days, when it apparently grazes through the surface of its blue-white companion star.

Evidence indicated that the entire universe is rotating at a rate that would enable it to complete one revolution every 63 trillion years. The evidence lay in observations of the polarization of radio sources and the direction of their magnetic fields; the chance that the alignments were random was calculated at one in 400. And speculations were advanced by two University of Chicago astronomers concerning the cosmological problem of "missing mass"; according to current theories, the universe does not have enough observable mass to hold it together as it expands. The scientists suggested that countless small black holes may have been formed in the first three millionths of a second after the initial "big bang," and that these could account for the apparently missing mass.   D.D.

AUSTRALIA. Numerous disputes in 1982 shook Australia's coalition government, led by Prime Minister Malcolm Fraser's Liberal Party. The economy was in recession, and a major tax-evasion scandal broke in August.

Domestic Affairs. Fraser's political troubles began in January when Sir William McMahon, the former Liberal prime minister, retired from parliament and made a bitter attack on the policies of the Fraser government. The by-election for McMahon's seat was held in March, and the opposition Labour Party won with a swing of 9 percent against the government. Labour was jubilant because, if the margin held in the next na-

AUSTRALIA

Australian Prime Minister Malcolm Fraser checks on the government's investment during a visit to a movie set in Sydney. The expanding Australian film industry, aided by grants and tax concessions, has turned out such recent international hits as Breaker Morant and Gallipoli.

tional election, the party would have a parliamentary majority of more than 20 seats. Then, in early April, Labour swept to power in state legislative elections in Victoria, Fraser's home state. In May, however, legislative elections in Tasmania ousted the Labour government and brought the Liberals to power.

Following the Victoria vote, Andrew Peacock, who had resigned from Fraser's cabinet in 1981, challenged the prime minister for leadership of the Liberal Party. The issue was brought to a head by Fraser, who called a special meeting to end speculation about the party's direction. When a poll was taken at the gathering, Liberal members of parliament voted 54–27 to return Fraser as party chief. Even so, the size of Peacock's vote indicated his popularity, and his return to the cabinet on Oct. 11, as minister for industry and commerce, was expected to strengthen the government's political standing.

A fresh controversy embarrassed the government in April. Health Minister Michael MacKellar returned to Australia from Hong Kong carrying a portable television set that he failed to declare for customs duty. Although told of the matter, Minister for Business and Consumer Affairs John Moore took no action against MacKellar. News of the affair, however, became public, and both men resigned from the Fraser cabinet. In May the prime minister made extensive cabinet changes.

Midyear economic figures proved to be a serious problem for the government. The world recession had struck normally prosperous Australia. Interest rates were high, unemployment stood at 6.7 percent, company profits were down, inflation was at a double-digit rate, and the Australian dollar was declining against its U.S. counterpart. The gross national product in 1982 was expected to rise by only 2 percent, and a devastating drought would cost at least $2.5 billion in lost production.

In the meantime, the opposition Labour Party was running into troubles of its own. In July Robert Hawke tried to dislodge William Hayden as party leader. At a meeting of Labour members of parliament, Hayden managed to win reelection by a margin of only 42–37. Controversy over nuclear policy also kept the party's ranks at odds.

With Labour embroiled in internal dispute, Fraser was tempted to call early national elections, although his term was not scheduled to end until October, 1983. In August the government presented a budget calculated more to win votes than to continue traditional monetarist policy. The budget's main features were personal tax cuts, a housing package lowering interest rates for home buyers, and increased spending for social security, welfare, and health.

Unfortunately for Fraser, scarcely had the budget been released than a major scandal broke. A Royal Commission report looking into alleged criminal activity by the Federated Ship Painters and Dockers Union uncovered the fact that massive tax-avoidance schemes had been common in many corporations in recent years, and that the Fraser government had been lax in dealing with the issue. As revelations began to mount, pressure increased for the resignations of Treasurer John Howard and Attorney General Peter Durack. Under the circumstances, Fraser thought it wiser to drop the notion of an election in 1982.

The aborigines, Australia's original inhabitants and its most disadvantaged people in modern times, staged militant protests on the occasion of the Commonwealth Games in Brisbane in September. Aboriginal demands included an end to discrimination and return of land taken by white settlers.

Foreign Affairs. Australia continued its close cooperation with Great Britain, the United States, and New Zealand. When the war in the Falkland Islands erupted in April, 1982, Australia temporarily recalled its ambassador from Buenos Aires and imposed trade sanctions on Argentina. Fraser played host to U.S. Vice-President George Bush in May, and later in the month visited Washington to confer with President Ronald Reagan. In a major speech during his U.S. visit, Fraser put forward a four-point plan to speed the growth of international trade by reducing protectionism.

The council of ANZUS, the Australia-New Zealand-U.S. defense pact, met in Canberra in June. Australia and New Zealand inched closer to economic union with an agreement on Nov. 10 to make almost all goods traded between the two countries tariff- and duty-free within five years.

While supporting Israel's right to exist within secure boundaries, the Australian government criticized Israel's continued use of force in Lebanon. The criticism came in an August statement by Fraser. To foster good relations in Asia, Fraser made official visits that same month to China, Malaysia, and the Philippines.

See STATISTICS OF THE WORLD.   F.W.

AUSTRIA. With national elections due in April, 1983, the key political question for Austrians in 1982 was whether Chancellor Bruno Kreisky would again run for office. Seventy-one years old and in none-too-robust health, Kreisky had been in office since 1970, longer than any other current Western European leader. His Socialist Party needed him badly if it were to compete vigorously against Austrian conservatives. Although Kreisky from time to time talked of retirement, he was thought to be leaning toward continuation in public life.

The Austrian economy remained sound, but it grew at a low rate in 1982. Unemployment stood at 2.3 percent of the labor force and inflation at 6 percent annually. The presence of 18,000 Eastern European refugees, most of them from Poland, presented a further burden to the national treasury. In September the government unveiled a long-term plan to invest more than $10,000,000 in industry in an effort to create between 30,000 and 35,000 new jobs.

In line with its neutrality, Austria attempted to maintain good working ties with nations of the East, West, and Third World. In March Chancellor Kreisky played host to Libya's controversial leader, Muammar el-Qaddafi, who arrived in Vienna after giving only short notice of his intention to visit. In his public remarks, Qaddafi attacked the United States, largely because of its recent embargo of Libyan oil. In response, Austria's three major political parties issued a joint statement reaffirming the "long-standing friendship" between the U.S. and Austria, and the government, shortly after, sent Foreign Minister Willibald Pahr to Washington.

Kreisky strongly condemned Israel's June invasion of Lebanon. In July he described as unrealistic the attempt by the administration of U.S. President Ronald Reagan to pressure the Soviet Union with economic boycotts. In April Austria joined other Western European countries in suspending arms shipments to Argentina during the Falklands war.

See STATISTICS OF THE WORLD.   F.W.

AUTOMOBILES. Sales by domestic automobile producers in 1982 plunged to their lowest level in two decades, under the grip of a long recession, high interest rates, and high prices. For the 1982 model year, which ended on Sept. 30, 5,543,006 U.S.-made cars were sold, down 15.9 percent from the 1981 model year and the lowest sales since the 1961 model year. Imports, affected by the recession and Japanese restraint in shipping autos abroad, also declined, to 1,979,100, down 27.9 percent.

Automakers gained new wage-saving labor contracts and cut costs by closing plants. Price rises moderated, while rebates had spotty impact.

Continuing Dismal Market. Sales forecasts for 1982 kept slipping, as the industry moved into its fourth straight year of depressed sales. At times, car sales trailed 1980 levels by 45 percent. Officials became anxious about the long-term outlook, as analysts warned that major reforms in car quality, technology, productivity, labor relations, and management attitudes were needed for domestic-industry survival. Even imports suffered, dropping to the lowest level since 1978. Japan acceded to U.S. pressure by agreeing to extend the annual ceiling of 1,680,000 units exported to the United States through March, 1983. Small-car import sales fell because motorists were less concerned about gasoline costs than previously.

New Ventures and Models. Domestic producers joined foreign automakers in joint ventures for building or selling cars for the U.S. market. General Motors Corp. (GM) in May agreed to import up to 200,000 subcompacts yearly from Isuzu Motors Ltd.; GM discussed similar plans with Suzuki Motor Co. and possible joint production with Toyota Motor Co. American Motors Corp. (AMC) moved to market cars under the banner of Renault, the French firm that owns nearly half of AMC, including the imported Renault and a new U.S.-built subcompact, the Alliance. Honda of America Manufacturing Inc. rolled out its first U.S.-assembled car, the Accord, on Nov. 1 in Marysville, Ohio.

Other new-model offerings were slim, as manufacturers avoided major costly changes.

Chrysler Corp. in October launched its new E-body front-wheel-drive cars, the Chrysler Gran LeBaron and Dodge 600. Ford Motor Co. departed from the "econoboxes" the industry had been selling, by introducing a smaller Ford Thunderbird with rounded body lines to improve handling and fuel economy. Convertibles, unseen since 1976, were revived by GM's Buick Riviera, Ford's Mustang, and two Chrysler models.

One recent model seemed headed for oblivion—the stainless-steel, gull-wing-door De Lorean. After the car, which cost more than $25,000, went on sale in July, 1981, its developer, John Z. De Lorean, a flamboyant former GM executive, ran into financing troubles. The Northern Ireland manufacturing subsidiary of his De Lorean Motor Co. was placed in receivership in February, 1982, and production ended on May 31. Federal agents arrested De Lorean on Oct. 19 in Los Angeles, on charges of conspiring to sell an estimated $24,000,000 worth of cocaine.

Prices, Rebates, and Earnings. Auto companies tried to attract buyers by holding down price increases and using sporadic rebates, special low-interest financing deals, and other sales incentives for dealers and customers. Sometimes these devices helped, but only slightly and only for a while. Prices rose up to 4 percent on many cars in May and June, but less than 2 percent on 1983 models in the fall.

The financial results of automakers improved, however, from lowered labor and other costs. GM earned $818,000,000 in the first nine months of 1982, up from $237,000,000 the previous year. Chrysler's net income for the period was $276,000,000, almost entirely from selling its profitable tank-making unit, Chrysler Defense Inc., to the General Dynamics Corp. in February to gain cash, and from a tax-loss credit. The company had lost $436,000,000 during the same period in 1981. Chrysler benefited from previous federally guaranteed loans, but still struggled, although boasting a $1 billion cash reserve. Ford omitted its dividend starting in the first quarter and sustained a $422,000,000 nine-month loss, although this sum was narrower than the $714,000,000 deficit in the same

With domestic auto sales running at a 20-year low and more than 200,000 auto workers unemployed, United Automobile Workers officials and Ford Motor Co. executives sign a contract freezing wages and deferring cost-of-living increases in return for job security and profit sharing provisions.

1981 period. AMC lost money in all three quarters, a total of $171,000,000.

Labor Pacts and Other Cost Cuts. Wage concessions spread to help automakers compete with imports. Members of the United Automobile Workers (UAW) ratified new agreements with Ford, GM, and AMC, generally giving up two annual 3 percent pay raises and deferring for 18 months three quarterly cost-of-living increases, among other concessions. Chrysler had a tougher time. There, workers had forgone wage hikes for two years, and in September they rejected a UAW agreement to give them quarterly wage bonuses, but only if Chrysler earned enough profit, although the proposed contract also called for quarterly cost-of-living adjustments. They voted against a strike on Oct. 26, but Chrysler workers in Canada walked out on Nov. 5. The strike ended in mid-December with approval of a contract that gave both U.S. and Canadian workers a 3 percent raise and a cost-of-living adjustment.

Auto firms took other steps to reduce their costs. Production cuts and layoffs occurred frequently, as sales lagged and inventories piled up. Output in early 1982 was at a 35-year low. The Commerce Department said that auto employment would stay low even if sales rebounded; more than 200,000 work-

ers were on "indefinite layoff." GM announced plans for widespread plant closings. Chrysler began halting car assembly several times daily. Ford said that it would trim another $1 billion in operating costs and began stretching out payments to suppliers, while GM got suppliers to cut prices 2 percent.

Deregulation. Some efforts by the administration of U.S. President Ronald Reagan to roll back auto-industry rules hit snags. A requirement that future cars be equipped with air bags or automatic safety belts, rescinded by the Transportation Department in late 1981, was reinstated by a federal appeals court on June 1. The Center for Auto Safety (a consumer group) and insurance interests sought court action to overturn an Administration decision reducing a requirement for crash-resistant bumpers. In Congress legislation backed by auto firms and the Administration to ease car emissions rules ran into stiff opposition.

Agencies moved in other ways to reduce the industry's regulatory burden. The Environmental Protection Agency (EPA) agreed in July not to require GM to recall 700,000 1979 cars with a fuel emissions rate higher than government-set levels; in October the EPA waived an emissions rule for some of GM's 1981-model cars.   A.R.K.

B

BAHAMAS. *See* STATISTICS OF THE WORLD.
BAHRAIN. *See* STATISTICS OF THE WORLD. *See also* PERSIAN GULF STATES.
BANGLADESH. The civilian government of poverty-stricken Bangladesh was overthrown by a military coup on March 24, 1982. The new regime, led by army chief of staff Gen. Hussain Muhammad Ershad, took steps to end corruption and to improve relations with neighboring India.

With the backing of the army, 75-year-old Abdus Sattar was overwhelmingly elected president in late 1981. Once in office, however, Sattar rejected pressure from Ershad to increase the military's role in government. Seizing power in a bloodless coup, Ershad named himself martial law administrator, suspended the constitution, banned political activity, dissolved parliament, and dismissed the president and his cabinet. Ershad replaced the judiciary with military courts in many instances, and he made criticism of the martial law administration punishable by prison sentences of up to seven years. He appointed retired judge A.F.M. Ahsanuddin Choudhury as a figurehead president.

Several former high government officials were arrested on charges of corruption and misuse of power, found guilty, fined, and sentenced to prison terms of up to 14 years. Ershad, who said that he had no political ambitions, promised to attempt to restore democracy within two years.

In 1982 Bangladesh remained one of the poorest countries in the world, with an average annual per capita income of $120; the country's economic outlook seemed dismal. Heavy oil import bills drained limited financial resources. Falling world prices for jute, the export that earns Bangladesh three fourths of its foreign exchange, as well as for tea and leather, sharply reduced export revenues. Despite vast, potentially fertile plains, capable of yielding at least two crop harvests annually, lack of water control continued to subject Bangladesh to both seasonal floods and drought. A poor rice harvest in 1982 forced Bangladesh to appeal urgently for foreign donations of food and money.

Relations with India improved markedly after Ershad took control of the government. In early October he visited New Delhi for a series of meetings with Indian Prime Minister Indira Gandhi, the first talks in eight years between the leaders of the two neighboring countries. A major issue was the question of sharing the waters of the Ganges River. As the first step, Ershad and Gandhi set an 18-month deadline for studying the feasibility of expanding the water flow in the 150-mi. Bangladesh portion of the river's course, an expansion regarded by Bangladesh as vital to its development. The two leaders also agreed to minor boundary adjustments and to further talks on New Moore, an island in the Bay of Bengal claimed by both countries.

See STATISTICS OF THE WORLD.   R.J.C.
BANKING AND FINANCE. High interest rates during most of 1982, the product of a tight monetary policy and massive federal budget deficits, inflicted a heavy toll on both the U.S. and international economies. The wreckage of failed banks, collapsed corporations, and insolvent debtor nations provided a harsh environment for any recovery to take root.

Interest Rates. Upward pressure on interest rates was building when 1982 began. The Federal Reserve Board was tightening credit by reducing the sharp growth in the money supply that had taken place during the early winter. The bank prime rate, the interest charged to these institutions' most creditworthy customers, held firm at 15.75 percent throughout January. But the rate on more market-oriented issues was already rising, with three-month Treasury bills, for example, ultimately hitting a high for the year of 14.1 percent in February. The prime rate held basically steady after February, at 16.5 percent, until late July.

The most extraordinary feature about the interest rates was that they were remaining so high despite falling inflation; this circum-

'QUICK COLLECTION. CUSTOMER OUT THERE WANTS TO CASH A TWENTY DOLLAR CHECK!'

This cartoon depicts the plight of the nation's thrift institutions. Much of their assets were in the form of mortgages yielding lower interest rates than they were paying out to attract and hold deposits.

stance defied time-honored economic theories that interest rates generally run only two or three percentage points ahead of inflation. A sharp slowdown in inflation during the first half of 1982 meant that three-month Treasury bills were a full six percentage points higher than the inflation rate at midyear. The spread between the inflation rate and interest rates was the widest since the 1930's. Interest rates at last fell from their plateau in July. The prime descended to 13.5 percent in August and to 11.5 percent in late October.

Government Policy. The high level of interest rates stemmed to a degree from business borrowing but seemed even more powerfully driven by the interaction of government monetary and budget policies. The Federal Reserve Board maintained a tight rein on the money supply until late July when, in response to indications that the economy was still mired in recession, it eased credit.

Meanwhile, however, the federal government was running a budget deficit for fiscal year 1982 that eventually reached a record $110.7 billion, and the Administration was compelled to abandon indefinitely its goal of a balanced budget. With even bigger deficits in store, financial analysts feared that the federal government's future demands for money would drive up interest rates again.

Business Borrowing. Business demand for credit remained unusually strong in a year of recession. Normally, businesses do less borrowing during a recession; as a result interest rates drop, which typically permits businesses to pay off high-cost, short-term debts accumulated during periods of growth and to lock in the lower rates of the recessionary period. But the last such period, in mid-1980, was so short that most businesses missed the opportunity and were trapped on a treadmill, forced continually to pay off short-term loans coming due with additional short-term loans. By the time interest rates began declining in July, business loans outstanding at banks amounted to 12.4 percent more than a year earlier.

Stocks and Bonds. Neither the bond market nor the stock market presented much opportunity for raising money during most of 1982. Corporations did get some help in March, however, when the Securities and Exchange Commission streamlined a ponderous system that required corporations to register bond sales in advance and then refile the registration before changing the amount or terms of the securities. The streamlined system was embodied in Rule 415, which permitted corporations to register a specified amount of bonds for an extended period and then bring all or part of the bonds to market whenever the corporation chose. The so-called shelf registration system permitted corporations to be more selective in timing bond issues to catch interest rates at their lowest point.

The Dow Jones average of 30 industrial stocks on the New York Stock Exchange was in the low 800s for most of the first half of 1982. After falling to a 27-month low of 776.92 on Aug. 12, a new high of 1070.55 was set on Dec. 27.

The bond market did well in 1982. In the 12 months ended on Oct. 31, prices of long-term Treasury issues rose about 29 percent. Top-rated 30-year corporate bonds and 30-year municipal bonds performed even better during this period. Both the stock and bond market rallies were fueled by the fall in the rate of inflation.

Bankruptcies. Many companies were devastated by a combination of high interest rates, recession-depressed profits, and the inability to continue raising prices. Corporations went bankrupt at a pace unrivaled since the Great Depression. In one flurry in the spring, a cluster of large, well-known firms declared bankruptcy: Saxon Industries on April 15, AM International on April 16, Wickes Companies on April 24, and Braniff International Corp. on May 13. With other large corporations, such as International Harvester Co., teetering on the edge of bankruptcy, banks wound up holding sizable amounts of bad debts. By June money set aside at banks to cover recent or expected loan losses had climbed to $1.04 billion, more than double the amount a year earlier. At least 35 commercial banks failed in 1982, the highest total since 1940.

But corporate bankruptcies were only one of the banks' problems. On May 17 an obscure firm, Drysdale Government Securities Inc., notified Chase Manhattan Bank that it was unable to make $160,000,000 in interest payments on repurchase agreements sold to and through Chase. Drysdale ultimately failed, exposing a weak spot in the financial system. Repurchase agreements—loans to financial institutions in which government securities are pledged as collateral—had long been a favored method by which banks collected funds and corporations and other large investors earned interest on idle cash. Furthermore, many financial institutions had entered into repurchase agreements with Chase, or so they thought, only to discover when Drysdale failed that Chase had put the deals together as a mere intermediary. Under pressure Chase took responsibility for Drys-

dale's losses, and new rules governing repurchase agreements were instituted.

Another blow to the image of the banking community occurred when federal bank regulators closed down the $465,000,000-deposit Penn Square Bank of Oklahoma City on July 5. Penn Square had increased its assets tenfold since 1976—through aggressive oil-field lending, making so many loans it had to sell $2 billion worth of them to other banks. About half went to the nation's sixth largest bank, Continental Illinois National Bank and Trust Co. of Chicago. But the glitter of energy lending—once considered the soundest investment possible following the sharp rise in oil prices after the Arab oil embargo of 1973—dimmed as oil prices fell in 1982.

By the time federal regulators closed Penn Square, they found problems involving more than just economics. It turned out that many loans had been undercollateralized; others had been made without adequate assurance that oil might actually be present in the tract involved. Bank examiners also found evidence of fraud and recommended prosecution of several individuals.

The major impact of Penn Square, however, was on the banks, credit unions, savings and loan associations, and other institutions that had dealt with Penn Square through a system in which all had become highly interdependent. Banks had for years taken comfort from syndications and participations, in which they shared the loans and risks and trusted the bank leading the syndicate or making the loan. But when Penn Square's loans turned sour, Continental Illinois and other large banks paid a heavy price. Continental Illinois had already run up large losses from the many corporate bankruptcies, and the Penn Square affair pushed it temporarily into the red. Moreover, several thrift institutions and credit unions discovered that they were unlikely to get back the total amount of their deposits placed with Penn Square.

Thrift Institutions. In 1982 the nation's thrift institutions—savings and loan associations and mutual savings banks—suffered through their second straight year in the red. Net worth declined in almost every month of the year as withdrawals outstripped deposits.

High Finance's Henry K.
Like another German-born Ph.D. with the same first name and last initial, Henry Kaufman is a man of influence. In Kaufman's case, the influence was brought to bear on the nation's financial markets. When on Aug. 17 Kaufman reversed his previous view that interest rates would remain high and predicted instead that they would decline, the Dow Jones industrial average on the New York Stock Exchange registered its largest single-day gain in history. Kaufman, who is chief economist for the investment firm Salomon Brothers, is a workaholic who spends his weekends writing his own speeches. He has been highly critical of large federal budget deficits because they force the government to compete for borrowing with businesses, thereby pushing up interest rates.

Henry Kaufman

The major problem for thrift institutions was that they held vast quantities of long-term mortgages at lower interest rates than the rates required to attract and hold deposits. About 400 thrifts were merged in 1982 in order to avoid failure. Citicorp of New York City became the first bank holding company allowed to acquire an out-of-state savings and loan association when federal authorities approved its acquisition of the failed Fidelity Savings and Loan Association of California on Sept. 28. In an effort to aid thrifts, on May 6 the Federal Home Loan Bank Board authorized savings and loan associations to offer investment and brokerage services to their customers.

Major legislation designed to aid the thrifts was passed by Congress on Oct. 1. It allowed, for the first time, federally chartered thrift institutions, including credit unions, to make consumer, commercial, and agricultural loans. Moreover, it permitted two federal agencies to issue government-guaranteed capital certificates in order to shore up the financial position of troubled thrift institutions. The agencies would have to make good on the notes if the institution actually failed.

In addition, the bill addressed a long-standing grievance of commercial banks by providing for an end to the ¼ percent interest rate advantage long accorded to thrift institutions for passbook savings accounts and Small Savers certificates. It also ordered federal regulators to create a federally insured deposit account that would enable banks and thrift institutions to compete with the extremely popular money market funds, which were paying interest of 10 to 13 percent for most of the year.

International. High U.S. interest rates had the effect of keeping interest rates high around the world, since foreign nations would suffer a debilitating loss of capital should their rates fall too far below the U.S. level. The high U.S. rates helped the dollar remain strong throughout the year. By late October the dollar had reached record highs against the French franc and Italian lira. At the same time it reached the highest levels in six years against the British pound, West German mark, and Swiss franc. It was also at a 65-month high against the Japanese yen. One effect of the strong dollar was to raise the price for foreigners of some key commodities, such as oil, that had to be paid for in terms of dollars.

With the economy of virtually every country in the world in weakened condition, several nations had trouble keeping up payments on their debts. Argentina, whose economic problems were intensified by the Falkland Islands war with Great Britain, had to renegotiate some of its nearly $40 billion in external debt. Mexico implemented a series of peso devaluations in an effort to redress its growing trade deficit and finally sought a loan from the International Monetary Fund (IMF) to make payments on its $80 billion in external debt, much of it owed to U.S. banks. Even France had to borrow $4 billion on the open market in September to support its currency, and, as of October, 28 nations were in arrears on their debt payments. The urgency of the international debt situation prompted the IMF to consider increasing its lending resources.

A major foreign banking scandal was the failure of Milan's Banco Ambrosiano—Italy's largest private bank—in August, following the mysterious death of its head, Roberto Calvi, whose body was found hanging under a London bridge on June 18. The bank was liquidated on Aug. 6, after having defaulted on $400,000,000 in losses by its Luxembourg-based holding company.

The Banco Ambrosiano was found to have made some $1.3 billion in unsecured loans to a number of companies registered abroad, most of them in Panama or the Bahamas, with the purpose of the loans and the whereabouts of the money unclear. The bank was known to have close ties with the Vatican's own bank, and there were reports that a number of the companies were in fact owned by the Vatican. The Vatican, however, refused to take responsibility for any of the bank's liabilities.　　　　G.D.W.

BARBADOS. See STATISTICS OF THE WORLD.

BEHAVIORAL SCIENCES. Advances made in 1982 in behavioral genetics, or the linking of heredity with behavioral patterns, included discoveries of evidence that suicidal behavior and shyness may both be inherited. The possibility that alcoholics might be retrained to drink socially remained a controversial subject, as did the nature of premenstrual stress. Behavioral scientists also continued to investigate child abuse.

Suicidal Behavior. Evidence that suicidal behavior can be inherited was provided by scientists at Wayne State University School of Medicine and at the National Institute of Mental Health (NIMH). The separate findings were made during comparison studies of the brains of suicides and those of victims of similar violent deaths.

The researchers found that levels of serotonin, a chemical messenger used by some nerves in the brain, varied according to whether the victim was a suicide or not. They determined this by measuring the ability of the antidepressant drug imipramine to bind to critical sites on the brain's frontal cortex. The degree of binding indicated the extent to which the brain used serotonin. Binding was reduced by about half in suicide victims, indicating a significant decrease in serotonin use by their brains.

Earlier research work had already shown that the binding of imipramine to blood platelets, the cells involved in clotting, is also abnormally low in depressed patients. Therefore an NIMH researcher, Frederick K. Goodwin, suggested that platelet-binding tests could be used to screen, at an early age, members of families with a history of suicidal behavior. In the meantime a drug called Zimeladine, which enhances the functional levels of serotonin, was being administered experimentally to NIMH patients who had previously attempted suicide.

Shyness. Shyness also appeared to be largely an inherited trait, according to the 1982 experimental findings of Robert Plomin of the University of Colorado Institute for Behavioral Genetics and David C. Rowe of Oberlin College. In a study of 1- and 2-year-old identical and fraternal twins, the researchers found that wariness toward strangers starts in infancy. Among identical twins, unlike the less genetically similar fraternal twins, both babies tended to be shy when a stranger approached. This was true only of reactions to strangers, however, not to the mother, which suggested that differences in behavior toward the mother seemed to be learned rather than inherited.

Alcoholics and Moderate Drinking. In 1970–71 a project organized by medical researcher Halmuth Schaefer aroused controversy by indicating that alcoholics could be

Studies of identical twins, who have identical genes, indicate that they also share a number of behavioral traits, such as shyness. From such evidence psychologists theorize that these traits are inherited.

trained to drink moderately. In 1982 Schaefer repudiated the findings of that study, citing more recent work by Mary Pendery, a psychologist at the Veterans Administration Medical Center at La Jolla, Calif. Her work convinced him that the earlier studies had reached false conclusions. During those experiments, alcoholics had drunk liquor in a simulated cocktail lounge at the Patton State Hospital near San Bernardino, Calif., with mild electric shocks administered to patients who drank too much or too quickly. In follow-up studies Pendery and other researchers found that some of the subjects later repeatedly went on alcoholic binges and underwent jailings and rehospitalizations.

Premenstrual Stress. A medical-legal controversy erupted in 1982 when women accused of violent assaults used the defense that premenstrual stress (PMS) had diminished their capacity to control such violence. PMS had been accepted as a mitigating factor during trials in Great Britain, but it was rejected as a legal defense by a British appeals court. The cause and nature of PMS appeared unclear, and no accepted way existed to diagnose or treat the condition. Some doctors had used

the hormone progesterone successfully in such cases, but why this kind of treatment worked in some cases and not in others was not known.

Child Abuse. A week-long conference was held at Cornell University in August, 1982, to study child abuse. An international forum of scientists in many fields discussed theories that sought to explain why some parents become child abusers. Sarah Hrdy, a Harvard University primatologist, noted that in all major groups of higher primates, including monkeys and great apes as well as humans, adult males have been observed to kill their infant young. Martin Reite, a psychiatrist at the University of Colorado School of Medicine, and Nancy Caine, a psychologist at Bucknell University, found what Reite called "remarkable similarities" between the child-abuse behaviors of pig-tailed macaques and humans. In both species about 18 percent of abused infants were abused repeatedly, and males were abused more than females. Failure of early mother-infant bonding led to infant abuse by the mother, and the young of abusive parents became abusive parents themselves.   M.K.

91

BELGIUM. A seriously declining economy dominated events in Belgium in 1982. To reverse the decline, the center-right government of Prime Minister Wilfried Martens adopted a strict austerity program, but efforts to put it into effect were complicated both by labor unrest and by external economic pressures.

On Feb. 2 the parliament granted the government (Belgium's 32nd in 38 years) special powers to rule by royal decree for a year. Martens had sought such authority in order to be able to come to grips with the country's grave economic problems. Chief among these were record unemployment, which by late 1982 had reached 13 percent of the labor force; soaring inflation, with wages indexed to price increases; and runaway government spending. No economic growth was expected in 1982.

Immediately after parliamentary approval the Martens government unveiled its austerity program. Designed to stimulate industrial activity, the program provided for broad tax cuts, curbs on wage increases, and significant reductions in public spending, including cuts in social security and other benefits. In late February the government devalued the franc by 8.5 percent.

The Socialist-led General Federation of Labor called a 24-hr. nationwide general strike on Feb. 8 in protest against the Martens plan. The strike paralyzed industrial activities in Wallonia, the French-speaking southern region of Belgium, but it gathered only partial support among workers in Brussels and in Flanders, the Flemish-speaking northern region.

In March steelworkers rioted in three cities to protest an order by the European Community (EC) that Belgium reduce employment in the steel industry by 10,000 under terms of a 1981 agreement to end government subsidies to steel companies by 1986. Another setback for the depressed industry came in October, when the EC agreed to cut steel exports to the United States.

See STATISTICS OF THE WORLD. L.A.S.

BELIZE. *See* STATISTICS OF THE WORLD.

BENIN. *See* STATISTICS OF THE WORLD.

BHUTAN. *See* STATISTICS OF THE WORLD.

BOLIVIA. After two years of political and economic turmoil under military dictatorships, civilian rule returned to Bolivia for the first time since 1965 when the congress overwhelmingly elected Hernán Siles Zuazo as president on Oct. 5, 1982. Bolivia thus became the third South American country in three years to turn to democratic rule, following Peru and Ecuador.

Early in the year, in an effort to restore some stability to Bolivia's failing economy, faced with a $3.8 billion foreign debt and a record payments deficit of $346,000,000, President Celso Torrelio Villa devalued the Bolivian peso and banned all meetings in order to maintain public order.

To offset growing popular unrest, Gen. Torrelio announced on July 15 that general elections, to be held in April, 1983, would permit Bolivia to return to constitutional rule. But a new military junta ousted Torrelio on July 19 and replaced him with Gen. Guido Vildoso Calderón two days later.

By mid-August the nation's major agricultural production center in Santa Cruz had declared bankruptcy. Bread and other basic foods became scarce, and prices nearly tripled during the year. Prices for the chief export, tin, were falling. Banks closed, and street sellers became the only source of pesos. Unable to meet payments on its foreign debt, Bolivia was refused additional loans by the International Monetary Fund unless drastic economic measures were imposed.

On Sept. 16 a wave of general strikes swept the country in protest against an emergency austerity program. Under pressure from the nation's military commanders, Vildoso resigned on Sept. 17.

Siles Zuazo, 68, was elected president by the congress elected in 1980 but meeting for the first time. This congress had been disbanded by the military after it seemed certain to elect Siles, who led the popular balloting for president in 1980 with 39 percent of the vote but fell short of the majority needed to choose a president without a runoff election in the congress. Siles had previously been president from 1956 to 1960.

Siles formed a three-party, left-of-center coalition government that included the

Communists, who received 2 of the 18 cabinet posts. On Oct. 11 he replaced the entire military high command in an effort to impose discipline on the armed forces.

See STATISTICS OF THE WORLD.   A.E.J.

BOTSWANA. See STATISTICS OF THE WORLD.

BRAZIL. The first free nationwide elections since 1962 were held in Brazil on Nov. 15, 1982, fulfilling a commitment made by President João Baptista de Oliveira Figueiredo. The nation's economy was beset by high inflation, slow growth, and difficulties in making payments on the huge foreign debt.

Politics. Although candidates of the government's Social Democratic Party polled only about 30 percent of the vote, they captured some 230 of the 479 seats in the national congress's Senate and Chamber of Deputies. The congress, as well as six representatives of the majority party in each state assembly, was to form an electoral college that would formally select the successor to Gen. Figueiredo in 1985. It seemed likely, therefore, that the military-run government would be able to designate its own choice to be the country's next president.

Voters also chose 22 governors, 25 senators, 947 state assembly members, 3857 mayors, and some 60,000 city council members. Candidates of the Social Democratic Party were elected governor in 12 states and candidates of the Brazilian Democratic Movement Party in nine. Leonel Brizola, the candidate of the Democratic Labor Party, was elected governor of the state of Rio de Janeiro. Brizola had been in exile for 15 years; the brother-in-law of the last civilian president, João Goulart, he had tried to mount armed resistance to the military takeover in 1964.

The nine states in which Brazilian Democratic Movement candidates were elected contained more than 60 percent of the population and produced 70 percent of the gross national product. Among them were Minas Gerais and São Paulo, the industrial centers. The elected candidates in these two states, Tancredo Neves and Franco Montoro, respectively, were members of the moderate faction of their party and said that they would not join any militant antigovernment movement.

The Economy. Despite belt-tightening measures, Planning Minister Antônio Delfim Netto was only barely able to hold the 1982 inflation rate under the three-digit mark, at about 99.5 percent. Further frustrating his efforts to revitalize the economy were sluggish world demand and low prices for such traditional Brazilian commodities as coffee, soybeans, and sugar. Despite catch-up wage increases equal to 110 percent of inflation, awarded to most workers, labor unrest grew during the year, and there were strikes in Belo Horizonte, Rio de Janeiro, and São Paulo. Moreover, bankers estimated that soccer fans who watched the World Cup competition on television during working hours cost Brazil more than $3 billion in lost production time.

A serious blow to Brazil's hopes for future prosperity was the decision, in January, by U.S. financier Daniel K. Ludwig to abandon his $1 billion development project in the Amazon basin. Known as Jari, the project was to be a vast agricultural, cattle, forestry, and mining undertaking located in the remote jungle. Prodded by the government, a group of Brazilian banks, contractors, insurance companies, and investment houses agreed to take over the project as "a service to the nation."

In 1982 Brazil ran into difficulties financing its estimated foreign debt of nearly $90 billion. The short-term debt was reported to have risen to nearly $14 billion, while foreign currency reserves were said to have fallen to less than $3 billion. In order to tide the country over, the government was forced to seek a loan from the International Monetary Fund (IMF) and direct assistance from the United States, two steps that it had long argued were against its interests. In return for IMF credits the government would probably be required to make cuts in a wide range of subsidies and put an end to the automatic semiannual adjustment of wages to price rises.

Foreign Policy. Figueiredo visited the U.S. in May and Canada in July, and he addressed the United Nations General Assembly in September. He stressed trade and financial issues and argued, in particular, that easier credit was needed to combat the world recession. In December U.S. President Ronald Reagan paid a visit to Brazil. He offered an emergency loan of $1.2 billion and said Washington would waive quotas limiting sugar imports from Brazil.

See STATISTICS OF THE WORLD.   A.E.J.

BRITISH COLUMBIA. See STATISTICS OF THE WORLD.

BULGARIA. Bulgaria remained the Soviet Union's most subservient European satellite in 1982. In January, however, Bulgarian Prime Minister Grisha Filipov announced the beginning of an economic reform unlike anything taking place in the Soviet Union. Called the New Economic Mechanism (NEM), it envisioned increased decision-making by individual enterprises and greater reliance on cost effectiveness and profits as tools in economic planning. Although less far-reaching than the experimentation that had taken place in Hungary in recent years, the reform marked a step away from rigid central control.

A scandal shook the ruling Communist Party during the year. Zhivko Popov, former deputy foreign minister and ambassador to Czechoslovakia, was expelled from the party Central Committee in March and was subsequently tried and convicted of misusing state funds. The court sentenced Popov to 20 years in prison and ordered the confiscation of his property.

Reports in the September issue of *Reader's Digest* and on NBC television speculated that Bulgaria's security forces had, with Soviet complicity, given aid to Mehmet Ali Agca, the Turk who shot and wounded Pope John Paul II in 1981. A Bulgarian was arrested in Rome on Nov. 25 and charged with complicity in the crime.

Bulgaria made efforts to maintain workable relations with its Balkan neighbors in 1982. The head of the National Assembly, Stanko Todorov, paid an official visit to Yugoslavia in March. In June President Todor Zhivkov played host to Greece's prime minister, Andreas Papandreou. Prime Minister Filipov visited Rumania for talks in July.

See STATISTICS OF THE WORLD.   F.W.

BURMA. Formerly, by its own choice, one of the world's most reclusive countries, Burma continued cautiously to open its doors to Western influence in 1982. Economically, the country sustained its modest boom of recent years.

Ne Win, who had come to power in a coup in 1962, announced his resignation from the presidency in 1981, and the office was turned over to an obscure functionary named San Yu. In 1982, however, Ne Win, who remained chairman of the country's only political party, the Burma Socialist Programme Party, continued to be regarded by Western diplomats as Burma's real political power. Political opposition was illegal, but it was not harshly dealt with in what was described as a "nonsinister police state."

Insurgent groups, including the China-backed Burmese Communist Party and tribal guerrillas such as the Karens, Kachins, and Shans, continued to be minor irritants. None of the insurgent movements, however, was considered a substantial threat to the Rangoon government.

Burma's economic gains were based primarily on the successful introduction of high-yield rice strains from the Philippines and on massive injections of foreign loans for capital investment. The excellent performance of agriculture was the main reason for an economic growth rate that reached 8.3 percent in 1981 and was expected to rise to 9 percent in 1982. During the fiscal year 1981–82, farmers harvested record crops, enabling Burma to boost its exports of agricultural products.

One of the founders of the "nonaligned" movement, Burma remained wary of foreign alliances and entanglements. Observers in international bodies such as the United Nations, however, discerned a slight shift toward the West. Relations with China remained cool, chiefly because of Chinese support for the Communist insurgents in Burma. Ties with Japan, the country's largest single aid donor, were close. Relations with the United States continued to improve, in part because of a $30,000,000 agreement for American agricultural assistance, which was signed in 1981.

See STATISTICS OF THE WORLD.   R.J.C.

BURUNDI. See STATISTICS OF THE WORLD.

C

CABINET, UNITED STATES. President Ronald Reagan's second year in office brought changes at the State and Energy departments and at the Council of Economic Advisers.

Cabinet Changes. Alexander M. Haig, Jr., resigned on June 25, 1982, as secretary of state, and President Reagan nominated George P. Shultz (see biography at PEOPLE IN THE NEWS) to succeed him. Although neither the President nor Haig gave specific reasons for Haig's departure, it was widely assumed that an important cause was dispute over U.S. policies in the Middle East and Europe. Secretary of Defense Caspar W. Weinberger and national security adviser William P. Clark (see biographies at PEOPLE IN THE NEWS) were said to have opposed Haig with increasing success on various policy and jurisdictional questions.

Shultz, president of the Bechtel Group, Inc., had served in the administration of President Richard M. Nixon as secretary of labor, director of the Office of Management and Budget, and secretary of the treasury. His nomination was unanimously confirmed by the Senate on July 15, and he took office the next day.

President Reagan sent to Congress on May 24 a new plan to abolish the Department of Energy, but it faced strong opposition from Democrats on Capitol Hill. Secretary of Energy James B. Edwards left his post Nov. 5 to assume the presidency of the Medical University of South Carolina. He was succeeded by Under Secretary of the Interior Donald Paul Hodel.

On July 20 Murray L. Weidenbaum submitted his resignation from the cabinet-level post of chairman of the Council of Economic Advisers. Harvard University Professor Martin Stuart Feldstein, president of the private, nonpartisan National Bureau of Economic Research, was named on Aug. 6 to replace him.

Officials under Fire. An apparent effort to put Secretary of the Interior James G. Watt on trial for contempt of Congress was blocked on March 18 when Congress and the Reagan administration agreed to a compromise. The House Committee on Energy and Commerce

---

A Frustrated Haig Exits

After only 17 months as secretary of state, Alexander M. Haig, Jr., resigned from office on June 25. Reportedly Haig, who had been fighting for preeminence over foreign policy since his appointment, threatened to quit once too often—and President Ronald Reagan, perhaps to Haig's surprise, finally accepted his offer. Haig's tenure in office was marked by continual policy differences and personal squabbling with White House officials, who found him abrasive, and also with Secretary of Defense Caspar W. Weinberger and Ambassador to the United Nations Jeane J. Kirkpatrick. Reagan's aides were said to consider Haig too soft on the Soviet Union and on Israel's invasion of Lebanon, and too accommodating toward China and Washington's European allies.

Alexander M. Haig, Jr.

had voted on Feb. 25 to ask the full House to decide whether Watt was in contempt for refusing, on President Reagan's orders, to give the committee some documents on Canadian energy and investment policies in the United States. Watt had said on Feb. 10 that he would go to prison rather than turn over such sensitive material. The compromise freeing Watt from the contempt threat permitted committee members to inspect the papers for no more than four hours and barred photocopying.

Secretary of Labor Raymond J. Donovan underwent intensive congressional and press scrutiny on various allegations, including charges that as an executive of the Schiavone Construction Co. of Secaucus, N.J., he had been involved with organized crime figures. Special prosecutor Leon Silverman reported on June 28 that he had found "insufficient credible evidence to warrant prosecution of Secretary Donovan on any charge." President Reagan said on June 30 that he was "sticking" with Donovan and considered the case "closed." After investigating additional allegations of a similar nature, Silverman reported on Sept. 13 that there still "was insufficient credible evidence to support a prosecution." A White House spokesman said that the case was "closed again."

Attorney General William French Smith announced on May 28 that he was abandoning about $117,600 in questionable tax deductions in connection with an oil and gas drilling venture. The Department of Justice said on July 21 that it was closing an investigation of Smith's behavior and was not recommending any action against him.

Membership. Cabinet-level officers (officials who hold cabinet rank without holding cabinet posts) included Feldstein; Jeane J. Kirkpatrick, U.S. representative to the United Nations; David A. Stockman, director of the Office of Management and Budget; William E. (Bill) Brock, U.S. trade representative; and William J. Casey, director of the Central Intelligence Agency.

The executive departments, the years of their establishment, and their heads during 1982 follow:

Department of State, 1789: Secretary, Alexander M. Haig, Jr., replaced by George P. Shultz.

Department of the Treasury, 1789: Secretary, Donald T. Regan.

Department of the Interior, 1849: Secretary, James G. Watt.

Department of Agriculture, 1862: Secretary, John R. Block.

Department of Justice, 1870: Attorney General, William French Smith.

Department of Commerce, 1913: Secretary, Malcolm Baldrige.

Department of Labor, 1913: Secretary, Raymond J. Donovan.

Department of Defense, 1949: Secretary, Caspar W. Weinberger.

Department of Health and Human Services, 1953: Secretary, Richard S. Schweiker.

Department of Housing and Urban Development, 1965: Secretary, Samuel R. Pierce, Jr.

Department of Transportation, 1966: Secretary, Andrew L. (Drew) Lewis, Jr.

Department of Energy, 1977: Secretary, James B. Edwards, replaced by Donald Paul Hodel.

Department of Education, 1979: Secretary, Terrel H. Bell.   L.A.S.

CALIFORNIA. *See* STATISTICS OF THE WORLD.

CAMBODIA, officially known as the PEOPLE'S REPUBLIC OF KAMPUCHEA. The government installed by Vietnamese troops in 1979 remained firmly in control of Cambodia in 1982. But the puppet regime was unable to eradicate guerrilla resistance to its rule or to gain international acceptance as the legitimate government in Phnom Penh.

Politics and Insurgency. Cambodians seemed resigned to a government kept in power by nearly 200,000 Vietnamese troops. Heng Samrin, as president of the Council of State and chairman of the Communist Party, held the two most powerful posts. In February Chan Sy, 50, another Cambodian with long-time ties to Vietnam, was named chairman of the Council of Ministers, a post roughly equivalent to prime minister. Vietnam's complete control of Cambodian affairs was confirmed by two Cambodian diplomats, who defected to Thailand in May.

In the countryside, however, three main guerrilla groups continued to fight against foreign domination. Of these three, the Khmer Rouge was the largest group, under the nominal leadership of Khieu Samphan. Numbering about 30,000 armed guerrillas, this seasoned force was the remnant of the extreme Communist regime of Pol Pot and Ieng Sary, which was held responsible for the deaths of several million Cambodians before being toppled by the Vietnamese in late 1978. The roughly 10,000 armed fighters of the Khmer People's Liberation Front were led by former conservative Prime Minister Son Sann. The Moulinaka resistance group, estimated at between 5000 and 9000 men, was led by former head of state Prince Norodom Sihanouk. Although militarily the weakest, its political influence was significant because of Sihanouk's international reputation and his popularity among the people of Cambodia. All three groups were based near western Cambodia's border with Thailand, although their influence extended to other parts of the country.

Early in the year the Vietnamese launched a major dry-season offensive against the insurgents and gradually drove them back. By mid-March up to 7000 Cambodian civilians had fled across the Thai border. Reports charged the Vietnamese with firing shells filled with "yellow rain," a chemical that caused nausea and itching. By May, however, the Vietnamese troops, having failed to take a key guerrilla mountain stronghold, were forced to withdraw by exceptionally heavy rains that blocked their supply lines.

Coalition Agreement. Throughout the first half of the year, the leaders of the three insurgent groups engaged in talks aimed at forging an anti-Vietnam coalition. Such a coalition was strongly backed by China, by the five countries of the Association of Southeast Asian Nations (Indonesia, Malaysia, the Philippines, Singapore, and Thailand), and, behind the scenes, by most Western countries. Despite ideological differences and personal antagonisms, the three rebel groups agreed, in the Malaysian capital, Kuala Lumpur, on June 22, to establish a new Cambodian government-in-exile, the Coalition Government of Democratic Kampuchea. Sihanouk was named president, Son Sann, prime minister,

Prince Norodom Sihanouk (right) inspects guerrilla forces fighting the Vietnam-backed regime in Cambodia. Leaders of three factions agreed in June to form a coalition government in exile, with Sihanouk as head of state and Son Sann as premier.

and Khieu Samphan, vice-president and foreign minister. Each of the three groups was to maintain its own identity and freedom of action.

In July Sihanouk met with Son Sann and Khieu Samphan in the guerrilla-held part of Cambodia to demonstrate the new coalition's territorial claim. In response, the Vietnamese proposed reducing their troops in Cambodia, but only on condition that Thailand agree to block aid to the insurgent groups.

Foreign Affairs. China was the only country openly sending arms to the insurgents, chiefly to the Khmer Rouge. Heng Samrin's government was recognized only by the Soviet bloc and by India. In the fall Sihanouk addressed the United Nations General Assembly in New York City; the assembly once again agreed to hold Cambodia's seat for the insurgent coalition. It also, once again, called for the withdrawal of foreign forces from Cambodia and for free elections.

See STATISTICS OF THE WORLD.   R.J.C.

CAMEROON. See STATISTICS OF THE WORLD.

While Canadian Prime Minister Pierre Elliott Trudeau watches, Queen Elizabeth II signs a proclamation in Ottawa enacting a new constitution for Canada. The action enables Canada to make changes in its constitution without petitioning the British Parliament.

CANADA. After many years of talks, Canada gained a new constitution in 1982, a historic event for the country and a political triumph for Prime Minister Pierre Elliott Trudeau (see biography at PEOPLE IN THE NEWS). The dismal state of the country's economy, however, caused the prime minister's popularity to plunge to an all-time low.

The Constitution. For the first time in its 115-year history, Canada assumed control of its own constitution. The British North America Act, signed by Queen Victoria to establish the Canadian federation in 1867, had served as the country's constitution. Although Canada gained full sovereignty in 1931, the constitution was never "brought home," because the federal and provincial governments were unable to agree on a formula to amend the document. Having been given a large amount of autonomy in the 1867 law, the provinces were wary of change.

Following years of talks, Trudeau finally induced the premiers of Canada's nine English-speaking provinces to accept a compromise in 1981. They agreed to an amending formula, whereby any constitutional change must have the consent of Ottawa and of seven of the ten provinces, provided that these represent at least 50 percent of the country's population, and included an "opting out" provision for those provinces rejecting certain changes. In exchange, the premiers agreed to accede to Trudeau's desire for incorporation in a new constitution of a charter of rights, including guarantees for the English-speaking minority in Québec and the French-speaking minority elsewhere to education in their own language, where numbers warrant. Later, other clauses were added guaranteeing equal rights for Inuit (Eskimo), Indians, mixed bloods, and women.

Only the premier of French-speaking Québec, René Lévesque, refused to accept the accord. Among his objections was the limitation put on Québec's right to legislate in favor of the French language.

Despite Québec's objections, a resolution asking the British government to approve these constitutional changes was passed by Parliament in December, 1981. The British Parliament approved the necessary legislation in March, 1982, and it received the royal assent on March 29. In an April 17 ceremony in Ottawa, Queen Elizabeth II formally transferred constitutional power from Great Britain to Canada, thereby giving Canada full control over its constitutional destiny. Lévesque boycotted the queen's visit.

Politics. A deeply troubled economy led to a steep decline in the popularity of Prime Minister Trudeau and his ruling Liberal Party. By midsummer, polls indicated that only 28 percent of the Canadian public supported the Liberals in the party's worst showing in the polls since 1943. The Progressive Conservatives, the main opposition party, were backed by 47 percent and the left-leaning New Democrats by 23 percent. One poll reported that 58 percent of Canadians hoped to see Trudeau resign as prime minister. Even some high-ranking members of the Liberal Party felt that Trudeau, Canada's prime minister for 16 years (except for an eight-month interval, during 1979–80), was a spent political force and should step aside.

In June Trudeau's government introduced a new budget aimed at bringing the country's double-digit annual inflation rate under control. Legislation quickly passed the Liberal-dominated parliament that imposed tax increases and provided for investment incentives. The key provision, however, was a wage restraint program limiting pay increases for Canada's 500,000 federal employees to 6 percent over the following 12 months and to 5 percent in the succeeding year. The government also appealed to public opinion in an effort to pressure provincial governments and the private sector into adhering to the "6 and 5" wage guidelines. In September Trudeau reshuffled his cabinet, naming one of his chief advisers, Marc Lalonde, to the key post of finance minister.

Job seekers in Vancouver, British Columbia, warm themselves by a makeshift fire while waiting for an employment office to open. The Canadian unemployment rate was about 12 percent in late 1982.

These moves, however, failed to halt the decline in the government's popularity. In October the Liberals were soundly defeated in three parliamentary by-elections in Ontario. Although Trudeau's party still retained a clear majority in parliament, opposition leaders demanded that Trudeau, little more than half-way through his five-year term, call for early elections.

Provincial elections also gave Trudeau no comfort. The Progressive Conservatives retained control in Alberta, Newfoundland, and Prince Edward Island, and they ousted the ruling New Democrats in Saskatchewan.

The Liberals did not control a single provincial government.

The Economy. Statistics made it clear that the Canadian economy suffered great difficulties in 1982. The Canadian dollar fell to an all-time low against its U.S. counterpart in June, dropping to U.S.76.86¢ in Toronto on June 21. In October the annual inflation rate stood at 11 percent, nearly twice that of the United States. Unemployment, at the highest level in nearly 50 years, was 12.2 percent of the labor force in August. From mid-1981 to mid-1982 the gross national product fell 6 percent, after adjustment for inflation.

Part of the reason for Canada's poor economic showing was the worldwide recession. Nevertheless, critics insisted that the Trudeau government itself deserved a large share of the blame. In particular, they charged that the government's economic nationalism, in the form of programs designed to reduce foreign ownership in Canada's critically important energy industry, was driving out badly needed investment and thus creating unemployment. At the same time, Canadian capital was slow to take up the slack. Moreover, Alberta and other oil-producing provinces alleged that federal controls over the oil industry had stifled exploration and production.

Two of the Trudeau government's most important projects, enterprises that were to have pumped billions of dollars into the Canadian economy and to have provided thousands of jobs, suffered devastating blows on April 30. The remaining members of a consortium of oil firms decided to abandon a four-year-old plan to extract more synthetic crude oil from oil sand deposits in northern Alberta. And a U.S. business consortium announced a two-year delay in planning for the construction of the northern section of the Alaska natural gas pipeline on the grounds that the necessary financing could not be found. The northern section of the pipeline was to have been linked with another section, already under construction, that was to cross Canada and link with two segments in the lower U.S. Delay of the project meant lost sales of Canada's own Arctic gas to U.S. customers.

Foreign Policy. Canada remained a staunch member of the Western alliance in 1982, standing alongside the U.S. and Western Europe on most critical international issues. A growing Canadian interest in hemispheric affairs was reflected in a special nonpartisan parliamentary committee recommendation in September that the country join the Organization of American States. A formal application for membership appeared likely to follow.

Relations with the U.S. remained the most important element in Canada's foreign policy. The Trudeau government continued to press Washington to act on the problem of acid rain. This phenomenon occurs when acidic gases, such as sulfur dioxide, usually emitted by power plants, smelters, and automobiles, combine with atmospheric moisture. Canadians were deeply concerned, because much of the acid rain deposited on Canadian territory, contaminating crops, forests, and lakes, originated in the U.S. in the form of air pollution. To the extreme annoyance of Ottawa, the administration of President Ronald Reagan opposed legislation requiring U.S. industry to install additional antipollution equipment.

The two countries also clashed on several economic issues. A major target of American criticisms was Canada's National Energy Program, introduced in late 1980, which discriminated against foreign investment in Canada's energy industry. The program was intended to ensure Canadians of half-ownership by 1990 in their nation's oil and gas industry, a large portion of which was owned by U.S. interests in 1982. Another major irritant to the U.S. was Canada's Foreign Investment Review Agency, established to screen all foreign investments for "significant benefit to Canada." In most instances, foreign investors were being admitted only if they promised to purchase Canadian goods and to export much of a new operation's product. In March the U.S. put the matter before the international forum of the General Agreement on Tariffs and Trade in Geneva, charging that the practices "distorted" international trade.

See STATISTICS OF THE WORLD.   R.J.C.

CAPE VERDE. *See* STATISTICS OF THE WORLD.

CARIBBEAN COUNTRIES. Unpopular measures aimed at halting the sharp economic decline in the region produced a rise in political and social tensions in many Caribbean countries in 1982. A rapid rise in population had increased the need for imports and outstripped the countries' ability to create jobs. Unemployment in much of the region stood at between 20 and 30 percent of the labor force. The worldwide recession caused prices for such traditional Caribbean exports as sugar, coffee, cocoa, and bauxite to plummet. Sugar import quotas, introduced by the United States in mid-1982, reduced the region's most important market for its exports.

Warning of the danger that "new Cubas will rise from the ruins of today's conflicts," U.S. President Ronald Reagan offered an economic plan for the Caribbean Basin on Feb. 24 that proposed expanded U.S. financial aid. His address called for an additional $350,000,000 in economic aid and $60,000,000 in military aid for the region during fiscal 1982, bringing the total to $996,000,000. Reagan also proposed duty-free status for almost all Caribbean products exported to the U.S., tax incentives for U.S. investment in the region, and U.S. technical assistance. The economic aid package was passed by Congress in September, with El Salvador, Costa Rica, Honduras, Jamaica, and the Dominican Republic expected to be the major recipients. The tax and trade incentives, however, did not gain legislative approval in 1982. Moreover, it was believed that the Caribbean region's lack of skilled labor and frequently unstable political conditions inspired little investor confidence.

Dominican Republic. In an election held on May 16, a huge voter turnout chose Salvador Jorge Blanco as the Dominican Republic's new president. Jorge Blanco, one of eight candidates for the presidency, handily defeated his strongest opponent, former President Joaquín Balaguer. In simultaneous balloting, voters also chose a new vice-president and candidates for the 27-seat Senate, the 120-member Chamber of Deputies, and for a number of municipal offices.

Little more than one month before Jorge

President Ronald Reagan and his wife pose with the prime ministers of five Caribbean nations in Barbados in April. In February the President had announced a new U.S. aid program for Central America and the Caribbean Basin.

Blanco was to be sworn in—July 3—outgoing President Silvestre Antonio Guzmán Fernández committed suicide. Despite a brief flurry of rumors of an impending military coup, power was swiftly transferred in an orderly fashion to Vice-President Jacobo Majluta Azar, who announced that he intended to turn over the government to the newly elected president on Aug. 16, as planned. The government offered no explanation for the suicide of the 71-year-old Guzmán. But it was later revealed that shortly before his death Guzmán had discovered that some trusted aides had skimmed large profits from government operations and had deposited millions of dollars from his economically crippled country in foreign bank accounts.

In his inaugural address Jorge Blanco bluntly declared that his nation was in "financial bankruptcy" and announced a program of austere economic measures.

Haiti. Bent on overthrowing the government of Haiti's President-for-life Jean-Claude Duvalier, a group of Haitian exiles invaded the offshore island of Tortuga in early January. The group's leader, Bernard Sansaricq, 37, an exile and a Miami gasoline station owner, said that the object of the invasion was to touch off a revolution in his native country. Although an undetermined number of invaders managed briefly to seize control of Tortuga, they were chased away by the Haitian army. Sansaricq himself and 25 companions never set foot on the island. Their boat sprang a leak at sea and was picked up by the U.S. Coast Guard, which returned the invaders to Miami, where they were charged with violating U.S. neutrality laws.

On Aug. 28 Silvio Claude, head of Haiti's tiny Christian Democratic Party, and 21 of his associates were sentenced to six years in prison. This was their second trial for antigovernment acts; an appeals court threw out their earlier sentences of 15 years at hard labor. Claude's party was one of the last remaining political opposition groups.

International human rights observers termed the trial "a farce," and declared that there was little credible evidence against most of the defendants. On Sept. 24 Duvalier granted a pardon to the 22, who had been in custody since 1980, but did not set a date for their release.

The donors of foreign aid, who pay 40 percent of Haiti's budget, forced President Duvalier to change some of his ways of doing business in 1982. As a condition for a $38,000,000 loan to help Haiti pay its foreign debts, the International Monetary Fund demanded strict controls on government borrowing, spending, and accounting.

Suriname. The four-man National Military Council of Suriname, headed by Lt. Col. Desi Bouterse, announced on Feb. 5 that it had taken over the government, following the resignation of civilian President Chin A. Sen and his entire cabinet. It was believed that the army takeover was prompted by resistance to the council's drift toward the Left.

A radio announcement on March 11 asserted that a "liberation council" of rebel forces had toppled the military government. The next day loyal government troops staged a predawn assault on the rebels at the military barracks outside Paramaribo, the capital. They captured the wounded Sgt. Maj. Wilfred Hawker, one of the two rebel leaders, who appealed to his followers to surrender, but was executed nonetheless. On Dec. 8, 15 opponents of the leftist government were killed by security forces.

See STATISTICS OF THE WORLD. See also CUBA; PUERTO RICO.   A.E.J.

CENTRAL AFRICAN REPUBLIC. See STATISTICS OF THE WORLD.

CEYLON. See SRI LANKA.

CHAD. The 17-year-long civil war in Chad took a surprising turn in 1982 when the forces of Hissène Habré overthrew the government of President Goukouni Oueddei in early June. Habré assumed the presidency on Oct. 21.

Habré and his Armed Forces of the North (FAN) had been driven out of the capital, N'Djamena, by Libyan forces supporting Oueddei in late 1980. The FAN retreated into western Sudan, where they began to rearm. Meanwhile, Oueddei, finding himself under increasing pressure from the West and from the Organization of African Unity (OAU) to remove the Libyans, did so in late 1981, and in their place accepted an OAU peacekeep-

Chadian leader Hissène Habré talks to reporters after his forces occupied the capital of this African nation in June. Habré declared his intention to seek a long-term solution to the strife that had racked his country for almost 20 years.

remain neutral in Chad's internal power conflict.

On June 7 the FAN, sweeping aside its opponents, entered N'Djamena. Oueddei fled, going first to Cameroon and then to Algeria. Habré, with his rule over the northern part of Chad now apparently secure, declared himself head of state on June 19. By the end of the month all OAU units had been withdrawn from Chad, leaving Habré's forces to seek revenge against their opponents; some 700 people were killed in the N'Djamena area. Thousands thereupon fled to Cameroon. In July, after an appeal for aid by the new Habré government, the United States began to airlift food to the country.

After being sworn in as president on Oct. 21, Habré named a 31-member cabinet that included former adversaries as well as longtime allies.

See STATISTICS OF THE WORLD.   J.T.S.

CHEMISTRY. Chemists in 1982 developed several interesting new products, ranging from insecticides to possible blood substitutes. Besides these practical achievements, they also conducted pure research into new molecules of unusual shape. These achievements represented a mere sampling of the ongoing work in chemistry, which is involved in nearly all areas of science and technology.

Möbius Strip Molecule. University of Colorado scientists David M. Walba, R. Curtis Haltiwanger, and Rodney M. Richards synthesized a new molecular form out of a chemical known as tris(tetrahydroxymethylethylene), or tris(THYME). They did this by taking the long, double-stranded molecule and joining its ends to create a closed form. Before joining the ends, however, they gave the molecule a half-twist so as to produce the shape of that familiar topological curiosity, a Möbius strip. The new molecule was found to obey the same rules as does such a strip; thus, when the scientists used ozone to split the molecule down the middle the long way, the result was a single ring twice as long and half as wide as before, rather than two separate rings.

The shape of a molecule often determines, at least in part, how that molecule would

ing force. But as soon as the Libyans withdrew, the FAN swept out of the Sudan, seizing abandoned Libyan arms and supplies, and captured the major towns of eastern Chad. By February, 1982, it became clear that the undermanned OAU force of some 3000, which was instructed to avoid combat, would be no match for Habré's troops, and that the cost of maintaining the force, estimated at $163,000,000 a year, was beyond the OAU's resources. The OAU called for a cease-fire and negotiations between the Oueddei government and the FAN; Oueddei, however, refused. In an effort to force negotiations, France cut off arms aid to Oueddei, and the OAU threatened to withdraw its force at the end of June. Disillusioned with the OAU efforts, Oueddei turned again to the Libyans, but in late May Tripoli declared that it would henceforth

At Los Alamos (N.Mex.) National Laboratory, analysis of a tiny sample of rare-earth elements is achieved by using a laser beam to selectively ionize one of the vaporized elements contained in the sample chamber of a mass spectrometer. Such analyses of elements produced at sites of underground nuclear weapons tests aid in evaluating weapons performance.

function in a given situation. What sort of function, then, would a molecule have that was shaped like a Möbius strip? No practical use was immediately determined for the odd new molecule, but researchers were at work synthesizing other topologically unusual molecules.

Insecticides and Repellents. An antibiotic insecticide called milbemycin B_3, which previously had been produced from cultures of a *Streptomyces* bacterium, was synthesized in 1982 by two different groups of researchers. The scientists, working independently, were led by Amos B. Smith 3rd of the University of Pennsylvania and David R. Williams of Indiana University.

The antibiotic in question is one of 13 known milbemycin antibiotics. Although milbemycins are fairly weak when used anti-

biotically, they are powerful when used to battle pests and parasites such as tent caterpillars, aphids, mites, and intestinal worms. The chemical synthesis of milbemycin B_3 might benefit agriculture, because small doses of the pesticide do not appear to be toxic to the plants and animals they are supposed to safeguard yet are potent pest killers.

One old-fashioned method of dealing with a household pest, the cockroach, was shown in 1982 to have some scientific basis. The method is the use of cucumbers or bay leaves to repel roaches, which appear to shun these substances. At Kansas State University, Clifton E. Meloan performed laboratory experiments to test the truth of that observation. The chemicals involved in this effect appeared to be the trans-2-noneal found in cucumber skins and the cineole, or eucalyptol, found in bay leaves. Meloan hoped to develop a new roach repellent, based on these chemicals, that would be safe for household use.

Better Artificial Blood. Fluosol-DA, a perfluorocarbon emulsion, is a chemical that is used as a hemoglobin substitute because it can carry oxygen in the blood to tissues that need it and can remove carbon dioxide from the tissues at the same time. Technically, the chemical is not a substitute for natural whole blood, but it can help anemic patients to survive surgery. In 1982 Fluosol-DA was used to treat five Jehovah's Witnesses who, because of their religious convictions, refused blood transfusions for surgery.

The chemical, however, has drawbacks. It must be kept frozen until used, the patient receiving it must be in a high-oxygen atmosphere, and the perfluorochemicals remain in the patient's body long after Fluosol-DA has done its work. Scientists, therefore, were searching for Fluosol-DA substitutes. One possible candidate, another fluorocarbon emulsion, can be safely stored at room temperature for months at a time and does not appear to linger in the body as long as does Fluosol-DA. Scientists also had recently found that blood substitutes already available might help patients suffering from heart attacks, strokes, shock, or cancer.

Bubble Bandages. Another recent chemical advance in medicine has been the development of new polyurethane surgical dressings. The new materials look more like pieces of household plastic wrap than the familiar bandage strips and patches, but they do not smother the wounds as those bandages can. Manufactured in Great Britain, West Germany, and the United States, they come in sizes to cover anything from a small cut to a wounded leg. One side of the bandage is completely covered with a special adhesive that does not stick to the wound but instead bubbles up around it. The special plastic is also permeable to oxygen, allowing the protected wound necessary access to air. The wound can thus heal faster and is less likely to become infected.   J.S.

CHILE. A faltering economy and growing social problems moved Chile's President Augusto Pinochet Ugarte to make two drastic cabinet changes during 1982. On April 19 Pinochet dismissed his entire cabinet and, in selecting replacements, reduced the number of civilians from 8 to 6 of the 16. The country's worsening economy was regarded as the main reason for the shake-up, but Pinochet overruled criticism of his economic policies and refused to devalue the peso, which had remained at 39.80 to the U.S. dollar for three years. Critics maintained that this exchange rate discouraged foreign investment and had drastically reduced Chilean exports. Industrial production fell by 14 percent during the first quarter of 1982 from the previous year.

On June 14, faced with the prospect of a prolonged recession, the Chilean authorities devalued the peso to 46 per dollar and later announced that it would float against the dollar. But after several months of continued economic deterioration, Pinochet again asked his cabinet to resign. On Aug. 30 he swore in six new cabinet ministers, unifying the nation's economics and finance ministries under a new minister, Rolf Luders. Luders was expected to adopt measures to increase production and to reduce unemployment, which had reached 21 percent of the labor force. The gross national product was expected to fall by at least 7 percent in 1982, partly due to the fall of world copper prices, since copper exports account for half of Chile's foreign income.

Following Argentina's defeat in the Falklands war (see MILITARY AND NAVAL AFFAIRS), Chileans were deeply worried that Argentina might renew its efforts to seize Chile's Beagle Channel islands at the southernmost tip of the continent. The territory consists of a group of remote rocky islands inhabited by a few sheepherders, fishermen, and kelpers. Chileans were further concerned by the fact that Argentina regularly sent its ships into Chile's South Atlantic waters without permission. In the continuing legal dispute, Chile opposed Argentina's contention that control of all territory on the Atlantic side of the Strait of Magellan and Cape Horn should be in Argentine hands and that Chile should control the Pacific side.

See STATISTICS OF THE WORLD.   A.E.J.

A new party constitution was adopted in September at the first national congress of the Chinese Communist Party to be held in five years. Many new members were elected to the 210-seat Central Committee of the party.

CHINA, PEOPLE'S REPUBLIC OF. China, under the leadership of Teng Hsiao-ping (Deng Xiaoping, see biography at PEOPLE IN THE NEWS), launched a major effort in 1982 to reduce the size of the central bureaucracy and of the Communist Party. Economic modernization was spurred by foreign investment. A new census revealed that China's population had passed the 1 billion level. Relations with the United States were strained by Washington's continuing military support for Taiwan. Signs of renewed interest appeared in improved relations between the Soviet Union and China.

Politics. The 12th Congress of the Chinese Communist Party, held in Peking, Sept. 1–11, approved a new party constitution to replace the one adopted in 1977. The new document outlined a changed administrative structure that resembled the Soviet model. The posts of party chairman and of vice-chairman were eliminated, and the role of secretary-general, held by Hu Yao-pang (Hu Yaobang), was strengthened, as was Teng's chairmanship of the central military commission. Teng, the real party leader and the architect of the new constitution, was also to remain on the Standing Committee of the Politburo, the party's ruling inner circle. Commissions were established to hasten the retirement of the party's many aging functionaries.

The new constitution pointedly downgraded the historic role of the late Mao Tsetung (Mao Zedong). Mao's handpicked successor, former party chairman Hua Kuo-feng (Hua Guofeng), was dropped from membership in the Politburo. Nearly 40,000,000 party members were placed on notice that they must reapply and be reconsidered for membership.

A similar trend was already under way in the government. Between March and the end of May the Standing Committee of the National People's Congress eliminated all but two vice-premierships, merged several ministries, abolished numerous state council organizations, and drastically reduced ministerial staffs. Twenty-three new ministers were appointed. Their average age was 58, considerably younger than that of their predecessors, which was 64. Several women emerged in high-level ministerial posts. Newly established rules, with some exceptions, required all ministers to retire at the age of 65. Although the changes were said to be designed to facilitate economic progress, many political foes of Teng were purged.

On Dec. 4 the National People's Congress ratified a new constitution, the third in seven years. It restored the post of head of state, limited top state officials to a maximum of two five-year terms, called on the Chinese people to practice birth control, and rescinded the right to strike.

The Economy. Economic reconstruction gained high priority. The ministries of foreign trade and external economic relations, and the state commissions on foreign investment and import-export affairs, were merged into one superministry. Chen Muhua, head of the powerful new agency, quickly reassured foreign nations that their commercial ties with China were not endangered by these changes.

In January the government announced that foreign investment was on the rise, having

Two curious Chinese women try out a Mickey Mouse telephone at the opening of the U.S. National Light Industry Exhibition in Peking. U.S.-Chinese relations remained strained, however, over the question of American military aid to Taiwan.

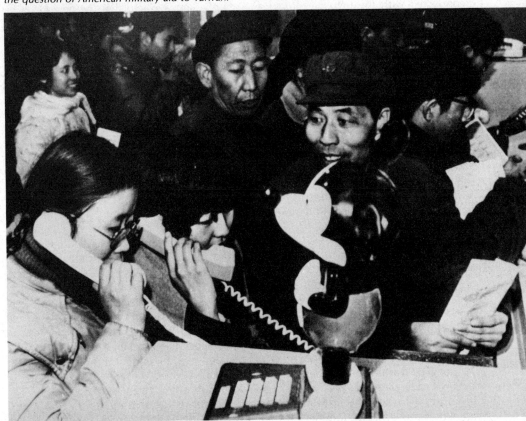

increased by 20 percent, to $1.2 billion, in 1981. The largest gains were made in small cooperative production agreements. On Nov. 4 China announced a bumper harvest, with total grain output for 1982 expected to exceed the record 332,100,000 tons in 1979.

To expand foreign economic ties, China opened its offshore waters for exploitation by foreign oil companies. The China National Offshore Oil Corp., formed on Feb. 15 to control drilling by foreign firms, invited bids from 46 companies, half of them American, representing 12 countries. Initial bidding was limited to areas in the Yellow Sea and the Pearl River estuary. It was estimated that by 1990 exploitation of China's offshore oil reserves could double its current crude oil production of about 2,000,000 bbl per day.

Census. On July 1 China undertook the task of registering its population, estimated at one fourth of the world's reported 4.5 billion inhabitants. The 1982 census was the first to be conducted with the help of computers, which were supplied by the United Nations. At a cost of $100,000,000, in addition to a further $15,600,000 from the U.N., and with the help of a staff of 5,100,000, the Chinese government was able to publish basic data in October. These showed a mainland population of 1,008,175,288, an increase of 313,000,-000 since the last census, held in 1964.

Military. On Oct. 16 the official New China News Agency reported that China had test-fired its first submarine-launched missile, making China the fifth country, after the U.S., the U.S.S.R., Great Britain, and France, to have achieved the successful development of such missiles.

Foreign Affairs. U.S.-Chinese relations were strained by the announcement on April 13 that the U.S. would sell $60,000,000 worth of spare parts to Taiwan to be used in the production of 60 F-5E fighter jets. Peking claimed that the sale was a clear violation of the Shanghai Communiqué of 1972 and of U.S. recognition of China in 1978. The U.S. countered that the Taiwan Relations Act of 1979 obliged Washington to help Taiwan maintain an adequate means of self-defense.

In an effort to heal the growing Peking-Washington rift, U.S. Vice-President George Bush visited China, May 5–9. Bush released letters from President Ronald Reagan to China's leaders, which pledged U.S. commitment to a one-China policy, and which also noted that the need for arms in Taiwan should diminish as Peking and Taipei progressed toward peaceful reunification.

On Aug. 17 the U.S. and China issued a communiqué in which the U.S. promised not to exceed current levels of arms sales to Taiwan and to reduce them gradually, without setting a timetable. China agreed to strive for a "peaceful resolution of the Taiwan question," as indicated in previous messages, including the nine-point proposal of Sept. 30, 1981, that invited Taiwan to submit to the central authority of the mainland. But Peking pointed out that it had not promised not to try to seize Taiwan by force. An Aug. 18 editorial in the Communist Party organ, *People's Daily,* strongly condemned the Taiwan Relations Act as a violation of Chinese sovereignty, and declared that the new U.S.-Chinese communiqué was only a beginning in settling the Taiwan issue.

The question of sovereignty also concerned the future of Hong Kong, a British colony. Great Britain holds a lease, expiring in 1997, on 90 percent of the colony's territory; the remainder, including the island of Hong Kong, was ceded to Britain in perpetuity by two 19th-century treaties that Peking regards as invalid. After a visit to China by British Prime Minister Margaret Thatcher in September, a joint communiqué said only that further talks would be held.

Soviet President Leonid I. Brezhnev appealed to Peking on March 24 to end two decades of hostility in Soviet-Chinese relations. He called for a resumption of long-interrupted border talks and for improved economic, cultural, and political ties. The first high-level talks in nearly three years were held in October with no details announced but more sessions scheduled to be held. In November Foreign Minister Huang Hua attended the funeral of Brezhnev and was warmly received by the new Soviet Communist Party chief, Yuri V. Andropov.

See STATISTICS OF THE WORLD.   T.L.K.

CHINA, REPUBLIC OF. *See* TAIWAN.

At the White House, before a group of congressional members, President Ronald Reagan signs into law an extension of the 1965 Voting Rights Act. A key provision of the original measure requires some states and localities to obtain federal clearance for changes in election procedure.

CIVIL RIGHTS AND CIVIL LIBERTIES. Groups advocating the rights of minorities and women repeatedly clashed with the administration of U.S. President Ronald Reagan over civil rights enforcement during 1982. In rulings on illegal aliens and mentally retarded persons, the U.S. Supreme Court took an expansive view of individual rights. The Equal Rights Amendment to the U.S. Constitution failed to win ratification, but the federal Voting Rights Act was renewed.

Civil Rights and the Reagan Administration. The Reagan administration's conservative economic policies and restrictive interpretation of civil rights laws and regulations led equal rights groups to complain of a retrenchment in civil rights enforcement. The biggest controversy was touched off on Jan. 8 when the Administration announced its intention to grant tax exemptions to private schools that discriminate on the basis of race. The decision, reversing an 11-year-old policy under which the Internal Revenue Service (IRS) denied tax-exempt status to such schools, applied specifically to Bob Jones University of Greenville, S.C., which segregated black and white students in various ways, including a ban on interracial dating, and the Goldsboro Christian Schools of Goldsboro, N.C., which refused to admit blacks.

A firestorm of criticism against the policy change prompted President Reagan to declare on Jan. 12 that he was "unalterably opposed to racial discrimination in any form."

Arguing that the IRS had been acting improperly by denying such tax exemptions in the absence of express legislative authority, the Administration called belatedly for Congress to act, but congressional leaders concluded that no new legislation was needed. The Justice Department on Feb. 25 asked the U.S. Supreme Court to decide whether the schools were entitled to tax exemptions and whether the original IRS decision to deny them reflected congressional intent. The Court was to hear testimony in the case during its 1982–83 term.

In September 33 state advisers to the U.S. Commission on Civil Rights charged the Administration with responsibility for "a dangerous deterioration in the federal enforcement of civil rights." President Reagan labeled this and similar charges "plain baloney."

Congress on June 23 approved extension for 25 years of key provisions of the federal Voting Rights Act of 1965. The compromise bill, which the Reagan administration endorsed only after a nationwide lobbying effort by civil rights groups, broadened the grounds on which the federal courts might decide suits alleging that voting rights had been infringed. The measure also permitted designated states and localities to "bail out" of the requirement that they submit changes in election procedures for federal approval, if they could show a ten-year history of nondiscrimination and of positive efforts to increase minority electoral participation. President

Reagan signed the extension into law on June 29.

Social Issues in Congress. On March 2 the Senate passed, by a vote of 57–37, the most restrictive antibusing bill in its history, severely limiting the ability of federal courts to order busing for the purpose of school desegregation. The measure failed to clear the House of Representatives, however.

Conservative legislators faltered in their efforts to pass legislation prohibiting abortion and allowing prayer in public schools. Although President Reagan indicated his personal support for such measures, filibusters and other parliamentary maneuvers by liberal Senators prevented definitive votes on pending bills by the Senate.

Sex Discrimination. The proposed Equal Rights Amendment (ERA), intended to bar discrimination on the basis of sex, fell three states short of approval before the June 30 deadline for ratification. ERA opponents celebrated its defeat, but the same proposed amendment to the Constitution was reintroduced in Congress on July 14. While prospects for the reintroduced amendment were uncertain at best, women on both sides of the ERA fight vowed to elect candidates of their choice. The National Organization for Women announced the formation of a $3,000,000 political action committee to further ERA prospects.

In two important sex discrimination rulings, a 5–4 majority of the Supreme Court on July 1 held unconstitutional the exclusion of men from a state-supported nursing school in Mississippi, and a 6–3 majority decided on May 17 that a federal law banning sex discrimination in federally financed education programs covers employees as well as students.

Rights of Aliens. On June 15 a 5–4 majority of the Supreme Court held that states cannot deny a free public education to the children of illegal aliens. The Court ruled, for the first time, that illegal aliens are "persons" entitled to protection under the Fourteenth Amendment's equal protection clause and that states therefore cannot deny to undocumented school-age children the same free education they provide for other children.

On June 29 a federal district court judge in Miami voided the procedures under which some 1900 Haitians who had entered the United States illegally were being held in detention camps. As a result of the ruling, the Haitians, many of whom had been detained for nearly a year, were released pending hearings on their petitions for political asylum in the U.S.

National Security. Upset over news leaks allegedly affecting national security, the Reagan administration sought to tighten its handling of classified foreign policy and defense information. New procedures announced on Feb. 2 restricted access to classified data, and an executive order on April 2 gave the government broader powers to classify sensitive material.

On June 10 Congress passed the Intelligence Identities Protection Act, which prohibits public identification of U.S. spies. The law bans anyone, including private citizens using public sources, from publishing the names of covert agents if there is "reason to believe" such disclosure would impair or impede U.S. foreign intelligence activities. Despite questions raised by legal scholars as to its constitutionality, President Reagan signed the bill into law on June 23.

Rights of the Mentally Retarded. In a unanimous ruling on June 18, the Supreme Court declared, for the first time, that mentally retarded persons in state institutions have the right to live in reasonably safe conditions, to be free from unreasonable physical restraints, and to receive "minimally adequate" training in caring for themselves. The decision was an important victory for mental health advocates. Although the Court did not rule that the retarded have a contitutional right to a particular form of treatment, it said that states must do more than provide adequate food, clothing, shelter, and medical care to persons involuntarily committed to state institutions.

Libel. A federal jury in Washington, D.C., held on July 30 that William P. Tavoulareas, president of Mobil Oil Corp., had been libeled by the Washington *Post* in a 1979 article alleging improper business dealings between Tavoulareas and his son. The father and son were awarded damages of more than $2,000,000.

Other Issues. In a decision announced on June 24, the Supreme Court held, 5–4, that a U.S. President may not be sued for damages for actions taken while in office. The ruling was expected to dissolve several pending civil lawsuits against former President Richard M. Nixon.

After a highly publicized trial, a federal district judge in Arkansas overturned that state's law requiring "balanced" teaching of the theories of evolution and "creation science" in public schools. In his Jan. 5 opinion, Judge William Ray Overton declared that the Arkansas law violated the First Amendment separation of church and state. On Nov. 22 a federal district judge struck down a similar Louisiana law on the ground that the legislature had overstepped its authority.

By a 6–3 majority, the Supreme Court on June 23 struck down a Massachusetts law requiring trial judges to exclude the press and public during the testimony of sex crime victims under the age of 18.

On July 2 the Court ruled that political boycotts are protected by the First Amendment. The 8–0 decision voided a judgment of more than $1,000,000 in damages imposed by Mississippi courts against the National Association for the Advancement of Colored People (NAACP) for a civil rights boycott against white-owned businesses in that state 16 years earlier.

In another important First Amendment ruling announced on July 2, the Court unanimously held that states can restrict the distribution of material depicting sexual activities of children under 16, whether or not the material is legally obscene.

U.S. Rights Groups and Leaders. On Jan. 18 National Urban League President John Jacob declared that the Administration's economic policies and "backtracking" on civil rights enforcement "created a feeling among many blacks that they were forgotten people." Some groups, however, recorded progress on the economic front. Operation PUSH (People United to Save Humanity) negotiated contractual agreements with several major U.S. companies for greater minority partici-

A jubilant Haitian refugee (seated) receives congratulations on his release from a federal detention camp. In June a judge in Miami ordered the federal government to parole most of the 1900 Haitian refugees being held in camps while seeking asylum in the U.S.

pation. Buoyed by the Supreme Court's decision upholding their right to boycott as a form of protest, delegates to the NAACP convention in July resolved to use boycotts more frequently—including one against the entertainment industry—to promote equal rights.

Joseph Paul Franklin, a self-avowed racist, was found not guilty on Aug. 17 of violating the civil rights of Vernon E. Jordan, Jr., former head of the National Urban League. Franklin, already serving life sentences for the murders of two black men, was accused of seriously wounding Jordan in a sniper attack in Fort Wayne on May 29, 1980.

See also NEGROES IN THE UNITED STATES; WOMEN.   D.C.

At a New York City auction in October, a $3 gold piece struck at the San Francisco Mint in 1870 is sold for $687,500. This coin, with the mint-mark "S," is thought to be the only one of its kind in existence.

COIN COLLECTING, *or* NUMISMATICS. The big news in the numismatic community during 1982 was the emergence of the remaining portion of the Virgil M. Brand collection. Brand, a wealthy Chicago brewer who died in 1926, owned perhaps the largest private collection ever assembled—some 368,000 coins—which passed to his heirs at his death. Most of the collection was dispersed in the 1930's, and it had been believed that the rest had also filtered through the trade anonymously. But in 1982 Sotheby & Co. of London and Zürich, Switzerland, announced that four major auctions of the remainder of the collection would be held over the next two years.

The first of these sales was held on July 1, 1982, in Zürich and realized more than

$2,000,000. It included a rare medallion of the Roman Emperor Galerius (d. 311) that sold for $160,000.

The Brand sale was atypical, since in general in 1982 the coin market suffered along with the rest of the economy. The enthusiasm for coins as an investment seemed to waver, just as it did for art objects and collectibles in general. Coin prices failed to advance at the pace of recent years, and some dealers, notably Seaby's of London and Sotheby Parke Bernet, Inc., of New York City, were forced to cut back on their operations. However, on Oct. 28 a $3 gold piece struck at the San Francisco Mint in 1870 was sold in New York for $687,500, the highest price ever paid at auction for a regular-issue U.S. coin. Minted with the letter "S," this coin was believed to be the only one of its kind extant. On the next day a half eagle, or $5 gold piece, minted in 1822—the only one in private hands—sold for the same price.

One striking feature of the recent coin market had been the increased interest in coins of the Islamic world. Since these coins normally bear only inscriptions and lack figural types, they are comprehensible only to those who possess at least an elementary knowledge of Arabic; nevertheless, three major auctions of Islamic material were held in the fall of 1982 in Cologne, West Germany, and in Basel and Zürich, Switzerland.

A consequence of the boom market of the 1970's was an increased differential between the bullion value and the numismatic value of precious-metal coins. This phenomenon in turn led to an ever-increasing number of forgeries, and with this the demand for a reliable authentication service. The American Numismatic Association, with headquarters in Colorado Springs, Colo., attempted to respond to this demand with a certification service. The association hired a qualified staff, acquired expensive equipment, and established guidelines for grading a coin's condition in addition to authenticating it. (Grade is as important as rarity in determining a coin's market value.) However, up to three months sometimes elapsed between a coin's submission for evaluation and its return, and grading did not take into account the quality of a coin's strike, color, contact marks, or general esthetic appeal. Procedures were revised after Kenneth E. Bressett took over as director of the certification service on Aug. 1, 1982.

The U.S. Bureau of the Mint named a new chief engraver in 1982. Elizabeth Jones succeeded Frank Gasparro, who had been associated with the mint for 38 years. Gasparro designed, among other things, the John F. Kennedy half-dollar and the ill-fated Susan B. Anthony dollar. His final work for the mint was the George Washington half-dollar, issued in 1982 to mark the 250th anniversary of the birth of the first President.   W.E.M.

COLOMBIA. Belisario Betancur Cuartas, Colombia's Conservative Party candidate, was elected president on May 30, 1982. More than 7,000,000 people out of an electorate estimated at nearly 13,000,000 cast ballots. With 47 percent of the vote, Betancur, 59, won easily over his three opponents, two of whom divided the vote of Liberal Party supporters. Betancur's nearest opponent was official Liberal Party candidate and former President Alfonso López Michelsen, with 40 percent of the vote. Earlier, in elections on March 14, the Liberals retained a majority in both houses of the nation's Congress.

Despite the presence of heavily armed military patrols, leftist guerrillas staged a violent campaign to discourage voters from going to the polls. In one incident, on May 26, a bomb attack in western Colombia killed a police officer and two constables. The governor of a Bogotá prison escaped unhurt when the M-19, Colombia's largest left-wing guerrilla organization, launched a machine gun attack on his car. The National University in Bogotá was forced to close on May 25, after leftist rioters clashed with police.

Earlier in the year, on Jan. 27, seven heavily armed members of M-19 seized an in-flight Colombian airliner, ordering the pilot to return to Bogotá and then to fly 300 mi. to Cali, in southwestern Colombia. The guerrillas issued a number of political demands that the government rejected. The hijacked Boeing 727 was severely damaged in a subsequent gun battle between the hijackers and government troops. The guerrillas later released the remaining hostages among passengers and crew in exchange for an escape plane and flew first to the island of San Andrés and from there to Cuba.

In his inauguration speech on Aug. 7, Betancur offered the "white flag" to leftist guerrillas who had been fighting against the government and the army for 33 years but stopped short of offering the general amnesty they had demanded. In June outgoing President Julio César Turbay Ayala lifted the 34-year-old state of siege that allowed the armed forces to curtail civil liberties. M-19 then announced a cease-fire and virtually halted armed activities. On Nov. 16 Congress passed a law pardoning guerrillas and those imprisoned for political crimes connected with rebellion and sedition.

To curb inflation, which stood at an annual rate of more than 30 percent, Betancur promised measures to provide tax incentives to industry, in order to promote development, and reduce unemployment.

Betancur moved Colombia toward a nonaligned stance in foreign policy. Greeting U.S. President Ronald Reagan, who stopped in Bogotá on Dec. 3, Betancur criticized U.S. policies relating to Latin America. He called for an end to "exclusions in the inter-American system," an apparent reference to Washington's exclusion of Cuba and Nicaragua from its Caribbean Basin aid initiative.

See STATISTICS OF THE WORLD.   A.E.J.

COLORADO. *See* STATISTICS OF THE WORLD.

COMMONWEALTH OF NATIONS. The major event in 1982 for members of the Commonwealth of Nations was the August meeting of finance ministers in London. The ministers welcomed their colleagues from the recent Commonwealth member countries of Belize and Antigua and Barbuda, who participated for the first time in a Commonwealth finance ministers conference.

The considerable time spent in discussing the problems of the developing world was strongly influenced by the large number of Third World countries represented at the conference. Many speakers deplored the growing trend toward protectionism among industrialized countries and called for a lowering of trade barriers on raw materials. The finance ministers, particularly those from developing countries, asked for a thorough reexamination of the international trade and payments system that was established at Bretton Woods, N.H., toward the end of World War II. They also questioned the practices of the two major international financial institutions, the International Monetary Fund (IMF) and the World Bank.

The Commonwealth ministers strongly criticized the IMF for what they saw as a slowdown in commitments and disbursements of funds to developing countries. They requested that the IMF pay particular attention to the payment problems of less developed nations.

The World Bank was also reproached. According to the ministers from the Third World, the bank was lagging significantly behind its target of a 5 percent increase in loans. The ministers urged industrialized countries to provide the bank with more funds for lending. They singled out the United States for particular criticism, noting that the administration of President Ronald Reagan had reduced U.S. contributions to the International Development Association, an arm of the World Bank. The ministers also requested that the bank be more "sensitive" toward the governments of developing countries in applying its conditions for granting loans.

On June 9 the Maldives became the 47th member of the Commonwealth. Composed of a chain of atolls situated in the Indian Ocean, the Maldives, which were formerly a sultanate and a British protectorate, gained their independence in 1965. It was not until 1982, however, that the group of some 160,000 inhabitants scattered over hundreds of islands decided to join the Commonwealth.   R.J.C.

COMMUNICATIONS. The major news story in the communications field in 1982 was the reorganization of the giant American Telephone and Telegraph Co. (AT&T), freeing the company for wider competition in a changing market and ending a long-standing antitrust lawsuit. The burgeoning areas of local network and data-base systems were also explored on several different fronts.

General Market Developments. Engineering advances in communications equipment took a back seat in 1982 to other kinds of developments. Major interest centered on the new commercial trends established by the actions of the U.S. government and the standards-setting communications organizations, both national and international. As these decision-makers considered how billions of dollars might be spent for decades to come, local communications networks were struggling to become established commercially and industrially. The purveyors of these networks had to deal with user confusion over the many kinds of networks available and the lack of standards governing their design and function. Similar problems were being faced in the field of consumer communications by promoters of such systems as teletext and videotex, in which the viewer uses a modified television set to tune in on text and graphics displays of various kinds of information.

Prospects in consumer communications rested partly on the potential success of direct broadcasting of television signals to the home by means of satellite. Such systems would first send hundreds of signals from many broadcasters to a geosynchronous satellite orbiting the earth. The signals would then be beamed down to antennas 1 m (3¼ ft.) wide, set up by private homeowners. The problem with this system was its cost to the consumer, but hope was expressed that the semiconducting material called gallium arsenide would help to meet the problem. Gallium arsenide, which can operate at the microwave frequencies used by satellites to transmit television signals, appeared to be suitable for constructing low-cost, mass-produced home receivers. By the end of 1982, however, such receivers were still only in limited use.

Antitrust Settlements. In January the administration of U.S. President Ronald Reagan opened a new chapter in the history of the communications industry by dropping two long-standing antitrust cases against the two giants in the field, AT&T and the International Business Machines Corp. (IBM). The agreements between the companies and the

These Washington, D.C., executives are conducting a business conference with their on-screen counterparts in New York City, who are viewing as well as listening to the Washingtonians in their own meeting room. The full-color system, called Picturephone Meeting Service, was inaugurated by AT&T in July.

federal government were expected to have far-reaching effects. Many predicted that the settlements would lead to greater competition in a variety of previously regulated areas of industry and would free IBM to become a formidable competitor to AT&T on several communications fronts.

AT&T agreed to divest itself of its 22 operating companies providing most of the nation's local telephone services and to make other adjustments in its fields of business activity. AT&T was freed, however, to enter the data-processing and equipment sales field. A new AT&T subsidiary, American Bell Inc., began operations by offering a communications package, the Advanced Information System, designed to be sold to firms with a need for extensive, nationwide, computer-based communications and data-processing services. The system would compete with some services being offered by IBM and other firms. American Bell and IBM also planned to furnish private branch exchanges that would handle voice and data transmissions for intra-office purposes, both firms thus taking advantage of the fact that computer and communications technologies had merged in recent years.

Although AT&T and IBM were the big names among those standing to benefit from this new environment of unregulated competition, smaller firms also planned to exploit the situation. For example, many communications firms in 1982 flocked to offer new cellular radio services that would make possible the installation of a telephone in any private car.

Local Networks. Communications firms of all sizes were also exploring the local communications network market. This market developed because of the dissimilarities between the equipment being made by manufacturers for sending or receiving voice or data transmissions or both. Local networks, which are based either on coaxial cable, twisted-pair wire, or fiber-optic links, were thought to offer an answer to this problem. The reasoning was that all the diverse gear of different manufacturers could be connected, at the local level, by means of suitable hardware and software adapters.

In 1982, however, confusion existed over the wealth of methods for making such connections and for operating the local networks. For example, there was uncertainty as to whether the so-called Ethernet system jointly proposed by Xerox Corp., Digital Equipment Corp., and Intel Corp. was the best way to do the job, compared with the approach known as token-passing that was advocated by IBM and Burroughs Corp. In the Ethernet approach, each equipment site connected to the network checks its connection whenever it wants to use the network to

This towering 55-m (180-ft.) Geosphere at Florida's Walt Disney World marks the entrance to a new exhibit by the Bell System called the Experimental Prototype City of Tomorrow (EPCOT). It houses a ride-through tour of communications history, including 65 Disney robots in historical dress that move about and talk.

living room. With teletext, a modified home television set can display text and graphics that provide such information as what merchandise is available at nearby shopping centers, or a food reviewer's opinion of a local restaurant. The videotex system also transmits such data-base information to a user, but in addition allows for greater interaction between the user and the transmitting source by means of telephone or cable connections. The viewer can stop the transmission, request different kinds of information, or focus on specific aspects of the data base as needed. A hand-held keypad or full keyboard may be used for more complicated interactions.

Videotex had made greater strides in Europe than in the United States, where such services mostly duplicated information readily available from other sources. In addition the Europeans were selling their data-base system in the U.S. using standards different from those developed by AT&T and the Canadian government's Department of Communications. Advances in integrated circuits and software design were, however, expected eventually to make both approaches compatible, so that in time a purchaser's reluctance to buy the "wrong" system might cease to be a market factor. H.J.H.

Get the Message?

New salvos in the war between the sexes were fired in 1982 by enterprising entrepreneurs in the United States and West Germany. Dump-a-Date, a Chicago-based service, offered to deliver personalized messages with accompanying dead flowers. A sample, delivered to one man, went: "Forty-one years old and still a mama's boy. You treated me like a worthless toy." Meanwhile, a company in Frankfurt released a tape cassette, titled "Telephone Alibi," containing authentic background noises for spouses trying to convince their mates that they have a valid excuse for not coming home. The noises include the rumble of subways, the bustle of airports, railroad stations, and street traffic, and the clacking of typewriters.

communicate with another piece of equipment elsewhere. If the communication line is busy, the sending equipment hangs up and tries again after a random period of time. In token-passing networks, by contrast, a computer or other piece of equipment that is to send a message must wait until its assigned time comes up. Proponents of both methods argued their respective merits in 1982, but most industry experts agreed that each scheme ultimately would have its own market.

Data-Base Systems. The home-consumer market also continued to be explored in 1982 by the communications industry. For example, the proponents of both the teletext and videotex data-base systems were pushing to place their services in the home consumer's

COMMUNISM. Seventeen nations made up the Communist world in 1982. The ruling parties in those countries, and Communist parties in nearly 80 other states, could count more than 77,000,000 members. Despite its size and strength, the Communist movement was badly divided by rival factions and national ambitions and was troubled by civil unrest, economic problems, and political uncertainty.

Death of Brezhnev. Leonid I. Brezhnev, president of the Soviet Union and general secretary of its Communist Party, died of an apparent heart attack on Nov. 10. Foreign observers had long speculated that a protracted power struggle could follow the death of the ailing Brezhnev. Two days later Yuri V. Andropov (see biography at PEOPLE IN THE NEWS) was named to succeed Brezhnev in the key post of party secretary. The first impression of U.S. government and academic analysts was that Andropov had formed a close alliance with the military establishment and would not face any immediate challenge to his authority.

Afghanistan. A fierce civil war continued to rage in Afghanistan during 1982. Muslim insurgents fought to unseat the regime of President Babrak Karmal, the Communist leader installed by the U.S.S.R. in late 1979. Although the Afghan army enjoyed the aid of 100,000 Soviet troops, the Muslim guerrillas controlled most of the countryside and some important towns. The economy was scarcely functioning; more than 2,000,000 Afghan refugees were camped in neighboring Pakistan. Few foreign nations outside the Soviet bloc had friendly dealings with the Afghan government, and there was little visible progress in 1982 on a negotiated solution to the war.

Poland. The Polish dilemma also remained unresolved. The Communist government, faced with a challenge to its rule by the Polish free trade union Solidarity, declared martial law in December, 1981. Lech Walesa and hundreds of other Solidarity leaders were taken into government custody, and the union was forced underground in 1982. Efforts by the Roman Catholic Church to mediate between the regime and the union brought only limited results. In October Warsaw authorities, backed by the Soviet Union, passed a law abolishing Solidarity altogether; strikes and demonstrations ensued. Shortages of food and other necessities continued to plague the country. In November the government suddenly released Walesa, who, although apparently unrepentant, nevertheless urged a constructive dialogue with the authorities. That development, together with a change of leadership in Moscow, offered a glimmer of hope for some accommodation in Poland.

Nonruling Parties. Soviet and Polish handling of events in Poland caused sharp disagreement among Communist parties. The parties of France and Portugal affirmed their support for the military crackdown. Other parties were sharply critical. Spanish Communist leader Santiago Carrillo declared that martial law in Poland was proof that the Soviet model of Communist rule was a failure. The Italian party, led by Enrico Berlinguer, denounced the Polish government move and defended Solidarity. The Japanese party described the imposition of martial law as a "coup d'etat."

The U.S.S.R. delivered a blistering attack on the Italian party in a private letter sent to Rome in January, 1982. Among other things, it said that the Italians "grossly violate the rules for relations between communist parties." In September Giancarlo Pajetta, the foreign affairs spokesman for the Italian Communists, reiterated that his party was "against repression" in Poland.

Comecon. The Council for Mutual Economic Assistance (Comecon) was shaken by economic difficulties in 1982. Its ten members—the Soviet Union, the nations of Eastern Europe, Mongolia, Cuba, and Vietnam—suffered the effects of the world recession, in addition to problems that stemmed from highly centralized planning and poor management. Economic growth rates had dropped, and political leaders largely lacked the daring to try reforms and experiments that would turn things around. Western governments and bankers, because of difficulty obtaining repayment of loans to Poland, hesitated to continue granting new loans to

Yuri V. Andropov (left), successor to the late Leonid I. Brezhnev as general secretary of the Soviet Union's Communist Party, chats with Fidel Castro (right), Cuban president and Communist Party leader. They conferred in the Kremlin after Brezhnev was laid to rest.

enable Comecon nations to supplement their domestic production with imports from the West. U.S. President Ronald Reagan's efforts to penalize Poland and the U.S.S.R. by means of trade barriers complicated the Eastern European economic picture. The Polish dilemma strained the Comecon countries as well. Since Polish production was slack, Moscow diverted machinery, spare parts, raw materials, and food to keep Poland functioning and fed. All these concerns dominated discussion at the June Comecon summit meeting in Budapest, Hungary, but no easy solutions emerged from the conference.

The Warsaw Pact. The European Communist military alliance, the Warsaw Pact, made no progress negotiating force-level reductions with the North Atlantic Treaty Organization (NATO) in 1982. A study issued by NATO in May reported that the Western alliance lagged behind the Soviet-led Warsaw Pact in almost every category of nuclear weaponry and conventional forces. According to the study, the Soviets had 600 intermediate-range nuclear missiles capable of hitting targets in Western Europe, while NATO would have no such similar missiles capable of striking the U.S.S.R. until the planned deployment in Europe of Pershing and cruise missiles. NATO had 800 aircraft capable of nuclear attacks on Eastern Europe, the study said, as against 2500 comparable planes for the Warsaw Pact. In long-range strategic nuclear delivery systems, it maintained that the Soviets had a combined missile and bomber force totaling 2704, compared with 2022 on the Western side. The Communist nations were said to have a manpower edge of 4,000,000 to 2,600,000 and 3-1 superiority in battle tanks.

The Sino-Soviet Split. Seeking to take advantage of differences between Peking and Washington over the issue of U.S. arms sales to Taiwan, President Brezhnev offered an olive branch to China in 1982. The Chinese, however, suspicious as ever of the Soviets, responded that they were interested in Soviet deeds, not words. By that, Western experts said, China was signaling that it still wanted a thinning of Soviet forces on its border, Soviet withdrawal from Afghanistan, and Soviet efforts to rein in the aggressiveness of the Vietnamese.

China did agree to broaden contacts with the U.S.S.R. In May the head of the Far Eastern Department of the Soviet foreign ministry traveled to Peking and held informal talks with Chinese officials. In October Soviet Deputy Foreign Minister Leonid Ilyichev visited the Chinese capital for further consultations. And in November Chinese Foreign Minister Huang Hua met briefly in Moscow with Soviet leaders during the Brezhnev funeral. Nevertheless, as the issues dividing the two countries involved ideology, territory, and national pride, it seemed unlikely that any deep thaw in their relationship would take place.

Indochina. To China's alarm, Soviet-backed Vietnam dominated all of Communist Indochina. The Vietnamese maintained troops in Laos to oversee the pro-Hanoi government there. In Cambodia nearly 200,000 Vietnamese troops propped up the puppet Heng Samrin regime and battled the 30,000-man Khmer Rouge rebel force. The Khmer Rouge reached agreement in June with former Cambodian Prime Minister Son Sann and Prince Norodom Sihanouk; the formation of their three-way coalition posed a fresh challenge for Hanoi. At home, meantime, the Vietnamese government was beset by economic troubles. With so much of its budget allotted to the military, Vietnam could neither develop its agriculture and industry nor repair the damage inflicted during the Vietnam war and Sino-Vietnamese fighting in 1979.

See articles on individual countries mentioned. F.W.

COMOROS. See STATISTICS OF THE WORLD.
CONGO. See STATISTICS OF THE WORLD.

CONGRESS OF THE UNITED STATES. The smooth relations that President Ronald Reagan had enjoyed with Congress during his first year in office became somewhat troubled in 1982. Especially as the November elections approached and the unemployment rate climbed, legislators exhibited more independence at the second session of the 97th Congress than they had at the first.

As in 1981, money issues dominated, but Congress did deal with other matters. A 25-year extension of the 1965 Voting Rights Act was signed into law on June 29. On Oct. 1 Congress cleared bills that provided help for ailing savings and loan associations (see BANKING AND FINANCE) and job-training assistance for the low-income unemployed (see LABOR). Efforts of Senate conservatives to enact a ban on abortion and to pave the way for the return of prayer to the public schools were defeated.

Taxation and Spending. Congress handed the President two major defeats on economic issues. His veto of a $14.1 billion fiscal 1982 supplemental appropriations bill was overridden on Sept. 10. Then, on Oct. 1, as members were heading out of Washington to campaign in their home districts, the House of Representatives rejected a proposed amendment to the U.S. Constitution that would have required a balanced federal budget. Reagan had campaigned hard for the measure.

Until those two votes, Reagan had been successful in pushing his economic programs through Congress. On Aug. 19, after a massive White House lobbying campaign, Congress approved a $98.3 billion tax increase and a $17.5 billion spending reduction package for fiscal years 1983–85. Approval of the measure was necessary to meet the deficit-reduction target in the fiscal 1983 budget resolution that Congress had adopted on June 23, 1982. That measure assumed deficit reductions of $76.8 billion in fiscal 1983 and $378.5 billion during fiscal 1983-85. The resolution projected spending at $769.8 billion and revenues at $665.9 billion in fiscal 1983, with a resultant deficit of $103.9 billion.

The fight over the tax hike and spending cut package was intense, and Reagan could

Speaker of the House of Representatives Thomas P. ("Tip") O'Neill (D, Mass.), at right, shakes hands with House Minority Leader Robert H. Michel (R, Ill.) after congressional passage on Aug. 19 of a $98.3 billion tax increase measure. The bipartisan effort to pass the legislation was intended to reduce sharply increasing federal budget deficits.

not have won without the assistance of House Speaker Thomas P. ("Tip") O'Neill (D, Mass.) and other Democratic leaders. In the House the vote was 226–207, with 89 of 192 Republicans voting against it and 123 of 241 Democrats voting for it. In the Republican-controlled Senate, the vote was 52–47, as 11 Republicans joined 36 Democrats in opposing the measure. This pattern was a notable departure from that of 1981, when a unified bloc of Republicans, joined by a number of defecting Democrats, produced Reagan's budget victories. The negative votes in 1982 came from legislators who faced close re-election races and were afraid to support tax increases, from liberal Democrats who opposed the bill's cuts in anticipated spending for social programs, from members who were uncomfortable with specific revenue measures (such as the doubling of cigarette taxes), and from some Republicans who argued that the middle of a recession was no time to repudiate Reagan's 1980 election mandate to cut taxes.

Reagan had scored another big victory in June when Congress gave in after he vetoed two versions of a special fiscal 1982 supplemental spending bill. The first version, vetoed on June 24, had an $8.9 billion price tag, including $3 billion for emergency housing

aid through mortgage subsidies, which Reagan opposed. An override attempt in the House failed 253–151, 17 votes short of the required two-thirds majority. A substitute measure, omitting the housing subsidy but still exceeding Reagan's spending request, also received a Presidential veto. On July 13 the House again failed to override; this time the vote was 242–169, 32 votes short of the required two thirds. Finally, a version that provided $5.4 billion in new spending was signed into law on July 18.

On the regular supplemental appropriation, however, Reagan's winning streak ended. The President had vetoed the $14.1 billion measure on Aug. 28, calling it a "budget buster" that cut his request for defense spending while providing too much for social programs. The measure was popular in Congress, however, because it contained funding for programs such as student loans, community service employment for the elderly, and education for the disadvantaged. Proponents argued that it actually provided nearly $2 billion less than the total $16.1 billion package Reagan had requested. On Sept. 9 the House voted 301–117 to override the veto, with 81 Republicans lining up against the President. The Senate vote the next day was 60–30, exactly the two-thirds majority needed to enact the measure over the President's veto.

Typically, Congress was unable to pass all its appropriations bills before fiscal 1983 began. When the new fiscal year actually arrived on Oct. 1 at 12:01 A.M., most government agencies technically were out of money. The government remained in limbo for nearly 24 hours, until the legislators finally passed a massive continuing appropriations resolution financing the government through Dec. 17.

Because of Congress's tardiness in acting on spending bills, Reagan asked that the legislators reconvene after the Nov. 2 elections to work on those measures. The congressional leadership agreed, and a four-week lame-duck session began on Nov. 29.

The postelection session provided $379 billion in fiscal 1983 for six departments and agencies. Included was $232 billion for the military, including money for two nuclear aircraft carriers. A 5¢-per-gallon increase in the gasoline and diesel fuel tax, in addition to higher user fees for heavy trucks, was to finance highway repairs and mass transit. A bill was also passed to establish a long-term system for the burial of radioactive wastes from nuclear power plants.

Balanced Budget Amendment. Even though he was presiding over the largest annual budget deficits in history, Reagan pushed hard for passage of the balanced budget amendment. He was successful in the Senate, which approved the measure on Aug. 4 by a vote of 69–31, 2 more than the two-thirds majority required. But he met defeat in the House on Oct. 1, when the amendment was voted down 236–187, 46 votes less than the two-thirds needed. Reagan immediately denounced the Democrats and promised to use their opposition to the amendment as a campaign issue. "This vote makes clear who supports a balanced budget and who does not," Reagan said. "Voters across America should count heads and take names."

The amendment would require the budget to be in balance at the beginning of each fiscal year. Deficit spending would be allowed by a three-fifths vote, however, and the amendment could be waived in wartime.

Voting Rights. On June 18, after a week-long filibuster, the Senate voted 85–8 to extend for 25 years certain key provisions of the 1965 Voting Rights Act. The extension had passed the House in 1981.

The extension measure required 9 states and portions of 13 others to continue requesting Justice Department approval for any changes they propose to make in their election laws. Beginning in 1984, they would be able to "bail out" from coverage if they could prove to a three-judge panel in the District of Columbia that they had had a clean voting-rights record for the previous ten years. The measure also made it easier to prove certain voting rights violations.

Abscam. Harrison A. Williams, Jr. (D, N.J.), the only Senator implicated in the 1980 Federal Bureau of Investigation's Abscam political corruption probe, resigned on March 11, 1982. His announcement came just hours before members were expected to vote to expel him. Williams, a 23-year Senate veteran, had been convicted by a federal jury on May 1, 1981, on bribery and conspiracy charges. A Republican, Nicholas F. Brady, was named to fill out the remaining months of Williams's Senate term.

See also ELECTIONS IN THE UNITED STATES. K.W.G.

CONNECTICUT. *See* STATISTICS OF THE WORLD.

CONSTRUCTION. Although construction starts were disastrously low in 1982, a hopeful indication for the U.S. construction industry was the moderation of cost increases for labor, equipment, and materials. U.S. Bureau of Labor statistics showed construction industry unemployment to be at the highest level since 1975, reaching 20.3 percent shortly after midyear. Industry wages increased only 7.3 percent in 12 months—one of the lowest gains in recent years. Official bidding volume indexes showed a zero percent change at the end of the third quarter of 1982.

New plans indexes showed a decline, down 12 percent for all types of construction. Manufacturing construction plans were down 64 percent, highway building plans were down 50 percent, and future bridge

Workers search for victims buried under concrete and steel debris after two spans of a bridge under construction in East Chicago, Ind., collapsed on April 15. Thirteen workers were killed and 17 others injured in the accident.

construction plans had fallen off 38 percent. Office construction was one area that was up—2 percent at the end of the third quarter.

The high cost of borrowing was blamed for most construction setbacks, both in the United States and abroad; many contractors could not afford to borrow money. Foreign work and joint ventures were resorted to by some contractors to overcome the effects of the recession.

Cost Rises Slow. The state of construction in general in 1982 slowed cost increases. Common labor rates rose 10 percent, 1 percent below the previous year's rate. Increases were higher in cities such as Dallas and San Francisco with several public projects under way, and lower in less busy areas. With a good market in office construction, iron workers' pay rose almost 10 percent above that of other skilled workers.

The overall building costs index rose 6.4 percent in the first three quarters of 1982, down 7 percent from the same period in the preceding year. The greatest rise in costs occurred in the Midwest, up 11.1 percent; the lowest rise was in the South, up 5.4 percent.

Earnings. Construction company stocks and profits also showed the effects of the recession in 1982. At the end of the third quarter, earnings were down about 6 percent for 45 publicly owned corporations in the industry, a smaller decline, however, than the overall industrial figure of 16 percent. Construction-firm stock prices fared less well, with those of general contractors showing a 9.8 percent decrease. Companies with high earnings often owed their gains to overseas work.

Foreign Markets. U.S. contractors who were still collecting money from foreign projects built in 1981 had fair, if slower, income in 1982. Middle East projects slowed, with new starts generally in Asia and to a lesser degree in Africa and Latin America. Middle Eastern construction continued to account for about 35 percent of international work, Asian contracts for 17 to 20 percent.

U.S. firms were hurt by President Ronald Reagan's ban on sales of equipment for construction of the 3700-mi.-long Siberia-to-West Germany pipeline; *see also* EUROPEAN COMMUNITIES; UNITED STATES OF AMERICA. Some foreign subsidiaries of U.S. companies fulfilled contracts, however, risking U.S. sanctions and possible prosecution of company officers.

Recession Remedies. Contractors found new ways, in addition to working abroad, to challenge the recession. The number of joint ventures increased, spreading out investment requirements. The use of joint ventures also allowed small- and medium-size contractors to join together to compete against industry giants.

Turning to specialty work was another antirecession method used by construction firms in 1982. Mechanical and electrical work remained high while other types of construction were down. A weakening in new bidding for specialty work at the close of the year suggested, however, that the trend might not continue into 1983.

Bridges. Several bridge shutdowns and other problems due to cracks in concrete were reported in 1982. One major project in difficulty was the Zilwaukee Bridge over the Saginaw River in Michigan, when Pier 11 of the bridge twisted and deflected. An investigation showed large cracks in the pile-supporting footing of the pier, with the top of the pier column about 7 in. out of plumb. Hairline cracks were found in the deck slabs of all winged box girders.

Thirteen construction workers were killed and 17 others injured when two steel-and-concrete road sections of an unfinished bridge collapsed on April 15 in East Chicago, Ind. The sections collapsed as concrete was being poured.

Steel, an alternative to concrete, was chosen for several bridge projects in 1982. The Farø bridge, a double-structure span across the Storstrøm Channel in Denmark, was to use all-welded, single-cell box girders, prefabricated and erected in 270-ft.-long segments.   R.W.S.

COSTA RICA. Luis Alberto Monge, a former union organizer, was overwhelmingly elected president of Costa Rica on Feb. 7, 1982, amid this Central American nation's worst financial crisis in 30 years. A major cause of the economic slump lay in the collapse of world prices for coffee, Costa Rica's major export. The country was unable to make more than nominal payments on either the principal or the interest on its foreign debt, which stood at $3.2 billion at the end of June. Foreign creditors refused to renegotiate Costa Rica's debt unless the government reached an agreement with the International Monetary Fund (IMF). The IMF, in turn, demanded harsh economic measures in exchange for a $100,000,000 standby credit.

Monge's belt-tightening measures, however, raised unemployment and underemployment to 20 percent of the labor force and threatened food shortages. The gross national product was expected to fall 6 percent in 1982. To forestall social unrest, Monge instituted an emergency plan to hand out food to the jobless.

Costa Rica was fearful of an increase in political violence, much of it emanating from right-wing opponents of neighboring Nicaragua's Sandinista regime and left-wing opponents of the El Salvador government. In January three leftist terrorists, two of them Salvadoran, were killed in the attempted kidnapping of a Salvadoran industrialist. The arrest of three other guerrillas led Costa Rican investigators to discover at least 20 terrorist cells and a "safe house" with a vast cache of arms. The guerrillas said that they had been trained in Nicaragua.

On May 22 Costa Rica expelled former Nicaraguan rebel leader Eden Pastora for his anti-Sandinista activities. On Aug. 9, 15 Nicaraguan rightist leaders were arrested. Three Nicaraguan diplomats involved in a bomb attack on the Honduran airline, Sahsa, were deported from Costa Rica. Soon afterward Costa Rica and Honduras concluded an agreement to oppose terrorism.

See STATISTICS OF THE WORLD.   A.E.J.

COUNCIL FOR MUTUAL ECONOMIC ASSISTANCE. *See* COMMUNISM.

CRIME AND LAW ENFORCEMENT. The overall volume of U.S. crime reported to the Federal Bureau of Investigation (FBI) during the first six months of 1982 dropped 5 percent in comparison to the same period in 1981. Violent crime dropped 3 percent, property crime 6 percent. The six-month decrease in the FBI crime index was the first since 1978. Nevertheless, Attorney General William French Smith cautioned that the fact that reported crimes had reached an all-time high in 1980 and had maintained that level in 1981 "should be of major concern to the nation."

Hinckley Verdict. On June 21, 1982, after a seven-week trial, John W. Hinckley, Jr., was found not guilty by reason of insanity in his attempted assassination of U.S. President Ronald Reagan on March 30, 1981. Although Hinckley, a 27-year-old drifter, admitted shooting the President, Presidential Press Secretary James S. Brady, and two others, the federal jury was apparently persuaded by lengthy defense testimony showing that Hinckley suffered from severe personality disorders.

The controversial verdict, which shocked and outraged many observers, prompted a reexamination of the insanity defense. Without commenting on the Hinckley verdict, the Reagan administration supported proposals to limit the insanity defense in federal trials to those defendants who did not know what they were doing when they committed crimes. Many critics of the insanity defense, including five of the Hinckley jurors who appeared before a U.S. Senate subcommittee on June 24, endorsed a verdict of "guilty but mentally ill," a formula ensuring punishment as well as treatment. Such a verdict was already permitted by several states.

On Aug. 9 Hinckley was committed for an indefinite period of time to St. Elizabeths Hospital, a federal mental facility in Washington, D.C., where he had been confined for psychiatric evaluation after the trial. Hinckley would be entitled to seek a hearing every six months to determine his eligibility for release, but he might only be released after satisfying psychiatrists and the court that he was no longer dangerous to himself and others.

Multiple Murders. Wayne B. Williams, a 23-year-old black free-lance television cameraman and self-styled talent scout, was convicted on Feb. 27 of murdering two young blacks in Atlanta. The verdict apparently ended a two-year reign of terror in the city, during which period 28 young blacks were slain. As a result of Williams's conviction, Atlanta police closed their files on 23 of the 28 murders. Williams was sentenced to two consecutive life terms in prison and would not be eligible for parole under Georgia law for 14 years.

In August prosecutors in Houston struck a bargain with Coral Eugene Watts, 28, an unemployed drifter suspected of murdering a number of women in Texas. Arrested in Houston after a bungled murder attempt, Watts confessed to more than a dozen murders in Texas, but because authorities lacked sufficient evidence to bring him to trial for the multiple homicides, they charged him with burglary with intent to commit murder. On Sept. 3 he received a 60-year prison sentence. In Florida Gerald Eugene Stano, 31, who was serving consecutive life sentences for murdering three women, confessed to having killed at least 22 other women since 1969.

On Sept. 23, 1982, Juan V. Corona, 48, was convicted for a second time of murdering 25 migrant farm workers in California. Corona's original conviction, in 1973, was overturned by a state appeals court five years later because he had received inadequate legal representation. He was sentenced on Dec. 15 to 25 years to life in prison.

Illegal Drugs. The Reagan administration launched a major offensive in 1982 against the illegal drug trade. Calling narcotics trafficking the nation's "most serious crime problem," Attorney General Smith formally announced on Jan. 21 that drug investigations would be handled jointly by the FBI and the Drug Enforcement Administration (DEA). FBI Director William H. Webster was given overall authority for coordinating the efforts of the two agencies.

On Oct. 14 President Reagan announced the formation of 12 special regional drug-related task forces, with agents from the FBI, DEA, U.S. Customs Service, and Internal Revenue Service, as well as federal prosecutors. The special task forces were to begin work in January, 1983, concentrating on the breakup of large drug distribution networks, particu-

Hard-Sell Salesman

A. Donald Fass, a Connecticut salesman of antitheft devices, had an impressive track record—because he provided the problem as well as the solution. First he made home visits to prospective customers, obtaining information about their vacation plans and the location of their valuables. While the occupants were away, he secretly made off with their goods. After they came back, he paid a follow-up call at which, not surprisingly, his victims expressed heightened interest in his pitch for antitheft protection. After Fass was apprehended escaping from a burglarized house, authorities uncovered a criminal record that included 26 felonies and 50 misdemeanors.

The Reagan administration announced a major effort to curb narcotics trafficking in 1982. Here a federal Drug Enforcement Administration agent weighs some of the 20 lb. of heroin seized in a February raid on three locations in the New York City metropolitan area.

larly those operated by organized crime, rather than on the investigation of street sales and local pushers. Implementation of the task-force plan would require 900 new agents, 200 new prosecutors, and additional space for 1260 inmates in the 11 federal prisons, at an estimated annual cost of from $160,000,000 to $200,000,000.

The prototype for this new antidrug effort was a task force organized in March, 1982, under U.S. Vice-President George Bush in southern Florida, through which flowed an estimated 70 percent of the nation's cocaine and marijuana traffic. Using federal agents as well as military personnel and equipment, the task force was credited with reducing the infiltration of drugs into that area.

Operation Tiburon, a 14-month joint investigation by the U.S. and Colombian governments, resulted in the seizure of more than 6,000,000 lb. of marijuana and the arrests of 495 persons in February. An investigation called Operation Swordfish netted indictments in October against 67 persons accused of drug smuggling and "money laundering" in Miami. Also in October automobile executive John Z. De Lorean, 57, was arrested in Los Angeles in connection with what federal investigators alleged was a multimillion-dollar heroin- and cocaine-smuggling scheme.

The federal crackdown on marijuana smuggling from overseas had the unintended result of spurring the growth of domestic production. By some estimates, marijuana had become the nation's third-leading cash crop and was valued at more than $10 billion. In October Attorney General Smith cited estimates that illicit retail drug sales in the United States had exceeded $79 billion in 1980.

White-Collar Crime. The FBI continued to devote the bulk of its resources to white-collar crime and corruption. The FBI's 1980 Abscam probe remained clouded in controversy, as a federal district judge on May 14, 1982, overturned the 1981 bribery conviction of former Rep. Richard Kelly (R, Fla.). Several courts, however, rejected similar motions to throw out convictions in other Abscam cases; a federal appeals court in Philadelphia, for example, reinstated the convictions, overturned in November, 1980, of two local city council members. Another Abscam defendant, Harrison A. Williams, Jr. (D, N.J.), resigned from the U.S. Senate on March 11, 1982, as a result of his 1981 conviction for bribery and conspiracy. Williams was sentenced on Feb. 16 to three years in prison and fined $50,000.

As a result of another FBI investigation, the president of the International Brotherhood of Teamsters, Roy L. Williams, went on trial in October with four codefendants on federal charges of conspiring to bribe U.S. Sen. Howard W. Cannon (D, Nev.) and defrauding a union pension fund. Williams was the third Teamsters president to be tried on corrup-

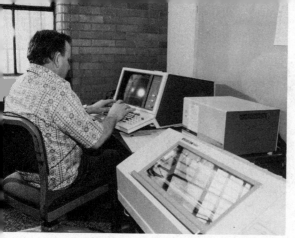

A $31,800,000 prison in Oak Park Heights, Minn., called the most innovative structure ever designed for housing criminals, was opened in March. Here an inmate learns to use a computer in the educational complex of the prison.

tion charges. All five defendants were found guilty on Dec. 15.

The value of high-technology information was emphasized when 18 employees of two Japanese companies, Hitachi, Ltd., and Mitsubishi Electric Corp., were indicted in June. The Justice Department alleged that officials of the firms had participated in two separate conspiracies to steal confidential computer information from the International Business Machines Corp. and transport the information to Japan. The indictments came at the end of an eight-month undercover operation by the FBI.

Organized Crime. In an extensive undercover penetration of organized crime by the FBI, special agent Joseph D. Pistone became for six-and-a-half years a trusted associate of the Bonannos, an alleged Mafia "family" in New York City. As a result of Pistone's infiltration and subsequent trial testimony, three members of the family were convicted on Aug. 27 of a racketeering conspiracy involving murder, robbery, gambling, and drug trading, and a fourth member was convicted of a related drug-selling charge.

Tylenol Scare. In October the U.S. public was alarmed by the deaths of seven Chicago-area residents who unknowingly took Extra-Strength Tylenol capsules that had been adulterated with cyanide. Law enforcement authorities concluded that the capsules were injected with the poison after they reached drugstore shelves, prompting drug manufacturers and federal food and drug officials to develop standards for making all over-the-counter medications tamper-resistant; *see also* HEALTH AND MEDICINE. Before these new standards could be implemented, allegations and stories abounded concerning the contamination of other pharmaceutical products in several other parts of the country.

Capital Punishment. Frank J. Coppola, 38, a convicted murderer, was executed by the state of Virginia on Aug. 10. He thus became the fifth person to be executed in the U.S. since 1976, and the first person executed in Virginia since 1962. Coppola, a former police officer who had maintained his innocence since his conviction in 1978, decided not to exhaust further appeals. Lawyers opposed to capital punishment won a last-minute stay of execution that was overruled by the U.S. Supreme Court shortly before Coppola was sent to the electric chair.

Convicted murderer Charles Brooks, Jr., was executed by the state of Texas on Dec. 7. He was the first person ever to be executed by lethal injection.

As of August, 1982, 37 states had enacted or revised death penalty statutes to conform to Supreme Court standards, and more than 1000 men and women were awaiting execution in 31 states. A report released by the Justice Department in July predicted that the U.S. would "witness a spate of executions beginning in 1983–84 without parallel in this nation since the Depression era." Noting that the Supreme Court was overturning fewer and fewer capital punishment statutes and that many death-row inmates were beginning to exhaust their appeals, the report forecast that the nation might soon witness executions "at a rate approaching the more-than-three per week that prevailed during the 1930's." The report concluded that the U.S. would then have "a grim arena in which to conduct our national debate on the efficacy of the death penalty."

On July 2 the Supreme Court held that the accomplice in a felony murder case who did not plan or directly participate in the murder could not be executed. Although the 5-4 ruling struck down laws in Florida and eight other states that allowed imposition of the death penalty for such accomplices, it only affected a few persons on death row.

See also CIVIL RIGHTS AND CIVIL LIBERTIES; SUPREME COURT OF THE UNITED STATES.   D.C.

CUBA. Cuba's economy faced serious problems in 1982. In a speech on July 26 President Fidel Castro told a large audience in Havana that "we must share" the coming hardships, which he blamed on the worldwide economic recession. He warned Cubans of possible shorter workweeks and lower salaries.

Some 80 percent of Cuban exports go to the Communist bloc, which pays subsidized prices, through bartering industrial equipment, raw materials, consumer goods, and food, for Cuban products. Only 20 percent of Cuba's exports are paid for in hard currency by its Western markets. A large portion of this foreign revenue was needed in 1982 to pay the interest on Cuba's $1.2 billion commercial debt; most of the remainder was earmarked for the purchase of medicine and food. As a result, Castro said: "We may lack the primary materials for industry and construction."

Plummeting world prices for sugar, Cuba's main export, and a decreasing demand for nickel, its second largest export, cut sharply into the country's export revenues in 1982. In September Castro asked Japanese and Western banks to reschedule debt payments, with repayment to be extended over ten years.

In an effort to broaden Cuba's financial base, the Castro regime sought to expand tourism and attract direct investment by offering favorable terms to foreign investors. In mid-April, however, U.S. President Ronald Reagan imposed restrictions aimed at banning all tourist and business travel from the United States to Cuba. Reagan also urged several European governments to reduce their trade with Cuba. These actions were dictated by U.S. displeasure with Cuba's involvement in the shipment of arms to Nicaragua and to left-wing guerrillas in Central America.

Cuba's "capitalist" experiment in free markets, begun less than two years earlier, came under severe criticism from the Castro government in 1982. These markets offered

A street in the heart of Old Havana is decorated with Cuban flags for the annual July 26 celebration commemorating President Fidel Castro's revolutionary movement. At the 1982 event Castro had bad news, warning of economic hard times ahead.

goods that were not available with ration cards. Intermediaries, however, were making small fortunes by marking up prices as much as 800 percent. It was also discovered that the raw materials for clothes and shoes sold on the free market were often stolen from state supplies. The government arrested some 200 of the intermediaries in an effort to "ferret out everyone who commits violations," according to Castro.

On Oct. 21 dissident poet Armando Valladares, 45, a former student leader and ally of Castro, was freed from prison and allowed to leave Cuba after serving 22 years of a 30-year jail sentence for breaking with the Communist regime. France's President François Mitterrand had personally sought the release of Valladares, who was described as in poor health.

Cuba was host to a meeting of the foreign ministers of the 94-nation Nonaligned Nations' Movement in early June. Cuban Foreign Minister Isidoro Malmierca Peoli delivered an address backing Argentina in its war with Great Britain over possession of the Falkland Islands.

See STATISTICS OF THE WORLD.   A.E.J.

CYPRUS. In 1982, eight years after Turkey's invasion of Cyprus, the Mediterranean island's Greek and Turkish communities remained as divided as ever, with no apparent progress in preliminary talks between the two sides. If there was anything new, it was the decision of the prime ministers of Greece and Turkey to pay unprecedented visits to the island.

Greek Prime Minister Andreas Papandreou visited Cyprus from Feb. 27 to March 1. In an address before the Greek Cypriot House of Representatives, he promised, in the name of "Hellenic solidarity," that Greece would support the Greek Cypriots' cause in world forums. He called for an international conference to settle the problem of Cyprus. Both Turkey and the United States opposed internationalizing the Cyprus issue, and Turkish Cypriot leader Rauf Denktash immediately criticized Papandreou's proposal.

Turkey's premier, Bülent Ulusu, made his visit to the occupied northern part of the island, the self-proclaimed Turkish Federated State of Cyprus, on May 20–23. He pledged Turkey's economic and political support but urged the Turkish Cypriots to make their distressed economy more self-sufficient through an increase in local revenues.

Political developments preoccupied both communities during the year. In the Greek sector, President Spyros Kyprianou announced that he would seek reelection early in 1983. His Democratic Party, which had won less than 20 percent of the vote in the 1981 parliamentary elections, agreed to form an electoral alliance with the Communist Party (AKEL), which had polled nearly 33 percent. In April Kyprianou carried out a major cabinet reorganization, changing all but 3 of his government's 11 ministers. In the Turkish sector, the government of Mustafa Cagatay fell in December, 1981, after a no-confidence vote. Cagatay, however, reassumed the premiership in March, 1982, with the formation of a new coalition.

See STATISTICS OF THE WORLD.   L.A.S.

CZECHOSLOVAKIA. The events of 1982 gave Czechs and Slovaks no grounds for cheer. The hard-line government of President and Communist Party leader Gustáv Husák, fearing public pressure for liberalization at home, applauded the imposition of martial law in neighboring Poland and continued its own harsh clampdown on dissent. It also rejected economic reform, even as the economic situation deteriorated badly.

Czechoslovak police kept a close watch on backers of the reform document Charter 77. Several leading charter supporters, including noted journalist Karel Kyncl and historian Jan Mlynarik, were released from prison, but charges against them were not formally dropped. Police and government plainclothesmen also harassed Catholic priests and churchgoers. To discuss this and other problems, Czech primate Cardinal Frantisek Tomasek traveled to Rome in March and met with Pope John Paul II.

Government refusal to reform the economy with decentralization measures stalled Czechoslovakia's growth. Poland's inability to deliver agreed amounts of coal and the rising cost of Soviet oil added to Czech economic woes. According to official figures, one in five of the country's enterprises failed to meet targets in the first half of the year; meat production was down 8.2 percent, and industrial output rose only 1.4 percent. In a belt-tightening move, the government decreed a 41 percent increase in the price of meat on Jan. 30.

At a trade union congress in April, Husák made clear his approval of martial law in Poland; the "great expectation" of Western imperialist countries, he said, had been thwarted by the suspension of the Polish free trade union Solidarity. In addition to maintaining close ties to Poland's military regime, Husák coordinated policy with Moscow, visiting the Soviet Union in June and again later in the summer. He paid a visit to neutral Austria in the autumn.

Relations between Czechoslovakia and the West remained cool. Under an agreement reached in late 1981, however, the United States and Great Britain in January, 1982, returned to Prague the 18.4 metric tons of Czech gold held since World War II. The gold had been captured from the Nazis, who had looted it from Czechoslovakia.

See STATISTICS OF THE WORLD.

D

DAHOMEY. *See* BENIN.

DANCE. A growing conservatism marked the dance world in 1982. Although there was no decline in productivity, dance troupes tended to feature repertories that looked to the past. Story ballets, the predominant mode of the 19th century, became the main fare of several companies. Revivals of old works were common. Choreographers with a modern viewpoint often applied a contemporary gloss on various aspects of dance history. Productions that referred to the past enjoyed both box-office success and much critical attention.

Dance Trends. The Dance Theatre of Harlem, originally known for its interpretation of the pure-dance ballets of George Balanchine, emphasized narrative dances in 1982. Its major new productions were revivals of Valerie Bettis's *A Streetcar Named Desire*, based on the Tennessee Williams play, and of Ruth Page and Bentley Stone's *Frankie and Johnny*, a satiric pantomime about the fabled lovers. The company's single new ballet, *The Firebird*, by John Taras, was a reworking of existing choreographies, but the story's magical allure made it an audience favorite. After appearing at the New York City Center from Jan. 12 to Feb. 14, the Dance Theatre of Harlem took these ballets on tour across the nation.

More and more regional ballet companies added such classics as *Giselle* and *Sleeping Beauty* to their repertories. The Boston Ballet, especially, was in great demand for its production of Rudolf Nureyev's version of *Don Quixote*, with Nureyev himself portraying the hero's role of Basilio. After the ballet bowed in Boston on March 11, the company took it to Chicago, New Orleans, Miami, Atlanta, Baltimore, Los Angeles, and Detroit for the remainder of the year.

The Martha Graham Dance Company presented the New York City premiere of Graham's Acts of Light *in June. The climax and ceremonial finale of this work celebrates the rising and setting of the sun.*

Cinderella, a story long favored by choreographers, received a much-praised new rendition by Paul Meija. Introduced by the Chicago City Ballet in late 1981, starring Suzanne Farrell, on loan from the New York City Ballet, the production promised to become an annual Thanksgiving event.

The public's interest in the era of Sergei Diaghilev's ballet companies (1909–29) continued to bring audiences to the Joffrey Ballet. The Oakland Ballet, a small troupe with a relatively local reputation, stepped into the national limelight when it revived Bronislava Nijinska's *Les Noces.* This masterpiece of the Diaghilev period, never before performed by an American company, was an important feature of the Spoleto Festival in Charleston, S.C.

In modern dance, two of the world's most forward-looking choreographers also cast their eyes backward. Martha Graham's *Dances of the Golden Hall,* premiered during her company's three-week engagement at the New York City Center in June, evoked the grandiose glamour of the Denishawn days of the 1920's. Paul Taylor's *Lost, Found and Lost,* first seen in Boston in March, was a humorous comment on the choreographer's youthful, avant-garde phase, when he called himself an "assembler" of movement. Although Taylor soon after dropped his interest in minimalist ideas, the stripped-down, assembled look of the choreography became a hallmark of the experimental Judson Church movement in the 1960's. The major event of the avant-garde movement in 1982 was not a new piece but a four-day festival of reconstructions from the Judson Church era.

Much of the new work created in 1982 was spurred by the celebration of the 100th birthday of Igor Stravinsky, whose compositions have inspired many dance classics of this century. The greatest interpreter of his music remained George Balanchine, whose New York City Ballet mounted an elaborate Centennial Celebration at the New York State Theater, June 10–18. Fourteen new ballets were staged for the occasion. Five of these were by Balanchine, the others by company associates Jerome Robbins, John Taras, Peter Martins, and Jacques d'Amboise. During April the San Francisco Ballet also honored the composer on a grand scale, with new ballets by Michael Smuin, John McFall, and Tomm Ruud.

The new work to receive most critical acclaim, however, was a modern adaptation of a 19th-century story ballet by Lev Ivanov, with music by Riccardo Drigo. This was Peter Martins's *The Magic Flute,* a delightful, often comic romance, premiered by the City Ballet on Jan. 21.

Financial Problems. Although the dance world as a whole did not yet feel the full impact of government cutbacks in the arts, many of the major ballet troupes faced financial problems. No longer able to afford New York City as a home base, the Joffrey Ballet was laid off for much of the year; its touring centered around fund-raising benefits. The company's outlook brightened in June, however, when it announced that it would become the first resident dance troupe of the Los Angeles Music Center as of mid-1983.

After a busy and successful first part of the year, the American Ballet Theatre's management canceled the company's fall seasons in Paris, Boston, and Washington, D.C., when contract negotiations with the dancers broke down at the end of August. The dancers, who were represented by the American Guild of Musical Artists, demanded parity with their counterparts at the New York City Ballet. A new contract was ratified by the dancers on Nov. 8.

The Pennsylvania Ballet also had to shut down for several months. In an attempt to reorganize its financial base, the board of directors forced company founder Barbara Weisberger to resign on March 2. Moreover, the board refused to rehire artistic director Benjamin Harkarvy on a long-term basis, instead hiring former City Ballet dancer Robert Weiss on a one-year contract.

Foreign Dance. Of the many foreign troupes visiting the United States, the most distinguished was the Royal Danish Ballet. Appearing at the John F. Kennedy Center for the Performing Arts in Washington, D.C., and at the Metropolitan Opera in New York City, in June, the Danes' repertory was largely devoted to the 19th-century master August Bournonville. Because Bournonville's work was virtually unknown to most Americans, the tour was considered of great artistic importance. N.G.

DELAWARE. See STATISTICS OF THE WORLD.

DEMOCRATIC PARTY. For the Democratic Party, 1982 was a year of rejuvenation. Only two years after losing the White House and the U.S. Senate to the Republicans and ceding effective control of the U.S. House of Representatives, the Democrats rebounded, exploiting voter disenchantment with President Ronald Reagan's economic policies

and thwarting Republican hopes of capitalizing on their 1980 landslide. The Democrats also moved to reform their Presidential nominating procedures in hopes of avoiding the sort of schism that helped doom President Jimmy Carter's 1980 reelection campaign.

Election Results. In the Nov. 2 elections, the Democrats failed to win back control of the Senate but made impressive inroads into Republican strength at the state and national levels. They lost only three incumbents while picking up a net gain of 26 seats in the House, effectively crippling the coalition of Republicans and conservative Democrats that had produced major legislative victories for Reagan in 1981. Democrats gained seven governorships and captured 11 more state legislative houses, giving them control of both houses of the legislature in 34 states.

The party's resurgence was in part the result of a major protest vote against the failure of "Reaganomics" to pull the United States out of recession. Hundreds of thousands of traditional Democrats who deserted the party in 1980 to vote for Reagan returned to the fold in 1982, producing heavy Democratic gains in the industrial states of the Midwest. See ELECTIONS IN THE UNITED STATES.

Party Reforms. Reversing a trend toward greater grass-roots participation in its Presidential nominating conventions, Democrats in March approved major changes in their delegate-selection process. Endorsing the recommendations of a commission headed by Gov. James B. Hunt, Jr. (D, N.C.), the Democratic National Committee approved a plan to set aside 550 seats at the 1984 convention for elected officeholders and party officials who would be allowed to come to the convention as uncommitted delegates. Proponents of the change maintained that previous party reforms had reduced the power of elected officials in favor of issues activists, who were outside the party's mainstream and whose disproportionate influence jeopardized Democrats' chances of winning the Presidency.

The party also decided to narrow the period for state primaries and caucuses from 20 to 15 weeks, eliminate compulsory proportional representation, and scrap the rule requiring convention delegates to vote for whichever candidate they were previously pledged to support. The new procedures were seen as enhancing the Presidential prospects of prominent potential candidates like Sen. Edward M. Kennedy (D, Mass.) and former Vice-President Walter F. Mondale at the expense of dark horse candidates like Jimmy Carter in 1976. The standing of Kennedy and Mondale as Presidential front-runners was evident in June at the party's three-day national conference, which—aside from a wholehearted embrace of the nuclear-freeze movement—provided no notable policy departures. However, Kennedy announced on Dec. 1 that he would not run for President in 1984.

Problems and Prospects. The election returns reaffirmed the Democrats' standing as the majority party in American politics and buoyed the spirits of party leaders as they looked ahead to the 1984 Presidential election. National Chairman Charles T. Manatt proclaimed that the Democratic coalition had been restored and that "the momentum is ours," a judgment partially supported by a September Gallup Poll finding that voters rated the Democrats better able to deal with the nation's problems than the Republicans. But many political analysts believed that Democratic gains were more a protest against the Administration than a vote of confidence in the Democrats. The party remained vulnerable to Republican charges that it offered no realistic policy alternatives of its own, and observers questioned whether the new Democratic strength could be translated into effective national leadership or would only produce a stalemate with a weakened Republican opposition.

See REPUBLICAN PARTY.   T.D.

DENMARK. The minority Social Democratic Party government of Prime Minister Anker Jørgensen fell on Sept. 3, 1982, after failing to win parliamentary support for its economic program. It was replaced on Sept. 10 by a right-of-center coalition headed by Conservative Party leader Poul Schlüter.

Schlüter formed a four-party government made up of the Conservative, Liberal, Center

Democrat, and Christian People's parties; together they held 66 seats in the 179-member parliament. The previous government had resigned after the parliament refused to approve its austerity program, which called for additional taxes and cuts in social services as a means of reducing the $8.5 billion budget deficit projected for 1983. The Danish gross national product was expected to rise by only 1.7 percent in 1982, and unemployment was at 10 percent of the labor force.

The change in government came about in the midst of a currency crisis, marked by heavy speculation against the krone as a result of the nation's political and financial problems. It was reported that Denmark's Central Bank had used up to one third of its foreign exchange reserves in the first nine days of September in an effort to prop up the krone. The currency had already been devalued by 3 percent on Feb. 22.

In October the new government presented to the parliament its own economic program. Consisting of 99 bills, the program was designed to reduce the debt by cutting public spending and increasing state revenues by more than $7 billion over the next two years. Among the provisions was a five-month freeze on wages, prices, and retail profit margins, and suspension of cost-of-living pay increases until 1985. The program aroused stiff opposition but was approved on Oct. 16 after Schlüter threatened to call new elections if it was rejected.

On Feb. 23 the Greenland electorate, in an advisory referendum, voted 12,615 to 11,180 against continued membership in the European Community (EC). Greenland, which has home rule but is a part of Denmark, would require Danish assent to withdraw. Those favoring withdrawal contended that EC membership had hurt the fishing industry by opening up Greenland's waters to other fishing fleets.

See STATISTICS OF THE WORLD.   L.A.S.

DISTRICT OF COLUMBIA. See STATISTICS OF THE WORLD.

DJIBOUTI. See STATISTICS OF THE WORLD.

DOMINICA. See STATISTICS OF THE WORLD.

DOMINICAN REPUBLIC. See STATISTICS OF THE WORLD. See also CARIBBEAN COUNTRIES.

E

EARTH SCIENCES. Major news stories on the earth sciences in 1982 included reports of volcanic eruptions and mysterious clouds in the upper atmosphere. Unusually bitter cold weather swept across much of the United States early in the year. Washington State's Mount St. Helens continued to test the ability of volcanologists to analyze its rumblings, and a Mexican volcano erupted for the first time in recorded history. Research continued on hydrothermal vents in the ocean floor, and seismologists offered an explanation for the eerie light seen during earthquakes.

CLIMATOLOGY

Weather records were broken repeatedly across the U.S. in January by bone-chilling blasts of arctic air and severe snowfalls. Jan. 10, in fact, became the coldest day thus far observed in the 20th century in most of the midwestern states. Atlanta dropped to its coldest temperature ever, −20.5° C. (−5° F.), and Florida citrus growers were hard pressed to protect their crops. Storms dumped up to about 0.3 m (1 ft.) of snow on New York City in early April. Such spring snowfalls, which battered much of the U.S., also established new records for snow cover in the nation. According to the National Earth Satellite Service of the National Oceanic and Atmospheric Administration (NOAA), about 16,300,000 sq.km. (about 6,300,000 sq.mi.) of North America were covered by snow from April 5 through April 11, which set a precedent for that time of year.

Nor did that end the bad-weather news for the U.S. In May 365 tornadoes whipped across the country, the highest number for any month since 1950, when the NOAA began keeping reliable tornado records. The figure topped by 90 the May, 1965, high of 275.

Antarctica also was subjected to an unusually severe winter. On June 23 scientists at the Amundsen–Scott South Pole station observed the coldest temperature ever recorded at the site, −85° C. (−117° F.), ac-

cording to the National Science Foundation, which supports and manages polar research. Previously, the coldest temperature recorded at the station was in July, 1965, when the mercury dipped to −80.5° C. (−113° F.).

Atmospheric Pollution. In 1982 possible connections between solar variability, climate, weather, and atmospheric pollution continued to be explored by various research groups. One panel of the U.S. National Research Council reaffirmed a 1979 report that

The prolonged winter of 1981–82 that held sway over much of the U.S. made possible this view of New York City's Times Square experiencing an Easter-week snowfall.

linked long-term global warming to a possible increase in atmospheric carbon dioxide as a result of human activity. In addition, the panel stated that no substantial revision was needed of an earlier estimate that global temperatures would probably increase by 3° C. (5.4° F.) should the amount of atmospheric carbon dioxide be doubled. This statement ran counter to recent research by other climatologists that appeared to refute the 1979 estimate.

The potential for studying the effects of another group of atmospheric pollutants, the fluorocarbons, was increased in September by a group of Harvard University scientists when they successfully tested a new research balloon over Texas. The giant balloon reached a height of 40 km (25 mi.) and then, by radio command, lowered and raised a capsule of instruments 12 km (7.5 mi.) through the stratosphere. The instruments measured the levels of atomic oxygen at varying heights, thus indicating the availability of atomic oxygen for producing the ozone layer that protects life on earth from harmful ultraviolet radiation. Fluorocarbons, which are used as refrigerants and for other purposes, are a potential threat to the ozone layer. The "yo-yo" balloon was made possible by a newly developed extremely strong but lightweight synthetic line.

Rising Seas and Longer Days. Scientists at the NOAA suggested in 1982 that shrinking polar ice caps may be causing the earth's sea level to rise, which in turn may be causing days to lengthen. Research by Robert Etkins and Edward Epstein showed that global sea levels have risen an average of slightly more than 2.5 mm (0.1 in.) each year since 1940, and the researchers estimated that more than 41,000 cu.km (10,000 cu.mi.) of polar ice had melted in the last 40 years. This thin layer of water added to the global oceans would tend to slow the earth's rotation and would lengthen each day by about 0.001 sec. The increase, it was suggested, would account for about 75 percent of the increase in length of day observed by scientists over the same time period.

On June 30, incidentally, the Bureau International de l'Heure (International Time Bureau) in Paris added another second to that day to allow the earth to catch up once again with the cesium-clock standard in international use—the eleventh time the bureau had done so since 1972.

GEOLOGY AND GEOPHYSICS

In the first months of 1982, earth scientists were intrigued by voluminous "mystery" clouds of suspended materials that they detected high above the earth in the Northern Hemisphere. Analysis of the materials in March showed that the clouds were clearly of volcanic origin, although scientists could not pinpoint the eruption that was the source. Later in the year, however, when similar clouds streamed across the hemisphere and yielded brilliantly colored sunsets, the origin was easily identified as El Chichón, a volcano in southern Mexico.

El Chichón's first eruption in historic times occurred on March 29, 1982, succeeded on April 3 and 4 by a major blast that produced a large, dense stratospheric cloud drifting west at first and then shifting north before moving toward the equator. Although the sulfur-rich cloud was probably 20 times more massive than the one produced by Mount St. Helens in 1980, the exact volume remained unknown. Because of its drift toward the equator, the cloud was not expected to affect North America's weather.

Other Volcano News. After 64 years of silence, Indonesia's Galunggung volcano began a series of eruptions on April 5. A dramatic moment during these explosive bursts occurred on June 24 when a British Airways jet airplane carrying 240 persons flew into one of the volcano's ash clouds. The cloud caused all four engines of the plane to stall, and the jet plummeted nearly 7700 m (25,000 ft.) before the engines could be restarted.

The number of known volcanoes in Antarctica was increased by two in March, when geologist Oscar González-Ferrán of the University of Chile spotted them from a helicopter while taking part in his nation's Antarctic program. The two small active volcanoes lie on the Weddell Sea side of the Antarctic Peninsula and may have been the product of the same plate-tectonics processes that formed the Andes mountains. Five volcanoes

Mexico's El Chichón volcano, erupting for the first time in recorded history, sent large dust clouds into the earth's atmosphere in 1982. Here explosion pits filled with boiling water and mud can be seen within the volcano's new crater.

are now known to be active on the southernmost continent.

Earthquake Lights. Researchers at the U.S. Geological Survey offered an explanation for the eerie glow that sometimes lights up the sky before, during, and after earthquakes greater than magnitude 7 on the Richter earthquake scale. James Byerlee, David Lockner, and Malcolm Johnston proposed that the glow is caused by electric fields produced when rocks slip along a fault in the earth's crust. The friction produced by the slipping heats the rocks and vaporizes the water trapped in the rocks' pores. According to this theory, the resulting electric charges at the rocks' surfaces are responsible for discharging an electric field that is then seen as earthquake lights.

OCEANOGRAPHY

Discoveries of petroleum and minerals on the ocean floor were reported at separate sites in 1982.

Hydrothermal Vents. Volcanically related vents on the ocean floor, where hot materials pour up into the sea, have been discovered regularly along midocean ridges. Recently, however, a group of hydrothermal vents was discovered in an ocean-floor subduction zone, where one of the earth's tectonic plates slips below another plate. The vents, found about 480 km (300 mi.) west of the Mariana Trench of the Pacific Ocean by a research team from the University of Tokyo and the Scripps Institution of Oceanography, were slated to be examined more closely in 1983 by means of the U.S. research submersible *Alvin*.

The first known petroleum formations in such hydrothermal vents were reported in 1982 by oceanographers from Oregon State University and Scripps. The find was made in the Guaymas Basin, about 70 km (about 40 mi.) off Mexico's northwestern coast. Although the petroleum could not be used

135

Detroit, on the left, and Windsor, Ont., on the right, are shown in this picture taken by Landsat-4, the latest in a U.S. earth resources satellite series. This satellite successfully tested a new sensing device that provides more than twice the resolution power of previous Landsats.

commercially, the discovery was expected to help scientists understand the formation of petroleum and minerals. This in turn could lead to better predictions of where commercially exploitable petroleum might be found in the future.

Manganese Deposit. A NOAA research expedition, using the *Alvin,* discovered a large mineral deposit on the ocean floor about 2900 km (1800 mi.) east of Miami. The deposit is rich in manganese, and scientists speculated that it might also contain large amounts of silver, copper, and zinc. Although such deep-ocean ores cannot be exploited profitably by current technology, they were generally considered to be valuable resources for the future.

See also ACCIDENTS AND DISASTERS. B.T.R.

ECONOMY AND BUSINESS. Both in the United States and worldwide, economic conditions were poor during 1982. In the U.S., the recession that began in mid-1981 appeared to bottom out during 1982, but there were few indications of recovery. Western Europe also suffered from slow growth or recession, and the output of 24 non-Communist industrial countries was expected to increase by only 0.5 percent in 1982.

High interest rates, which helped to curb inflation, also had the effect of slowing economic activity. The U.S. dollar reached an 11-year high as capital from abroad flowed into the U.S., attracted by high interest rates. In July the Federal Reserve Board began easing credit, and interest rates dropped, but the value of the dollar remained high.

U.S. Recession. The U.S. gross national product declined at an annual rate of 5.1 percent during the first quarter of 1982. It grew at an annual rate of 2.1 percent in the second quarter of the year, but there was no growth in the third quarter. Unemployment rose to 10.8 percent of the labor force in November, the highest jobless level since 1940. Inflation declined significantly, however. The cost of living, as reflected by the consumer price index, rose at an annual rate of 4.8 percent in the first nine months of 1982, about half the inflation rate for 1981.

U.S. factories were operating at less than 68.4 percent of productive capacity in October, the lowest level since the federal government began keeping such records in 1948. With businesses carrying high inventories and operating so far below capacity, investment in new plants and equipment was meager, falling from 1981 levels—the first such yearly decline since 1975.

Manufacturing industries were hard hit by the recession, particularly the steel industry.

Sales of automobiles, as expressed by totals for the 1982 model year, were the lowest in more than 20 years. Oil company profits declined as the demand for petroleum dropped. The housing and construction industries performed poorly. Net income for farmers fell sharply as bumper harvests depressed commodity prices.

A few sectors of the economy did well, however. With farm prices lower, profits for the nation's big grocery chains rose sharply. A third-quarter surge in Wall Street stock trading sent profits for the nonbank financial sector soaring. Service industries generally maintained profit levels.

Taxes. The tax cuts mandated by legislation in 1981 seemed, at best, to keep the economy from sliding further than it would have otherwise. One reason was that the fear of unemployment kept consumers from spending rather than saving. Another was that the record federal budget deficit of $110.7 billion in fiscal year 1982, in large part a result of tax cuts, helped raise interest rates to levels that retarded recovery. With government borrowing increased in order to finance the deficit, companies were unable to obtain low-rate loans in order to expand facilities or pay off earlier short-term loans.

With still higher deficits predicted in fiscal year 1983, Congress passed legislation in August raising taxes. The amount of added revenue to be gained from businesses as a result of this legislation was estimated at $8.6 billion in fiscal 1983, $17.7 billion in fiscal 1984, and $22 billion in fiscal 1985.

As of 1984, businesses would lose a 1981 tax break that allowed firms with concessions from investing in equipment to sell unused benefits to other firms through so-called safe-harbor leasing deals. Corporations were required to make bigger estimated tax payments and settle their final tax bills faster. Oil firms were limited in using foreign tax credits to offset U.S. tax. Expanded tax credits and depreciation write-offs for plant and equipment, enacted in 1981, were scaled back. New curbs were imposed on the use of tax-exempt bonds issued by state and local governments to support commercial and industrial ventures.

Where Inflation Is Slowing Down

	Change, 1980 to '81*	Change, 1981 to '82*
Potatoes	+ 5.1%	−17.2%
Eggs	+ 4.9%	− 7.2%
Gasoline	+10.2%	− 4.1%
Women's dresses	+ 1.4%	− 3.3%
Hamburger	− 2.3%	− 1.8%
Chicken	− 7.8%	− 1.3%
Mortgage rates	+26.1%	− 1.2%
Sofas	+ 5.2%	− 1.2%
Chuck roast	+ 0.6%	− 0.9%
Television sets	− 0.4%	− 0.9%
Car tires	+ 6.1%	− 0.6%
Milk	+ 4.9%	+ 0.4%
Sirloin steak	+ 0.4%	+ 1.2%
Flour	+ 4.7%	+ 1.4%
Men's suits	+ 5.4%	+ 1.7%
Soft drinks	+ 8.0%	+ 2.0%
Butter	+ 4.6%	+ 2.1%
Sugar	−18.6%	+ 2.8%
Cheese	+ 6.4%	+ 2.9%
Photo supplies	+ 2.7%	+ 2.9%
New cars	+ 5.3%	+ 3.3%
White bread	+ 8.5%	+ 3.3%
Wine	+ 7.0%	+ 3.4%
Beer	+ 6.7%	+ 3.8%
Baby clothes	+ 9.9%	+ 3.9%
Long-distance calls	+12.5%	+ 4.2%
Haircuts	+ 8.4%	+ 4.3%
Home purchases	+ 5.0%	+ 4.5%
Cookies	+10.8%	+ 4.9%
All items	**+11.0%**	**+ 5.0%**
Restaurant meals	+ 8.6%	+ 5.1%
Coffee	−19.0%	+ 5.2%
Soap	+10.3%	+ 5.2%
Rent	+ 8.6%	+ 7.1%
Cereal	+12.4%	+ 7.2%
Refrigerators	+ 7.7%	+ 7.2%
Electricity	+15.1%	+ 7.3%
Property taxes	+ 7.8%	+ 8.5%
Apples	−10.9%	+ 8.6%
Doctor bills	+11.2%	+ 9.0%
Airline fares	+20.0%	+ 9.9%
Hotel rooms	+13.7%	+11.3%
School supplies	+14.1%	+11.3%
Prescriptions	+12.1%	+11.7%
Used cars	+27.1%	+11.7%
Cigarettes	+ 8.4%	+11.8%
Pork chops	+ 9.2%	+12.2%
College tuition	+11.9%	+12.7%
Hospital room	+15.5%	+15.3%
Natural gas	+13.5%	+19.9%
Bacon	+ 7.7%	+33.1%
Oranges	+16.8%	+49.1%

* September–to–September

Boss of Construction Empire

The third-generation leader of a worldwide construction empire, 57-year-old Stephen Bechtel, Jr., is chairman of the Bechtel Group, a family-owned enterprise that in 1981 alone won new contracts worth $10.6 billion. Bechtel's 113 major projects in 21 countries included building the Washington, D.C., subway system, cleaning up the Three Mile Island nuclear power plant near Harrisburg, Pa., and constructing Jubail, a $20 billion city in Saudi Arabia. Two former top company executives, Caspar W. Weinberger and George P. Shultz, were secretary of defense and secretary of state, respectively; a third, W. Kenneth Davis, was deputy secretary of energy. Despite these political connections, industry observers said that the company's success was built on accomplishment, not influence peddling.

Stephen Bechtel, Jr.

Bankruptcies and Mergers. Through the first eight months of 1982, Dun & Bradstreet Corp. reported 15,829 business failures, up 47 percent from the same period in 1981. In the last week of August alone, 696 commercial and industrial companies failed—the highest weekly total since the depths of the Great Depression. Among the companies filing bankruptcy petitions were AM International, one of the nation's oldest suppliers of office equipment and information processing systems; Wickes Companies, the nation's largest merchandiser of lumber and building materials and the second largest furniture dealer; and Braniff International Corp., the nation's eighth largest airline. Penn Square Bank, an Oklahoma City bank that made many bad oilfield loans, was declared insolvent. Drysdale Government Securities Inc. defaulted on its debts, and another government securities trader, Lombard-Wall Inc., filed for bankruptcy. *See also* BANKING AND FINANCE. In August the Manville Corp., the world's largest asbestos producer, filed for bankruptcy in an action apparently not related to any current problem of profitability but rather to the financial drain of contesting more than 16,000 lawsuits related to the risks of inhaling asbestos. UNR Industries, another firm being sued by former workers exposed to asbestos, had filed for bankruptcy in July.

In the biggest merger of the year, Occidental Petroleum Co. acquired Cities Service Co., a smaller oil company, for about $4 billion in August. A complicated takeover struggle ended in September with Allied Corp. acquiring Bendix Corp. for $1.9 billion after Bendix had tried to acquire Martin Marietta Corp., provoking a counterbid for Bendix by Martin Marietta. Before the struggle was resolved, Bendix had acquired 70 percent of Martin Marietta, and Martin Marietta owned about 50 percent of Bendix. A stock swap kept Martin Marietta independent, but Allied held 38 percent of its stock.

In other merger activity, Stroh Brewery Co. acquired Jos. Schlitz Brewing Co. for nearly $500,000,000; R. J. Reynolds Industries, the nation's largest cigarette producer, bought Heublein Inc., a company with large holdings in fast foods and liquor, for $1.3 billion; and Xerox Corp. announced an agreement to acquire Crum & Foster, a leading property and casualty insurer, for $1.6 billion. Several railroad mergers proposed earlier were approved in 1982 by the Interstate Commerce Commission, including that of the Union Pacific Railroad with the Missouri Pacific and

Braniff International Corp. filed for bankruptcy on May 13; it was the first major U.S. airline to fail. After hearing the news, many Braniff pilots simply parked their jet aircraft at the corporate headquarters at the Dallas–Fort Worth Regional Airport and went home.

Western Pacific railroads; *see* TRANSPORTATION.

An eight-year antitrust battle ended in 1982 as the Department of Justice ended its suit against the American Telephone and Telegraph Co. (AT&T) with an agreement under which AT&T would divest itself of its 22 fully owned local telephone companies. Under the terms of the agreement about two thirds of AT&T's $138 billion in assets would be divided among the reorganized local phone companies. *See* COMMUNICATIONS.

Trade. The strength of the U.S. dollar made U.S. exports more expensive, translating into the loss of an estimated 250,000 jobs. The merchandise trade deficit of $13.1 billion in the third quarter was the largest quarterly shortfall ever, and the deficit for the entire year was likely to exceed the record of $33.8 billion set in 1978. However, a large surplus in financial transactions and trade in services, including income from investment overseas, was expected to result in a surplus for the third straight year in the current account of overall balance of payments.

Productivity. For the first year since 1976, it was likely that productivity in the nation's private businesses would increase in 1982. The reason was the decline in working hours and employment, meaning fewer workers were doing more to produce output. Productivity measures the volume of goods and services the nonfarm private sector produces in each hour of paid working time.

World Outlook. France, Great Britain, and West Germany were all experiencing slow or negative economic growth in 1982. In November unemployment in the ten-member European Community was at a postwar high of 10.3 percent of the labor force. Inflation rates were falling, however, to the lowest levels in almost ten years.

Eastern Europe also experienced economic difficulties, stemming from the Polish crisis and the reluctance of Western banks to make new loans. The Soviet bloc owed about $80 billion to Western banks and governments in 1982. Poland, with debts estimated at about $24 billion, was unable to pay principal or interest in 1982. Rumania rescheduled 1982

The Reagan administration took the brunt of blame for the high unemployment arising from poor economic conditions. Here a tent city erected for the homeless by Washington, D.C., community organizations—one of 15 such settlements across the country, dubbed "Reaganvilles"—faces the White House.

payments on its debts of about $11 billion.

In the Middle East, reduced demand for oil and lower oil prices meant that the oil producing countries had smaller trade surpluses. Some countries had deficits for the first time in years, but the situation remained basically healthy.

Although the economic slowdown also affected the non-Communist nations of the Far East and Southeast Asia, this region performed better than any other, with growth estimated at almost 5 percent in 1982. But barriers to Japanese exports increased as recession-battered industrial nations tried to protect their key industries.

Latin America was in deep trouble in 1982. It experienced its first drop in real gross national product since the 1930's and had a staggering $247 billion debt. A problem for all was the recession-caused decline in the prices of the raw materials and agricultural products that they exported. Mexico was in arrears of payment on the principal and interest owed on much of its estimated $80 billion in debt. Argentina and Brazil needed further loans to make payments on a combined total of about $125 billion in debts.

Black African countries recorded growth of about 1.5 percent, but those heavily dependent on exporting commodities performed

From the Grain to the Grape

Vintage wines are coming to moonshine country, according to investors who hope to grow European grapes in northern Georgia. In August they announced plans to produce high-priced red and white wines on more than 500 acres in Jackson County, noted in the past as a source of "white lightning"— homemade whiskey. Officials of Chateau Elan, the new winery, said that the land was hospitable to good grapes and much cheaper than the increasingly expensive wine country of California.

poorly. The need to import ever-larger quantities of food resulted in growing foreign debts.

See also articles on individual countries and the various sectors of the U.S. economy in UNITED STATES OF AMERICA.   R.W.S.

ECUADOR. The world oil glut, falling export prices, and a decline in Ecuador's oil production impelled the government of President Osvaldo Hurtado Larrea to seek aid in 1982 in order to help meet payments on a foreign debt estimated at about $5.5 billion. From European credit markets Hurtado requested loans of $1.2 billion for Ecuador's public sector and $900,000,000 for its private sector. During the year important industrial development projects had to be canceled, and speculative trading in world money markets caused Ecuador's sucre to plunge in value against the dollar.

In an effort to shore up the sucre, to reduce imports, and to promote exports, the government introduced austerity measures, as well as a multitiered system of exchange rates, which Hurtado's opponents regarded as "a disguised devaluation" of the sucre. Dissatisfaction with the government's austerity measures, which included raising domestic energy prices, forced the resignation of the finance minister, and, on Sept. 8, of the oil minister, following a vote of censure against him by the nation's Congress. Strikes and rioting to protest the austerity measures took place in October.

See STATISTICS OF THE WORLD.   A.E.J.

EDUCATION. The year 1982 saw the apparent passing of some old controversies concerning education. In the fall there were only 65 major teachers' strikes in the United States, down from a record 242 three years earlier; among the longest walkouts in 1982 were strikes of 22 days in Detroit and 19 days in Teaneck, N.J. Busing for racial integration was less of a preoccupation than in years past, in part because the nation's most segregated urban systems, in the Northeast and Midwest, had so few white children as to render integration within city limits all but impossible. On the other hand, proposed school prayer and government aid to private schools remained controversial issues, as did the Administration's decision to seek an end to the denial of tax exemptions to schools practicing racial discrimination.

School Prayer. In May President Ronald Reagan proposed a constitutional amendment that would allow voluntary prayer in public schools, thus reversing a 20-year-old U.S. Supreme Court ban on school prayer. The Constitution, said Reagan, guaranteed freedom *of* religion, not freedom *from* religion. His declaration sparked renewed debate on the issue, with supporters claiming that voluntary prayer was a right the Supreme Court should never have taken away and opponents maintaining that reinstatement of school prayer would inevitably breach the First Amendment separation of church and state. A Gallup Poll found that 79 percent of the American public favored the return of school prayer.

U.S. Sen. Jesse Helms (R, N.C.) attempted to bypass the complex and time-consuming amendment process by proposing a law that would simply prohibit the Supreme Court from reviewing any state laws that allow voluntary school prayer. However, U.S. Senate liberals trying to avoid a showdown on a controversial issue in an election year mounted a two-week filibuster that kept the Helms proposal from reaching the floor. The issue seemed certain to return in the next congressional session.

Meanwhile, several states took steps to return prayer to their classrooms. In Alabama Gov. Forrest H. ("Fob") James, Jr. (D), signed a new law that allowed teachers to lead willing students in prayer and even offered a model prayer written by the governor's son. When a federal judge barred implementation of the law, Gov. James defied the order and encouraged teachers across the state to ignore the court injunction. That stand earned the governor a contempt-of-court citation.

Race, Religion, and Tax Exemptions. On Jan. 8 the Reagan administration suddenly reversed an 11-year-old policy of the Internal Revenue Service (IRS) denying tax exemptions to schools that practice racial discrimination. The action provoked immediate opposition from civil rights advocates. A federal appeals court order on Feb. 18 prevented the IRS from carrying out the new directive, but the issue was already headed for the Supreme Court.

The major case involved two religious institutions, Bob Jones University in Greenville, S.C., and Goldsboro Christian Schools in Goldsboro, N.C., both of which had sued to challenge the IRS policy. Goldsboro did not admit black students; Bob Jones had admitted them only since 1975 and still barred interracial dating. Both schools claimed that their racial policies were religiously ordained; therefore, they said, for the government to deny their tax exemptions would violate their religious freedom.

When the case was argued before the Supreme Court in October, the U.S. Justice Department supported the plaintiffs' contention that the IRS had been acting without proper legislative authority. This meant that no party to the case was prepared to argue for the defense. In an unusual step, the Court authorized a special advocate, former Transportation Secretary William T. Coleman, Jr., to defend the IRS policy the Administration had abandoned. The Court's ruling, expected in the spring of 1983, might hold significant implications not only for civil rights policy but also for church-state relations.

Tuition Tax Credits. Another issue with religious overtones came to the fore in April when President Reagan told a meeting of the National Catholic Educational Association in Chicago that he would introduce legislation to allow most parents who send their children to private schools to deduct half the tuition, up to $500 by 1985, from their federal income taxes. The idea of tuition tax credits was particularly attractive to Roman Catholics because a majority of the nation's private-school children attend Catholic schools. Many public school teachers and administra-

The Reagan administration aroused protests in January by seeking to allow tax-exempt status to schools previously ruled ineligible on grounds of practicing racial discrimination. Here Bob Jones 3rd (left), president of Bob Jones University—one of the schools involved in the controversy—and his father, Bob Jones, Jr., appear outside the U.S. Supreme Court to appeal for tax exemption.

This cartoon depicts the problem of paying for college costs, rising faster during a period of economic recession than at any time in a decade. College students and their parents received some comfort when Congress rejected new cuts in federal aid for university students that had been proposed by the Reagan administration.

tors opposed the idea, saying that it would amount to a government subsidy of private education at the expense of the public schools. Some opponents also claimed that such tax credits were unconstitutional because tax dollars would be going, indirectly, to religious schools. The Supreme Court agreed to hear a challenge to a similar state law in Minnesota.

Testing. Falling scores on the Scholastic Aptitude Test (SAT) had long been cited as evidence of deterioration in U.S. secondary schools. In 1982, however, average scores on the SAT, which is taken annually by about 1,000,000 high school students, rose for the first time since 1963. The increase, although slight—only 2 points on the verbal section and 1 point on the mathematics section—was viewed by educators as an encouraging sign.

For the first time, the College Board, which sponsors the SAT, released an analysis of test scores along racial and social lines. White students on average scored higher than Asians, Mexicans, Puerto Ricans, or American Indians, with black students' scores the lowest. Family finances apparently had much to do with students' test results. Within each racial or ethnic group, scores rose with family income, and the relative scores of the various groups coincided with their relative median family incomes. In releasing the data, the College Board said that it hoped recognition of the discrepancies would prompt schools to do better by nonwhite students, particularly blacks. A week later the College Board released another study, this one suggesting that the overall increase in 1982 resulted mainly from an improvement in black and Puerto Rican students' scores.

143

Financial Aid. The Reagan administration unsuccessfully sought new cuts in federal aid for university students, proposing reductions of about 30 percent over two years. By one estimate, had the Reagan proposals passed Congress, one third of needy students would have been denied federal grants, graduate students would have been cut off from guaranteed loans (on which they now rely heavily), and the college work-study program (which helps students find part-time work in return for scholarship aid) would have been curtailed. Higher education lobbyists fought against the cuts. So did the students, who at times displayed a level of political activism that was unseen since the era of the Vietnam war.

In the end, President Reagan signed a bill that held student-aid funding roughly at existing levels. But some educators suggested that publicity about the proposed cuts had already done some damage. With college costs rising faster than at any time in a decade, prolonged uncertainty over financial aid in a time of recession probably contributed to a "trickle-down" phenomenon in college enrollment: Some students (especially those in low- and middle-income brackets) who might once have aspired to an expensive private college began to look to state universities, while those same state schools saw some of their potential students decide to attend community colleges instead.

See also CIVIL RIGHTS AND CIVIL LIBERTIES.   D.A.W.

EGYPT. Egyptian President Hosni Mubarak (see biography at PEOPLE IN THE NEWS) marked his first year in office on Oct. 14, 1982. A cautious and low-key leader, Mubarak won praise for having guided Egypt safely through the turmoil that followed the assassination in 1981 of President Anwar el-Sadat. But his inability to play more than the role of a helpless and frustrated onlooker during Israel's invasion of Lebanon left Egypt still in an isolated position in Arab politics. Moreover, although Mubarak brought stability to Egypt, he was unable to devise and implement any formula of his own for tackling the country's pressing political, social, and economic problems.

Domestic Affairs. Egypt's staggering economic difficulties remained the leading domestic problem for the Mubarak government. Revenues from both oil production and tourism were down sharply, reflecting the troubled world economy. Remittances from Egyptian workers abroad were also off. Foreign investment declined, indicating frustration with Egyptian bureaucracy as well as uncertainty over the nation's political stability. The cost of subsidizing such staples as oil, sugar, rice, and flour rose to $2.4 billion in 1982. Meanwhile, the population, estimated at more than 43,000,000, continued to grow at an alarming rate.

Mubarak's leadership style was in deliberate contrast to the grand and imperious manner of Sadat. He canceled the annual Oct. 6 military parade at which Sadat had been killed a year earlier, and he continued to live in the same suburban house he had occupied as Sadat's vice-president. He freed many of the opposition political figures whom Sadat had sent to jail, and he lifted the ban on the publishing of opposition newspapers. Nevertheless, the threat from Islamic militants remained a continuing source of concern. On Sept. 16 Egyptian police arrested at least 58 members of an underground religious group that had vowed to overthrow the Mubarak government. And on Oct. 3 the government asked parliament to extend for another year the emergency powers invoked after Sadat's assassination, allowing police to detain suspects indefinitely without a court hearing.

Foreign Affairs. On April 25, under terms of the Egyptian-Israeli peace treaty, Egypt regained the last strip of the Sinai Peninsula still under Israeli occupation. Militant Israeli settlers in Yamit, the largest of the Jewish settlements in northern Sinai, threatened to block the final handover of territory, but Israeli soldiers forced them to leave, and Israel returned the Sinai to Egypt on schedule. A 2500-man, 11-nation peacekeeping contingent, known as the Multinational Force and Observers and including a battalion of the U.S. 82nd Airborne Division, was formed to patrol the demilitarized zone of the eastern Sinai.

On April 25, 15 years of Israeli occupation ended with complete withdrawal from Egypt's Sinai Peninsula, under the terms of a 1979 treaty. Egyptian military police celebrate the pullout by waving flags.

Mubarak remained committed to the peace process affirmed by President Sadat in negotiations at Camp David, Md., with U.S. President Jimmy Carter and Israeli Prime Minister Menachem Begin in September, 1978. However, Mubarak also sought to mend Egypt's fences in the Arab world. He promoted closer ties with Jordan's King Hussein. On June 14 he flew to Saudi Arabia to pay his respects following the death of King Khalid. This was the first meeting of Saudi and Egyptian leaders since Saudi Arabia and most other Arab countries broke ties with Cairo in 1979 to protest the peace treaty with Israel. On Oct. 12 he signed an agreement with Sudan aimed at coordinating the political and economic policies of the two Arab neighbors.

Israel's invasion of Lebanon on June 6 and the subsequent siege of Beirut severely strained Egyptian-Israeli relations. Mubarak condemned the invasion as "a flagrant violation of international law" and suspended talks with Israel on Palestinian autonomy. After the mid-September massacre of Palestinian civilians in Beirut refugee camps, Mubarak declared Israel "fully responsible" for the carnage, canceled all official visits between Egypt and Israel, and on Sept. 20 recalled Egypt's ambassador from Tel Aviv. In a speech to the Egyptian parliament on Oct. 3, he denounced Israel for "sounding the drums of war and flexing the muscles of tyrannous force" in Lebanon. Mubarak endorsed U.S. President Ronald Reagan's Mideast peace plan as a "basis for dialogue among all parties in the region," but he also strongly criticized Washington for not restraining Israel in Lebanon.

See STATISTICS OF THE WORLD.   A.D.

Clockwise from top left: Governors elected or reelected in November included Anthony S. Earl (D, Wis.), George C. Wallace (D, Ala.), and James R. Thompson (R, Ill.). H. John Heinz 3rd (R, Pa.) and Paul S. Trible, Jr. (R, Va.) were reelected and elected, respectively, to the Senate. Katie Hall (D, Ind.), elected to the House of Representatives, became the first black from the state to serve in Congress.

ELECTIONS IN THE UNITED STATES. The Nov. 2, 1982, elections showed a clear Democratic tide. The Democrats gained seven governorships and 26 seats in the U.S. House of Representatives, jeopardizing President Ronald Reagan's working majority in Congress. The results were interpreted neither as a complete repudiation of Reagan nor as a vote of confidence in the Democrats but as a protest against the recession which "Reaganomics" had failed to alleviate.

Senate Standoff. With 33 U.S. Senate seats at stake, the results were a standoff. The Democrats gained seats in New Jersey and New Mexico but lost seats in Nevada and Virginia, leaving the Senate with a 54–46 Republican edge. Only two incumbents were defeated: Howard W. Cannon (D, Nev.), who lost to former Republican State Sen. Jacob ("Chic") Hecht, and Harrison ("Jack") Schmitt (R, N.M.), a former astronaut upset by State Attorney General Jeff Bingaman. Hecht and Bingaman were two of only five new faces elected in 1982. The others were Pete Wilson

(R, Calif.), Frank R. Lautenberg (D, N.J.), and Paul S. Trible, Jr. (R, Va.). Lautenberg, a millionaire businessman, outspent and upset Rep. Millicent Fenwick, (R, N.J.), one of the three women who ran—all unsuccessfully—for the Senate as major-party candidates. Wilson, the mayor of San Diego, defeated California Gov. Edmund G. ("Jerry") Brown, Jr. (D), successfully exploiting Brown's negative ratings and thwarting Brown's national ambitions. Trible, a conservative congressman from Newport News, edged out Virginia Lt. Gov. Richard J. Davis (D), a reluctant candidate drafted at the urging of Gov. Charles S. Robb (D).

Democratic incumbents were reelected in Arizona, Florida, Hawaii, Maine, Maryland, Massachusetts, Michigan, Mississippi, Montana, Nebraska, New York, North Dakota, Ohio, Tennessee, Texas, Washington, West Virginia, and Wisconsin. Republican incumbents held onto their seats in Connecticut, Delaware, Indiana, Minnesota, Missouri, Pennsylvania, Rhode Island, Utah, Vermont, and Wyoming.

While Republicans avoided a net loss in the Senate, political analysts regarded their shrinking margins of victory as an unpleasant omen for the GOP. Five moderate Republicans won by an average of only 51 percent, and a combined shift of only 43,000 votes in those contests would have given the Democrats control of the Senate. The Democrats also appeared to have an advantage in 1984, when 19 Republicans but only 14 Democratic incumbents would face reelection.

Gubernatorial Contests. The Democrats made a strong showing in state races, winning nine governorships while losing two, for a net gain of seven; their statehouse margin thus increased from 27–23 to 34–16. In Alabama former Gov. George C. Wallace (D), with heavy support from blacks and liberal voters (despite his segregationist past), won an unprecedented fourth term over Montgomery Mayor Emory Folmar (R), who campaigned on a law-and-order platform. Ohio Lt. Gov. Richard F. Celeste (D), a former director of the Peace Corps, defeated Rep. Clarence J. ("Bud") Brown (R) to succeed retiring Gov. James A. Rhodes (R). Texas Attor-

ney General Mark White (D) offset a huge fund-raising disadvantage to upset incumbent Gov. William Clements (R).

In New York, Lt. Gov. Mario M. Cuomo (D), a liberal, beat conservative drugstore magnate Lewis E. Lehrman by an unexpectedly narrow margin of 51–49 percent. Former Gov. Bill Clinton (D, Ark.) regained the job he lost to Frank White in the 1980 Reagan landslide, and Nebraska Gov. Charles Thone (R) was ousted by Robert Kerrey (D), a Medal of Honor winner in Vietnam. In Michigan, where the unemployment rate exceeded 16 percent, James J. Blanchard (D) beat insurance executive Richard H. Headlee (R). The Democratic sweep in the Midwest included Wisconsin, with Anthony S. Earl (D) swamping GOP businessman Terry J. Kohler. Democrats also took control of statehouses in Alaska, Minnesota, and Nevada. In Massachusetts former Gov. Michael S. Dukakis (D) easily bested John Winthrop Sears (R) after beating incumbent Gov. Edward J. King in the Democratic primary; King had unseated Dukakis in a 1978 primary battle. The New Mexico governorship went to a Hispanic American, State Attorney General Toney Anaya (D).

The only gains for Republicans came in California, where State Attorney General George Deukmejian (R) defeated Los Angeles Mayor Tom Bradley (D), who had hoped to become the country's first elected black governor, and in New Hampshire, where incumbent Gov. Hugh J. Gallen (D) lost to Tufts University engineering professor John H. Sununu (R). Illinois Gov. James R. Thompson (R) survived a stiff challenge from former Sen. Adlai E. Stevenson 3rd (D) in what was expected to be a Thompson runaway. Stevenson lost by only about 5000 votes out of more than 3,600,000 cast.

House Races. Democrats bounced back from their 33-seat loss in 1980 to recapture 26 seats in the House in 1982, scoring most of their gains in the economically depressed Northeast and Midwest. More than a score of other GOP incumbents narrowly won reelection, including House Minority Leader Robert H. Michel (R, Ill.), whose district was particularly ravaged by the recession. The composition of the new House, with 81 freshman members, would be decidedly more moderate-to-liberal. Nine Hispanics were elected, an increase of three; women added one seat to 20 previously held. Black representation increased from 17 to 20, but Robert Clark (D) failed in his bid to become the first black congressman from Mississippi since Reconstruction.

Though the Republicans had expected to pick up seats from redistricting mandated by the 1980 census, the Democrats gained the upper hand instead. Of 17 new House districts created in the South and West, Democrats won ten. And of the six races where incumbent Democrats and Republicans were thrown against each other by redistricting, Democrats won four.

Financial Impact. An enormous fund-raising advantage almost certainly saved some Republican candidates who might otherwise have lost, though several heavily financed candidates were defeated. Both Texas Gov. Clements, whose campaign spent an estimated $14,000,000, and New York gubernatorial challenger Lehrman, who reportedly spent at least $8,000,000 of his own money in a $13,500,000 campaign effort, lost their races. Among Democrats, Minnesota senatorial candidate Mark Dayton spent more than $6,000,000 of his personal fortune in a losing cause, and Adam Levin was unable to oust a New Jersey Republican congressman despite spending more than $1,000,000, or at least $14 for each vote he received; however Lautenberg's $2,700,000 personal investment helped him win New Jersey's U.S. Senate seat.

Democrats were cheered by the poor showing of two far-right organizations, the National Conservative Political Action Committee (NCPAC) and Senator Jesse Helms's (R, N.C.) Congressional Club. Both groups successfully targeted several liberals in the 1980 elections but failed badly in 1982, despite fund-raising efforts that netted each committee some $10,000,000. Of 17 senators on NCPAC's target list, all but one were reelected. And all five candidates backed by the Congressional Club in Helms's home state of North Carolina were defeated.

Ballot Questions. Voters in 42 states and the District of Columbia confronted more than 230 referendums, initiatives, and propositions on Nov. 2. A proposal for a U.S.-Soviet nuclear arms freeze was approved by eight states (California, Massachusetts, Michigan, Montana, New Jersey, North Dakota, Oregon, and Rhode Island), the District of Columbia, Chicago, Philadelphia, and Denver, losing on a statewide level only in Arizona. A tough handgun control law was rejected in California, and New Hampshire and Nevada voters approved constitutional amendments reaffirming the right to bear arms. Massachusetts passed a measure requiring voter approval before any new nuclear power or waste-processing plant could be constructed, but Maine voted to keep its only nuclear plant operating. The death penalty was restored in Massachusetts, and Arizona and Colorado voted to keep violent-crime suspects in jail while awaiting trial. Massachusetts voters refused to repeal a state law mandating a 5¢ deposit on returnable beverage containers, but "bottle bills" lost in Arizona, California, Colorado, and Washington. The District of Columbia approved a proposed constitution, a preliminary step toward possible statehood, while Alaska voters refused to ban state funding for abortions and rejected a proposal to move the state capital from Juneau.

See also STATE GOVERNMENT REVIEW.   T.D.

GOVERNORS, U.S. SENATORS, AND U.S. REPRESENTATIVES ELECTED IN 1982

Governors

ALABAMA
George C. Wallace (D)
ALASKA
William Sheffield (D)
ARIZONA
Bruce Babbitt (D)
ARKANSAS
Bill Clinton (D)
CALIFORNIA
George Deukmejian (R)
COLORADO
Richard D. Lamm (D)
CONNECTICUT
William A. O'Neill (D)
FLORIDA
Robert Graham (D)
GEORGIA
Joe Frank Harris (D)
HAWAII
George R. Ariyoshi (D)
IDAHO
John V. Evans (D)
ILLINOIS
James R. Thompson (R)
IOWA
Terry Branstad (R)
KANSAS
John W. Carlin (D)
MAINE
Joseph E. Brennan (D)
MARYLAND
Harold R. Hughes (D)
MASSACHUSETTS
Michael S. Dukakis (D)
MICHIGAN
James J. Blanchard (D)
MINNESOTA
Rudy Perpich (D)
NEBRASKA
Robert Kerrey (D)
NEVADA
Richard H. Bryan (D)
NEW HAMPSHIRE
John H. Sununu (R)
NEW MEXICO
Toney Anaya (D)
NEW YORK
Mario M. Cuomo (D)
OHIO
Richard F. Celeste (D)
OKLAHOMA
George Nigh (D)
OREGON
Victor G. Atiyeh (R)
PENNSYLVANIA
Richard L. Thornburgh (R)
RHODE ISLAND
J. Joseph Garrahy (D)
SOUTH CAROLINA
Richard W. Riley (D)
SOUTH DAKOTA
William J. Janklow (R)
TENNESSEE
Lamar Alexander (R)
TEXAS
Mark White (D)
VERMONT
Richard A. Snelling (R)

WISCONSIN
Anthony S. Earl (D)
WYOMING
Ed Herschler (D)

Senators

ARIZONA
Dennis DeConcini (D)
CALIFORNIA
Pete Wilson (R)
CONNECTICUT
Lowell P. Weicker, Jr. (R)
DELAWARE
William V. Roth, Jr. (R)
FLORIDA
Lawton M. Chiles, Jr. (D)
HAWAII
Spark M. Matsunaga (D)
INDIANA
Richard G. Lugar (R)
MAINE
George J. Mitchell (D)
MARYLAND
Paul S. Sarbanes (D)
MASSACHUSETTS
Edward M. Kennedy (D)
MICHIGAN
Donald W. Riegle, Jr. (D)
MINNESOTA
David F. Durenberger (R)
MISSISSIPPI
John C. Stennis (D)
MISSOURI
John C. Danforth (R)
MONTANA
John Melcher (D)
NEBRASKA
Edward Zorinsky (D)
NEVADA
Jacob ("Chic") Hecht (R)
NEW JERSEY
Frank R. Lautenberg (D)
NEW MEXICO
Jeff Bingaman (D)
NEW YORK
Daniel P. Moynihan (D)
NORTH DAKOTA
Quentin N. Burdick (D)
OHIO
Howard M. Metzenbaum (D)
PENNSYLVANIA
H. John Heinz, 3rd (R)
RHODE ISLAND
John H. Chafee (R)
TENNESSEE
James R. Sasser (D)
TEXAS
Lloyd Bentsen (D)
UTAH
Orrin G. Hatch (R)
VERMONT
Robert T. Stafford (R)
VIRGINIA
Paul S. Trible, Jr. (R)
WASHINGTON
Henry M. Jackson (D)
WEST VIRGINIA
Robert C. Byrd (D)

WISCONSIN
William Proxmire (D)
WYOMING
Malcolm Wallop (R)

Representatives

ALABAMA
1. Jack Edwards (R)
2. William L. Dickinson (R)
3. William Nichols (D)
4. Tom Bevill (D)
5. Ronnie G. Flippo (D)
6. Ben Erdreich (D)
7. Richard C. Shelby (D)
ALASKA
At large: Donald E. Young (R)
ARIZONA
1. John McCain (R)
2. Morris K. Udall (D)
3. Bob Stump (R)
4. Eldon D. Rudd (R)
5. Jim McNulty (D)
ARKANSAS
1. William V. ("Bill") Alexander, Jr. (D)
2. Edwin R. Bethune, Jr. (R)
3. John P. Hammerschmidt (R)
4. Beryl F. Anthony, Jr. (D)
CALIFORNIA
1. Douglas H. Bosco (D)
2. Eugene A. Chappie (R)
3. Robert T. Matsui (D)
4. Vic Fazio (D)
5. Phillip Burton (D)
6. Barbara Boxer (D)
7. George Miller (D)
8. Ronald V. Dellums (D)
9. Fortney H. ("Pete") Stark, Jr. (D)
10. Don Edwards (D)
11. Thomas P. Lantos (D)
12. Ed Zschau (R)
13. Norman Y. Mineta (D)
14. Norman D. Shumway (R)
15. Tony Coelho (D)
16. Leon E. Panetta (D)
17. Charles Pashayan, Jr. (R)
18. Richard Lehman (D)
19. Robert J. Lagomarsino (R)
20. William M. Thomas (R)
21. Bobbie Fiedler (R)
22. Carlos J. Moorhead (R)
23. Anthony C. Beilenson (D)
24. Henry A. Waxman (D)
25. Edward R. Roybal (D)
26. Howard L. Berman (D)
27. Mel Levine (D)
28. Julian C. Dixon (D)
29. Augustus F. Hawkins (D)
30. Matthew G. Martinez (D)
31. Mervyn M. Dymally (D)
32. Glenn M. Anderson (D)
33. David T. Dreier (R)
34. Esteban Torres (D)
35. Jerry Lewis (R)
36. George E. Brown, Jr. (D)
37. Al McCandless (R)
38. Jerry M. Patterson (D)
39. William E. Dannemeyer (R)

40. Robert E. Badham (R)
41. William D. Lowery (R)
42. Daniel E. Lungren (R)
43. Ron Packard (R)
44. Jim Bates (D)
45. Duncan L. Hunter (R)

COLORADO
1. Patricia Schroeder (D)
2. Timothy E. Wirth (D)
3. Ray P. Kogovsek (D)
4. Hank Brown (R)
5. Kenneth B. Kramer (R)
6. Jack Swigert (R)

CONNECTICUT
1. Barbara B. Kenelly (D)
2. Samuel Gejdenson (D)
3. Bruce A. Morrison (D)
4. Stewart B. McKinney (R)
5. William R. Ratchford (D)
6. Nancy L. Johnson (R)

DELAWARE
At large: Thomas R. Carper (D)

FLORIDA
1. Earl D. Hutto (D)
2. Don Fuqua (D)
3. Charles E. Bennett (D)
4. William V. Chappell, Jr. (D)
5. Bill McCollum, Jr. (R)
6. Kenneth H. ("Buddy") MacKay (D)
7. Sam M. Gibbons (D)
8. C. W. Young (R)
9. Michael Bilirakis (R)
10. Andrew P. Ireland (D)
11. Bill Nelson (D)
12. Tom Lewis (R)
13. Connie Mack (R)
14. Daniel A. Mica (D)
15. E. Clay Shaw (R)
16. Larry Smith (D)
17. William Lehman (D)
18. Claude D. Pepper (D)
19. Dante B. Fascell (D)

GEORGIA
1. Lindsay Thomas (D)
2. Charles F. Hatcher (D)
3. Richard Ray (D)
4. Elliott H. Levitas (D)
5. Wyche Fowler, Jr. (D)
6. Newt Gingrich (R)
7. Lawrence P. McDonald (D)
8. J. Roy Rowland (D)
9. Edgar L. Jenkins (D)
10. D. Douglas Barnard, Jr. (D)

HAWAII
1. Cecil Heftel (D)
2. Daniel K. Akaka (D)

IDAHO
1. Larry E. Craig (R)
2. George V. Hansen (R)

ILLINOIS
1. Harold Washington (D)
2. Gus Savage (D)
3. Martin A. Russo (D)
4. George M. O'Brien (R)
5. William O. Lipinski (D)
6. Henry J. Hyde (R)
7. Cardiss Collins (D)
8. Dan Rostenkowski (D)
9. Sidney R. Yates (D)
10. John E. Porter (R)
11. Frank Annunzio (D)
12. Philip M. Crane (R)
13. John N. Erlenborn (R)

14. Tom Corcoran (R)
15. Edward R. Madigan (R)
16. Lynne M. Martin (R)
17. Lane Evans (D)
18. Robert H. Michel (R)
19. Daniel B. Crane (R)
20. Richard J. Durbin (D)
21. Charles Melvin Price (D)
22. Paul Simon (D)

INDIANA
1. Katie Hall (D)
2. Philip R. Sharp (D)
3. John P. Hiler (R)
4. Daniel R. Coats (R)
5. Elwood H. Hillis (R)
6. Daniel L. Burton (R)
7. John T. Myers (R)
8. Francis X. McCloskey (D)
9. Lee H. Hamilton (D)
10. Andrew Jacobs, Jr. (D)

IOWA
1. James A. S. Leach (R)
2. Thomas J. Tauke (R)
3. Cooper Evans (R)
4. Neal Smith (D)
5. Thomas R. Harkin (D)
6. Berkley W. Bedell (D)

KANSAS
1. Charles P. ("Pat") Roberts (R)
2. Jim Slattery (D)
3. Larry Winn, Jr. (R)
4. Dan Glickman (D)
5. Robert Whittaker (R)

KENTUCKY
1. Carroll Hubbard, Jr. (D)
2. William H. Natcher (D)
3. Romano L. Mazzoli (D)
4. Marion Gene Snyder (R)
5. Harold D. Rogers (R)
6. Larry J. Hopkins (R)
7. Carl D. Perkins (D)

LOUISIANA
1. Robert L. Livingston, Jr. (R)
2. Corinne C. ("Lindy") Boggs (D)
3. William J. Tauzin (D)
4. Charles E. Roemer 3rd (D)
5. Thomas J. ("Jerry") Huckaby (D)
6. W. Henson Moore (R)
7. John B. Breaux (D)
8. Gillis W. Long (D)

MAINE
1. John R. McKernan, Jr. (R)
2. Olympia J. Snowe (R)

MARYLAND
1. Royden P. Dyson (D)
2. Clarence D. Long (D)
3. Barbara Ann Mikulski (D)
4. Marjorie S. Holt (R)
5. Steny H. Hoyer (D)
6. Beverly B. B. Byron (D)
7. Parren J. Mitchell (D)
8. Michael D. Barnes (D)

MASSACHUSETTS
1. Silvio O. Conte (R)
2. Edward P. Boland (D)
3. Joseph D. Early (D)
4. Barney Frank (D)
5. James M. Shannon (D)
6. Nicholas Mavroules (D)
7. Edward J. Markey (D)
8. Thomas P. ("Tip") O'Neill, Jr. (D)
9. John J. Moakley (D)
10. Gerry E. Studds (D)
11. Brian J. Donnelly (D)

MICHIGAN
1. John Conyers, Jr. (D)
2. Carl D. Pursell (R)
3. Howard E. Wolpe (D)
4. Mark Siljander (R)
5. Harold S. Sawyer (R)
6. M. Robert Carr (D)
7. Dale E. Kildee (D)
8. Bob Traxler (D)
9. Guy A. Vander Jagt (R)
10. Donald J. Albosta (D)
11. Robert W. Davis (R)
12. David E. Bonior (D)
13. George W. Crockett, Jr. (D)
14. Dennis M. Hertel (D)
15. William D. Ford (D)
16. John D. Dingell (D)
17. Sander Levin (D)
18. William S. Broomfield (R)

MINNESOTA
1. Timothy J. Penny (D)
2. Vin Weber (R)
3. William E. Frenzel (R)
4. Bruce F. Vento (D)
5. Martin O. Sabo (D)
6. Gerry Sikorski (D)
7. Arlan Stangeland (R)
8. James L. Oberstar (D)

MISSISSIPPI
1. Jamie L. Whitten (D)
2. Webb Franklin (R)
3. Gillespie V. Montgomery (D)
4. Wayne Dowdy (D)
5. Trent Lott (R)

MISSOURI
1. William L. Clay (D)
2. Robert A. Young (D)
3. Richard A. Gephardt (D)
4. Ike Skelton (D)
5. Alan Wheat (D)
6. E. Thomas Coleman (R)
7. Gene Taylor (R)
8. William Emerson (R)
9. Harold L. Volkmer (D)

MONTANA
1. Pat Williams (D)
2. Ronald C. Marlenee (R)

NEBRASKA
1. Douglas K. Bereuter (R)
2. Hal Daub (R)
3. Virginia Smith (R)

NEVADA
1. Harry Reid (D)
2. Barbara Vucanovich (R)

NEW HAMPSHIRE
1. Norman E. D'Amours (D)
2. Judd Gregg (R)

NEW JERSEY
1. James J. Florio (D)
2. William J. Hughes (D)
3. James J. Howard (D)
4. Christopher H. Smith (R)
5. Margaret S. Roukema (R)
6. Bernard Dwyer (D)
7. Matthew J. Rinaldo (R)
8. Robert A. Roe (D)
9. Robert G. Torricelli (D)
10. Peter W. Rodino, Jr. (D)
11. Joseph G. Minish (D)
12. James A. Courter (R)
13. Edwin B. Forsythe (R)
14. Frank Guarini (D)

NEW MEXICO
1. Manuel Lujan, Jr. (R)

2. Joseph R. Skeen (R)
3. Bill Richardson (D)

NEW YORK
1. William Carney (R)
2. Thomas J. Downey (D)
3. Robert J. Mrazek (D)
4. Norman F. Lent (R)
5. Raymond J. McGrath (R)
6. Joseph P. Addabbo (D)
7. Benjamin S. Rosenthal (D)
8. James H. Scheuer (D)
9. Geraldine Anne Ferraro (D)
10. Charles D. Schumer (D)
11. Edolphus Towns (D)
12. Major R. Owens (D)
13. Stephen J. Solarz (D)
14. Guy V. Molinari (R)
15. S. William Green (R)
16. Charles B. Rangel (D)
17. Theodore S. Weiss (D)
18. Robert Garcia (D)
19. Mario Biaggi (D)
20. Richard L. Ottinger (D)
21. Hamilton Fish, Jr. (R)
22. Benjamin A. Gilman (R)
23. Samuel S. Stratton (D)
24. Gerald B. Solomon (R)
25. Sherwood Boehlert (R)
26. David O. Martin (R)
27. George C. Wortley (R)
28. Matthew F. McHugh (D)
29. Frank Horton (R)
30. Barber B. Conable, Jr. (R)
31. Jack F. Kemp (R)
32. John J. LaFalce (D)
33. Henry J. Nowak (D)
34. Stanley N. Lundine (D)

NORTH CAROLINA
1. Walter B. Jones (D)
2. I. T. ("Tim") Valentine, Jr. (D)
3. Charles O. Whitley (D)
4. Ike F. Andrews (D)
5. Stephen L. Neal (D)
6. Charles R. Britt (D)
7. Charles Rose (D)
8. W. G. ("Bill") Hefner (D)
9. James G. Martin (R)
10. James T. Broyhill (R)
11. James M. Clarke (D)

NORTH DAKOTA
At large: Byron L. Dorgan (D)

OHIO
1. Thomas A. Luken (D)
2. Willis D. Gradison, Jr. (R)
3. Tony P. Hall (D)
4. Michael Oxley (R)
5. Delbert L. Latta (R)
6. Bob McEwen (R)
7. Michael DeWine (R)
8. Thomas N. Kindness (R)
9. Marcy Kaptur (D)
10. Clarence E. Miller (R)
11. Dennis E. Eckart (D)
12. John R. Kasich (R)
13. Donald J. Pease (D)
14. John F. Seiberling (D)
15. Chalmers P. Wylie (R)
16. Ralph Regula (R)
17. Lyle Williams (R)
18. Douglas Applegate (D)
19. Edward F. Feighan (D)
20. Mary Rose Oakar (D)
21. Louis Stokes (D)

OKLAHOMA
1. James R. Jones (D)
2. Mike Synar (D)
3. Wesley W. Watkins (D)
4. Dave McCurdy (D)
5. Marvin H. Edwards (R)
6. Glenn English (D)

OREGON
1. Les AuCoin (D)
2. Bob Smith (R)
3. Ronald L. Wyden (D)
4. James Weaver (D)
5. Denny Smith (R)

PENNSYLVANIA
1. Thomas Foglietta (D)
2. William H. Gray 3rd (D)
3. Robert A. Borski (D)
4. Joseph P. Kolter (D)
5. Richard T. Schulze (R)
6. Gus Yatron (D)
7. Robert W. Edgar (D)
8. Peter H. Kostmayer (D)
9. E. G. ("Bud") Shuster (R)
10. Joseph M. McDade (R)
11. Frank Harrison (D)
12. John P. Murtha (D)
13. Lawrence Coughlin (R)
14. William J. Coyne (D)
15. Donald L. Ritter (R)
16. Robert S. Walker (R)
17. George W. Gekas (R)
18. Doug Walgren (D)
19. William F. Goodling (R)
20. Joseph M. Gaydos (D)
21. Thomas J. Ridge (R)
22. Austin J. Murphy (D)
23. William F. Clinger, Jr. (R)

RHODE ISLAND
1. Fernand J. St. Germain (D)
2. Claudine Schneider (R)

SOUTH CAROLINA
1. Thomas F. Hartnett (R)
2. Floyd D. Spence (R)
3. Butler C. Derrick, Jr. (D)
4. Carroll A. Campbell, Jr. (R)
5. John Spratt (D)
6. Robert M. Tallon, Jr. (D)

SOUTH DAKOTA
At large: Thomas A. Daschle (D)

TENNESSEE
1. James H. Quillen (R)
2. John J. Duncan (R)
3. Marilyn L. Bouquard (D)
4. Jim Cooper (D)
5. William H. Boner (D)
6. Albert Gore, Jr. (D)
7. Don Sundquist (R)
8. Ed Jones (D)
9. Harold Ford (D)

TEXAS
1. Sam B. Hall, Jr. (D)
2. Charles Wilson (D)
3. Steve Bartlett (R)
4. Ralph M. Hall (D)
5. John Bryant (D)
6. Phil Gramm (D)
7. W. R. ("Bill") Archer (R)
8. Jack M. Fields (R)
9. Jack Brooks (D)
10. J. J. ("Jake") Pickle (D)
11. J. Marvin Leath (D)
12. James C. Wright, Jr. (D)
13. Jack E. Hightower (D)

14. William N. Patman (D)
15. E. Kika de la Garza (D)
16. Ronald Coleman (D)
17. Charles W. Stenholm (D)
18. George T. ("Mickey") Leland (D)
19. Kent R. Hance (D)
20. Henry B. Gonzalez (D)
21. Thomas Loeffler (R)
22. Ronald Paul (R)
23. Abraham Kazen, Jr. (D)
24. Martin Frost (D)
25. Mike Andrews (D)
26. Tom Vandergriff (D)
27. Solomon P. Ortiz (D)

UTAH
1. James V. Hansen (R)
2. David D. Marriott (R)
3. Howard C. Nielson (R)

VERMONT
At large: James M. Jeffords (R)

VIRGINIA
1. Herbert Bateman (R)
2. G. William Whitehurst (R)
3. Thomas J. Bliley (R)
4. Norman Sisisky (D)
5. W. C. ("Dan") Daniel (D)
6. James Olin (D)
7. J. Kenneth Robinson (R)
8. Stanford E. Parris (R)
9. Frederick Boucher (D)
10. Frank R. Wolf (R)

WASHINGTON
1. Joel Pritchard (R)
2. Al Swift (D)
3. Don L. Bonker (D)
4. Sid W. Morrison (R)
5. Thomas S. Foley (D)
6. Norman D. Dicks (D)
7. Mike Lowry (D)
8. Rodney Chandler (R)

WEST VIRGINIA
1. Alan B. Mollohan (D)
2. Harley O. Staggers, Jr. (D)
3. Robert E. Wise (D)
4. Nick J. Rahall (D)

WISCONSIN
1. Les Aspin (D)
2. Robert W. Kastenmeier (D)
3. Steven C. Gunderson (R)
4. Clement J. Zablocki (D)
5. James Moody (D)
6. Thomas E. Petri (R)
7. David R. Obey (D)
8. Toby Roth (R)
9. F. James Sensenbrenner, Jr. (R)

WYOMING
At large: Richard Cheney (R)

Despite guerrilla opposition and a leftist boycott, the people of El Salvador turned out in unprecedented numbers on March 28 to elect representatives to a Constituent Assembly. Here soldiers keep a watchful eye during voting in the capital city of San Salvador.

EL SALVADOR. As a result of legislative elections held on March 28, 1982, President José Napoleón Duarte was succeeded on May 2 by Alvaro Alfredo Magaña. The civil war produced continuing violence on both sides. The country's economy suffered severe hardships, and the worst natural disaster since 1965 befell the nation in September.

Politics. Despite violence and threats of violence from guerrillas and a boycott by the leftist opposition, the turnout was heavy as Salvadorans elected a Constituent Assembly. Duarte's centrist Christian Democratic Party won 41 percent of the vote and 24 of the 60

seats but was outpolled by the combined weight of five right-wing parties, which won the remaining 36 seats.

Official results, which, however, were widely recognized as inflated, indicated that 74 percent of the total electorate cast ballots. About 12 percent of the ballots were blank or spoiled.

The Constituent Assembly was empowered to appoint a new government, draft a new constitution, and provide for a presidential election scheduled for 1983. The rightists locked the Christian Democrats out of all key legislative posts and chose as the assembly's president Maj. Roberto d'Aubuisson, head of the extreme right-wing Nationalist Republican Alliance (ARENA) and a man said to be implicated in terrorist activities. Following heavy pressure, reportedly from both the United States and the armed forces, the body elected Magaña, an independent centrist, president. The number of vice-presidents was increased to three, representing one man each from the Christian Democrats, ARENA, and the National Conciliation Party, which had broken ranks with the other rightist parties to help elect Magaña. In early May Magaña installed a cabinet with virtually equal representation from the three leading parties.

The Economy. Aid from the U.S. and international lending agencies helped this small Central American nation avoid bankruptcy arising from continued political uncertainty, a lack of capital investment, high prices for imported oil, and the cost of prolonged fighting.

Continued U.S. military aid had been made dependent, in part, on progress in the land reform program instituted in 1980. On May 18, however, the assembly voted to suspend Decree 207, a phase of the program under which peasants would have been allowed to purchase plots of land of up to 17 acres that they had been renting or sharecropping. More than 30,000 of perhaps 150,000 potential beneficiaries had received provisional titles to these plots, but no one had received clear title. Opponents of the program blamed it for sharp drops in the production of coffee, sugar, and grain since 1980. After suspension of the decree, thousands of peasant families were reported to have been evicted by landowners.

The assembly also repealed Phase 2 of the land reform program, intended to expropriate with compensation farms of between 247 and 1250 acres for use as peasant cooperatives. This phase, covering more than 23 percent of all farmland, had been deferred indefinitely in 1981.

Civil War. By midyear it seemed apparent that the guerrillas were as strong as ever, yet no closer to a military victory. They held vast sections of the sparsely populated Chalate-nango and Morazán provinces, and government troops were unable to dislodge them. Large areas of the country were blacked out more than a dozen times in 1982, sometimes for up to a week, by attacks on power stations. The U.S. trained three army battalions and sent supplies that included helicopters, jets, ammunition, and trucks. Three battalions of Honduran troops attempted to dislodge guerrillas in the mountainous area along the border between El Salvador and Honduras.

According to Defense Minister José Guillermo García, government troops suffered 3801 casualties, representing roughly one-fifth the army's strength, in the 12-month period ending on June 30. The death toll for noncombatants for the first half of the year was estimated at 2658, compared with 4383 in the previous six months. Many of these were victims of the armed forces, other security forces, or rightist "death squads."

In September President Magaña was said to be considering peace negotiations between his government and guerrilla forces. With the quiet support of the administration of U.S. President Ronald Reagan, Magaña began an indirect "dialogue" with guerrilla leaders, when he met with Costa Rican Foreign Minister Fernando Volio in San Salvador on Sept. 3.

Exiled Salvadoran leftist opposition leaders stated repeatedly that they were prepared to return home "to work for a political settlement of the war." Among the demands of the Democratic Revolutionary Front, headed by Guillermo Manuel Ungo, was amnesty for some 500 political prisoners. El Salvador's conservative leaders rejected the overtures, saying that the only dialogue possible was "the dialogue with the people in the next elections."

Disaster. During five days of torrential rains in September, floods and mud slides killed at least 700 persons, with hundreds more presumed dead. Whole villages were virtually swept away in what was described as the worst natural disaster to strike El Salvador since an earthquake in 1965. The crop loss was estimated at $200,000,000.

See STATISTICS OF THE WORLD.   A.E.J.

Solar One, the largest operating solar energy plant in the world, was dedicated in April in Daggett, Calif. Its 72-acre field of mirrors focuses sunlight, heating water to generate enough electricity during peak daylight hours to serve about 6000 customers.

ENERGY. Following through on a promise to dismantle the Department of Energy (DOE), the administration of U.S. President Ronald Reagan sent a message to Congress in May, 1982, proposing that the DOE's chief functions be transferred to the Department of Commerce. The White House claimed that the proposed reorganization would save more than $1 billion in the first year and reduce the federal work force by more than 3000 persons. This claim was disputed in Congress, however, and the plan made no headway in 1982.

Donald Paul Hodel, under secretary of the interior, was nominated secretary of energy on Nov. 5. The 47-year-old Oregonian had been administrator of the Bonneville Power Administration (1972–77) and head of the Electric Reliability Council (1978–80), a private industrial group. Energy Secretary James B. Edwards had announced on May 12 that he intended to resign in order to accept the post of president of the Medical University of South Carolina.

Citing a need to refine the federal government's focus on basic and long-term research, President Reagan in his fiscal 1983 budget message sought to cut research outlays for fossil fuels by 74.3 percent, solar energy by 65.4 percent, geothermal energy by 84.1 percent, and conservation by 77.8 percent. In all, he proposed that funding for nonnuclear research programs be cut $1 billion, to $700,000,000. By way of contrast, funds for fusion energy research were to be cut by only 2.2 percent. Reagan proposed a doubling of money for the Clinch River breeder reactor in Tennessee and more than a 700-fold increase for research on the nuclear fuel cycle and used reactor fuel, including its disposal.

Coal. The National Coal Association estimated that coal production for 1982 would reach 837,000,000 short tons—up 22,000,000 short tons from 1981. The increase reflected a slight rebound following the 1981 United Mine Workers coal strike. But the lowest industrial output since 1977, stagnation in the steel industry, and zero growth in the electrical industry all combined to leave U.S. coal consumption below the 1981 mark. Exports also trailed 1981 levels.

Adding to the industry's uneasiness was a lawsuit filed on Sept. 28 by the National Resources Defense Council on behalf of seven other groups. The suit charged that the Interior Department's coal-leasing program was invalid and threatened to kill the program. The leasing scheme had been proposed to ensure that mineable coal would be available as demand increased. The environmentalists charged, however, that not only did the plan violate three major environmental statutes but also permitted coal companies to engage in speculative leasing of coal stocks.

Under one of the more novel agreements to deliver coal supplies, the Interior Department accepted, on Oct. 13, W. R. Grace and Co.'s plan to float crushed coal, packed in waterproof bags, from Colorado to the West Coast. Grace's $2–$3 billion "Aquatrain" pipeline was expected to deliver coal by 1987 to its destination at a cost of $18 per ton—$10 per ton less than the 1982 cost of moving coal between Craig, Colo., and Long Beach, Calif.

Synfuels. On Aug. 20 the Exxon Research and Engineering Co. announced successful completion of a two-year test of a process for converting coal into petroleumlike liquid fuels. Large-scale liquefaction tests in Baytown, Texas, involved processing 250 tons of coal per day into liquids that could be refined for fuel oil, gasoline-blending stock, domestic heating oil, and diesel fuel. The pilot plant used three types of coal—Illinois high-sulfur bituminous, Wyoming low-sulfur subbituminous, and Texas lignite (a soft coal). Exxon hoped to license the technology for commercial use.

These tests were part of a spectrum of activities within the nascent synthetic-fuels industry, which had a goal of developing synthetic substitutes for oil and natural gas. But the Exxon tests may have been the industry's sole success story in 1982. High interest rates, low oil prices, and slumping energy demand throughout the year prompted the closing of one major synfuel venture and threatened the viability of others.

Exxon stunned the industry on May 2 when it announced its withdrawal from a joint venture with Tosco Corp. to develop the Colony oil shale project in Colorado. Tosco could not continue the project alone, despite a $1.1 billion loan guarantee from the federal government. As a result, Exxon was forced to buy back Tosco's 40 percent share in the project. Exxon claimed the project's escalating price—pegged at an eventual total of $6 billion—no longer made the experiment justifiable.

A month later Chevron Oil Corp. announced that it had decided to delay work on its $7 billion Clear Creek oil shale project in Colorado. It too cited the economy as grounds for scaling back. In October Standard Oil Co. of Ohio withdrew from its partnership with four other companies to develop a $2 billion coal-liquefaction plant in Gillette, Wyo. The plant's remaining backers pledged to continue, albeit at a slower pace. On Nov. 22 Ashland Oil Co. withdrew its sponsorship of a proposed multibillion dollar project to produce synthetic oil from coal in Breckenridge County, Kentucky.

The high costs and speculative nature of synthetic-fuels development were what led the administration of former President Jimmy Carter to propose the Synthetic Fuels Corp. (SFC). However, by 1982, two years after its establishment, SFC had yet to fund a single project. By October only 13 of the first 90 applicants were still in the running for consideration for grants or loans. And most were having severe difficulties meeting the SFC's demand for 25 percent private financing.

Solar Energy. The solar energy industry achieved several firsts in 1982, among them a ground breaking in Golden, Colo., for the Solar Energy Research Institute. The $8,000,000 facility, expected to be completed in August, 1983, would house 60 scientists conducting research in such areas as thermochemical-energy conversion and biotechnology.

A 10-megawatt solar-central receiver near Daggett, Calif., named Solar One, was dedicated in April. Its field of identical and slightly curved mirrors arranged in 32 circular arcs tracks the sun daily, focusing sunlight onto a central solar energy absorber, 250 ft. atop a tower set within the 72-acre field of mirrors. Cold water pumped up the tower returns as superheated steam to generate power. It was the largest operating solar energy plant in the world.

See also NUCLEAR POWER; PETROLEUM AND NATURAL GAS.   J.A.R.

ENVIRONMENT. International attention was focused on environmental problems in 1982 at a United Nations conference held in Nairobi, Kenya. A separate U.N. survey indicated that the oceans of the world appeared to be in better health than ten years earlier, mainly because of laws passed by industrial nations against several toxic chemicals. In the United States, environmentalists continued to object to what they felt were regressive changes in policy by the administration of President Ronald Reagan, particularly in its reinterpretation of the Clean Water Act of 1972 and in its reduction of funds for environmental agencies.

International Conference. Environmental leaders from 105 nations met for eight days in May in Nairobi to celebrate the 10th anniversary of the U.N. Conference on the Human Environment and the creation of the U.N. Environment Programme (UNEP). A focal issue for the Nairobi participants was how the UNEP would structure its role for the coming decade. Although many developing nations lobbied for the agency to adopt a more active stance by both managing and financing environmental conservation, that turnabout would have required greater contributions from the U.N.'s wealthier and more developed members. The latter nations had instead reduced their outlays for programs aimed at ameliorating global environmental problems, according to a consensus declaration issued by participants at the meeting's close. The conference therefore settled on trying to make the UNEP a catalyst for action.

Many of the Nairobi participants, angered over what they perceived as a lack of U.S. attention to environmental matters, criticized the policies of President Reagan's administration, which had decreased U.S. contributions to the UNEP. Since 1972 the U.S. had given the UNEP close to $10,000,000 annually, but President Reagan wanted to reduce this amount to $2,000,000. Although Congress thwarted the plan, the ultimate figure settled on for 1982 was $7,850,000.

"New Federalism." Environmental Protection Agency (EPA) administrator Anne M. Gorsuch, one of the leaders of the U.S. delegation to Nairobi, touted the global application of President Reagan's "new federalism" tenets. She stated that free-market economics offered a better approach to solving environmental problems than did government regulation. Within the U.S. as well as at Nairobi, however, environmental leaders took issue with this line. Their feeling, expressed by the Conservation Foundation in its 440-page report, *State of the Environment 1982,* was that there was "no market for clean air or water or for wilderness, and no market is likely to develop."

Another aspect of the new federalism drew heavy fire both from the National Governors' Conference and from individual state officials. Gorsuch had announced that 75 percent of all federal environmental programs would be turned over to the states for administration before the end of Reagan's first term in office. Although fewer than half had been turned over by the end of 1982, state officials were already protesting that cutbacks in many federal aid programs, coupled with a drop in state tax revenues because of the economic recession, had made it impossible for them to maintain their former responsibilities, much less to take on new ones.

Purple loosestrife, a plant brought to the U.S. in the 19th century, threatens to dominate the wetlands of the northeastern and upper midwestern parts of the country. Although incursions of foreign plants and animals are upsetting the ecology of many areas, a redeeming quality of loosestrife, aside from the beauty of its rose-purple flowers, is demonstrated in this picture: Abundant nectar attracts bees.

When wild deer in Florida's Everglades grew too numerous in 1982, federal and state agencies permitted hunters to try to thin the herd by 1500. Environmentalists, protesting the "mercy killings," attempted to move the deer to less crowded areas.

Blood-Lead Levels. The accumulation of lead in the human body, mainly from airborne pollutants, continued to be an area of health concern. The first national estimate of blood-lead levels for a statistically representative sample of the U.S. population was formally published in 1982. Joseph Annest and colleagues at the National Center for Health Statistics developed the figures from data collected as part of the second national Health and Nutrition Examination Survey (HANES II). Among their more worrisome findings was that one out of five inner-city black children five years old or younger carried a burden of lead that could affect his or her intellectual and behavioral development. For white children in the same age group the ratio was only one in 20. No clear-cut explanations were found for this difference. Affected children exhibited lead levels of 30 micrograms or more per deciliter of blood. In young children, blood-lead levels on this order correlate with a reduction in learning skills, a lower score on intelligence tests, and a decreased ability to concentrate on classroom tasks.

Against the backdrop of these HANES II findings, however, the EPA proposed on Feb. 18 to relax limits on an earlier federal order to refiners to phase out the amounts of lead that they placed into each gallon of leaded gasoline. At hearings on the proposed change in April, nearly 100 people turned out to testify, virtually all of them arguing against the measure. Many refiners were there as

well, and because most of them had already made adjustments to comply with the standards set in 1975, they also argued that firms that still lagged in compliance should not be excused. In response, the EPA issued a statement in August that it had reversed its position and would strengthen its lead-in-gasoline rules. The EPA acknowledged that health risks indeed justified maintaining a tough stance on leaded gasoline, the major contributor of airborne lead. In the meantime, however, the Division of Environmental Hazards Research, which had performed major research on the effects of lead from gasoline on children's health, was dismantled by the Department of Housing and Urban Development as part of general budget cutting.

Other Metal Pollutants. Other heavy metals besides lead also made news. For example, H. Mitchell Perry and his colleagues at the St. Louis Veterans Administration Hospital reported in the Aug. 27 issue of *Science* magazine that high blood pressure in humans might be caused in part by eating or inhaling small amounts of cadmium, an industrial pollutant that often contaminates animal livers and shellfish, particularly oysters. Until Perry's report, cadmium was believed to be biologically harmless in amounts that humans might be expected to encounter by eating such foods or breathing polluted air. Perry cautioned that the work, conducted on rats, was preliminary, but he noted that if the results were confirmed in humans, smokers would be at elevated risk because they in-

Acid rain damaged this statue at the Field Museum of Natural History in Chicago. In 1982 environmentalists claimed that a new Environmental Protection Agency (EPA) report indicated that rain acidified by pollutants was a much more widespread hazard in the U.S. than previously estimated. The EPA disputed this interpretation.

hale almost twice as much cadmium as do nonsmokers.

As for other heavy metals, a study of rural American households found that one in four used water contaminated with levels of mercury exceeding the EPA's drinking-water standards, one in six used drinking water exceeding the EPA's lead standards, and more than one in seven used drinking water exceeding the EPA's recommended limit for selenium. The survey was prepared by Cornell University as part of the first nationwide analysis for rural drinking-water quality.

The Problem of Noise. Beginning in February the Occupational Safety and Health Administration (OSHA) began phasing in changes to federal noise-pollution rules. Part of the Hearing Conservation Amendment, these new provisions established that firms covered by OSHA regulations must survey their work environment to establish the decibel level to which employees were being exposed; farms and construction sites were exempted. Any workers exposed to noise that, on the average, was 85 decibels (dB) or

higher had to be assigned to a hearing-conservation program, offered hearing protectors, and given free annual hearing tests. These measures still offered less than 100 percent protection. According to the EPA, 75 dB is the maximum sound intensity to which most adults can be exposed for 8 hr. daily throughout a 40-year career without risk of hearing loss. Yet OSHA estimated that 53 percent of the nation's production workers employed in 1981 were exposed to noise of 80 dB or higher, and at least 5,100,000 worked in environments where the sound exceeded the legally permissible 90 dB.

Research also began to show that noise can affect blood pressure, body chemistry, susceptibility to disease, and even the ability to acquire knowledge. Much of this ongoing research financed by the EPA came to an end on Oct. 1, however, when the agency eliminated its noise office. One of the last reports completed by the office concluded that the 24-hr. din of street noise in many urban neighborhoods approaches or exceeds the legal limits for workers, especially in neighborhoods near subways and airports.

Another intriguing noise study was reported by James Willott and Shao-Ming Lu of Northern Illinois University in the June 18 issue of *Science*. In a study of mice, they found that "moderate" noise levels, equivalent in humans to listening to a passing freight train or jet, can affect individual brain cells. The response evoked was a form of confusion whereby the brain inaccurately interpreted its sound environment. The researchers said that their results might at long last offer an explanation for such human afflictions as "ringing in the ears" and impairment of sound comprehension. In addition, at the American Psychological Association meeting in August, a panel of scientists reported that the intellectual development of infants and small children may be delayed by exposure to noisy households or classrooms. Purdue University's Theodore Wachs found that children characterized as temperamentally "difficult" were most affected.

Endangered Whales. One international problem appeared to be solved in July when the International Whaling Commission (IWC) voted an end to all commercial whaling and developed quotas for a four-year phaseout of such harvests. Concern was expressed, however, as to whether the seven countries that voted against the ban, including Japan and the Soviet Union, would in fact respect it. Under amendments to U.S. fisheries legislation, the U.S. was empowered to restrict by at least 50 percent the catch permitted a foreign nation in U.S. territorial waters if that nation disregarded IWC recommendations. Tom Garrett, U.S. deputy commissioner to the IWC, noted that such restrictions on Japanese fishing vessels "could knock out close to a quarter of all jobs in the Japanese offshore fishing industry—a loss of jobs many times the loss if the whaling industry shuts down."

Ozone Studies. In April members of the National Academy of Sciences ozone-depletion study reduced by half the earlier estimates of how much ozone was being stripped from the atmosphere largely as a result of releasing fluorocarbons, once widely used as propellants for aerosol sprays. Because ozone in the atmosphere protects the earth from excessive ultraviolet radiation, the EPA had earlier banned the use of fluorocarbons in nonessential aerosols. An American Chemical Society panel on ozone reported 19 studies that were largely in agreement with this lowering of the estimates. Another hazard with respect to ozone was discussed by the congressional Office of Technology Assessment at a symposium in February. It was estimated that ozone causes as much as a 5 percent loss of the total annual U.S. crops of corn, wheat, soybeans, and peanuts alone, amounting to a possible $4.5 billion per year.

Radiation. In Utah 11 sheep ranchers were given a second chance to claim compensation from the U.S. government for damages that they said they sustained in the early 1950's. The ranchers claimed that fallout from nuclear weapons detonated at the Nevada Test Site in 1953 had killed 4490 sheep. When the ranchers first went to court in 1956, virtually all data on nuclear-test fallout patterns, readings, and health effects had been classified secret by the Atomic Energy Commission (AEC), and Judge A. Sherman

Watt Next?

Virginia Clark Clarkson of Glen Head, N.Y., so enjoyed her 1981 vacation at the National Audubon Society's ecology camp on Hog Island, Maine, that in 1982 she offered to send Secretary of the Interior James G. Watt to the summer camp. Presumably she hoped the experience would give Watt, the bane of environmentalists (who accused him of seeking to ravage America's natural resources), "an understanding of the interconnectedness of all living things"—in the words of the camp brochure. When Watt did not reply, the society next offered the Clarkson scholarship to any other "deserving person" in the government.

Christensen was forced to rule that insufficient evidence existed to point to radiation as the cause for the ranchers' losses. Since that time, however, much of the AEC's fallout data was declassified, and the ranchers petitioned for a new trial. On Aug. 4 Judge Christensen ruled that the government had "perpetrated a fraud upon the court" by withholding and misusing data and that the initial case of *Bulloch et al. vs. the United States* was to be retried. In an unrelated case the federal government was taken to court by persons seeking compensation for personal injuries, including cancers, that they claimed they had sustained from weapons-test fallout. No verdict was reached by the end of 1982.

In June Alice Stewart of the University of Birmingham, England, reported a reevaluation of previous interpretations of Japanese atomic-bomb survivor statistics. The new data appeared to contradict earlier analyses finding no delayed effects of radiation, other than cancer, and indicated that cancer deaths attributable to bomb radiation had been underestimated by a factor of three. More important, Stewart found the incidence of all radiation-related deaths, including cancers, to be one in four, a figure ten times higher than the earlier estimate. In another challenge to established views on radiation effects, Edward Martell and Kevin Sweder of the National Center for Atmospheric Research reported in February that they had found preliminary evidence that radioactive radon, a naturally occurring decay product of radium, may, when cycled through a burning cigarette, present a health hazard sufficiently potent to account for all lung cancers associated with smoking.

Lastly, research from the London School of Hygiene and Tropical Medicine established an apparent link between nonionizing radiation given off by fluorescent lights and an increased risk of melanoma, a skin cancer. According to Valerie Bernal and colleagues, it was not yet clear whether radiation from the lights acts alone in doubling the melanoma risk or whether it acts in conjunction with other chemicals present, such as indoor chemical pollutants.

Love Canal Update. On July 14 the long-awaited results of the EPA's investigation into the hazardous-waste landfill known as Love Canal, in Niagara Falls, N.Y., were finally published. The EPA stated that the region was as habitable as the control areas, elsewhere in Niagara Falls, with which it was compared. Since all of Niagara Falls was highly polluted, the study implied that environmental contamination around Love Canal was probably attributable to sources other than chemicals from the canal. Critics quickly challenged the methodology, and therefore the validity, of the work. Meanwhile the EPA committed itself to spending $7,000,000 more for work to contain the site, to ensure that the site was monitored regularly, and to investigate measures for cleaning up contaminated storm sewers and drains.   J.A.R.

EQUATORIAL GUINEA. See STATISTICS OF THE WORLD.

ETHIOPIA. The stalemate between the central government of Lt. Col. Mengistu Haile Mariam and those forces seeking to dismember Ethiopia continued in 1982. In January the government declared that the Eritrean secessionist movement had been effectively destroyed, and on Feb. 1 Mengistu announced a plan for the economic reconstruction of the province. Nevertheless, despite the presence of some 140,000 troops in Eri-

trea and Tigre provinces, guerrilla activity continued. A new government offensive was launched in February to capture Nafka, the major town controlled by the Eritrean People's Liberation Front. But by May it became clear that the offensive had collapsed, with government casualties estimated as high as 20,000 killed or wounded.

In the Ogaden, where Somali-backed guerrillas were fighting to wrest the province from Ethiopia, the central government strengthened its hold and began a new series of reprisal attacks on Somali border towns. Some 9000 Ethiopian troops and dissident Somalis were involved in a two-week battle in early July. Fighting continued at a lower level until mid-September, when it intensified again; more than 500 Ethiopians were believed killed or wounded in a new border clash.

Meanwhile, in an attempt to deal with the threat at its source, the Mengistu government launched a military campaign of its own to topple Somalia's Western-backed leader, Muhammad Siad Barre. On June 30 a group of Somali rebels, supported by a mechanized force of at least 10,000 Ethiopian troops, invaded Somalia and seized two towns along the border. The invaders, believed to include Cuban and East German advisers, met greater resistance than expected, and by early October they had failed to make any headway and withdrew from one of the towns. Somalia received emergency military aid from the United States.

Ethiopia's relations with the U.S. remained cool throughout the year, despite speculation that the administration of U.S. President Ronald Reagan was seeking an improvement. In January the Administration announced the end of special refugee status for the estimated 15,000 Ethiopian exiles in the U.S. Claiming that human-rights conditions in Ethiopia had improved, it announced that Ethiopians who could not meet the standards for political asylum would be deported. The new U.S. policy, however, provoked a storm of protest in Congress, and the Administration reversed its decision in July.

See STATISTICS OF THE WORLD. *See also* SOMALIA.   J.T.S.

EUROPEAN COMMUNITIES, a supranational organization comprising the European Economic Community, the European Atomic Energy Community, and the European Coal and Steel Community. Because these communities share the same institutional framework, they are frequently referred to as the European Community (EC), or Common Market. In 1982 the ten member countries were Belgium, Denmark, France, Great Britain, Greece, Ireland, Italy, Luxembourg, the Netherlands, and West Germany.

External Affairs. Relations between the EC and the United States soured during 1982. A major sore point was the U.S. attempt to thwart construction of a natural gas pipeline connecting Siberia with Western Europe by banning the sale to the Soviet Union of oil and natural gas equipment produced by foreign subsidiaries and licensees of American firms. After France, Italy, and Great Britain announced their decision to ignore the ban and honor all contracts with the Soviets, the EC issued a formal protest on Aug. 12, calling the American sanctions a violation of international law. U.S. President Ronald Reagan rescinded the ban on Nov. 13.

A second source of contention was the claim by U.S. steel manufacturers that European producers, subsidized by their governments, were selling their products on the American market at unfairly low prices. The U.S. steelmakers rejected as "neither fair nor equitable" an agreement announced on Aug. 6 under which the European firms agreed to reduce their exports to the U.S. of certain steel products by about 10 percent below 1981 levels. The dispute was resolved by a new accord, announced on Oct. 21, in which EC members agreed to make further cuts in their share of the U.S. market; in return, the American firms dropped their complaints of unfair trade practices, which could have resulted in the imposition of U.S. penalty duties on steel imports from Europe. The EC countries also announced reductions in their own steel imports, to permit the sale within Europe of steel that would no longer be shipped to the U.S.

Still another source of friction was the American threat that unless the EC phased

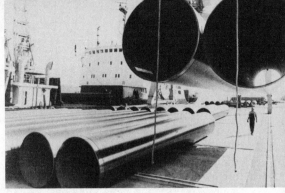

In Hamburg a Soviet freighter receives a shipload of pipe for the pipeline that will eventually bring Siberian natural gas to Western Europe. In 1982 the European Community successfully resisted an American effort to stop the pipeline by banning sales of oil and gas equipment.

out its program of farm export subsidies (which gave European agricultural exports a competitive boost), the U.S. would retaliate by dumping surplus dairy products and grain at subsidized prices on the European market. The Geneva conference of 88 nations that had signed the General Agreement on Tariffs and Trade ended in late November without any clear resolution of this conflict.

The EC supported Great Britain in the Falklands war, agreeing on April 9 to impose an embargo on arms shipments to Argentina and on April 14 a month-long ban on imports from that country. When the import sanctions were renewed indefinitely on May 24, however, Ireland and Italy refused to go along. The import ban was lifted in June by all the remaining EC members except Britain.

Internal Affairs. Britain was the odd-man-out in an institutional crisis that pitted the principle of unanimity against that of majority rule in the EC Council of Ministers. Traditionally, a unanimous vote had been required on any issue upon which a member state believed its "vital interests" were at stake. On May 18, however, the agriculture ministers of seven EC countries adopted by majority vote a 10.7 percent rise in farm prices that Britain, a food-importing country, opposed. The British were mollified the following week when the EC foreign ministers agreed on an $850,000,000 rebate on Britain's 1982 contribution to the EC budget.

See also articles on individual countries mentioned. W.M.

F

FASHION. During 1982 the importance of American fashion as an international force, on a par with its European equivalent, was established. Top American labels gained ready acceptance in new boutiques opened by designers in London, Paris, and Milan, Italy. In the United States, several large department stores celebrated American fashion with the kind of full-scale promotions that had previously been devoted only to other countries. Signs of new creative activity appeared also in Japan. More buyers went to Tokyo to see the innovations of young, hitherto unknown Japanese designers.

Like their European counterparts, the Americans offered great variety. No single style, silhouette, or length was imposed as the one-and-only choice. The hemline could be short, medium, or long; the shape attenuated, cocoon, or flared; the look a matter of personal preference. Some clothes were reminiscent of Victorian or medieval times, others of the eras preceding and following World War I.

Within this diversity of choices certain across-the-board changes could be observed. Extremes were avoided, and nothing was so different that it made existing wardrobes unwearable. Ostentatious opulence was less frequent. Stylish, elegant conservatism prevailed, with an aura of good breeding.

Most noteworthy was the move away from voluminous layers to slimmed-down elongated lines. Influenced by the much-admired costumes of the 1920's and 1930's in the television series *Brideshead Revisited* and the film *Chariots of Fire,* many designers expressed nostalgia in their well-mannered tweeds, intricately patterned hand-knit sweaters, delicate voile and georgette afternoon dresses, and alluring evening metallics and velvets recalling the days before World War II among Great Britain's privileged classes.

Narrower clothes were introduced for spring. Some dresses had hip sashes and ended at flapper length; others reached to below the middle of the calf. Oversize stripes of contrasting colors (black and white were favorites) were featured, and prints included neat windowpane checks, miniature plaids, paisleys, and tiny florals. Two-color treatments remained modish, and turquoise, often paired with flaming red or coral, was a leading color, although khaki was still popular. Linen and seersucker enjoyed revivals.

Seen everywhere—and in every conceivable fabric from denim to pincord—was the ruffle-hemmed prairie skirt, given its fashion send-off by Ralph Lauren the season before. The skirt was generally accompanied by a white cotton Gibson-girl blouse with leg-of-mutton sleeves. Hip-yoked gathered shorts, as full as a dirndl skirt, also sold extremely well. Worn by younger customers with loose T-shirts or tank tops, the new flared shorts came in sweat-shirt jersey as well as poplin and other cottons.

By fall, the watchwords were "long" and "lean" as the trend toward pencil-line clothes gathered strength. Narrow suit jackets with lowered waistlines, straight skirts, and slinky evening gowns with bared backs framed by cowled drapery reflected the 1920's and 1930's. Other slim suits and coats had accentuated shoulders and were nipped in at the waist.

Many alternatives to the bean-pole silhouette existed, including princess coats with fitted bodices and flared skirts. Suits that combined a midcalf circular skirt with a cropped bandmaster jacket were widely available. Dresses varied from bubble-shaped tunics over skinny knee-grazing skirts and plumb-line chemise styles to jersey tents held in at the waist with broad cummerbunds. The miniskirt accompanied by a blouson top and colored opaque tights, worn under a long greatcoat, provided yet another option.

In sportswear, classic pleated-top trousers outnumbered culottes, although the latter

Above, left: The Western look, with ruffle-hemmed prairie skirt, was seen everywhere in 1982. Above, right: Narrower clothes included such items as this pleated silk overblouse and skirt ensemble. Left: An alternative to the beanpole silhouette popular in fall was this corduroy dress combining laced bodice with a full flounced skirt.

were still in evidence. Enlarged argyles, Fair Isle stripes, and cable stitches were dominant among Shetland sweaters. Mixtures of patterns (herringbones with checks and paisleys, for instance) and textures (tweeds with velvets) characterized fall separates. A so-called stone-washed distressed denim put new life into the lagging jeans market.

Earth and autumn-leaf tones, along with wine, teal, forest green, black with bright red, black with white, and solid black, all ranked high on the color scale. A resurgence of black-tie, or tuxedo, evening wear for women had its side effects. Wing collars with

bow ties were universal. They appeared on expensive cashmere sweater dresses as well as on moderately priced blouses and became an identifying mark of the 1982 fall season. **Accessories.** Jewelry, millinery, and scarves, striking in color or design, enhanced the simplicity of the fashions. A single bold accessory was often considered enough. Jewelry, for example, a large diamanté ornament embroidered on the shoulder of a stark black dinner dress, was sometimes an integral part of a costume. Pearls of sizable dimensions came into their own again, especially the one-strand matinee-length necklace. Another accent for both daytime tweeds and evening velvets was the lace fichu, knotted at the neck like an ascot. Renaissance-inspired costume jewelry of colored cabochon stones in antiqued gilded settings was high fashion, as were abstract sculptural pieces of lucite and brass. Scarves came in rich colors on dark grounds. Shawls had less importance, and metallics were limited to discreet trimmings. Hats of dramatic shape with higher crowns added dash to daytime outfits. Gloves were allotted generous counter space in the stores. Patterned and textured stockings, including a foulard print and openwork laces, complemented the year's leading shoe, an unadorned patent or colored leather pump with a rounded pointed toe and a low curved heel.

Menswear. Men's clothes benefited from freer use of color. Such tones as mauve and olive were combined with browns, navies, and grays in conservative, smooth-surfaced suitings. Jewel colors—garnet, amethyst, lapis, turquoise—were added to camels and grays to enrich the effect of sportier glenurquhart plaids and herringbones, which often had a nappier finish. Nevertheless, stripes, from hairline to chalk, were the outstanding pattern. Blazers came in dozens of solid hues. The selection of nonwhite shirts was generous, many of them with white collars, which could be button-down, spread, rounded, or pointed.

Brideshead Revisited had perhaps more influence on men's clothes than on women's. Double-breasted suits, vested suits, cuffed trousers, Norfolk sports jackets, fedora hats, silk shirts, and French cuffs were some of the revivals inspired by the television series. Moderation in shoulder and lapel widths was the rule, and jackets were a little longer. A dressier look predominated for business, and town coats like the chesterfield remained popular. In casual outerwear, the bomber jacket was most popular, and new ones had longer lines. Down- or fiber-filled garments accounted for 75 percent of all winter outerwear sales; the most fashionable quilted downs were roomy in the armholes and reached the ankle in length.   P.F.

FIJI. *See* STATISTICS OF THE WORLD.

FINLAND. A new president, Mauno Koivisto, took office in Finland on Jan. 27, 1982. One immediately perceptible result of the change was a greater openness among Finns as they discussed not only domestic problems but what had seldom, if ever, been mentioned publicly before—the country's foreign policy, including its special relationship with the Soviet Union.

Koivisto, the prime minister, had been serving as acting president since September, 1981. The Social Democratic Party nominee in an eight-candidate contest, he received 43 percent of the popular vote on Jan. 17 and 18 in the first round of the presidential elections, in which electoral college members were chosen. In the second round, on Jan. 26, he won 167 of the electoral college's 301 votes. His majority was provided by 21 electors of the Communist-dominated Finnish People's Democratic League. Significantly, Koivisto's showing in the first round had been hailed by the Soviet Union on Jan. 22 as a "clear shift to the left."

Koivisto took office on Jan. 27, and on Feb. 17 he announced a new cabinet, composed of the same four parties that had formed the previous government. They were the Social Democrats, the Center Party, the Swedish People's Party, and the Finnish People's Democratic League. Kalevi Sorsa, who had been chairman of the Social Democrats, became prime minister.

From March 9 to 11 Koivisto paid a "working visit" to the Soviet Union, where he met with President Leonid I. Brezhnev and other Soviet officials. He promised to continue the policy of his predecessor, the late Urho Kekkonen, which consisted of warm relations with Finland's powerful neighbor and neutrality in international affairs.

Nevertheless, the change in presidents brought into the open issues that had been present but not discussed publicly. These included the view, held by many Finns, that the nation's future depended as much on cooperation with the Nordic countries (Sweden, Norway, and Denmark) as on Soviet goodwill. Observers also noted with interest Koivisto's downplaying of a plan, proposed by Kekkonen and supported by the U.S.S.R.,

Man of the People
When 58-year-old Mauno Koivisto, a Social Democrat, was elected president of Finland in January, it was the first elective office for the carpenter's son who inspired trust, polls attested, as a man of the people. Koivisto, though, was no stranger to national responsibility: A banker by training, he had served in several Finnish cabinets as finance minister and prime minister, and had been acting president since September, 1981. Tall and craggy, the taciturn leader made few promises but, when he did speak, was often remarkably candid. Koivisto, who worked on the docks and as a teacher to pay for his university education, occupied an unpretentious log cabin that he largely built himself. Photographers found him engaged in his regular Monday night volleyball game as election returns came in.

Mauno Koivisto

to establish a nuclear-free zone in the Nordic countries.

In economic matters, in October the government devalued Finland's currency twice within a week, by a total of 10 percent. At the same time, it imposed a comprehensive price freeze to last until mid-December and announced that it would raise the sales tax from the current 14 percent to 16 percent in July, 1983. The economy grew slowly in 1982, and unemployment exceeded 6 percent of the labor force.

See STATISTICS OF THE WORLD.   L.A.S.

FISHERIES. Commercial landings of edible and industrial fish by U.S. fishers at ports in the 50 states during 1981, the latest year for which data were available, were 6.0 billion lb. and were valued at $2.4 billion—down 8 percent in quantity but up 7 percent in value as compared with 1980. Although there were increased landings of anchovies, clams, cod, Pacific mackerel, rockfish, salmon, and squid, declines were recorded in such major groupings as crabs, flounder, menhaden, Atlantic sea herring, and tuna.

Only 53 percent of the domestic supply of edible fish and shellfish was produced in the United States in 1981. Imports of edible and nonedible fishery products rose 14 percent to a record $4.2 billion. Exports increased 15 percent to a record $1.2 billion, but the trade deficit continued to grow.

Despite a decline in the menhaden catch, Cameron, La., maintained its position as the leading port in the U.S. in quantity of commercial fishery landings. With 447,600,000 lb., Cameron was well ahead of the Los Angeles area where 373,600,000 lb. were landed. Two other Gulf Coast menhaden ports, Empire–Venice, La., and Pascagoula–Moss Point, Miss., ranked third and fourth in volume. In terms of value, Kodiak, Alaska, was first with a record $132,900,000. Los Angeles and San Diego were next, followed by New Bedford, Mass.

Because of the menhaden catch for industrial purposes, Louisiana was by far the leading state in volume of landings with almost 1.2 billion lb. followed by Alaska, California, and Virginia. Alaska was far in front in terms of value, with a 1981 total of $639,797,000. California was second, followed by Massachusetts and Louisiana.

Fisheries Zone. The foreign catch (excluding tuna) in the U.S. 200-mi. fisheries zone during 1981 totaled 1,700,000 metric tons, up 2 percent from 1980. Most of the catch consisted of underutilized bottom fish off the coast of Alaska (91 percent). Japan led all other nations fishing in the U.S. zone. With the Soviet Union excluded since its invasion of Afghanistan in 1979, South Korea took the second largest catch. On April 26, 1982, the U.S. cut Japan's allowable catch off the Alaska coast by 10 percent, a restriction to remain in force until U.S. fish processors were allowed greater access to Japanese markets.

Joint ventures, with U.S. boats harvesting and foreign vessels processing, continued to increase rapidly; despite the loss of their direct fishing quotas, the Soviets were allowed to participate in these joint ventures. Joint-venture volume in 1981 was 307,800,000 lb. valued at $21,000,000, well over twice the 1980 figures.

World Landings. A record 72,200,000 metric tons for world commercial fishery landings was recorded in 1980, the most recent year for which data were available. Japan was first with 14 percent of the total, followed by the Soviet Union, 13 percent; China, 6 percent; the U.S., 5 percent; and Chile, 4 percent.

Recreational Fishing. According to a 1980 National Survey of Fishing, Hunting and Wildlife Associated Recreation, about one in every four Americans 6 years or older went fishing at least once during the year. The estimated total of anglers 16 years or older was 42,100,000. Recreational fishers spent $17.24 billion in 1980 while fishing an estimated 857,500,000 days. Excluding the Great Lakes, freshwater anglers favored various panfish, black bass, and catfish. Sportfishers in the Great Lakes opted for yellow perch, salmon, steelhead, walleye, and sauger. About 30 percent of all anglers did at least some fishing in salt water, and their total catch may have rivaled the U.S. commercial landings of edible finfish. On the Atlantic and Gulf coasts (taken together), bluefish provided the largest recreational catch both in numbers and weight.

Law of the Sea. A provision of a wide-ranging treaty, adopted at the United Nations on April 30, 1982, to govern the use and exploitation of the seas, declared that every coastal nation has exclusive rights to the fish and other marine life in the waters extending 200

mi. beyond its shores. When nations are separated by a body of water less than 400 mi. in extent, they must establish dividing lines for the zones.   A.J.R.

FLORIDA. *See* STATISTICS OF THE WORLD.

FRANCE. The popularity of President François Mitterrand (see biography at PEOPLE IN THE NEWS) ebbed somewhat in 1982, as did the political power of France's Socialist government, in the wake of local elections and signs of economic decline. In foreign affairs France reaffirmed its close working relationship with West Germany and tried to strengthen its influence in the Third World, while its relations with the United States continued on a rocky course.

Politics and Terrorism. The year opened inauspiciously for the Socialists. In January, in four by-elections to the National Assembly for the Paris region, they lost to conservative opponents. The results, even though they caused consternation in some Socialist ranks and led critics to speak of popular disillusionment with the Mitterrand government, did not affect the Socialists' comfortable majority in parliament. Yet they were a portent. On March 14 and 21, in a two-round election for departmental assemblies, the Socialists suffered a more serious setback. The opposition, which had made the Socialists' policies of nationalization and higher taxation campaign issues, gained control of 58 assemblies, while the Socialists held 37 assemblies.

Nevertheless, the Mitterrand government pressed ahead with its plans to decentralize France's administration, designating Corsica as the first of 22 regions that would ultimately be allowed to exercise control, albeit limited, over local affairs. In early August elections were held on the island for a new regional assembly. Corsican separatists, who captured only 8 of 61 seats, again resorted to violence to make their case, launching a wave of bombings across the island on Aug. 20.

Terrorism was not confined to Corsica. Paris became the scene of several violent attacks. In January a U.S. Embassy military attaché was shot dead in front of his home. In April a car bomb exploded in a crowded street, killing a woman passerby and injuring

46 other people. Authorities believed that Arab terrorists were responsible for both incidents. Armenian terrorists bombed Paris cafes in July. The worst attack, part of a series of violent anti-Semitic acts, occurred on Aug. 9, when masked gunmen fired submachine guns and hurled a grenade into a kosher restaurant, Chez Jo Goldenberg. Six people were killed and 22 wounded. An extreme leftist organization, Direct Action, claimed credit for the attack. Another bomb blast in Paris, in September, wounded an Israeli diplomat and 40 other people; police arrested two members of the now-banned Direct Action. Because of domestic and international reaction to the August terrorist attack, the Mitterrand government took steps to tighten internal security and said that it would reexamine France's traditionally liberal policy of political asylum. The country's Jewish community, the largest outside Israel and the U.S., although alarmed by the outbreak of anti-Semitism, seemed divided in its response; it did, however, reject Israeli Prime Minister Menachem Begin's suggestion that French Jews might have to take their defense into their own hands.

The Socialists' nationalization program was temporarily postponed by an adverse court decision in January, but the government made minor modifications and proceeded with the takeover of most of the country's banks, and it negotiated with various companies on appropriate compensation.

Economic Woes. Other parts of the Socialists' domestic program suffered greater reverses. In June the government was obliged to devalue the franc for the second time in eight months, and Premier Pierre Mauroy announced a four-month freeze on wages and prices. The proposed budget for 1983 also reflected a slowdown in social and military spending. On the other hand, the government scheduled massive funding for long-range research and technology to bring France to third place, after the U.S. and Japan, in high technology; as part of its plan, it also made the import of foreign electronic products, especially from Japan, more difficult. The government in addition set aside $2.51 billion, compared with $2.09 billion in 1981, for investment in the state sector, which represents about 25 percent of France's competitive industry.

A low rate of production, record trade deficits, and high interest rates accompanied mounting unemployment, creeping inflation, and a declining franc. Valued at about U.S.$0.22 in 1981, the franc fell to about U.S.$0.14 by the last quarter of 1982. To stave off a third devaluation, the government used its dwindling reserves and sought access to multinational funds. At the same time, the new retrenchment policy was expected to bring inflation down from an annual rate of 14 percent. Jobs were at a premium, with unemployment approaching 9 percent of the labor force. The gross national product was expected to increase by only 1 percent in 1982.

Selling its technological and military wares abroad offered France some opportunity of economic relief. It held talks with Pakistan and Egypt on the sale to those countries of nuclear fuel processing plants. It also contracted to sell to India telephonic equipment, nuclear fuel, and Mirage airplanes. Paris shipped nonoffensive weapons to Nicaragua. And it negotiated with China for the sale of Mirage jets, capping off previous sales of helicopters and airbuses to the Peking government. France also maintained commercial links with black Africa, links that Mitterrand sought to strengthen on a tour he made in the latter part of the year to several French-speaking African countries.

Foreign Policy. The explosive situation in Lebanon, the unrest in Central America, the building of the Soviet gas pipeline, and the Argentine seizure of the Falkland Islands were among the international developments commanding French attention.

Even before the Lebanese conflict broke out in June, Franco-Israeli relations, after initial improvement under the Mitterrand government, had once again taken a turn for the worse. In February, for example, Foreign Minister Claude Cheysson, on a trip to Arab countries in the Middle East, declared that the Palestinians had a right to their own homeland, which would in all likelihood include the West Bank, and that France did not see why they should not be represented in future negotiations by the Palestine Liberation Organization (PLO). France had also called for a halt to further Israeli settlements on the West Bank. Cheysson's remarks infuriated the Israeli government. When, therefore, President Mitterrand visited Jerusalem in March, he met a very critical Prime Minister Begin. In late November Mitterrand made a state visit to Cairo, where, at a joint news conference with Egyptian President Hosni Mubarak, he reiterated his government's view that the Palestinian problem could not be resolved as long as the PLO called for the destruction of Israel.

Israel's invasion of southern Lebanon and siege of west Beirut led France to join Egypt and other states, both inside and outside the United Nations, in condemning Israel. The Mitterrand government's public statements on the war, interpreted by some observers as being uncommonly critical of Israel, led to further strains in French-Israeli relations. The Begin government, not given to mincing words, accused Mitterrand of contributing, because of his remarks, to what it saw as a rising wave of anti-Semitism in France. It was thus that Begin, in August, begrudgingly agreed to the inclusion of the French in a multinational force, composed also of Italian and U.S. troops, to oversee the evacuation of PLO units from west Beirut. French paratroopers returned to the Lebanese capital in September, after the massacre of Palestinian refugees, as part of the reconstituted multinational force.

France's relations with the U.S. also fared poorly. Although the French joined with the Americans in the Beirut peacekeeping force, and although Mitterrand and President Ronald Reagan viewed with the same alarm the Soviet role in Afghanistan and Poland, the two allies nevertheless found themselves on opposite sides of several important issues, and did not even pretend to conceal the rift between them. At the annual summit of the leaders of the major non-Communist industrial powers, held in June at Versailles, the two presidents, instead of smoothing over their differences, exacerbated them. The French resented the monetary policy of the Reagan administration; they argued that at a

time of economic interdependence, no country, especially a friendly one, could pursue a financial policy without considering the consequences it would have on the economies of other countries. Bringing down high interest rates in the U.S., they said, would improve French and other Western European currencies, industries, trade, and employment. The French were angered, too, by the U.S. threat to impose penalties against Western European steel exporters subsidized by their governments, because of their competition with U.S. steel producers. The Americans listened politely amid the clinking of champagne glasses (French and other critics complained of the summit's lavish setting), but did not appear persuaded to change U.S. policies.

The issue that divided Paris and Washington the most was the question of the West's economic relations with the Soviet Union. After the imposition of martial law in Poland in late 1981, the Reagan administration cut off the sale of American turbines and other equipment to the Soviet Union in order to slow down the construction of the Soviet gas pipeline to Western Europe. Washington followed that move by imposing sanctions on foreign subsidiaries that continued to supply the Soviets with comparable technology. The French were the first to defy the American President and order their firms to honor their existing contracts with the Soviets; they were followed by the British, Italians, and West Germans. At stake for the Western Europeans were jobs, sales, and energy sources for their lagging economies. The sanctions were lifted by Reagan in November, with Paris insisting that it had made no concessions to Washington.

France also stood united with its partners in the European Community (EC) when, at Great Britain's request, the EC imposed an embargo on arms shipments to Argentina after that country seized the Falkland Islands. Ironically, many of the successes scored by the Argentines against the British in the brief South Atlantic war were scored with previously purchased French Exocet air-to-surface missiles.

See STATISTICS OF THE WORLD.   D.J.H.

G

GABON. *See* STATISTICS OF THE WORLD.
GAMBIA, THE. *See* STATISTICS OF THE WORLD.
GEORGIA. *See* STATISTICS OF THE WORLD.
GERMAN DEMOCRATIC REPUBLIC, *or* **EAST GERMANY.** East Germany remained a loyal and prosperous satellite of the Soviet Union in 1982. In August the Soviets marked the 70th birthday of East German Communist Party leader and head of state Erich Honecker by awarding him the Order of Lenin and the title of Hero of the Soviet Union. Two issues, however, troubled Honecker and his government: the emergence of an East German peace movement and signs of economic difficulty.

Politics. Like other Communist regimes, the East German government had applauded the growth of youthful peace movements in Western Europe that lobbied to eliminate from the continent nuclear weapons of the North Atlantic Treaty Organization (NATO). In 1982, however, young people in East Germany began to emulate their counterparts in the West, and East Berlin officials reacted with alarm.

East Germany's pacifist movement was less an organized lobby than an amorphous collection of church-oriented young people and dissident intellectuals. Adopting jacket badges bearing the words "Swords into Plowshares," they condemned the growing militarization of East Germany and the stockpiling of nuclear weapons by both NATO and the Warsaw Pact. On Jan. 25 the pacifists issued a document, "The Berlin Appeal," urging a nuclear-free zone in Europe; it was written by an East Berlin Protestant pastor, Rainer Eppelmann. Hoping to gain influence in the budding movement, the Protestant Evangelical Church sponsored a peace forum in Dresden on Feb. 13. At its close, several thousand young people held an impromptu demonstration at a nearby church destroyed in World War II.

To the Communist government, the emergence of a movement that questioned official military policy was deeply troubling. Authorities banned the wearing of the peace emblem, and security officials detained Eppelmann for two days. These actions brought a protest from the Evangelical Church. In a letter read by pastors at Easter, the church accused Communist leaders of alienating East Germany's youth.

East German head of state and Communist Party leader Erich Honecker (left) greets Polish Prime Minister Wojciech W. Jaruzelski in East Berlin in March. East Germany warmly supported the Polish government's military crackdown in December, 1981.

The government refused to make any overt gesture to appease the pacifists. On March 25 it passed a new military law, which decreed for the first time that women could be drafted and reemphasized the requirement that men must be prepared for service. Both the government and the church attempted to damp down polemics on the peace issue thereafter, but pacifist activities continued throughout the year.

The Economy. The domestic economy, good in recent years, began to show the ill effects of international economic problems. East Germany was especially hard hit by the Soviet Union's decision to cut oil sales to its satellites in order to sell more oil for Western hard currencies. The East Berlin government ordered energy conservation and the stepped-up production of lignite (a form of coal), but growth began to slow. Figures for the first half of 1982 showed the national income increasing at an annual rate of 3 percent, compared with the targeted 4.8 percent. At the same time, East Germany's debt to the West rose to more than $10 billion, and Western bankers, badly burned by overlending to Poland, hesitated to extend further credit.

Foreign Policy. East Germany received a major credit grant from West Germany in June. The government of Chancellor Helmut Schmidt hoped that East Berlin would in return ease currency restrictions imposed since 1980 on visitors from the West, but no such concession was forthcoming. Relations between Bonn and East Berlin appeared even more uncertain after the fall of the Schmidt coalition government in October. East German officials expressed concern over Chancellor Helmut Kohl's public references to "German unity."

On March 29 Polish leader Gen. Wojciech Jaruzelski was received with full military honors during a one-day visit to East Berlin. The East Germans had strongly supported the military crackdown in Poland.

In line with East Germany's efforts to expand its influence in the Third World, Honecker visited Syria in October, where he held talks with President Hafez al-Assad.

See STATISTICS OF THE WORLD.   F.W.

GERMANY, FEDERAL REPUBLIC OF, *or* **WEST GERMANY.** Thirteen years of Social Democratic government in West Germany ended in October, 1982. Chancellor Helmut Schmidt and his Social Democratic Party (SPD) fell from power not in an election but as a result of a unique parliamentary maneuver in which the SPD's coalition partner, the Free Democratic Party (FDP), joined the opposition Christian Democratic Union (CDU) in unseating Schmidt and making Helmut Kohl (see biography at PEOPLE IN THE NEWS) the new chancellor.

Politics. The ruling national SPD-FDP coalition had won a majority in national elections in late 1980. But by the start of 1982 the partnership was experiencing severe strains. East-West tensions, a slumping economy, squabbling within and between the allied parties, and a general national feeling of malaise led to dissatisfaction with the leadership of Chancellor Schmidt, although he remained the most popular politician in the country. The FDP began to discuss openly whether to forsake the SPD and line up with the CDU. Hoping to keep his own unruly party and the FDP in line, Schmidt repeatedly threatened to resign. On Feb. 5 he demanded, and got, a parliamentary vote of confidence from the coalition deputies.

Schmidt's troubles, however, were only starting. A small party, the Green-Alternative List, known as the Greens, loomed increasingly large on the West German political scene. A coalition of protest groups, the Greens were opposed to nuclear power, nuclear missiles, environmental pollution, and business-as-usual by traditional political parties. In local elections the Greens were making steady gains among supporters of both the SPD and FDP.

The year's first major electoral test for Schmidt, and the Greens, took place in Lower Saxony on March 21. The results were a crushing defeat for Schmidt. The CDU won an absolute majority, while the runner-up SPD made its worst showing in decades. The FDP came in fourth, behind the Greens, who got more than the minimum 5 percent of votes needed for representation in the state legislature.

West Germany received a new government in October. Helmut Kohl (right), leader of the Christian Democratic Union (CDU), became chancellor. The CDU led a coalition that included its Bavarian affiliate, the Christian Social Union, headed by Franz Josef Strauss (left), and the Free Democratic Party, headed by Hans-Dietrich Genscher (center).

Schmidt's fortunes did not improve when the year's second state election was held in Hamburg in June. Running on the slogan "Hamburg won't leave Helmut in the lurch," the SDP fell from 51.5 percent of the vote to 42.8 percent. The FDP failed to win the crucial 5 percent and took no seats. The CDU gained, but lacked a majority. The Greens entered the state legislature for the first time, with 7.7 percent of the vote. Months of negotiation to build a working coalition in Hamburg eventually failed, and a further election was held in December, in which the SDP won a majority. Meanwhile, the June results led the FDP in Hesse to announce that in the state election there in September, it would drop its local alliance with the SPD and ally itself with the CDU.

Preparation of the annual national budget resulted in a sharp SPD-FDP conflict in July. Schmidt wished to cut the deficit to $12 billion but also to fight the economic slump with government spending based on borrowing; the FDP wanted to slash the deficit to $10.4 billion through cuts in welfare spending. Only a last-minute compromise—a deficit of $11.4 billion—saved the coalition.

As polls, however, showed rising sentiment for the Greens, many FDP leaders concluded that their national partnership with the SPD could lead to their party's demise. Economics Minister Otto Lambsdorff, a Free Democrat, brought matters to a head by criticizing the government budget. Schmidt, exasperated by the FDP's increasing truculence, made a dramatic speech to parliament on Sept. 9, challenging both the FDP and the CDU to use against him the parliamentary tactic known as "constructive vote of no-confidence"—a vote through which the *Bundestag* (the lower house of parliament) may remove the chancellor if it simultaneously names his successor. On Sept. 17 Hans-Dietrich Genscher, FDP leader, deputy chancellor, and minister of foreign affairs, together with Lambsdorff and two other FDP members, dropped out of Schmidt's cabinet, leaving him with a minority government. The FDP and the CDU then agreed to invoke, for the first time in West German history, the constructive no-confidence vote on Oct. 1.

As parliament prepared for the balloting, national attention focused on the election in Hesse, which many observers regarded as a barometer of the public's reaction to the unprecedented goings-on in Bonn, the capital. The results indicated a large sympathy vote for Schmidt. His party won 42.8 percent of the tally, down slightly from the SPD's previous total but above predicted results. The CDU dropped from 46 percent to 45.6 percent. The Greens gained 8 percent, taking votes from the FDP, which fell short of the 5 percent needed to maintain representation in the state. Despite its loss, however, the FDP decided to go ahead with its pact with the CDU. On Oct. 1, therefore, the Bundestag, by 256 to 235, voted to transfer power from Schmidt to Helmut Kohl, the 52-year-old CDU leader. Kohl, goaded by criticism

171

The Green-Alternative List, a loosely organized political party made up of environmentalist and antiwar groups, loomed increasingly large in West German politics. The Greens, opposed to nuclear power and nuclear missiles, won representation in three states during 1982.

from Schmidt, pledged to hold elections in March, 1983.

On Oct. 13 Chancellor Kohl made his first policy address to the parliament. He asked the German public to accept sacrifices in a package of tax increases and welfare cuts; he said that the new coalition would ease taxes for small business and seek to limit immigration of foreign workers. His foreign policy promised little change from that of Schmidt.

The formation of the Kohl government provoked more political maneuvering. Members of the left wing of the FDP criticized Genscher for deserting Schmidt and declared that they would contest Genscher's party leadership; but at the party's convention, held in West Berlin in early November, Genscher was able to beat back the left wing's opposition, winning reelection as FDP leader by a vote of 222 to 169. (Later that month, however, more than 1500 FDP members bolted the party to form a new party, the Liberal Democrats.) Meanwhile, Franz Josef Strauss, head of the Christian Social Union (CSU), the CDU's ally, attacked the FDP during the October state election in Bavaria, the CSU's stronghold. Both the FDP and the Greens failed to win parliamentary seats in Bavaria, which returned the CSU to power.

The most significant repercussion of the Bundestag move was Schmidt's decision, announced on Oct. 26, not to run again as chancellor. Three days later the SPD nominated Hans-Jochen Vogel, 56, former mayor of West Berlin, as its leader.

The Economy. West Germany was hard hit by the worldwide recession. As 1982 began, unemployment stood at 1,700,000, the highest level since 1956. Industrial output was dropping, and export orders were slack.

Statistics later in the year brought no better news. In August the Federal Labor Office reported unemployment at 1,760,000, or 7.4 percent of the labor force. In November it exceeded 2,000,000 and economists predicted that it would reach 2,500,000 by early 1983. Corporate bankruptcies were taking place at an unprecedented rate. On Aug. 9 AEG-Telefunken, the electronics giant, declared itself insolvent. In October the West German Council of Economic Experts predicted in a special report to the government that the gross national product would fall by 1 percent in real terms in 1982.

Foreign Affairs. Partnership with the United States remained the bedrock of West German foreign policy under both Schmidt and Kohl. But significant bilateral differences surfaced in 1982. Seeking to preserve good working relations with Eastern Europe, the Schmidt government initially reacted less harshly to the imposition of martial law in Poland than did the administration of U.S. President Ronald Reagan, causing Washington to criticize Bonn. To be sure, Schmidt imposed new strictures against the Soviet Union in February, barring the opening of new Soviet consulates in West Germany and curtailing official Soviet visits. But in Washington, in March, Foreign Minister Genscher made it clear that Bonn would proceed as planned with the building of a major new Soviet gas pipeline to West Germany.

President Reagan visited West Germany in June. In an address to the Bundestag he sought to allay West German fears that

Washington was overemphasizing an arms buildup and underemphasizing negotiations with Moscow. Although militant leftists protested Reagan's stopover in West Berlin, both the West German and U.S. governments counted the trip a success. Some days later, however, Schmidt was shocked by Reagan's sudden expansion of the embargo on U.S. equipment for the Soviet pipeline to include foreign subsidiaries of U.S. companies. Like other European governments, the Bonn coalition ignored the Reagan ban, which was lifted in November. Kohl planned no change in West Germany's policy, although he underlined the continuing importance of close ties with the U.S.

West Germany worked closely with its partners in the European Community (EC) in 1982. Schmidt conferred with French President François Mitterrand in Paris in February, and he backed Great Britain during the Falklands war. After taking office, Kohl flew to Paris, Brussels, London, and Rome for strategy sessions with EC leaders; he also visited Washington, where he conferred with President Reagan.

West Germany did not win the key concession it hoped for in its dealings with East Germany. Although Bonn agreed in June to continue interest-free credits for East Berlin, the Communists would not ease currency-exchange requirements imposed since 1980 on Western visitors; such requirements significantly cut the number of visits by West Germans to East Germany. Adding to the strain in relations between the two German states was East German wariness of the new conservative government in Bonn.

See STATISTICS OF THE WORLD.   F.W.

GHANA. On Dec. 31, 1981, the civilian government of President Hilla Limann was overthrown in a military coup led by Flight Lt. Jerry J. Rawlings, 34, and his supporters. Rawlings, who had seized power through another coup in June, 1979, but had stepped down three months later after the election of Limann, accused the country's civilian leaders of corruption and incompetence. Indeed, Limann's relatively brief rule was characterized by continuing economic decline, a collapse of the standard of living because of in-

flation (estimated at 150 percent a year), and mismanagement.

In his first acts after taking over, Rawlings suspended the constitution, banned all political parties, and imposed tight control over Ghana's newspapers, which are government owned. He also ordered Limann and about 100 other officials and businessmen arrested (most of them were subsequently released). On Jan. 13 Rawlings announced the creation of a seven-man Provisional National Defense Council (PNDC) to rule the country. As chairman of the PNDC, he appointed a 16-member civilian cabinet on Jan. 22.

Recognizing the economy as the major problem, Rawlings, who enjoyed wide popularity, mobilized a populist, self-help campaign to repair bridges and roads in order that the harvest of cocoa, Ghana's chief export, could be shipped abroad, and to repair or replace worn-out industrial facilities. To help bring inflation under control, the PNDC devised, among other measures, a plan to cut food imports by 50 percent in 1982, and it reduced the number of Ghana's overseas missions. It declared cocoa smuggling a crime punishable by death and promised farmers fair prices for their crops. Rent and price controls were introduced in February. While the government sought ways to reduce its dependency on oil, the importation of which consumed 50 percent of the country's export earnings, Rawlings reestablished diplomatic relations with Libya and benefited from Libyan aid in the form of cheap oil, machinery, and import credits.

These and other short-term measures helped bolster the economy and increased Rawlings's popularity among workers and students. But Ghana's self-appointed young guardian, whose rhetoric since 1979 had become noticeably more Marxist, was distrusted by members of the bureaucracy, the middle class, and the military, many of whom were reported to have left the country. Such an exodus raised the specter of a Ghanaian brain drain. Another grave problem confronting Ghana's rulers was internal instability. According to persistent rumors, a handful of army officers had plotted to carry out a coup in March, on the 25th anniversary

A wave of patriotism swept Great Britain in 1982 as its armed forces went to war and regained the Falkland Islands, which had been seized by Argentina. Here fighting men returning home on the luxury liner Canberra are welcomed by flag-waving Britons.

of independence. In July three judges of the country's high court were found murdered in Accra, and in November there was an attempted military coup.

See STATISTICS OF THE WORLD. J.T.S.

GREAT BRITAIN. In 1982 the people of Great Britain celebrated victory in the Falklands war and the birth of a son to the Prince and Princess of Wales. They also welcomed a pope for the first time. But the government of Prime Minister Margaret Thatcher (see biography at PEOPLE IN THE NEWS) failed to solve the unemployment crisis.

The Falklands War. The Falklands, a group of windswept islands in the South Atlantic, were seized by Argentina on April 2; *see* MILITARY AND NAVAL AFFAIRS. On April 3 a stunned Thatcher, breaking relations with Argentina and calling Parliament to its first weekend session since 1956, declared that Britain would take military action to regain the islands (called the Malvinas in Argentina), whose inhabitants wished to remain British. Foreign Secretary Lord Carrington resigned, taking responsibility for not having anticipated the crisis; Francis Pym replaced him. U.S. Secretary of State Alexander M. Haig, Jr., attempted to negotiate a settlement of the dispute through shuttle diplomacy.

In the wake of the Argentine action, the British public in the main rallied to Thatcher. Some criticism, however, was heard in Parliament. The right wing of Thatcher's Conservative Party pressed her not to make concessions to Argentina; the left wing of the opposition Labour Party counseled against Britain's going to war over a "colonial possession." After Haig's mission ended in failure—and the United States, laying aside its momentary neutrality, came out strongly for Britain in the dispute—the House of Commons on May 17 voted 296–33 to approve Thatcher's policy.

British forces, transported to the South Atlantic by a task force of about 30 British warships, including the *Invincible* with Prince Andrew aboard, landed in the Falklands on May 21. After bitter fighting, the commander of Argentina's forces on the islands surrendered to the British on June 14. Thatcher, having won back the Falklands at a cost of 255 British lives (including civilians) and $1.19 billion, ruled out any future talks with Argentina on the ownership of the islands. On July 6, in accordance with the wishes of Parliament, she appointed a six-man board of inquiry, under Liberal Party member Lord Franks, to examine the causes of the war and to ascertain why the British government had been caught apparently unprepared by the Argentine invasion.

Politics. Thatcher's approval rating among voters shot to a new high as a result of the Falklands victory, although it dipped somewhat in ensuing months. In late October a poll showed that the Conservative Party had the backing of 43 percent of a sample of voters, with Labour drawing 32 percent and the alliance of Liberals and Social Democrats 23 percent.

Both the Labour Party and the Liberal–Social Democratic alliance experienced internal difficulties in 1982. Within Labour a left-wing Trotskyist-Marxist faction called the Militant Tendency had challenged leader Michael Foot; members of the group advocated the overturning of Parliament and the monarchy. Foot sought to deprive the organization of affiliation with Labour; his hand was strengthened in September with the election of right-wing members to the party's powerful national executive committee. A month later the committee stripped Tony Benn, the radical Labourite leader and Foot's nemesis, of many of his important party posts. The action was preceded that same month by the defection of two Labour members of Parliament to the Social Democrats.

The Social Democratic Party (SDP) lost ground in the polls, compared with its 1981 standing. Roy Jenkins, a founder of the party and a former Labourite, won election to Parliament from Glasgow in a March by-election. After that victory, Jenkins defeated David Owen, also a former Labourite and at one time foreign secretary, in a contest for party leadership. Looking ahead to the next national election, the SDP and the Liberal Party attempted to divide the country's 635 parliamentary constituencies between them so that their candidates would not be competing against each other. Since some constituencies were considered far more likely than others to be won by an alliance candidate, the division process caused sharp Liberal-SDP disagreement.

Royalty. Queen Elizabeth II marked the 30th anniversary of her accession to the throne on Feb. 6. Among the royals, however, it was Diana, Princess of Wales, who stole the headlines. The 20-year-old princess gave birth on June 21 to a 7-lb.-1½-oz. son, who thus became second in line to the throne, after his father, Prince Charles. The baby was christened William Arthur Philip Louis.

Espionage. Familiar with earlier spy scandals, Britons learned in July that Geoffrey Arthur Prime, a 44-year-old linguist at the country's main electronic intelligence agency, had been arrested on charges of passing secrets to the Soviet Union over many years. Prime, who was first arrested on sex charges, pleaded guilty to espionage charges on Nov. 10 and was sentenced to 35 years in jail. Adding to a new wave of criticism over the competence of security procedures was the trial in London in late 1982 of a Canadian professor with a British passport, Hugh Hambleton, who was charged with passing economic secrets to the Soviet Union while working in Paris for the North Atlantic Treaty Organization. Hambleton pleaded guilty on Dec. 7 and was sentenced to ten years in prison.

Papal Visit. On May 28 Pope John Paul II began a six-day pastoral visit to Britain, the first ever by a reigning pope. His trip marked a historic reconciliation with the Anglican Church, headed by Queen Elizabeth, who received him at Buckingham Palace. Roman Catholicism had been Britain's religion until King Henry VIII broke with the papacy in the 16th century. In all, more than 2,000,000 Britons saw John Paul during his travels in England, Scotland, and Wales. See RELIGION.

Ulster. The Catholic-Protestant conflict in Northern Ireland continued to torment Britain. Terrorist incidents took more than 55 lives in Ulster during 1982. In London itself the militant Irish Republican Army wrought havoc in July, setting off bombs in two London parks that killed 11 soldiers and injured more than 50 persons. James Prior, secretary of state for Northern Ireland, put into effect a new plan to create a provincial Ulster assembly of both Catholics and Protestants. Elections for the 78-member assembly, essentially an advisory body, were held on Oct. 20. Two Protestant-dominated parties won 48 seats; a moderate Catholic group gained 14 seats; and a nonsectarian party took 10 seats. Sinn Fein, the political wing of the Provisional Irish Republican Army, captured 5 seats. When the assembly opened, however, on Nov. 11, all the Catholic members stayed away.

The Economy. Britain's economy remained the most controversial part of the Thatcher record. As the year began, inflation had dropped to an annual rate of 12 percent and unemployment had risen to 11.5 percent of the labor force. Thatcher held that, despite the high level of joblessness, her tight-

Several thousand unemployed young people march in London in a demonstration sponsored by the Trades Union Congress. About 3,300,000 Britons, or almost 14 percent of the nation's working force, were unemployed in late 1982.

money policies were solving long-term problems, and that she intended to stick with them. In March the government presented a budget that included a reduction in the payroll tax, an increase in personal income tax allowances, and higher taxes for alcohol, tobacco, and gasoline. Economists said that the budget was aimed primarily at aiding business.

By November inflation had dropped to an annual rate of around 7 percent, but unemployment had risen to nearly 14 percent, with 3,300,000 people jobless. Although the gross national product was expected to increase by 1.5 percent in 1982, industrial output remained flat; the Confederation of British Industries reported that 78 percent of manufacturing companies had less than four months' worth of work on order. An awareness of how seriously troubled the economy still was apparently permeated the trade unions, as well. Although the year began with a crippling railway strike, renewed in July, it drew to a close with relative quiet on the labor front, as union leaders acceded to pay increases of about 7 percent (compared with 16.6 percent two years before) and workers

(for example, the miners, traditionally Britain's most militant) voted down calls to strike. To Thatcher the unions' seemingly more conciliatory attitude represented, as she told Parliament, a "vote of confidence" in her government's economic policy.

Foreign Relations. Britain and the U.S. remained close allies, despite some differences. In addition to backing Thatcher on the Falklands issue, President Ronald Reagan made a state visit to Britain in June. Invited to address Parliament, Reagan surprised many listeners by launching a harsh attack on the Soviet Union. Although the Thatcher government condemned Soviet policy in Afghanistan and Poland, it refused to go along with Reagan's subsequent decision to try to block the building of a major Soviet gas pipeline to Western Europe. In September it ordered British-based U.S. subsidiaries to ignore Reagan's ban on supplying pipeline parts to the Soviets. (Subsequently, the Reagan administration dropped the ban.)

Thatcher visited Asia in September. In Tokyo she urged Japan's government to take steps to cut the country's trade surplus with Britain. In Peking she began bilateral discussions on the future of Hong Kong. In 1997 Britain's lease with China, involving parts of Hong Kong, would run out; China wanted unequivocal acknowledgment of its sovereignty over all Hong Kong.

See STATISTICS OF THE WORLD. See also COMMONWEALTH OF NATIONS.   F.W.

GREECE. Greece's first Socialist government, led by Prime Minister Andreas Papandreou, had its popularity put to the test in nationwide municipal elections in October, 1982.

Politics and the Economy. In two rounds of elections, held on Oct. 17 and 24, Greek voters in effect cast their ballots in a referendum on the national government in Athens, which had come to office 12 months earlier promising radical reforms. Papandreou's Panhellenic Socialist Movement (PASOK) captured 173 major mayoralties, including those of Athens, Piraeus, and Thessaloníki. The Communist Party won 45, the conservative New Democracy Party 44, and independents 14. (In the previous municipal elections, in 1978, the results were almost the reverse:

New Democracy 150, PASOK 70, and Communists 33.)

Many critics of the government, especially the left wing of PASOK and the Communists, were disappointed by the relatively slow pace of change. The Socialists in 1981 had promised to nationalize banks and key industries such as shipbuilding. Instead, the government in 1982 only proposed to offer workers a say in company management; it actively sought to promote private investment and considered plans to aid ailing companies. The government also abandoned talk about withdrawing from the European Community (EC); instead, it sought more favorable terms from the EC, especially for Greek farmers. The area in which Papandreou moved swiftly was social programs, which he increased, along with state employees' wages. To pay for such increases, the Socialists called for higher personal and corporate income taxes, but expenditures were projected to exceed revenues by $3.8 billion in the annual budget.

In July, as unemployment rose and inflation hovered at an annual rate of 25 percent, Papandreou appointed 17 new ministers and deputy ministers, among them Gerasimos Arsenis, governor of Greece's central bank. Arsenis was brought into the cabinet to head the new ministry of national economy.

In other domestic areas, the Papandreou government achieved more visible progress. It legalized civil marriage, moved to separate church and state, abolished government censorship, passed laws strengthening civil liberties, and went ahead with plans to decentralize the country's administration.

Foreign Affairs. Despite his 1981 campaign pledge, Papandreou did not move to withdraw Greece from the North Atlantic Treaty Organization (NATO); nor did he close down U.S. military bases in Greece. In February Papandreou visited Cyprus, where he pledged solidarity with Greek Cypriots. In June he conferred with U.S. President Ronald Reagan in Bonn, West Germany, during the annual meeting of NATO government heads. On Sept. 1 Papandreou greeted Yasir Arafat, leader of the Palestine Liberation Organization (PLO), who made Athens his first stop

after the PLO's expulsion from Lebanon. In early November Papandreou made a trip to Rumania, where he joined President Nicolae Ceauşescu in proposing that the Balkans be made a nuclear-free zone. Later that month the Greek prime minister attended the funeral of Soviet President Leonid I. Brezhnev in Moscow; there he met with Polish leader Wojciech W. Jaruzelski, who asked him to act as mediator between Poland and the EC.

See STATISTICS OF THE WORLD. *See also* CYPRUS.   L.A.S.

GRENADA. *See* STATISTICS OF THE WORLD.

GUAM. *See* STATISTICS OF THE WORLD.

GUATEMALA. Amid charges of fraud in the conduct of Guatemala's March 7, 1982, elections, and with the promise to restore "peace and authentic democracy," dissident army officers overthrew the government of outgoing President Romeo Lucas García on March 23. A three-man military junta was named to lead the country, headed by retired Gen. Efraín Ríos Montt. On June 9 Ríos Montt ousted his two fellow junta members and declared himself president.

The bloodless March 23 coup by young officers followed balloting in which Gen. Angel Aníbal Guevara, the government candidate, polled 39 percent of the vote for president in a contest in which fewer than half of the registered electorate took part. Moreover, leftists did not participate and the three unsuccessful presidential candidates charged that the election was fraudulent. On March 13, however, the Congress chose Guevara as president in a runoff made necessary by his failure to win a majority of votes.

Immediately following the coup, the junta suspended Guatemala's constitution, disbanded Congress, and banned the activities of all political parties. On May 17 Ríos Montt said that he planned to call elections at the end of the year for a constituent assembly to rewrite the constitution and that general elections would be held, "probably within two years."

Three weeks later Ríos Montt placed Guatemala under a state of siege for what he declared to be the final battle against leftist guerrillas. He said that special three-man military courts were to be empowered to or-

Born-Again Christian Strongman

A military coup in March brought to power Guatemala's new strongman, Gen. Efraín Ríos Montt, 55, a born-again fundamentalist Christian and a lay preacher in the Church of the Christian Word. After rising to become chief of staff of the army, he ran unsuccessfully for president in 1974 in an election widely regarded as rigged in favor of the government candidate. In 1982, after an election again considered fraudulent, dissident army officers overthrew the regime on March 23 and made Ríos Montt head of a three-man junta. In June he dismissed the other junta members, proclaiming himself president, and suspended many civil liberties. "It is time to do what God orders," he declared, as he launched a new effort to halt the leftist insurgency that, along with right-wing and government terrorism, was taking hundreds of lives each month.

Efraín Ríos Montt

der the public execution of all guerrillas found guilty of murder, terrorism, sabotage, or treason. All political and union activities were banned. Press censorship included a ban on all reports concerning the civil war, except government-approved news.

In order to clear guerrilla strongholds, Guatemala's army was increased to 25,000 men, supplemented by 5000 reservists and an additional, newly created 25,000-member Civil Defense Force. Since, however, these forces were generally unable to come to grips with the guerrillas, their chief targets were Indian villagers. Indians make up more than half of Guatemala's inhabitants, and many Indian communities were providing manpower or other support to the guerrillas. The civilian death toll was at least 400 a month, many of them Indian women and children, and about 100,000 people had fled to Mexico. (All U.S. military sales to Guatemala were banned in 1977 because of the country's poor human rights record.)

On Feb. 8 the country's four major guerrilla groups, which were believed to have 6000 men and women under arms, announced the creation of a unified military command. It was announced that a broad political front was formed on Feb. 16 with the objective of overthrowing the regime.

Guatemala's economy suffered in 1982 from a fall in the price of coffee, its chief export, and the near cessation of tourism because of guerrilla activity.

See STATISTICS OF THE WORLD.   A.E.J.

GUINEA. *See* STATISTICS OF THE WORLD.

GUINEA-BISSAU. *See* STATISTICS OF THE WORLD.

GUYANA. *See* STATISTICS OF THE WORLD. *See also* VENEZUELA.

H

HAITI. *See* STATISTICS OF THE WORLD. *See also* CARIBBEAN COUNTRIES.

HAWAII. *See* STATISTICS OF THE WORLD. *See also* STATE GOVERNMENT REVIEW.

Health and Medicine

Researchers continued in 1982 to make progress in the treatment and prevention of cancer, heart disease, and other maladies. The trial of John W. Hinckley, Jr., on charges of trying to assassinate President Ronald Reagan raised interesting medical as well as legal issues.

MEDICINE

A major event in the health and medicine field in 1982 was the inception of changes in packaging requirements for nonprescription drugs after national alarm over the adulteration of a popular pain reliever. Others included the identification of an epidemic among male homosexuals, the discovery that two experimental agents were effective against colds and influenza, the development of new tests for genetic diseases in unborn children, and the removal of a new arthritis drug from the market after it had caused at least 72 deaths. Government officials announced in August that U.S. medical costs increased 15 percent in 1981 compared with the previous year and that the nation's health-care bill consumed almost 10 percent of the gross national product, or an average of $1225 per person.

Tylenol Scare. A wave of fear swept the United States in the early fall of 1982 after seven persons in the Chicago area were killed by cyanide that had been injected into capsules of the nonprescription pain reliever Extra-Strength Tylenol. The drug was quickly withdrawn from the shelves while a search began for the culprit. Although Tylenol's manufacturers were soon absolved of blame, the incident had enormous implications for the entire nonprescription drug industry in terms of federal and local regulations for the labeling and packaging of such drugs. Chicago passed a law that required tamper-resistant packaging by the end of the year, and in November the federal government passed a regulation requiring such packaging on almost all nonprescription drugs within 15 months and within 90 days for drugs in capsule and liquid form. By November Extra-

Strength Tylenol capsules were being returned to the shelves with the required new packaging.

The Food and Drug Administration (FDA) began to develop a more effective system for the rapid reporting of deaths from poison. The system in use provided only for incomplete and scattered monitoring, so that

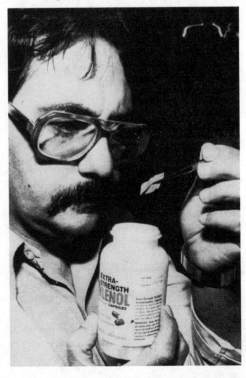

Chicago Board of Health chemist John Rasho inserts a treated paper strip into a bottle of Extra-Strength Tylenol, after cyanide-laced Tylenol capsules killed seven people. The presence of cyanide or some other oxidizer is indicated if the paper turns blue-green, making further testing necessary.

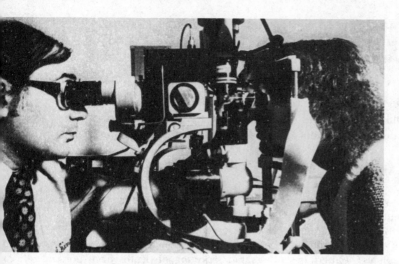

Cleveland ophthalmologist L. J. Singerman uses this laser device for halting the abnormal growth of blood vessels in the macular region of the retina. Scientists announced in 1982 that such therapy is highly effective against senile macular degeneration, a disease that causes blindness in thousands of people each year, mainly the elderly.

national figures on poisoning deaths were sometimes unavailable to federal officials for years.

Genital Herpes. Five known herpes viruses are believed to cause more human illnesses than any other group of viruses. The diseases include cold sores, infectious mononucleosis, chicken pox, and genital herpes, as well as a number of related complications such as encephalitis, shingles (or herpes zoster), infant deaths, and possibly several forms of cancer. The viruses are insidious in their ability to lodge within the body for years, and no drug is yet known that will completely dislodge them. Genital herpes, caused mainly by herpes simplex virus type 2, was believed to have become the leading cause of venereal disease in the U.S. Accurate statistics were lacking in 1982, but the National Institute of Allergy and Infectious Diseases awarded a grant to develop such data and determine whether the disease was a true epidemic.

In April the FDA approved a drug, acyclovir, that effectively treats primary cases of genital herpes. The ointment, however, does not kill off the latent viruses that lodge within the body's nervous system and is less useful against recurrent infections; oral and intravenous forms that were being tested might prove more effective. Many other drugs were also being studied, including interferon and a cottonseed oil extract called

gossypol that was being investigated in Finland with U.S. support.

Innovative Therapy. Striking new methods were used by medical researchers in 1982 in attempts to improve on existing treatments for cancer, Parkinson's disease, blindness, and premature sexual maturation. In the first instance, physicians at Stanford University Medical School used a laboratory-grown antibody to treat a patient with lymphoma, a cancer of the blood-forming organs. The preparation contained pure antibody that attacked only the surface of the patient's cancer cells. The doctors found the results of this therapy dramatic and relatively long-lasting, indicating its potential if the preparation of the special antibody could be simplified.

In Sweden a team of doctors, joined by a U.S. researcher, undertook a dramatic surgical approach in April to treating Parkinson's disease, a condition in which victims lose voluntary control of their movements and develop tremor and difficulty in walking. The disease is due to a deficiency in dopamine, a brain chemical produced by the adrenal gland. Ordinarily the deficiency is corrected with medication. When one Swedish patient continued to have symptoms even with the medication, however, a medical team attempted to provide him with a built-in lifetime supply of dopamine by transplanting into his brain a small amount of tissue from his own adrenal gland, a method previously used only on laboratory animals. The patient's symptoms improved, and he was not harmed by the operation.

In May scientists at the National Eye Institute announced that laser-beam therapy can prevent or substantially delay 90 percent of the blindness due to senile macular degeneration (SMD). Each year SMD causes blindness among 16,000 Americans, most of them elderly, because of abnormal growth of blood vessels in the macula, a small circle in the center of the retina. The laser treatment, a 10-min. procedure, halts this growth, and early detection of the condition enhances the effectiveness of the treatment.

Finally, tests of the National Institute of Child Health and Human Development demonstrated the efficacy of a laboratory-produced version of a human hormone, called luteinizing hormone-releasing hormone (LHRH), in halting premature puberty. Children with this condition grow tall quickly but stop growing before reaching their full potential. They can also develop breast enlargement or beard growth any time between the ages of 1 and 10. These traits were decreased or reversed in 90 percent of the children given daily injections of LHRH.

New Syndrome in Male Homosexuals. U.S. public health officials uncovered a mysterious epidemic of unusual and lethal diseases, primarily among young male homosexuals but also among heterosexual abusers of intravenous drugs, refugees from Haiti, and a few hemophilia patients being treated with replacement blood products. The two most common illnesses observed were a rare kind of cancer called Kaposi's sarcoma and a form of pneumonia caused by the protozoan parasite *Pneumocystis carinii.* Many of the patients also were severely infected with other parasites such as the protozoan *Toxoplasma,* fungi that attack the brain and lungs, and herpes viruses of the cold-sore type. In healthy people these organisms may have only mild effects, but the victims of the observed outbreak seemed to have no defense against them and usually died.

Doctors already knew that severe infections from such agents occur in patients receiving drugs to suppress the body's immune system. Therefore investigators of the epidemic studied the functioning of the immune systems of the victims and found them to be profoundly depressed. The illness thus became known as acquired immune deficiency syndrome, or AIDS. Unlike patients receiving drugs to suppress the immune system, AIDS patients had no known cause for deficient immunity, and scientists looked for one. Meanwhile the number of new cases in 1982 increased to almost 1000.

Oral Contraceptives. Studies published in 1982 showed that the most common oral contraceptives, those containing low amounts of the hormones estrogen and progestin, protect women from several serious illnesses, including two forms of cancer. According to a study by doctors at the Boston University School of Medicine, one of the

James Curran heads a federal team investigating the acquired immune deficiency syndrome, or AIDS, that has stricken homosexual males and several other groups in the U.S. Here, he and two colleagues work with blood samples taken from victims of the mysterious disease.

major protective effects is the reduction of the risk of ovarian cancer by about half, even for some years after the oral contraceptives are no longer taken. The contraceptives reduce even more greatly the incidence of uterine cancer and are responsible for a 70 percent reduction in severe pelvic inflammatory disease, an infection of the fallopian tubes that can lead to sterility. In addition, use of oral contraceptives prevents most cystic disease of the breast and ovaries as well as eliminating ectopic pregnancy (the implantation of the fertilized egg outside the uterus).

For these reasons, a specialist at the federal Centers for Disease Control concluded that the beneficial effects of oral contraceptives are greater than their potentially harmful ones, which include strokes and heart attacks, mostly among women who smoke.

Drugs for Colds and Flu. In a study published in 1982 in a British medical journal, scientists reported that synthetic interferon completely prevented the development of symptoms in volunteers exposed to a type of virus that causes 30 to 50 percent of all adult colds. Because of interferon's promise as an antitumor agent, several pharmaceutical companies had been working to make large amounts of the rare substance more inexpensively by genetic-engineering techniques. The British work suggested that such interferon would also be useful in preventing and possibly treating colds.

In a study at the University of Vermont, volunteers took an experimental anti-influenza drug called rimantidine during an outbreak of the disease. The volunteers suffered only one third as much illness as a comparison group. Rimantidine was thus shown to be as effective in preventing flulike illness as a related, currently available drug called amantidine, and in addition causes almost no side effects, whereas amantidine can produce insomnia and jitters.

Cardiovascular Disease. Among a number of developments in the cardiovascular field in 1982, a report at a November meeting of the American Heart Association in Dallas indicated that men suffering from the condition known as unstable angina could reduce the incidence of heart attacks by half if they took one buffered aspirin every day. The research, headed by H. Daniel Lewis, was based on studies made at 12 Veterans Administration hospitals.

Scientists at Duke University's medical center reported evidence that men with "Type A" personalities, who are high-strung and compulsive workers with a greater likelihood of having heart attacks than are calmer "Type B" men, show higher levels of the hormones cortisol, adrenaline, and noradrenaline in their bodies. The scientists suggested that these hormones, which help the body adapt to stress, may also be a factor in the higher heart attack rate because they may cause more fat to be released into the blood for deposit in the heart.

Two separate sources of evidence in 1982 indicated that a healthy life-style protects against heart disease. The first, a seven-year federally funded study of almost 13,000 men, showed that persons at risk of heart disease can alter their habits and thereby decrease their chances of dying of a heart attack. The men had been chosen because of their predisposition to heart attacks due to smoking, high blood pressure, and high serum cholesterol. Half the men were counseled intensively by special teams to reduce these risk factors; the others continued to receive care from their community physicians. Based on previous experience, it was anticipated that those in the special intervention group would improve their health habits and that the men in the usual-care group would not, leading to a major difference in mortality from heart disease. Instead both groups reduced all three risk factors considerably, and both groups enjoyed a reduced rate of heart attack mortality compared with the average rate prevailing in the U.S. at the time. The study suggested that the change in the usual-care group resulted from the broad influence of health education in the U.S.; the results apparently spoke well for the ability of patients to change and of practicing physicians to do their jobs effectively.

In a separate study conducted at the University of North Carolina, epidemiologists found that higher education may be a factor in increased protection from heart disease.

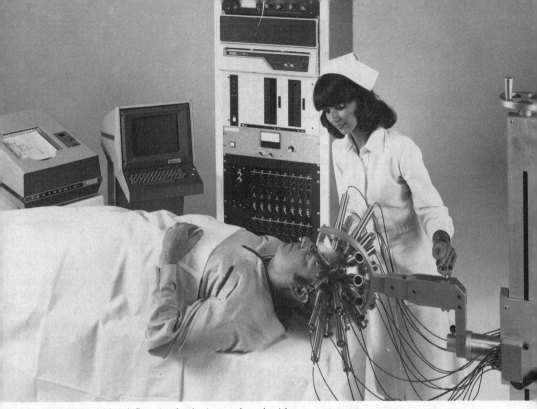

Areas of impaired blood flow in the brain are found without exploratory surgery by using this new Cerebral Blood Flow Analysis System. As the patient breathes in air containing slightly radioactive gas, sensors in the 16 cylinders jutting from the transparent helmet record the gas's circulation through the brain's blood vessels.

Among 10,000 subjects studied over ten years, those who were more highly educated tended to have blood cholesterol levels suggesting a lower risk of heart attack. It appeared that better educated persons ate a healthier, less fatty diet. The improvement of diet with education was greater for men than for women.

Cancer. Life-style and diet also received major attention in 1982 in the area of cancer prevention. The American Cancer Society launched a major six-year study to discover how life-style and environmental factors influence cancer development. More than 1,000,000 citizens were to be questioned about what they ate, what drugs they took, what types of commercial chemicals they were exposed to, and other possible factors. Each volunteer questioner was to be responsible for ten families and would obtain information from those people every two years.

On June 16 the National Academy of Sciences (NAS), the official national scientific advisory group, issued a report called "Diet, Nutrition and Cancer," which advised people of dietary practices that could delay the onset and progression of cancer. The guidelines represented the first time that the NAS had discussed fully the current status of knowledge about diet and cancer. The two-year study led to the general conclusion that there was increasing evidence to suggest that diet can affect the chances of contracting cancer. Some specific suggestions were made: (1) Reduce fat intake by 25 percent by decreasing consumption of beef and other fatty meats, deep-fried foods, and cheese and other high-fat dairy products; (2) decrease intake of smoked or pickled foods such as sausage, ham, smoked fish, and hot dogs; and (3) eat foods high in carotene (apricots, broccoli, carrots, leafy green vegetables, tomatoes) and vitamin C (citrus fruits, broccoli, tomatoes, green peppers, peas). The study also concluded that insufficient evidence existed concerning the cancer-causing potential of several suspect substances such as food additives and preservatives, saccharin, and coffee. It found no convincing evidence that ingesting dietary fiber, vitamin E, or the element selenium could prevent cancer.

Further doubts were cast on the cancer-causing ability of coffee by a Norwegian research group. In contrast to a 1981 Harvard University Medical School study widely criticized by epidemiologists, the Norwegian researchers found no relationship between coffee drinking and cancer of the pancreas among the more than 13,000 people that they had studied for 11 years.

In February the U.S. surgeon general called cigarette smoking the chief preventable cause of death in U.S. society and linked it as a factor in cancers of the bladder, kidney, and pancreas as well as of the lungs and respiratory tract. Scientists reported a possible explanation of how cigarette smoking may cause cancer. Trapped in the cigarette smoke, they found, are particles that release radioactivity of a type known to cause lung cancer in uranium miners, who are exposed to much lower concentrations of the material than are smokers. Smoking one and a half packs of cigarettes every day is equivalent to having 300 X rays taken every day. The radioactive material passes from the lungs and travels throughout the body, which may also explain the connection between cigarette smoking and cancers other than those of the lungs.

As a result of a report at an International Cancer Congress in Seattle in September, a dispute broke out about the safety of low-tar, low-nicotine cigarettes. Researchers from the American Cancer Society reported that switching to filtered cigarettes should reduce deaths from cancer, but the NAS responded in a report that evidence for this conclusion was doubtful. The NAS reasoned that persons who switch to low-tar, low-nicotine brands tend to offset most or all of the potential benefits by smoking more, inhaling more deeply, and holding the smoke in their lungs longer, apparently to maintain a certain amount of nicotine in the blood.

Prenatal Diagnosis Advances. Scientists announced two new tests in 1982 for detecting severe genetic diseases in unborn children. The first, described by public health researchers in New York State, is a method for determining whether a fetus carries a chromosomal defect, called "fragile X," that is thought to be responsible for at least 20 percent of mental retardation in males. The test is done on cells withdrawn from the amniotic fluid surrounding the fetus. Previous attempts had foundered on the problem of growing these cells in the laboratory in such a way that the abnormal chromosomes would be visible through a microscope. The scientists solved this problem by growing the cells in special nutrients.

The other new test, designed to detect the presence of sickle-cell anemia in fetuses, also was done on amniotic fluid but used more sophisticated recombinant DNA (deoxyribonucleic acid) procedures. Sickle-cell anemia is caused by a defect in the structure of the oxygen-carrying blood protein hemoglobin; any critical reduction of oxygen in the blood can cause red blood cells to assume a sickle shape and block the blood vessels, leading to extreme pain and often death. When both parents carry one sickle-cell gene, each of their children has a one-in-four chance of having the disease. For such pregnancies, DNA can be removed from amniotic cells and analyzed for normal or abnormal hemoglobin genes.

Attack on Starch Blockers. For the third year in a row a diet aid came under fire from the medical community. This time the target was the so-called starch blockers, kidney-bean extracts that were supposed to block the ability of the body to use food starches. The starch blockers became the focus of many commercial diet programs during the year and accounted for about $1,000,000 per week in over-the-counter sales. Manufacturers claimed that the substances were food supplements, but the FDA ruled in July that starch blockers were unapproved new drugs and prohibited their further distribution or sale until their efficacy and safety were approved. In fact, 27 persons were reported hospitalized for intestinal problems related to use of the pills, and in October the FDA seized more than 1,000,000 pills from distributors in five states.

Arthritis Therapy. Clinical researchers from Stanford and Harvard reported success in 1982 with a form of intensive X-ray therapy for rheumatoid arthritis patients who were not helped by the customary drugs. The X-ray treatment, called total lymphoid irradiation, was devised many years ago at Stanford to treat persons with a form of cancer called Hodgkin's lymphoma, by killing most of the cells of the immune system. Lymphoid irradiation was then tried on arthritis patients, whose disease is largely caused by immune cells reacting against the patient's own tissues. This therapy caused the arthritis to abate for up to 12 months.

A second radical new treatment was found effective by physicians at the Medical College of Wisconsin. They combined three powerful drugs: hydroxychloroquine, originally used to treat malaria, and cyclophosphamide and azathioprine, two agents that suppress immune cells. Most patients had remarkable remissions, and some were even able to stop taking aspirin. In some patients, damaged joints became nearly normal after six months.

A heavily promoted new drug for arthritis was voluntarily withdrawn from the market two months after it was introduced. The drug, Oraflex, came under attack in June because it had been associated with 12 deaths in Great Britain from kidney and liver disease and intestinal bleeding, and with nonfatal kidney and liver damage in many other arthritis patients. In July the FDA reprimanded the drug's manufacturer for overstating the drug's effectiveness in advertisements and press conferences. The company withdrew the product on Aug. 4, hours after the British government suspended its sale. In all, the drug was associated with 61 deaths in Britain and up to 20 in the U.S.

Regulatory Actions. In 1982 the Federal Trade Commission launched an investigation into the promotion and sale of cardiac pacemak-

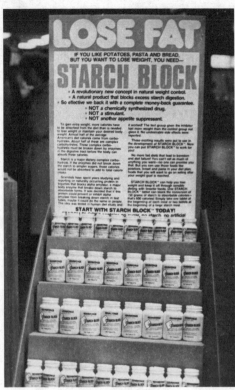

Kidney-bean extracts called starch blockers, which supposedly keep the body from metabolizing starches in foods, became popular with many dieters. In 1982 the FDA ruled that the patent medicines were drugs, however, and prohibited their sale until approved.

ers. The manufacturers were found to have resorted to giving kickbacks to surgeons and subsidizing their vacations in order to obtain sales. As a result, possibly one fourth of the total number of pacemaker implantations may have been unnecessary, and the waste may have cost Medicare hundreds of millions of dollars a year.

In February the Consumer Product Safety Commission banned the use of foam insulation, already installed in 500,000 homes. The insulation releases formaldehyde gas as it decomposes, and formaldehyde has been shown to cause cancer in laboratory animals.

Several government agencies and medical societies united to warn the public about the danger of aspirin for children with fever or flulike illness. Epidemiological studies had raised the possibility that aspirin may cause a severe and sometimes fatal brain disease called Reye's syndrome in a small number of these children. Aspirin was also implicated as a possible cause of excessive bleeding in mothers and their newborn if taken within a few days of delivery, according to the Upstate Medical Center in Syracuse, N.Y.

New Drug Approvals. In 1982 the FDA approved Auranofin, a gold-containing drug used to treat arthritis. Although gold injections had been available for several years, Auranofin was the first gold compound in pill form. The FDA also approved an old drug, Benadryl, best known as an antihistamine, for a new use—insomnia. In addition, three new penicillin-derived antibiotics—piperacillin, azlocillin, and mezlocillin—were released. The new antibiotics are active against bacteria resistant to older types of penicillin.

In July scientists from France, Senegal, and the U.S. reported that a new drug called ivermectin might prove highly effective against onchocerciasis, or river blindness, a major roundworm disease of tropical regions. The drug was a modification of a natural substance, avermectin, that is produced by fungi. In October Brazilian and U.S. scientists announced successful trials of an FDA-approved drug, moxalactam, for use against

---

The Age of Anxiety

Among the trendy maladies of 1981 were sprained wrists from playing too many video games and "Rubik's sore thumb" from too much cube twisting. In 1982 two southern California psychologists, John Flowers and Bernard Schwartz, reported some contemporary "newroses" symptomatic of our times. Their list of "newrotics" included metaphiliacs, who search for more meaning in life than there really is; cataclonics, who are happy only when creating problems; inverse paranoids, who feel they are unworthy of being persecuted; and sufferers from pretraumatic-stress syndrome, who feel anxious because nothing bad has happened to them yet.

---

acute bacterial meningitis that is resistant to the standard drugs.

Dentistry. The National Institute of Dental Research announced in 1982 that dental caries among schoolchildren had declined by more than one third during the past ten years. It estimated that 37 percent of all children between the ages of 5 and 17 had no cavities in permanent teeth; fluoridation of municipal drinking water was widely credited with this gain. At the 70th Annual World Dental Congress, held in Vienna, scientists noted similar reductions in caries among children of other industrialized nations. Developing countries, however, showed opposite trends, with caries occurring in almost epidemic proportions. W.A.C.

MENTAL HEALTH

The use of the insanity plea as a criminal defense was made prominent in 1982 when a would-be assassin of President Ronald Reagan was found not guilty by reason of insanity. Evidence was reported during the year of brain-wave differences among persons suffering from multiple personality disorder.

Insanity Defense. The acquittal of John W. Hinckley, Jr., the man accused of trying to assassinate President Reagan in 1981, attracted much national attention in 1982. The trial, resulting in his acquittal by reason of insanity on June 21, added a new dimension to the old debate over the merits and demerits of the insanity defense. For the first time, attorneys for both the defense and the prosecution drew heavily on research findings from the new field of biological psychiatry.

The trial turned largely on one scientific question: Do structural abnormalities in the brain reliably indicate a mental disorder? Radiologists and psychiatrists who argued for the defense testified that computerized axial tomography scanning, a sophisticated X-ray technique, revealed enlarged ventricles and diminished brain tissue in the defendant's brain. Such abnormalities, they held, provided solid evidence that Hinckley suffered from an organic brain disorder, probably schizophrenia, that precipitated his irrational act. The prosecution summoned its own stable of experts, however, who testified that slight brain atrophy is not uncommon in the

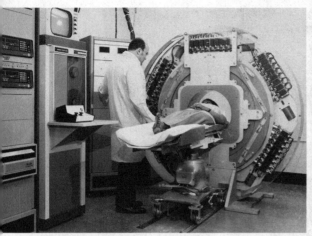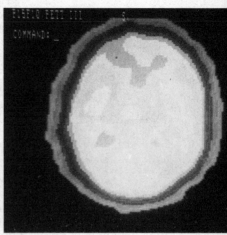

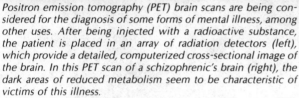

Positron emission tomography (PET) brain scans are being considered for the diagnosis of some forms of mental illness, among other uses. After being injected with a radioactive substance, the patient is placed in an array of radiation detectors (left), which provide a detailed, computerized cross-sectional image of the brain. In this PET scan of a schizophrenic's brain (right), the dark areas of reduced metabolism seem to be characteristic of victims of this illness.

normal population. The fact that Hinckley had a marginally abnormal cortex was meaningless in terms of assessing his mental health, one radiologist stated.

How much this conflicting neurological testimony influenced the jury's decision to find the 27-year-old Hinckley not guilty by reason of insanity was uncertain. The decision, however, seemed destined to have an impact that would go far beyond the fate of Hinckley alone. U.S. Senate committee hearings were held in July in response to public outcry over the decision, and at least one bill was introduced that would all but eliminate mental illness as a legal defense.

Multiple Personalities. In May a National Institute of Mental Health researcher, psychiatrist Frank W. Putnam, released some preliminary but promising findings about one of the most bizarre forms of mental illness: multiple personality disorder. Putnam reported data indicating that each of the alternative personalities of such patients was associated with a unique pattern of brain activity, suggesting that fundamental differences in sensory processing may underlie the reported shifts in personality. Putnam measured the electrical brain activity for four different personalities of ten patients. He also tested control subjects, who were invited to create and "fake" an alternative personality. Whereas the brain patterns of the control subjects were unchanged, indicating that they could not fake a personality change, the brain activity of the patients' alternative personalities varied significantly. The neurological variability might indicate that different personalities actually use different brain circuitry, said Putnam.

Even though the public had long been fascinated by popularized multiple-personality cases in books and films such as *Sybil* and *The Three Faces of Eve,* psychiatrists had in general been doubtful of the validity of such diagnoses. If different personalities actually do process sensory stimuli differently, however, this fact could explain the markedly altered self-perceptions and behavior of multiple personalities. Thus some mental-health professionals viewed Putnam's data as vindicating their work in this area.

See also BEHAVIORAL SCIENCES; CIVIL RIGHTS AND CIVIL LIBERTIES; CRIME AND LAW ENFORCEMENT. W.H.

A U.S. Air Force officer addresses Honduran troops being piloted by American airmen to military maneuvers near the border with Nicaragua. With encouragement and aid from Washington, Honduras took an active part in resisting the spread of communism in Central America.

HONDURAS. Roberto Suazo Córdova, a former country doctor elected president in November, 1981, took office on Jan. 27, 1982, as the first civilian president of Honduras in a decade. The military, however, under army commander Gen. Gustavo Alvarez Martínez, remained visible and powerful.

In 1982 Honduras, long believed to be a transit point for the shipment of weapons from Nicaragua to guerrillas in El Salvador, took an active part in resisting the spread of communism in Central America. U.S. aid to Honduras increased to $89,000,000 in fiscal year 1982, and the number of U.S. military advisers rose to about 90, even more than in El Salvador. In late June some 3000 Honduran troops joined the Salvadoran army in attempting to crush Salvadoran guerrillas in a mountainous region claimed by both countries. The Honduran army also collaborated

with armed Nicaraguan exiles who sought to overthrow the leftist Sandinista regime in Nicaragua.

Gen. Alvarez established a network of civil defense committees to deal with domestic leftists committing acts of antigovernment violence. The most serious such act in 1982 was the Sept. 17 capture by 12 men of 105 business and government leaders attending a conference in San Pedro Sula. The leftists' demands, which were denied, included the expulsion of foreign military advisers and the release of 60–80 Latin American leftists allegedly being held in Honduras. After releasing the hostages, their captors were allowed on Sept. 25 to fly to Panama, from where they continued to Cuba.

Honduras was expected to record a decline in gross national product in 1982. In order to pay for imports and meet payments on the foreign debt of $1.4 billion, the government undertook such austerity measures as reduced spending for social welfare and major public projects, and reduced subsidies for essential foods and medicines.

See STATISTICS OF THE WORLD.   A.E.J.

HOUSING. The U.S. housing industry's performance in 1982 was probably its worst since 1945, with bidding volume down 13 percent at the end of the third quarter. Housing contracts were down 16 percent for the same period.

Housing starts picked up in the third quarter, however, to an adjusted annual rate of 1,060,000. As interest rates fell, housing starts rose to an annual rate of 1,430,000 units in November.

High interest rates, often blamed for the housing industry slump, dropped after midyear. Conventional mortgage rates were running at 16 percent at the end of the third quarter, but the government dropped Federal Housing Administration and Veterans Administration mortgage ceilings one point below their previous 15 percent, to 14 percent. The new-construction capital index showed a cumulative gain of 55 percent at the end of the third quarter, another hopeful sign for the industry.

Construction Starts. The increase of housing starts in the third quarter brought hope of a recovery for the industry. Housing starts increased 31.4 percent in July to a seasonally adjusted rate of 1,195,000. The rise, which was the largest in the 23 years for which records had been kept, was spearheaded by a boom in multifamily housing starts. Much of the increase in multifamily starts was due to the beginning of work on projects subsidized by the Department of Housing and Urban Development (HUD).

Mortgages. With buyers unable to obtain mortgages at an affordable rate, some housing contractors made sales by providing the financing themselves. At least 30 housing builders offered mortgages, including all of the 10 largest home builders. U.S. Homes, the nation's largest housing builder, lost $1,100,000 on housing construction in the first half of 1982, but reported a $2,800,000 profit. Profits from the firm's mortgage subsidiary ($1,400,000), land sales, and a trade of debts for common stock accounted for the profit. The firm's mortgage profits were an estimated 50.5 percent of its total profits in the first half of 1982.

The increase in seller mortgages continued in 1982, as housing prices declined in many areas of the country. High interest rates, responsible for the stagnant market in existing housing, were increasingly overcome by balloon mortgages, buy-downs, and land contracts.

Balloon mortgages allow the buyer to pay the seller his or her house payments for a period of 5 to 10 years, based on a 25- or 30-year amortization, with interest rates usually 11 percent to 13 percent. At the end of the balloon, the buyer refinances and pays the seller the balance. Buy-downs consist of the seller assuming a part of the new mortgage payment for a short period, such as one year, to ease the buyer's financing costs until his or her income rises. With land contracts, the seller accepts a down payment and monthly payments, but retains title to the property until the loan is paid.

Spokespeople for the real estate industry were disturbed by a U.S. Supreme Court ruling on June 28 holding that federally chartered savings and loan associations may refuse to allow home buyers to assume existing mortgages. The 6–2 decision stated that these thrift institutions may enforce clauses in the mortgages they write requiring a homeowner to pay off the balance owed on a mortgage when the home is sold, regardless of any state laws to the contrary. The ruling thus limits the ability of homeowners to pass on their mortgages at the lower interest rates of previous years.

Government Housing. A hopeful sign of recovery in the housing industry was a $90,000,000 housing rehabilitation program to be financed through HUD. The program would rehabilitate 10,000 housing units in 162 cities. Half the money would come from community development block grants and the rest from private sources.

Public housing funding came under fire in June, when the National Association for the Advancement of Colored People took fed-

Despite high interest rates and economic recession, housing starts picked up in the second half of 1982. This new home was one of several being built in Gwynedd, Pa.; prices started at $119,500.

eral court action against HUD. The move was intended to force HUD to intervene more aggressively on behalf of minorities in giving block grant funds to the city of Boston. The city was receiving about $25,000,000 per year in HUD grants and, like all recipient cities, had to certify that the funds were used to meet the needs of low and moderate income level residents.   R.W.S.

HUNGARY. János Kádár, the Communist leader of Hungary, marked his 70th birthday in May, 1982. As architect of government policy for 26 years, Kádár was chiefly responsible for making Hungary unique in Eastern Europe for its relatively relaxed domestic atmosphere, its economic pragmatism, and its

emphasis on ties with the West. Kádár continued on course in 1982.

The government permitted dissent, within limits. *Beszelo* (The Talker), a dissident publication that first appeared in late 1981, issued a new installment in 1982; it discussed student criticism of the government, opinion on the Polish crisis, and a new pacifist movement among Hungarian Catholics.

The budding Catholic pacifist movement was inspired by Father György Bulanyi, a priest who counseled youth to do social service work rather than compulsory military service. Although Bulanyi's followers numbered only several thousand, the movement aroused concern in both government and official Catholic Church circles. With Communist backing, the Bench of Hungarian Bishops warned Bulanyi to suspend his activities. In June they withdrew his right to celebrate Mass and submitted his case to the Vatican for review.

Reform decrees effective in 1982 allowed aspiring businessmen to form small private companies and to set up shops and restaurants. The move was intended to improve the supply of goods and services, but Western analysts said that it also served to legitimize underground economic activity already taking place.

Hungary formally joined the International Monetary Fund and World Bank, which improved the country's creditworthiness; it subsequently gained a loan of $260,000,000 from a consortium of private Western banks and $300,000,000 in short-term credit from government banks. In line with the wishes of Western banks, to which Hungary owed more than $8 billion, the regime acted vigor-

ously to keep national spending in line. In a series of decrees, it raised the price of household fuels, bread and other food, and public transport. In September it imposed new restrictions on the import of raw materials and industrial components.

Hungary followed the basic foreign policy line of the Soviet Union. Even so, Kádár managed to maintain cordial ties with the West. In April he paid a two-day working visit to West Germany and met with Chancellor Helmut Schmidt. In July Kádár played host to President François Mitterrand, the first French head of state ever to visit Communist Hungary. In November Kádár attended the funeral of Soviet President Leonid I. Brezhnev in Moscow. Brezhnev's successor as Soviet Communist Party boss, Yuri V. Andropov, had been ambassador to Hungary during the Hungarian uprising of 1956. He was allegedly instrumental in suppressing the revolt and installing Kádár in power.

See STATISTICS OF THE WORLD.　　　　F.W.

I

ICELAND. Local elections, a lingering dispute over a North Atlantic Treaty Organization (NATO) base, and an international whaling decision were the main concerns of Iceland in 1982.

Elections were held on the local level on May 22. The results showed the right-wing Independence Party regaining strength, with about 43 percent of the popular vote, some 15 percent above what it polled in the 1978 local elections. The votes of the Communist and the Social Democratic parties declined about 25 percent each, while that of the centrist Progressive Party remained virtually unchanged.

Opposition to Iceland's membership in the Atlantic alliance remained strong among many Icelanders. Left-wing parties proposed that the government close the U.S.-manned NATO air base at Keflavík. In March about

150 people demonstrated peacefully at the base. The left-wing People's Alliance charged that a government decision to move several NATO oil storage tanks out of Keflavík was part of a NATO "offensive" strategy that would drag Iceland into a war.

On July 23, at a meeting of the International Whaling Commission at Brighton, England, Iceland joined six other whaling nations in voting against a worldwide ban on whaling, starting in 1985. The ban was adopted by a 25–7 vote, but the commission had no powers of enforcement.

President Vigdís Finnbogadóttir visited the United States in September to participate in "Scandinavia Today," a celebration of the cultural achievements of the Nordic nations.

See STATISTICS OF THE WORLD.　　　L.A.S.

IDAHO. *See* STATISTICS OF THE WORLD.

ILLINOIS. *See* STATISTICS OF THE WORLD.

Zail Singh (right), the first Sikh to become president of India, is congratulated by outgoing President N. Sanjiva Reddy. Singh, an aide to Prime Minister Indira Gandhi, was chosen for the largely ceremonial post by an electoral college.

INDIA. As India celebrated its 35th year of independence in 1982, Prime Minister Indira Gandhi (see biography at PEOPLE IN THE NEWS) remained firmly at the helm of the government in New Delhi. But political squabbles, violence in the streets, poor grain crops, and delicate foreign policy maneuvering presented the world's largest democracy with its usual abundance of problems.

Politics. The chief opposition parties posed little threat to the prime minister in 1982, although state elections in May showed some waning of public support for the prime minister's Congress-I Party. In July Zail Singh, Gandhi's candidate for the largely ceremonial position of president, won 73 percent of the vote in indirect balloting by India's state and national legislators.

The most startling political challenge to Gandhi came literally from within the family.

The challenger was Maneka Gandhi, the widow of the prime minister's favorite son and heir apparent, Sanjay, who was killed in an air crash in 1980. The quarrel between Maneka, 26, and Gandhi, 64, gained public notoriety in March, when Maneka addressed a meeting of Sanjay's old friends, in defiance of the prime minister's orders. After what was described as a "dreadful scene" at her mother-in-law's house, Maneka was asked to move out.

In August Maneka made it clear that she intended to form a political movement to rival the ruling Congress-I Party. The new group, temporarily called Sanjay Vichar Manch, or Platform for the Propagation of Sanjay's Ideas, started with few supporters. Nevertheless, Maneka predicted the desertion from the prime minister's side to her own of many members of parliament. She also announced her intention to challenge Rajiv, Gandhi's surviving son, in the next parliamentary elections.

Domestic Turmoil. At least 12 people died and 60 others were seriously injured in violence connected with a one-day national strike, called in January, to protest laws outlawing strikes in essential services and providing for detention without trial. Nearly 25,000 persons were arrested and held for questioning. Most of them were later released. In May, more than 350 people were arrested in the state of Punjab when bands of Hindus and Sikhs attacked each other. The Dal Khalsa, or Association of the Pure, was seeking to establish greater autonomy in the Punjab, the home state of the Sikhs. In October up to 5000 Sikhs armed with swords and spears launched an assault on Parliament House in New Delhi to demand a judicial inquiry into the deaths of 34 comrades killed when a train hit the bus taking them to jail for defying a ban on demonstrations. They were repulsed after a bloody battle with police, in which four people were reported killed. At least 60 policemen were injured. Further incidents of violence in the Punjab followed.

In August thousands of police officers, protesting labor conditions, led an all-day rampage of arson and looting in the streets of

Bombay. On Sept. 6 rioting broke out between Muslims and Hindus in a dispute over use, for religious purposes, of an empty building in Meerut, 40 mi. northeast of New Delhi. By early October at least 30 persons had died in continuing violence, and more than 795 had been arrested.

The Economy. India's economic performance in 1982 was mixed. In June the World Bank praised the Gandhi government's efforts to reduce inflation, increase investment, and stimulate exports. The bank warned, however, that a liberalized attitude toward foreign capital was an essential factor in generating significant economic growth during the 1980's.

Erratic monsoon rains caused widespread damage to India's grain crops in 1982 and forced the government to abandon its claims of food self-sufficiency. In August it reluctantly announced a decision to import 2,500,-000 tons of wheat from the United States. The corn, barley, and rice harvests were also poor, leading economists to predict a decline in the growth rate of India's gross national product for the year.

Foreign Affairs. Although Prime Minister Gandhi maintained a close relationship with the Soviet Union in 1982, she also sought to improve India's ties with the U.S., China, and Pakistan.

Prospects for an India-Pakistan détente on the subcontinent appeared to fade in February, when India abruptly withdrew from talks scheduled in Islamabad between the foreign ministers of the two countries. In the ensuing months, however, Pakistani President Zia ul-Haq and Gandhi exchanged letters, and senior civil servants met in August. At the two-day session, the two countries discussed a nonaggression pact proposed by Pakistan. In early November Zia met briefly with Gandhi in New Delhi. They agreed to establish a joint commission to resolve problems between the two countries.

India's long-standing border dispute with China remained unresolved in 1982, although representatives of the two most populous nations in the world held four days of talks in May in what was described as "the most cordial atmosphere in decades."

In late July Prime Minister Gandhi paid her first official visit in 11 years to the U.S. She and President Ronald Reagan announced a wide range of agreements designed to improve scientific, economic, and cultural cooperation. Gandhi and Reagan also appeared to resolve a dispute dating to 1974, when India surprised the world by exploding an atomic device. In question was the fuel supply for the U.S.-built nuclear reactor at Tarapur, India. In 1978 the U.S. Congress barred shipments of nuclear fuel to any country that refused to submit to full international safeguards. India had consistently resisted pressure to allow international inspection of all its nuclear facilities. By agreeing in July that France could supply India's fuel needs, although India would not be allowed to reprocess the spent fuel without U.S. permission, Gandhi and Reagan reached a compromise solution.

India's decision in April to buy 40 Mirage fighter bombers, with an option to buy 110 others, was described in France as "the first step" in French-Indian industrial cooperation. It was also seen as a reduction in India's dependence on Soviet arms.

In September Prime Minister Gandhi visited Moscow for talks with President Leonid I. Brezhnev, who offered Soviet construction of a 1000-megawatt nuclear power station in India. Diplomats, however, pointed out that Soviet regulations concerning nuclear fuel were at least as stringent as those of the U.S.

See STATISTICS OF THE WORLD.   R.J.C.

INDIANA. *See* STATISTICS OF THE WORLD.

INDIANS, AMERICAN. In a major political upheaval on the nation's largest reservation, Navaho tribal chairman Peter MacDonald, 53, was defeated for reelection to a fourth four-year term by Peterson Zah, 44. Also notable in 1982 were the restoration of Jim Thorpe's Olympic honors, a U.S. Supreme Court ruling that tribes may tax non-Indian businesses, and a precedent-setting settlement of Papago water claims in Arizona.

Navaho Election. MacDonald, one of the most powerful Indian leaders in the United States, was a founder and board chairman of the Council of Energy Resource Tribes (CERT), an Indian oil and natural gas cartel.

However, with federal aid sharply cut by the government and an unemployment rate on the reservation approaching 80 percent, MacDonald polled only 24,665 votes to 29,208 for Zah. Zah was director of a legal services organization on the 24,000-sq.mi. reservation in northeastern Arizona, northwestern New Mexico, and southeastern Utah. He criticized leases on the reservation's minerals that provided the Navaho with as little as 25¢ a ton for coal as "outrageous" and pledged to renegotiate the contracts.

New Indian Policy? At conventions and meetings of Indian organizations in October, the U.S. Department of the Interior's assistant secretary for Indian affairs, Kenneth L. Smith, announced an imminent new federal policy toward Indians. Smith gave no date for the White House announcement of the policy but indicated that it would be soon— probably within a few weeks at most. The policy statement, however, was not made. At the end of the year, the assistant secretary was still awaiting the statement.

In 1970 President Richard M. Nixon declared: "We must make it clear that Indians can become independent of federal control without being cut off from federal concern and federal support." Indian leaders continued to seek reinforcement and support for this concept from subsequent Presidents.

A policy statement from President Ronald Reagan was likely to support the concept of less federal intervention in tribal affairs, but also to provide less financial support for reservation programs. Speaking as the Administration's top Indian affairs official, Smith had consistently emphasized increased autonomy and responsibility for tribal governments and less dependence on the federal government.

Thorpe's Honors Restored. In an act of symbolic significance to American Indians, the Olympic honors stripped in 1913 from Jim Thorpe, a Sac and Fox Indian born in 1888 in Indian Territory (now Oklahoma), were fully restored in 1982. Thorpe, who was named in a 1950 Associated Press poll as the greatest athlete of the half-century, reached the summit of his athletic career at the 1912 Olympics in Stockholm, where he won gold medals in both the decathlon and the pentathlon. Seven months later, however, Thorpe's victories were struck from the record books and his Olympic medals taken from him because he had played baseball in 1910 for $60 a month, voiding his amateur status.

After Thorpe's death in 1953, members of his family and others sought the restoration of his Olympic honors on the grounds that his violation had been a minor technicality. That approach failed, but a new appeal, also based on a technicality, succeeded. On Oct. 13 the International Olympic Committee voted to restore Thorpe's name to the official record books and to present new medals— the originals were distributed in 1913 to the second-place finishers—to Thorpe's daughter Charlotte.

Taxing Authority. In the most important 1982 court decision affecting Indian tribes, the U.S. Supreme Court ruled on Jan. 25 that the Jicarilla Apache tribe of New Mexico, and by extension other Indian tribes, had the authority to impose a severance tax on oil and gas taken from reservation lands by non-Indian companies. In a 6–3 decision, the Court said that the right to tax "derives from the tribe's general authority, as sovereign, to control economic activity within its jurisdiction. . . ." The Court noted that Congress could limit tribal taxing powers, but had not done so. The case pitted a dozen of the nation's biggest oil companies against the 2100-member tribe.

Water Rights. On July 14 Interior Secretary James G. Watt announced the formulation of a plan for settling by negotiation more than 50 outstanding lawsuits over Indian water claims. The following month, a negotiator from the Interior Department helped Arizona state officials, the Papago tribe, and other parties to the Papago litigation reach an accord that was expected to set a precedent for other water claim settlements.

President Reagan had vetoed an earlier Papago settlement on June 1, describing it as "a multimillion-dollar bailout of local public and commercial interests at the expense of federal taxpayers." The President contended that the mining companies and other local users in southern Arizona who had pumped

Peterson Zah does some campaigning in his successful bid to become tribal chairman of the Navahos. On his election, Zah vowed that the natural resources of the nation's largest Indian reservation would no longer be "exploited."

groundwater from under the Papago reservation should share in the cost of the settlement. The new Papago agreement, signed by President Reagan on Oct. 12, gave the Indians the same amount of water as in the previous accord but reduced the federal outlay from $112,000,000 to $18,500,000. The state of Arizona, the city of Tucson, and various companies were to make up the difference.

Economic Developments. The Choctaw tribe of Mississippi arranged a unique $2,600,000 financing plan to bring a new greeting card industry and some 300 new jobs to the reservation. It was the first time that state industrial bonds were being used to finance a project on an Indian reservation.

In 1982 the Gila River Indian community of Arizona was pioneering a domestic rubber industry. In 1975 the tribespeople began research and development for the production of rubber from the guayule shrub, which grows in the southwest deserts. They produced a shrub that yields three times the

normal amount of rubber. In October they received a Defense Department contract to expand production to 5000 acres and build a processing plant.

The Indian growth industry of 1982—and one likely to grow in the future—was bingo and other forms of gambling. In Florida the Seminole Indians, who had pioneered commercial bingo on reservations, made an estimated $6,000,000 profit from this enterprise. The Shakopee Sioux built a $950,000 bingo palace on their reservation outside Minneapolis; it opened on Oct. 16 with a full house and $10,000 jackpots. In North Dakota, the Three Affiliated Tribes of the Fort Berthold reservation announced a proposal to allow $100-limit blackjack and other gambling at the reservation's Four Bears Lodge as a means to raise money for day-care centers and programs for senior citizens. Because reservations are not generally subject to state gambling regulations, other tribes were also considering this business opportunity.   V.L.

INDONESIA. The military-backed 15-year rule of President Suharto won a resounding endorsement from Indonesia's electorate in 1982. Violence during the 45-day election campaign cost more than 58 Indonesian lives. However, when some 82,000,000 voters went to the polls throughout the southwestern Pacific archipelago on May 4, the election was uneventful. Foreign observers in Djakarta, the capital, reported that the balloting, called by the government a "festival of democracy," appeared to be fair.

The ruling Golkar Party, improving on the record it set in the previous national elections in 1977, accounted for slightly more than 64 percent of the vote. The Muslim-dominated Development Unity Party took about 28 percent of the vote, and the coalition Indonesian Democratic Party won 7.9 percent. The result provided Gen. Suharto's Golkar Party with some 244 of the 364 parliamentary seats. An additional 100 seats were to be filled by Suharto appointees, many of them drawn from the military.

Indonesia's unprecedented economic growth of recent years appeared to slow down in 1982. Largely responsible was the worldwide decline in oil demand and prices; oil revenues had been accounting for almost 70 percent of Indonesia's budget. Japan, the chief importer of Indonesian oil, threatened to buy petroleum elsewhere unless the Indonesian government lowered its prices. In August Indonesia reluctantly agreed that it would do so.

Indonesia remained a staunch member of the non-Communist Association of Southeast Asian Nations (ASEAN) that also includes Malaysia, the Philippines, Singapore, and Thailand. ASEAN repeatedly called for the withdrawal of Vietnamese troops from Cambodia, and for elections, sponsored by the United Nations, in that country; see INTERNATIONAL CONFERENCES.

In October Gen. Suharto received a warm welcome in Washington, D.C., where he requested additional military aid. He was also assured that U.S. plans for the Japanese navy to play a more active role in Southeast Asian waters did not include bringing Japanese warships near Indonesia.

The administration of U.S. President Ronald Reagan chose to deal through what a U.S. official called "quiet diplomacy" with charges of Indonesian abuses of human rights—particularly against the people of East Timor, a Portuguese colony that Indonesia invaded in 1975 and later annexed. The issue had led to strained relations between Suharto and former U.S. President Jimmy Carter.

See STATISTICS OF THE WORLD.   R.J.C.

INTERNATIONAL CONFERENCES. As in most years, a wide variety of international conferences took place in 1982. For conferences not included under the headings below, *see* ARAB LEAGUE; COMMONWEALTH OF NATIONS; COMMUNISM; NORTH ATLANTIC TREATY ORGANIZATION; ORGANIZATION OF AMERICAN STATES; ORGANIZATION OF PETROLEUM EXPORTING COUNTRIES; UNITED NATIONS. See also articles on individual countries mentioned.

Conference on Security and Cooperation in Europe. The two-year-old 35-nation East-West conference, designed to review and expand the provisions of the 1975 Helsinki accords on territorial security, human rights, and economic exchanges in Europe, reconvened in Madrid in February. Talks became deadlocked, however, when the United States and its Western European allies insisted that continuing human rights violations under martial law in Poland made negotiations impossible with the Soviet Union and Eastern European nations.

In March the conference was recessed, and the delegates agreed to reconvene on Nov. 9. Although reluctant to resume talks, the U.S. consented to do so when its allies agreed to make martial law in Poland a major issue and to press for expanded human rights in Eastern Europe. Included among the latter were the forming of free trade unions, the right to political self-determination, an end to radio interference, and protection for foreign journalists. Observers saw little likelihood, however, of an agreement between the Soviet bloc and Western nations.

Summit at Versailles. In early June the leaders of the world's most powerful non-Communist industrial nations gathered at Versailles,

Leaders of seven major industrial nations gather at Versailles, France, in June for their annual meeting. Left to right: Japanese Prime Minister Zenko Suzuki, British Prime Minister Margaret Thatcher, U.S. President Ronald Reagan, French President François Mitterrand, West German Chancellor Helmut Schmidt, Canadian Prime Minister Pierre Elliott Trudeau, and Italian Premier Giovanni Spadolini.

outside Paris, for their annual conference. The countries represented were Canada, France, West Germany, Great Britain, Italy, Japan, and the U.S. The three-day conference achieved little more than an exchange of ideas on economic cooperation. U.S. President Ronald Reagan won a measure of agreement on the need to limit export credits and technology sales to the Soviet Union, but the joint communiqué was vaguely worded.

ASEAN Foreign Ministers. In June the foreign ministers of the Association of Southeast Asian Nations (ASEAN), composed of the non-Communist countries of Indonesia, Malaysia, the Philippines, Singapore, and Thailand, held a three-day meeting in Singapore. ASEAN renewed its demand for Vietnam's withdrawal from Cambodia and for Vietnamese agreement to Cambodian elections, monitored by the United Nations. The minis-

ters also appealed to the industrial powers to resist pressures to protect their home industries against foreign imports and to pay a fair price for their purchases of raw materials from developing countries.   R.J.C.

IOWA. *See* STATISTICS OF THE WORLD.

IRAN. After months of stalemate in the Persian Gulf war, Iran seized the initiative in mid-1982 by driving Iraqi forces out of Khuzistan Province and then sending an Iranian invasion force into Iraq. Within Iran itself, executions and political violence continued to take a heavy toll.

War with Iraq. In early 1982 Iranian forces began pushing back Iraqi invaders all along the battlefront. On April 30 Iran launched an offensive to recapture Khorramshahr, a major Iranian oil port that had been in Iraqi hands for more than a year. The Iranians completed the reconquest of the city on May 24. The loss of Khorramshahr—renamed Khunin-

197

Shouting "God Is Great," a teenage Iranian volunteer prepares for action in the war against Iraq. Such youthful zealots often rushed headlong into enemy minefields and machine-gun fire.

shahr (City of Blood) by the Iranians—was a major setback for Iraq's President Saddam Hussein, who had launched the war against Iran on Sept. 22, 1980, in hopes of making Iraq the dominant power in the Persian Gulf region. The Khorramshahr offensive demonstrated that the Iranian army, badly disorganized after the fall of Shah Mohammed Riza Pahlavi in January, 1979, had reemerged as a comparatively potent fighting force.

On June 10 Hussein announced a unilateral cease-fire, but Iran's leader, Ayatollah Ruhollah Khomeini (see biography at PEOPLE IN THE NEWS), responded with a stiff new set of demands. Khomeini called for nothing less than the establishment of an Islamic republic in Iraq to replace the secular regime of Hussein and his Arab socialist Ba'ath Party. Iran also demanded $150 billion in repara-

tions from Iraq, as well as condemnation of Iraq as the aggressor by an international tribunal. Ayatollah Hussein Ali Montazeri, a hard-line mullah (Islamic cleric) who was considered a likely successor to the 82-year-old Khomeini as Iran's spiritual leader, went so far as to urge that an Islamic army 20,000,000 strong go forth to "liberate" not only neighboring Iraq but the holy city of Jerusalem as well.

Iranian tanks and troops crossed the Shatt-al-Arab waterway on July 14 and plunged into Iraqi territory toward Basra, a key oil center. But Iraqi troops, who had generally performed poorly in Iran, put up stiff resistance. The Iranian offensive bogged down near the border, after hundreds of Iranian tanks were destroyed and thousands of Iranian troops were killed. Iran attempted a second push across the Iraqi border on Sept. 30, some 100 mi. northeast of Baghdad, but it, too, ground to a halt.

Casualties were heavy throughout the summer offensive. Iraq claimed that 28,000 Iranians had been killed; some Western military analysts estimated the toll at 6000–8000 dead and 20,000–24,000 wounded, missing, or taken prisoner. Losses were particularly severe among youthful religious zealots belonging to Iran's Revolutionary Guards (Pasdaran), who rushed headlong into Iraqi minefields and machine-gun fire shouting Islamic slogans.

Iran's invasion of Iraq stunned and alarmed moderate rulers throughout the Arab world, particularly the oil-rich but militarily weak sheikhdoms and hereditary monarchies of the Persian Gulf. Saudi Arabia, Kuwait, and other Gulf countries had loaned at least $25 billion to Iraq since the start of the war.

Politics and the Economy. Iran's militantly Islamic regime grew increasingly repressive in 1982. Iranian exiles alleged that Iran's prisons held as many as 40,000 political prisoners and that 8000 people had been executed in 1981–82. The regime's principal opposition, the left-wing underground group known as the Mujahedeen, claimed that 15,000 Iranians were executed in the 11 months ending in April, 1982. The mullahs themselves admitted to having executed 4000.

Before a cheering crowd of followers, Ayatollah Ruhollah Khomeini (seated) announces a new military offensive against Iraq. The guiding force of the Iranian revolution, Khomeini continued in 1982 to brand foes of the regime as enemies of Islam.

The most prominent victim of the mullahs' wrath in 1982 was Sadegh Ghotbzadeh, 46, who was executed by a military firing squad in Tehran on the night of Sept. 15. A confidant of Khomeini when the ayatollah lived in exile in France, Ghotbzadeh had become foreign minister after the fall of the shah. During the hostage crisis, he had advocated a negotiated settlement with the United States. Accused of leading a plot to overthrow Iran's regime, the former foreign minister was condemned to death, as were some 70 Iranian army and air force officers implicated in the same alleged conspiracy.

Supported by the largely illiterate masses, the mullahs continued to stamp puritanical Islamic values on Iranian society. For example, in September the Majlis (parliament) passed a law specifically prohibiting kissing for sexual pleasure. Meanwhile, political violence continued to devastate the country. On Oct. 1 at least 60 persons were killed and 700 injured when a huge bomb exploded in Tehran's main square.

Iranian factories limped along at a fraction of their productive capacity in 1982, and many staple food items were in chronic shortage. Iran's oil production was thought to exceed 2,500,000 bbl a day (compared to 6,000,000 bbl under the shah), but Tehran said that it wanted to raise the figure to 3,000,000 bbl. At a meeting in Ecuador in May of the Organization of Petroleum Exporting Countries (OPEC), Iran refused to accept OPEC production limits, and Iranian delegates made bitter personal attacks on other OPEC ministers.

See STATISTICS OF THE WORLD. A.D.

Iraqi soldiers bathe in a canal during a break in fighting against the Iranian forces that invaded Iraq in mid-1982. The Iranian assault soon bogged down.

IRAQ. In 1982 Iraq suffered serious reverses in its protracted war against Iran. The cancellation of a summit meeting of nonaligned nations in Baghdad in September was a bitter blow to Iraqi President Saddam Hussein.

War with Iran. The war that Hussein launched against Iran in September, 1980, in order to make his nation the dominant power in the Persian Gulf region, began going badly for Iraq in the spring of 1982. After months of stalemate, Iran began an offensive on March 22; by the end of May, Iraqi units had been driven out of the salient they had held in western Iran for almost 20 months. Iraq suffered a humiliating defeat at Khorramshahr, a major Iranian oil port that

Iraq had captured early in the war but that Iranian forces recaptured May 22–24 in a swift assault. With his army reeling, Hussein on June 10 proclaimed a unilateral cease-fire. But Iran's militant Islamic leaders rejected the peace gesture, and on July 14 Iranian forces invaded Iraqi territory for the first time in the conflict. The invaders' immediate objective was Basra, an important Iraqi oil center and port southeast of Baghdad. Iran's ultimate aim, however, was nothing less than the overthrow of Hussein and the establishment of an Iranian-style Islamic republic in Iraq. Fortunately for Hussein, Iraqi troops resisted stubbornly, and the Iranian offensive bogged down.

Iran's invasion of Iraq caused deep concern among moderate, pro-Western Arab regimes such as Egypt, Jordan, and the oil-producing Persian Gulf states. The Sudan, a Muslim nation closely allied with Egypt, promised in October to send troops to fight alongside the Iraqis. Egypt supplied Iraq with ammunition and spare parts, and Jordanian "volunteers" were encouraged by their government to join the Iraqi side against Iran.

Effects of the War. The bad news from the war front forced Hussein to scale back sharply his most cherished political and economic ambitions. For months Hussein had followed a guns-and-butter policy. Loans totaling $25 billion from Persian Gulf states such as Saudi Arabia and Kuwait enabled Iraq to press ahead with a massive industrialization and agricultural development program. New, Western-style offices and apartment buildings sprouted all over Baghdad. But the war was costing Iraq an estimated $1 billion a month, and Iraq's oil revenues, once estimated at $30 billion a year, dwindled to around $5 billion. In April Iraq's oil exports suffered a severe cutback when Syria, an ally of Iran, closed the Iraqi oil pipeline running through Syrian territory to the Mediterranean Sea. Soon after that Hussein, for the first time, proclaimed the need for austerity on the home front, and in June he carried out major reshuffles of the cabinet, the ruling Ba'ath Party leadership, and the Revolutionary Command Council, which is Iraq's supreme political body.

Hussein's international prestige suffered when it was announced in August that a summit meeting of nonaligned nations scheduled for Baghdad the following month had been canceled for "security reasons" and would be held instead in New Delhi in 1983. The Iraqi government had invested vast sums in preparation for the meeting, erecting luxury hotels and modern conference sites in Baghdad. As host of the gathering, Hussein would have become unofficial spokesman for the nonaligned bloc for the ensuing three years. He thus would have established himself as a Third World leader of the first rank. Despite this and other setbacks, there was no evidence that Hussein was in any immediate danger of losing his grip on power in Iraq.

See STATISTICS OF THE WORLD.   A.D.

IRELAND, NORTHERN. See GREAT BRITAIN.

Beleaguered Iraqi Leader

In September, 1980, Saddam Hussein, president of Iraq, made his bid for preeminence in the Arab world by invading neighboring Iran. By mid-1982, 22 months later, Hussein's forces had been expelled and Iranian troops, exhorted by Ayatollah Ruhollah Khomeini, had pushed into Iraq, vowing to overthrow Hussein. This turn of events threatened to end Hussein's 14-year iron grip over his country, but his past indicated he would be equal to the challenge. Involved in his youth in an abortive coup, he was wounded but cut a bullet out of his leg with a penknife and escaped. As the power behind the scenes from 1968 to 1979 and as head of state thereafter, he dealt ruthlessly with all opposition, executing some of his closest comrades.

Saddam Hussein

Garret FitzGerald returned to power as prime minister of Ireland in December, following parliamentary elections—the second in 1982. Deteriorating economic conditions resulted in political instability.

IRELAND, REPUBLIC OF. A deteriorating economy provoked more political instability in Ireland in 1982, as two governments fell in their attempts to put austerity measures through parliament. Called to the polls twice in nine months, a weary electorate was unable to decide conclusively between the country's two major parties.

On Jan. 27 the seven-month-old minority cabinet of Prime Minister Garret FitzGerald, leader of the Fine Gael Party, was evicted from office by vote of the Dáil (lower house of parliament). It was replaced in March by a Fianna Fáil government headed by Charles J. Haughey.

The FitzGerald coalition fell after the Dáil voted 82–81 against its austerity budget. The government's budget had called for deep cuts in public spending and large tax increases, including a raise, to 30 percent, in the standard sales tax. FitzGerald insisted that stern measures were needed in the face of rising unemployment, double-digit inflation, and a $15 billion foreign debt. New par-

liamentary elections were called, the second in seven months.

In the elections, held on Feb. 18, Fianna Fáil increased its strength in the 166-member Dáil from 78 seats to 81, 3 short of the majority needed for parliamentary control. The strength of FitzGerald's Fine Gael Party dropped from 65 seats to 63. Fine Gael's partner in the outgoing coalition, the Labour Party, retained its 15 seats.

On March 9, after more than two weeks of negotiations with independent and minority-party members, largely over ways of modifying austerity demands, Haughey was able to win enough support in the Dáil to be elected prime minister, by a vote of 86 to 79. On March 26 the new government presented its budget. It differed from the FitzGerald budget in several respects. It provided for new government spending of $157,000,000, primarily for construction, and it proposed several tax changes, among them the exemption of clothing and footwear from the value-added tax.

Although James Joyce left his native Dublin at the age of 22, the Irish author depicted his native city in many works, most prominently in *Ulysses*. Dublin reciprocated in 1982 by celebrating the 100th anniversary of Joyce's birth on June 16, the day Joyce called "Bloomsday" because on that date in 1904, Leopold Bloom, the hero of *Ulysses*, wanders through Joyce's imagined city. Irish radio broadcast a nonstop 31-hr. reading of the novel, scenes were performed on the streets, and scholars gathered to discuss Joyce's works. Crowds also gathered at the Ormond Hotel, where beer was offered at 1904 prices. "I don't know anything about Joyce," said one man, "but I do know you can get a pint here for tuppence."

By fall the economy had shown few, if any, signs of improvement. The annual rate of inflation was 17 percent; unemployment was 13 percent of the labor force. The Haughey government, with only tenuous support in parliament, met growing dissatisfaction within its own ranks.

In August it came under a cloud when authorities revealed that a house guest of Attorney General Patrick Connolly had been arrested for murder. Connolly resigned. Two more cabinet ministers resigned in October, and 22 members of Fianna Fáil attempted unsuccessfully to oust Haughey as party leader, and thus as prime minister. On Nov. 4 a no-confidence vote in the Dáil brought down the government.

New elections were held on Nov. 24. Fianna Fáil led with 75 seats, but Fine Gael was close behind, with 70; Labour trailed with 16. FitzGerald formed a new government with Labour support on Dec. 14.

As a member of the European Community (EC), Ireland joined in the EC decision to impose economic sanctions against Argentina on April 16, following Argentina's occupation of the British-held Falkland Islands. Ireland, along with Italy, lifted the sanctions on May 24, however, an action that angered the British government.

See STATISTICS OF THE WORLD.   L.A.S.

ISRAEL. Israel's invasion of Lebanon overshadowed all other events during 1982. It raised questions about Israel's relations with the United States, shook the foundations of Prime Minister Menachem Begin's governing coalition (see biography at PEOPLE IN THE NEWS), and moved hundreds of thousands of Israeli citizens to protest their government's policy.

Operation "Peace for Galilee." The de facto cease-fire in Lebanon negotiated by U.S. envoy Philip C. Habib in July, 1981, between Israel and the Palestine Liberation Organization (PLO) nearly collapsed on April 21, when Israeli planes heavily bombed Palestinian outposts following the death of an Israeli soldier by a land mine in southern Lebanon. The crisis came to a head six weeks later, with the attempted assassination of Israel's ambassador to Great Britain, Shlomo Argov. Although the PLO disclaimed responsibility for the attack on Argov, Israeli jets again struck at PLO positions in Lebanon, and the PLO retaliated with a rocket and artillery bombardment of northern Israel. On June 6 Israeli troops crossed the Lebanese border, ostensibly to clear the PLO from a 25-mi.-deep zone of southern Lebanon. But the Israelis, meeting little resistance, did not stop at the 25-mi. limit. Instead, they pushed forward, reaching the outskirts of Beirut in less than a week.

The operation the Israelis called Peace for Galilee also led to fighting with Syrian forces in Lebanon. Between 60 and 80 Soviet-built fighter planes, nearly all of Syria's antiaircraft missiles in the Bekaa Valley, and scores of tanks were destroyed in the most severe setback suffered by Damascus since the 1973 war with Israel. As the fighting progressed, Israel's objectives were extended to include the departure of Syria as well as the PLO from Lebanon.

By the end of June, Israel held most of the territory south of the road linking Beirut with the Syrian border, except for Syrian outposts in the Bekaa Valley. PLO and Syrian forces in west Beirut were besieged, and Israeli troops controlled the area surrounding the presidential palace. From July onward, the Israelis intermittently banned the entry into west

Before Israel could fulfill its peace treaty with Egypt by withdrawing from the Sinai Peninsula, it had to remove forcibly 2500 protesters from Yamit, the most prosperous of several Jewish settlements in the Sinai. Israeli troops broke their resistance by spraying them with firefighting foam, then removed the diehards by putting them in cages hoisted away by cranes.

Beirut of food, water, and fuel. Even medical supplies were strictly limited.

While pursuing its military objectives, Israel ignored several United Nations Security Council and General Assembly resolutions calling for an Israeli withdrawal. Negotiations for a PLO pullout from Lebanon were conducted not through the U.N. but through Habib, who shuttled between Beirut and Jerusalem, with side trips to other Middle Eastern capitals. In mid-August an agreement was reached for a cease-fire and total withdrawal of some 14,000 Palestinian and Syrian fighters from Beirut, under supervision of an international force from the U.S., France, and Italy. The evacuation proceeded smoothly, and by Sept. 1 was officially complete. Israel

then declared that it would not leave Lebanon until all other foreign troops were evacuated and until Lebanon agreed to a bilateral security arrangement.

Massacre in Beirut. On Sept. 15 Israeli troops suddenly moved into west Beirut, following the assassination of Lebanese President-elect Bashir Gemayel. As chief of the Maronite Christian Phalangist forces, Gemayel was closely allied with Israel, which for several years had been supplying his men with military and other assistance. During Operation Peace for Galilee, Phalangist troops collaborated with Israeli forces. Israel authorized the Phalangists to enter Palestinian refugee camps in west Beirut to "cleanse" them of any remaining PLO forces. By Sept. 19 it was revealed that Phalangist forces had massacred hundreds of Palestinian men, women, and children trapped in the camps.

The massacre fed rising criticism of the war both within the Begin government and among the public at large. Reservists who had been at the front were among the leaders of the antiwar movement, which reached its climax on Sept. 25 in Tel Aviv, when an estimated 350,000 Israelis (nearly 10 percent of the population) took part in the largest political rally in the nation's history. Within the cabinet, Defense Minister Ariel Sharon was criticized by several ministers for initiating important operations without cabinet approval. Many Israeli newspapers, army officers, and opposition political spokesmen held Begin and Sharon at least indirectly responsible for the Beirut carnage.

Initially, Prime Minister Begin labeled as a "blood libel" the accusation that Israel was in any way to blame for the massacre, and he refused to authorize the appointment of a full-scale, independent judicial investigation. But after Energy Minister Yitzhak Berman and several other officials resigned in protest, the cabinet authorized Supreme Court Chief Justice Yitzhak Kahan to head a formal commission of inquiry. The three-member panel, which began gathering evidence in October, was not expected to conclude its inquiry until early 1983.

Costs and Consequences. The war, which Prime Minister Begin said in October had established, "for the first time," a state of security on all of Israel's borders, exacted a high price militarily, economically, and diplomatically as well as politically. By early October the number of dead was 368, with nearly 2400 wounded. Another 75 Israelis were killed in southern Lebanon on Nov. 11 when a military headquarters building collapsed. The economic costs were estimated at more than $3 billion, with about $2 billion (more than 10 percent of the annual gross national product) necessary to replace war matériel. Tourism, one of Israel's major foreign currency sources, fell by more than 20 percent. To help pay for the war, subsidies on basic foods such as milk, eggs, and bread were cut, and a special 4 percent income tax in the form of a compulsory loan was imposed. The annual rate of inflation, which had decreased to 101.5 percent in 1981, shot back up to 130 percent. Even so, the gross national product was expected to rise by 2 or 3 percent in 1982, and the unemployment rate was less than 6 percent.

The war rekindled opposition to the government among Arabs on the West Bank and Gaza Strip, as well as on the Golan Heights, which Israel had annexed in December, 1981. Even before June, military authorities had increased the severity of their rule in the occupied areas. Curfews and economic reprisals were imposed on striking Druze inhabitants in Golan who refused to comply with regulations resulting from annexation. On Sept. 5, four days after U.S. President Ronald Reagan announced a plan calling for "self-government for the Palestinians of the West Bank and Gaza in association with Jordan," the Begin government authorized $18,500,000 to build new Israeli settlements in the occupied lands. By a vote of 50–36, the Knesset (parliament) on Sept. 8 endorsed Begin's rejection of the Reagan peace plan.

Relations with Egypt were soured by events in Lebanon, and further autonomy negotiations were suspended despite Israel's final withdrawal from the Sinai Peninsula on April 25. The withdrawal, in compliance with the Israel-Egypt peace treaty of 1979, aroused intense opposition from fervent nationalists. Several times during March and April the government had to use military force in Sinai to dislodge Jewish settlers unwilling to leave, although many were paid a large subsidy for their losses.

See STATISTICS OF THE WORLD. *See also* LEBANON; MIDDLE EAST; MILITARY AND NAVAL AFFAIRS.   D.P.

Israel's Tough Commander
A hard-nosed, hard-line nationalist, Defense Minister Ariel ("Arik") Sharon, 54, staked his political career on the invasion of Lebanon in June—"Arik's war," as a senior official told reporters. Sharon, who owned a 1000-acre ranch in the Negev desert, was born at a farm cooperative near Tel Aviv. Severely wounded in the 1948 struggle for independence, he became a career officer, commanding forces in the 1956, 1967, and 1973 wars, as well as a counterterrorist unit in the early 1950's. While winning praise for his daring and strategic brilliance, he was accused by his detractors of recklessness, brutality, and insubordination. His aggressive prosecution of the Lebanese campaign at times exceeded government policy, and many Israelis held him responsible for the massacre of Palestinians by Christian militiamen in mid-September.

Ariel Sharon

ITALY. Amintore Fanfani, 74, formed a new Italian government on Dec. 1, 1982, following the failure of the previous prime minister, Giovanni Spadolini, to resolve disagreements between his coalition partners over austerity measures. Despite formidable political and economic problems, including a bank scandal that put a strain on relations between Rome and the Vatican, the government assumed a more assertive role in foreign affairs and stepped up its campaign against terrorism.

Politics. Spadolini and his five-party coalition—composed of members of the dominant Christian Democrats, the Socialists, the Liberals, Social Democrats, and Spadolini's own small Republican Party—fell for the first time on Aug. 7, when the Socialists withdrew their support because the Christian Democrats rejected a Socialist-supported proposal to impose a higher tax on oil companies. President Sandro Pertini, although himself a Socialist, ordered Spadolini to try to put together a new government. On Aug. 23 the Republican leader announced the formation of Italy's 42nd post-World War II government, consisting of the same ministers who had served in the previous cabinet.

Once again divisions occurred over economic policy. While the Christian Democrats favored deep cuts in public spending, the Socialists advocated spending increases to stimulate the economy. On Nov. 13 Spadolini resigned for the second time. After about two weeks of feverish negotiations, veteran Christian Democrat Fanfani formed a coalition of Christian Democrats, Socialists, Social Democrats, and Liberals. The four partners commanded a majority of 353 seats in the 630-member Chamber of Deputies. Fanfani, who was serving as president of the Senate (upper house of parliament), had been prime minister four times before.

The Economy. An annual inflation rate of 17 percent, an unemployment figure of more than 2,000,000, declining industrial production, and increased public borrowing, reaching 15 percent of the gross national product, highlighted Italy's serious economic plight in late autumn. The Fanfani government put forth a 28-point austerity program that called for, among other measures, a drastic reduction in public spending and a two-year wage freeze. Unions voiced their opposition by threatening a general strike.

Terrorism. The dreaded Red Brigades were dealt a crippling blow in the wake of their daring abduction of U.S. Brig. Gen. James L. Dozier in Verona on Dec. 17, 1981. Special antiterrorist commandos raided their hiding place in Padua on Jan. 28, 1982, and rescued the general, a staff officer of the North Atlantic Treaty Organization, after 42 days of captivity. The police had assigned an unprecedented 5000 agents to the case, and some 375 suspected leftist terrorists had been arrested since Dozier's kidnapping. After a two-week trial in Verona, an Italian court on March 25 convicted 17 terrorists for the abduction; almost half of them, who were still at large, were tried in absentia.

On Aug. 5 a court convicted 87 members of the Front Line, a radical group associated with the Red Brigades, for armed assaults perpetrated from 1976 to 1979. On Oct. 3, police arrested ten Red Brigades suspects in Naples.

Other terrorist outrages shocked Italy. Mafia killings of prominent officials in Sicily culminated in the murder in Palermo of Communist Deputy Pio La Torre, an outspoken opponent of the Mafia, on April 30 and of Gen. Carlo Alberto Dalla Chiesa and his wife on Sept. 3. The general, one of Italy's top police officials, had been named on May 1 as prefect of Palermo to lead the fight against the Mafia. Prime Minister Spadolini appointed Emanuele de Francesco as the general's successor and invested him with the power to tap telephones, search bank records, and interrogate witnesses in private, but by late November 130 people had been murdered in Sicily during 1982.

On Oct. 9 five gunmen hurled grenades and fired submachine guns at Jewish worshipers as they were leaving Rome's main synagogue; one 2-year-old was killed and 38 other people were injured. Police searched for five suspects, reportedly of Middle Eastern origin. The assault prompted Jewish leaders to condemn Italy's, and the Vatican's, reception of Yasir Arafat, head of the Palestine

U.S. Army Brig. Gen. James Dozier arrives at a church to attend services with his family after Italian commandos rescued him from 42 days of captivity by the terrorist Red Brigades. Seventeen persons were convicted of responsibility for the abduction.

Liberation Organization (PLO), after the PLO's evacuation from Beirut.

Bank Scandal. On June 18 Roberto Calvi, president of the Banco Ambrosiano of Milan, Italy's largest privately owned banking group, was found dead in London, an apparent suicide. Soon after, it was learned that Banco Ambrosiano had made unsecured loans of about $1.3 billion, primarily to Panamanian- and Bahamian-registered companies indirectly owned by the bank. In July a Luxembourg subsidiary of the bank defaulted on some $400,000,000 in foreign loans it had received. Banco Ambrosiano was liquidated and reconstituted on Aug. 6, apparently to put its debts, including those of the Luxembourg bank, out of the reach of creditors.

The unsecured loans were endorsed by the head of the Vatican's bank in a so-called letter of patronage, but the Vatican, which held an interest in Banco Ambrosiano, disclaimed responsibility. Reports of organized crime involvement added to the scandal, which hurt the entire Italian financial system.

Foreign Affairs. A member of the European Community (EC), Italy joined in the economic sanctions imposed by the EC after Argentina occupied the British-held Falkland Islands in April. On May 24, however, Italy, along with Ireland, withdrew the sanctions. (Argentina has a large population of Italian origin.)

In August Italian troops were sent to Lebanon to serve with U.S. and French peacekeeping forces in Beirut. The Italian contribution grew to 1100 soldiers in September.

The arrest in Rome in November of a Bulgarian airline representative, part of the continuing investigation into the 1981 assassination attempt against Pope John Paul II, threatened to affect Italian-Bulgarian relations. Bulgaria sternly protested the arrest.

On July 11 Italians celebrated the national team's victory in the World Cup soccer tournament in Madrid. Italy defeated West Germany 3–1.

See STATISTICS OF THE WORLD.   J.N.

IVORY COAST. *See* STATISTICS OF THE WORLD.

J

JAMAICA. *See* STATISTICS OF THE WORLD.

JAPAN. Yasuhiro Nakasone (see biography at PEOPLE IN THE NEWS) became prime minister of Japan on Nov. 26, 1982, succeeding Zenko Suzuki, who announced on Oct. 12 that he would step down. Suzuki's decision followed party factional disputes and growing criticism of his economic policies during a year in which the Japanese economy performed poorly.

Politics. Nakasone, 64, director general of the Administrative Management Agency, was backed to succeed Suzuki by the two largest factions of the ruling Liberal-Democratic Party (LDP), including Suzuki's own faction. In a victory for the conservative mainstream of the party, he received 58 percent of the mail-in ballots cast by eligible members of the party in a four-candidate contest. The LDP parliamentary members then elected him party president, thus making him the party's candidate for prime minister. Since the LDP, which had been in power since 1955, held majorities in both houses of the parliament, Nakasone was easily elected prime minister.

Nakasone's cabinet of 22 members included 6 supporters from the party faction led by Kakuei Tanaka, a former prime minister who was standing trial on charges arising from a bribery scandal involving Lockheed Corp. Although he was forced to give up his party membership after he was indicted, Tanaka nonetheless continued to be a powerful figure.

Nakasone said that he would give priority to increasing defense spending and improving relations with the United States, issues that took on growing political importance in 1982. In April 158 government and academic leaders called for Tokyo to seek a revision of the 1960 U.S.-Japan security treaty, in order for Japan to take on more responsibility for its own defense.

The government's budget proposal for the fiscal year beginning in April, 1983, released in July, called for a 7.3 percent increase in defense spending and for cutting most other programs by 5 percent. This action was seen as a direct response to growing pressure at home and from the U.S. for Japan to rearm, and to mounting apprehension among government leaders over the Soviet military buildup in the Far East. Japan's level of military spending remained below the 1 percent ceiling of the gross national product (GNP) imposed by the 1947 constitution and was the lowest of all major industrialized nations.

The Economy. The pressure for accelerated defense spending came in a year when Japan's economy performed poorly. During the fiscal year ending on March 31, 1982, Japan's GNP grew by only 2.7 percent, the lowest annual growth figure since 1974. The decline was attributed in part to a slowdown in exports resulting from the worldwide recession, low consumer spending, and a drop in housing construction. The number of unemployed reached a postwar high, although the unemployment rate was only 2.2 percent of the labor force. The government revised its economic growth forecast for the 1982–83 fiscal year from 5.2 to only 3.4 percent.

After several years of substantial deficits, foreign trade showed a $9.2 billion surplus for the fiscal year ending in March. In trade with the U.S., Japan's surplus stood at a record $14.4 billion, as a result of a 20 percent gain in exports to the U.S. Trade with the European Community (EC) registered a surplus of $10.2 billion. In early 1982 the U.S. and the EC began to press Japan to reduce its import barriers. Although Tokyo removed tariffs from a number of industrial goods and reduced levies on selected farm and fishery products, U.S. authorities were guarded in their reactions. Forecasts from Washington suggested that the Japanese measures were mere palliatives. These forecasts indicated a possible Japanese surplus in trade with the U.S. of up to $20 billion in the fiscal year ending in March, 1983.

Trade issues were an important feature of Japan's foreign relations in 1982. Here Japanese farmers picket the U.S. embassy in Tokyo to protest American demands for the liberalization of quotas on farm imports.

Foreign Affairs. On March 26 U.S. Secretary of Defense Caspar Weinberger, during a visit to Japan, voiced a proposal that Tokyo build up its military forces to enable Japan to defend sea lanes and air space within 1000 mi. of its home islands. Weinberger observed that this required increased defense spending substantially above the modest increases in the 1982–83 austerity budget. He further urged the Japanese to achieve self-sufficiency in defense by 1990. On Sept. 30 Weinberger and Japanese Defense Minister Soichiro Ito signed an agreement to deploy U.S. Air Force F-16 fighter-bombers in northern Honshu, only 350 mi. from Soviet territory.

Angry outcries from Japan's Asian neighbors followed the publication, in July, of Japanese history textbooks that minimized Japan's military aggression and atrocities committed prior to and during World War II. Protests from China, Taiwan, South Korea, and other Asian countries that were formerly occupied by Japan linked the rewritten history to a resurgence of Japanese militarism.

Cabinet reaction in Japan was mixed. Officials pointed out that it was too late to correct the 1,300,000 copies already printed and due for distribution to schools in April, 1983. On Aug. 26 Chief Cabinet Secretary Kiichi Miyazawa, the spokesman for Prime Minister Suzuki, promised that "the government will undertake on its own responsibility to make necessary amendments." He failed to mention when or how this was to be done, although officials noted that the earliest time was about 1985. Until then, schools were instructed to teach such versions of Japan's role in World War II as were acceptable to the country's Asian neighbors.

Peking promptly rejected these moves as inadequate. The dispute was tentatively settled in early September, when both China and South Korea conditionally approved Japanese efforts toward amending the offensive passages.

See STATISTICS OF THE WORLD.　　T.L.K.

JORDAN. Geographically and politically, Jordan, under King Hussein, played a pivotal role in 1982 in the search for peace in the Middle East and in the region's complex rivalries.

Hussein, who had consistently refused to join the Camp David peace process, appeared to be moving closer to entering future negotiations on the Palestinian problem. Hussein labeled as "a very constructive and a very positive move" U.S. President Ronald Reagan's Sept. 1 peace proposal, which called for Palestinian self-rule "in association with Jordan." The Jordanian monarch also said that he intended to play "a very active part" in promoting peace in the area. Although the Administration was encouraged by Hussein's response, the king—never a risk taker—maintained that he still lacked a mandate from the other Arab states and from the Palestine Liberation Organization (PLO) to negotiate on behalf of the Palestinian people. The Israeli government had consistently refused to recognize the PLO but had indicated willingness to negotiate the future of the Palestinians with Jordan, which has a large Palestinian population.

Hussein appeared to seek a reconciliation with the PLO, with which Jordan's relations had long been strained. Jordan took in several hundred Palestinian guerrillas after the PLO was forced to evacuate Beirut following the Israeli siege of the Lebanese capital. On Oct. 6 Hussein announced an amnesty for hundreds of Palestinians accused by Jordan of committing "crimes against state security" during the 1970 civil war. Less than a week later, Hussein received PLO chairman Yasir Arafat in Amman, the first meeting there between the two former archenemies in a decade. Their talks, which dealt in part with the Reagan peace plan, were reportedly inconclusive.

Hussein also played a role in the Iran-Iraq war, turning the Jordanian port of 'Aqaba into a supply lifeline to Iraq. Imports through 'Aqaba—largely routed overland to Iraq—rose by 90 percent in 1981; during the first three months of 1982 they increased 40 percent over the same period a year earlier. At the urging of King Hussein, hundreds of young Jordanians enlisted in the war against Iran.

See STATISTICS OF THE WORLD.   A.D.

K

KAMPUCHEA. See CAMBODIA.
KANSAS. See STATISTICS OF THE WORLD.
KENTUCKY. See STATISTICS OF THE WORLD.
KENYA. On Aug. 1, 1982, a group of junior air force officers, charging that the government of President Daniel arap Moi of Kenya was "corrupt" and "dictatorial," tried to overthrow it. The attempted coup, the first in Kenya's 19-year history as an independent nation, was supported by university students and urban workers. Fighting broke out in Nairobi and at the Nanyuki air force base, about 125 mi. north of the capital, but after initial rebel successes, the army rallied to Moi, and the rebellion was crushed by evening. During the brief rebellion more than

500 people were believed killed; more than 3000, including almost the entire 2100-member air force, were arrested.

Looting, however, aimed primarily at Asian merchants, continued until Aug. 4, with losses estimated at more than $100,000,000. In a speech in February Moi had accused some Asian businessmen of currency smuggling and corruption. His remarks caused consternation among Kenya's Asian—mostly Indian and Pakistani—community of about 100,000.

Discontent with Moi's rule had been growing among many Kenyans in the face of a faltering economy, apparently widespread corruption, and political repression. Another alienating issue was Kenya's close ties with the United States. The Moi government had been unsuccessful in reversing the country's high unemployment and inflation. At the same time Moi's Kenya African National Union (KANU) had solidified its power by expelling opponents, including former Vice-President Oginga Odinga (who reportedly had been considering forming a socialist-oriented opposition party). On June 9 Kenya became a one-party state by unanimous vote of parliament. (All members of parliament were from KANU, the only opposition party having been dissolved in 1969.)

In the aftermath of the coup Moi took further steps to retard political opposition. Military trials occurred throughout the fall as air force members were sentenced for their roles in the rebellion. In late September an editor of the *Sunday Standard,* a dean of the University of Nairobi, and Oginga Odinga's son were arrested and charged with treason.

On Oct. 1 the International Monetary Fund suspended the remaining $67,600,000 of a loan to Kenya approved in January. It cited the lack of serious reform efforts as the reason. On Oct. 5 Moi, reacting to charges of corruption, announced the formation of a committee to establish a code of conduct for government officials.

See STATISTICS OF THE WORLD.   J.T.S.

KHMER REPUBLIC. *See* CAMBODIA.

KIRIBATI. *See* STATISTICS OF THE WORLD.

KOREA, DEMOCRATIC PEOPLE'S REPUBLIC OF, *or* **NORTH KOREA.** The secrecy surrounding affairs in North Korea continued to baffle foreign observers in 1982. President Kim Il Sung, North Korea's ruler since 1948, and the first Marxist-Leninist leader to espouse the concept of hereditary leadership, went on grooming his son Kim Jong Il to become his eventual successor. Some foreign analysts believed that the president planned to use his 70th birthday, on April 15, to announce a major promotion for his son. When he did not, there was speculation about possible opposition within President Kim's family against the further advancement of Kim Jong Il.

General elections for the Supreme People's Assembly were held on Feb. 28. It was claimed that every vote had been cast for the 615 candidates who were on the single official list.

From meager evidence gleaned by outside experts, North Korea's economy remained seriously troubled in 1982. The government was careful to meet its obligations to Japan, with which it does $500,000,000 worth of business annually. For the second time in recent years, however, North Korea fell behind in its payments to Western creditors.

Although reluctant to align itself either with China or the Soviet Union, North Korea appeared to tilt slightly toward China in 1982. In September President Kim paid his first visit in seven years to Peking, where he was warmly greeted. Contrary to Soviet wishes, Kim agreed to allow China to use the port of Ch'ŏngjin, near the Soviet border, to transship export products bound for Japanese markets. Analysts regarded the visit as the forerunner of a further pro-China tilt in North Korea's foreign policy.

After rejecting in January a South Korean proposal for reunification, the North Korean government issued its own proposal in February. The statement called for a conference of 100 political figures, representing both sides, to discuss "reunification and national salvation, irrespective of their past doings."

See STATISTICS OF THE WORLD.   R.J.C.

KOREA, REPUBLIC OF, *or* **SOUTH KOREA.** Despite a financial scandal that seriously damaged his image as a fighter against corruption, President Chun Doo Hwan retained a firm grasp on power in South Korea in 1982. The country continued its recovery from the economic recession of 1980.

Dissidents. In early 1982 Chun lifted a curfew that had been in effect since 1945, and he also abolished government-enforced student dress codes. On March 3 Chun reduced the prison sentence of South Korea's leading dissident, Kim Dae Jung, from life to 20 years. Moreover, Chun either freed, or granted reduced sentences to, almost 3000 other prisoners. Critics, however, pointed out that few of those released were political prisoners. Another amnesty, granted on Aug. 15, freed 1251 convicted criminals and 35 political dissidents. On Dec. 24 Chun freed 1200 prison-

Despite the world recession, South Korea was one of several Far East countries registering satisfactory economic growth in 1982. The new $500,000,000 Okpo Shipyard is among a number of new heavy industry projects.

ers, among them Kim and 47 other political detainees. Kim came to the U.S.

In February and March Christian activists had challenged Chun to release jailed political dissidents, charging the military-backed government with sanctioning widespread torture of prisoners. Protesters also demanded a revision of labor laws that all but prevented workers from organizing. On March 18 one Korean died when arsonists set fire to the American Cultural Center in Pusan. Following a nationwide search, the government put 16 people on trial in June; all were convicted and two were sentenced to death.

Financial Scandal. In May a major scandal came to light in Seoul, the capital, when a former member of parliament, his wife, and other influential persons were charged in connection with a fraudulent multimillion-dollar moneylending scheme that threatened the solvency of several industrial firms. The scheme involved $79,000,000 in cash loans to six companies, in return for bank-guaranteed promissory notes amounting to $361,000,000, issued on the understanding that they would not be cashed. More than half of these notes were sold for cash, however. When banks stopped honoring them, a credit crisis seriously affected South Korea's money market.

An investigation led to the trial and conviction of 31 persons in all, variously charged with fraud, embezzlement, and bribery. Most damaging to the Chun government were the charges against an uncle of the president's wife. The uncle, who had earlier been appointed by Chun to head the governmental Korean Mining Promotion Corp., received a four-year prison term. Although few people thought that Chun himself was involved in wrongdoing, the president sought to restore public confidence by replacing most of his cabinet. Many South Koreans nevertheless remained convinced, despite a lack of evidence, that some of the money had been funneled into political party coffers.

The Economy. During the 1970's South Korea's consistently high growth rate earned the country, along with Taiwan and Singapore, the designation of "newly industrialized country." The world recession, however, deflated the South Korean economy in 1980, although it recovered in 1981, with a growth rate of 7.1 percent. In 1982 the real growth in gross national product was expected to reach about 7 percent. Inflation was down, and South Koreans looked forward to another period of rapid economic expansion.

Foreign Affairs. In 1982 South Korea strengthened its ties with the United States, its major ally. Vice-President George Bush and Secretary of Defense Caspar Weinberger visited Seoul during the year and pledged U.S. support for South Korea. Chun tried unsuccessfully to draw North Korea into meaningful talks. He also made friendly gestures toward China and the Soviet Union, and he traveled to Africa to reinforce South Korea's position in the Third World.

See STATISTICS OF THE WORLD.   R.J.C.

KUWAIT. A wealthy, stable, yet highly vulnerable Persian Gulf country, Kuwait was increasingly fearful in 1982 of being caught up in the Iran-Iraq war. A next-door neighbor of both combatants, Kuwait feared that an Iranian victory would upset the balance of power in the region and unleash a dangerous tide of Islamic fundamentalism. Kuwait had lent Iraq some $6 billion since the start of the war. That made it a conspicuous target for threats from Iran. In the spring, Tehran let it be known that Iran would consider itself at war with Kuwait if Kuwait did not stop supporting Iraq.

Despite Kuwait's vast oil wealth—the people enjoy one of the highest per capita incomes in the world—the government in April announced an austerity program involving cutbacks in subsidies. Oil provides 92.5 percent of government revenues. But with a world oil surplus, Kuwait's oil output fell in 1982 to an estimated 650,000 bbl a day, the lowest level since the 1950's. The budget for the fiscal year ending June 30, 1983, anticipated petroleum income at about $10.4 billion, down 42 percent from the previous year. Because of falling oil revenues, Kuwait expected its first trade deficit in modern times, from $2 billion to $3 billion.

Scandal struck Kuwait in August when a period of irresponsible speculation ended with the collapse of the over-the-counter stock exchange. The government established a rescue fund of $2 billion in order to limit the impact on the economy.

See STATISTICS OF THE WORLD.   A.D.

L

LABOR. Mounting joblessness brought on by an entrenched recession dominated news of labor in the United States in 1982. Workers settled for smaller wage gains than in the past; in some cases they received no pay boosts at all.

Unemployment. The nation's seasonally adjusted unemployment rate passed the double-digit level in September and reached 10.8 percent of the labor force in November. These were the highest jobless levels since 1940, when the U.S. was recovering from the Great Depression. Hardest hit in 1982 were workers in the durable-goods manufacturing sector of the economy. Various labor force experts believed that employment in manufacturing would not pick up significantly even after the recession ended because of long-term changes in the U.S. economic structure. These changes included competition from abroad and increasing automation of U.S. industry.

The number of jobless Americans totaled nearly 12,000,000 in November, over 4,000,000 more than when the recession took hold in the late summer of 1981. Statisticians said that it was difficult to draw analogies between the recession of 1982 and the depression of the 1930's, mainly because no official job data and no monthly figures were collected by the government in the earlier era.

Settlements. In the first nine months of 1982, the major collective bargaining agreements in the private sector provided pay boosts averaging 3.8 percent in the first contract year, less than half the 7.7 percent average first-year wage gains won by the same workers in their previous collective bargaining agreements. By September at least 85 separate labor agreements had been reached containing cost-cutting union concessions aimed at bolstering job security. The once mighty United Automobile Workers (UAW) and International Brotherhood of Teamsters set the year's bargaining pace by granting major economic concessions to management.

The UAW sanctioned broad-ranging wage and benefit "givebacks" in negotiating new two-and-a-half-year accords with the Ford Motor Co. and General Motors Corp. In the

Unemployed rubber tire plant workers listen in Philadelphia to plans for unemployment benefits. By late 1982 the jobless rate had exceeded 10 percent of the U.S. labor force. Hardest hit were blue-collar workers in durable-goods manufacturing.

new contracts auto workers gave up annual wage increases and nine paid days off a year, and deferred cost-of-living increases. But auto workers balked at making similar concessions to the Chrysler Corp., which had won substantial concessions to avoid bankruptcy in an earlier bargaining situation. In December Chrysler workers accepted an 11-month contract that gave them a 3 percent wage increase and a cost-of-living raise.

Some 300,000 Teamsters truckers and warehouse workers accepted a 37-month accord with the financially strained unionized trucking industry on March 1. The Teamsters agreed to forgo wage increases for at least two years, settling for continuation of cost-of-living raises. The agreement provided for reopening the pact in the third year if conditions in the trucking industry improved or declined further.

Toward the end of the year, management and labor in the depressed U.S. steel industry were searching for a new contract agreement that would help both sides survive a welter of problems resulting from the recession and heightened international competition.

The United Rubber Workers signed new three-year contracts with the four largest U.S.

tiremakers. Although there was no general wage increase, the existing cost-of-living formula was retained, and improvements were made in insurance, health, and medical benefits and in funding for supplemental unemployment benefits. It was the first settlement without a strike in the industry since 1965.

Strikes. Because of lessened corporate profits and high unemployment, strike activity was generally at a low ebb in 1982.

The Brotherhood of Locomotive Engineers conducted a four-day walkout against many of the nation's railroads in September. U.S. President Ronald Reagan had invoked emergency provisions of the Railway Labor Act to forestall the strike by some 26,000 engineers in July. But at the end of a 60-day cooling-off period, the engineers idled virtually all privately owned railroads on Sept. 19. Reagan won congressional enactment of emergency legislation imposing a fact-finding board's proposed settlement, thereby forcing an end to the strike.

Left unresolved was the issue that had precipitated the walkout—the engineers' fears that they would lose their 15 to 20 percent pay differential over other rail workers. They objected particularly to a clause in the contract that called for a strike moratorium.

The National Football League Players Association, following a course pursued by professional baseball players in 1981, walked out on Sept. 21 and stayed out until Nov. 16. It was the first strike within the actual playing season in the league's 63-year history, and for a time it threatened cancellation of the season. The strike ended with agreement on a five-year contract providing substantial salary, bonus, and benefit increases. However, the players failed to win one important objective—a fixed percentage of the owners' gross revenues or revenues from television. *See also* SPORTS.

Court Decisions. The Supreme Court handed down several decisions important to labor in 1982. The Court held on April 5 that seniority systems were legal as long as they had not been adopted with the intention of discriminating against minorities or women. On June 14 the High Court ruled that a labor union could prohibit candidates for union office from accepting campaign funds from outside sources. On April 20 the Court ruled unanimously that the International Longshore-

men's Association violated federal law in 1980 when it took part in a secondary boycott for political reasons by refusing to handle Soviet cargo after the Soviet invasion of Afghanistan.

Job Training Bill. The job training program funded under the Comprehensive Employment and Training Act of 1973 expired on Sept. 30, 1982. Congress enacted—and Reagan signed—a scaled-back program designed to provide training to some 1,000,000 people in fiscal 1983. The new bill turned most responsibility for the training programs over to the states, through a system of block grants. None of the funds would go for public service jobs.

AFL-CIO. On Feb. 15 the executive council of the American Federation of Labor and Congress of Industrial Organizations (AFL-CIO), meeting in Bal Harbour, Fla., endorsed a plan to end budget cuts of government social programs, raise corporate taxes, and reduce unemployment by expanding public works and public employment efforts. In a reversal of the group's traditional support of military spending, the council questioned increased government defense expenditures,

Surviving the Flak

Perhaps no member of Ronald Reagan's cabinet—even Alexander Haig—had traveled a rockier road than Secretary of Labor Raymond J. Donovan. Charges of ties with organized crime figures and illegal payoffs to union officials dogged the New Jersey construction contractor from the moment he was appointed. On June 28, however, and again on Sept. 13, a special prosecutor found no persuasive evidence to support allegations that he had been involved in illegal activities. A confident Donovan told reporters: "I like sitting here, and I'm going to be sitting here for another six and a half years." Although often at odds with labor leaders, Donovan shared the President's commitment to cut federal spending, citing a reduction of almost $14 billion in spending for his department's programs in the 1982 and 1983 budgets and a 20 percent reduction in personnel.

Raymond J. Donovan

215

Don't Hassle a Teamster

For the actors and actresses who portrayed Mickey and Minnie Mouse, Donald Duck, Goofy, and other cartoon characters at Walt Disney World in Florida, enough was enough. Their uniforms, they complained, were hot and dirty, and company rules forced them to endure abuse from amusement park patrons without talking back. So, in August, they voted, 45–41, to be represented by the Service Trades Council, which administered a contract with seven unions, including the International Brotherhood of Teamsters. "They wanted respect in their working rights," explained a Teamsters business agent. "They are actors and they are professionals, and they want to be treated as such."

charging that they were being made at the expense of workers and the poor. On Aug. 5 the council voted to seek, by December, 1983, a labor movement consensus for a 1984 presidential candidate. Under the leadership of the late George Meany, the AFL-CIO had withheld endorsement until after the parties had selected their candidates. The labor federation's desire to play a part in the process of selection stemmed in part from dissatisfaction with the last two Democratic Party nominees, George McGovern and Jimmy Carter.

Leadership Changes. Patrick J. Campbell, 64, general vice-president of the United Brotherhood of Carpenters and Joiners of America, was named to succeed retiring president William Konyha, 67.

Marvin J. Boede, 54, was elevated to the helm of the United Association of Journeymen and Apprentices of the Plumbing and Pipe Fitting Industry of the United States and Canada. He succeeded Martin J. Ward, who died on Oct. 9 at age 64.

Richard L. Trumka, 33, an insurgent candidate, was elected president of the United Mine Workers of America (UMWA) on Nov. 9. Trumka defeated incumbent Sam M. Church, Jr., 46. About 20 percent of the UMWA coal miners were out of work in late

1982, and many members were dissatisfied with the contract that followed a 72-day strike in 1981. That contract, with the Bituminous Coal Operators Association, permitted unionized operators to process coal from nonunion mines without paying the royalties that support union miners' health benefits.   M.H.

LAOS. Premier Kaysone Phomvihan continued to guide the fortunes of impoverished Laos in 1982. At the third congress of the ruling Lao People's Revolutionary Party, held in April, Kaysone retained his position as premier and as secretary general of the party. He thus continued as the undisputed leader of the country's hard-line Communist government, despite earlier rumors of his possible replacement.

The congress adopted the country's first five-year plan, concentrating on the development of agriculture and trade and on a reduced pace of socialization. The plan called for the use of more incentives to win the support of the peasants. Kaysone admitted that the government had erred in trying to force small farmers into cooperatives. He also called for a slowdown in the program to persuade mountain tribesmen to settle in lowland villages.

In September Deputy Premier Nouhak Phoumsavan resigned as finance minister and was replaced by an expert in economics. Other top party figures lost their ministerial positions to officials with technical skills rather than ideological purity.

Laos generally adhered to the policies of the Soviet Union and Vietnam, its two chief backers. The Vietnamese maintained about 40,000 troops in Laos to support the government against feeble but persistent attacks by rebel forces. A warmer attitude toward the United States appeared to emerge. In early 1982 the U.S. supplied equipment to improve a large hospital in Vientiane, the capital. Laos responded by permitting a visit by a U.S. group seeking information about 576 Americans still listed as missing in action in Vietnam. During that visit, Laotians expressed an eagerness for U.S. aid, especially in the areas of health and agriculture.

See STATISTICS OF THE WORLD.   R.J.C.

LEBANON. Violent warfare raged in Lebanon throughout the summer of 1982 as Israel waged a massive air, land, and sea campaign against Palestinian forces. The fighting resulted in high casualties and massive property damage, and Israeli forces occupied much of the country. In September Lebanon's president-elect, Bashir Gemayel, was assassinated and hundreds of Palestinians were massacred in Beirut refugee camps. Amin Gemayel, Bashir's brother, became president on Sept. 23.

Israeli Invasion. On June 6 Israel invaded southern Lebanon in an attack aimed at crushing strongholds of the Palestine Liberation Organization (PLO). The long-expected assault was triggered by an assassination attempt against Israeli Ambassador Shlomo Argov in London three days earlier, but Israel said that the objective of its offensive—code-named Operation Peace for Galilee—was to free northern Israel from the threat of PLO rocket and artillery attacks. Israel's conquest was swift: PLO outposts at Hasbeya, Nabatiyeh, and the Beaufort Castle, a medieval Crusader fortress, fell within two days. Sidon fell the next day and Damur was quickly surrounded. Israeli invading forces were soon fighting Syrian troops based in Lebanon. Syria and Israel fought huge air battles, but Israel established total air supremacy. Israelis, flying American-made F-15 and F-16 fighters, downed more than 60 Syrian MiG-21's and MiG-23's in two days. Israeli warplanes also destroyed all 19 Syrian antiaircraft missile batteries in eastern Lebanon's Bekaa Valley, without the loss of a single Israeli plane. Israel declared a cease-fire on June 11, but the truce quickly broke down and Israeli troops encircled Beirut, trapping more than 10,000 PLO guerrillas.

Siege of Beirut. From mid-June until the withdrawal of PLO forces at the end of August, west Beirut was under fierce siege—cut off by Israeli tanks and troops and pounded relentlessly by Israeli jets, artillery, and warships. In an effort to negotiate a halt to the fighting and save west Beirut—the Muslim half of the city—from destruction, U.S. special envoy Philip C. Habib shuttled between Beirut and Jerusalem. As the complex nego-

Saida was one of the Lebanese cities under Palestine Liberation Organization control that fell to Israeli troops in June. At least 60,000 Palestinians lost their homes.

tiations dragged on, Israel stepped up its pressure on Beirut. In early July Israeli forces completely sealed off west Beirut, cutting off water and electricity and preventing food and medicine from passing through the "green line" separating the city's Muslim and Christian sectors. Eventually, PLO leader Yasir Arafat agreed to a plan negotiated by Habib whereby the PLO would withdraw by land and sea to other Arab countries, under the protection of a force made up of French and Italian troops and a contingent of U.S. Marines. On Aug. 21, brandishing assault rifles and flashing victory signs, the first PLO guerrillas were evacuated from Beirut by ship. By Sept. 1, two days ahead of schedule, the last of approximately 14,000 Palestinian

217

Lebanon's New President
Amin Gemayel, a 40-year-old Maronite Christian, was elected on Sept. 21 to a six-year term as president of Lebanon. He replaced his brother Bashir, who had been assassinated a week earlier after becoming president-elect on Aug. 23. Unlike Bashir, who had headed the country's largest Christian militia, Amin, who was elected to parliament in 1970, had the support of Muslim as well as Christian leaders. An eloquent speaker, he promised in his inaugural address to work to get all foreign troops out of Lebanon and to maintain the nation's ties to other Arab countries. His immediate goal was to reorganize and expand the Lebanese army.

Amin Gemayel

fighters and Syrian soldiers in west Beirut had left the city.

Massacre and Aftermath. The assassination on Sept. 14 of Lebanese President-elect Bashir Gemayel, 34, leader of a powerful Maronite Christian militia force, plunged war-weary Lebanon into another crisis and led to a new round of bloodshed. Gemayel had been elected on Aug. 23 by a special session of parliament boycotted by almost all Muslim members. He was killed by an explosion that ripped his Phalangist party headquarters in east Beirut.

Israeli tanks and troops then thrust into west Beirut. On Sept. 16 troops of the Phalangist militia—allies of Israel since the 1975–76 Lebanese civil war—were ordered by Israel to carry out a mopping-up operation against PLO guerrillas said to be hiding in the Sabra and Shatila refugee camps on the outskirts of Beirut. Instead, the Phalangists killed hundreds of Palestinian men, women, and children. Whole families were lined up and shot. Others were buried in the rubble of their dynamited homes. Rescue workers later found 328 bodies in the camps, but Israeli intelligence estimated that at least 700 or 800 Palestinians died in the bloodbath.

After the massacre the Lebanese government called for the withdrawal of the Israelis

from west Beirut and the return of the multinational force. Israeli forces left the city by Sept. 29 and were replaced by a force of French, Italians, and Americans.

Precise casualty figures for the summer-long war in Lebanon might never be known. Israel said that 368 Israeli soldiers were killed and almost 2500 were wounded; another 75 died in November when a headquarters building in Tyre collapsed. Lebanese police estimated that 6775 people, many of them civilians, died during the siege of Beirut and that 12,310 died outside the city, for a total of 19,085. Israel considered the Lebanese figures too high.

Prospects for Peace. Amin Gemayel, Bashir's brother, was elected president on Sept. 21 and was inaugurated on Sept. 23. Unlike his brother, Amin had Muslim support and was elected almost unanimously. On Nov. 9, by a 58–1 vote, parliament gave him the power to rule Lebanon by decree for six months. One of Gemayel's first priorities was to establish the small and ill-equipped army's authority over the nation's 40-odd warring and armed factions. The leftist and Muslim militias in west Beirut were largely disarmed, but the Christian militias remained untouched.

Another of Gemayel's prime objectives was the withdrawal of all Israeli, Syrian, and

Palestinian forces still in Lebanon. But Israel's occupation troops in southern Lebanon were dug in for the winter and its government refused to withdraw them unless the estimated 8000 PLO fighters in northern and eastern Lebanon left first. Syria, which kept troops in northern and eastern Lebanon, insisted that the Israelis leave first.

See STATISTICS OF THE WORLD. See also ISRAEL; MIDDLE EAST; MILITARY AND NAVAL AFFAIRS; PALESTINE LIBERATION ORGANIZATION; SYRIA. A.D.

LESOTHO. See STATISTICS OF THE WORLD.

LIBERIA. See STATISTICS OF THE WORLD.

LIBRARIES. Federal budget cuts affected nearly all libraries in the United States during 1982. The administration of President Ronald Reagan proposed the elimination of library support programs funded by the Department of Education. Libraries responded by stepping up efforts to gain renewed backing from both the public and private sectors, and Congress approved funding at previous levels.

Book Banning. The U.S. Supreme Court ruled 5–4 on June 25 that students were entitled to challenge in court the banning of books from school libraries by a local school board. The case, *Board of Education vs. Pico,* originated in the Island Trees Union Free School District in Nassau County, N.Y. The Supreme Court ordered that the case proceed to trial.

The High Court's ruling did not touch on the merits of the suit brought by the students against the banning of nine books. The ruling did indicate, however, that the suit involved First Amendment rights and that federal courts were an appropriate forum for the issue. The books, banned six years earlier after a conservative parents' group complained about them, were: *Go Ask Alice,* by an anonymous author; *A Reader for Writers,* edited by Jerome Archer; *A Hero Ain't Nothin' but a Sandwich,* by Alice Childress; *Soul on Ice,* by Eldridge Cleaver; *Best Short Stories of Negro Writers,* edited by Langston Hughes; *The Fixer,* by Bernard Malamud; *The*

This new library on the campus of the University of Wisconsin/ Stout in Menomonie provides microcomputers and terminals with access to the university computer center.

Naked Ape, by Desmond Morris; *Down These Mean Streets,* by Piri Thomas; and *Slaughterhouse-Five* by Kurt Vonnegut, Jr. In removing the books from the high school library, the board of the Island Trees district ruled that they contain "indecent matter, vulgarities, profanities, explicit descriptions of sexual relations . . . or disparaging remarks about blacks, Jews or Christ."

On Aug. 12 the school board voted 6-1 to restore the banned books to library shelves. It said that it did so to avoid a trial that "would have the effect of surrendering local control of the schools to the courts."

New Buildings. A new $6,700,000 library at the University of Wisconsin/Stout in Menomonie was dedicated on April 24, 1982. The 123,000-sq.ft. library provides microcomputers and terminals with access to the university computer center, and an in-house telephone system for requesting assistance from the circulation and reference desks.

- Ground was broken for a three-story, $11,500,000 library at Drexel University in Philadelphia. Study carrels would be provided on all levels of the library for up to 1350 users.
- Residents of Anchorage, Alaska, approved the sale of $17,100,000 in general obligation bonds to finance construction of a 140,000-sq.ft. library headquarters.
- Voters in Corpus Christi, Texas, approved $5,000,000 to build a new central library.
- The University of Texas at El Paso announced plans to build a $28,800,000 library. It would house 1,200,000 volumes and seat 2420 users.
- The Birmingham, Ala., Public Library announced plans for a $12,000,000 four-level addition to its central building.

Library Meetings. The Canadian Library Association held its annual conference in Saskatoon, Sask., June 10-15. The International Federation of Library Associations' 48th general conference met in Montréal, Aug. 23-28. The 101st annual conference of the American Library Association convened in Philadelphia, July 10-15. The theme of this conference was "Responsiveness: Key to Developing Library Awareness/Awareness: Key to Meeting Fiscal Challenges."   R.J.S.

LIBYA. Despite efforts to shed his image as a promoter of international terrorism, Libya's Col. Muammar el-Qaddafi faced growing international isolation in 1982.

Foreign Relations. Qaddafi's attempts at improving relations with the West were largely unsuccessful. In March, suddenly accepting an invitation that had been extended by Chancellor Bruno Kreisky seven years earlier, Qaddafi paid a visit to Austria—his first visit to the West in nine years. But the visit touched off a storm of controversy in Austria, and one opposition parliamentarian accused Kreisky of "breaking the international quarantine" of Qaddafi. A follow-up trip to Greece was canceled.

Relations between Libya and the United States remained acrimonious. The administration of U.S. President Ronald Reagan muted its public denunciations of Qaddafi. But on March 10, the day Qaddafi arrived in Vienna, the Reagan administration announced an embargo on oil imports from Libya and banned exports of U.S. technology to Libya. The move meant a loss of an estimated $5,000,000 a day in oil revenues for Libya.

Although Qaddafi had been a vociferous opponent of Israel, he made no move to assist the Palestine Liberation Organization (PLO) during the Israeli invasion of Lebanon. Instead, during the siege of Beirut, he advised PLO leader Yasir Arafat to "commit suicide rather than accept shame" by withdrawing PLO forces from Beirut. Libya absented itself from an Arab League summit meeting, held in September, that adopted a Middle East peace plan.

Qaddafi's biggest diplomatic setback was in Africa. Twice in four months, in August and in November, the Organization for African Unity (OAU) met in Tripoli for its annual summit conference, but on both occasions failed to convene—thus dashing Qaddafi's hopes, as official host of the gathering, of becoming the OAU's next chairman. In August the summit collapsed over the question of seating the Polisario guerrilla movement, which has been fighting Morocco for control of the Western Sahara, with Libya backing the Polisario. In November the OAU again

Short of Petrodollars—and Influence

For Libyan leader Muammar el-Qaddafi, 1982 was a year of setbacks. The militant Arab spokesman was supposed to have become chairman of the Organization of African Unity during a summit conference in Tripoli, but almost half the African heads of state boycotted the August meeting, paralyzing the organization throughout the year. Long distrusted by moderate Arabs, Qaddafi also angered Palestine Liberation Organization leaders by advising them to "commit suicide" rather than accept expulsion from Lebanon after the Israelis besieged Beirut. At the same time, he scorned other Arab leaders as cowards. The United States, charging that Qaddafi was supporting terrorist and subversive activities, imposed an embargo on Libyan oil products. With world demand slack, Libya's petroleum earnings declined, leaving Qaddafi short of cash to finance foreign adventures.

Muammar el-Qaddafi

failed to produce a quorum because of the question of which of two rival leaders from Chad should be seated at the summit. A slight majority of the 51-nation organization favored pro-Western President Hissène Habré. Qaddafi favored Goukouni Oueddei, the deposed president. After three days of intense efforts to find a compromise, the summit collapsed on Nov. 25, leaving the OAU in disarray and confusion—and resentful of Qaddafi.

The Economy. The continuing world oil glut caused serious problems for Libya's economy. In early 1982 Libyan oil output dropped to 600,000 bbl a day from a 1981 high of 1,700,000 bbl a day. In an effort to close the gap, Qaddafi offered customers a discount of $2 per barrel below official Organization of Petroleum Exporting Countries prices; as a result production returned to 1981 levels. Even so, oil revenues had slumped to $15 billion in 1981—compared with annual revenues of $25 billion envisioned in Libya's five-year development plan—and were expected to total still less in 1982. Libya's gov-

ernment-run supermarkets were still well supplied with luxury items, such as television sets, imported suits, and furniture. But staples such as fruit, meat, and eggs were in short supply. Despite such hardships in an oil-rich country, and despite a number of diplomatic setbacks, there was no clear indication of mounting political opposition to Qaddafi in Libya itself.

See STATISTICS OF THE WORLD. *See also* ORGANIZATION OF PETROLEUM EXPORTING COUNTRIES.   A.D.

LIECHTENSTEIN. *See* STATISTICS OF THE WORLD.

LIFE SCIENCES. Life scientists in 1982 continued their pioneering research into the new techniques of genetic engineering. Work on pest control suggested new methods of dealing with insects such as gypsy moths, termites, and pine beetles. The nearly extinct American chestnut tree was successfully cloned for the first time, and seeds were developed for growing potatoes. Fossils found in Antarctica supported a major geological theory.

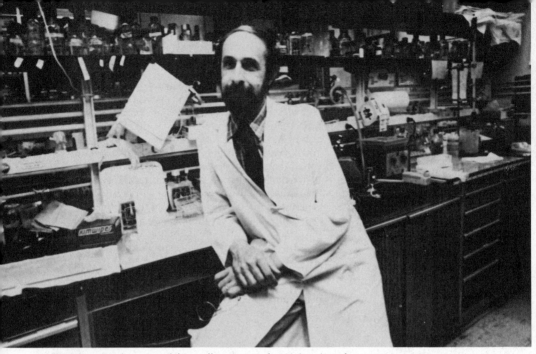

Theodore Friedmann and his colleagues at the University of California at San Diego have isolated the human gene that is involved in two inherited diseases, Lesch-Nyhan syndrome and gouty arthritis. Their achievement is significant not only for the future treatment of genetic diseases but also for gene research in general.　　.

BIOLOGY

Major news stories on biological research in 1982 centered on developments in genetic engineering, ranging from possible new ways to deal with a wide variety of diseases to the large-scale manufacture of artificial insulin. Research suggested that insecticides might not be the best way to battle gypsy moths, and that termites might be controlled by means of a natural hormone.

Genetic Research on Thalassemia. Biological researchers continued their attack on various human diseases by using the methods developed in the rapidly expanding field of genetic engineering. These methods involved the manipulation of genetic materials such as deoxyribonucleic acid (DNA) and ribonucleic acid (RNA). In particular, the basic research reported by Gary F. Temple of Bethesda Research Laboratories in Maryland, Andree M. Dozy and Yuet Wai Kan of the University of California at San Francisco, and Kenneth L. Roy of the University of Alberta appeared to hold promise for the eventual

treatment of an inherited blood disease called beta-thalassemia, one of a family of thalassemia diseases. This disorder, which is most common among people of Mediterranean origin, is caused by an abnormal gene that dictates the construction of faulty molecules of the body protein hemoglobin. In red blood cells, hemoglobin molecules constitute the red pigment that carries oxygen throughout the body. The faulty hemoglobin molecule in thalassemia victims can lead to the retardation of growth, malformed bones, frequent bone fractures, and the inhibition of sexual development; most of the victims die before the age of 30.

Although no effective treatment existed for the family of thalassemia diseases, including the more severe beta-thalassemias, the molecular nature of their cause was known. A defect in the cellular genetic material that normally directs the manufacture of a vital part of the hemoglobin molecule causes the production of that part to stop before completion. In the construction of hemoglobin, a special substance called transfer RNA, or tRNA, carries the specific amino acid molecules that make up the protein to the hemoglobin "assembly line" in the cell. This tRNA does its job according to the "blueprint" laid down by the DNA of the cell; therefore, if the DNA carries an erroneous "stop" order, the tRNA will not complete a normal hemoglobin molecule. Such a stop signal exists in the abnormal DNA molecule that causes thalassemia disorders.

The first efforts to correct these disorders, consisting of direct attempts to repair the faulty DNA blueprint, were notably unsuccessful. Temple and his colleagues therefore considered another approach: trying to build a human gene that would instruct the tRNA to disregard the stop signal in the faulty DNA blueprint, so that hemoglobin construction could proceed normally. Using highly sophisticated genetic engineering techniques, the team of researchers did in fact accomplish this feat. The next problem was to determine whether the new tRNA gene would function in a living cell. To do this the scientists incorporated the new gene in developing frog eggs, and then painstakingly analyzed the proteins produced by the egg cells. One of the proteins they found was indeed human hemoglobin; what is more, the hemoglobin was normal.

Although elated by their discovery, the researchers were quick to point out that human cells are far more complex than frog eggs. Much work remained to be done before a human cell that manufactures abnormal hemoglobin could be redesigned to produce normal hemoglobin.

Other Genetic Research. Progress was also made in investigating two other inherited human diseases: Lesch-Nyhan syndrome and gouty arthritis. The former affects children and causes mental retardation, self-mutilation, and cerebral palsy. The latter is largely a disease of male adults that affects bones at their joints. Both ailments are caused by the absence or partial deficiency of the same enzyme—enzymes being the protein catalysts without which certain chemical processes in the body cannot proceed. Because enzymes are manufactured in accordance with genetic blueprints, scientists studying these two diseases had sought to locate and identify the gene that directs the production of the enzyme, whose complex name is abbreviated HPRT.

In 1982 a team of researchers at the University of California at San Diego was rewarded with a notable success in this effort. The researchers, Theodore Friedmann, Douglas J. Jolly, Abby C. Esty, and H. Uli Bernard, isolated the HPRT gene from a human X-chromosome. This discovery had further implications, because in addition to carrying the HPRT gene and others, the X-chromosome contributes to the determination of the sex of a baby. Females carry two X-chromosomes and males carry one X- and one Y-chromosome; a mother will always contribute one X-chromosome to her offspring whereas a father will contribute either one X- or one Y-chromosome. Assuming that a woman carries a defective gene for HPRT on one of her X-chromosomes, in the case of Lesch-Nyhan syndrome approximately half of her sons are likely to develop the disease. Female offspring generally do not suffer from the disease, because a normal X-chromosome donated by the father provides a functional blueprint for HPRT production; and most affected males will not live long enough to donate their defective X-chromosome to a daughter.

In a series of intricate steps, the University of California researchers took a human X-chromosome and isolated fragments of genetic material that they hoped contained the basic building blocks of the HPRT gene. Using mouse and bacterial cells as a kind of assembly factory, the researchers attempted to construct a functional HPRT gene from the fragments. They succeeded in synthesizing a new material that might or might not have been the elusive gene; to find out, they inserted the material into mouse cells previously unable to produce HPRT. Careful analysis then revealed that the cells did indeed produce HPRT.

The feat had a number of consequences, among them the potential for studying how genes in general affect neurological function and human behavior. It was believed that the technique might also lead to a better understanding of the genetic organization of the human X-chromosome, which is responsible for determining many vital human traits. Lastly, it appeared likely that the success of the San Diego researchers might open a path to the development of gene-transplant methods that could one day be used to treat victims of Lesch-Nyhan syndrome and other abnormal-gene diseases.

Practical Genetic Engineering Achievements. Perhaps the most striking practical result of genetic engineering in 1982 was the large-scale production of human insulin, which regulates blood-sugar levels and whose deficiency in the body results in diabetes. Genetically engineered human insulin became the first such substance to be commercially marketed. It was produced in England by Eli Lilly International Corp. under the trade name Humulin. Lilly applied to the U.S. Food and Drug Administration in May, 1982, for permission to market the product in the United States, and it received approval in October. Because bacterially produced human insulin is identical in structure to naturally occurring human insulin, the likelihood of allergic reactions is small. Such reactions are relatively common in the use of animal insulins, which heretofore had been the major source of insulin for diabetes treatment. Moreover, bacterially produced human insulin promised to relieve the short supply of the drug and, possibly, also reduce the cost of treatment.

In 1982 genetic engineers also produced a vaccine against foot-and-mouth disease, a devastating disease of livestock. In addition, they found and artificially produced two human growth hormones, substances essential in various ways to normal growth and development. Finally, researchers used bacteria to manufacture human interferon, an antiviral and possibly anticancer substance.

Battling the Gypsy Moth. Biological researchers in 1982 sought to deal with the growing menace of the gypsy moth. In 1981 gypsy-moth larvae completely stripped the leaves from nearly 5,300,000 hectares (nearly 13,000,000 acres) of New England forests. Nor did the voracious insect pests restrict themselves to this region; they ranged across the U.S., leaving paths of denuded trees in their wake. The insects were attacked with about a dozen chemical insecticides and various natural parasites; techniques aimed at interrupting the reproductive cycle of the adults were also employed. Only limited success was achieved in the control of local infestations, however, and few practical effects were observed on a larger scale.

Research reported in 1982 by two Dartmouth College entomologists, Jack C. Schultz and Ian T. Baldwin, suggested that the gypsy-moth infestation might instead be halted by natural forces. They observed that many trees, including the red oak and the copper beech, are stimulated to produce a second growth of leaves when the first growth has been completely eaten away by gypsy-moth larvae. Frequently the larvae, still hungry, cling to the bare branches and seemingly await this second growth. The new leaves, however, as observed by Schultz and Baldwin, do not make nearly as good a meal for the larvae. Through chemical analysis, the scientists discovered that the second-growth leaves of red oaks, in particular, contain increased levels of certain phenolic compounds, including tannin. The leaves also contain less water and are less tender than the first-growth leaves. All these characteristics, said the scientists, contribute to making the leaves more difficult to eat and digest. This limits the growth of the gypsy-moth population and makes the survivors an easier prey to their hunters and to disease organisms.

Studies of plant tannins revealed why these substances adversely affect larval growth. The tannins combine with the proteins synthesized by the leaves, and proteins bonded to tannins are virtually indigestible. According to Schultz and Baldwin, this may account for the observation that gypsy-moth outbreaks are usually followed by a number of years of relative calm. The outbreaks may yield many trees that are resistant because of the high tannin content of their second-growth leaves, producing an environmental status quo for perhaps eight to ten years until the next outbreak. Schultz pointed out that

This caterpillar, the larva of the gypsy moth, was among the countless numbers of the hungry insects that denuded millions of acres of trees in New England and other areas of the U.S. in 1982. Research shows that some trees develop a chemical defense against this insect pest.

in the long run the practice of spraying gypsy moths with insecticides may be self-defeating, because trees deprived of the natural stimulation of periodic defoliation may end up being more vulnerable to gypsy-moth larvae attacks and may succumb to repeated low-level assaults.

Termite-Control Proposal. A novel method of biological control of another insect pest, the termite, was also proposed in 1982. Termites are wood-eaters; more precisely, the protozoa that inhabit their intestines endow their hosts with the ability to destroy any structure made of wood. Termites are also highly social insects that live in colonies numbering in the millions. Each colony consists of a king, a queen, workers that care for and nourish the colony, and soldiers that defend it against predators. Each of these castes has adaptations that enable it to do its job efficiently. Thus the mouth parts of soldier termites have developed into weapons of defense that are useless in devouring wood, so that soldiers rely on workers to feed them. Clearly, then, upsetting the balance of the number of workers to soldiers could have a devastating effect on a termite colony.

This concept led scientists of the U.S. Department of Agriculture (USDA) Forest Service at Gulfport, Miss., to experiment with a chemical, called methoprene, that mimics a natural hormone of termites. When ingested, methoprene induces workers to be transformed into soldiers, resulting in a decreased number of workers and an increased number of soldiers, many of whom starve because of the lack of workers to feed them. Moreover, methoprene has a toxic effect on the wood-digesting protozoa in the workers' intestines, further weakening the colony's ability to survive. In addition, although methoprene works slowly it does not contain toxic substances that might be a danger to pets, livestock, or human beings.

As of 1982, however, USDA researchers restricted their experiments with methoprene to small groups of termites under laboratory conditions. Ralph W. Howard, who headed the research team, suggested that the final verdict on the efficacy of methoprene in termite control awaited field experimentation.   C.P.

BOTANY

Botanical research in 1982 yielded developments in many areas, from discoveries of chemical warfare among simple algae and their magnetic properties to the cloning of a chestnut tree.

Algae Research. In 1982 scientist Donald Cheney of Northeastern University came close to producing a hybrid between two algae, one of which grows quickly, the other being a producer of high-quality agar, a material in which microorganisms and tissues are grown. The hybrid could not be produced sexually, so Cheney prepared protoplasts, or cells minus the cell wall, which he hoped to fuse and thereby regenerate the new hybrid; the process had been successful with a few land plants. The hybrid would be valuable because agar had become quite expensive, ranging up to $1500 a pound.

Another alga, the blue-green *Scytonema hofmanni,* was found to produce a chemical

225

For centuries the only way to grow potatoes was to plant small tubers or potato pieces. In 1982 a seed company at last developed potato seeds that breed true and yield a hardy potato of good quality.

that is toxic to other blue-green and green algae. The chemical was named cyanobacterin by its Minnesota discoverers, Charles P. Mason of Gustavus Adolphus College, K. R. Edwards of the H. B. Fuller Co., and F. K. Gleason of the Gray Freshwater Biological Institute. The chemical was believed to have the potential to remove undesirable algae from lakes.

A green unicellular alga of the genus *Chlamydomonas* was found in 1982 to have magnetic properties; that is, the directions in which the alga moved responded to changes in an applied magnetic field. This response, called magnetotaxis, was the first to be observed in a nonanimal organism more highly evolved than bacteria. The finding was announced by three Brazilian scientists, Henrique Lins de Barros, Darci Motta Esquivel, and Jacques Danon, who had been working at the Francis Bitter National Magnet Laboratory at the Massachusetts Institute of Technology.

Energy and Food. Certain plants such as sunflowers produce oil-rich seeds of commercial importance for both energy and food. Such seeds can be processed into chemical raw materials, gasoline, and liquefied petroleum gas. One plant under active investigation in 1982, by horticulturist William P. Bemis of the University of Arizona, was the buffalo gourd, *Cucurbita foetidissima.* Because the plant grows in arid areas of little value for conventional crops, it could become a valuable crop on lands otherwise unused. According to Eugene Shultz, Jr., of Washington University in St. Louis, the buffalo gourd is capable of producing oil yields comparable to those of sunflowers. It was believed that the plant would be grown for commercial use if the proposed Arid Lands Renewable Agricultural Resources Corporation Act were passed by the U.S. Congress.

A more conventional food crop, spinach, was implicated in the lowering of the body's supply of available zinc. Zinc deficiency was shown by Ananda S. Prasad of Wayne State University to cause lowered sperm counts and weight loss in males. According to June L. Kelsay of the U.S. Department of Agriculture, the effect is noticed when spinach is eaten by people on a high-fiber diet. Kelsay suggested that the oxalic acid in spinach leads to the zinc reduction.

Pest Control. A number of natural plant chemicals were shown in 1982 to be effective against insects. For example, the bitter-tasting liminoids that occur in grapefruit seeds were found to deter serious pests such as the fall armyworm and the cotton bollworm, as reported by Isao Kubo of the University of California at Berkeley. Research conducted in Israel by Ilan Sela and Patricia Orchansky of Hebrew University and Menachem Rubinstein of the Weizmann Institute of Science showed that human interferon can help protect tobacco plants from viral attack. In addition, R. Marshall Wilson of the University of Cincinnati produced a synthetic pheromone that interferes with the normal sensing abilities of pine beetles, pests capable of causing serious damage in the lumber industry. For information about a natural roach repellent, *see* CHEMISTRY.

Chestnut Tree Cloning. The first cloning of an American chestnut tree was reported by Franklin C. Cech and Roy N. Keys of the Agricultural and Forestry Experiment Station at West Virginia University. Blight had reduced the number of these valuable wood trees to about 50; it was believed that if a blight-resistant form could be found and cloned it would mean the return of the chestnut. The scientists cloned some hybrids with Chinese and Japanese chestnuts; although the hybrids still appeared blight-susceptible, they recovered and kept growing.

Other Plant News. Until 1982, potatoes and strawberries were reproduced vegetatively rather than from seed, because the seeds did not reproduce true. The Pan-American Seed Co. of West Chicago, Ill., developed such seeds, however, and their SweetHeart strawberry seeds were to be marketed in 1983. One quarter-ounce of their Explorer potato seeds was found capable of producing as many potatoes as a ton of tubers or cut potato pieces could.

Fossils of the primitive seed fern, the earliest known seed plant, were reported in 1982 to have been discovered in West Virginia. They were identified by William H. Gillespie and colleagues of the U.S. Geological Survey; Gillespie dated them as being some 360,000,-000 years old. R.P.P.

This handsome botanical drawing is one of a long-lost set of 2000 sketches and watercolors recently refound in Barcelona, Spain, and purchased by Pittsburgh's Hunt Institute for Botanical Documentation. The collection was the work of a research expedition sent to Mexico in 1787 by King Charles IV of Spain.

ZOOLOGY

Fossils found in Antarctica in 1982 were of major interest to zoologists and earth scientists in general. Research on frogs revealed a surprising adaptation to cold temperatures; studies of fruit flies gave support to an old evolutionary hypothesis; and an experiment with chimpanzees suggested a revision of theories on the effects of crowding.

Antarctic Fossils. In the spring of 1982 a scientific expedition discovered fossil remains of a land mammal in Antarctica for the first time. The find provided the first solid evidence to support a theory much disputed by scientists: that marsupials originated in South America and reached Australia by crossing Antarctica in the geological past. Until this discovery of the jawbones of a small, rodent-like marsupial by Michael Woodbine, a vertebrate paleontologist from the University of

California at Riverside, the fossil record provided no support for the theory. The marsupial belonged to the genus *Polydolops*. Researchers suggested that the 23–25-cm (9–10-in.)-long animal survived on berries that grew near the shore.

The theory that marsupials spread by the Antarctic route rests on the hypothesis that Antarctica, Australia, and South America once formed a single enormous landmass, called Gondwanaland by geologists. The newly discovered fossils provided good evidence that the continents were indeed attached about 65,000,000 years ago, during the late Cretaceous and early Tertiary periods,

Notes from Underground

Perhaps the most persistent myth about New York City is that alligators live in the 6500 mi. of the municipal sewer system. The story goes that New Yorkers visiting Florida brought back baby alligators for pets but later flushed them down toilets into the sewers, where they now thrive in an environment cool in summer, warm in winter. But John T. Flaherty, chief of design in the New York City Bureau of Sewers, says that there is not enough space in the sewers for alligators and not enough food. "The vast majority of it has been, to put it as delicately as possible, predigested," he says.

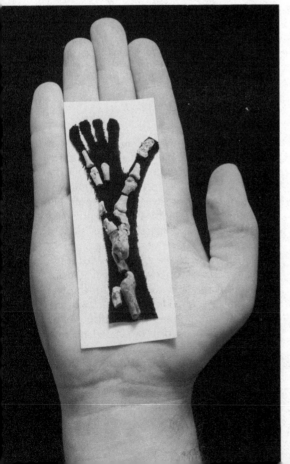

These foot bones of an early primate, Cantius trigonodus, *were found in Wyoming by a fossil-hunting team led by Robert Bakker of Johns Hopkins University. About 50,000,000 years old, they are the first fossils sufficiently complete to prove that the cat-sized* Cantius *had a grasping big toe and is therefore the earliest-known true primate.*

according to William Zinsmeister of Ohio State University, who led the expedition.

Frozen Frogs. Zoologists discovered in the 1970's that some insects and fish that live in very cold waters survive because they can produce chemicals that lower the temperature at which they would freeze. The zoologists speculated that the same was true of frogs. A discovery reported in February, 1982, however, indicated that a different mechanism enables frogs to survive the cold; the animals actually freeze and then revive, apparently showing no ill effects from the experience.

The report, by zoologist William Schmid of the University of Minnesota, examined the tolerance to cold of three species: the gray tree frog, the wood frog, and the spring peeper. These animals normally hibernate each winter beneath the fallen leaves of the previous autumn. Schmid collected frogs in the fall and then gradually cooled them in his laboratory. He found that the frog's body fluids, unlike those of other cold-adapted animals, did not remain liquid at temperatures below freezing; instead, about 35 percent of their body fluids froze. After keeping the frogs frozen for about a week, Schmid slowly thawed them, and the animals returned to normal by the end of four days. According to the study, frogs are able to withstand subfreezing temperatures because in the winter their bodies accumulate glyc-

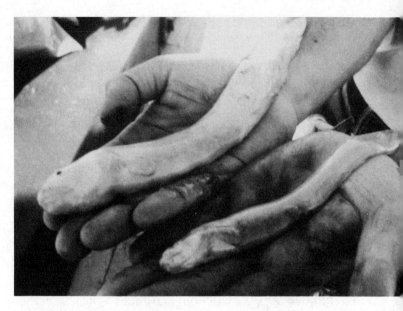

These odd fish, members of a newly discovered species related to the cusk eel, were inadvertently caught by scientists who were exploring deep-ocean volcanic vents off the Pacific coast of Mexico. Still a mystery is how these fish survive in extremely hot water and without sunlight to supply energy or help create food supplies.

erol, a viscous, cold-resistant alcohol used industrially as a lubricant and in the making of plastics. The study suggested that frogs produce glycerol in response to the arrival of cold weather in the fall.

Changing Traits. According to an evolutionary hypothesis proposed three decades ago, traits that neither enhance nor detract from the chance that an organism will survive should eventually be eliminated at the genetic level by the cumulative effect of naturally occurring mutations. Abundant examples in nature, such as the vestigial wings on flightless birds, suggest that this is so, but genetic evidence for the theory was lacking. In the fall of 1982, however, a University of Hawaii researcher reported strong genetic evidence for the hypothesis. Hampton L. Carson and colleagues found that the sexual performance of female fruit flies, *Drosophila mercatorum,* declines when the flies undergo no pressures that favor successful mating.

The researchers carried out the study on a strain of all-female fruit flies developed by scientists 20 years ago; isolated from males, the flies reproduced through the process of parthenogenesis. According to the researchers, the all-female flies existed without natural selection operating to maintain the ge-

netic basis of female mating behavior. In 1973 the researchers first studied the flies' propensity to mate, comparing that with the percentage of a group of ordinary fruit flies that mated within 30 min. after being placed with males. They found that the unisexual flies showed only slightly lowered propensity to mate. In 1981, however, when they again ran the experiment, they found a dramatic change; the unisexual females showed a markedly lower propensity to mate. The researchers favored a genetic interpretation of this change in behavior.

Effects of Crowding. Because rats and other animals confined in crowded quarters often react by becoming more aggressive, many researchers believed that the same would hold true for primates as well, including humans. In the summer of 1982, however, two Dutch researchers reported that the theory does not, at least, apply to chimpanzees. During their study of a colony of 20 chimpanzees, Kees Nieuwenhuijsen and Frans M. B. de Waal found that moving the animals to small winter quarters brought about only a slight increase in aggressive behavior. The researchers suggested that the findings may mean that humans are less severely affected by crowding than data from studies of other species had suggested.   S.P.W.

LITERATURE

LITERATURE. Among the major literary developments of 1982 were:

AMERICAN

Many of America's most respected novelists published new books in 1982. The first volume of an eagerly awaited biography of former U.S. President Lyndon B. Johnson was greeted with wide acclaim, and several outstanding young poets emerged with superior collections. Despite these accomplishments, however, it seemed likely that 1982 would be remembered for a number of excellent memoirs—individual lives recollected with amusement, nostalgia, bitterness, or a mixture of any and all of these.

Fiction. With the death of John Cheever, the United States lost one of its finest fiction writers. Cheever's last novel, *Oh What a Paradise It Seems,* was a fitting requiem, a quietly lyrical book in which many of the author's familiar themes (love versus lust, in particular) are reexamined. Familiar themes were also evident in the long-awaited *Collected Stories of Isaac Bashevis Singer,* which provided a testament to the enduring work of a unique artist.

Bernard Malamud's latest novel, God's Grace, *is a dialogue between God and the sole survivor of a nuclear holocaust.*

Major books by important novelists appeared in 1982. Saul Bellow's *The Dean's December* looks at social conditions in Chicago and in Eastern Europe, in the context of an aging academic's personal crisis. Bernard Malamud's *God's Grace,* about an attempt to build a new civilization after a nuclear war, displays the author's fondness for allegory and fable. John Updike's *Bech Is Back,* a sequel to his earlier *Bech: A Book,* explores the often comic contradictions in a writer's life.

Like Updike, Mary Lee Settle returned to familiar territory in 1982. *The Killing Ground,* which completed her *Beulah Quintet,* involves a woman's coming to terms with her brother's death. Paul Theroux's *The Mosquito Coast,* set in remotest Honduras, concerns a New England inventor whose vision of self-sufficiency runs tragically amok.

John Barth and William Wharton came out with novels that departed from their recent preoccupations. Barth's *Sabbatical,* his most life-affirming and least experimental novel since *The Sot-Weed Factor,* is a cerebral but very touching love story involving a man, a woman, and a sailboat; Wharton's *A Midnight Clear,* unlike his cult favorite *Birdy,* is a realistically told, introspective tale about the responses of a group of sensitive young people to the horrors of war.

First novels of note in 1982 included Sonia Gernes's *The Way to St. Ives,* about the agonized sexual awakening of Rosie Deane, a 41-year-old virgin who "never even had a date"; W. P. Kinsella's *Shoeless Joe,* a bewitching combination of fantasy and baseball; and Angela Davis-Gardner's *Felice,* in which a young orphan growing up in a convent school develops her own approach to matters of the spirit.

Contemporary Issues. Perhaps the most talked about book of 1982 was Jonathan Schell's *The Fate of the Earth,* which looks carefully at nuclear war from a variety of perspectives—political, biological, and moral.

Violent crime continued to be a topic on writers' minds. Gary Kinder's *Victim* retells the story of a grisly 1974 murder, calling attention to the failures of the U.S. justice system. Richard Levine's *Bad Blood,* an equally frightening book, investigates the killing of a teenage girl's stepparents from the point of view of the murderers (the girl and her boyfriend).

Saudi Arabia in all its complexity is the subject of *The Kingdom,* by Robert Lacey, and *The House of Saud,* by David Holden and Richard Johns. Lacey avoids straight reporting, striving instead to communicate through anecdotes the majesty of the Saudi world; Holden and Johns provide fascinating background on the rise to power of the Saudi royal family.

The Arab world also figured prominently in two important examinations of recent U.S. policies. Jimmy Carter's *Keeping Faith,* the former President's memoirs of his term in office, discusses the 1979–81 hostage crisis in Iran and its effects on his Presidency; Hamilton Jordan's *Crisis* offers a surprisingly candid journal of the last year of the Carter administration, as seen from the point of view of the former White House chief of staff.

Richard Reeves's *American Journey* takes the reader across the country, following in the footsteps of Alexis de Tocqueville and comparing the contemporary U.S. with the nation that Tocqueville observed in the 1830's.

History and Biography. Richard Rodriguez's *Hunger of Memory,* perhaps the freshest, most remarkable book of the year, combines a critique of modern education with an absorbing account of the author's realization that his success in English-speaking America estranged him from his Spanish-speaking family. Other superior memoirs in 1982 included *Last Stands,* in which Hilary Masters, the son of poet Edgar Lee Masters, writes with great sensitivity of a youth spent largely in the shadow of a famous father; *A Margin of Hope,* in which critic Irving Howe eloquently recounts his development as an intellectual and left-wing spokesman; and *Growing Up,* in which newspaper columnist Russell Baker recalls his early years, a time spent under the protective, and sometimes smothering, wing of a domineering mother.

The lives and works of several modern American poets came under scrutiny in two outstanding biographies. Eileen Simpson's *Poets in Their Youth* is a fascinating account

In Hunger of Memory, *Richard Rodriguez's autobiographical essay, the author argues that his advancement in the English-speaking world was won at the inevitable price of alienation from his Mexican-born, Spanish-speaking parents.*

of the early careers of a group of poets—including John Berryman, once Simpson's husband—who came to prominence in the 1950's. The same era is the focus of Ian Hamilton's *Robert Lowell,* which looks at the tragic life of one of America's finest lyric poets.

Readers of U.S. history were also well served in 1982. In *The Years of Lyndon Johnson: The Path to Power,* the first volume in a five-volume study, Robert Caro examines in meticulous detail the 36th President's early forays into politics. *The Vineyards of Liberty,* the first volume of historian James MacGregor Burns's *American Experiment,* assesses the State of the Union from its beginnings to the Civil War. James M. MacPherson's *Ordeal by Fire: The Civil War and Reconstruction* presents a painstaking reappraisal of the war between the states.

Two 1982 books were unclassifiable in form and approach. Ivor Noel Hume's *Martin's Hundred,* a captivating blend of archeology, anthropology, history, and the detective novel, re-creates the excitement of excavating a 17th-century Virginia settlement. Jean Stein's *Edie: An American Biography,* composed of interconnected interviews with a wide variety of people who knew Edie Sedgwick (a New England heiress turned underground-film star), forms a stunning amalgam of the energies and excesses of the 1960's.

Poetry. American poetry lost one of its most distinctive voices with the death of James Wright. *This Journey,* the poet's ninth collection, published posthumously, displays Wright's splendid gifts—a striking lyricism, a refreshing clarity, and a warmth that transcends subject matter. Among other new

Edie: An American Biography tells the story of the late Edie Sedgwick (below), a beautiful but disturbed and self-destructive "superstar" of the New York scene who died of a barbiturate overdose at the age of 28.

collections from major American poets were *PM/AM,* in which Linda Pastan's remarkable command of metaphor once again is in evidence; *A Glass Face in the Rain,* more of William Stafford's spare yet always beguiling musings; and *Our Ground Time Here Will Be Brief,* in which Maxine Kumin shows her ability to deal with difficult issues in language both vivid and penetrating.

Denis Johnson was one of several less well established poets whose work in 1982 showed great promise. In *The Incognito Lounge,* Johnson captures the alienation of urban life and the resiliency of the human heart, with gripping images evoking the squalor of bus terminals, all-night diners, and fleabag hotels. Jay Parini's *Anthracite Country* contains grim depictions of accidental death while recalling in the most celebratory of terms the blossoming of youth.

Katha Pollitt and Mark Perlberg are poets who achieve eloquence through understatement and forceful directness. Pollitt's *Antarctic Traveller,* her first collection, displays a rare talent for observing objects and events intensely. Perlberg, in *The Feel of the Sun,* writes of the pleasures of the senses with a special lucidity and economy.   B.O.

AUSTRALIAN

Several good novels displaying the Australian preoccupation with the problem of national identity appeared in 1982. A number of poets published novels, continuing a recent trend and demonstrating that rather than plot and theme, the nature of language itself had become important in Australian fiction. Women writers were again prominent.

Fiction. Journalist and author Ian Moffitt published an interesting first novel, *The Retreat of Radiance,* about an Australian on a mission of revenge to China. Gerald Murnane's *The Plains* proved to be an original and satiric vision of Australians who are obsessed with their own character, surroundings, and history. David Malouf, the poet turned novelist and one of the country's finest writers, published two books—*Child's Play,* a masterful analysis of a terrorist and his victim, a man of letters; and *Fly Away Peter,* a philosophical, highly literary novella about war. *Just Relations,* poet Rodney Hall's third novel, evoked universal admiration. It tells of the aged denizens of a sleepy country town whose peace is disturbed by the Australian Aesthetic and Historical Resources Commission. Jean Bedford's *Sister Kate* is about the sister of notorious bushranger Ned Kelly; the author here relates a grim story of women as victims. Barbara Hanrahan, a writer of tremendous vitality, explores a similar theme in *Dove*. Elizabeth Jolley, another talented novelist, creates a strange, appealing character, an old cleaning woman, in *The Newspaper of Claremont Street.*

Poetry. Although there was a significant drop in the number of books of poetry in 1982, the top titles were of a high standard. Fay Zwicky's *Kaddish and Other Poems* enjoyed acclaim for its characterization, humor, and detail. John Tranter's *Selected Poems* was praised as the poetic event of the year, and Andrew Taylor's *Selected Poems 1960–1980* was also well received.

Awards. Geoffrey Serle's biography of *Sir John Monash,* who commanded Australian forces in World War I, won first prize in the National Book Council's Awards. Second prize went to Peter Carey for his novel *Bliss,* which according to the judges has "the inventiveness, the subtlety, the originality of the author's short stories." The prestigious Patrick White Award, which acknowledges writers who have not received due recognition, was given to the poet Bruce Beaver. Great Britain's most coveted fiction award, the Booker Prize, went to the prolific Australian writer Thomas Keneally for a mainly factual work. His *Schindler's Ark* (published in the U.S. as *Schindler's List*) is the story of a real person, Oskar Schindler, who during World War II turned his factory in Poland into a benign concentration camp and thereby saved the lives of more than 1000 Jewish employees.   I.K.

CANADIAN

Several Canadian short-story writers produced notable work in 1982 and won attention for their perfection of this literary form. Alice Munro, Carol Shields, Veronica Ross, and Edna Alford were particularly praised for their ability to deal with the intricacies of the familiar and evoke a strong sense of place.

In *Dancing Girls and Other Stories*—a collection of 14 stories—Canadian author Margaret Atwood displays her precise narrative style.

Two distinguished authors received the Governor-General Award in 1982. The prize for English-language fiction was won by Mavis Gallant for her collection *Home Truths: Selected Canadian Stories.* Gallant had long been neglected, partly because of her move to Paris in the 1940's; but her irony, subtle instinct for the "Canadian way," and fine style were becoming appreciated. The award for English-language poetry was given to F. R. Scott for his *Collected Poems.* Scott, well known, too, as a lawyer, university professor, and social critic, began this body of poetry more than 60 years ago. The collection also includes his superb translations of the French-Canadian poet Anne Hébert.

University of Toronto professor and man of letters Northrop Frye came out with *The Great Code: The Bible and Literature.* In this volume Frye "decodes" the Bible and interprets its role in Western culture, seeing it as another *Divine Comedy* or proclamation of hope.

Novels. Hugh Hood's *Black and White Keys* was the fourth episode in his cycle, *The New Age/Le Nouveau Siècle,* about Canadian intellectual life. The first three novels (*The Swing in the Garden, A New Athens,* and *Reservoir Ravine*) view the Scottish-Protestant ethic of rural Ontario with realism tempered with affection. The new novel, shifting over 60 years, is more diffuse but still smoothly written, and it presents once again Hood's concern with the lack of myth in the Canadian psyche.

In his third novel, *La Duchesse et le Roturier* ("The Duchess and the Commoner"), Michel Tremblay delights in theatrics and characterizes his people with humor and tolerance.

Poetry. Two notable books by George Bowering, *A Way with Words* and *West Window,* express the joy of experiment and freedom of response in postmodern poetry. Poetry *is,* Bowering writes; and he advises: "Listen to it go by, the way we do with a movie or a piece of music." Ten years of fine writing of English-language poets was collected in *Crosscuts,* edited by Peter van Toorn. His introduction praises Québec writers for having supplied Canada with "a model for a novel and imaginative approach to itself." B.M.P.

BRITISH

As in 1981, names new to the novel-reading public dominated the fiction list in 1982. In nonfiction, several remarkable works filled in some of the background to the modern political scene.

Fiction. The battle for the £10,000 Booker Prize for Fiction centered on two novels—Thomas Keneally's *Schindler's Ark,* about an actual person, a German industrialist who managed to save more than 1000 Jews from the extermination camps of World War II; and William Boyd's *An Ice Cream War,* a rather fierce comedy about the English in German East Africa during World War I. *Schindler's Ark* won the prize, but many critics complained that it could not be called fiction at all. The judges defended themselves by saying that Keneally brought the fictional arts of shaping and storytelling to an admittedly factual, historical account.

Among established novelists, the 78-year-old Graham Greene stood out with his *Monsignor Quixote,* in which a couple of elderly Spaniards, a Roman Catholic parish priest and a Communist mayor, go off on a trip in the priest's old car, called Rosinante (like Don Quixote's nag). Their adventures help them to discover in what ways they really differ and what, in spite of appearances, they have in common. Lawrence Durrell's *Constance* was another volume in his "quincunx" of novels that give a phantasmagoric picture of Europe during World War II. John Fowles's difficult *Mantissa* seems to be an attempt to understand the nature of his own inspiration; it is about a novelist in a psychiatric hospital struggling in his mind with a vengeful, mythical woman.

The playwright John Arden published his first novel, *Silence Among the Weapons;* set in ancient Italy when the Roman general Sulla was fighting the populist leader Marius, the story is told as seen through the eyes of a theater manager of dubious character.

Still practicing his trade, 78-year-old Graham Greene came out in 1982 with a new novel, Monsignor Quixote, *the adventures of two elderly Spaniards—a parish priest and a Communist mayor.*

Constance, *another volume in a series on Europe during World War II, is the latest novel by British author Lawrence Durrell.*

Nonfiction. The novelist Nicholas Mosley, the son of Sir Oswald Mosley (leader of the British Union of Fascists), wrote *The Rules of the Game,* a frank and critical account of his father's early life and character. Taking readers back still further into the origins of 20th-century political history, the first volume of *The Diary of Beatrice Webb* reveals this mother-figure of English socialism to have been a brilliant, lively girl.

Attlee, a full, fascinating biography of Great Britain's first post-World War II prime minister, was written by Kenneth Harris. And Susan Crosland, the American widow of one of the most gifted Labour Party politicians of recent years, wrote *Tony Crosland,* a remarkable account of her husband's life in politics; he died in 1977 at the age of 58.

Theatrical life was evoked in two books—*The Noel Coward Diaries,* which seem to bring back to life that witty and subtle man; and *Confessions of an Actor* by Laurence Olivier, which was criticized for saying too much about his former wife, Vivien Leigh, and not enough about acting.

Two important biographies of poets appeared in 1982. *Thomas Hardy,* by Michael Millgate, drew on much unpublished material; *Robert Graves,* by Martin Seymour-Smith, was a somewhat polemical portrait.

Another absorbing literary biography was the authorized life, by Frances Donaldson, of *P. G. Wodehouse,* whose Jeeves and Bertie Wooster stories were still as popular as ever. The novelist Anthony Powell published his latest volume of autobiography under the title *The Strangers All Are Gone.* Like the earlier volumes, it contains many perceptive vignettes of well-known people.

The fourth volume of Virginia Woolf's *Diary* was as dashing and illuminating as its predecessors had been.

Poetry and Plays. The poet Thom Gunn, who moved to California, brought out an attractive new volume of poems largely with an American setting, *The Passages of Joy.* Two young poets made a mark: James Fenton, with his austere, intelligent volume *The Memory of War;* and Christopher Reid, with his light, inventive *Pea Soup.* The two most remarkable new plays of 1982 were *A Kind of Alaska,* an uncharacteristic work by Harold Pinter about a girl with sleeping sickness; and Julian Mitchell's *Another Country,* about the forming, in his school days, of an upper-class spy.   D.M.

FOREIGN

Biographies and memoirs were among the most significant books published in 1982 in several countries. Also during the year, a

LITERATURE

number of distinguished works by foreign writers became available in English translation.

French. One of the most ambitious French novels of 1982 was Claude Simon's *Les Géorgiques* ("Georgics"). The subject of Simon's intricate narrative is the Spanish Civil War and the occupation of France by the Germans in 1940—two events of crucial importance to Simon's generation—but the novel also returns to earlier historical events and alludes to famous literary treatments of these events. Another, older writer, Marguerite Yourcenar, talks about her life and art in *Les Yeux Ouverts* ("Open Eyes"). Ostensibly responses to an interviewer's questions, *Les Yeux Ouverts* is really a confessional in which Yourcenar, the only woman member of the French Academy, reflects on her formative years as well as on her experiences as a writer. An extraordinary first novel, *Les Chambres du Sud* ("The Rooms of the South"), was published by Laurence Cossé, a young Paris journalist. Cossé's novel is a highly sensitive and insightful account of a young girl's passage from childhood to adolescence.

A Colombian novelist, Gabriel García Márquez, received the 1982 Nobel Prize in literature. The award citation hailed his "richly composed world of imagination."

Works by and about important French writers also appeared in English during the year. Patrick McCarthy's biography of Albert Camus (*Camus*) offers a reevaluation of the Nobel Prize-winning French author who died in 1960. *A Barthes Reader* contains selections from the writings of Roland Barthes, one of the most influential French critics and thinkers of recent times. Another legendary French literary figure, Simone de Beauvoir, had a collection of stories published in 1982. *When Things of the Spirit Come First* makes available, for the first time in English, her semiautobiographical stories, originally written in the 1930's, about young women struggling against the restrictions and hypocrisies of middle-class morality. A literary event, and to some extent a political event also, was the publication, in English, of François Mitterrand's journal, *The Wheat and the Chaff*. Written before Mitterrand became France's president, the journal contains a gifted essayist's reflections on politics and culture. The Socialist Party politician surprised his American critics by writing admiringly of many facets of U.S. life.

Spanish. An important although internationally little-known Spanish writer, Camilo José Cela, contributed in 1982 a revealing new work about his country. Known primarily as a novelist, Cela writes journalism as well, and his *Vuelta de Hoja* ("Turning a New Leaf") is a collection of articles about post-Franco Spain—perceptive comments on the reestablishment of the monarchy as well as on the introduction of democratic reforms. The noted Latin American writer José Donoso published a highly acclaimed short novel, *El Jardín de al Lado* ("The Patio Next Door"), a finely crafted work about an unsuccessful novelist's fight to stay afloat. However, the best literary news for the Spanish-speaking world in 1982 came from Stockholm. A Latin American, Gabriel García Márquez, born in Colombia, won the Nobel Prize in literature; *see also* PRIZES AND AWARDS. García Márquez's latest novel, *Crónica de una Muerte Anunciada* ("The Chronicle of an Announced Murder"), is based on an actual murder that took place years ago in a Colombian village.

The literary scene in Latin America was illuminated, too, by the Peruvian Mario Vargas Llosa. His novel *Aunt Julia and the Scriptwriter,* the zany story of a young writer's love affair with his aunt and his relationship with an eccentric author of radio soap operas, appeared in English in 1982 and was enthusiastically received by critics. Vargas Llosa's 1981 novel, *La Guerra del Fin del Mundo* ("The War at the End of the World"), about a 19th-century massacre of thousands of peasants in the Brazilian wilderness, created a sensation in Spanish-speaking countries, and had already been translated into a number of other European languages.

Italian. A fascinating novel that turns out to be also a mystery story was published by Mario Soldati in 1982. Entitled *L'Incendio* ("The Fire"), the novel relates the adventures of an unknown but talented painter whose works are one day acquired by a sharp-eyed art dealer. The Sicilian Angelo Fiore contributed *L'Erede del Beato* ("Heir of the Blessed"), a narrative about life in his native region; the novel was judged by critics to be a remarkably authentic evocation of the Sicilian scene, including its many social tensions. Books by and about the late Pier Paolo Pasolini, one of the most influential and controversial cultural figures in postwar Italy, still appeared in great numbers in his native country and in the U.S. Among them, in 1982, were English translations of Enzo Siciliano's biography of the famed filmmaker-poet-journalist and of Pasolini's hard-edged poems.

German. New works by established writers in German enlivened the literary scene in 1982. Temporarily abandoning his customary genre, Swiss playwright Friedrich Dürrenmatt published a lengthy three-part prose work entitled *Stoffe I-III* ("Subjects I-III"). Partly autobiographical, Dürrenmatt's narrative contains a number of absorbing—and puzzling—parables. Siegfried Lenz's new novel, *Der Verlust* ("The Loss"), is similarly a curious work, about a young man trying to make his way in the world after losing the ability to speak. Günter Grass's whimsical *Headbirths,* a trenchant satire on German institutions and the German character, became available in English.

Peruvian novelist Mario Vargas Llosa was represented in English translation in 1982 by Aunt Julia and the Scriptwriter.

Russian and Eastern European. Two of the most noteworthy literary works to be published in the Soviet Union in 1982 were Valentin Rasputin's *Farewell to Matyora,* which concerns an island village about to be swept away by a hydroelectric project; and Daniil Granin's *Portrait,* which describes the struggles of a valiant mayor to save a quaint old home from demolition. Both works imply a criticism of the drab uniformity of the Soviet system. A number of important works on Russian literature were published outside the U.S.S.R. during the year. For example, two volumes of Boris Eikhenbaum's pioneering biography of Leo Tolstoy—*Tolstoi in the Sixties* and *Tolstoi in the Seventies*—at last appeared in English. *The Correspondence of Boris Pasternak and Olga Freidenberg 1910-1954,* which was also translated, is notable for the light it sheds on the early years of the much maligned Russian poet.

The most exciting Polish book of the year was *Courier from Warsaw* by Jan Nowak, a spellbinding autobiographical account of World War II. Nowak was a Polish patriot who smuggled messages and people out of Warsaw. Czech literature was represented by two outstanding works of fiction: Milan Kundera's astute political novel, *The Joke,* which was republished in an unabridged edition and in a new English translation; and Jiří Gruša's *The Questionnaire,* in which a Czech boy gives a whimsically elaborate account of his life, although his starting point is a list of standard questions on a job application. Because of its political overtones, Gruša's novel could not be published in his native Czechoslovakia. *The Loser,* a new novel by the Hungarian George Konrád, also had to be published abroad, for it, too, deals outspokenly with political matters. Its hero, a disillusioned Hungarian intellectual, offers an ironic and bitter survey of his country's recent history.

Japanese. Western interest in Japanese society resulted in, among other things, the increased availability in 1982 of modern Japanese literary works in translation. Shusaku Endo's *The Samurai,* which deals with a 17th-century Japanese expedition to Europe, appeared in English. The revealing memoirs of Japanese filmmaker Akira Kurosawa were also translated. Entitled *Something Like a Biography,* Kurosawa's book considers the dilemmas of an artist who is a master of an essentially Western medium.   I.S. & A.E.

BOOKS FOR CHILDREN

Poetry received deserved attention in the children's books of 1982. Like fine graphic art in picture books, poetry reached sensibilities that were shared by children and adults alike. In several of the year's collections the poet's probing spirit, expressive language, and inner vision provided a heightened experience of life for young readers. For example, the poems of D. H. Lawrence compiled by Donald Hall in *Birds, Beasts, and the Third Thing* are simple in form but many-layered in their implications.

The contemporary poet Barry Wallenstein collected a small group of his own poems in *Roller Coaster Kid and Other Poems.* They are sometimes clever and sometimes a blend of the somber and lyrical.

In a more comical vein, Judith Viorst's *If I Were in Charge of the World and Other Worries: Poems for Children and their Parents* is thoroughly modern in mood and offers a modern insight into children. *A Green Place: Modern Poems,* compiled by William Jay Smith, contains poems by many 20th-century writers who should be well known, but have never before been represented in publications for children. As a prelude to Smith's anthology, children may become acquainted with poetic devices by reading X. J. Kennedy and Dorothy M. Kennedy's *Knock at a Star.* This work, subtitled *A Child's Introduction to Poetry,* organizes a wide range of poems under the heading "What Do Poems Do?" and another group of poems in terms of poetic elements: "Images, Word Music, Beats that Repeat, Likenesses."

Fiction. The poetic impulse is important also in a 1982 novel that portrays a purely imaginary world. Carol Kendall devises a new language, a new geographical terrain, and a fully developed social structure in *The Firelings.* Her civilization of little people lives at the foot of an erupting volcano and is as terrified and superstitious as any group of mortals might be. Kendall makes excellent use of narrative suspense and a humorously improvised vocabulary.

The Darkangel by Meredith Ann Pierce has a plot like a gothic romance, but is carefully restrained in tone. It also is ingenious in its evocation of a mythical world and in the creation of a unique language and a host of symbolic characters. The "darkangel" entraps young brides, who are finally liberated from a network of evil forces by the efforts of one dauntless girl.

Realistic novels stem from a different kind of imagination, the sort that can penetrate beneath surface appearances and deal with enigmas of personality. In *The Animal, the Vegetable, and John D. Jones,* Betsy Byars illuminates a situation that many children know at first hand: The children of one divorce meet those of another and everyone is tense about the prospect of becoming a united family. *This Strange New Feeling* by Julius Lester presents three short stories about three slave marriages. Each narrative is based upon an actual happening and focuses on the brutality that American slaves endured. Readers need some background in antebellum U.S. history to feel the full impact of these fictionalized struggles.

Two works by British writers are ideal read-aloud stories when the child is not yet ready for such complex issues. *Pigs Might Fly,* by Dick King-Smith, is a short novel and *The Tiger Who Lost His Stripes,* by Anthony Paul, is a brief fable. In their satiric characterizations and whimsical style, the writers are reminiscent of Rudyard Kipling and A. A. Milne. Paul's book contains handsome watercolor illustrations by Michael Foreman.

Other notable picture books of 1982 included *Selina, the Mouse and the Giant Cat,* by Susi Bohdal; *My Uncle,* by Jenny Thorne; and *Ming Lo Moves the Mountain,* by Arnold Lobel. Bohdal uses intricate black-on-white etchings for her story about a child mastering her fears in order to rescue a mouse. Thorne draws upon Art Nouveau conventions in a comical tale about strange beasts and a rather daft English uncle. Lobel's nonsense narrative shows how a couple "danced" backward until they were some distance from a mountain, and when they opened their eyes were sure they had moved the obstacle. The charm of picture books was evident, too, in a well-designed nursery rhyme collection, *The Parrot in the Garret and Other Rhymes about Dwellings,* by Lenore Blegvad and illustrator Eric Blegvad.

In the realm of folktales, Al-Ling Louie's *Yeh Shen: A Cinderella Story from China* is a mystical, lyrical version of this favorite story. Yeh Shen's godfather is a fish who supplies her magical ball dress and golden shoes. Everything looks suitably mysterious and elegant in Ed Young's illustrations. Harold Courlander's *The Crest and the Hide* offers folk narratives from Africa, a collection of 20 tales about tribal chiefs, hunters, heroes, and common folk.

Nonfiction. An unusual work of nonfiction—*The Brooklyn Bridge: They Said It Couldn't Be Built,* by Judith St. George—could be recommended, as well as works on natural history (*The Fox,* by Margaret Lane) and timely issues (*God and Government: The Separa-*

tion of Church and State, by Ann E. Weiss).
Prizes. For the first time, a collection of poems won the Newbery Medal for best text—*A Visit to William Blake's Inn: Poems for Innocent and Experienced Travelers,* by Nancy Willard; it was also named a Caldecott Honor book for its illustrations. The Caldecott Medal for illustration went to Chris Van Allsburg for *Jumanji.*   D. MAC.

LOUISIANA. *See* STATISTICS OF THE WORLD.

LUXEMBOURG. In 1982 the government of Prime Minister Pierre Werner imposed a wage freeze and other austerity measures to help combat inflation and stabilize the economy after a currency devaluation by Belgium, with which Luxembourg is allied in a monetary union.

The first general strike in Luxembourg in 60 years took place on April 5 as unionized workers protested the austerity measures, specifically the ban on wage increases. Manufacturing, public transportation, and postal services were virtually halted for the day. Cross-border traffic was stopped as pickets kept workers outside the grand duchy from commuting to their jobs.

Seven U.S. steel companies lodged charges of unfair trade practices against the steelmakers of Luxembourg and ten other countries. The complaints, filed with the U.S. Department of Commerce and the International Trade Commission, accused Luxembourg and other producers of selling steel in the United States that was either unfairly priced below the cost of production or unfairly subsidized. The Commerce Department affirmed the subsidy charges and warned that it would impose countervailing duties; but it absolved Luxembourg of the pricing charge. The dispute ended with an agreement on Oct. 21 between the U.S. and the European Community. *See* MANUFACTURING INDUSTRIES.

The failure of Banco Ambrosiano, Italy's largest private banking group, put a strain in relations between Rome and Luxembourg. Banking Commissioner Pierre Jaans demanded that Italy accept responsibility for the liabilities of the bank's Luxembourg subsidiary, Banco Ambrosiano Holdings S.A., but Italian officials refused.

See STATISTICS OF THE WORLD.   L.A.S.

M

MADAGASCAR. *See* Statistics of the World.

MAINE. *See* Statistics of the World.

MALAWI. *See* Statistics of the World.

MALAYSIA. The government of Malaysian Prime Minister Datuk Seri Mahathir bin Mohamad gained a popular mandate in 1982. In March, more than a year before the parliament's term was to expire, Prime Minister Mahathir called for national elections. His National Front, the ruling coalition of 11 ethnic parties, already held an overwhelming majority of the seats. Mahathir, however, sought a mandate for his controversial, aggressive style of leadership.

On April 22 the National Front, of which Mahathir's United Malays National Organization (UMNO) was the largest component, won 132 of the 154 seats in the federal house of representatives, a gain of two. The opposition Democratic Action Party lost 7 of its 16 seats. Mahathir again invited the other major opposition group, the Pan-Malaya Islamic Party, which retained its 5 seats, to join forces with his own UMNO.

Following the election, Mahathir introduced "new-style" leaders into his government, drawing on university-trained experts and managers. With unusual bluntness, he told the country's military men to do without expensive weapons systems. Mahathir's belief in the work ethic irritated many bureaucrats when he insisted that they clock in for work, wear name tags, and make a full disclosure of their assets. The prime minister also urged Malaysians to emulate the work habits of the Japanese and South Koreans.

Falling prices for oil, rubber, timber, palm oil, and tin affected Malaysia's economy in 1982, although unemployment remained negligible and inflation was low. Citing deteriorating trade conditions, officials predicted a fall in the economic growth rate in 1982 from 6.1 percent in 1981 to between 3.5 and 4.5 percent in 1982. In a protective effort against the uncertainties of fluctuating world tin prices, Malaysia moved in 1982 to form a tin producers' association with Indonesia and Thailand. An announcement that Malaysia planned a 22 percent reduction in tin production was interpreted as part of a strategy to keep tin prices from falling further.

On most foreign policy issues, Malaysia was closely aligned with its fellow members in the Association of Southeast Asian Nations, Indonesia, the Philippines, Singapore, and Thailand. Relations with Great Britain were cool. Mahathir particularly resented British criticism of Malaysia's Internal Security Act, which permits preventive detention without trial and provides the death penalty for possessing unauthorized arms.

See Statistics of the World.   R.J.C.

MALDIVES. *See* Statistics of the World.

MALI. *See* Statistics of the World.

MALTA. A one-day general strike in Malta on June 29, 1982, called by the opposition Nationalist Party to protest the victory of the Labour Party government of Prime Minister Dom Mintoff in parliamentary elections in December, 1981, was only partly successful. Most shops were closed, and many teachers and students stayed home; but in factories and government offices most employees appeared for work after the government warned of possible disciplinary action against absentees. The Nationalist Party had won 51 percent of the popular vote, but the Labour Party had a three-seat majority in the house of representatives. Nationalist leaders charged that Labour had won its parliamentary margin through gerrymandering, and unsuccessfully sought new elections.

On Feb. 16 the house of representatives elected Agatha Barbara, 59, president of Malta. Barbara, the first woman chosen for the largely ceremonial five-year post, had also been the first woman elected to parliament (in 1947).

Almost 8 percent of the work force was unemployed in late 1982. The government blamed the world recession, which had re-

U.S. Steel Corp. demolishes its blast furnace in Youngstown, Ohio, as part of its program of reducing outmoded capacity. In October the domestic steel industry's output was only 37 percent of its productive capacity, the lowest level since 1933.

sulted in a drop in exports and a slump in tourism. In November it banned the importation of 49 items, including products made locally, and announced plans to promote local industry.

Libyan leader Muammar el-Qaddafi visited Malta in March. He and Mintoff agreed to refer their often bitter dispute over oil-drilling rights in the Mediterranean Sea to the International Court of Justice at The Hague, the Netherlands. Malta and Libya also resumed negotiations on the creation of a joint commission to supervise industrial, commercial, tourist, and other previously planned enterprises suspended by the oil-drilling squabble.

See STATISTICS OF THE WORLD.   L.A.S.

MANITOBA. *See* STATISTICS OF THE WORLD.

MANUFACTURING INDUSTRIES. At the close of 1982's third quarter, U.S. manufacturers in several key categories were confirmed in their late 1981 fears that the economy would continue to decline.

In October the nation's factories were operating at only 68.4 percent of capacity when figures were adjusted seasonally—the lowest level since the federal government began keeping such records in 1948. In the same month new factory orders fell by 2.8 percent (about $4.5 billion).

Steel. Production dropped precipitously from 1981's average output, declining during the first seven months of 1982 to a level 37.1 per-

cent below that point in the previous year. As reported by the American Iron and Steel Institute (AISI), July production was 5,719,000 net tons; in July, 1981, the figure was 10,160,-000 tons. The total for the seven months was 47,527,000 tons, compared with 75,591,000 tons for the same period in 1981.

Domestic steel mill shipments through July (37,705,000 tons) were off 31 percent from the same period in 1981 and at their lowest level in 20 years. July shipments totaled 4,514,000 tons, as against 7,115,000 tons in July, 1981. July's raw steel output was 43.8 percent of production capability compared with 77.6 percent in July, 1981, and the lowest since the 39.6 percent recorded in 1938. By the end of August, output was down to 39.9 percent of capability, and in the last week of October it fell to 36.8 percent, the lowest level since 1933.

Steel industry employment for July, 1982, registered 283,000—the 14th straight month of decline and substantially below the 402,000 for July, 1981. An informal AISI survey indicated an additional 8000-person drop between the July posting and the end of August—an industry unemployment rate of about 40 percent. The workweek for those employed eroded from 35.6 hr. in July, 1981, to 30.2 hr. for mid-1982. Meanwhile, total employment cost per hour reached $24.30, up $4.58 from July, 1981.

Steel imports claimed a 22.4 percent share of the U.S. market during the first seven months of 1982. Imports had reached 19.1 percent in 1981.

Much import steel—especially from Europe—came from nationally subsidized mills and was "dumped" in the United States at prices below fair market value, which was defined as below U.S. production costs. In protest, major U.S. producers filed a series of countervailing (antisubsidy) and dumping complaints, directed mainly at the European Community (EC) nations. Preliminary International Trade Commission findings of injury to the steel industry were followed by a U.S. Department of Commerce pledge to impose penalties in the form of duties.

In August Commerce Secretary Malcolm Baldrige announced a tentative agreement with the EC calling for a 10 percent cutback in steel imports to the U.S., based on the 1981 level of shipments (6,500,000 tons). But implementation of the agreement depended upon the withdrawal of complaints and suits by U.S. steel producers, who flatly rejected the proposal, contending that the proposed cutback was not deep enough.

On Oct. 21 the EC countries agreed to reduce carbon and alloy steel shipments to the U.S. by an estimated 13 percent from the 1981 level, a reduction from about 6.3 percent to about 5.4 percent of projected U.S. consumption. EC exports of pipe and tube products were restricted to 5.9 percent of expected U.S. demand. The agreement was to run from Nov. 1 through the end of 1985. U.S. producers accepted the offer and formally withdrew 45 charges of unfair trade practices that they had brought against the EC producers. The agreement did not cover specialty steel, however, another issue of contention.

Meanwhile, nearly $7.7 billion in capital expansion plans—announced in the year following the 1980 election—were canceled or deferred, because major producers had incurred substantial operating losses. The causes of the steel industry's depressed state included not only foreign dumping but high interest rates and reduced demand from auto manufacturers, capital goods producers, steel

service centers and distributors, and the construction industry—steel's four largest customers.

Throughout 1982, domestic steel companies continued efforts to improve their competitive position. A number of marginal steel facilities were closed, including U.S. Steel Corp.'s Fairfield plant, largest in the South and one of the biggest employers in Birmingham, Ala., with a peak payroll of more than 7500. Another changeover slated for 1982–83 involved the Ford Motor Co.'s Rouge Steel Co., once part of the car-builder's integrated production operation and the eighth largest U.S. steel company. It was expected to be acquired by Nippon Kokan, Japan's second largest steel producer.

Some steel companies negotiated deferral of labor cost increases, due under current contracts, at individual steel plants. But efforts to reopen the national contract between major producers and the United Steelworkers of America failed; the contract was not due to expire until Aug. 1, 1983.

Steel producers continued efforts to diversify throughout 1982. A major development was U.S. Steel's acquisition of the Marathon Oil Co., owner of extensive proven petroleum reserves. The $6 billion merger was the second largest in U.S. history.

Machine Tools. The sharp slide in this bellwether industry continued through the first nine months of 1982. New orders for September totaled just $86,800,000, 53.7 percent below that of September, 1981, according to the National Machine Tool Builders' Association. This figure—a reflection of overall manufacturing cutbacks—was only 20 percent as large as in August, 1979, when orderbook volume began its long descent. Shipments—38 percent below September, 1981, but more than three times the size of new orders—cut into the industry's backlog.

Foreign pressures compounded the industry's problems. Exports to two major markets—Canada and Mexico—were off 39 percent in the first six months of 1982 to $353,000,000, a phenomenon traceable to a strong U.S. dollar and weakening economies in those countries. Imports, on the other hand, declined only 2 percent to $712,000,-

000, with Japan alone devouring 45 percent of the U.S. import market.

Industry technological advances were in evidence at 1982's biennial Machine Tool Show in Chicago. More manufacturers appeared to employ computerized numerical control machines and robotics. Multimillion-dollar flexible manufacturing centers also highlighted robot control systems.

Paper. Sales from paper and paperboard products declined in the first half of 1982 by 7.9 percent compared with the same period of 1981, while production remained fairly steady. However, after-tax profits dropped by $560,000,000 (49.4 percent) for the first six months of 1982, before adjustments for such items as the sale of mills, plant, and property, or write-downs of closed facilities.

Commerce Department projections for capital expenditures were set at $6.28 billion for 1982, a near half-billion-dollar drop from the 1981 level. First and second quarter outlays were running behind even that estimate, indicating possible excessive optimism by forecasters.

Textiles. Overall textile production for the first and second quarters of 1982 remained about equal to the last two quarters of 1981 (2.6 billion lb.) but below the first two quarters of 1981 (3 billion lb.). Total shipments, according to the American Textile Manufacturers Institute, dropped in the second quarter of 1982 to $11.7 billion from an average of $12.6 billion in the first half of 1981.

Fiber consumption showed an 18 percent drop (561,000,000 lb.) during the second quarter of 1982 compared with the same period in 1981, with first-half figures totaling 5 billion lb., off 17 percent. Synthetic fibers led the decline (20 percent), followed by cotton (10 percent). The U.S. Department of Agriculture estimated a sharp curtailment in cotton crops for 1982–83, but carry-over stocks—some 6,600,000 bales—were double the previous season's level.

Meanwhile, synthetic fiber shipments for the first half of 1982 were just under 3.6 billion lb., a 21 percent decline from the same period in 1981. At the end of June, inventories for fiber producers were 669,000,000 lb., up 4 percent from the previous year.

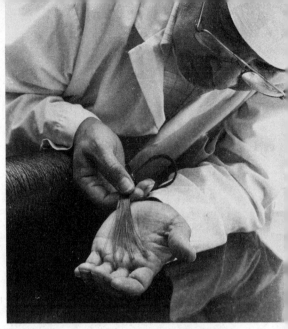

Carbon-fiber composites are being used in manufacturing aircraft parts to form material as strong as steel but lighter than aluminum. A Northrop Corp. technician displays graphite fibers that are combined with other materials to make airframe parts.

Industry unemployment soared 19.3 percent in July, leaving 163,000 textile employees out of work and doubling the figure of one year earlier; 52,000 more were working on reduced workweeks.

Textile average prices rose only a half percent in the first half of 1982, but profits dropped 68 percent for the first quarter. Hence, the projected $1.3-billion capital expenditure outlay for 1982 was expected to be curtailed considerably. Rising imports and falling exports produced a trade deficit that was 43 percent higher in the first half of 1982 than in the first half of 1981. The $3.2 billion deficit resulted from a 9 percent rise in imports and a 21 percent decrease in exports.

Federal regulations on textile mills eased somewhat in 1982 as three federal agencies (the Food and Drug Administration, Environmental Protection Agency, and Occupational Safety and Health Administration [OSHA]) agreed that no action was to be taken on formaldehyde. However, revised rules on mill wastewater discharge were expected to be issued by the end of 1982. Results of an OSHA review of cotton dust standards were not expected until the spring of 1983. L.R.H.

MARYLAND. *See* STATISTICS OF THE WORLD.
MASSACHUSETTS. *See* STATISTICS OF THE WORLD.
MAURITANIA. *See* STATISTICS OF THE WORLD.
MAURITIUS. *See* STATISTICS OF THE WORLD.
MEXICO. Following his July 4 election by an overwhelming majority, Miguel de la Madrid Hurtado (see biography at PEOPLE IN THE NEWS) assumed the presidency of Mexico on Dec. 1, 1982. Outgoing President José López Portillo handed him administration of a country that was gripped by its worst financial crisis in memory.

Elections. De la Madrid, 47, the candidate of the ruling Institutional Revolutionary Party (PRI), was chosen as Mexico's 21st president by 74 percent of the popular vote. Of the other six contenders, National Action Party nominee Pablo Emilio Madero was a distant second, with 16 percent of the vote. In third place, with 3.7 percent of the vote, was the Unified Socialist Party's candidate, Arnoldo Martínez Verdugo. In simultaneous elections for both houses of Congress, PRI candidates won all but one seat chosen by direct election. A system of proportional representation allotted 100 of the 400 seats in the Chamber of Deputies to other parties.

Mexicans place paper ballots in receptacles during July 4 elections. The ruling Institutional Revolutionary Party once again dominated the voting, and its presidential candidate, Miguel de la Madrid Hurtado, was easily elected.

Financial Crisis. After four years of unprecedented prosperity as a result of rising oil exports, Mexico's economy plummeted into a state of chaos in 1982. The country had achieved an annual growth rate of 8 percent for four consecutive years, but was expected to record virtually no growth in its real gross national product in 1982. Mexico had contracted huge foreign debts in order to finance an ambitious economic development policy, but its export earnings fell dramatically when world demand for oil began declining in 1981. Nonoil exports, as well as tourism, Mexico's second largest industry, also dropped because of the worldwide recession and soaring inflation within the country.

In order to spur exports and to reduce the drain on the nation's financial reserves, the government on Feb. 17 announced that it would cease intervening on exchange markets to support the peso, which had been trading at about 26 to the U.S. dollar. It was allowed to "float"—find its own level in free trading—and had dropped to 47.3 to the dollar by June 1, when the government started supporting the currency again.

Hardest hit by the peso's loss of buying power were Mexico's lower- and middle-income groups. To counteract the impact of inflation, the government in March announced emergency salary increases for all workers. This measure, however, forced many small businesses to reduce their staffs. An annual inflation rate of more than 30 percent in March climbed to 60 percent by July; in all, prices were expected to rise 95 percent in 1982. Although the government at first imposed strict price controls on more than 5000 consumer products, on Aug. 2 the prices of bread, corn tortillas, and gasoline were sharply increased.

A new crisis developed in July as European bankers declined to refinance loans falling due. Perhaps $7 billion in private capital left the country as Mexicans anticipated another devaluation since the government was falling short of foreign exchange needed to support the value of the peso.

On Aug. 5 the peso, officially quoted at 49 to the dollar, was again allowed to float freely; a week later it was trading at about 80 to the dollar. However, a preferential rate, initially set at 49 pesos to the dollar, applied to essential imports, such as food and medicine, and to payments to foreigners on public debt.

With the flight of capital continuing, the government took the unprecedented step on Aug. 12 of temporarily closing foreign exchange markets and declaring that about $12 billion worth of foreign currency—mainly dollars—held in Mexican banks would be convertible only to pesos. Exchange markets reopened on Aug. 16, but only to buy dollars at a fixed rate of 69.5 pesos. After seekers of dollars were allowed to buy them legally again on Aug. 19, a rate of 125 pesos to the dollar was soon established.

Banks Nationalized. In his final state of the union address, delivered on Sept. 1, López Portillo announced the nationalization of Mexico's 59 private banks and ordered them closed until Sept. 6. He accused a group of wealthy Mexicans, encouraged by the banks, of draining the country's wealth by investing it abroad. Mexicans held a reported $14 billion on deposit abroad and another $30 billion invested in U.S. real estate.

López Portillo's step was applauded by Mexico's labor unions and left-wing groups. The action amounted to a vast nationalization of the economy, since private banks also owned hotels, real estate, manufacturing plants, and supermarket chains. The president pledged that bank shareholders would receive "a just economic compensation" and assured depositors that their funds were safe.

The banks and exchange markets reopened on Sept. 6 under a restored two-tier system, with a preferential rate of 50 pesos to the dollar for foreign debt payments and indispensable imports and an "ordinary" rate of 70 to the dollar for all other transactions, such as exports, most imports, and tourist activity. In September Mexicans were told that they could take only 5000 pesos—worth about $71—in or out of the country at one time. Limits were also imposed on dollars available to Mexicans traveling abroad. Foreign investors were allowed to repatriate profits and royalties at the rate of 70 pesos to

Policemen posted outside the entrance to a Mexico City bank turn away tourists in enforcing the closing ordered by President José López Portillo after he had decreed the nationalization of privately owned Mexican banks. These actions were taken to stem currency speculation and a flight of capital from Mexico.

the dollar. New rules adopted Nov. 3 allowed trading in towns along the border at a floating rate averaging 116 pesos to the dollar.

Neither interest nor principal was being paid on the private sector's $20 billion foreign debt, and a 90-day postponement, ending on Nov. 23, had been granted Mexico on payments of principal, though not of interest, on the $60 billion public sector foreign debt. On Aug. 30 the government banks of the United States and 11 other major industrialized countries agreed to lend Mexico $1.85 billion. The U.S. also provided $2 billion in advance payments for crude oil and credits to finance Mexico's grain imports.

The International Monetary Fund agreed on Nov. 10 to extend $3.84 billion of credit to Mexico over the next three years. In return, however, the government was committed to such austerity measures as slashing public spending, raising taxes, and curbing imports.

See STATISTICS OF THE WORLD.   A.E.J.

MICHIGAN. See STATISTICS OF THE WORLD.

MICRONESIA. See PACIFIC ISLANDS.

Middle East

A new war broke out in the Middle East in 1982, with Israeli troops occupying much of Lebanon. Another war, between Iran and Iraq, continued. But Israel observed its peace treaty with Egypt by completing its withdrawal from the Sinai Peninsula.

Collapse of the de facto cease-fire between Israel and Palestinian forces negotiated in 1981 by U.S. Presidential envoy Philip C. Habib led to war in Lebanon from June to September, 1982. The fighting resulted in the expulsion of Palestine Liberation Organization (PLO) and Syrian fighters from Beirut, the launching of new Middle East peace plans by the United States and by the Arab world, and major political changes in Lebanon.

Invasion of Lebanon. On June 6 the Israeli army launched a large-scale invasion of Lebanon, with the stated purpose of driving out all Palestinian forces within 25 mi. of the border in order to prevent artillery attacks on northern Israel. The operation, called Peace for Galilee, quickly reached far beyond the 25-mi. zone, and in less than a week Israeli troops had penetrated the outskirts of Beirut. As the war expanded, fighting broke out between Israelis and Syrians, and Israel broadened its aims to include removal of all Palestinian and Syrian troops from Lebanon. When the fighting ended in September, Israel controlled most of southern Lebanon and several strategic points north of the capital, as well as the road linking Beirut with the Syrian frontier. Syrian losses were heavy, including between 60 and 80 Soviet-made warplanes, nearly all antiaircraft missiles in the Bekaa Valley, and scores of tanks. Syria also suffered the loss of several strategic outposts in the Lebanese hinterlands of Damascus, Syria's capital, and a decline in its political influence among the Palestinians and other Arab countries.

In its effort to drive Palestinian and Syrian troops from Beirut, Israel laid siege to the western sectors of the city not held by its Christian Phalangist allies. Food, water, fuel, and medical supplies were prevented from entering west Beirut, raising the specter of epidemic and of the breakdown of all but the most rudimentary services. Agreement was reached in mid-August on a cease-fire to include total withdrawal of Syrian and Palestinian forces from Beirut. Nearly all the 14,000 Palestinian and Syrian fighters were evacuated by Sept. 1, under the supervision of a new international force made up of U.S., French, and Italian troops. The Palestinians were taken by sea or by land to several Arab countries, including Syria, Tunisia, and South Yemen. The agreement, negotiated by Habib, raised hopes that all foreign forces could be evacuated from Lebanon and that an overall peace settlement could be achieved.

Tragedy in Beirut. Even as Israeli troops surrounded the capital, the Lebanese parliament met on Aug. 23 to elect a new head of state. Among the many Lebanese factions, the Phalangist Party was in the strongest position by virtue of its large militia, its close alliance with Israel, and the power wielded by its chief, Bashir Gemayel, son of the party's founder, Pierre Gemayel. Unable to meet in a regular session, the parliament convened under emergency conditions in a makeshift barracks to choose Bashir as the nation's next president. However, on Sept. 14, Bashir was assassinated in an explosion at Phalangist headquarters that also killed more than two dozen of his colleagues. The following day, Israeli troops moved into west Beirut, ostensibly to maintain order. However, the Israelis, believing that hundreds of PLO fighters were

An Israeli guard in southern Lebanon keeps watch over a camp holding thousands of Palestinian fighters. After Israel achieved its stated purpose of securing northern Israel from artillery attacks, it sought to remove all Palestinian and Syrian troops from Lebanon.

still hiding in the city, authorized Phalangist troops to enter Palestinian refugee camps to "cleanse" them of any remaining guerrillas.

During the next few days, until the Israeli military stopped them, the Phalangists massacred several hundred Palestinian men, women, and children. When news of the massacre spread, it raised a storm of protest in Israel and throughout the world. Although there were also expressions of horror in Lebanon, the new Lebanese government of President Amin Gemayel (the late Bashir's brother) seemed far less anxious than the Israelis to locate responsibility for the massacre and to explain why and how it happened.

New Peace Proposals. Following the PLO departure from Beirut, U.S. President Ronald Reagan announced a new plan for settling the Palestinian conflict. The crux of the problem, he stated, was "how to reconcile Israel's legitimate security concerns with the legitimate rights of the Palestinians." He called for negotiations leading to security arrangements for Israel, and he urged the Arab states and the Palestinian people to accept the "reality" of Israel's existence. Following the outlines of a Camp David agreement, negoti-

ated in 1978 by President Jimmy Carter, Reagan's plan proposed full autonomy for the Palestinians in the West Bank and Gaza Strip, giving "due consideration . . . to the principle of self-government." The U.S. would support neither the establishment of an independent Palestinian state in the West Bank and Gaza nor annexation or permanent control by Israel. While the "final status of these lands must . . . be reached through the give-and-take of negotiations," Reagan said that it was the "firm view of the United States that self-government by the Palestinians of the West Bank and Gaza in association with Jordan offers the best chance for a durable, just, and lasting peace." Reagan also called for the immediate adoption of a freeze by Israel of Jewish settlements established on the West Bank as a way to "create the confidence needed for wider participation" in the peace talks. Jerusalem, he stated, "must remain undivided, but its final status should be decided through negotiations."

Israel's cabinet unanimously rejected Reagan's plan, calling it a "serious danger" to the country's security. Contending that the plan seriously deviated from the Camp David

247

Paratroopers of the U.S. Army's 82nd Airborne Division arrive in the Sinai Peninsula to join an 11-nation peacekeeping force. This force patrolled the Sinai after Israeli forces withdrew in April.

agreement, the Israeli government refused to enter into any negotiations with any party on the basis of the proposal. Israel's Labor Party opposition was less hostile, with many of its leaders expressing cautious approval. A vote on Sept. 8 in the Israeli Knesset (parliament) supported the government's position by 50–36.

Arab reaction was mixed. Egypt said that the plan contained "positive aspects" and could provide momentum to the peace process, and Jordan's King Hussein likewise called the Reagan proposal a "positive move." At a summit meeting in Fez, Morocco, of the Arab League, including the PLO and 19 Arab states, members on Sept. 9 adopted a counterproposal incorporating parts of a 1981 Saudi Arabian plan and earlier Tunisian suggestions. It called for a United Nations Security Council guarantee of peace for all states in the Middle East, establishment of an independent Palestinian state with Jerusalem as its capital, Israeli withdrawal from territory seized in the 1967 war, and dismantling of Jewish settlements established in these areas. Although he described

the Fez proposals as "at considerable variance" from Reagan's plan, U.S. Secretary of State George P. Shultz commended them as a step forward.

In October a six-nation Arab League delegation came to the U.S. to confer with Reagan on the various proposals. Its leader, King Hassan II of Morocco, said the delegation's presence in the U.S. "shows that we also want ourselves to live in peace with Israel." Peace based on the Reagan plan, the Fez proposals, and U.N. resolutions could be achieved, the king asserted, provided Israel returned to its 1967 borders. Also in October, PLO leader Yasir Arafat (see biography at PEOPLE IN THE NEWS) visited King Hussein in Amman for extended discussions on the Reagan plan, especially its proposal for Palestinian self-government in association with Jordan. The talks, though reportedly inconclusive, appeared to open possibilities for eventual PLO recognition of Israel and participation by the organization in the peace process.

Political Repercussions. The war had serious repercussions within several Middle East countries. For the first time, Israelis took part in large public protests against an ongoing war; several antiwar rallies were led by returning veterans. Following the mid-September massacre in Beirut, there was a protest demonstration in Tel Aviv by an estimated 350,000 Israelis of most political persuasions, the largest mass rally since the state was established. After resignations of several high officials, including one cabinet member, Supreme Court Chief Justice Yitzhak Kahan was asked to establish an independent commission to investigate the Israeli government's responsibility, if any, for the Beirut killings. Many observers believed that the war, although a military success, was a political setback for the government of Prime Minister Menachem Begin (see biography at PEOPLE IN THE NEWS) and a serious blow to the presumed ambition of Defense Minister Ariel Sharon to become prime minister should poor health force Begin to step aside.

In Lebanon Amin Gemayel, inaugurated as president on Sept. 23, received wide support from most factions in his efforts to extend

Meeting in the royal palace at Fez, Morocco, Arab League members announced a Middle East peace plan in September that called for an independent Palestinian state with Jerusalem as its capital and United Nations guarantees of peace for all states of the region.

central government control over a unified Lebanon. His relations with Israel cooled considerably after he resisted Begin's pressures to sign an immediate peace treaty and as the new government began to pressure Israel to withdraw its forces.

Relations between Syria and the PLO worsened. The Palestinians complained that Damascus had not given as much assistance as it should have to help the PLO resist the Israeli invaders. Relations between Syria and its neighbors, Jordan and Iraq, also remained distant. However, Syria was among the Arab League members to support the Fez peace proposals.

Israel completed its withdrawal from nearly all of Sinai on April 25, as scheduled, as a multinational peacekeeping force stood guard along the Israeli-Egyptian border. But continuation of the Camp David peace process, including extension of normalization measures between Egypt and Israel and resumption of Palestinian autonomy talks for the West Bank and Gaza, was suspended as a result of the Lebanese war. The only Egyptian move toward continued relations with Israel was a demand for talks to settle the dispute over a small area of Sinai remaining in Israeli hands.

Iran-Iraq Conflict. In the spring fighting was renewed in the Gulf war, as Iran took the offensive in an attempt to drive the last Iraqis from its territory. In mid-July, Iranian forces, having earlier retaken Khuzistan Province, crossed the border into Iraq. Continued efforts to resolve the dispute through the U.N. and a conference of some 40 Muslim nations were to no avail. Iran adamantly demanded that Iraq pay war damages of about $150 billion, restore the prewar territorial status quo, and allow Iraqi President Saddam Hussein to be tried as a war criminal. The Gulf war continued to divide the Arab world, with Syria and Libya supporting Iran, while Jordan and Saudi Arabia backed Iraq. Hostilities within the region spilled over into the ministerial meetings of the Organization of Petroleum Exporting Countries, at which Iran threatened to seek to break what it called Saudi domination of the oil cartel. Within Iran, arrests and trials of dissidents continued. Among the victims was former Foreign Minister Sadegh Ghotbzadeh, who had played an important role in negotiations leading to release of the U.S. hostages held in Tehran from November, 1979, to January, 1981; he was executed on Sept. 15.

See Arab League; Military and Naval Affairs; Palestine Liberation Organization; and articles on individual countries mentioned and other Middle Eastern countries. D.P.

Smoke pours from the British destroyer Sheffield *after it was hit by a missile fired by an Argentine aircraft somewhere off the Falkland Islands. The loss of a $50,000,000 destroyer to a single aircraft firing a $200,000 missile from 20 mi. away led some naval analysts to conclude that surface ships were becoming obsolete.*

MILITARY AND NAVAL AFFAIRS. Wars between Great Britain and Argentina over the Falkland Islands and between Israel and Palestinian and Syrian forces in Lebanon dominated military affairs in 1982. The Iran-Iraq war remained a stalemate, and the United States and the Soviet Union accelerated their arms shipments to other nations.

Falklands War. War erupted in the South Atlantic on April 2 when several thousand Argentine marines stormed ashore at Stanley and seized the Falkland Islands, a remote British colony whose sovereignty had been disputed by Argentina (which calls the territory the Malvinas) since 1833. The invasion touched off the most intensive fighting between major world powers since the Arab-Israeli war of 1973. After intense diplomatic efforts by U.S. Secretary of State Alexander M. Haig, Jr., failed to settle the conflict, the U.S. threw its support to Great Britain and suspended economic credits and military sales to the Argentine military government of Gen. Leopoldo Galtieri.

Assuming that the 8000 mi. between London and Stanley made direct British retaliation unlikely, Argentina established military rule over the islands' 1800 British subjects. However, British Prime Minister Margaret Thatcher (see biography at PEOPLE IN THE NEWS) sent a naval task force, including the aircraft carriers *Hermes* and *Invincible* and thousands of troops, steaming toward the Falklands. Within three weeks the Falklands dependency of South Georgia had been recaptured, and on April 30 the British fleet imposed an air and sea blockade of the islands.

Battle for the Falklands. While the main force of British ground troops steamed toward the battle zone, the combatants engaged in a furious air and naval battle. British forces attacked Argentine positions on East Falkland on May 21 and quickly established a bridgehead at Port San Carlos. Argentine soldiers, mostly young conscripts, proved no match for Britain's elite combat troops, and in three days the British had extended their bridgehead to 50 mi. and had begun a steady land

and helicopter assault on Stanley. Despite heavy casualties, the British retook Darwin and Goose Green on May 28, capturing 1400 prisoners, and by June 12 the advance had reached within 5 mi. of Stanley. After the British captured three strategic hills within 2 mi. of the capital, Argentine forces surrendered on June 14, and the Galtieri government was toppled by a new military junta.

More than 11,000 Argentine prisoners of war were soon repatriated by the British, who intended to maintain a garrison of several thousand troops in the Falklands indefinitely to deter another invasion. A total of 237 British troops were killed in action. The Argentine death toll was estimated at 746.

Implications for Naval Strategy. The Falklands war, which produced the first major naval combat since World War II, prompted considerable debate over the future of naval forces in an era of advancing technology. Both sides suffered heavy losses during the 74-day war. The first casualty was the Argentine cruiser *General Belgrano,* sunk on May 2 by two torpedoes from the British submarine *Conqueror;* more than 350 crew members died in the attack. Two days later, in an Argentine counterattack, a Super Etendard fighter-bomber penetrated the British defense perimeter and launched a French-made Exocet missile; it scored a direct hit on the British destroyer *Sheffield,* starting a fire that burned out of control and forced the crew to abandon ship. Argentine air attacks also subsequently sank the destroyer *Coventry* and the frigates *Antelope* and *Ardent.* A British supply ship was also sunk and the frigate *Plymouth* heavily damaged by Argentine bombs and missiles; more than 50 British soldiers were killed when Argentine jets bombed and strafed two landing ships.

The heavy naval losses gave impetus to the arguments both of seapower advocates and their critics. The loss of a $50,000,000 destroyer to a single aircraft firing a $200,000 missile from 20 mi. away led some naval analysts to conclude that surface ships, especially large aircraft carriers, were becoming obsolete. But others viewed the naval encounter as a powerful argument for even larger ships. U.S. government officials main-

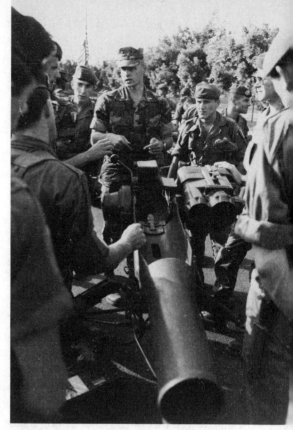

In Beirut, a U.S. Marine platoon commander demonstrates an antitank missile launcher to French Foreign Legion paratroopers. American, French, and Italian forces patrolled Lebanon's capital to keep the peace there.

tained, for example, that the presence of giant U.S. carriers with their large complement of high-performance fighters would have provided sufficient combat air patrol to prevent Argentine jets from penetrating British defenses. (The two British carriers were able to accommodate only small numbers of limited-capability Harrier jets.) Some naval experts contended that the *Sheffield* might have survived if its superstructure had not been made of aluminum (which burns more easily than steel but has been used on many modern ships as a weight-saving device).

Israel-Arab Conflict. The fragile peace between Israel and Egypt remained intact for another year. In keeping with the 1978 Camp David accords, Israel returned the remaining 7500 sq. mi. of the Sinai Peninsula to Egypt in April and withdrew its troops from the desert territory it had occupied since the 1973 war. But the simmering conflict between Israel and the Palestine Liberation Organization (PLO) over control of southern Lebanon exploded into full-scale war in June, as Israel launched a massive offensive, laying siege to Beirut within days. By the time a political settlement was negotiated by American envoy Philip C. Habib in August, thousands of civilians had died in the fighting, the war had expanded into aerial combat between Israeli and Syrian forces, and relations between the U.S. and Israel had been severely strained.

The uneasy cease-fire observed by Israel and the PLO in southern Lebanon since July, 1981, began to break down in April, as the PLO launched rocket attacks against towns in northern Israel, and Israeli jets bombed suspected PLO strongholds. Determined to destroy the PLO as a military and political force, Israeli Prime Minister Menachem Begin (see biography at PEOPLE IN THE NEWS) ordered a massive air and land invasion of southern Lebanon on June 6. Israeli armored columns swept through the demilitarized zone, policed by United Nations troops, and within 24 hr. had captured several PLO garrisons, including Beaufort Castle, built by the Crusaders.

Although the Israelis originally claimed their intention was to pacify only a 25-mi.-deep zone of southernmost Lebanon, it soon became apparent that PLO headquarters in west Beirut was the primary objective of what Israel called Operation Peace for Galilee. As Israeli jets engaged in furious combat with Syrian planes, winning an overwhelming victory in the skies and destroying Syria's Soviet-built antiaircraft missile defenses in the Bekaa Valley of east-central Lebanon, an amphibious landing of artillery and ground forces near Beirut linked up with several armored columns advancing from the south. Within a week, the PLO had been crushed in southern Lebanon. Israeli troops completely encircled west Beirut, trapping the PLO political leadership and thousands of Palestinian fighters. Before a lasting cease-fire was eventually reached in the middle of August, Israeli forces had advanced along the coast 25 mi. north of Beirut.

While Habib shuttled among Mideast capitals frantically attempting to negotiate a political settlement, the Israelis besieged west Beirut, cutting off electricity and restricting supplies of food, water, and medicine while periodically renewing massive air strikes against suspected PLO positions in the city. As civilian casualties mounted, U.S. government officials warned that continued bombing of Beirut could force the U.S. to reassess its support for Israel.

After several weeks of delicate negotiations, an interim settlement was reached in mid-August. The plan called for U.S., French, and Italian troops to monitor a two-week phased evacuation of some 14,000 Palestinian fighters, PLO officials, and Syrian and other Arab troops from west Beirut to eight Arab countries. The withdrawal began on Aug. 21, as paratroopers of the French Foreign Legion watched the evacuation of 400 PLO soldiers to Cyprus. On Aug. 25, 800 U.S. Marines arrived in Beirut; they withdrew on Sept. 10 but were ordered back less than three weeks later, after Israeli troops, who had moved into the capital after the assassination of Lebanese President-elect Bashir Gemayel, failed to prevent the massacre of several hundred Palestinian civilians in Beirut refugee camps.

During the fighting, Israeli U.S.-built F-15 and F-16 warplanes reportedly downed 79 Syrian Soviet-made MiG-21 and MiG-23 jets without suffering a single combat loss. Israel demolished Syria's 19 Soviet-built surface-to-air missile batteries in the Bekaa Valley with a combination of air-mounted missiles and electronic-warfare systems.

As of Oct. 11, the number of Israeli war dead in the campaign was given as 368. Lebanese police gave the number of Arab deaths—including Syrian troops, Palestinian fighters and civilians, and Lebanese civilians—as 19,085, but Israel said this count was much too high.

American troops were also deployed in a peacekeeping role to the Sinai Peninsula. About 1100 U.S. troops, mostly from the 82nd Airborne Division, formed the vanguard of a 2600-member, 11-nation force that began policing a 300-mi.-long zone between Egypt

An M-1, the U.S. Army's first turbine-powered main battle tank, is assembled in Warren, Mich. The M-1 can move across country at speeds twice as fast as previous combat models and has a cruising range of 275 mi. It holds a crew of four.

and Israel on April 25, when Israel's return of the Sinai to Egypt was completed.

Iran-Iraq Stalemate. The war between Iran and Iraq entered its third year, with both sides trading territory but unable to generate a decisive offensive. The war of attrition shifted in Iran's favor during 1982, however, as counterattacks drove Iraqi forces from most of the territory they had captured in 1981. A new Iranian counteroffensive in late March pushed the Iraqis from most of the land they had occupied for more than a year in Khuzistan Province, and a second offensive in May saw the Iranians reclaim the strategic port of Khorramshahr.

Emboldened by their successes, the Iranians invaded Iraq for the first time in July, and within a week were threatening the strategic refinery city of Basra. The Iraqis soon claimed to have repelled the invasion, and both sides periodically cited major (though dubiously authenticated) victories.

Observers concluded that neither side had the military strength to produce a clear victory. As the year ended, casualties continued to mount, and both countries were suffering from the war's financial drain.

Pentagon Budget. President Ronald Reagan submitted a Department of Defense budget request to Congress on Feb. 8. Maintaining that a substantial U.S. military buildup was necessary to keep pace with the Soviets, Reagan asked for $215.9 billion for fiscal year 1983, a sum $33.1 billion more than the previous year's outlays and an increase of 10.5 percent after inflation. This record peacetime increase in defense spending provided huge jumps in funding for major weapons systems. The Pentagon proposed to spend $6.9 billion for two nuclear aircraft carriers, $4.8 billion for the B-1 bomber, $4.5 billion for the MX strategic missile, $4.2 billion for the Trident submarine and missile system, $3 billion for the F-18 attack jet, and $2 billion for the M-1 tank. The budget request also funded a military establishment of 16 Army and 3 Marine divisions, 26 Air Force tactical wings, 13 Navy and 3 Marine air wings, and a Navy fleet of 482 ships. Strategic forces included 450 Minuteman II and 550 Minuteman III missiles, 53 Titan II missiles, and 496 Poseidon and 72 Trident I submarine-launched missiles.

Congressional critics maintained that the budget proposal was excessive in light of the

A child holds a placard demanding a freeze on nuclear weapons during a massive disarmament rally in New York City's Central Park on June 12. A reported 750,000 people attended the rally.

fiscal austerity Reagan was imposing on other federal programs. In June Congress adopted a budget resolution that set a ceiling on defense spending $5.4 billion less than Reagan had sought, and it adjourned without voting production funds for the proposed MX missile system or the Pershing II missile. Reagan said that he would not be bound by congressional objections to his military spending plans, and he served notice that future budget proposals would carry even steeper price tags. Pentagon officials disclosed in August that the fiscal 1984 defense budget would approach $250 billion.

U.S.-Soviet Balance. A new U.S. five-year strategic defense plan, completed in August, broke with precedent by directing the Pentagon to prepare to win a prolonged nuclear war against the Soviet Union. Previous U.S. war plans had assumed that a nuclear conflict would be over quickly, but the new Reagan policy was based on the assumption that a nuclear war might last as long as six

months. Answering strong criticism of the plan by members of Congress and leaders of the peace movement, Secretary of Defense Caspar W. Weinberger (see biography at PEOPLE IN THE NEWS) insisted that the U.S. had no interest in fighting a protracted nuclear war and did not believe such an exchange was "winnable." But he maintained that the Soviets were developing the capability to win just such a conflict and that a Soviet attack could only be deterred by improving U.S. nuclear readiness.

The Falklands fighting gave new impetus to the buildup in seagoing forces by the U.S. and the U.S.S.R., with most impartial observers again concluding that the Soviets maintained a slight edge in naval power. U.S. naval analysts estimated Soviet fleet strength at 84 ballistic missile submarines; 286 attack and cruise missile submarines; 2 *Kiev*-class aircraft carriers; a battle cruiser; 2 helicopter carriers; 274 cruisers, destroyers, and frigates; and 81 amphibious warfare ships. U.S. fleet strength included 32 ballistic missile submarines; 90 attack submarines; 13 aircraft carriers; 193 cruisers, destroyers, and frigates; and 59 amphibious warfare ships.

The U.S. Navy had more than 100 warships authorized or under construction in 1982. Ships joining the fleet or being commissioned during the year included the second Trident missile submarine, the *Michigan;* the nuclear attack submarines *Baltimore* and *Houston;* and four *Perry*-class frigates. The first of the giant Trident submarines, the *Ohio,* launched its first Trident missile in January. Modernization continued on four *Iowa*-class battleships scheduled to rejoin active fleet duty in 1983. The fiscal 1983 shipbuilding request totaled $19 billion.

Arms Talks. Strategic arms reduction talks (START) between the U.S. and the U.S.S.R.

opened in Geneva on June 29. In a speech delivered on May 9, Reagan proposed cuts in missiles and warheads that would fall most heavily on Moscow's land-based arsenal. Soviet President Leonid I. Brezhnev replied that the proposal was designed to insure "military superiority" over the Soviet Union, and a *Pravda* editorial objected to Reagan's omitting any constraints on the development of the proposed B-1 bomber and on cruise missiles.

U.S.-U.S.S.R. talks in Geneva on limiting medium-range nuclear weapons in Europe, which began in 1981, continued through 1982. The U.S. had offered to cancel plans to deploy cruise and Pershing medium-range weapons in Western Europe by the end of 1983 if the U.S.S.R. dismantled its SS-20 missiles. The Soviets proposed an immediate

An army officer candidate from war-torn El Salvador undergoes training at Fort Benning, Ga. Washington also provided arms and advisers to help Salvadoran government forces in their struggle against leftist insurgents.

freeze, which the U.S. contended would leave a Soviet advantage in place.

Arms Sales. Both the U.S. and the U.S.S.R. continued to escalate their arms exports in 1982. The U.S. Arms Control and Disarmament Agency reported in April that the Soviets were by far the world's leading arms merchant, selling $9.6 billion in military equipment to other countries in 1979, compared with $5.1 billion by the U.S. A study issued by the State Department in August maintained that during the last decade, the Soviet Union sold twice as much military hardware to developing nations as its closest competitor.

The Administration made plans for a significant increase in U.S. arms sales, seeing weapons shipments as a way of gaining influence and access to new foreign military bases for American forces. U.S. arms sales for fiscal 1982 were estimated at $25 billion, triple the total for the previous year. The U.S. announced plans to sell $1 billion in artillery to India, jet fighters to Bahrain, antitank missiles to Saudia Arabia, and billions of dollars worth of other weaponry to a dozen nations. The Administration also went forward with previously announced plans to sell advanced jets to Venezuela and Pakistan and to modernize Egypt's armed forces.

In a decision with far-reaching policy consequences in Asia, the U.S. announced in mid-August that it would "reduce gradually" its arms sales to Taiwan as the price for improving relations with the People's Republic of China. The U.S. said that it would continue to supply Taiwan with defensive weapons but that the quantity and quality of those weapons would not be improved. While rejecting Taiwan's request to buy advanced jet fighters, the U.S. agreed to sell replacement parts for F-5E jets to the Taiwanese.

The world's third-largest arms supplier, France, also expanded its exports. The French arms industry was given a major boost by the performance of French weapons in the Falklands war, notably the destruction of the *Sheffield* by a single Exocet missile fired from a French-built jet fighter.

China. The official New China News Agency reported on Oct. 16 that Peking had success-

fully test-fired its first submarine-launched missile in the East China Sea. The successful test made China the fifth country, after the U.S., U.S.S.R., Great Britain, and France, to have developed submarine-launched missiles. Western experts said that the Chinese navy remained essentially a coastal defense force.

Military Coups. Several governments were overthrown by military coups during the year. A military junta controlled Ghana after Air Force Lt. Jerry Rawlings on Dec. 31, 1981, seized power for the second time in two years. Retired Gen. Efraín Ríos Montt commanded Guatemala after a coup by junior army officers in March. That same month, troops loyal to Gen. Hussain Muhammad Ershad toppled the newly elected government of Bangladesh in a bloodless coup. An attempted coup by air force officers in Kenya was foiled by the government in August.

Other U.S. Developments. Reversing the position he had taken during the 1980 presidential campaign, President Reagan on Jan. 7 ordered an indefinite extension of compulsory draft registration for 18-year-old men. Reagan said that the continuation of peacetime registration did not foreshadow a return to the draft and that he would consider a return to conscription "only in the most severe national emergency." But continued registration, he contended, would save the U.S. up to six weeks in mobilizing reserve manpower for a military emergency.

Despite Reagan's assurances, an estimated 700,000 young men had refused to register. After repeated warnings that violators would be prosecuted, the government began criminal proceedings against 160 men in June. On Oct. 4 a California college student, Benjamin H. Sasway, became the first American since the Vietnam war to be sentenced to jail for failing to register for the draft.

Hyman G. Rickover, the controversial father of the U.S. nuclear Navy, was forcibly retired from active duty by President Reagan in January. The 82-year-old admiral had logged 59 years of naval service.

See NORTH ATLANTIC TREATY ORGANIZATION and articles on the individual countries mentioned. T.D.

A hydrometallurgical process, employing aqueous solutions at relatively low temperatures, is used to extract copper from sulfide ore at a Duval Corp. facility near Sierrita, Ariz. Hydrometallurgy is being applied increasingly as an alternative to pyrometallurgy, or smelting.

MINERALS AND METALS. President Ronald Reagan submitted to Congress on April 5, 1982, a plan to open public lands to exploration and mining for minerals. He said that the plan was intended to reduce "America's minerals vulnerability by allowing private enterprise to preserve and expand our minerals and materials economy." In addition to promising a continued review of regulations to identify those that were unnecessarily burdensome to the mining industry, he called on Congress to approve the purchase of at least $12.5 billion of strategic minerals, such as bauxite, chromium, cobalt, and tungsten, and the sale of excess materials, such as tin.

The President's message endorsed legislation earlier proposed by Interior Secretary James G. Watt that would withdraw federal wilderness areas from leasing for oil drilling and mining for the rest of the 20th century but would permit the President to use any wilderness land for development in time of "urgent national need." Other provisions would allow proposed wilderness lands under the jurisdiction of the National Forest Service and the Bureau of Land Management to be released for nonwilderness uses in two to six years unless Congress specifically

voted to protect them. According to the President's message, 40 to 68 percent of public lands were closed to mineral exploration and development, contributing, he said, to dependence on foreign sources for many strategically important materials. Many of these lands, he maintained, were withdrawn from mining "by obsolete and unnecessary executive action."

Law of the Sea Treaty. After more than a decade of discussion, United Nations delegates voted 130–4, on April 30, to adopt a wide-ranging treaty to govern the use and exploitation of the world's seas. Israel, Turkey, the United States, and Venezuela voted against the treaty; 16 Soviet bloc and Western nations abstained. It would come into force when ratified by 60 nations.

The U.S. opposed the treaty because of objections to limits on future seabed mining. The treaty declared that the nodules of manganese, copper, nickel, cobalt, and zinc lying on the ocean floor under the high seas were "the common heritage of mankind." To let contracts to mine these deposits, a complex global authority would be established that would make decisions by a three-fourths vote of a 36-nation council. It would fix a

257

In Silver Bell, Ariz., many of the homes stood empty in 1982, vacated by out-of-work copper miners. The open pit mine in the background was closed because of low demand, as part of a cutback in mining operations in Arizona, the nation's leading copper-producing state.

production ceiling to support present prices and to ensure that they would not be reduced by seabed yields. Private mining concerns or their governments would be obliged to sell their technical knowledge to the enterprise. Essentially, Washington was unhappy at the prospect of having to share seabed mining technology and decision making with smaller Third World countries that would contribute little financially to the enterprise.

Metals Production. Most aspects of the mining and metal producing industries in the U.S. were seriously affected in 1982 by the recession. Midyear statistics indicated a major reduction in production of most commodities. Exceptions were gold, silver, and other precious metals, production of which was equal to or only slightly less than in 1981. However, Bunker Hill Co., which produced 20 percent of the nation's lead, zinc, and silver, went out of business in January, and the 98-year-old Sunshine silver mine in Idaho was shut down in June.

Aluminum production was down 20 percent to about 4,000,000 tons. Only 6 out of 31 aluminum plants stayed at full capacity during the year. Several plants were shut down completely. About one fourth of the aluminum metal produced in 1982 came from recycling used beverage cans.

The copper industry also reduced operations because of the poor market situation. The Anaconda Copper Co. closed down the Berkeley Pit, one of the world's largest open pit mines, at Butte, Mont., in April. By the end of August, 15 of the top 25 domestic copper mines were closed, and 9 had curtailed production; one was producing near the previous year's rate. Seven of the 15 primary domestic copper smelters were closed, and production had dropped at 6 of the other 8. Copper production was expected to drop about 35 percent in 1982 from the 1981 level. At one point during the year more than 40 percent of the work force had been laid off.

Lead mining was one of the few mining industries that maintained production at close to the level of the previous year. Lead smelters operated at about 85 percent of capacity, producing 600,000 tons. Almost 75 percent of lead production goes into batteries for auto, industrial, and home use.

Zinc also was produced at near 1981 levels of 350,000 tons, but only 5 primary smelters were in operation compared with as many as 14 in recent years. St. Joe Minerals Corp., however, began production of zinc ore at its newly developed Pierreport mine in St. Lawrence County in New York. Daily production of almost 500 tons of ore, averaging 16 percent zinc, was planned from the 2,500,000-ton ore body.

Production of iron ore declined about 20 percent in 1982 to 56,800,000 tons. During one interval the monthly mining rate was the lowest since 1959, only about 10 percent of production capacity. As many as 11,000 of the 12,000 miners in the iron range area of northern Minnesota were unemployed.

The nation's only integrated nickel operation was closed at Riddle, Oreg., on April 19 by the Hanna Mining Co., leaving relatively small amounts of nickel being produced in the U.S. The decision to close resulted from the recession, increased power and labor costs, and a declining grade of crude ore mined.

International Titanium Inc. became the fourth domestic producer of the light metal when it opened its new plant in Moses Lake, Wash., in February. The plant had the potential to produce 10,000,000 lb. a year. Markets for the metal decreased as orders for new aircraft dropped in 1982, but a rising defense budget was expected to increase orders in the next few years.

Phosphate. Production of phosphate rock was off almost 25 percent from 1981 levels, at 40,600,000 tons. Although exports were at 1981 levels, they were a third less than in 1980. Decreased need for fertilizers also affected the production of sulfur, which dropped around 25 percent from 1981 to 4,900,000 tons. Sulfur is used in the processing of phosphate rock into fertilizer.

Asbestos. The Manville Corp., the world's largest asbestos producer, petitioned for bankruptcy on Aug. 26. Although Manville reported only a minor loss for the first nine months of 1982 and an actual profit in the third quarter, it was seeking protection because of the financial drain of contesting more than 16,000 lawsuits. Inhaling asbestos, a mineral fiber that has been used in thousands of insulation and industrial products, can cause asbestosis, a chronic disease of the lungs, and several forms of cancer. It was thought that total liabilities to asbestos companies from lawsuits could reach $40 billion to $200 billion, according to various estimates. Some industry officials suggested that the federal government assume at least part of the payments awarded.   K.B.H.

MINNESOTA. See STATISTICS OF THE WORLD.

MISSISSIPPI. See STATISTICS OF THE WORLD.

MISSOURI. See STATISTICS OF THE WORLD.

MONACO. See STATISTICS OF THE WORLD.

MONGOLIAN PEOPLE'S REPUBLIC. See STATISTICS OF THE WORLD.

MONTANA. See STATISTICS OF THE WORLD.

MOROCCO. King Hassan II of Morocco played an increasingly visible role during 1982 in the search for peace in the Middle East.

Hassan was host to the Arab League summit conference at Fez, Sept. 6-9, which produced the Arab world's first common peace plan; see ARAB LEAGUE. Subsequently, Hassan led an Arab League delegation to Washington, D.C., to explain the Fez accord to the administration of U.S. President Ronald Reagan and to explore ways in which the Fez plan and Reagan's own Sept. 1 peace initiative might be reconciled. At a meeting in the White House on Oct. 22, Hassan told Reagan and U.S. Secretary of State George P. Shultz that "peace and coexistence" in the Middle East were possible. But he said that Israel would first have to "evacuate" all the territory seized in the 1967 war—including the Golan Heights, the West Bank, and East Jerusalem—before being recognized by the Arabs. When those steps were taken, Hassan told the press the following day, Israel could live "in peace and with security."

On May 27 Morocco and the United States completed an agreement that would allow American military planes to use Moroccan air bases during emergencies in the Middle East and Africa. The military side of Casablanca's international airport and the military base at Sidi-Slimane, northeast of Rabat, were reportedly covered by the accord. The pact was seen as evidence of closer U.S.-Moroccan military, economic, and political ties under the Reagan administration. During Hassan's state visit to Washington May 18-19, the President hailed the king as "a firm friend of the United States."

Hassan reiterated his refusal to negotiate a settlement with the Polisario Front, a Marxist-led guerrilla group that was fighting Moroccan forces for control of the phosphate-rich Western Sahara. The war continued to drain Morocco's resources at a time when the country's economy was already afflicted by severe droughts, high oil bills, and a slump in the European demand for phosphates, Morocco's chief export. Morocco suffered a diplomatic setback in February when the Organization of African Unity recognized the Polisario-led Saharan Arab Democratic Republic as its 51st member.

See STATISTICS OF THE WORLD. See also AFRICA.   A.D.

Children display their tickets to the motion picture hit of the year, Steven Spielberg's E.T.—the Extra-Terrestrial. *During the summer it became the fastest-drawing attraction in film history.*

MOTION PICTURES. Attendance rose and fell dramatically at movie theaters in 1982. After posting average figures for the early months, ticket sales soared in May and stayed high through Labor Day. Admissions for the summer period were estimated at nearly $1.4 billion, more than 14 percent above the same period in 1981. A record 444,300,000 tickets were sold between May 26 and Sept. 7 at a national average price of $3.14. Moviegoing then declined in the autumn months, with October figures the lowest in six years; a combination of weak films and a weak economy was blamed for the slump. Total box-office revenues for the year were projected at $3.36 billion, a 13 percent increase over 1981, with about half the improvement attributable to price inflation.

Films of 1982. Continuing a trend of recent years, a handful of hits accounted for much of the year's earnings, with eight movies drawing half of Hollywood's revenue during the peak summer months. The most success-

ful was *E.T.—the Extra-Terrestrial,* a science-fiction fantasy directed by Steven Spielberg, which took in nearly $13,000,000 in its first three days and went on to become the fastest-drawing attraction in motion picture history, grossing a daily average of $3,500,000 in its first three weeks. Another fast starter, Sylvester Stallone's boxing drama *Rocky III,* earned more than $16,000,000 in its first four days. Together, *E.T.* and *Rocky III* drew 25 percent of the summer's total box-office earnings. *E.T.* continued strong into the fall.

Close behind them was another science-fiction adventure, *Star Trek II: The Wrath of Khan,* which drew a record $14,300,000 in its first three days, but then dropped in popularity.

Other midyear hits were *Poltergeist,* a fantasy directed by Tobe Hooper; *Firefox,* a melodrama directed by Clint Eastwood; and two musicals, *Annie* and *The Best Little Whorehouse in Texas,* both based on Broadway shows. *An Officer and a Gentleman,* a drama about a young man's coming of age, became one of the biggest 1982 hits despite an old-fashioned story and modest budget.

Other fantasy and science-fiction films included *The Thing* and *Cat People,* remakes of earlier Hollywood pictures, and *Blade Runner,* an ambitious drama set in the future. *The Dark Crystal,* directed by Jim Henson and Frank Oz, was a fantasy created entirely through puppet and special-effects techniques. *Conan the Barbarian* took place in the distant past, as did *Quest for Fire,* a naturalistic melodrama directed by French filmmaker Jean-Jacques Annaud. *The Road Warrior,* directed by Australian George Miller, dealt with a future society plunged into primitive life after a nuclear holocaust.

Among comedies released in 1982, *My Favorite Year* featured Peter O'Toole as a dissolute movie star preparing to appear on a 1950's "live" television show. Steve Martin starred in *Dead Men Don't Wear Plaid,* a spoof that blended excerpts from old movies with new footage. Julie Andrews masqueraded as a man in *Victor/Victoria,* and Dustin Hoffman dressed as a woman in *Tootsie,* both comedies about performers looking for work. Woody Allen directed and starred in *A Midsummer Night's Sex Comedy.* *Deathtrap* was based on the long-running Broadway mystery-comedy with a convoluted murder plot. *Diner* dealt with young people in the manner of *American Graffiti,* while *Eating Raoul* satirized middle-class mores. *Porky's,* a deliberately vulgar farce, was aimed at a teenage audience. *The Toy* starred Richard Pryor in a comedy based on a French film.

The most popular literary adaptation of 1982 was *The World According to Garp,* with Robin Williams as the hero of John Irving's tragicomic novel. Alan J. Pakula's film version of *Sophie's Choice* opened late in the year, starring Meryl Streep as the title character of William Styron's best-seller about a Polish concentration camp survivor. Other films based on books included the unsuccessful *Cannery Row,* from John Steinbeck's novel, and *Evil under the Sun,* with Peter Ustinov returning as Agatha Christie's detective hero, Hercule Poirot. *Gandhi,* based on a biography by Louis Fischer, was Richard Attenbo-

rough's lengthy chronicle of the Indian statesman's life. *That Championship Season* was directed by Jason Miller from his own Broadway play.

Other dramas included *Shoot the Moon,* with Diane Keaton and Albert Finney as a newly separated couple, and *Five Days One Summer,* with Sean Connery as a middle-age man having a love affair with his young niece. *The Verdict* starred Paul Newman as a down-and-out lawyer who takes a courageous stand on a difficult case. Mary Tyler Moore and Dudley Moore had leading roles in *Six Weeks,* about the last days of a little girl's life. *Personal Best* and *Making Love* dealt with homosexual relationships. *I'm Dancing as Fast as I Can* starred Jill Clayburgh as an executive with a drug problem. *Still of the Night* was an Alfred Hitchcock-style

The prizefight drama Rocky III *was a sequel to a sequel—and a box-office smash. Sylvester Stallone (left) once again portrayed Rocky Balboa.*

Indestructible and Irrepressible
Only two years after nearly burning himself to death in a drug-related accident, Richard Pryor was hotter than ever in 1982, having starred in four hit movies, including, most recently, *Some Kind of Hero* and *Richard Pryor Live on the Sunset Strip.* The talented actor and stand-up comic draws his material from ghetto life, but he also "plays in Peoria"—the Illinois city where he was born in 1940. He honed his act in clubs and on TV before making his mark through his best-selling comedy albums and in films such as *Lady Sings the Blues* (1972). Pryor's private life has included four stormy marriages, several brushes with the law, and a heart attack in 1977. "When they bury me," he told one interviewer, "they better dig the hole deep, because I may get out of that, too."

Richard Pryor

thriller with Roy Scheider as a sleuthing psychiatrist and Meryl Streep as a woman who may have murdered one of his patients.

Walt Disney Productions continued an effort to broaden its audience beyond very young viewers. *Tron* used new techniques of computer animation to put across its thin story of a man trapped in a video-game machine. By contrast, *Tex* was notably restrained in its realistic depiction of a teenager growing up with only an older brother to guide him. Other films aimed at youngsters included *The Escape Artist* and *Night Crossing,* neither of which fared very well at the box office.

One of the most popular European imports was *Fitzcarraldo,* Werner Herzog's tale of a man obsessed with building an opera house in the jungles of Peru. *Das Boot,* also from West Germany, was a World War II submarine adventure. Two films from Rainer Werner Fassbinder, *Lola* and *Veronika Voss,* which opened shortly after his death in June, completed his trilogy on postwar West German economic life. France contributed *Diva,* a visually inventive thriller, and *Le Beau Mariage,* Eric Rohmer's gentle story of a young woman seeking a husband. *Time Stands Still* was a Hungarian drama about teenagers. *Yol,*

the story of several men on parole from jail, was the work of Turkish dissident Yilmaz Guney, who smuggled filmmaking instructions from prison to director Serif Goren. *Gregory's Girl,* about a student looking for romance, was a popular import from Scotland.

Academy Awards. The Academy of Motion Picture Arts and Sciences held its 54th annual awards ceremony in Los Angeles on March 29. The Oscar for best picture went to *Chariots of Fire,* a British film about two runners in the 1924 Olympics. In all, the drama earned four awards, including that for best original screenplay. Henry Fonda and Katharine Hepburn were named best actor and actress for their work in *On Golden Pond,* which also garnered the Oscar for best adapted screenplay. Warren Beatty was named best director for *Reds,* in which he played journalist John Reed. Maureen Stapleton was chosen best supporting actress for her performance in *Reds,* and John Gielgud was named best supporting actor for his performance in the comedy *Arthur.* The prize for best foreign-language film went to *Mephisto,* a Hungarian drama directed by Istvan Szabo.

Industry News. Former Columbia Pictures president David Begelman was the subject of a best-selling nonfiction book, *Indecent Ex-*

posure, by David McClintick. The book focuses on Begelman's central role in a check-forging scandal during his tenure at Columbia. On July 12 the recently formed Metro-Goldwyn-Mayer/United Artists Entertainment Co. (MGM/UA) announced Begelman's departure as chairman and chief executive officer of its UA subsidiary. It was speculated that Begelman's ouster was due to his lack of success at UA, where only one of 11 pictures he authorized for production was a box-office hit.

In another development at MGM/UA, the firm announced on July 14 that it had reached agreement with seven major banks on realignment of $525,000,000 in long-term debt. The firm's total outstanding debt was put at $670,000,000, not counting quarterly interest charges. MGM/UA had reported a loss of $4,400,000 in the third quarter of its 1982 fiscal year. Problems were attributed to a group of box-office failures and the cost of financing MGM's 1981 acquisition of UA.

Columbia Pictures Industries Inc. and the Coca-Cola Co. signed an agreement on March 19 by which the soft-drink maker acquired the motion picture and television production company. The transaction was valued at $723,800,000. Meanwhile, Lucasfilm Ltd., the production company of filmmaker

In Quest for Fire, *Everett McGill, Nameer El-Kadi, and Ron Perlman (left to right) are treed by marauding beasts. The film, set 80,000 years in the past, dramatized the discovery of fire.*

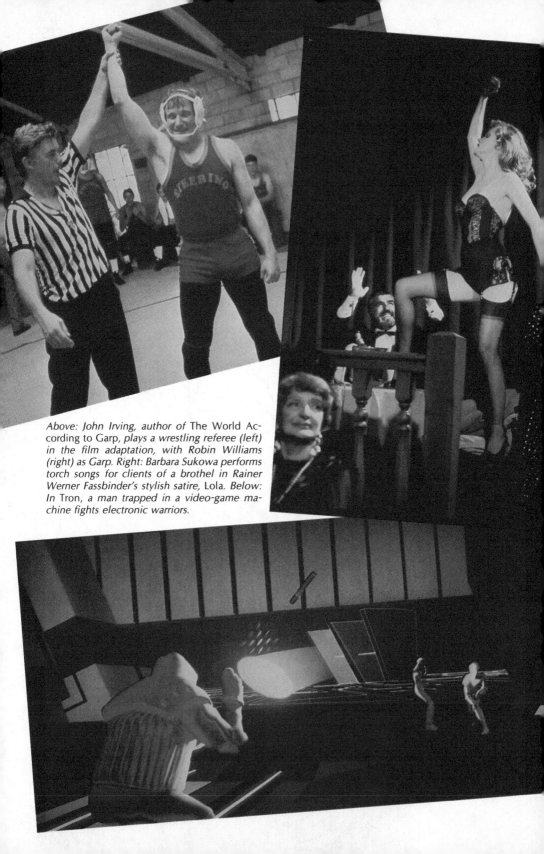

Above: John Irving, author of The World According to Garp, *plays a wrestling referee (left)
in the film adaptation, with Robin Williams
(right) as Garp. Right: Barbara Sukowa performs
torch songs for clients of a brothel in Rainer
Werner Fassbinder's stylish satire,* Lola. *Below:
In* Tron, *a man trapped in a video-game machine fights electronic warriors.*

George Lucas of *Star Wars* fame, formed a joint venture with Atari Inc. to market video games and related home-entertainment products. This marked the first venture of its kind between a film studio and a manufacturer of video games and home computers. As its first project, the firms planned to offer a home video cartridge based on *Raiders of the Lost Ark,* a film produced by Lucas.

Another of Hollywood's younger moguls, Francis Ford Coppola, previewed his expensive film *One from the Heart* in January at New York City's Radio City Music Hall, without consulting the film's distributor, Paramount Pictures. Paramount then dropped plans to release the picture, which was eventually distributed with poor box-office results by Columbia Pictures. In April, beset by millions of dollars in bank debt and the failure of *One from the Heart,* Coppola announced his intention to sell his Zoetrope Studios for a minimum bid of $20,000,000.

Columbia Pictures, CBS Inc., and Home Box Office (HBO) announced plans on Nov. 30 to create a motion picture company expected to begin operations early in 1983. CBS hoped to fulfill its intention of becoming a power in the film industry, and HBO, a unit of Time Inc. and the dominant company in the pay television field, would guarantee itself an additional source of feature films. HBO, which had earlier agreed to license Columbia films for pay television, agreed to license all the films produced by the new studio.

Fatal Accident. Actor Vic Morrow and two child performers, aged 6 and 7, were killed on July 23 when they were hit by a helicopter's rotor blade during filming of a Vietnam war scene for *The Twilight Zone,* a Warner Bros. film. Special-effects explosives damaged the helicopter's main rotor, apparently because the aircraft was flying too close to the ground. The accident occurred at 2:30 A.M. in a park 40 mi. north of Los Angeles. California Labor Commissioner Patrick Henning said that employment of the youngsters at that hour violated state laws, which prohibit children from working after 6:30 P.M. Warner Bros. and several of the film's production chiefs were fined $5000 each. In Au-

gust members of Hollywood's guilds and craft unions proposed establishment of a union-management safety commission to prevent such incidents in the future.   D.S.

MOZAMBIQUE. Armed opposition to the Marxist government of President Samora Machel increased in 1982. The Mozambique Resistance Movement (MRM), led by former Portuguese colonial agents, spearheaded the resistance, which took the form of widespread sabotage of railway lines, bridges, and government facilities, as well as assassination of government supporters and abduction of foreign technical advisers. In February Machel appointed a military commander for each province, and in the south, where guerrilla activity was greatest, he began to arm a civilian militia. He also brought in 200 Tanzanian military advisers to replace Soviet-bloc personnel in combating the MRM.

Documents captured in a raid on an MRM camp provided support for the government's contention that neighboring South Africa was providing arms and money for the rebel forces. South Africa denied the charge, but a South African radio station broadcast MRM propaganda into Mozambique and MRM training bases operated in South Africa and Malawi. In June the army launched a major offensive against rebel bases in Manica Province, with inconclusive results.

Fostering the insurgency was the country's economic plight, which Western analysts attributed in part to the government's experimentation with communal farms and tight market controls. Two years of drought and floods aggravated the problem of poor agricultural production. As a result, the government had to buy grain to supplement what Mozambique received in aid from other countries, among them the United States.

Although the government continued to adhere to Marxist theory, it turned increasingly to the West in 1982 for financial and other assistance. In late June Machel signed several economic agreements with visiting Portuguese Prime Minister Francisco Pinto Balsemão, thus adding to previous agreements with Lisbon for arms and military training.

See STATISTICS OF THE WORLD.   J.T.S.

The $40,000,000 Roy Thomson Hall was opened in Toronto in September. The circular, flat-topped building contained a 2812-seat auditorium to serve as the new home of the Toronto Symphony. It would also be used for recitals.

MUSIC. Of the many remarkable events in the music world in 1982 the following were outstanding:

CLASSICAL MUSIC

Leon Fleisher's return to the two-handed piano repertory, on Sept. 16, was both a personal and a musical triumph for the pianist, following a long illness that had kept him from using his right hand. Fleisher played César Franck's *Symphonic Variations* with the Baltimore Symphony in a gala concert that opened the city's Joseph Meyerhoff Hall. The renowned pianist Vladimir Horowitz made his first European appearance in 31 years at London's Royal Festival Hall on May 22. Making his first important mark on the world of music was 13-year-old pianist Pavel Pskarsky, who won the National Symphony Orchestra's Young Soloists Competition. Other contest winners included Andrew Litton, of New York City, in the British Broadcasting Corp.'s Sixth International Young Conductors' Contest; Thomas Reibl, violist, the Naumburg

Competition; and Horacio Gutiérrez, pianist, the Avery Fisher Prize.

New and refurbished concert halls opened in many cities during 1982. In March London unveiled its Barbican Centre, the largest arts complex in Western Europe. On Sept. 10 New Orleans socialites turned out in record numbers for the first concert in the beautifully restored Orpheum Theater, and in Toronto Roy Thomson Hall opened on Sept. 13. Of special interest was the Sept. 24 inauguration in Eugene, Oreg., of Silva Concert Hall, whose electronically controlled acoustics were designed by Christopher Jaffee. The New York City Opera began its fall season on Sept. 7 in a newly renovated New York State Theater. Critics who reviewed the performance judged the theater's acoustics to be improved but not yet perfected. The City Opera, however, lost a familiar hall on April 4, when the Filene Center at Wolf Trap Farm, Vienna, Va., where the company often played, was destroyed by fire. This disaster forced one of the nation's major summer music festivals to use a temporary structure.

As in other years, there were several changes among music directors and administrators. Christoph von Dohnányi, the director of the Hamburg State Opera, was named music director of the Cleveland Orchestra, beginning in 1984. Christopher Keene took over as artistic supervisor of the New York City Opera, to assist Beverly Sills. In Florida Emerson Buckley, the artistic director of the Greater Miami Opera, resigned on June 1 after 32 years of service. On May 23 Sergiu Comissiona conducted his final concert with the American Symphony Orchestra before leaving for Europe to become the permanent guest conductor of the Radio Philharmonic Orchestra of the Netherlands. On the administrative side, Seymour Rosen, the Philadelphia Orchestra's executive director, resigned in March and was appointed to be the artistic director of New York City's Carnegie Hall on July 1. Stephen Sell replaced him in Philadelphia. Adrian Gnam, an oboist and conductor, was appointed to be the director of the music program of the National Endowment for the Arts.

In New York City, in a surprise announcement, John Mazzola resigned as president of Lincoln Center. Benjamin S. Dunham, of Chamber Music America, was named executive director of the American Symphony, and Joanne Hubbard Cossa took over the leadership of the Chamber Music Society of Lincoln Center. In March trumpet player and conductor Gerard Schwarz agreed to become permanent music adviser to Lincoln Center's Mostly Mozart Festival, whose orchestra signed a three-year contract specifying that such a position be established.

Other orchestral events also made news in 1982. On March 7 the New York Philharmonic performed its 10,000th concert, a world record. In February the instruments of Israel's Kibbutz Chamber Orchestra and the van transporting them were stolen from a parking place in New York City. They were recovered on Feb. 19. A public outcry followed the Boston Symphony's decision to cancel its April 2 performance of Igor Stravinsky's *Oedipus Rex*. Protesters had objected to the appearance of Vanessa Redgrave, the scheduled narrator, for her support of the Palestine Liberation Organization. On July 1 the board of directors of the Kansas City (Mo.) Philharmonic voted to disband the orchestra. A new organization, however, the Kansas City Symphony, began to operate on Sept. 16, under the management of the Lyric Opera of Kansas City.

Opera News. Operatic premieres provided a rich musical tapestry in 1982. Among them were Robert Ward's *Minutes Till Midnight,* which opened at the Greater Miami Opera on June 4, with Emerson Buckley conducting. Ward's *Abelard and Heloise* was performed at the Charlotte (N.C.) Opera on Feb. 19, with Richard Marshall conducting. Two operas for young people were heard for the first time in April: Gian-Carlo Menotti's *A Bride from Pluto,* at the Kennedy Center Terrace Theater in Washington, D.C.; and Charles Strouse's *The Emperor and the Nightingale,*

Zubin Mehta conducts the New York Philharmonic on March 7 in its gala 10,000th concert performance, a world record. Singers Maureen Forrester (foreground) and Kathleen Battle flank the podium during the performance of Gustav Mahler's Resurrection Symphony.

at Wolf Trap Farm Barns. Other American world premieres included Henry Mollicone's *The Mask of Evil,* performed by the Minnesota Opera on April 30; Alice Parker's *The Ponder Heart,* in Jackson, Miss., on Sept. 10; Stephen Paulus's *The Postman Always Rings Twice,* by the Opera Theater of St. Louis on June 17; and George Rochberg's *The Confidence Man,* by the Santa Fe (N.Mex.) Opera on July 31. No less intense was the operatic scene in Europe, where audiences heard world premieres of Luciano Berio's *La Vera Storia,* performed by La Scala Opera, of Milan, Italy, on March 9, and Maurizio Kagel's *Présentation* and *Der Tribun,* given in Munich on Jan. 30.

The Concert World. A variety of world premieres of orchestral and chamber music demonstrated the continuing vitality of contemporary classical music. As part of the New York Philharmonic's program of commissioned works for its principal players, George Walker's Concerto for Violoncello was played by Lorne Munroe on Jan. 14, with Zubin Mehta conducting. Paula Robison introduced Leon Kirchner's *Music for Flute and Orchestra* at Carnegie Hall on March 7 with the American Symphony Orchestra, Michael Tilson Thomas conducting. In California James Galway premiered John Corigliano's *Pied Piper Fantasy* on Feb. 4 with the Los Angeles Philharmonic, Myung-Whun Chung conducting. The Sept. 29 world premiere of Lou Harrison's Symphony No. 3 by the Cabrillo Music Festival was conducted by Dennis Russell Davies. The world premiere of Ernst Křenek's *Arc of Life* was performed by the Los Angeles Chamber Orchestra on Feb. 24, with Gerard Schwarz conducting.   J.B.B.

RECORDINGS

The classical music recording industry's financial retrenchment of recent years became increasingly apparent in 1982. With notable exceptions, such costly large-scale projects as operas were giving way to inexpensive solo and chamber albums. The industry's mood was nevertheless guardedly optimistic at the end of the year. The imminent release on the American market of fully digital Compact Discs and Compact Disc players for home use promised to revitalize the industry.

Anniversaries. Centenary celebrations contributed to the year's releases. By far the most impressive single package was the 31-disc CBS tribute to Igor Stravinsky (1882–1971), which offered most of the composer's performances of his own works. This release was, however, poorly documented. Far greater acclaim was accorded to the arrival from Hungary of Hungaroton's meticulously researched 13-disc release of all the recordings of Béla Bartók (1881–1945).

Two works commissioned for the Boston Symphony's 100th anniversary in 1981, Roger Sessions's Concerto for Orchestra and Andrzej Panufnik's *Sinfonia Votiva,* were ignored by American companies but released by the small British label Hyperion in performances led by Seiji Ozawa. German labels rallied around the Berlin Philharmonic for its 1982 centenary. Historical surveys of the orchestra were released by EMI Electrola, on five discs in a single box, and by Deutsche Grammophon (DG), which offered 33 discs in six sets. Both surveys began with Arthur Nikisch's 1913 version of Ludwig van Beethoven's Fifth Symphony, the earliest recording of a complete symphony. DG followed with a five-disc package of new performances by various conductorless Philharmonic chamber ensembles.

The Berlin Philharmonic's anniversary was also attended by an extraordinary number of other major releases, some of them representing significant new directions for its 74-year-old music director, Herbert von Karajan. DG symphony recordings included Anton Bruckner's First and Second, completing the cycle; Camille Saint-Saëns's Third; Carl Nielsen's Fourth; Dimitri Shostakovich's Tenth; Richard Strauss's *Alpine;* and a three-disc set of Joseph Haydn's *Paris* symphonies. Also from DG came the violin concertos of Johannes Brahms, Max Bruch, and Felix Mendelssohn, with soloist Anne-Sophie Mutter; the piano concertos of Edvard Grieg and Robert Schumann, played by Krystian Zimerman; and Wolfgang Amadeus Mozart's C minor *Mass* ("the Great"), performed by the Vienna Singverein.

In Search of Authenticity. Efforts to resurrect the performance styles of past eras multi-

plied steadily. Possibly the most eccentric manifestation in 1982 of this tendency was conductor Joshua Rifkin's recording, without chorus, of Johann Sebastian Bach's B minor *Mass.* This Nonesuch release exemplified Rifkin's controversial theory that many of Bach's "choruses" were originally performed by only one singer for each part. Peter Schreier's recording of the same *Mass* (Eurodisc) adhered to a more conservative interpretation, using "original" instruments, but larger forces. The "traditional" modern-instrument approach found its advocate in Eugen Jochum, who recorded the Bach work for Angel.

Christopher Hogwood's scintillating series of Mozart symphonies on original instruments neared its end with the appearance of Volume I, the fifth to be released, which contained a performance of the newly discovered F major, K.19a (L'Oiseau-Lyre). Joining it was a similar series devoted to the symphonies of Haydn, with spirited performances by L'Estro Armonico, Derek Solomons directing. Volumes 1 and 2 were released by Saga, Volume 3 by CBS. Baroque specialist Nikolaus Harnoncourt added a sparkling performance of the *Prague* Symphony to his releases of late Mozart symphonies, with the Concertgebouw Orchestra of Amsterdam (Telefunken). Harnoncourt used his own Concentus Musicus and the Vienna State Opera Chorus for his recording of Mozart's *Requiem* (Telefunken).

Archiv offered enticing packages of *German Chamber Music Before Bach,* by the Cologne (West Germany) Musica Antiqua, and of Bach harpsichord concertos, by Trevor Pinnock and the English Concert. L'Oiseau-Lyre uncovered John Ward's delightfully idiosyncratic *1613 Madrigals,* performed by Anthony Rooley and his Consort of Musicke. **Piano.** No classical artist had been so closely identified with the recording medium as Canadian pianist Glenn Gould, a lifelong Bach specialist. Gould's death in October followed shortly after the release of his extraordinary digital recording of Bach's *Goldberg Variations* (CBS). Ironically, it was a CBS release of the same work that launched Gould's recording career in 1955. That issue continued to be available. Gould, however, also explored other areas, as captured in the 1982 release of the pianist's fascinating two-disc recording of late Haydn sonatas (CBS).

The Audiofon label, based in Florida, made its debut with a series of fine nondigital piano recordings that stressed sound as well as performance. Most notable were the performances by Leonard Shure of Franz Schubert's Sonata in B flat and of Beethoven's opus 110 Sonata and the *Diabelli Variations.* Another superior *Diabelli* recording featured Peter Serkin (RCA). Rudolf Serkin, Peter's father, continued his Beethoven concerto cycle, with a performance of the Concerto No. 4 with the Boston Symphony, under Ozawa's direction (Telarc). The elder Serkin also launched a Mozart concerto cycle, playing Nos. 12 and 20 with the London Symphony under Claudio Abbado (DG).

Two splendid two-disc sets documented concert performances, both given on Nov. 1, 1981: Earl Wild's *Art of the Transcription* (Audiofon), at Carnegie Hall, and Vladimir Horowitz's *Live from the Met* (RCA).

Hoping to spur a major revival of Charles Valentin Alkan's music, Arabesque began a project devoted to his piano works, with three discs performed by Ronald Smith.

Symphonic and Chamber Works. In two admirable British sets, from Unicorn and Chandos, respectively, Eric Fenby led the Royal Philharmonic in works by Frederick Delius, who had originally dictated them to Fenby after having lost his sight, and Australian Geoffrey Simon conducted the London Symphony in previously unknown music by Pëtr Ilich Tchaikovsky, including the original version of *Romeo and Juliet*. Recent interest in Shostakovich resulted in additions to Bernard Haitink's continuing cycle of the composer's symphonies with the London Philharmonic (London). A recording of Shostakovich's 14th came from Leonard Bernstein with the New York Philharmonic (CBS), and a striking 13th from Kiril Kondrashin with the Moscow Philharmonic Symphony (Philips). Angel continued its Jean Sibelius cycle.

Chamber music recordings produced a remarkable number of Brahms releases. The Juilliard Quartet's digital recording of the six Bartók string quartets (CBS) represented the group's third release of these works.

Opera, Choral, and Solo Vocal Works. With a few exceptions, the year's operatic recordings were not centered on standard repertory. Among noteworthy releases were Beethoven's *Fidelio*, with Hildegard Behrens, Kurt Masur conducting (Eurodisc); the second installment, *Die Walküre*, in the first completely digital *Ring des Nibelungen* cycle of Richard Wagner, with Jeannine Altmeyer, Jessye Norman, Theo Adam, and Marek Janowski (Eurodisc); and two recordings of Wagner's *Tristan und Isolde*, one with Reginald Goodall leading the Welsh National Opera (London), the other the long-awaited release conducted by Carlos Kleiber, with

Margaret Price and René Kollo (DG). More esoteric fare included Leoš Janáček's *Cunning Little Vixen*, with Lucia Popp and Charles Mackerras (London); Jean Martinů's *Greek Passion*, with John Mitchinson and Mackerras (Supraphon); excerpts of Modest Musorgski's *Salammbô*, with Zoltán Peskó (CBS); Jaromir Weinberger's *Schwanda*, with Popp, Hermann Prey, and Heinz Wallberg (CBS); and Virgil Thomson's *Four Saints in Three Acts*, with Clamma Dale and Joel Thome (Nonesuch).

Two of the year's major collections of song recitals were especially striking. They were the three-disc release of Elly Ameling singing the complete Haydn (Philips) and the four-disc recording of Dietrich Fischer-Dieskau singing music of Franz Liszt (DG).

Innovations. The giant distributor PolyGram introduced a "special import" service (PSI) to make available items too limited in appeal to interest American PolyGram branches. For the buyer of classical music this meant access to a wide range of additional DG, Philips, and London recordings. London inaugurated a new medium-price Jubilee reissue line with impressive first releases. CBS Masterworks adopted new packaging, designed to stress label identity and call attention to recent quality-control improvements. CBS also announced that it had allowed its longtime exclusive contract with the New York Philharmonic to lapse, and that it planned to restrict itself to occasional individual releases by the orchestra.   J.R.O.

POPULAR MUSIC

Although popular record sales continued to slip in 1982, a large number of best-selling discs by new artists indicated that, from an artistic point of view, the record business was healthier than ever.

Among newcomers who received platinum awards from the Recording Industry Association of America in 1982, for sales of more than 1,000,000 long-playing records, were the Go-Go's, Quarterflash, Loverboy, Asia, Joan Jett, Rick Springfield, Vangelis, Juice Newton, John Cougar, Richard Simmons, and Survivor. The award also went to the Royal Philharmonic Orchestra for its "disco-beat" medley album, "Hooked on

Classics." The orchestra's follow-up record, "Hooked on Classics II," received the gold award when sales exceeded 500,000 units.

Trends and Comebacks. A significant shift in taste became apparent when AM top-40 radio stations began to play "modern rock" by several groups that had formerly been considered "new wave." In this largely British vanguard were such acts as A Flock of Seagulls, Haircut 100, Soft Cell, the Motels, the Clash, the Human League, and Missing Persons. This change in programming seemed to be related to the arrival of a new generation of listeners, as well as to the competition from album-oriented (AOR) FM stations.

The AOR stations, however, continued to dominate the airwaves, and the record charts still reflected the popularity of 1970's-style mainstream rock. Among the established groups that enjoyed big successes in 1982 were AC/DC, Foreigner, Journey, the Rolling Stones, the J. Geils Band, Hall and Oates, Van Halen, Billy Squier, the Steve Miller Band, Fleetwood Mac, and the Who.

Moreover, several older artists returned to the top. Most surprising of these comebacks was that of Crosby, Stills and Nash. After a decade of following their separate careers and returning from a very different kind of musical era, they joined the top 10 in 1982 with their recording of "Daylight Again." Paul Simon and Art Garfunkel enjoyed a popular revival with their double album of old favorites, recorded at a concert in New York City's Central Park in September, 1981. Chicago returned to the top, following a period of obscurity. Both Paul McCartney and Aretha Franklin also enjoyed their biggest recording successes in several years. Among the artists from existing or former groups who released solo LP recordings, the most successful were Michael McDonald (Doobie Brothers), Stevie Nicks (Fleetwood Mac), and Robert Plant (Led Zeppelin).

Country, Jazz, and Rhythm and Blues. In the realm of rhythm and blues, as well as jazz, the biggest-selling artists of 1982 included Diana Ross; Prince; George Benson; Earth, Wind and Fire; Al Jarreau; Shalamar; Ray Parker, Jr.; Stevie Wonder; Cameo; the Dazz Band; Rick James; the Gap Band; and Skyy.

The Us Festival, called the Woodstock of the 1980's, was held in California in September. About 200,000 people turned out for the three-day festival of nearly continuous electronic music and a bazaar of video games and home computers.

Top country-music artists were Hank Williams, Jr., Willie Nelson, Alabama, Kenny Rogers, the Oak Ridge Boys, Johnny Lee, and Crystal Gayle. Among those who spearheaded a resurgence of traditional country music was newcomer Ricky Skaggs.

Concerts and Festivals. On the concert scene, the two most important events of 1982 were the Us Festival in San Bernardino County, Calif., and the farewell tour by the Who. At a press conference in New York on Aug. 20, the Who's lead singer, Roger Daltrey, revealed that although the veteran British group intended to go on recording together, their autumn tour through the United States would "probably" be their last. As a result of this announcement, tickets for the Who concerts were sold out as soon as they became available at stadiums across the country.

Above, left: Roger Daltrey sings and Pete Townshend plays guitar as the Who perform to capacity crowds during their fall tour of the U.S., which the veteran British group said would "probably" be their last. Above, right: Among the hottest groups of the year was the Go-Go's, a 1960's-style rock 'n' roll girl group.

The Us Festival, proclaimed the "Woodstock of the '80's," was held at the Glen Helen Regional Park near San Bernardino, Sept. 3–5. A total of 200,000 spectators came to hear such acts as Jackson Browne, the Kinks, Fleetwood Mac, Santana, the Police, Talking Heads, Oingo Boingo, the English Beat, the Ramones, the Gang of Four, Tom Petty and the Heartbreakers, Jimmy Buffett, Eddie Money, Jerry Jeff Walker, the B-52's, the Cars, Dave Edmunds, and Pat Benatar. In addition to the music, festival organizer Steve Wozniak, a cofounder of Apple Computer Inc., offered a "technology fair" designed to acquaint the visitors with the latest developments in the world of high technology.

Business Trends. Technology seemed to promise an entirely new product line, as the Sony Corp. and its partner, Philips, prepared to introduce the digital audio player and its laser-read Compact Disc. Scheduled to appear in the U.S. in the spring of 1983, the Compact Disc was expected to offer sound of considerably better quality than that of conventional records and tapes. Because of the high price of the player, at between $700 and $800, however, the initial market was expected to be limited.

Another Sony product, the Walkman portable cassette player, sparked a veritable revolution in the U.S. marketplace in 1982. Together with its many imitators, the popular Walkman vastly accelerated the demand for prerecorded cassettes, as well as for blank tapes. Although record companies welcomed the former trend, they deplored the latter. As record sales in 1982 threatened to drop by more than 12 percent, a coalition of music industry groups decided to seek legislative action in order to combat home taping of prerecorded products. As a result, the Coalition to Save America's Music began to lobby Congress in April in an effort to gain the passage of bills designed to add a special tax on blank tape and/or on tape hardware intended for home recording. Assuming the passage of such bills, the Copyright Royalty Tribunal in Washington, D.C., was then expected to determine the amount of tax to impose and on which products to levy it. Tape and equipment manufacturers vehemently opposed such measures, and a fierce battle raged between the two groups both in the press and in Congress.

Home taping, however, was not the only cause for concern among the record companies. Such factors as the economic recession, the aging of their market, the competition of video games, and the opening of record rental shops contributed to the industry's ills.

In an effort to improve their profits, the record companies retrenched considerably by reducing their work forces and by closing some pressing plants and sales offices. The cutbacks at CBS Records, one of the industry's two largest companies, were especially drastic. Approximately 350 label staffers were laid off in the course of 1982. In December 1250 additional workers lost their jobs when CBS discontinued its manufacturing operations at its Terre Haute, Ind., plant.

The rapid decline of record sales led many labels to emphasize prerecorded cassettes. Various marketing schemes were introduced during the late summer and fall, ranging from two-album cassettes for the price of one record to "cassingles" at $2.98.

The record companies also tried to combat record counterfeiting by placing easily identifiable, nonduplicable labels on their product. In an attempt to reverse the steady erosion of singles sales, CBS started in September to release one-sided singles at less than half the price charged for the two-sided variety.

Pop People. Thelonious Monk, the great jazz pianist, died on Feb. 17 at the age of 64. And Neil Bogart, president of Boardwalk Records and Entertainment Co., died on May 8 at the age of 39. Bogart had been responsible for building the careers of Donna Summer, Kiss, and several other artists who rose to prominence in the 1970's.

Other events in the music business included the following: Rod Stewart severed his ties with longtime manager Billy Gaff; Jim Steinman sued his songwriting partner and frontman, Meat Loaf, over back royalties; RCA signed Kenny Rogers, reportedly for $20,000,000; *Dreamgirls,* the Broadway musical loosely based on the career of the Supremes, generated the biggest-selling original-cast album in recent history; soul singer Teddy Pendergrass was seriously injured in an automobile accident; Glenn Frey, Don Henley, and Randy Meisner of the former supergroup the Eagles all released solo albums; and Ricky Skaggs became the youngest member of the Grand Ole Opry.   K.T.

N

NAMIBIA. *See* SOUTH-WEST AFRICA.
NAURU. *See* STATISTICS OF THE WORLD.
NEBRASKA. *See* STATISTICS OF THE WORLD.
NEGROES IN THE UNITED STATES. To black Americans, 1982 was a year of hopes deferred, as problems of racial discrimination were shunted aside and the federal government continued to cut back on social services. For these negative signs, blacks placed much of the blame on President Ronald Reagan. They accused his Justice Department of neglecting civil rights enforcement, and they felt his promise of a "safety net" for the truly needy had not been kept.

Economic Outlook. The economic slump that persisted throughout most of 1982 fell with special severity on blacks. Business failures, more numerous among white-owned firms than at any time since the depression of the 1930's, took a crippling toll on the far weaker black business community. Struggling black businesses also found themselves in competition with newly established firms that posed as minority-owned in order to win equal employment contracts. Black farmers were also hard-hit: The U.S. Commission on Civil Rights reported that although all farmers were threatened by loss of their land, such loss had "occurred most severely among black farm operators." For urban blacks the unemployment figures rose to new highs, leading many young blacks to drop out of the employment market. Others joined the armed services, accounting for

A giant replica of a stamp commemorating the late Jackie Robinson is unveiled by Rachel Robinson, widow of the first black to play major-league baseball. Assistant Postmaster General Gordon C. Morison (left) and Los Angeles Mayor Tom Bradley look on.

more than 33 percent of Army recruits and 22 percent of Marines, far in excess of black Americans' 12 percent share of the general population. Overall, the unemployment rate among blacks reached 20.2 percent in September. In July the Census Bureau acknowledged that 34.2 percent of blacks were officially classified as poor in 1981, compared with 26.2 percent of Hispanics and 11.1 percent of whites.

To improve their economic lot, blacks continued to boycott businesses that did not employ blacks or carry goods purchased from black manufacturers. Prospects for the success of such tactics improved on July 2, when the U.S. Supreme Court unanimously upheld the legality of a 1960's boycott by blacks against merchants in Port Gibson, Miss., to provide more jobs for blacks. Operation PUSH (People United to Save Humanity), headed by the Reverend Jesse L. Jackson, successfully used the threat of a boycott in winning major concessions from such firms as the Coca-Cola Co., Seven-Up Co., and Heublein, Inc., owners of Kentucky Fried Chicken. At its annual midyear meeting, the National Association for the Advancement of Colored People set in motion a selective boycott of Hollywood motion pictures, charging that film producers had been slow to employ black actors, screenwriters, cameramen, and technicians. Black leaders also accused both the film and the television industries of continuing to cast blacks in clownish or negative roles, thus perpetuating old stereotypes.

Education. Although not as lively an issue as in previous years, controversy over the use of busing to desegregate the public schools did not go away. Early in the year, a bill to deny jurisdiction to the federal courts in school busing cases passed in the U.S. Senate, but did not pass in the House of Representatives. On June 30 the Supreme Court upheld a California voter initiative that limited the power of local school boards and state judges to mandate busing where some prior intent to segregate was not at issue. That same day, however, the Court struck down a Washington state initiative that had barred voluntary as well as mandatory school busing; the ruling thus upheld a Seattle area program of voluntary busing for the purposes of racial balance.

Another issue facing the Supreme Court was that of tax exemptions for private schools and colleges that discriminated against blacks. In January President Reagan drew a storm of protest by ordering the restoration of tax-exempt status to two private institutions, Bob Jones University of Greenville, S.C., and Goldsboro Christian Schools of Goldsboro, N.C., that acknowledged practicing racial discrimination. Reagan subsequently backtracked, leaving the question of whether the Internal Revenue Service had been justified in denying the exemptions up to the Court. Another Presidential recommendation that blacks regarded as racially motivated was a proposed tax tuition credit for parents paying private school fees.

In a case concerning discrimination in housing, an issue closely related to integration in the public schools, the Supreme Court left standing a lower court decision that Parma, Ohio, a predominantly white suburb of Cleveland, must revise its housing and zoning laws so as to encourage blacks to become residents.

Voting Rights. To blacks the most important political development of the year—indeed, of many years—was the passage in June of a law extending the Voting Rights Act of 1965 for 25 years. Like its predecessor, the new measure establishes standards and procedures designed to safeguard minorities against discrimination in election practices. The 1965 law required proof of intention to discriminate, but the new measure more broadly prohibits any procedure or practice that results in racial discrimination, even where such discrimination may have been unintentional. Another distinctive feature of the new measure is a "bail out" provision whereby a state or locality that has a history of discrimination but that can show a current ten-year record of fairness in election practices would be exempt from the requirement of "preclearing" any new voting procedures with the Justice Department.

Heartened by the new law, black leaders redoubled their efforts to get out the black vote in the November elections. They knew, however, that the struggle for voting equality was far from won. Blacks in some rural Georgia and Alabama communities still had trouble in registering to vote. Some southern counties still retained their at-large election practices, thereby keeping whites in control; voting-rights advocates pointed as an example to Burke County (Ga.), with its predominantly black population and its all-white elected board of commissioners. (The Supreme Court upheld on July 1 a federal appeals court ruling that the county voting sys-

tem was discriminatory.) In September the Justice Department charged seven states and the city of Chicago with redistricting their voting boundaries so as to dilute the political strength of their minorities.

Newsmakers. Two black mayors of major cities were reelected in 1982, Ernest N. ("Dutch") Morial in New Orleans and Kenneth A. Gibson in Newark, N.J., the latter for an unprecedented fourth term. Brooklyn's Shirley Chisholm (D, N.Y.), the first black woman elected to Congress, decided not to seek reelection after 14 years in the House.

In the November elections, Tom Bradley lost his bid to become the first popularly elected black governor of California, and Robert Clark lost his attempt to become the first black elected to Congress from Mississippi since Reconstruction days. However, 20 blacks were elected to the House, a pickup of three seats and a new high.

Lt. Gen. Roscoe Robinson, Jr., commanding general of the U.S. Army in Japan and decorated for valor in the Korean and Vietnam wars, was promoted to four-star general, the first black to attain that Army rank. Lt.

Loretta Thompson Glickman was inaugurated in May as the first black mayor of Pasadena, Calif. Glickman, 38, had formerly been a schoolteacher and entertainer.

Gen. Julius W. Becton, commanding general of the VII U.S. Army Corps in Stuttgart, West Germany, for 30 months, received the Knight Commander's Cross of the Order of Merit, the Federal Republic's highest award. James H. Costen, dean of Johnson C. Smith Seminary in Atlanta, was elected moderator of the 194th General Assembly of the United Presbyterian Church. Oscar Adams was elected in November to Alabama's supreme court, the first black man to win election to a statewide office in Alabama since the Reconstruction era. Charles Fuller won the Pulitzer Prize for his drama *A Soldier's Play,* produced by the New York–based Negro Ensemble Company.

Setting a record for black golfers, Calvin Peete won championships in four tourneys on the Professional Golfers' Association circuit. And Jackie Robinson, the first black in major league baseball, appeared on a U.S. postage stamp, a first for any baseball player.

See also CIVIL RIGHTS AND CIVIL LIBERTIES. B.Q.

NEPAL. *See* STATISTICS OF THE WORLD.

NETHERLANDS, THE. Ruud Lubbers became prime minister of a center-right Netherlands government on Nov. 4, 1982, following parliamentary elections held on Sept. 8.

On May 12 the three-party center-left coalition government of Prime Minister Andreas van Agt fell apart when the Labor Party members resigned in opposition to proposals to reduce government spending and simultaneously cut taxes on industry. A minority government made up of Christian Democrats and Democrats-66 was formed by van Agt on May 29. The two parties held only 65 of the lower house of parliament's 150 seats, but Liberal Party support enabled the government to stay in power until general elections on Sept. 8.

In the September voting, no grouping won a majority. Labor, which raised its strength in the lower house of parliament from 44 seats to 47, emerged as the strongest party by a scant two seats. The Christian Democrats fell from 48 seats to 45. The right-wing Liberals made the greatest gains, especially among young voters, increasing their total from 26 seats to 36.

Lubbers, 43, a former economics minister, formed a government composed of his Christian Democrats and the Liberals. In late November the new government unveiled an economic plan that called for spending cuts amounting to about $12.3 billion over the next four years. (Public spending in 1982 consumed more than 65 percent of the country's gross national product.) The Lubbers plan also called for a freeze on public employees' wages, which unions vowed to fight.

In the area of defense, the new government indicated that it would be willing to accept deployment of 48 cruise missiles by the North Atlantic Treaty Organization if current East-West arms talks in Geneva failed. According to public opinion polls, however, about 75 percent of the Dutch people opposed the stationing of such missiles on their soil.

The gross national product was expected to increase by only 1 percent in 1982. The unemployment rate was 13 percent in late 1982 and was increasing.

Queen Beatrix visited the United States in April and June to help commemorate a yearlong celebration of 200 years of friendly relations between the Netherlands and the U.S.

See STATISTICS OF THE WORLD. L.A.S.

NEVADA. *See* STATISTICS OF THE WORLD.

NEW BRUNSWICK. *See* STATISTICS OF THE WORLD.

NEWFOUNDLAND. *See* STATISTICS OF THE WORLD.

NEW HAMPSHIRE. *See* STATISTICS OF THE WORLD.

NEW JERSEY. *See* STATISTICS OF THE WORLD.

NEW MEXICO. *See* STATISTICS OF THE WORLD.

NEW YORK. *See* STATISTICS OF THE WORLD.

NEW ZEALAND. With a working parliamentary majority of only one following 1981 elections, the government of New Zealand's Prime Minister Robert Muldoon experienced a difficult year in 1982.

The economy was Muldoon's chief problem. New Zealand continued to have difficulty in finding the new markets for its goods made necessary by Great Britain's entry into the European Community, which had caused a drop in British purchases of New Zealand products. Inflation stood at an annual rate of 17 percent, and unemployment was at 3.7 percent and rising. The gross national product was expected to increase by only 1 percent in 1982. "Think Big" was the slogan for Muldoon's program to develop domestic energy resources as substitutes for imports and as new exports, but the plan was increasingly criticized as being too slow and too expensive a means to economic stability. One of Muldoon's own cabinet ministers, Derek Quigley, spoke out against the government's economic strategy and, rejecting a demand from Muldoon to apologize, resigned his post on June 14.

The prime minister made two major attempts to improve the economic situation. He announced a 12-month wage and price freeze on June 22 as a means of containing inflation. Interest rates and the exchange rate of the New Zealand dollar were also frozen. On Aug. 5 the government introduced a budget that gave substantial income tax cuts to most citizens. It planned to recoup revenue through sales taxes and curbs on tax avoidance and evasion.

In the chief opposition party, Labour leader Wallace Rowling faced problems of his own. Convinced that union militancy had cost Labour some popularity among voters in the 1981 elections, Rowling suggested in a February speech that the party loosen its long-standing ties to the unions. The idea became the subject of bitter attack from many party members, and political analysts predicted that Rowling would vacate the top party job in the near future.

Following the outbreak of the war over the Falkland Islands, New Zealand provided a frigate to the British navy, thereby releasing a British ship for duty in the Falklands. U.S. Vice-President George Bush visited Wellington in May as part of the celebration of the 30th anniversary of the ANZUS defense pact, which links Australia, New Zealand, and the United States. On Nov. 10 Australia and New Zealand announced an agreement to phase out within five years all tariff and duty restrictions on almost all goods traded between the two countries.

See STATISTICS OF THE WORLD.   F.W.

NICARAGUA. The revolutionary government of Nicaragua's nine-member Sandinista National Directorate, headed by Daniel Ortega Saavedra, faced continuing political pressures within and outside its borders in 1982. **Politics.** Early in the year, the Sandinista regime was reported to have launched a campaign to regain the support of the 120,000 Miskito Indians in eastern Nicaragua. The isolation and neglect of the largely English-speaking Miskitos had long fostered their resentment toward Nicaragua's central government.

It was revealed in March that in what U.S. officials described as "a campaign of systematic violence" against the Miskitos, the Sandinista government had forcibly removed some 10,000 of them to five settlement camps farther south. Several Indian villages were burned, and the area bordering Honduras was militarized. Another 9000 Miskitos were said to have fled to Honduras. The Sandinistas maintained that their action was necessary in order to secure the region against increasing raids into Nicaragua by armed exiles based in Honduras.

On March 14 rightist guerrillas, believed to have entered from Honduras, bombed two major bridges in northern Nicaragua. In response, Ortega announced the suspension of all individual rights for 30 days. The Roman Catholic Church's radio station was closed indefinitely for reporting the incident before the government announced it.

In April, from exile in Costa Rica, Sandinista revolutionary hero Edén Pastora Gómez, known as Commandante Zero, denounced his former Sandinista colleagues as "traitors and murderers." Saying that he remained a dedicated leftist, Pastora decried the Cuban influence on the Sandinista regime and the Soviet-Cuban military presence in Nicaragua. His challenge to the Nicaraguan leadership was seen as signaling the emergence of a centrist movement-in-exile to overthrow the Sandinista regime. He won support from two former members of Nicaragua's ruling junta who had gone into exile, Arturo Cruz and Alfonso Robelo Callejas. How or when Pastora planned to seize power remained unclear.

A makeshift ferry over the Río Negro in Nicaragua, close to the border with Honduras, carries workers and goods. A nearby bridge was destroyed in March by antigovernment insurgents based in Honduras.

The Economy. Many Nicaraguans were disillusioned by the Sandinistas' failure to improve the country's economy. Inflation stood at an annual rate of 30 percent in August, with unemployment rising. The Sandinistas were forced to seek $450,000,000 in new foreign loans in order to keep making payments on the country's $2.4 billion foreign debt.

In March the government announced several capitalist-style economic measures. These gave Nicaraguan exporters of cotton, coffee, meat, and sugar a foreign exchange rate that was more favorable than the official rate of 10 córdobas to the U.S. dollar.

Foreign Affairs. U.S. officials said on Nov. 1 that the Central Intelligence Agency (CIA) was providing money, training, and equipment to paramilitary units of Nicaraguan exiles conducting raids from Honduras. The operation, these officials claimed, was intended to apply pressure on Nicaragua to stop providing aid to guerrillas in El Salvador, not to overthrow the Nicaraguan government itself. U.S. President Ronald Reagan had also approved distribution through the CIA of millions of dollars in covert financial aid to "moderate" individuals and private organizations within Nicaragua.

The Reagan administration asserted that aerial photographs it made public in March proved that Nicaragua was creating the largest military force in Central America, with Soviet and Cuban help. Nicaragua protested the aerial reconnaissance as "a flagrant violation of international law."

In April, in an effort to mend its relations with Nicaragua, the United States proposed an eight-point plan, including the resumption of American economic aid. In return, among other demands, the plan called for an end to Nicaragua's aid to guerrillas in El Salvador. The Sandinista government's 17-point counterproposal included a "sincere disposition to begin serious negotiations," preferably in Mexico, and invited the U.S. to set a date.

In early May the Soviet Union signed its first major aid agreement with the Sandinista regime. The five-year pact, involving $166,800,000 in technical assistance and credits for Soviet-built projects, made the U.S.S.R. one of Nicaragua's main benefactors, along with Cuba, Libya, Mexico, and Venezuela.

See STATISTICS OF THE WORLD. See also HONDURAS. A.E.J.

NIGER. See STATISTICS OF THE WORLD.

NIGERIA. Worsening economic conditions and intensified political rivalries posed problems for the Nigerian government of President Shehu Shagari in 1982. Shagari began to prepare for the 1983 presidential election by reshuffling his cabinet in February to bring more dynamic administrators into key posts. In May he sought to broaden his appeal by granting a pardon to Odumegwu Ojukwu, former leader of the Biafran war of secession, who had been living in exile. Ojukwu remained popular among the large Ibo ethnic group. In June Shagari was renominated as the presidential candidate of the National Party.

Meanwhile, in January, Shagari's political rivals proposed a merger of the four major opposition parties. Chief Obafemi Awolowo, leader of the Yoruba people, was selected to run for the presidency in March under the Unity Party's banner. Rivalries between the coalition parties led to serious splits by autumn, however.

The economy continued to suffer in 1982 from a fall in earnings because of the world oil glut. Oil production, as low as 650,000 bbl a day in March, rebounded to close to 1,500,000 bbl a day in late 1982, but projected export earnings for 1982 were only $16 billion compared with more than $26 billion in 1980. Since oil revenues accounted for about 80 percent of government income, the government had to cut back on spending for various development projects. It also suspended some imports and restricted others. In June Nigeria drew a $740,000,000 loan from the International Monetary Fund and secured a six-month $1 billion loan from Saudi Arabia.

Pope John Paul II visited Nigeria Feb. 12–16. A new outburst of religious unrest in northern Nigeria erupted in November, when at least 206 persons died in rioting blamed on an extremist Islamic sect.

See STATISTICS OF THE WORLD.   J.T.S.

NORTH ATLANTIC TREATY ORGANIZATION, abbreviated NATO. In 1982, under the leadership of Secretary-General Joseph Luns of the Netherlands and U.S. Army General Bernard W. Rogers, the supreme military commander, NATO—the Western political and military alliance—concentrated on up-grading its military strength to keep pace with forces of the Soviet-bloc Warsaw Treaty Organization (Warsaw Pact). The alliance was strengthened in May when Spain became NATO's 16th member nation. But the severe strains caused by a growing wave of pacifism in Western Europe and serious disagreement between the United States and Europe over détente were exacerbated during much of the year by U.S. sanctions against some European firms trading with the Soviets. As a result, relations between the NATO allies plummeted to what many diplomatic observers considered a new low.

Friction. At the heart of the discord within the alliance was a fierce debate over the value of détente with the East. The administration of U.S. President Ronald Reagan continued to maintain that détente had been a one-way street, permitting the Soviets to expand their military power in Europe without challenge. In this view, the Europeans placed more emphasis on expanded trade with the Soviets than meeting the military threat. But many Western European leaders believed that the hard-line stance of the Americans was the product of simplistic cold war thinking, which threatened the stability of East-West relations and made war on the continent more, rather than less, likely.

The Soviet-inspired crackdown in Poland in December, 1981, triggered a new crisis within NATO as the U.S. and its allies, while deploring the suspension of civil liberties by the Polish military rulers, were unable to agree on a unified Western response. In December, 1981, Reagan embargoed U.S. exports of oil and natural gas equipment to the Soviets. He also attempted to persuade the allies to cancel their lucrative commercial participation in the construction of a natural gas pipeline from Siberia to Western Europe. The allies refused to pull out of the pipeline deal, pointing out that the Reagan administration had agreed to sell U.S. grain to the Soviets while asking Europe to curtail its own trade. Reagan then asked the allies at an economic summit meeting in France in June to make the cost to the Soviets of trading with the West more expensive. When his attempt apparently failed, Reagan extended the Ad-

Secretary-General Joseph Luns (foreground, center) poses with U.S. President Ronald Reagan (left) and the·government heads of Canada, Great Britain, and Italy and the foreign ministers of the U.S. and West Germany at a NATO summit meeting held in Bonn in June. At this meeting particular stress was laid on improving NATO's conventional defenses.

ministration's embargo on pipeline exports to foreign subsidiaries of U.S. firms and European businesses using licensed American technology. Several European nations promptly defied Reagan's order, which they called illegal. The embargo sanctions were lifted by Reagan on Nov. 13.

NATO Summit. NATO heads of government convened in Bonn, West Germany, on June 10 for a one-day summit meeting called in an attempt to paper over, in the interest of Western solidarity, the hard feelings within the alliance. The summit leaders released a broadly worded communiqué in which they reaffirmed their commitment to a stronger common defense, stressing the need to improve the readiness and capability of NATO's military forces. In language designed to defuse Europe's antinuclear movement, which drew more than 200,000 demonstrators at the summit, the communiqué also stressed NATO's willingness to participate in arms reduction talks with the Soviet bloc and pledged "to develop substantial and bal-

anced East-West relations aimed at genuine détente."

Nuclear Maneuverings. Responding to the growing antinuclear movement in Western Europe and the U.S., American and Soviet leaders sought to gain the propaganda advantage with proposals to reduce military tensions in Europe. Soviet President Leonid I. Brezhnev, in a speech in February, suggested a two-thirds reduction in U.S. and Soviet medium-range nuclear weapons on the continent, declaring that it was "madness for any country to build its policy with an eye to nuclear war." Reagan countered in May, proposing that both superpowers reduce their strategic nuclear strength by at least one third, with land-based missiles limited to one half the total nuclear force. Reagan followed up with a suggestion that both sides institute a seven-year phased reduction of conventional forces in central Europe to 900,000, with a 700,000 limit on ground forces. This second plan was formally submitted by U.S. negotiators in Vienna in July at the force-reduction talks, which remained stalemated after nine years.

Despite the rhetorical emphasis on arms reductions, NATO proceeded with plans to deploy 464 U.S. ground-launched cruise missiles and 108 Pershing II medium-range nuclear missiles by 1984 to counter the Soviet buildup of SS-20 missiles in Eastern Europe. But Reagan's November, 1981, pledge to cancel the NATO deployment plan if Moscow dismantled its SS-20's remained on the table.

Military Affairs. A study issued by NATO defense ministers in May claimed that the Soviet bloc Warsaw Pact forces had achieved superiority in nearly all categories of military power but that the alliance's nuclear strength remained a powerful deterrent to war in Europe. The report concluded that the military balance had moved steadily in the Warsaw Pact's favor over the last decade and provided support for the Reagan administration's contention that a major expansion of NATO military strength was overdue. U.S. Secretary of Defense Caspar Weinberger told a defense seminar in Munich in February that the 1978 NATO agreement to increase defense spending by 3 percent annually beyond inflation had become inadequate, and Gen. Rogers called for a 4 percent increase in real terms beginning in 1983. Several NATO members, however, again failed to meet the 3 percent target, intensifying U.S. complaints that the allies were foot-dragging for fear of offending the Soviets.

Dozier Freed. Italian antiterrorist police stormed an apartment in Padua on Jan. 28 and rescued U.S. Army General James L. Dozier from his Red Brigades captors. Dozier, a staff officer at a NATO installation in Verona, had been held 42 days before being rescued after the most intensive Italian police dragnet in history.

See also COMMUNISM; MILITARY AND NAVAL AFFAIRS; and articles on NATO member nations.   T.D.

NORTH CAROLINA. See STATISTICS OF THE WORLD.

NORTH DAKOTA. See STATISTICS OF THE WORLD.

NORTHWEST TERRITORIES. See STATISTICS OF THE WORLD.

NORWAY. Unemployment became increasingly serious in Norway in 1982, reaching a postwar high of 2.6 percent of the labor force in August. Inflation, at an annual rate of 11.5 percent, compounded the problem.

The minority government of Conservative Prime Minister Kaare Willoch took several steps in its effort to revitalize the economy and put people back to work. Most significantly, it devalued the krone twice, in August and September, in an effort to make exports more competitive in world markets. The second of the monetary adjustments, a 3 percent devaluation effective on Sept. 6, together with the August devaluation and a recent decline in the value of the krone in foreign exchange markets, reduced the value of Norway's currency by a total of 10 percent. The government's move was intended ultimately to increase the volume of exports, but an immediate result was a deepening of the country's already troublesome inflation.

The plans of the Oslo government, moreover, seemed to go awry only a month later. It anticipated, as a result of the decrease in the krone's value, a growth in exports of Norwegian products, especially to the other Scandinavian countries, which are among Norway's chief trading partners. But on Oct. 8 Sweden devalued its own currency, by 16 percent. Sweden's action precipitated a flurry of anxiety among all the other Nordic countries. As a result, Norway on Oct. 11 reduced the duty-free allowance for Swedish imports.

Finance Minister Rolf Presthus issued a budget proposal for 1983 on Oct. 6 that called for corporate income tax cuts in order to improve the competitive position of Norwegian industry. It also called for individual income tax cuts designed principally to benefit higher wage brackets, and it proposed raising alcohol and tobacco taxes. A Conservative Party spokesman indicated that the government might resign if parliament rejected the budget.

Norway was one of the dissenters as the International Whaling Commission, by a 25–7 margin, voted on July 23 for a worldwide ban on commercial whaling, starting in 1985. The decision was not enforceable.

See STATISTICS OF THE WORLD.   L.A.S.

Radioactive steam is vented from the Rochester Gas & Electric Corp.'s Robert E. Ginna nuclear power plant in Ontario, N.Y., on Jan. 25. The mishap was regarded as the most serious accident at a commercial nuclear plant since the 1979 near disaster at Three Mile Island.

NOVA SCOTIA. See STATISTICS OF THE WORLD.

NUCLEAR POWER. The U.S. nuclear power industry continued to experience hard times in 1982. Eighty-two nuclear power reactors had been licensed for operation, another 68 were under construction, and 8 more were on order. But no new orders had been placed since 1978, and at least eight projects were canceled in 1982. Public unease about safety was one reason; continuing steep rises in the cost of building, operating, and maintaining nuclear power plants was another.

On Jan. 22 the Washington Public Power Supply System (WPPSS) announced that it was killing plans to complete its partially constructed WPPSS 4 and 5 plants, near Richland and Satsop, Wash., respectively. On April 29 it voted to suspend construction of WPPSS 1, in Richland. On Feb. 16 the Public Service Co. of Oklahoma canceled work authorizations for two plants. On Feb. 23 Duke Power Co. in North Carolina terminated purchase agreements for three plants.

Ten days later, the Tennessee Valley Authority (TVA) announced "indefinite deferral" of its Yellow Creek 1 plant at Corinth, Miss., and Hartsville 1 and 2 plants in northern Tennessee. The TVA had already spent $2.1 billion on the three plants, which made the decision costly. By the end of May the TVA said that it was planning to cancel work on eight reactors it had until then postponed. Philadelphia Electric Co. was in a similar situation, unable to decide whether to shelve construction of its Limerick 2 plant for three years or to kill it outright.

Mishaps. A ruptured steam-generator tube triggered bursts of slightly radioactive steam and caused a shutdown of the Robert E. Ginna plant in Ontario, N.Y., on Jan. 25. An investigation disclosed that a spear-shaped scrap of steel plate accidentally left inside a steam generator after 1975 design changes might have been responsible.

Other incidents further tarnished the industry's image. Among them was a report prepared for the Nuclear Regulatory Commission (NRC) by Oak Ridge National Laboratory and Science Applications. The report reviewed 19,400 "off-normal" events at nuclear plants between 1969 and 1979. An analysis rated 169 of the mishaps as serious.

In addition, 111 errors and possible errors were discovered in March at the $2.3 billion Diablo Canyon nuclear plant near San Luis Obispo, Calif. The design flaws raised questions as to whether the reactor could withstand an earthquake—something the NRC requires of plants in quake-prone regions. Diablo Canyon had received a low-power operating license in September, 1981, but the license was suspended in November of that year after discrepancies were uncovered in its design and construction.

Three Mile Island. In April the Department of Energy (DOE) signed an agreement with General Public Utilities Corp. (GPU), owner of the Three Mile Island No. 2 reactor damaged in 1979, to acquire its core for federal study. However, the core would not be ready for removal for at least three more years. In fact, it was not until July 21 that engineers responsible for cleanup at the plant got their first look at the damaged core through videotapes of a 2-hr. camera inspection performed that day. Though the tapes only pictured the gross condition of the core, there was sufficient detail to establish that much of it had been reduced to rubble.

In September GPU announced that the second phase of its cleanup program had begun. Approximately three times a week engineers entered the plant to spray water on building surfaces. The water, carrying away radioactive deposits, drained into a basement sump, where it was collected for decontamination.

Clinch River. Ground-breaking ceremonies were held on Sept. 22 for the much delayed Clinch River breeder reactor near Oak Ridge, Tenn. The breeder reactor had been approved in 1972, and $1.3 billion had already been spent on its development. In September the General Accounting Office (GAO) concluded that the project's cost could exceed $8 billion, more than double the federal government's current estimate. (Cost projections had been revised six times in the plant's 11-year history.) But the Breeder-Reactor Corp. disputed the GAO figure and also disputed the contention that the reactor's design was not only obsolete but a "technological turkey." Attempts were made to kill appropriations for the project in both the U.S. House of Representatives and Senate. They failed, in the Senate by a single vote.

Nuclear Wastes. Congress approved a bill on Dec. 21 that called for building a permanent underground repository before the year 2000 for storing radioactive wastes from nuclear power plants. It called for temporary storage sites until that date.

International Developments. Nuclear troubles were not confined to the United States. Yugoslavia announced in April that it had scaled down energy production and opted for coal instead of nuclear power. Work on the nuclear plant at Lemoniz, near Bilbao,

Spain, was suspended following the assassination of the plant's director, Angel Pascual Mugica, by Basque terrorists in May. Mexico announced on May 18 that its ambitious nuclear power development program was being shelved because of the nation's financial crisis. Companies from five nations had been bidding on the construction of 20 reactors.

In France the nation's first experimental breeder reactor, Rapsodie, was shut down permanently after 15 years of service. The reactor was closed in January because of a nitrogen leak; by October the government had decided that repair costs could not be justified. Also in January, Superphoenix, planned to be France's first full-scale breeder reactor, was hit by antitank rockets. Responsibility was claimed by a group calling itself the Pacifist and Ecologist Committee.

On Sept. 8 the administration of U.S. President Ronald Reagan announced that it would tighten controls on the export of nuclear technology by issuing a new list of countries for which specific approval of shipments would be necessary. The list of 63 countries offered a few surprises. South Korea and Taiwan, formerly a source of worry owing to their keen interest in nuclear technology, were omitted, ostensibly because they had signed the Nuclear Nonproliferation Treaty. However, Iran, Iraq, Libya, and Syria—also signatories to the treaty—were listed. The Administration said that Communist bloc nations would remain on the list, as would "unstable" nations.

China announced in September that it had started construction of its first nuclear power station. Its two 300-megawatt generators were expected to begin operation in 1988.

The U.S. had declined to resupply an Indian atomic power plant after Congress passed a bill in 1978 (in the wake of India's detonation of an atomic device in 1974) barring resupply by the U.S. of nuclear fuel to any nation that refused to permit full international inspection of its nuclear facilities. In a compromise announced on July 29, France was to supply the fuel for India's Tarapur power plant, but India would not be allowed to reprocess the spent fuel without U.S. permission. J.A.R.

283

O

OBITUARIES. Each entry below contains the name of a notable person who died in 1982. It also contains a brief description of the accomplishments and events that contributed to making each person notable.

Abdullah, Mohammad, Indian politician. Known for more than four decades as the "Lion of Kashmir," he was a Muslim leader in the movement for independence from Great Britain. He was chief minister of Jammu and Kashmir (1947–53), but was deposed for urging independence for Kashmir and spent the next 20 years in jail, under house arrest, or in exile before becoming chief minister again in 1975. Died Sept. 8, age 76.

Ace, Goodman, American comedy writer. *Easy Aces,* a radio show starring himself and his wife, was on the air from 1928 to 1945. Later he was probably television's highest-paid writer. Died March 25, age 83.

Adams, Harriet Stratemeyer, American writer. She was the author or editorial director for nearly 200 children's books written under various pseudonyms, including books of the Nancy Drew, Hardy Boys, Bobbsey Twins, and Tom Swift, Jr., series. Died March 27, age 89.

al-Bakr, Ahmed Hassan, Iraqi statesman. An army officer, he took part in the 1958 military coup that overthrew the monarchy. In 1968 he led another coup and served as president until 1979. Died Oct. 4, age 68.

Aragon, Louis, French poet and novelist. First a dadaist and later a surrealist, he became a Communist after a visit to the Soviet Union in 1930. His work thereafter emphasized class struggle. Died Dec. 24, age 85.

Balmain, Pierre, French fashion designer. His ball gowns were worn by royalty and film stars. Died June 29, age 68.

Barnes, Djuna, American writer. Among her works, which included short stories, poems, novels, and a play, was the avant-garde novel *Nightwood* (1937), told Greek-chorus style by a physician. Died June 18, age 90.

Belushi, John, American comedian. He was a hit on television's *Saturday Night Live* and in such films as *National Lampoon's Animal House* and *The Blues Brothers.* Died March 5, age 33.

Benelli, Giovanni, Italian Roman Catholic prelate. A conservative, he was Pope Paul VI's principal aide and adviser as deputy secretary of state of the Vatican (1967–77). He became archbishop of Florence and a cardinal in 1977. Died Oct. 26, age 61.

Bergman, Ingrid, Swedish actress. Noted for her beauty and acting ability, she starred in such films as *Intermezzo* (1939), *Casablanca* (1943), *For Whom the Bell Tolls* (1943), and *Notorious* (1946). She received Oscars as best actress for her performances in *Gaslight* (1944) and *Anastasia* (1956) and as best supporting actress in *Murder on the Orient Express* (1974). Later films included *Autumn Sonata* (1978), and she also appeared on the stage and on television. Died Aug. 29, age 67.

Irreverent comic John Belushi starred on television's Saturday Night Live *and in such films as* National Lampoon's Animal House.

Swedish actress Ingrid Bergman became one of Hollywood's most popular film stars and won three Oscars.

Berlin, Don R., American aircraft designer. During World War II he designed and developed the Curtiss P-36, P-40, and Hawk 75 fighter planes. Died May 17, age 83.

Bettis, Valerie, American dancer and choreographer. Her works included experimental ballets incorporating dancing, singing, and acting. Died Sept. 26, age 62.

Biemiller, Andrew J., American labor leader. Chief lobbyist for the American Federation of Labor and Congress of Industrial Organizations from 1956 to 1978, he was involved in drafting many major pieces of social legislation. Died April 3, age 75.

Bloomingdale, Alfred S., American businessman. A key figure in the growth of the credit card field, he was president of the Diners Club (1955–64) and chairman of its board (1964–70). Died Aug. 20, age 66.

Brezhnev, Leonid Ilyich, Soviet statesman. As head of his nation's Communist Party since 1964, he sought to make his country the military equal of the United States. Although Brezhnev supported the concept of détente with the U.S., during his years in power Moscow stamped out a liberal reform movement in Czechoslovakia, invaded Afghanistan, and pressured Polish authorities to impose martial law. During the late 1970's, repression increased in the Soviet Union and economic conditions seemed to become more difficult.

The son of a steelworker, Brezhnev was an engineer before taking a government post in 1937. During World War II he served in the Red Army as a political commissar. He rose to become president (1960–64; he again took the post in 1977) before joining with others to oust Nikita S. Khrushchev from power in 1964. *See* UNION OF SOVIET SOCIALIST REPUBLICS. Died Nov. 10, age 75.

Butler, Richard Austen, British politician. He served in seven Conservative Party governments and, as first minister of education, was responsible for a 1944 act that gave every British child the right to free secondary education. In 1965 he was made a life peer. Died March 8, age 79.

Canham, Erwin Dain, American editor. He was editor (1945–64) and editor in chief (1964–74) of the acclaimed Boston-based newspaper *The Christian Science Monitor.* Died Jan. 3, age 77.

Carr, Edward Hallett, British historian. Chief among his works was the 14-volume *History of Soviet Russia.* Died Nov. 3, age 90.

Case, Clifford Philip, American politician. A liberal New Jersey Republican, he served in

Leonid I. Brezhnev was the Soviet Union's leader, serving as head of its Communist Party from 1964.

285

Acclaimed for his short stories and novels about suburban dwellers, John Cheever won many honors, including a Pulitzer Prize.

the U.S. House of Representatives (1945–55) and U.S. Senate (1955–79). Died March 5, age 77.

Chapman, Colin, British auto designer and manufacturer. He founded Lotus Cars Ltd., which produces sports cars, and his Lotus racing cars were prominent on the Grand Prix circuit. Died Dec. 16, age 54.

Cheever, John, American writer. His more than 100 short stories and four novels stress memory and desire among upper-middle-class residents of New York and New England. He received a National Book Award in 1958 for *The Wapshot Chronicle* and a Pulitzer Prize in 1979 for a collection of short stories. Died June 18, age 70.

Chenoweth, Dean, American hydroplane racer. A four-time national champion, he was killed during a qualifying run for the annual Columbia Cup race. Died July 31, age 44.

Chuikov, Vasily I., Soviet army officer. He commanded the Soviet troops in the successful defense of Stalingrad, considered the turning point of World War II. After spearheading the Soviet drive that culminated in the capture of Berlin, he commanded the Soviet occupation force in Germany until 1953. Later he was commander of all Soviet land forces and deputy minister of defense. Died March 18, age 82.

Cody, John Patrick, American clergyman. As archbishop of Chicago, the nation's largest Roman Catholic diocese, since 1965, he

stressed strongly centralized church authority, alienating many priests who called him arbitrary in his use of power. He was made a cardinal in 1967. Earlier, as head of the New Orleans diocese, he carried out the integration of Catholic schools there. In 1981 a federal grand jury began investigating allegations that Cody had misappropriated church funds. Died April 25, age 74.

Curzon, Sir Clifford, British pianist. He was considered the leading British pianist of his generation. Died Sept. 1, age 75.

Dannay, Frederic, American writer. He was coauthor of more than 35 Ellery Queen detective novels between 1928 and 1971. Died Sept. 3, age 76.

Deutsch, Babette, American writer. A poet and novelist, she also wrote five books of literary criticism. Died Nov. 13, age 87.

Deutsch, Helene Rosenbach, Polish-American psychoanalyst. Among her works was *The Psychology of Women* (1944). Died March 29, age 97.

Devi, Ragini, American dancer. Born Esther Sherman, she introduced India's classical dances to the U.S. and helped to revive them in India itself. Died Jan. 23, age 86.

Cardinal John P. Cody was archbishop of Chicago—the nation's largest Roman Catholic diocese—for 17 years.

David Dubinsky fought to eliminate sweatshops as president of the International Ladies Garment Workers Union for 34 years.

Dick, Philip K., American writer. He was the author of 35 science-fiction novels and six collections of short stories. Died March 2, age 54.

Dietrich, Noah, American businessman. He was financial adviser to and chief executive of Howard Hughes's business empire for more than 30 years. Died Feb. 15, age 92.

Dubinsky, David, Polish-American labor leader. As president of the International Ladies Garment Workers Union, (1932–66), he greatly increased its membership and brought a standard 35-hr. week to a sweatshop industry. He helped organize the Liberal Party, a force in New York politics, in 1944. Died Sept. 17, age 90.

Dubos, René Jules, French-born American bacteriologist and writer. He was the author of 20 books on environmental and scientific questions. He received a Pulitzer Prize in 1969 for *So Human an Animal*. Died Feb. 20, age 81.

Eldjárn, Kristján, Icelandic statesman. An archeologist, he was curator of the National Museum of Iceland (1947–68) before serving as president of Iceland (1968–80). Died Sept. 13, age 65.

Engel, Lehman, American musician. He was musical director for more than 100 stage musicals and won two Tony Awards. He also composed operas, choral works, and other orchestra works, wrote seven books, and worked in radio, films, and television. Died Aug. 29, age 71.

Fassbinder, Rainer Werner, West German film director. In a career of only 13 years, he made 43 feature-length films, melodramas about individuals crushed by social institutions. Found dead June 10, age 36.

Feldman, Marty, British comedian. After performing on his own British weekly television series, he came to the U.S. in 1974 and appeared in such films as *Young Frankenstein*. Died Dec. 2, age 49.

Fitzgerald, Albert J., American labor leader. He was president of the United Electrical, Radio and Machine Workers of America (1941–78). Died May 1, age 75.

Fitzmaurice, David Joseph, American labor leader. He had been president of the International Union of Electrical Workers since 1976. Died Nov. 12, age 69.

Fonda, Henry, American actor. He appeared in many plays and in more than 80 motion pictures, playing a quiet, decent

One of Hollywood's finest actors and most popular leading men, Henry Fonda also starred on stage during a career that spanned nearly 50 years. He is shown here in the film The Grapes of Wrath.

American hero in such films as *Young Mr. Lincoln* (1939), *The Grapes of Wrath* (1940), *Mister Roberts* (1955), and *The Best Man* (1964). He received an Academy Award in 1982 for his performance in *On Golden Pond.* Died Aug. 12, age 77.

Ford, O'Neil, American architect. He was best known for integrating the architectural styles of his native Texas with modern technology. Died July 20, age 76.

Fortas, Abe, American lawyer and jurist. A founding partner of one of Washington's most successful law firms, he was appointed to the U.S. Supreme Court in 1965 after serving as an adviser to President Lyndon B. Johnson, who attempted unsuccessfully to make him chief justice in 1968. The following year Fortas resigned after it was disclosed that he had accepted a fee from a foundation operated by a former client under federal investigation. Died April 5, age 71.

Frei Montalva, Eduardo, Chilean statesman. A Christian Democrat, he promoted land reform and nationalization of the copper industry as president (1964–70). Later he opposed the military government. Died Jan. 22, age 71.

Freud, Anna, Austrian-British psychoanalyst. A daughter of Sigmund Freud, she be-

An eminent Washington lawyer and confidant of President Lyndon B. Johnson, Abe Fortas served on the U.S. Supreme Court for four years before resigning under fire.

came a specialist on the emotional and mental life of children and founded a clinic in London. Died Oct. 9, age 86.

Friedman, Benny, American football player. He was an all-American quarterback at the University of Michigan in 1925 and 1926. Later he played professional football and coached college football. Died Nov. 23, age 76.

Gardner, John, American writer. *Grendel* (1971), *The Sunlight Dialogues* (1972), and *October Light* (1976) were among his novels. Died Sept. 14, age 49.

Garroway, David Cunningham ("Dave"), American television personality. He was the first host of the popular *Today* show. Died July 21, age 69.

Gaver, John M., American horse trainer. Head trainer of Greentree Stables (1933–77), he was elected to thoroughbred racing's Hall of Fame in 1966. Died July 11, age 81.

Gemayel, Bashir, Lebanese Christian leader. He headed his country's largest militia force, the 25,000-man Phalangist army. In an election boycotted by most Muslim leaders, he was chosen president on Aug. 23 but was killed in a bomb explosion. *See* LEBANON. Died Sept. 14, age 34.

The original host of television's news and talk show Today, *Dave Garroway often appeared with sidekick J. Fred Muggs.*

Ghotbzadeh, Sadegh, Iranian politician. Foreign minister during the American hostage crisis, he fell under the disapproval of Islamic fundamentalists and was shot for allegedly plotting to kill Ayatollah Ruhollah Khomeini and establish a secular government. *See* IRAN. Died Sept. 15, age 46.

Giauque, William F., American chemist. In 1949 he received the Nobel Prize in chemistry for his contributions to the study of substances at extremely low temperatures. He also discovered two isotopes of oxygen. Died March 28, age 86.

Goldmann, Nahum, Lithuanian-born Zionist leader. He helped organize the World Jewish Congress in 1936 and was its president (1951–78). Died Aug. 29, age 87.

Gomulka, Wladyslaw, Polish politician. Gomulka led his country's Communist Party (1956–70). Promising a "Polish road to socialism," he initially loosened political and cultural restrictions and improved relations with the Roman Catholic Church. Economic conditions failed to improve, however, and he was ousted when riots and disorders broke out among shipyard workers. Died Sept. 1, age 77.

Gould, Glenn Herbert, Canadian pianist. Best known for his interpretations of the music of Johann Sebastian Bach, Gould's provocative and mannered style was highly influential. He abandoned the concert stage in 1964 and devoted himself instead to making recorded performances put together from edited tapes. Died Oct. 4, age 50.

Before becoming Princess Grace of Monaco, Grace Kelly starred in several films and won an Oscar.

Grace, Princess of Monaco. The Philadelphia-born Grace Kelly was an actress who starred in such films as *High Noon* (1952), *Rear Window* (1954), and *The Country Girl* (1954); she received an Oscar for her performance in the latter. She married Prince Rainier III in 1956. Died Sept. 14, age 52.

Gregory, Horace, American poet and scholar. In 1965 he received the Bollingen Prize, regarded as the highest honor in American poetry. Died March 11, age 83.

Grosman, Tatyana, Russian-American printmaker. She founded Universal Limited Arts Editions, which published a high proportion of classic prints in the 1960's and 1970's. Died July 24, age 78.

Widely regarded as one of the finest classical pianists of the century, Glenn Gould was especially known for his innovative interpretations of the music of Johann Sebastian Bach.

OBITUARIES

Gross, Courtland S., American businessman. He and his brother Robert founded Lockheed Aircraft Corp., parlaying a $40,000 investment into a business that grossed more than $5 billion in 1981. Died July 15, age 77.

Grumman, Leroy Randle, American aviation pioneer and businessman. Founder in 1929 of what became the Grumman Aerospace Corp., he designed fighter planes during World War II and saw his company grow to sales of almost $2 billion in 1981. He relinquished the presidency in 1946 but remained chairman of the board for another 20 years. Died Oct. 4, age 87.

Guzmán Fernández, Silvestre António, Dominican Republic statesman. Elected president of the Dominican Republic in 1978, he was credited with removing the military from politics. *See* CARIBBEAN COUNTRIES. Died July 4, age 71.

Hall, Joyce Clyde, American businessman. In 1910 he founded what became Hallmark Cards Inc., the world's largest greeting card concern and one of the world's largest privately held companies. He was its chief executive officer until 1966. Died Oct. 29, age 91.

Harkness, Rebekah West, American philanthropist. Although a generous contributor to medical research, she was best known for her support of dance, including New York City's Harkness Ballet company from 1964 to 1975. Died June 17, age 67.

Hicks, Granville, American writer and critic. Among his works was *The Great Tradition* (1933), an examination of American literature written from a Marxist point of view. Died June 18, age 80.

Hillenkoetter, Roscoe H., American naval officer. He rose to the rank of admiral, served as commander of a task force in the Korean War, and was first director of the Central Intelligence Agency (1947–50). Died June 18, age 85.

Hofheinz, Roy Mark, American businessman. After serving as mayor of Houston in the 1950's, he proposed the building of the Astrodome, the world's first domed stadium, which opened in 1965. Hofheinz held a 40-year lease on the building. Died Nov. 21, age 70.

Hopkins, Sam ("Lightnin' "), American blues singer who also had great influence on rock guitar players. Died Jan. 30, age 69.

Irish, Edward S. ("Ned"), American sports promoter. During a 40-year association with New York City's Madison Square Garden, beginning in 1934, he helped in the development of college and professional basketball. Died Jan. 21, age 76.

Jakobson, Roman, Russian-American linguist. An authority on Slavic languages and literature, he was the founder of modern phonology, the study of abstract properties of speech, and was called the father of modern structural linguistics. Died July 18, age 85.

Jaworski, Leon, American lawyer. He was best known as the second of three special prosecutors charged with investigating the Watergate scandal. A Houston lawyer, he was president of the American Bar Association (1971–72) and served as a prosecutor at the Nuremberg trials of Nazi war criminals. Died Dec. 9, age 77.

Jeritza, Maria, Czech-American opera singer. A highly acclaimed soprano, she performed at the Imperial Opera House in Vienna before coming to America for a new career at New York City's Metropolitan Opera (1921–32). Died July 10, age 94.

Johnson, Dame Celia, British actress. A star of the British stage and screen, she was best known in the U.S. for her role in the film *Brief Encounter* (1946). Died April 26, age 73.

Jurgens, Curt, German actor. He appeared in more than 160 films, many of them World War II melodramas. Died June 18, age 66.

Khalid ibn Abdul-Aziz, King of Saudi Arabia since 1975. He became king in 1975 when his half-brother Faisal was murdered. Along with his designated successor, Prince Fahd, Khalid maintained the 4000-member extended family's control of the oil-rich kingdom. *See* SAUDI ARABIA. Died June 13, age 69.

Khan, Fazlur R., Bangladesh-born American engineer. He was the creator of a system of skyscraper design, first used for Chicago's Sears Tower, in which a group of tubelike structures are grouped together to form a thicker tower. Died March 27, age 52.

Kistiakowsky, George B., Russian-American chemist. He worked on the development of the first atomic bomb during World War II and was science adviser to President Dwight D. Eisenhower (1959–61). As chairman of the Council for a Livable World, he was a leading advocate of banning nuclear weapons. Died Dec. 7, age 82.

Kleinsinger, George, American composer. His works ranged from tunes for youngsters such as "Tubby the Tuba" (1946) to the chamber opera *Archy and Mehitabel* (1954), and its sequel, the musical *Shinbone Alley* (1957). Died July 28, age 68.

Kogan, Leonid, Soviet violinist. Acclaimed for his virtuosity and tone, he performed frequently abroad as well as in the U.S.S.R. and appeared as a soloist with many major U.S. orchestras. Died Dec. 17, age 58.

Lay, Herman W., American businessman. He turned Lay's Potato Chips into the first national potato chip brand in 1961, when he formed Frito-Lay Inc. In 1965 he negotiated a merger with the Pepsi-Cola Co. to form Pepsico, becoming its chairman of the board. Died Dec. 6, age 73.

Leek, Sybil, British journalist and writer. A self-proclaimed witch, she wrote more than 60 books dealing with the occult. Died Oct. 26, age 65.

Lockridge, Richard, American writer. He and his first wife, Frances, wrote many mystery novels featuring the sleuths Mr. and Mrs. North. Died June 19, age 83.

Loring, Eugene, American dancer and choreographer. He created *Billy the Kid* (1938), one of the earliest and best-known works of the folklore genre in modern American ballet. Died Aug. 30, age 72.

Loughran, Tommy, American boxer. He was world light-heavyweight champion (1927–29), and a member of the Boxing Hall of Fame. Died July 7, age 79.

Lynd, Helen Merrell, American sociologist. With her husband, Robert S. Lynd, she wrote *Middletown* (1929), said to be the first sociological study of an American community. She taught social philosophy at Sarah Lawrence College (1928–64). Died Jan. 30, age 85.

Macdonald, Dwight, American author. His magazine essays on politics and culture appeared in *Against the American Grain* (1963) and in other books. Died Dec. 19, age 76.

Sometimes called the unofficial American poet laureate, Archibald MacLeish received three Pulitzer Prizes for his verse.

MacLeish, Archibald, American poet and playwright. He won two Pulitzer prizes for poetry that tended to draw themes from social and political issues, and a third for *J.B.*, a verse drama based on the Book of Job. MacLeish had been head of the Library of Congress (1939–44). Died April 20, age 89.

Marsh, Dame Ngaio, New Zealand novelist. She was the author of 31 mystery novels, featuring Chief Inspector Roderick Alleyn of Scotland Yard. Died Feb. 18, age 82.

McCabe, Thomas Bayard, American business executive. He was chief executive officer of the Scott Paper Co. for 39 years and chairman of the Federal Reserve Board (1949–51). Died May 27, age 88.

McGivern, William P., American writer. Fourteen of his 23 mystery novels were made into films, including *The Big Heat* (1952) and *Odds Against Tomorrow* (1955). Died Nov. 18, age 60.

Mendès-France, Pierre, French political leader, lawyer, and economist. While premier (1954–55), he negotiated an end to the war in Indochina, relinquishing French colonial rule. A leader of the Left, he served with Free French forces during World War II. Died Oct. 18, age 75.

Jazz pianist and composer Thelonious Monk was noted for his innovative style.

Merrill, Henry Tindall ("Dick"), American aviator. In 1936 he made the first transatlantic round-trip flight in an airplane. He and the entertainer Arthur Godfrey flew a corporate jet around the world in 1966, setting 21 world speed records. Died Oct. 31, age 88.

Monaco, Mario del, Italian opera singer. Considered the most famous tenor of post–World War II Italy, he sang at New York City's Metropolitan Opera from 1951 to 1959. Died Oct. 16, age 67.

Monk, Thelonious Sphere, American jazz pianist and composer noted for his unusual harmonies and rhythms. Died Feb. 17, age 64.

Moore, Stanford, American chemist. He shared the 1972 Nobel Prize for chemistry for research into the chemical structure of pancreatic nuclease, a human enzyme. Died Aug. 23, age 68.

Morton, Thruston Ballard, American politician. A Republican from Kentucky, he served in the U.S. House of Representatives (1947–53) and U.S. Senate (1957–68) and was Republican national chairman in 1960. Died Aug. 14, age 74.

Mueller, Reuben H., American clergyman. A Methodist bishop, he was a leading spokesman for interfaith unity and racial justice. He was president of the National Council of Churches (1963–66). Died July 6, age 85.

Namgyal, Palden Thondup, former King of Sikkim. He headed this Himalayan protectorate from 1964 to 1975, when the monarchy was abolished and Sikkim annexed as an Indian state. Died Jan. 29, age 58.

Nicholson, Ben, British painter. He was noted for abstract all-white reliefs carved into or raised from wood and synthetic board. Died Feb. 6, age 87.

Noel-Baker, Philip John, British statesman and peace advocate. A Labour Party member of the House of Commons (1929–70), he received the Nobel Peace Prize in 1959 for relief work during the Soviet famine of the 1920's, his lifelong efforts for disarmament, and his support of the League of Nations. He was made a life peer in 1977. Died Oct. 8, age 92.

O'Gorman, Juan, Mexican painter and architect. His major works included murals and frescoes at the National Museum of Anthropology and Mexico City's airport. Found dead Jan. 18, age 76.

Olson, Harry Ferdinand, American engineer. His research for the RCA Corp. (1928–67) won him more than 100 patents and many advances for the recording and broadcasting industries. Died April 1, age 81.

Orff, Carl, German composer. The best known of his works is *Carmina Burana* (1937), a music drama combining music, dance, and text. He also devised a popular method for the musical education of children. Died March 29, age 86.

Paige, Leroy Robert ("Satchel"), American baseball player. A pitcher, he was a star of the Negro leagues and was elected to the Baseball Hall of Fame in 1971. In 1948, after blacks were admitted to organized baseball, he helped Cleveland to a world championship. Died June 8, age 75.

Pepper, Art, American jazz musician. He was a leading saxophonist, usually with Stan Kenton's orchestra, until drug addiction eclipsed his career in 1953. Died June 15, age 56.

292

Perhaps baseball's greatest pitcher, Satchel Paige did not play in the major leagues until age 42.

credentials of 1000 teachers he described as "morally unfit" and advocated "a little bit of censorship" in public school libraries. Died June 13, age 65.

Rambert, Dame Marie, Polish-born British ballet director. As director of the Ballet Club (later the Ballet Rambert) from 1931, she presented works by nearly every important British choreographer of the time. Died June 12, age 94.

Rand, Ayn, Russian-American writer. Best known as author of the novels *The Fountainhead* (1943) and *Atlas Shrugged* (1957), she espoused "objectivism" or "rational selfishness" based on laissez-faire capitalism. Died March 6, age 77.

Rawls, Katherine, American swimmer. She won 33 national swimming and diving titles in the 1930's and was elected to the Swimming Hall of Fame. Died April 8, age 64.

Rexroth, Kenneth, American poet. One of the most political of American poets, he was elected in 1969 to the National Institute of Arts and Letters. Died June 6, age 76.

Pollock, William, American labor leader. He was general president of the Textile Workers Union of America (1956–72). Died March 3, age 82.

Poulson, Norris, American politician. As mayor of Los Angeles (1953–61), he brought baseball's Brooklyn Dodgers to Los Angeles. A Republican, he served in the U.S. House of Representatives (1943–45 and 1947–53). Died Sept. 25, age 87.

Powell, Eleanor, American dancer. A tap-dancing star, she appeared in Hollywood musicals of the 1930's and 1940's. Died Feb. 11, age 69.

Primrose, William, British musician. He was regarded as the greatest violist of his time, giving concerts and appearing with orchestras around the world. He moved to the U.S. in 1937. Died May 1, age 77.

Rafferty, Maxwell Lewis, Jr., American educator. As California's state superintendent of public education (1963–71), he gained national attention for his opposition to busing for racial balance, sex education, and the theory of evolution. He revoked the teaching

Hollywood's top female tap dancer in the 1930's and 1940's was Eleanor Powell.

Pianist Arthur Rubenstein was acclaimed throughout the world during a career of concert performances that spanned nearly 80 years.

Robbins, Marty, American singer. He won two Grammy Awards and was elected to the Country Music Hall of Fame. Died Dec. 8, age 57.

Rubinstein, Arthur, Polish-American pianist. One of the most acclaimed pianists of the 20th century, he was noted for a distinctive, sonorous tone, and for his command of romantic works, particularly those of Frédéric Chopin. He began performing publicly at the age of 4, and during a career that lasted into the late 1970's he toured the world. Died Dec. 20, age 95.

Ryan, T(ubal) Claude, American aviation pioneer. In 1925 he established the first year-round regular passenger air service in the U.S., and in the same year produced the first high-wing monoplane, the M-1. He built *Spirit of St. Louis* in 1927 for Charles A. Lindbergh, who made the first solo nonstop transatlantic flight. The Ryan Aeronautical Co., founded in 1933 and sold in 1969, provided many of the armed services' training aircraft. Died Sept. 11, age 84.

Sackler, Howard, American playwright. His play *The Great White Hope* received the 1969 Pulitzer Prize for drama. Died Oct. 14, age 52.

Sánchez, Salvador, Mexican boxer. He had been World Boxing Council featherweight champion since 1980. Died Aug. 12 in a car crash, age 23.

Schneider, Romy, Austrian actress. She appeared in more than 60 films, many of them in France, where she had lived since the 1960's. Died May 29, age 43.

Scholem, Gershom, German-born Israeli scholar widely regarded as the world's foremost authority on Jewish mysticism. Died Feb. 20, age 84.

Selye, Hans, Austrian-Canadian biochemist and physician. Director of the International Institute of Stress at the University of Montréal, he was credited with pioneering studies on the effect of psychological stress, which he considered a causal factor in certain diseases. Died Oct. 16, age 75.

Sillman, Leonard, American theatrical producer. He produced 13 Broadway editions of the revue *New Faces* between 1934 and 1968. Died Jan. 23, age 72.

Simmons, Calvin, American symphony conductor. In 1978 he became music director of the Oakland Symphony, the only black music director of a major symphony orchestra in the U.S. Died in a canoeing accident Aug. 21, age 32.

Smith, Dan Throop, American economist. He was a leading tax expert and the principal architect of the Internal Revenue Code, which was restructured in 1954. Died May 29, age 74.

Smith, Walter Wellesley ("Red"), American journalist. As a sports columnist for the New York *Herald Tribune* (1945-66), he became widely syndicated; in 1971 he joined the New York *Times.* He won a Pulitzer Prize for distinguished commentary in 1976. Died Jan. 15, age 76.

Sobhuza II, King of Swaziland. The world's longest-reigning sovereign, he was king of his African country from age 1. Four years after Swaziland became independent from Great Britain, he abolished the British-drafted constitution in 1973 and assumed absolute rule. Died Aug. 21, age 83.

Stitt, Edward ("Sonny"), American jazz musician. An acclaimed saxophonist, his style was similar to that of Charlie Parker. Died July 22, age 58.

Strasberg, Lee, Polish-born American acting teacher. As artistic director of the Actors Studio since 1948, he popularized the "Method" in the American theater, encouraging actors to employ their subconscious in preparing for a role. Earlier, he cofounded the Group Theater in 1931 and was a stage director. Died Feb. 17, age 80.

Sunay, Cevdet, Turkish statesman. He was president of Turkey from 1966 to 1973. Died May 22, age 82.

Suslov, Mikhail A., Soviet statesman. He was the chief ideologist of the Soviet Communist Party and one of the most influential members of the Politburo. He reputedly argued for military intervention whenever he felt the Soviet sphere of influence was being threatened. *See* UNION OF SOVIET SOCIALIST REPUBLICS. Died Jan. 25, age 79.

Swart, Charles Robberts, South African statesman. He was the first president of the Republic of South Africa (1961–67). As minister of justice (1948–59), he drafted some of the nation's apartheid laws. Died July 16, age 87.

Swinnerton, Frank, British novelist, critic, and journalist. Among his 60-odd novels were *Nocturne* and *Quadrille.* Died Nov. 6, age 98.

Tati, Jacques, French actor, writer, and director. He created and portrayed the bumbling Mr. Hulot in *Mr. Hulot's Holiday* (1954), *My Uncle* (1958), *Playtime* (1967), and *Traffic* (1971). Died Nov. 5, age 75.

Terry, Walter, American dance critic. The author of 22 books, he also championed modern dance and ballet in writing for the

Mikhail Suslov, chief ideologist of the Soviet Communist Party, was one of his nation's most influential figures.

New York *Herald-Tribune* and the *Saturday Review.* Died Oct. 4, age 69.

Theorell, (Axel) Hugo (Teodor), Swedish biochemist. He received the 1955 Nobel Prize for medicine for discoveries related to the nature and action of oxidative enzymes, which are vital to all animal life. Died Aug. 15, age 79.

Thompson, Thomas ("Tommy"), American writer. All six of his books were financially successful, including the nonfiction *Blood and Money* (1976) and *Celebrity* (1982), a novel. Died Oct. 29, age 49.

Tjader, Cal, American jazz musician. A vibraphonist and percussionist who played Latin-influenced music, he won a Grammy Award in 1981. Died May 5, age 56.

Townsend, William Cameron, American missionary. Cofounder of Wycliffe Bible Translators, Inc., in 1935, he brought the Bible to previously illiterate peoples in Latin America by establishing written forms of their languages and then teaching them to read. Died April 23, age 85.

Truman, Elizabeth Virginia ("Bess"), American First Lady. The wife of President Harry S. Truman (1945–53), she was credited by him as being his "chief adviser always." Died Oct. 18, age 97.

Tuve, Merle Anthony, American physicist. His work on short-pulse radio waves was instrumental in the development of radar. Died May 20, age 80.

Twining, Nathan Farragut, American military officer. During World War II he commanded U.S. Army air forces. He was U.S. Air Force chief of staff (1953–57) and chairman of the joint chiefs of staff (1957–60). Died March 29, age 84.

Tworkov, Jack, Polish-born American painter. An abstract expressionist, he was known for his flamelike brush strokes. Died Sept. 4, age 82.

Vidor, King Wallis, American film director. *The Big Parade* (1925) depicted World War I; *The Crowd* (1928) realistically described the lives of ordinary people; and *Our Daily Bread* (1934) dealt with the Great Depression. In 1979 he received a special Academy Award. Died Nov. 1, age 88.

Villeneuve, Gilles, Canadian auto racing driver who won several Grand Prix Formula One events. Died May 8 in a racing crash, age 30.

Wallenberg, Marcus, Swedish financier and industrialist. With his brother Jacob he headed a family empire that encompassed one third of Sweden's industry. Died Sept. 13, age 82.

Waner, Lloyd, American baseball player. He was an outfielder in the major leagues for 18 years and was elected to the Baseball Hall of Fame in 1967. Died July 22, age 76.

Ward, Martin J., American labor leader. He had been president of the 380,000-member United Association of Journeymen and Apprentices of the Plumbing and Pipe Fitting Industry since 1971. Died Oct. 9, age 64.

Warner, Leslie H., American businessman. As president, chief executive officer, or chairman (1961–76) of the General Telephone and Electronics Corp. (now GTE Corp.), he presided over a fivefold growth in earnings for the large communications firm. Died Aug. 19, age 71.

Webb, Jack, American actor. He starred as a Los Angeles police detective in the *Dragnet* television series (1952–59 and 1967–71). Webb also produced *Dragnet* and other television shows and acted in films. Died Dec. 23, age 62.

Weiss, Peter, German-born Swedish playwright. He was the author of *Marat/Sade* (1964), a political play that won a Tony Award in 1966. Died May 10, age 65.

Wheeler, Raymond M., American physician. He was president of the Southern Regional Council (1969–74), and his research into hunger and malnutrition spurred the first food-stamp legislation in the late 1960's. Died Feb. 17, age 62.

Whitney, John Hay ("Jock"), American entrepreneur. Through Whitney Communications Corp., he held interests in newspapers, magazines, and television and radio stations. He was also a world-class polo player, art collector, philanthropist, and ambassador to Great Britain (1957–61). Died Feb. 8, age 77.

Woods, George David, American banker. As president of the World Bank (1963–68), he pursued a policy of freer access to loans for developing countries. Died Aug. 20, age 81.

Ydígoras Fuentes, Miguel, Guatemalan statesman. While president (1958–63), he allowed Cuban exiles to launch the abortive Bay of Pigs invasion in 1961. Earlier he was an army officer, rising to the rank of general. Died Oct. 6, age 86.

Zaturenska, Marya, Ukrainian-born American poet. She won a Pulitzer Prize in 1938 for *Cold Morning Sky*. Died Jan. 19, age 80.

Zworykin, Vladimir Kosma, Russian-American scientist and inventor. He was often called the father of television for his inventions, patented in 1923 and 1924, of the iconoscope camera tube and the kinescope picture tube. He was also credited with helping to develop the electron microscope. Zworykin was director of the Radio Corp. of America's electronic research laboratory (1929–54). Died July 29, age 92.

OHIO. *See* STATISTICS OF THE WORLD.

OKLAHOMA. *See* STATISTICS OF THE WORLD.

OMAN. *See* STATISTICS OF THE WORLD.

ONTARIO. *See* STATISTICS OF THE WORLD.

OREGON. *See* STATISTICS OF THE WORLD.

ORGANIZATION OF AMERICAN STATES, abbreviated OAS. Relations between the United States and its Latin American neighbors were severely strained in 1982 by Washington's support for Great Britain in its war with Argentina to retain possession of the Falkland Islands. Most Latin American countries backed Argentina in voting on resolutions adopted at OAS meetings.

An OAS resolution, approved at a meeting on April 28 in Washington, D.C., supported Argentina's claim of sovereignty over the Falkland Islands. The vote was 17 to 0, with Chile, Colombia, Trinidad and Tobago, and the U.S. abstaining, and the other eight members not participating. The resolution deplored the economic sanctions imposed on Argentina by European Community members and other countries. However, the resolution also supported United Nations Security Council Resolution 502, passed immediately following Argentina's April 2 invasion of the Falklands, which demanded the withdrawal of Argentine forces and an end to hostilities. The OAS resolution did not support more active pressures against Britain, under the so-called Rio Treaty. This mutual defense pact, the 1947 Inter-American Treaty of Reciprocal Assistance, calls on the countries of the Western Hemisphere to regard an attack on any nation in the region as an attack on all of them.

After lengthy deliberations and some harsh language against the U.S. for its support of Great Britain, representatives of the OAS member states passed another resolution in Washington, on May 29, by a vote of 17 to 0. Again abstaining were Chile, Colombia, Trinidad and Tobago, and the U.S. This resolution condemned Britain's "acts of war" against Argentina, and urged the U.S. to stop aiding the British and to respect the concept of "hemispheric solidarity." It also called on members to offer whatever aid to Argentina they found appropriate.

Earlier, on Feb. 24, in a speech before the OAS in Washington, U.S. President Ronald Reagan proposed a broad plan of U.S. economic and military assistance and trade and investment incentives for the Caribbean area; see CARIBBEAN COUNTRIES.   A.E.J.

ORGANIZATION OF PETROLEUM EXPORTING COUNTRIES, abbreviated OPEC. Continuation of the world oil glut aggravated the already intense political and economic rivalries among OPEC's 13 members in 1982.

In early 1982 it became evident that to prevent a decline in petroleum income, OPEC members would have to agree on production quotas and a price floor. At an emergency meeting in Vienna, OPEC oil ministers agreed on March 20 to limit aggregate production to 17,500,000 bbl a day, 700,000 bbl less than the current daily output and about 43 percent below the 1979 average. Iran, Iraq, and Libya were exempted from the cutbacks. The basic price of $34 per barrel for Saudi light crude, or "market" oil, was retained, but price differentials for higher-quality oil were cut in half. In December the price was again retained but the production ceiling was raised to 18,500,000 bbl a day.

By midyear several members were greatly exceeding their assigned production quotas, Iran by an estimated 1,000,000 bbl daily, Nigeria by at least 300,000 bbl, and Libya by about 250,000 bbl. In July the oil ministers again met in Vienna, but this time the talks broke down in acrimony. Libya accused Saudi Arabia of flooding the oil market to force prices down and impose its will on other members, even though Saudi Arabia cut production in 1982 to a ten-year low of 5,300,000 bbl a day. Iran's oil minister also accused Saudi Arabia of "stealing Iran's share" of the market and threatened to "use force" to rectify the situation. Iraq and Iran brought their animosities to the meeting, accusing each other of cheating. Syria's seizure in April of Iraqi oil in Syrian ports and its closure of the pipeline linking Iraq with the Mediterranean Sea also sparked a dispute.

These conflicts erupted as OPEC faced an aggregate 1982 payments deficit of $9.5 billion, compared with a trade surplus of nearly $60 billion in 1981. Oil costs fluctuated, but by July the spot price had fallen to $31.50 for Saudi light crude, 7 percent below the benchmark price. Kuwait's oil minister, Sheikh Ali al-Khalifa al-Sabah, predicted in September that OPEC would be unable to raise its prices until 1985. Until the end of the century, he said, increases would barely keep up with inflation.

Mexico, the world's fourth-largest oil producer, agreed in 1982 to accept observer status. OPEC's sister association, the Organiza- tion of Arab Petroleum Exporting Countries, approved Tunisia as a new member.

See PETROLEUM AND NATURAL GAS and arti- cles on individual countries mentioned.

D.P.

P

PACIFIC ISLANDS. The Marshall Islands and the Federated States of Micronesia, which are two of the four units of the U.S. Trust Territory of the Pacific Islands, signed agree- ments with the United States in 1982. The pacts, signed in Honolulu by the Marshall Is- lands on May 30 and by the Federated States of Micronesia on Oct. 1, were to make these islands independent in domestic and foreign affairs, with the U.S. retaining exclusive mili- tary rights.

The Trust Territory consists of 2141 west- ern Pacific islands and atolls seized from Ja- pan by U.S. forces during World War II and administered by the U.S. since 1947 under a United Nations trusteeship. Besides the Mar- shalls and the Federated States, the territory consists of the Palau Islands and the North- ern Mariana Islands; the Northern Marianas voted in 1975 to become a commonwealth of the U.S., like Puerto Rico. Any change in the status of these island groups would require,

Queen Elizabeth II receives a whale's tooth on her yacht before stepping ashore on Fiji's Bau Island. Fiji was the queen's last stop on an autumn tour of the South Pacific.

Relations between long-time rivals India and Pakistan improved in 1982. Early in the year Pakistani Foreign Minister Agha Shahi (right) met Indian External Affairs Minister P.V.N. Rao (left) in New Delhi. On Nov. 1 Pakistani President Muhammad Zia ul-Haq conferred with Indian Prime Minister Indira Gandhi.

in addition to approval by plebiscite, approval by the U.S. Congress and the U.N.

Under the new agreement with the Federated States of Micronesia, the U.S. expected to spend about $1 billion in financial subsidies over 15 years. Under the pact with the Marshall Islands, Washington promised to provide an estimated $1.5 billion in various subsidies over a 50-year period. Moreover, up to $9,000,000 annually was to be paid to property owners on Kwajalein for use of a missile test range on their atoll. Protesting the inadequacy of the proposed payments, however, more than 800 Kwajalein landowners occupied parts of the missile range and demanded a development fund for Ebeye, 2 mi. away, where Kwajalein residents had been relocated when the U.S. military took over their island in the 1950's. In October, 1982, the U.S. agreed to cut 20 years from its 50-year pact for use of the test range and also agreed to increase aid payments to island residents. The islanders agreed to halt demonstrations.

The ruling party of Fiji's Prime Minister Ratu Sir Kamisese Mara narrowly defeated the Indian-led opposition in July elections. General elections returned Michael Somare to power as prime minister of Papua New Guinea on Aug. 2.

See STATISTICS OF THE WORLD.   R.H.

PACIFIC ISLANDS, TRUST TERRITORY OF THE. *See* PACIFIC ISLANDS.

PAKISTAN. In 1982 the military government of Pakistan's President Muhammad Zia ul-Haq maintained its authoritarian rule and strove for improved relations with India, its longtime adversary.

Politics. In what appeared to be a sign of a gradual return to civilian rule, Pakistan's 288-member Consultative Assembly convened in early January for the first public debate on government in the four and a half years of Gen. Zia's rule. As constituted, however, the assembly was powerless in matters of policy, able only to make recommendations to Zia's government. At the same time, Zia lifted the press censorship he had imposed after his takeover in 1977, but a ban on press coverage of political activities was later reimposed. In August Zia promised to install a new "Islamic system of government" within a year.

Pakistan's political opposition was totally powerless, although the Zia government did permit the existence of an opposition grouping called the Movement for the Restoration of Democracy (MRD), an ineffectual alliance of parties that had little popular support. The MRD's main component was the Pakistan People's Party (PPP) of the late Prime Minister Zulfikar Ali Bhutto, who was executed by Zia's government in 1979. The PPP was headed by Bhutto's widow, Nusrat Bhutto, who was released from house arrest but not allowed to leave the country until late 1982.

Violence. In February a shoulder-fired missile was launched at Zia's plane while it was taxiing at Rawalpindi airport. A series of assassination attempts followed in August and September. And on Sept. 13 a pro-Zia politician, Zahur Hassan Bhopali, was shot to death in his office in Karachi.

The violence was blamed on the clandestine Al Zulfikar group that sought to overthrow the military government. Said to be based in Afghanistan, Al Zulfikar was led by Mir Ghulam Murtaza Bhutto, the older son of the late prime minister. The government arrested thousands of suspected "subversives" in a drive against the organization. Zia also issued a new martial law order decreeing the death penalty for anybody convicted of destroying government property, acquiring arms illegally, or contributing to lawlessness.

In a 54-page report, issued in January, the London-based organization Amnesty International charged that Pakistan's human rights violations had steadily increased during 1981. Pakistan claimed that the report was exaggerated and contained lies.

The Economy. Generous monsoon rains played a major role in improving Pakistan's food supply. The economy was also boosted by remittances from 1,500,000 Pakistani workers in the oil-rich Persian Gulf states, and by large amounts of foreign aid from the United States, Saudi Arabia, the International Monetary Fund, and the World Bank. A dependence on foreign oil, however, together with sluggish world demand for Pakistan's exports, created severe payments problems.

Foreign Affairs. Relations with India, with which Pakistan had waged three wars in 35 years, were of paramount importance. The foreign ministers of both countries met to explore the possibility of a nonaggression treaty and of increased trade, travel, communications, and cultural exchange. In early November President Zia met briefly with Indian Prime Minister Indira Gandhi in New Delhi. They agreed to establish a permanent joint commission to deal with problems between the two countries as they arose.

Zia strengthened Pakistan's ties with two of its strongest allies by visiting China in October and the U.S. in December. Among the chief topics discussed were the Soviet occupation of neighboring Afghanistan and the potential Soviet threat to Pakistan. In November Zia said that at least 2,800,000 Afghan refugees were in Pakistan.

See STATISTICS OF THE WORLD. R.J.C.

PALESTINE LIBERATION ORGANIZATION, abbreviated PLO. During 1982 the PLO, led by Yasir Arafat (see biography at PEOPLE IN THE NEWS), passed through its most severe crisis since the organization was established in 1964. In Lebanon the PLO suffered its greatest military defeat, but abroad it scored several diplomatic coups.

Escalation of hostilities began in April when Israeli planes bombed Palestinian outposts in retaliation for the death of an Israeli soldier killed by a land mine while on patrol in Lebanon. Arafat announced that he would not respond to the bombing but would maintain the precarious truce between Israel and PLO forces negotiated by U.S. envoy Philip C. Habib in July, 1981. Tensions continued to rise, however, and on June 6 Israel launched a full-scale invasion of southern Lebanon, with the intent of destroying Palestinian bases that threatened northern Israel. The Israeli government said that the attack was partly in reprisal for the attempted assassination in London of Ambassador Shlomo Argov—an attack for which the PLO disclaimed any responsibility. British officials later asserted that Argov's assailants were guerrillas who were hostile to the PLO leadership.

By the end of June, Israel had driven PLO forces from southern Lebanon and had encircled west Beirut, where the PLO leadership

PLO members leave Beirut, en route to Syria, as part of an evacuation of 14,000 Palestinian fighters and Syrian troops from Lebanon's capital. The Israeli invasion of southern Lebanon eliminated the Palestinian movement's independent base of operations.

and some 14,000 Palestinian and Syrian fighters were dug in. The Israeli siege lasted until late August, when, under an accord reached through U.S. mediation, the pro-Palestinian forces were evacuated, some by land to Syria, the rest by ship via Cyprus and Greece to other Arab countries. Arafat was among the last to leave—by ship to Greece and then to Tunisia. Terms of the evacuation agreement also called for the closing of PLO civilian offices in Beirut, including its information center and diplomatic posts. An estimated 8000 Palestinian fighters remained in northern and eastern Lebanon, however.

The number of Palestinian military casualties was uncertain, but most estimates cited several hundred killed and thousands wounded. Israel also captured some 7000 prisoners whom it classified as members of Palestinian terrorist groups. On Sept. 16–18, after the assassination of Lebanese President-elect Bashir Gemayel, several hundred Palestinians living in west Beirut refugee camps were massacred by Christian militiamen.

After the PLO's withdrawal from Lebanon, Arafat sought through diplomacy to rebuild the organization's political base. He was received by the highest officials in Greece, whose socialist government had earlier upgraded PLO representation in Athens to ambassadorial status. In Rome Pope John Paul II followed a statement of support for Palestinian rights by granting a personal audience with Arafat on Sept. 15. Arafat's Rome visit occurred within the framework of a conference of the 98-nation Interparliamentary Union, which had granted observer status to the PLO. In October Arafat met in Amman with Jordan's King Hussein to discuss, among other matters, U.S. President Ronald Reagan's Middle East peace plan, which provided for Palestinian self-government in Gaza and the West Bank "in association with Jordan."

See STATISTICS OF THE WORLD. D.P.

PANAMA. Panama's President Arístides Royo Sanchez resigned on July 30, 1982, two years before the end of his term, and Vice-President Ricardo de la Espriella was sworn in hours later as his successor. Hundreds of Panamanian officials, including all ten cabinet ministers, also resigned in a massive government reorganization.

Although Royo gave "health reasons" for his resignation, observers considered his ouster an illegal action that resulted from friction between the president and the 10,000-member National Guard, Panama's only armed force. Long considered the country's major source of power, this military body was headed by Brig. Gen. Rubén Darío Paredes del Río, who had ousted Col. Florencio Flórez Aguilar as its commander in March. Paredes was said to have opposed Royo's left-wing, anti-U.S. foreign policy, and to have charged the administration with economic mismanagement.

Within minutes of de la Espriella's inauguration, Paredes offered the new president a series of "suggestions" and "recommendations." Among these was a call for the resignation of all ministers, ambassadors, mayors, and provincial officials. A new cabinet, with three holdovers, was named on Aug. 3. Moreover, Paredes announced a seven-day closing of the nation's eight newspapers, as well as a policy of future government censorship by in-house "moralizers." *La Prensa,* the country's major opposition newspaper, appeared to be a particular target. Heavily armed troops expelled staff members and seriously damaged the paper's machinery and presses.

On April 1 the United States formally transferred to Panama law enforcement and judicial duties in the Canal Zone, as provided by treaty. This action gave Panamanian police and courts full authority in the area. De la Espriella met with U.S. President Ronald Reagan in Washington, D.C., on Oct. 1. While in Washington he signed a treaty aimed at promoting U.S. investment in Panama.

See STATISTICS OF THE WORLD. A.E.J.

PAPUA NEW GUINEA. *See* STATISTICS OF THE WORLD.

PARAGUAY. On a continent beset by strife, poverty, and huge foreign payments deficits, Paraguay, under its longtime president, Gen. Alfredo Stroessner, offered a positive economic outlook in 1982. The country's economic growth was expected to reach about 6 percent for the year. The agricultural sector prospered, benefiting from new investments that continued to come in, largely from Europe.

The $18.5 billion Itaipú water power plant, built jointly with Brazil, was formally opened on Nov. 5. This huge hydroelectric dam, stretching across almost 5 mi. of the Paraná River, which along this portion divides Paraguay and Brazil, was expected to produce electricity in excess of Paraguay's own needs, thereby allowing sales of surplus production to neighboring countries.

The construction of Paraguay's Yacyretá dam, however, a joint venture with neighboring Argentina, came to a virtual standstill in 1982, partly because of the worldwide economic slump. Moreover, Argentina was forced to divert necessary funds from the project to its military operations in the conflict with Great Britain over the Falkland Islands.

On Sept. 18 Stroessner was nominated by his Colorado Party for reelection in 1983 to another five-year term. In accepting the nomination, Stroessner, president since 1954, lashed out at human rights advocates who had criticized his government's treatment of political dissidents. "They are nothing but instruments in the Communist world domination plans," he said.

See STATISTICS OF THE WORLD. A.E.J.

PENNSYLVANIA. *See* STATISTICS OF THE WORLD.

People in the News

Queens and knaves, princes and presidents, dancers, acrobats, and sailors made news in 1982. From the Atlantic Ocean to the Sahara, from the South Pole to the North Pole, flying through midair or posing before spotlights and cameras, the year's personalities played to a fascinated public.

The public appetite for details of the lives of the famous continued in 1982. People in the worlds of entertainment, sports, and the arts, and in the darker world of crime, grabbed the headlines. The biggest spotlight, however, was on the people who held the greatest power and on those around them, beginning with the family that occupied the White House.

As President **Ronald Reagan** entered his second year in office, First Lady **Nancy Reagan** was still the target of criticism for her expensive tastes. She agreed to stop her practice of accepting dresses as gifts from designers after much adverse publicity. When her new White House china arrived, her office went to pains to disclose figures—converted to the current dollar—that previous Administrations had spent on new china, so that Nancy Reagan's choice, at $209,000 for the set, seemed more reasonable. In other ways, her image was given a high polish. She undertook a visible program of battling drug abuse among young people by sponsoring a national conference at the White House in March and by making visits to drug rehabilitation centers in Texas and Florida. A book, *To Love a Child,* was published under her name in October to promote another pet project, the Foster Grandparents program. In June the First Lady accompanied her husband on a ten-day state visit to Western Europe, where she drew generally favorable comments from the foreign press—except when she wore a pair of high-fashion knickers to a reception in Paris.

As unemployment topped the 10 percent mark, joblessness hit home. The President's son **Ron Reagan,** 24, who had been promoted from the Joffrey II ballet troupe to the main company, was laid off in October for four weeks, along with all the other dancers—and he turned up on New York City unemployment lines to collect his $125-a-week benefit. His sister, **Patti Davis,** 30, continued to pursue a screen acting career and landed her first motion picture role, a small part in *The Curse of the Pink Panther,* which was filmed on the French Riviera in the spring. **Maureen Reagan,** daughter of the President by his first wife, actress **Jane Wyman,** lost her bid for the Republican Party nomination for U.S. Senator from California.

The Carter family, settled back in Plains, Ga., also made the news. Former President **Jimmy Carter** published his memoirs, *Keeping Faith,* in early November and went on a whistle-stop tour to promote the book. He also joined the faculty of Emory University in Atlanta in September as distinguished professor of government. His daughter, **Amy Carter,** 14, spent the summer in a highly visible job: as a $175-a-week page in the U.S. Senate. During the course of the job she appeared as a guest on *Late Night with David Letterman* on NBC television, where she said that the worst thing she did as a child growing up in the White House was to carve her initials on a windowsill.

Ten years after his historic first trip to the People's Republic of China, former President **Richard Nixon** went back in September to celebrate the anniversary. The crowds that attended his 1972 journey were missing, but the welcome from Chinese officials was warm. Later in the fall another 10th anniversary party was held, this time in Washington, D.C., where former Nixon aides gathered to mark the landslide election of 1972 in which Nixon won his ill-fated second term. Among

Charles and Diana, Prince and Princess of Wales, pose with their infant son, Prince William Arthur Philip Louis, at his christening on Aug. 4. The baby, second in line to the throne, was born on June 21.

those in attendance was former Secretary of State **Henry Kissinger,** who had a busy (and lucrative) year as a consultant and lecturer after undergoing triple-bypass heart surgery at Boston's Massachusetts General Hospital in February.

In Great Britain, on the heels of the nation's victory over Argentina in the Falkland Islands, came another piece of news to prompt public rejoicing: the birth of a son to **Charles** and **Diana,** the Prince and Princess of Wales. The 7-lb.-1½-oz. baby arrived on June 21, about ten days ahead of schedule, with his father in attendance at the hospital birth—a break from royal tradition. Named **Prince William Arthur Philip Louis,** the baby was second in line to the throne, after his father.

A few weeks later, the British public was shocked to learn that an intruder had gained access to Buckingham Palace in the early hours of July 9 and had entered the bedroom of **Queen Elizabeth II. Michael Fagan,** 30, an unemployed laborer, sat on the foot of her bed and chatted with her for 10 min. until she was able to summon help. He was not

charged in the incident, but it turned out that he had entered the palace about a month earlier, on which occasion he had drunk half a bottle of wine. He was charged with burglary in the earlier incident—for taking the wine—but was acquitted. Both incidents prompted an uproar in Parliament and an immediate investigation into the lax security precautions surrounding the royal family.

With Prince Charles no longer a bachelor, his younger brother, **Prince Andrew,** 22, who served with the British forces in the Falklands, became the focus of attention. "Randy Andy," as the British press had dubbed him, caused quite a stir when he went on holiday with a young American actress, **Koo Stark,** 25, who had once starred in a soft-core pornographic movie. The queen, reported the Fleet Street tabloids, was not amused.

Another Briton who caused his mother a good deal of worry was **Mark Thatcher,** son of Britain's Prime Minister **Margaret Thatcher.** Young Thatcher, an amateur race car driver, spent six days in January lost in the Sahara after an axle casing cracked on his Peugeot 504 during the third annual Paris–Dakar (Senegal) auto rally. He and his co-driver, **Anne Charlotte Verney,** and their mechanic were found safe in southern Algeria. "All I need is a beer and a sandwich," said Thatcher, "a bath and a shave."

The death of **Princess Grace** of Monaco on Sept. 14 sent shock waves not only through the tiny Mediterranean principality that her husband, **Prince Rainier III,** ruled, but also through Hollywood and the world that had followed her fairy-tale life. The princess, driving her Rover automobile, plunged off a winding Riviera road. Her daughter **Princess Stephanie,** 17, who had accompanied her, was injured in the accident.

Twice in 1982 **Queen Beatrix** of the Netherlands visited the United States to commemorate 200 years of Dutch-American relations. A highlight of her first trip, in April, was a private meeting, at her request, with the Dutch-born artist **Willem de Kooning,** 78, at which she discussed with him several of his abstract expressionist paintings, which had been assembled for the occasion.

One of the world's royal households contained a particularly reluctant prince. Japan's **Prince Tomohito,** 36, seventh in line for the throne, had hinted in a Japanese magazine interview that his duties interfered with his sports and charitable activities. In the spring the Oxford University-educated prince, a world-class skier known for his love of night-life, skipped several state functions and wound up checking into a Tokyo hospital for "fatigue."

For movie queen **Sophia Loren,** 47, the role of inmate was all too real. The Academy Award-winning star of *Two Women,* who had been absent from her native country since 1980, returned to Italy in May to face a 30-day sentence for income-tax evasion that she blamed on a since-deceased accountant.

Queen Beatrix of the Netherlands and her husband, Prince Claus, visited the U.S. in 1982. The royal tour commemorated the bicentennial of relations between the U.S. and the Netherlands, which was the first country to grant official recognition after the American Revolution.

Actress Sophia Loren leaves an Italian prison after serving part of a 30-day sentence for income-tax evasion. A few weeks later she was back at work filming a picture set in Florence.

Loren was released after serving 17 days in a small women's prison outside Naples, a stay she described as "interminable" but "enriching."

Fiery Greek actress **Melina Mercouri** also had a nonacting role: As minister of culture in the Greek government, she seized many opportunities to press for the return of Greek art treasures to her country, especially the Elgin marbles in the British Museum. No stranger to controversy, **Vanessa Redgrave** blamed "blacklisting" when the Boston Symphony Orchestra canceled her contract to narrate Igor Stravinsky's opera-oratorio *Oedipus Rex* after patrons protested. Known for her support of the Palestine Liberation Organization, Redgrave said that she was being denied participation in a "purely artistic" performance for "purely political" reasons.

Back together again—at least for photographers—were **Elizabeth Taylor** and **Richard Burton** at the actress's 50th birthday party in London in March. Although both had recently separated from their respective spouses, the couple, married to each other twice, denied any intention of trying it a third time. "We love each other with a pas-sion so furious that we burn one another out," explained Burton. Longtime friends **Mary Martin,** 68, and **Janet Gaynor,** 77, were both injured—Gaynor more seriously—when a taxi in which they were riding in San Francisco in September was hit broadside. Martin's companion and manager was killed, and Gaynor's husband suffered injuries.

A personnel change proved highly personal when **Mikhail Baryshnikov,** artistic director of the American Ballet Theatre, dismissed fellow Russian émigré-dancer **Aleksandr Godunov** from the company in June. A spokesman for the company said that the action was taken simply because the next season's repertory did not have appropriate roles for Godunov, but the dancer complained that Baryshnikov "threw me away like a potato peel."

Playboy Enterprises, Inc., might not appear to be a company with a feminist consciousness, but it acquired a woman at its helm—the boss's daughter. **Hugh Hefner,** founder and chairman of the board, promoted **Christie Hefner,** 29, a Phi Beta Kappa graduate of Brandeis University, to president of the company in April.

A major scandal struck corporate America in 1982 when **John Z. De Lorean,** 57, the maverick former General Motors Corp. executive, was arrested in Los Angeles in October after a federal "sting" operation implicated him, according to law enforcement authorities, in a deal to acquire 220 lb. of cocaine. The speculation was that De Lorean hoped to bail out his financially crippled motor company with the $24,000,000 to be realized from the alleged deal.

A jury in Newport, R.I., found **Claus von Bülow,** 55, guilty on March 16, after a sensational nine-week trial, of twice attempting to murder his wealthy socialite wife, **Martha ("Sunny") von Bülow.** The victim was in a coma with no hope of recovery after what the prosecution charged was injection of insulin. Von Bülow, sentenced to 30 years in prison, was freed on $1,000,000 bail, pending appeal.

Jack Henry Abbott, 38, author of *In the Belly of the Beast* and a protégé of writer **Norman Mailer,** was convicted of first-degree manslaughter in the 1981 slaying of a waiter in New York City. Having already spent 25 years of his life in prison, Abbott

Claus von Bülow had many courtroom sympathizers; nevertheless, the Danish-born socialite was convicted of attempting to murder his wealthy wife. He was sentenced to 30 years in prison.

was sentenced in 1982 to a minimum of 15 years and a maximum of life.

The world of journalism was tinged by an ethics breach when **"Ann Landers"** admitted on May 3 that she had recycled old letters and answers in her nationally syndicated advice column. A week later her twin sister, who wrote the rival "Dear Abby" column under the name **Abigail Van Buren,** admitted that she did the same thing. Neither thought the practice terribly harmful, but both agreed to stop.

Most "feats" are merely attempts to appear in a book of records, but a few are accomplished by real adventurers under risky conditions. On Aug. 29 two British explorers became the first to circumnavigate the globe via both the North and South poles, completing a 52,000-mi., three-year expedition. **Sir Ranulph Twisleton-Wykeham Fiennes** and **Charles Burton** were greeted in Greenwich, England, by a trumpet fanfare and by their patron, Prince Charles, who had once termed their voyage "gloriously, refreshingly mad." The very same day in Falmouth, England, **Bill Dunlop,** a truck driver from Mechanic Falls, Maine, stepped shakily onto dry land, having crossed the Atlantic in the smallest craft ever to do so, a 9-ft.-1-in. sailing yacht called *Wind's Will.*

For the 12-member crew of the *Hjemkomst,* the Atlantic crossing was a sentimen-

Maine truck driver Bill Dunlop gets a big hug from his wife and a big stein of beer after sailing across the Atlantic Ocean in a 9-ft.-1-in. boat, the smallest craft ever to accomplish the journey.

The Hjemkomst, a replica of a 1000-year-old Viking ship, lies in New York City's East River prior to its journey across the Atlantic Ocean, heading for Norway. The voyage was intended as a tribute to the Scandinavians who migrated to the New World.

Miguel Vazquez, 17-year-old member of a circus trapeze team, became the first aerialist ever to achieve the quadruple somersault in public. He was traveling at a speed of 75 mi. an hour when he was caught by his brother.

tal journey. The dream of a Minnesota man, **Robert Asp,** who died before he could see the ship launched, the voyage of the replica Viking ship reversed the Atlantic route that the Vikings took 1000 years ago. The ship, which left Duluth, Minn., in May, arrived in Oslo in August. Crossing the Atlantic in an even less conventional way was **Christian Marty,** 35, a pilot for Air France who sailed on a wind surfer from Senegal and arrived in French Guiana in January. How did he amuse himself on the tedious trip? He listened to the music of Wolfgang Amadeus Mozart and Claude Debussy.

For a sports feat, where records seem to be broken almost as soon as they are set, the performance of **Miguel Vazquez** was astounding. The Mexican trapeze artist became the first ever to execute a quadruple somersault in public (a triple somersault had been accomplished by only 12 people) on July 10 before an audience of 7000 at the Ringling Brothers and Barnum & Bailey Circus in Tucson, Ariz. The 17-year-old member of the Flying Vazquez circus team was going 75 mi. an hour in the fourth turn as he flew into the waiting hands of his brother.

Some people are just plain lucky. **Alberta Joyce Kidd,** 49, a divorced mother of six,

Allan Bakke chats with classmates after graduating from the medical school of the University of California at Davis. Bakke's suit for admission to the medical school produced a landmark U.S. Supreme Court decision in which he was found to be the victim of "reverse discrimination."

scored the biggest jackpot ever from an Atlantic City (N.J.) slot machine when after 20 min. of playing, she suddenly won $919,559. But her luck soured a bit with the outpouring of criticism that followed: She had been gambling although on welfare. Kidd, who insisted that she was using her boyfriend's money in the slot machine, not welfare funds, said that she would pay back the $2000 she had received in public assistance during the year.

In June **Allan Bakke,** 41, graduated from the University of California Medical School at Davis, to the loud cheers of his classmates and spectators. Bakke, who is white, was admitted to the medical school after a landmark U.S. Supreme Court decision in 1978 in which the Court agreed that he had been the victim of reverse discrimination in being denied admittance because of the school's policy of maintaining an admissions quota for the benefit of minority applicants. Bakke went on to an internship at the Mayo Clinic in Rochester, Minn.

The sister of **Fidel Castro,** who helped her brother to overthrow the regime of Fulgencio Batista in 1959 and assume power in Cuba, became a citizen of the U.S. on Feb. 4. A U.S. resident for 17 years, **Juanita Castro** said that it took her a long time to make the decision. "My heart is in Cuba, but my life is here," she said.

Wedding bells rang in 1982 for entertainer **Marie Osmond,** 22, and **Steve Craig,** 25, a former star basketball player for Brigham Young University. They were married in the Mormon Temple in Salt Lake City on June 26. **William Agee,** 44, chairman of the Bendix Corp., married **Mary Cunningham,** 30, the former Bendix executive who resigned in 1980 after a wave of publicity about her relationship with Agee, in San Francisco on June 5. It was the second marriage for both. **Robert F. Kennedy, Jr.,** 28, and his law school classmate, **Emily Black,** 24, were married in the bride's hometown of Bloomington, Ind., on April 3. British actress **Diana Rigg,** 43, best known as Emma Peel on television's *The Avengers* series, was wed to producer **Archibald Stirling** on March 25; the couple were the parents of a 4-year-old daughter. Former Olympic figure skating champion **Dorothy Hamill,** 25, and **Dean Paul Martin,** 30, a professional tennis player, sometime actor, and son of entertainer Dean Martin, were married in Beverly Hills, Calif., on Jan. 8.

Sen. Edward M. Kennedy (D, Mass.), announced on Dec. 1 that he would not run for the presidency in 1984, to spare his children the pressures of another political campaign while he and his wife, **Joan Kennedy,** were undergoing a divorce.

Actor **Lee Majors,** who fought a long divorce battle to regain the house he had

Several weddings made news in 1982. In April Robert F. Kennedy, Jr., was married to a law school classmate, Emily Black.

owned when he married **Farrah Fawcett,** decided after their divorce on Feb. 16 that she could keep the $2,500,000 home anyway—for free. "She deserves it," said Majors. "She's a nice lady and I still love her very much."

Hope springs eternal, at least for **Glenn de Moss Wolfe** of Blythe, Calif., an ordained Baptist minister who was, according to the *Guinness Book of World Records,* the most-married and most-divorced man in the monogamous world. Recently divorced from his 24th wife, Wolfe, 73, who had 40 children, disclosed in April that he kept two wedding dresses of different sizes in his closet, ready for instant use. "Everybody's looking for love," he said. "I've been doing this over half a century, and I'm still as game as ever, if not gamer." C.McG.

ANDROPOV, YURI V(LADIMIROVICH)

General Secretary of the Soviet Communist Party, born June 15, 1914, in the village of Nagutskoye, in the northern Caucasus. On Nov. 12, two days after the death of Leonid I. Brezhnev, the party's Central Committee chose Yuri Andropov for the Soviet Union's top leadership post. Although Andropov had been prominent in the Soviet hierarchy for 15 years as head of the KGB, the Soviet security agency, he remained a little-known figure to reporters and diplomats. Some described him as intelligent, informed, witty, sophisticated—a bibliophile with a taste for Western popular literature (he was said to know English). Others noted that he had shown himself to be a loyal and efficient apparatchik, or party servant, tough but not inflexible, and, in view of his surprising rise to the top, a skillful politician. The British weekly *Economist* described him as an "enlightened conservative."

The son of a railway worker, Andropov attended Petrozavodsk State University and at 22 began his political career as an organizer for the Young Communist League. During World War II and after, he held several minor posts before being appointed ambassador to Hungary in 1954. He was reported to have played a major role in helping the Soviets to suppress the Hungarian uprising of 1956 and in installing the relatively liberal regime of János Kádár. At the KGB he won high marks

Yuri V. Andropov became general secretary of the Communist Party, the most powerful post in the Soviet Union, on the death of Leonid I. Brezhnev.

for modernizing the agency and bringing it under strict party control. He left the agency in May, 1982, to fill the important Secretariat post made vacant by the death of Mikhail A. Suslov, a hard-line party ideologue. From that vantage point, apparently, Andropov maneuvered his way to the top party job, ahead of such other contenders as Konstantin U. Chernenko, 71, Brezhnev's reported favorite.

In his first public pronouncements, Andropov called for greater effort and efficiency in industry and agriculture at home and for a lessening of tensions abroad.

ARAFAT, YASIR

Chairman of the Palestine Liberation Organization (PLO), born in 1929 near Jerusalem. Israel dealt the PLO a crippling blow by invading southern Lebanon in June and overrunning its strongholds there. PLO headquarters in west Beirut were encircled and its lifeline to Syria severed. The Palestinian encampments of west Beirut suffered intensive bombardment. Finally, on July 3, after hours of wrangling with Lebanese leaders, Arafat gave them the written commitment they were looking for. "The PLO," he wrote, "does not wish to remain in Lebanon." By early August, through the mediation of U.S. special envoy Philip C. Habib, general agreement had been reached on the terms of the PLO withdrawal. On Aug. 21 the pullout from Beirut began. And on Aug. 30 Arafat himself departed. He faced the formidable task of rebuilding and maintaining control over the now-scattered Palestinian movement.

Arafat's exodus from Beirut was the latest in a series of moves that had taken him from Palestine, the land of his birth, to Egypt, where he received his civil engineering degree from the University of Cairo and served in commando and regular army units, and then to Kuwait, where he made his living from 1958 to 1965 as a contractor and engineer. In Kuwait he joined Al Fatah, a militant Palestinian group. By 1965 Arafat was head of its guerrilla operations. When Al Fatah became the dominant faction of the PLO four

Yasir Arafat's "V" sign could not conceal the defeat of his Palestine Liberation Organization, which was compelled to leave Lebanon in order to avoid destruction by Israeli forces.

years later, Arafat emerged as the organization's executive chairman.

BEGIN, MENACHEM

Prime Minister of Israel, born Aug. 16, 1913, in Brest Litovsk (now Brest), Russia. If the Middle East was the storm center of world politics, then Menachem Begin was the storm center of the Middle East. Few events in recent Arab-Israeli history were so hotly debated as Begin's decisions first to send troops into southern Lebanon, then to allow Israeli ground forces to surround Beirut, and finally to authorize Defense Minister Ariel Sharon to besiege the Lebanese capital until PLO forces were compelled to withdraw under international supervision.

More than any other war Israel had fought, the invasion of Lebanon provoked dissent both in Israel and among American Jews, although most observers agreed that Begin still commanded majority support among both constituencies. The U.S. Congress had long been generous to Israel and cordial to its emissaries, but when Begin came before committees of the House of Representatives and Senate on June 21–22, the legislators' questions were insistent and sometimes hostile.

U.S. support for Israel waned further after the Beirut massacre of Palestinians in mid-September. The discovery of the killings, and allegations of Israeli army complicity in them, gave rise to the establishment of a state investigatory commission in Israel. Meanwhile, relations with the U.S. suffered new strains when the Begin government summarily rejected a U.S. Mideast peace plan announced by President Reagan.

Begin was careful to keep the peace with Egypt, carrying out the Sinai pullout as scheduled on April 25. Nevertheless, Egypt recalled its ambassador to Israel in the wake of the Beirut massacre and spoke vaguely of a deterioration in relations. In domestic affairs, Begin maintained his fragile governing coalition despite sharp challenges in the Knesset (parliament).

BOTHA, P(IETER) W(ILLEM)

Prime Minister of South Africa, born Jan. 12, 1916, in Paul Roux, Orange Free State. On July 30, at a convention of the ruling National Party, Botha outlined his government's long-anticipated plan of power sharing between whites, Asians, and Coloureds, or people of mixed race. Under the plan, the present unicameral parliament would be replaced by three ethnically constituted lower chambers, with the President's Council functioning as an upper house. Critics on the Left were quick to complain that the plan continued to exclude blacks (who make up about 70 percent of the population) from power, while Botha's right-wing foes warned that it was a dangerous step toward racial integration. For their part, leaders of Asian and Coloured groups contended that Botha's plan did not go far enough.

Botha, South Africa's prime minister since September, 1978, entered politics as a National Party organizer at the age of 20. Elected to parliament in 1948, he first attained cabinet rank 13 years later, as minister of Coloured affairs and of community development and housing. Named defense minister in 1966, he presided over the expansion of South Africa's military budget from about

South African Prime Minister P. W. Botha faced criticism for his plan to replace the parliament with new bodies representing the nation's whites, Asians, and Coloureds.

$100,000,000 to nearly $2 billion within a decade. In that post and as prime minister, Botha was deeply involved in South Africa's attempt to hold on to South-West Africa (Namibia) in defiance of the United Nations and a guerrilla insurgency. Negotiations toward a peaceful settlement of the South-West Africa question dragged on throughout 1982.

CLARK, WILLIAM P(ATRICK)
Assistant to the President for National Security Affairs, born Oct. 23, 1931, in Oxnard, Calif. President Reagan's choice on Jan. 4 of Clark to replace Richard V. Allen as his national security adviser came as no surprise to Washington insiders. For months, Allen had been a controversial figure, as federal investigators and the media probed his financial dealings. Even though the Justice Department cleared him in December, 1981, of any criminal misconduct, he had become an embarrassment to the Administration. Moreover, his lack of direct access to the President had limited his effectiveness as a Presidential adviser.

Clark, although lacking in foreign policy experience, did not suffer the same handicap. The California lawyer had known Reagan since the 1966 gubernatorial campaign. In 1967 then-Gov. Reagan made Clark his chief of staff, in 1969 a state superior court judge, and in 1973 a California supreme court justice. Clark came to Washington in 1981 as deputy secretary of state, serving as liaison between the White House and Secretary of State Alexander M. Haig, Jr. In his national security post, Clark reportedly clashed with Haig and was said to have played a key role in the backstage maneuverings that led to Haig's resignation on June 25.

The White House schedule called for Clark to brief the President daily on foreign affairs, but there were many indications that his counsel also extended to domestic politics and other matters. Like Reagan, Clark was a part-time rancher, and they were known to take time out from the cares of state to swap horse catalogs and ranching lore.

DE LA MADRID HURTADO, MIGUEL
President of Mexico, born Dec. 12, 1934, in Colima, Mexico. Surprise and suspense have

rarely intruded on a Mexican presidential campaign. In national balloting on July 4, de la Madrid polled about 74 percent of the vote, swamping six rivals. His election had been considered a virtual certainty since Sept. 25, 1981, when he was nominated for the presidency by the Institutional Revolutionary Party, which had ruled Mexico uninterruptedly since 1929.

De la Madrid, who held a master's degree in public administration from Harvard University, had been a bureaucrat since the age of 19, when he entered the legal department of a state bank. During the 1960's and 1970's, he held positions with the Bank of Mexico; Petróleos Mexicanos (Pemex), the national oil monopoly; and the ministry of finance. In 1979 he became planning and budget minister under President José López Portillo, whom he succeeded as the country's 21st chief executive on Dec. 1, 1982.

As Mexico's chief economic planner, de la Madrid was credited with using the nation's oil wealth to fuel rapid economic growth. As president, he would have to cope with some of the consequences of that policy—high inflation, a huge foreign debt, and a widening gap between rich and poor—along with such chronic problems as overpopulation, malnutrition, unemployment, and government corruption. Observers interpreted his unusually vigorous presidential campaign schedule as a sign that he was willing to come face-to-face with Mexico's social and economic ills and hoped to build his own broad following rather than rely on his party's residual popularity.

GANDHI, INDIRA (PRIYADARSHINI)

Prime Minister of India, born Nov. 19, 1917, in Allahabad. Gandhi took pains to demonstrate throughout 1982 that her nation was not committed to the Soviet camp and remained open to Western technology and investment. "We are friends with the Soviets," she told one interviewer. But, she added, "that does not prevent us from . . . trying to be friends with China or with the United States, and we don't think it should come in the way of other friendships." Observers pointed to her growing personal rapport with British Prime Minister Margaret Thatcher, In-

Prime Minister Indira Gandhi devoted much time in 1982 to improving India's relations with the West. At home she faced opposition from an unexpected source—her daughter-in-law—who was ordered out of the prime minister's home.

dia's continued cultivation of close ties with France, and a steady movement in talks toward normalization of ties with Pakistan and China as evidence of progress on the diplomatic front.

Probably the boldest diplomatic initiative that Gandhi took was her midsummer journey to the U.S., her first official visit in 11 years. After she met with President Reagan in Washington, D.C., on July 29, she announced agreement on increasing U.S.-Indian cooperation in scientific, cultural, and economic affairs. More substantively, the two leaders resolved a thorny nuclear issue: Blocked by U.S. law from supplying low-enriched uranium fuel to India's Tarapur power plant, near Bombay, because India does not allow full international inspection of all its nuclear installations, the Reagan administration agreed to let France be the supplier instead.

Within India, Gandhi continued to dominate political affairs. She carefully dissociated herself from the former colleagues and protégés of her son Sanjay, who died in a plane crash in 1980. Sanjay's widow, Maneka Gandhi, ordered out of the prime minister's residence because of political disagreements, later formed a new party to rival her mother-in-law's Congress-I (for Indira) political organization.

JARUZELSKI, WOJCIECH W.

First Secretary of the Polish United Workers' (Communist) Party and Chairman of the Council of Ministers (Prime Minister), born July 6, 1923, in Kurów, Poland. After more than a year as leader of Poland's government and Communist Party hierarchy, Jaruzelski remained something of a mystery man. As a deportee to the Soviet Union during World War II, he was converted to Communism and commissioned as an infantry officer in the Russian-sponsored Polish army. After the war, he rose steadily in both Communist and military ranks, emerging as a member of the party's Central Committee in 1964 and as chief of the general staff in 1965. Three years later he was promoted to minister of defense, a post he retained when he assumed the premiership in February, 1981, and became party first secretary the following October. Little was known about his personal life and interests; his wife was said to be of Soviet origin. His dark glasses, worn because he suffered from an eye ailment, seemed to mask his face from public scrutiny.

Throughout the year, sporadic efforts to relax the martial law restrictions imposed by Jaruzelski on Dec. 13, 1981, proceeded in tandem with a growing militarization of Polish society. Observers reported that generals had taken over many provincial party posts and that military commissars were overseeing factories and government offices. In March and August Jaruzelski visited the Soviet Union and conferred with Soviet President Brezhnev. In November Jaruzelski attended Leonid I. Brezhnev's funeral in Moscow. Martial law was suspended in December, but many of the restrictions imposed as emergency measures were made permanent by legislation.

JOHN PAUL II

Pope of the Roman Catholic Church, born Karol Wojtyła on May 18, 1920, in Wadowice, Poland. John Paul II dramatized his quest for peace by journeying to Great Britain and Argentina during the height of the Falkland Islands crisis. "Today the scale and horror of modern warfare—whether nuclear or not—makes it totally unacceptable as a means of settling differences between nations," he told a crowd of 300,000 worshipers at an open-air Mass near Coventry, England, on May 29. As if to demonstrate the gap between the papal vision of peace and the realities of world politics, no sooner had the pope arrived at Buenos Aires on June 11 than the British launched their climactic drive to recapture the Falklands.

World peace was not the only issue to preoccupy John Paul. In January he denounced the imposition of martial law in his native Poland; the following month he gave his explicit support to Solidarity, the Polish trade union movement, before a visiting delegation of labor leaders that included some Solidarity officials. Also in February, John Paul spent eight days in west Africa, addressing the faithful in Nigeria, Gabon, Benin, and Equatorial Guinea. The ecumenical highlight of the pope's British visit came on May 29, when John Paul (the first pontiff ever to set foot on British soil) worshiped at Canterbury Cathedral alongside Robert Runcie, the archbishop of Canterbury; this act, culminating in an embrace between the two men after the service, symbolized the narrowing of a 450-year breach between the Anglican and Roman churches.

The pope barely escaped injury, while on pilgrimage to Portugal's Basilica of Our Lady of Fátima, when a 32-year-old Spanish rebel priest lunged at him with a bayonet. The attack, foiled by police, came on May 12—almost a year to the day after John Paul was shot in St. Peter's Square, in Rome, by a Turkish terrorist. In the fall he paid a ten-day visit to Spain.

KHOMEINI, AYATOLLAH RUHOLLAH (MUSSAVI)

Iranian spiritual leader, born May 17, 1900, in Khomein, Persia (now Iran). Ayatollah Khomeini continued to make headlines in 1982, but to what extent he actually controlled events in Iran was a matter of speculation. On Feb. 18 the Iranian government made it known that Khomeini would eventually give up his role as guiding force of the Islamic revolution and that a three- to five-man council would succeed him. The announcement sparked rumors that the ayatollah (an honorific meaning "reflection of God") was already dying or incapacitated—rumors the Tehran regime labeled "imperialist and Zionist lies." In April the New York *Times* reported that the power struggle around the ayatollah was so intense that action on land redistribution and on choosing a successor to Khomeini could not be taken.

On the other hand, when Iranian troops launched an invasion of Iraq in mid-July, *Time* magazine's correspondent portrayed Khomeini as the leader who made the ultimate decision to seek the overthrow of Baghdad's Ba'athist regime as retribution for Iraq's 22-month-old war on Iran. How could Iran punish Iraq and at the same time fulfill Khomeini's pledge to aid Lebanese Muslims against Israel? "We shall get to Lebanon, and to Jerusalem, through Iraq," the ayatollah answered.

Whatever the long-term merits of that strategy, Iraq's defenses did not crumble, nor did the Iranian invasion inspire an Islamic fundamentalist uprising within Iraq, as Khomeini may have expected. The result of what Western observers saw as Khomeini's miscalculation was the prolongation of a bloody and inconclusive conflict.

KOHL, HELMUT
Chancellor of the Federal Republic of Germany, born April 3, 1930, in Ludwigshafen. On Oct. 1 the Christian Democratic Union (CDU), in alliance once again, after 13 years, with the Free Democratic Party (FDP), brought down the government of Chancellor Helmut Schmidt, leader of the Social Democratic Party (SDP). Helmut Kohl, leader of the CDU, was elected chancellor in parliament.

Kohl differed from Schmidt more in appearance and temperament than in fundamental policy. Unlike his somewhat aloof and intellectual predecessor, the new chan-

Helmut Kohl, leader of West Germany's Christian Democratic Union, became chancellor in October, succeeding Helmut Schmidt. Little change was expected in West Germany's fundamental policies.

cellor (who held a Ph.D. in political science from the University of Heidelberg) was a towering (6 ft. 4 in.), folksy politician who enjoyed mingling with crowds. He served as minister-president (governor) of Rhineland-Palatinate (1969–76). In 1976, when he was the CDU candidate for chancellor, his party lost narrowly to the SDP-FDP coalition in parliamentary elections.

A staunch supporter of the Western alliance and particularly of West Germany's close ties with the U.S., Kohl was expected to continue Schmidt's foreign policy, but perhaps with less emphasis on good relations with Eastern Europe and the Soviet Union. He was expected to institute cuts in government spending in order to keep the federal budget deficit from widening.

MITTERRAND, FRANÇOIS M(AURICE) M(ARIE)
President of France, born Oct. 26, 1916, in Jarnac. When Mitterrand hosted a summit meeting of the seven major non-Communist

industrial nations at Versailles, June 4–6, he warned the conferees that austerity programs "hinder technological development by discouraging long-term investments that generate new demand." Only a week later, however, Mitterrand and his ruling Socialist Party abandoned their program of economic stimulation and announced a four-month freeze of wages and prices, coupled with other measures aimed at curbing inflation and propping up the franc.

The turnaround came in the wake of a June 12 European currency realignment that devalued the franc by 5.75 percent (and by 10 percent against the revalued West German mark). The devaluation, an annual inflation rate of 14 percent, and an unemployment rate of 8.7 percent of the labor force were taken as signs by many observers that the Socialists' aggressive program of economic reform was in desperate trouble.

Under President Hosni Mubarak, Egypt's relations with Israel cooled. Mubarak declined to visit Jerusalem and withdrew Egypt's ambassador from Israel after the massacre of Palestinians in Beirut.

On March 3 Mitterrand became the first French head of state to visit Israel. In a speech to the Knesset the following day, he endorsed the concept of a Palestinian state— a stance that Israeli Prime Minister Menachem Begin called the main obstacle to improved relations between France and Israel. Israeli officials later blamed Mitterrand's public support of the Palestinians for a rash of anti-Semitic incidents in France during the summer. Meanwhile, relations with the U.S. continued to sour. Mitterrand openly expressed opposition to U.S. policies in Central America, and Paris took a leading role in European defiance of Washington's attempt to thwart construction of a gas pipeline between Siberia and Western Europe.

MUBARAK, HOSNI (MUHAMMAD)

President of Egypt, born May 4, 1928, in Minufiya. On April 25, as Israel completed its withdrawal from the Sinai Peninsula, Mubarak chose not to take part in the official Egyptian flag-raising ceremony at Rafah. Characteristically, Mubarak, who became president in October, 1981, after the assassination of Anwar el-Sadat, elected instead to lay a wreath at Sadat's grave, near Cairo. Three days later, the Sinai town of Yamit was renamed Sadat in the late president's honor.

During his first full year in office, Mubarak, as reserved as his predecessor was effusive, carefully laid the foundations for the post-Sadat era. On Jan. 2 he relinquished the premiership to Ahmed Fuad Mohieddin, a veteran Egyptian bureaucrat. Mubarak paid his first official visit to Washington, D.C., on Feb. 2. At the White House, where he received a warm welcome, he pledged to abide by the Camp David accords (which Sadat had negotiated) and urged the U.S. to negotiate directly with the Palestinians in an effort to reach a comprehensive Middle East settlement. Later, back in Egypt, Mubarak ordered the release of hundreds of Muslim militants whom Sadat had arrested in September, 1981, but he turned down appeals for clemency by five men sentenced to death for their roles in Sadat's assassination; the men were duly executed on April 15.

Under Mubarak, Egypt's relations with Israel were noticeably cooler than they had

New Japanese Prime Minister Yasuhiro Nakasone celebrates his accession with a serving of wild boar. He planned an early visit to Washington, D.C., to ease strains in relations with the U.S.

been in Sadat's last years. Plans for Mubarak to go to Israel were shelved after he declined to visit Jerusalem, whose status remained a matter of international dispute. In September he laid full blame on Israel for the massacre of Palestinians in west Beirut by Christian militiamen, and he recalled Egypt's ambassador to Israel.

NAKASONE, YASUHIRO

Prime Minister of Japan, born May 27, 1917, in Takasaki. A veteran member of the Liberal-Democratic Party (LDP), Japan's ruling party since its inception in 1955, Nakasone was elected prime minister on Nov. 26. He succeeded Zenko Suzuki, who apparently tired of trying to resolve differences within the faction-ridden party. In the four-candidate race within the party to succeed Suzuki as LDP president, and therefore as prime minister, Nakasone had the crucial support of Suzuki and former Prime Minister Kakuei Tanaka, leaders of the party's two largest factions in parliament.

The son of a lumber dealer, Nakasone served as a lieutenant in the Japanese navy during World War II. He won a seat in parliament in 1947 and retained it in every suc-

ceeding election. He was appointed to the first of several cabinet posts in 1967 and also served as LDP secretary-general (1974–76) and chairman (1977–80).

Nakasone indicated that in a visit to Washington, D.C., scheduled for January, 1983, he would try to ease strains with the U.S. over military questions and the growing Japanese trade surplus with the U.S. He planned, according to aides, to hold down government spending in order to cut the budget deficit, reduce regulatory controls on business, and open Japan's markets to more foreign products.

PÉREZ DE CUÉLLAR, JAVIER

Secretary-General of the U.N., born Jan. 19, 1920, in Lima, Peru. If Javier Pérez de Cuéllar learned one lesson in his years of U.N. service, it was how to accept disappointment. Prior to his election by the U.N. Security Council as secretary-general in December, 1981, Pérez had been seeking to persuade the Soviet Union to remove its troops from Afghanistan—an effort that by the end of

In his first year as secretary-general of the United Nations Javier Pérez de Cuéllar experienced the frustrations inherent in his job. The world body was unable to resolve many long-standing disputes.

1982 had still borne no fruit. Earlier, in 1976, acting on behalf of then-Secretary-General Kurt Waldheim, he succeeded in bringing leaders of the Greek and Turkish Cypriot communities to the conference table—but their differences, too, remained unresolved six years later.

"This is what happens with the U.N.," Pérez told an interviewer in 1981. "You have an improvement in the atmosphere. You are so close to a solution. Then you are frustrated." The frustrations continued after Pérez began his five-year term as secretary-general on Jan. 1, 1982. His major new effort at crisis handling—an attempt to mediate the Falkland Islands dispute—collapsed on May 20, when the British, accusing Argentina of bad faith, resorted to a military solution.

Pérez, a veteran diplomat who had served four years as Peru's ambassador to the U.N. and then two more as Waldheim's under secretary for special political affairs, did not lobby for his new post. In fact, when the Security Council chose him as a compromise candidate on Dec. 11, 1981, breaking a prolonged deadlock, he was reading and relaxing at a beach house near Lima. The author

Steady, soft-spoken George P. Schultz succeeded his temperamental opposite, flamboyant Alexander M. Haig, Jr., as secretary of state. Shultz exercised his influence behind closed doors, avoiding the limelight.

of two books on international diplomacy, he was also considered well versed in the literatures of France, Spain, and Latin America.

SHULTZ, GEORGE P(RATT)

U.S. Secretary of State, born Dec. 13, 1920, in New York City. When Alexander M. Haig, Jr., resigned as secretary of state on June 25, President Reagan's choice to replace him was generally regarded as the abrasive Haig's temperamental opposite. Steady, soft-spoken, and unflamboyant, George Shultz had a reputation for seeking compromise rather than conflict.

Shultz, a professional economist who received his Ph.D. from the Massachusetts Institute of Technology in 1949, was no stranger to Republican politics or to government service. The former dean of the University of Chicago's Graduate School of Business came to Washington, D.C., in 1969 to join the Nixon administration as secretary of labor. He served subsequently as budget director and Treasury secretary before leaving the capital in 1974 to sign on with the Bechtel Corp., a construction and engineering conglomerate based in San Francisco. (Another former Bechtel executive was Secretary of Defense Caspar Weinberger.)

By late summer Shultz was making his mark on U.S. foreign policy, according to some news accounts. The Israeli government considered him less well disposed than Haig to its policies, an opinion that deepened after President Reagan offered a Middle East peace plan on Sept. 1 that called for, among other things, a freeze on Jewish settlements in the West Bank area. Israel quickly rejected the plan, which Shultz reportedly had helped prepare. Shultz was also credited with persuading the President to remove a major irritant in U.S.-European relations by revoking the sanctions Reagan had earlier imposed in order to impede construction of a Siberian natural gas pipeline to Western Europe.

TENG HSIAO-PING (DENG XIAOPING)

Vice-Chairman of the Communist Party of the People's Republic of China, born Aug. 22, 1904, in Kuang-an (Guangan), Szechwan (Sichuan) Province. Teng's 37-day absence from Peking, beginning in mid-January, fueled speculation that the 77-year-old Chinese leader was unburdening himself of his political responsibilities. In fact, however, Teng continued to be China's top leader, even as a massive purge was under way that could cost the jobs of as many as 200,000 of China's 600,000 central government bureaucrats.

Among the targets of the purge were radical holdovers from the Great Proletarian Cultural Revolution of the 1960's, corrupt officials, and elderly officeholders ("veteran comrades"). The latter group, however, apparently did not include Teng, who in September was elected chairman of the newly created Central Advisory Commission to the Communist Party. He also retained control of the party's central military commission, which oversees the armed forces, and he remained on the party Politburo and the Politburo's Standing Committee, its six-man inner circle. The various party committees all received an infusion of new members regarded as sympathetic to Teng's policies. Moreover, Teng was considered the architect of the new party constitution that banned "all forms of personality cult"—an obvious criticism of the late Mao Tse-tung (Mao Zedong) and the era of adulation of Mao during which Teng was purged from power.

THATCHER, MARGARET (HILDA ROBERTS)

Prime Minister of Great Britain, born Oct. 13, 1925, in Grantham, England. Showing remarkable resilience, Thatcher rebounded from her political nadir at the close of 1981, raising her approval rating in the polls from 25 percent to 59 percent by midyear. Her government's budget, submitted on March 9 and providing for a cautious economic recovery, a payroll tax reduction, and modest increases in certain social programs, was a popular success: A poll taken later that month showed her Conservative Party leading the opposition for the first time since she took office in 1979.

The event that galvanized British opinion behind her, however, was Argentina's seizure of the Falkland Islands on the morning of April 2. Thatcher's response was resolute: Within days, a British naval task force set out for the South Atlantic. The prime minister cooperated in attempts by U.S. Secretary of State Alexander M. Haig, Jr., and U.N. Secre-

Margaret Thatcher's popularity soared as British forces went to war to recover the Falkland Islands from Argentina. Observers wondered whether the British prime minister could maintain her standing with the public in the face of massive and growing unemployment.

tary-General Javier Pérez de Cuéllar to mediate the dispute; but when diplomatic efforts collapsed, she gave the go-ahead for the victorious assault.

By late in the year Thatcher still maintained her popularity, even as unemployment continued to climb, to 14 percent. With the Labour Party preoccupied with internal ideological struggles, with the Liberal–Social Democratic alliance slipping, and with the unions turning surprisingly conciliatory, Thatcher appeared to be in no immediate political peril. Yet, "can such luck hold," asked the Economist in November, "and until when?"

PEOPLE IN THE NEWS

TRUDEAU, PIERRE ELLIOTT

Prime Minister of Canada, born Oct. 18, 1919, in Montréal. On April 17 Queen Elizabeth II, standing on a massive wooden platform atop Ottawa's Parliament Hill, signed the Constitution Act, 1982. The measure, terminating the British North America Act of 1867 and transferring to Canada full constitutional powers, marked one of the major triumphs of Prime Minister Trudeau's political career. Canada, he said, had "at long last . . . acquired full and complete sovereignty."

Euphoria was not, however, boundless. Nine of Canada's ten provinces had approved the terms for the transfer of sovereignty, but Premier René Lévesque of Québec had not. He denounced the new constitution and vowed that Québec would change none of its laws or policies to conform to the federal mandate. And, in August, all ten provincial premiers rejected Trudeau's program to limit price and wage increases to 6 percent in 1982 and 5 percent in 1983.

When both unemployment and inflation reached 12 percent levels in late summer, Trudeau blamed the world recession and high U.S. interest rates, but critics blamed his restrictions on foreign investment. In September Trudeau's popularity with the public reached an all-time low of 28 percent. Con-

During his previous stint in federal government service, Caspar Weinberger described himself as a "fiscal Puritan." As secretary of defense, however, he lobbied hard for increased military spending.

fronting a crowd of hostile demonstrators, he defiantly raised his middle finger before television cameras. The incident spurred other demonstrators to pelt Trudeau's car with tomatoes, eggs, and rocks.

WEINBERGER, CASPAR W(ILLARD)

U.S. Secretary of Defense, born Aug. 18, 1917, in San Francisco. At the Office of Management and Budget (OMB), which he headed from May, 1972, to February, 1973, in the Nixon administration, Caspar Weinberger was known as "Cap the Knife." There, the self-described "fiscal Puritan" relentlessly pruned each agency's budget request. A decade later, the shoe was on the other foot. As President Reagan's defense secretary, Weinberger administered the largest U.S. military budget ever. And he lobbied hard in Congress to keep intact his proposed defense spending plan of $1.6 trillion for fiscal years 1982–86.

Weinberger rarely missed an opportunity to warn Congress and the American public of the Soviet military threat. In April he asserted that the Soviets had "a missile which basically has a greater accuracy than ours by a significant amount"—an admission of Russian qualitative as well as quantitative superiority that no U.S. official had ever before felt compelled to make. Some defense experts challenged his claim, and a Weinberger-approved Pentagon document, completed in August, discussing U.S. preparations for a "protracted" nuclear war with the Soviet Union, drew even harsher fire. The defense secretary later softened his rhetoric.

Weinberger, who graduated from Harvard University Law School in 1941, entered Republican Party politics in California after serving in World War II. After a brief stint as then-Gov. Reagan's state finance director, he was named to the Federal Trade Commission; after serving as OMB director, he was secretary of health, education, and welfare (1973–75). Before his confirmation as defense secretary in January, 1981, Weinberger was vice-president and general counsel of the Bechtel Corp., where he was a colleague of Secretary of State George P. Shultz, another Nixon administration cabinet member.

G.M.H.

Qabus bin Said, sultan of Oman, attends a banquet in his honor at London's Buckingham Palace on March 16. To the right stands Queen Elizabeth II, wearing on the end of her sash the Order of al-Said, a gift from the sultan. Also shown are the Queen Mother and Prince Philip.

PERSIAN GULF STATES. Alarmed and shaken by Iran's counteroffensive against Iraq in the Persian Gulf war and by Israel's invasion of Lebanon and siege of Beirut during the summer, the six members of the Gulf Cooperation Council (GCC), consisting of Bahrain, Kuwait, Oman, Qatar, Saudi Arabia, and the United Arab Emirates, forged an increasingly cohesive alliance in 1982. When 73 Shi'ite Muslim militants were arrested in Bahrain in December, 1981, on charges of having taken part in an Iranian-inspired coup attempt against the Bahraini government, many Arab leaders in the region saw confirmation of their underlying fear: that Iran's Shi'ite rulers were determined to export their Islamic revolution and undermine the ruling Sunni Muslim regimes of the Gulf. On May 22, 1982, following a three-month trial, Bahrain's Supreme Court found all 73 defendants, who were members of the Islamic Front for the Liberation of Bahrain, guilty as charged; the

three ringleaders were sentenced to life imprisonment, and the others received lesser sentences.

Hoping to reduce their extreme vulnerability to outside attack, GCC members moved toward the establishment of an integrated air-defense system centered around Saudi Arabia's American-built Airborne Warning and Control Systems (AWACS) surveillance planes and Hawk antiaircraft missiles. Under GCC auspices, the pro-Western Sultanate of Oman and the People's Democratic Republic of Yemen (South Yemen), a Marxist state, began reconciliation talks on Oct. 25. The talks came after reports that the Soviet Union might reduce its use of South Yemen as a military base. At a Nov. 16–17 meeting in Bahrain, GCC leaders signed an economic accord, effective on March 1, 1983, that would remove tariff barriers between the six member states and ensure freedom of movement of labor within the GCC area.

Clear evidence of the GCC's cohesiveness was also seen in the field of oil production and pricing. At a GCC meeting in Oman on Oct. 14, council members issued an angry ultimatum denouncing oil-producing states inside and outside the Organization of Petroleum Exporting Countries (OPEC) whose overproduction, the GCC declared, had caused oil prices to weaken. Some GCC members pushed for the formation of a "mini-OPEC" to reestablish the dominance of the Gulf oil producers in world markets.

See STATISTICS OF THE WORLD. *See also* KUWAIT; ORGANIZATION OF PETROLEUM EXPORTING COUNTRIES; SAUDI ARABIA.   A.D.

PERU. Increased leftist guerrilla violence forced the government of Peru's President Fernando Belaúnde Terry to declare several states of emergency in 1982. These measures were apparently intended, in part, to allay press and popular criticism and to dispel public fears of a possible military coup.

On March 3 between 60 and 100 guerrillas stormed a prison in the Andean city of Ayacucho, and freed 230 inmates. Fourteen people were killed in the fighting. In other actions, a guerrilla assault on a police post in the town of Quinua was repelled, but guerrillas killed one policeman and wounded three others in an attack on a police station in Trujillo Province. The guerrillas were said to belong to a Maoist group, known as Sendero Luminoso, or Luminous Path, with an estimated membership of between 500 and 1000. Four provinces in the central Andes mountains were placed under a state of emergency.

By far the most serious incident occurred on Aug. 19, when saboteurs bombed Lima's power installations, blacking out the capital for two days. Several shops and official buildings were also attacked. On Aug. 20 the Belaúnde government imposed a 60-day state of emergency in greater Lima, suspending civil liberties and giving the police the power of entry and arrest without a warrant. Of 34,107 people arrested and questioned by police, all but 33 "suspected terrorists" were released.

Plummeting world prices for metals exports damaged Peru's economy in 1982. In order to save many mining companies from bankruptcy, the Belaúnde government announced a six-month emergency measure in July that granted tax exemptions to small- and medium-size mining companies and suspended all collective bargaining in the industry until the end of that term. The slump in prices was expected to cost Peru $600,000,-000 in export revenues in 1982, doubling the projected trade deficit for the year. Earlier in July the International Monetary Fund approved a three-year, $975,000,000 loan to Peru to help the country meet payments on its debts. In return, the government was obligated to postpone economic development projects.

See STATISTICS OF THE WORLD.   A.E.J.

PETROLEUM AND NATURAL GAS. In 1982 oil availability again proved no problem. A recession affecting most of the world's industrial nations helped curb demand. The economic downturn, coupled with the inability of the often fractious Organization of Petroleum Exporting Countries to maintain a ceiling on production, resulted in a global oil glut.

In the United States a lagging economy and high energy prices continued to encourage conservation. U.S. petroleum consumption fell for the fourth consecutive year. In fact, the Department of Energy expected consumption in 1982 to fall to a ten-year low. It was also estimated that American dependence on imported oil would reach a ten-year low. The 4,900,000 bbl imported per day represented only 30 percent of the nation's petroleum use, a decline of nearly 15 percent from 1981. Falling demand helped stabilize prices, a boon for consumers but not for the oil industry, whose profits fell.

When the administration of U.S. President Ronald Reagan decontrolled oil prices in early 1981, some analysts predicted that gasoline would jump to $2 per gallon by the end of 1981. The 1981 yearly average price for all grades, however, was $1.33 per gallon. For the first half of 1982, the average was slightly lower, and the year ended with the average price being $1.22 per gallon.

Production. A leading argument for decontrolling oil prices was that this action would

Controversies over proposed oil drilling on federally owned acreage continued in 1982. Environmentalists opposed any further leasing or drilling in this wilderness area of California, which is a sanctuary for the endangered California condor.

spur the exploration and development of domestic oil resources. In 1981 oil and gas companies spent more than $30 billion for exploration. The number of drilling rigs in operation—generally the most accepted measure of industry activity—averaged 3970 per month in 1981, with a December high of 4530. But with oil and gas revenues slowing in 1982 due to the slump in demand and prices, companies spent only $24 billion for exploration, down 20 percent from 1981. The number of drilling rigs in operation dropped steadily all year; the September average of 2526, for example, was off 40 percent from a year earlier. Not surprisingly, the big industry losers were oilfield goods and service companies that supply drilling rigs and related equipment. Their revenues were expected to fall $8 billion by the end of 1982.

Leasing. In February Interior Secretary James G. Watt made a controversial proposal with regard to the leasing of federal wilderness areas for oil drilling and mining; *see* MINERALS AND METALS.

In July the Interior Department released the final version of a five-year offshore-leasing program. The plan, involving roughly 1 billion acres, called for 41 lease sales through June, 1987. Tracts were to be opened up for leasing at a rate of 200,000,000 acres a year, more than a 13-fold increase over the yearly rate that would have been available through an earlier version of the plan, although only a small percentage of the available acreage was likely to be drilled.

Critics said that the accelerated program would cut the time available for environmental studies, as well as reduce the ability of state and local officials to participate in the leasing process. Environmentalists were most disturbed by the plan's opening up of vast amounts of so-called frontier acreage off Alaska, where marine life might be jeopardized.

The Administration estimated that leasing-program revenues could total $15.7 billion in fiscal year 1983. A leasing sale held on Oct. 13 for tracts in Alaska's Beaufort Sea—a prime region northeast of oil-rich Prudhoe Bay—was seen as a test of the plan's capacity to yield such revenues. Twenty-three oil companies bid a near-record $2.1 billion for Beaufort Sea drilling rights. Earlier in the year the Congressional Budget Office (CBO) had

323

Lower demand for petroleum cut into oil company profits in 1982. In August Exxon Corp. announced that it was closing 850 service stations in the Northeast and Middle West.

charged that Interior's revenue estimates were inflated by at least a third. Other critics had charged that by holding the sale during an oil glut, the Interior Department would give industry prized acreage at bargain prices. But the bid total turned out to be four times the figure that had been projected by the CBO.

While interest was high in the Alaska offshore area, oil-industry enthusiasm waned for the Baltimore Canyon and Georges Bank regions off the Atlantic coast. Nine oil companies wound up a four-year effort to find crude oil in those regions. The $2.9 billion spent yielded nothing but 35 dry holes.

More promising, according to reports in the fall, was an area of the Pacific Ocean 65 mi. northwest of Santa Barbara, Calif. Test drilling on a tract leased by two companies was said to have yielded results indicating as much as 1 billion bbl of recoverable crude oil in this area.

Natural Gas. U.S. consumption of natural gas fell moderately in 1982; but at 10 trillion cu.ft., it was off only 1.5 percent from 1981. Imports to the U.S., however, were up to 504 billion cu.ft.—11.5 percent above 1981. The cost of domestic gas rose—up almost 14 percent over the average price for 1981 in just the first four months of the year.

Under the provisions of the Natural Gas Policy Act (NGPA) of 1978, prices for "new"

gas—reserves discovered after April, 1977—rose gradually throughout 1982. This gas was slated for full decontrol under the act by 1985. Prices for "old" gas—reserves contracted for prior to April, 1977—stayed controlled as before, though some adjustments were made for inflation.

The NGPA was designed to eliminate the gap between oil and gas prices. (In 1977 natural gas sold at the wellhead for half the cost of an equivalent amount of domestic crude oil.) However, falling oil prices and rising gas prices brought gas to parity far sooner than had been anticipated. The Reagan administration, saying that gas decontrol "remains the essential component of a sound energy policy," wanted to accelerate the pace of gas decontrol, much as it had accelerated oil-price decontrol. But unlike the oil measure, accomplished by executive order, gas decontrol required legislation. Though the subject was much discussed in 1982, Congress never got around to tackling it directly.

Uncertainty about the future cost of natural gas appeared to doom the $43 billion Alaska natural gas pipeline. In late 1981 Congress had granted the project's sponsors special waivers. Among other provisions, the waivers would allow pipeline operators to bill consumers for some costs of the project even before any gas was delivered. Project sponsors said that the waivers were needed to attract financing. Despite the waivers, however, financing could not be arranged in 1982. By year-end, the project was considered unlikely to survive because estimates of the cost of the gas it would deliver were believed to be too high to attract buyers.

On Nov. 13 President Reagan lifted the ban he had imposed a year earlier on the sale of U.S. oil and gas equipment to the Soviet Union. At the same time he lifted sanctions later imposed on foreign affiliates of U.S. companies that were intended to bar them from fulfilling their contracts for construction of a 3700-mi. natural gas pipeline linking Siberia with West Germany. *See* EUROPEAN COMMUNITIES; UNITED STATES OF AMERICA.

See also ENERGY; ORGANIZATION OF PETROLEUM EXPORTING COUNTRIES. J.A.R.

The Tonkinese cat, a blend of the Siamese and Burmese, received provisional recognition in 1982 from the Cat Fanciers Association. It is described as outgoing and affectionate.

PETS. The Tonkinese cat, a breed resulting from crosses between Siamese and Burmese, was given provisional recognition in 1982 by the Cat Fanciers Association (CFA), largest of the purebred feline registry associations in the United States. The Tonkinese would have to be judged and ranked under its provisional status at CFA shows; other national cat societies had already recognized the breed.

According to the American Kennel Club, more than 1,000,000 purebred dogs were registered in the U.S. during 1981. Cocker spaniels moved into second place behind poodles in number of dogs registered, replacing Doberman pinschers. Among the top 30 breeds, the greatest increase in popularity was shown by the chow chow, the greatest decline by the Irish setter. The greatest loss in popularity among all breeds, however, was registered by the Australian cattle dog, down from 55th place to 81st place.

In February, 1982, the Pekingese bitch Ch. St. Aubrey Dragonora of Elsdon won best in show at the Westminster Kennel Club annual event.

At midyear a dwarf hamster (*Phodopus*) from northern China, a different species from the regular pet hamster (*Mesocricetus*), became much sought after. Only about half the size of the normal hamster and a good deal more docile, the newly introduced rodent was in very short supply, but breeders hoped to produce it in quantity.

Parrots such as budgerigars, lovebirds, and cockatiels maintained their popularity among bird fanciers, and were much more important economically than canaries and finches. Beginning in March the U.S. Department of Agriculture required that all parrots shipped from California be identified by leg bands and accompanied by a waybill or a similar document signed by a department inspector. The regulation was promulgated to combat the trade in illegally imported parrots, many of which came into the U.S. through California; illegally imported parrots had been implicated as carriers of Newcastle disease, a killer of poultry.

Tropical fish hobbyists who specialize in the keeping and breeding of anabantid fish responded with enthusiasm to the first breeding in captivity of a beautiful species from Brunei. Known as *Betta macrostoma*, the vividly marked, aggressive newcomer is closely related to the Siamese fighting fish, an aquarium favorite for years, but differs from it markedly in breeding behavior. N.P.

Putting the Bite on Dog Owners

The U.S. Postal Service claims to be ready to deliver the mail in all eventualities—even nuclear war—but it seems to be losing the war against dogs. By August an average of 21 mail carriers had been bitten by dogs each working day in 1982, well ahead of the pace that resulted in 5700 attacks in 1981. Under a new policy outlined by Postmaster General William F. Bolger, mail carriers, who have the right to sue when injured on private property but often balk because of high legal costs, may ask Postal Service attorneys to file lawsuits on their behalf, with the federal government receiving a share of the proceeds.

PHILIPPINES. Despite opposition to his authoritarianism and speculation concerning his health, President Ferdinand E. Marcos continued his firm rule of the Philippines in 1982.

Politics. Twelve opposition parties, including the Liberals and the Nationalists, both of which had dominated pre-Marcos politics, formed a coalition front in April. Nationalist Party leader Salvador Laurel was named interim president of the coalition, whose announced intention was to mount a strong campaign for the 1984 parliamentary elections.

A major scandal in May led to the resignation of all 14 Philippine supreme court justices, following repeated allegations that the court had fixed the bar examination results of a judge's son in order to allow him to pass. Marcos swore in a new supreme court on May 14, including 12 of the justices who had resigned.

Longtime government efforts to quell a rebellion of the Moro National Liberation Front, a secessionist Muslim organization in the southern Philippines, appeared to show gains following June elections in the region. Government-backed Muslim candidates won overwhelming victories, although militant Muslims, who boycotted the voting, claimed that the results did not reflect the Muslim community's feelings.

In a nationwide sweep against what it considered "terrorist plotters," the government began in August to arrest dozens of labor leaders. They were charged with seeking to disrupt the government through strikes, assassinations, and bombings, in connection with the tenth anniversary of Marcos's declaration of martial law. Most Filipinos discounted the charges, and opposition leaders called for Marcos's resignation.

Persistent rumors of the president's ill health appeared to gain credence in August, when Marcos entered a Manila hospital with what was described as a mild case of pneumonia. In September Marcos, 65, sought to resolve repeated questions concerning his successor. He signed a new law that formally bequeathed his powers to a 15-member executive committee including his wife Imelda.

In the event of his death, resignation, or incapacitation, the committee would be required to organize presidential elections within 90 days of assuming control.

The Economy. With a per capita income of more than $700 per year, the Philippines ranked among the more affluent of Third World countries. However, the high price of imported oil, together with depressed world prices for exports such as sugar, coconut products, and timber, had created severe payment deficits and a soaring foreign debt. Real economic growth for 1982 was expected to be minimal.

Foreign Affairs. In a visit to Washington, D.C., in September Marcos met with members of the U.S. Congress and the press, in an effort to defend his government against charges of human rights abuses. Marcos was warmly welcomed by U.S. President Ronald Reagan, who pledged a $204,500,000 loan to help finance a Philippine nuclear power plant. The United States also agreed to enter new talks, starting in April, 1983, concerning U.S. military facilities at Subic Bay and Clark Air Force Base. Among the issues to be discussed was Marcos's desire to quadruple the $100,000,000 annual rent paid by the U.S. for use of the bases.

See STATISTICS OF THE WORLD. R.J.C.

PHOTOGRAPHY. In 1982 photography shows proliferated at major art institutions in the United States; some museums expanded their photography collections and allocated more space and time to photography exhibitions. The work of several contemporary photographers explored the possibilities and intentions of the medium. New camera equipment to suit a variety of needs was introduced by Eastman Kodak Co., Timex Corp., Nimslo, and Sony Corp.

Major Shows. In the spring of 1982 the Art Institute of Chicago opened a new 8000-sq.ft. exhibition and storage space devoted entirely to photography. Curator David Travis was instrumental in developing the space, which presented at its first show 287 pictures exploring the history of photography, from masters such as Eugène Atget and Man Ray to the work of current photographers. "Counterparts: Form and Emotion in Photographs" was brought together by Weston J. Naef at the Metropolitan Museum of Art in New York City. More than 100 photographs were shown in pairs, allowing comparisons between works by such eminent photographers as Margaret Bourke-White, Harry Callahan, Lisette Model, and László Moholy-Nagy. "Color as Form: A History of Color Photography," at the Corcoran Gallery of Art in Washington, D.C., included rare color work as well as examples of unsuccessful or now obsolete color processes; a second part of the exhibition was a sampling of the uses of color photography in science and the mass media, and by amateurs.

Images from the European past figured in many 1982 exhibitions. Magnum, the distinguished photographers' cooperative, presented "Paris/Magnum: Photographs 1935-1981" at New York's International Center for Photography (ICP). Magnum members selected the 100 black-and-white photographs, representing the work of 28 photographers including Robert Capa, Henri Cartier-Bresson, Inge Morath, and Marc Riboud. The ICP also presented the work of Erich Salomon, who photographed politicians and government leaders at nearly every important international conference between 1928 and 1939. The Prakapas Gallery in New York showed a view of a past era, the work of Cas Oorthuys, a World War II Resistance fighter in Amsterdam; his photographs, taken surreptitiously in 1944-45, documented the barbarities of the Nazi occupation.

Non-Western cultures were the subject matter of several photography exhibitions. The most ambitious was the ICP survey "Through Indian Eyes," comprising 200 19th- and 20th-century photographs of people of all levels of society in India, taken and often brilliantly hand-colored by local photographers. Photographs of Mayan monuments, taken in the 1880's by the English archeologist A. P. Maudslay, were shown at the Brooklyn Museum along with very similar wash drawings of the same architectural works done in 1843 by the painter Fredrick Catherwood. The show was called "Discovering the Maya." At the ICP "The Last and First Eskimos: Photographs by Alex Harris"

"Landowner's Wife, Rajasthan, c. 1895," an albumen print, was one of 200 photographs in the 1982 exhibition "Through Indian Eyes" at New York City's International Center of Photography.

explored contemporary Inuit (Eskimo) culture in transition.

Important exhibitions of news photography also emphasized distant or non-Western places. "Micha Bar-Am: Israel Diary, 1956-1982," another ICP show, included 70 photographs by this New York *Times* photographic correspondent in the Middle East. Images of war outnumbered landscapes and portraits in a reflection of Israel's turbulent history. The temple architecture at Angkor in Cambodia was the subject of a 50-photograph exhibition at the United Nations General Assembly building. A *National Geographic* team headed by the magazine's editor, Wilbur E. Garrett, who took most of the photographs, showed the sad deterioration of the neglected temples and their carved ornamentation.

Shows by several photographers in 1982 challenged the limits of both form and content. Irving Penn, best known for his fashion work, exhibited black-and-white photographs at the Marlborough Gallery, New York. Still lifes composed of medicine bottles, skulls, and objets d'art, the photographs were intended as a meditation on death. A retrospective of 60 prints by conceptual art-oriented photographer Eve Sonneman was organized by Bruce Kurtz for the Hudson River Museum in Yonkers, N.Y. Sonneman's double-frame format—two images of the same subject taken seconds apart—showed a concern with the limits of the camera as it records movement in time and space.

Technological Advances. In February the Eastman Kodak Co. introduced a compact new motorized camera, called the Disc, which uses a rotating 2½-in. film disk instead of a roll of film. The three pocket-sized models of the Disc are only ¾ in. thick. Lithium cells with a life of more than 2000 exposures provide power to set exposure, automatically activate the flash, and advance film as soon as the picture is taken. Everything from 4 ft. to infinity is in focus at all times. The film negative is one sixth the size of a postage stamp. Each film disk contains 15 exposures.

Timex Corp., the watchmakers, and Nimslo Technology Inc., a photography company in Atlanta, promoted a new 3-D camera. Lightweight, with four fixed lenses, and using conventional 35-mm color film, the new system shoots four simultaneous pictures. A computerized process develops and prints the four images as one 3-D image.

In 1981 Sony Corp. introduced the Mavica, an electronic camera that uses a magnetic videodisk instead of film. The 50 color images recorded on the disk are viewed when the disk pack is inserted into a player attached to a television set. The Mavigraph, unveiled in March, 1982, is a color video printer for use with the Mavica. The Mavigraph's thermal printing head receives video signals and generates different levels of heat based on a signal's intensity. Dye on four dye sheets then evaporates and is transferred onto paper. A color print appears in five minutes. The Mavigraph can also produce prints from such sources as X-ray machines, television sets, videotape recorders, and personal computers.   R.M.

In February the Eastman Kodak Co. introduced three pocket-sized camera models that use a rotating film disk instead of a roll of film. Lithium cells set the proper exposure, activate a flash if needed, and advance the film as soon as the picture is taken.

PHYSICS. Physicists in 1982 were excited by the reported detection of the theoretical basic unit of magnetic force, the magnetic monopole, although the observation remained to be verified. Another impressive, although more predictable, achievement was the brief creation of a new element, number 109, by scientists in West Germany.

Magnetic Monopole. Great interest was aroused in the scientific community over the announcement by physicist Blas Cabrera that he may have detected a magnetic monopole on Feb. 14, in the course of an elaborate experiment at Stanford University. Magnetic monopoles had been predicted to exist in theory, but none had as yet been observed in fact. A similar report of such an observation, made in 1975, had gone unverified and was never generally accepted.

All known magnets, however small, are at least dipoles—that is, they have at least two magnetic poles, north and south. No matter how finely a magnet is divided, the resulting pieces are still dipoles. Magnetism and electricity are related, however, in that a moving electric current creates a magnetic field, and a moving magnetic field creates an electric current. Therefore, because unit electric charges are "monopole" in nature, being either positive or negative, physicists proposed that magnets could in theory also be reduced to monopole units of either north or south.

Magnetic monopoles form an important part of certain so-called Grand Unification theories that attempt to show that the known forces at work in nature are all aspects of a single force. These forces include electromagnetism, gravity, and the strong and weak interactions at work inside atoms. In their efforts to develop such theories, physicists have long sought to find out whether magnetic monopoles actually exist.

The search has not been easy. According to theory, magnetic monopoles should have a charge about 69 times that of the charge on an electron, but theories differ as to their probable mass. It has been suggested that very light monopoles exist in great number, but none has ever been detected. Much heavier monopoles have also been proposed, by physicists such as Gerard t'Hooft of the

Stanford University physicist Blas Cabrera examines equipment used in his apparently successful attempt to detect the elusive theoretical particles called magnetic monopoles. His results, if verified, would be of profound significance for physics.

Netherlands and Alexander Polyakov of the Soviet Union. According to theory, such monopoles would be about 10^{16} times as massive as a proton, or about as massive as some protozoans, but they would be slow-moving and few in number.

Cabrera decided to search for the latter kind of monopoles, which would be traveling about 1000 times more slowly than the speed of light. He devised an experiment that would detect a monopole solely by its charge and would screen out spurious charges. The experiment was so designed that, should a monopole pass through his apparatus, it would cause a change in the electric current moving through a superconducting loop of niobium metal. On Feb. 14 his detector recorded a current jump that correlated extremely well with the current change that would have been caused by the magnetic monopole. Cabrera looked for other explanations for the current jump, such as a

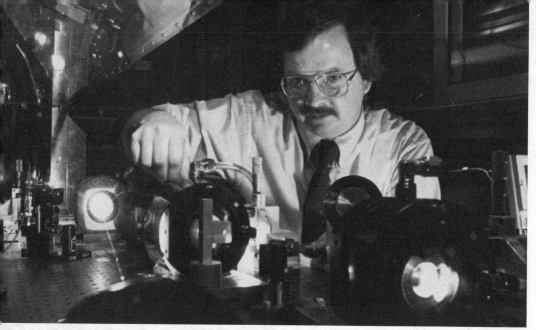

Bell Telephone Laboratories physicist Charles Shank uses a new laser device that he and colleagues developed to produce the shortest light pulse yet achieved, only 30 femtoseconds, or 30 × 10⁻¹⁵ sec., long—the time light takes to cross half the thickness of a human hair. The laser, to be used in semiconductor studies, could also explore changes taking place in the course of many chemical and physical processes.

loose wire, electrical interference, or a small earthquake, but all were ruled out.

No one could be certain that the observed effect was indeed caused by a magnetic monopole, but physicists planned different kinds of experiments to detect the elusive particle. Cabrera himself began to construct a larger detector that was expected to be 50 times more sensitive than his first one.

Element 109. Scientists working in West Germany reported the creation of a new element, number 109, in the transuranium region of the periodic table of elements. On Aug. 29 the researchers, who were using the Unilac accelerator in Darmstadt, bombarded a layer of bismuth (element 83) with billions of ions of iron (element 26) and produced an atom of the new element. Predictably, the element was extremely unstable. Within five milliseconds (.005 sec.) after it was formed, it began to decay radioactively by emitting alpha particles, thereby changing into a lighter element. The Darmstadt team then began plans to create another superheavy element, number 116, by bombarding curium (ele-

ment 96) with ions of calcium (element 20).

Ion Microscope. Physicist Riccardo Levi-Setti of the University of Chicago made a significant addition to scientific instrumentation in 1982 by devising a new kind of microscope. The instrument, called a scanning ion microscope, can magnify objects that are no wider than 0.00001 cm (0.000004 in.). It does this by bombarding a target object placed in the microscope with ions, and then mapping the collisions that result. Scanning electron microscopes work in a similar manner, but because ions are much more massive than electrons, the resulting images from the scanning ion microscope are different. The scanning ion microscope produces high-contrast images as its bombarding ions knock atoms off the surface of the target, whereas the scanning electron microscope provides less contrast but shows more surface detail. The new microscope, said Levi-Setti, would be useful for studying crystal structures and for observing tissues one layer at a time. The microscope might also be used to produce circuits on silicon chips for microprocessors.   J.S.

POLAND. Poland spent 1982 under the martial law regime declared on Dec. 13, 1981, by Prime Minister and Communist Party leader Wojciech W. Jaruzelski (see biography at PEOPLE IN THE NEWS). Aware of the government's overwhelming strength, citizens remained largely quiescent but sullen. The suspended free trade union Solidarity, which was formally outlawed on Oct. 8, operated underground but gradually lost active public support as the year wore on. In December Communist authorities felt secure enough in their victory over Solidarity to ease martial law and free many internees.

Politics. Gen. Jaruzelski outlined his policy for Poland in a speech to parliament in January. He attacked Solidarity for provocative actions, promised that a less politicized union movement would be permitted provided the country remained calm, and appealed for Poles to work together. With Solidarity leader Lech Walesa in government detention, Zbigniew Bujak replied for the underground union by demanding an immediate end to martial law. The Roman Catholic Church took a position between the adversaries; primate Archbishop Jozef Glemp agreed that the state of emergency must be lifted, but he counseled the Polish people to engage in dialogue with their rulers, not confrontation.

In early April Catholic lay leaders formulated a proposal for conciliation between the government and Solidarity; among other things, the document accepted that Solidarity must bear some of the responsibility for bringing on the military crackdown and that Poland's position in the Communist bloc must not be challenged. Bujak promptly endorsed the document. In response, Jaruzelski freed 1000 internees and lifted the nationwide nightly curfews. For the public, however, the pace of normalization seemed too slow. On May Day, and again on May 3, violent clashes took place in Poland's major cities between Solidarity sympathizers and

Defiant Poles took to the streets several times in 1982 to protest the imposition of martial law and the suspension of free trade unions. Here Polish riot police release tear gas to disperse thousands of demonstrators in Gdańsk.

A Polish army officer watches transactions in a Warsaw food store to guard against black marketeering. The regime raised food prices substantially in February.

police. In response, the regime reinstated the curfew in nine cities.

Both Bujak and Jaruzelski had to struggle against hard-liners in their own camps. Solidarity radicals demanded a campaign of sabotage and strikes; Communist conservatives demanded tougher measures against underground Solidarity. In July Jaruzelski won a significant victory over a powerful rival by securing the removal of leading conservative Stefan Olszowski from the post of party secretary for ideology. Jaruzelski next announced that more internees would be released and that martial law could be lifted by year's end if the situation were "favorable," but at the same time he made it clear that he would not allow an August visit to Poland by Pope John Paul II.

On Aug. 13, the second anniversary of Solidarity's founding, and again on Aug. 31, union sympathizers took to the streets to vent their frustrations. But that proved to be Solidarity's last major show of force, although there was scattered unrest in October. Parliament formally abolished Solidarity in October and laid the groundwork for new, weaker unions. With Glemp urging moderation upon both sides and with the collapse of an underground Solidarity attempt to stage a nationwide strike and demonstrations on Nov. 10, Jaruzelski agreed in early November to permit a 1983 papal visit and to free Walesa. Arriving home in Gdańsk on

Nov. 14, Walesa promised to be "prudent," but he later called for the regime to restore the legal status of free trade unions and to free all internees. Underground Solidarity leaders on Nov. 27 called off the strike they had planned for the first anniversary of martial law.

On Dec. 13 parliament met to pass legislation ending such practices as internment, domestic travel restrictions, and routine monitoring of mail and telephone calls. However, the legislation, which was approved on Dec. 18, preserved press censorship, prison sentences for distributing leaflets and creating a "public disturbance," and the deployment of riot police. The military administration of some 200 factories, mines, and transport facilities would continue, and their workers would not be able to quit without permission. Military courts would continue to try civilians in many cases. Hundreds of political internees were released in December, and martial law was suspended on Dec. 31.

The Economy. Martial law solved few of Poland's grave economic difficulties. Economic reforms discussed during Solidarity's heyday were shelved. Western sanctions and lack of funds to import machinery and raw materials crippled industry, with overall production dropping 7.8 percent in the first six months of 1982. To cut the budget deficit, the regime increased food prices substantially in February. Higher prices, rationing, and the greater efficiency of distribution achieved by military rule served to eliminate many of the long consumer lines, but the standard of living plummeted. Poland remained unable to repay principal or interest on about $24 billion borrowed in the West; in November Western banks agreed to defer payment of the $3.5 billion due from Warsaw in 1982. Coal mining provided almost the only bright spot. With miners working overtime for large bonuses and required to work on Saturdays, 1982 hard coal output ran about 15 percent above the 1981 level.

Foreign Affairs. Poland's relations with the West remained frosty in 1982. In October U.S. President Ronald Reagan suspended Poland's "most favored nation" trade status, thereby raising tariffs on Polish imports.

Jaruzelski maintained close but uneasy relations with the Soviet Union, which insisted that he bring Solidarity to its knees. He visited the U.S.S.R. in March and August to report to Soviet President Leonid I. Brezhnev, and in November he traveled to Moscow again to confer with Brezhnev's successor as Communist Party leader, Yuri V. Andropov. The Soviets provided Poland with cash and raw materials to keep its economy functioning.

See STATISTICS OF THE WORLD.　　　　F.W.

PORTUGAL. Portuguese politics in 1982 focused on the continuing struggle between President António Ramalho Eanes and the ruling Democratic Alliance (AD) coalition headed by Premier Francisco Pinto Balsemão. On Dec. 19 Pinto Balsemão resigned because of losses suffered in local elections by his Social Democratic Party.

The AD and the Socialist Party, which together commanded 197 of the 250 seats in the National Assembly, voted on Aug. 12 to revise the 1976 constitution by disbanding the Council of the Revolution, a committee composed of left-leaning military officers and the president. This committee had held broad powers to veto legislation and had used its power to block parliamentary attempts to expand the scope of the private sector in the economy, much of which was nationalized after the 1974 revolution. The constitutional revision provided for the creation of a tribunal composed of judges chosen by the parliament to take over the council's responsibility for ruling on the constitutionality of legislation. Other functions of the council would be assumed by a council of state and a council of national defense. The military came under the direct control of the government.

The constitutional revision was the high point of an otherwise difficult year for Pinto Balsemão and the AD government. A general strike called in February by the Communist-controlled CGTP union confederation shut down some industries and rail services in Lisbon, although it did not succeed in forcing the government to resign. Pinto Balsemão named new ministers of foreign affairs, education, labor, and parliamentary relations in a cabinet reshuffle in June. The cabinet changes set off a brief constitutional dispute because Eanes had not been informed ahead of time about the shake-up.

The Portuguese economy remained stagnant during 1982. Public sector expenditures mounted and produced a budgetary deficit, while the import of fuel as well as of foodstuffs contributed to a payments deficit. Responding to this crisis, the government announced a 9.5 percent devaluation of the escudo in June, and it ordered fuel price increases and a wage-price freeze in July. Prices for food and other key items remained frozen through the end of the year.

Portuguese foreign policy aimed at entry into the European Community by early 1984 and the establishment of better political and commercial ties with the former colonies in Angola and Mozambique. Eanes visited Angola in April, where he pledged development aid. Pinto Balsemão went to Mozambique in June and visited the United States in December.

Pope John Paul II paid a three-day visit to Portugal in May. While at the shrine of Fátima on the evening of May 12, he was the target of an assassination attempt by a 32-year-old dissident Spanish priest. The priest, who was armed with a bayonet, was seized by security agents and charged with attempted murder.

See STATISTICS OF THE WORLD.　　　　E.M.L.

President Ronald Reagan admires an 800-lb. boar on an Iowa hog farm after addressing the National Corn Growers Association. With his personal popularity still high but confidence in his economic program eroding, the President sought in personal appearances and radio and television addresses to reassure Americans that the nation was "recovery bound."

PRESIDENT OF THE UNITED STATES. Ronald Wilson Reagan, 40th President of the United States, was born Feb. 6, 1911, in Tampico, Ill. In his second year as President, Reagan continued to preach the gospel of less government spending, lower taxes, and a strong national defense. But what his partisans called the "Reagan revolution" sputtered in 1982, as the President's economic policies failed to produce the prosperity he had promised in his 1980 campaign. Through several nationally televised speeches and a series of Saturday afternoon radio broadcasts, Reagan sought to reassure the nation that "America is recovery bound." But as unemployment reached double-digit levels, substantial Democratic gains in the November elections placed Reagan's congressional coalition in jeopardy. At the midpoint of his first term, Reagan remained personally popular with voters. Nevertheless, his job approval rating

eroded, as a majority of Americans appeared to believe that his policies favored the privileged at the expense of the less fortunate. **Economic Problems.** In his State of the Union message on Jan. 26, Reagan predicted that his programs would "pull the economy out of its slump and put us on the road to prosperity and stable growth by the latter half of this year." But while inflation dropped significantly, business failures soared, consumer spending and industrial production lagged, and unemployment figures reached a postwar high of 10.8 percent.

Critics claimed that Reagan's fiscal policies were the primary cause of the continued recession. In 1981 Reagan had argued that reductions in federal tax rates and government spending would stimulate the economy and that the tax revenues from this economic resurgence would keep budget deficits under control. But when the recovery failed to materialize, enormous deficits were inevitable. Reagan's fiscal 1983 budget, unveiled on Feb. 6, showed a deficit of $91.5 billion and projected a three-year shortfall of more than $246 billion. The deficits were politically so unpalatable that even Republicans rejected Reagan's 1983 budget and sought to bridge the gap through tax increases. Though Reagan repeatedly protested that "raising taxes won't balance the budget," in August he reluctantly backed a Republican bill raising revenues by $98.3 billion over three years.

Domestic Policy. With the exception of a Jan. 7 decision to resume military draft registration, Reagan's domestic initiatives kept faith with his 1980 campaign pledges. In March he sent Congress a plan to reinvigorate decaying urban areas through the creation of tax-favored "urban enterprise zones," and in April he proposed a scheme of tuition tax credits for families with children attending private elementary and secondary schools. He proposed various reforms to the criminal justice code in September, including restrictions on the insanity defense and the exclusionary rule, provisions that he contended frequently allowed criminals to escape punishment. In October the President announced plans to escalate the government's assault on narcotics trafficking and organized crime; *see* CRIME AND LAW ENFORCEMENT. Sensitive to complaints from conservatives that he had strayed from his principles, Reagan reiterated his support for the "social issues," endorsing antiabortion legislation, a law permitting prayer in public schools, and a constitutional amendment requiring a balanced federal budget.

Reagan's most ambitious domestic proposal was for a sweeping transfer of social programs from the federal government to the states. Under the "new federalism" plan, Reagan proposed eventually to turn back to the states responsibility for more than 40 social programs. The plan also contained a "financially equal swap" in which the federal government would pay all Medicaid costs, with states assuming the cost of food stamps and most government welfare programs. The plan met with resistance from the nation's governors, and submission to Congress was deferred until 1983.

Foreign Policy. Despite his emphasis on economic policy, Reagan became more actively engaged in foreign affairs during 1982, moving on a variety of fronts to implement what

some aides described as a policy of conservative pragmatism.

In August an agreement was reached with China on a plan to reduce gradually the sale of U.S. military equipment to Taiwan. The Chinese were angered, however, when Reagan refused to agree to a specific cutoff date for all arms shipments to the Taipei government. In a May 9 speech, the President called for "significant reductions" in U.S. and Soviet nuclear arsenals; strategic arms reduction talks with the Soviets began in late June. But little progress was evident, and Soviet-American relations remained frigid.

Controversy over the proposed natural gas pipeline linking the Soviet Union with Western Europe strained the Western alliance during much of 1982. Rebuffed in attempts to persuade the Europeans to cancel their lucrative financial participation in the pipeline, Reagan prodded allied European governments to impose more stringent credit terms on the Soviets. When that failed, Reagan ordered foreign subsidiaries of U.S. companies not to sell oil and gas equipment to the U.S.S.R. The ban was defied by the Europe-

One stop on President Ronald Reagan's June visit to Western Europe was West Germany, where he and Secretary of State Alexander M. Haig, Jr. (far left), conferred with West German Chancellor Helmut Schmidt (second from right) and Foreign Minister Hans-Dietrich Genscher.

ans, incensed that Reagan would allow U.S. farmers to sell grain to the Russians while attempting to restrict their own trade with the East. When Reagan decided in November to lift the ban, his move was less a conciliatory gesture to Moscow than an attempt to ease tensions with the Western allies.

Reagan's major foreign policy achievement was in the Middle East. On Sept. 1, after U.S. diplomacy produced a negotiated settlement to the fighting in west Beirut between Israel and pro-Palestinian forces, Reagan unveiled plans for a comprehensive peace agreement. His "fresh start" proposed a freeze on Israeli settlements as well as some form of self-government for Palestinians living in the territories occupied by Israel since the 1967 war. The proposal was vigorously opposed by Israel but favorably received by moderate Arab states.

Hoping to counter Cuba's influence in Latin America, Reagan in February proposed a major increase in economic and military aid to Caribbean Basin countries. Reagan's foreign travel included trips to the Caribbean, Europe, and Latin America.

Election Campaign. Persuaded that the 1982 election results would be interpreted as a referendum on his policies, Reagan campaigned extensively for Republican candidates, repeatedly urging voters to "stay the course" and support his economic program. The strong showing by Democratic candidates on Nov. 2 was seen by political analysts as a protest against his failure to produce an economic recovery, and the loss of 26 Republican seats in the House of Representatives called into question Reagan's ability to work his will with the new Congress. Some observers suggested that he would have to compromise to a greater degree with the Democratic opposition in 1983 than he had during his first two years in office.

Personnel Changes. Several prominent Reagan administration officials resigned during the year, including Secretary of Energy James B. Edwards, domestic policy adviser Martin C. Anderson, national security assistant Richard V. Allen, and Murray L. Weidenbaum, chairman of the Council of Economic Advisers. The most controversial departure was that of

Secretary of State Alexander M. Haig, Jr., whose resignation was announced abruptly on June 25. Haig's partisans claimed that he had resigned as a matter of principle to protest the alleged drift of U.S. foreign policy. But White House aides passed the word that Haig was discharged after repeated power struggles with other officials. Haig was replaced by George P. Shultz (see biography at PEOPLE IN THE NEWS), former secretary of the treasury (and also of labor) in the administration of President Richard M. Nixon.

See also CABINET, UNITED STATES. T.D.

PRINCE EDWARD ISLAND. *See* STATISTICS OF THE WORLD.

PRIZES AND AWARDS. The following is a selected listing of prizes awarded during 1982 and the names of the persons who received them. For awards given in specific fields, see the appropriate subject entry, such as MOTION PICTURES.

NOBEL PRIZES

A Colombian novelist and a Swedish diplomat were among the best-known Nobel laureates in 1982. Also among the prizewinners were two Americans, one a physicist, the other an economist. The prizes, announced in October and presented on Dec. 10, each carried a cash value of $157,000.

Chemistry. For his "development of crystallographic electron microscopy and his elucidation of biologically important nucleic acid–protein complexes":

Aaron Klug (1926–), coleader of the division of structural studies at the Medical Research Council's Laboratory of Molecular Biology in Cambridge, England. Born in Dunbar, South Africa, Klug came to Cambridge University as a doctoral candidate in 1949. His studies of how oxygen combines with hemoglobin and of the protein crystallographic structure of viruses attracted the attention of Francis Crick (who shared the 1962 Nobel Prize in medicine for his work in determining the molecular structure of deoxyribonucleic acid, or DNA), and he was invited to join the council as a research scientist.

Economics. For "seminal studies of industrial structures, functioning of markets, and the causes and effects of public regulation":

Seven 1982 Nobel Prize winners pose in Stockholm prior to receiving their awards. Seated are Gabriel García Márquez (left), literature, and Sune K. Bergstrom, medicine. Standing, from left, are George J. Stigler, economics; Bengt I. Samuelsson, medicine; Aaron Klug, chemistry; John R. Vane, medicine; and Kenneth G. Wilson, physics.

George J. Stigler (1911–   ), Charles R. Walgreen Distinguished Service Professor of American Institutions, at the University of Chicago. Of the 12 Americans who have won the economics prize since it was established in 1969, Stigler was the eighth to have been associated in some way—as faculty member, student, or researcher—with that university. Born in Renton, Wash., he received his doctorate from Chicago in 1938 and returned to teach there 20 years later. As a member of the politically conservative "Chicago school" of economics, he has long been associated with Milton Friedman, who won the Nobel economics prize in 1976.

Literature. For his novels and short stories, "in which the fantastic and the realistic are combined in a richly composed world of imagination, reflecting a continent's life and conflicts":

Gabriel García Márquez (1928–   ), born in Aracataca, Colombia, and a resident of Mexico for most of the last two decades. Unlike some writers honored by the Swedish Academy's selection committee in recent years, García Márquez enjoys a wide popular following, as the academy itself pointed out: "Each new work of his is received by expectant critics and readers as an event of world importance, is translated into many languages, and published as quickly as possible in large editions." Known for his leftist sympathies, the Latin American author has been a longtime friend of French President François Mitterrand and Cuban President Fidel Castro. The novels of García Márquez, originally written in Spanish, have appeared in English translation as *One Hundred Years of Solitude* (1970), *The Autumn of the Patriarch* (1976), and *In Evil Hour* (1979).

Peace. Hoping to stimulate "the climate of peace that has emerged in recent years, first and foremost in the Western world," the Nobel committee awarded the peace prize to two diplomats—one Swedish, the other Mexican—who have represented their respective countries at United Nations disarmament talks in Geneva.

Alva Reimer Myrdal (1902–), born in Uppsala, Sweden, is a sociologist who has held numerous diplomatic posts and served as minister in charge of disarmament and church affairs in the Swedish cabinet from 1966 to 1973. Her husband, Gunnar Myrdal, won the economics prize in 1974; the Myrdals were the first married couple to win Nobel prizes in different disciplines.

Alfonso García Robles (1911–), born in Zamora, Mexico, is a career diplomat who has headed the Mexican delegation at Geneva since 1977. He was the guiding force behind the 1967 Treaty of Tlatelolco, which banned nuclear weapons from Latin America, and he coauthored the 1968 Nuclear Nonproliferation Treaty.

Physics. For solving "in a definite and profound way the critical phenomena" entailed by basic changes in matter, changes that may involve untold billions of particles, atoms, or molecules:

Kenneth G. Wilson (1936–), professor of physics at Cornell University. Born in Waltham, Mass., Wilson earned his doctorate at the California Institute of Technology in 1961 and assumed his Cornell professorship ten years later. In making the award, the Swedish Academy of Sciences cited his development of a method of solving such problems as how a metal liquefies or how water changes into steam by "dividing the problem into a sequence of similar problems in which each part could be solved." This technique, called renormalization, helps simplify calculations by eliminating complex variables that are shown to be insignificant.

Physiology or Medicine. Two Swedes—including the chairman of the Nobel Founda-

tion, which grants the award—and one Englishman were honored for their research on prostaglandins. These hormonelike substances, formed by the body's cells from fatty acids, play a key role in regulating the response of humans and animals to illness, injury, or stress.

Sune K. Bergstrom (1916–), born in Stockholm, served as rector of the Karolinska Institute from 1969 to 1977; since then, he has headed the Nobel Foundation while serving as chairman of the World Health Organization's advisory committee on medical research.

Bengt I. Samuelsson (1934–), born in Halmstad, is dean of the medical faculty at the Karolinska Institute, where he has been Bergstrom's student and colleague. Working with his mentor, he determined the chemical structure of the fatty acid from which prostaglandins are primarily formed; his subsequent achievements included discovering and explaining the process by which animals and humans produce and metabolize prostaglandins.

John R. Vane (1927–), a native of Worcestershire, England, earned his doctorate at Oxford University in 1953 and became research director of a British pharmaceuticals firm, Wellcome Research Laboratories, 20 years later. Vane discovered prostaglandin X, now known as prostacyclin, which can prevent the formation of blood clots that can cause heart attacks and strokes. Earlier he had recognized and explained the way in which aspirin reduces fever and inflammation by inhibiting the formation of prostaglandins.

PULITZER PRIZES

The 1982 Pulitzer prizes were announced on April 12. John Updike won the fiction award for *Rabbit Is Rich*, the third novel in a trilogy that also includes *Rabbit, Run*, published in 1960, and *Rabbit Redux*, published in 1971. The music prize, not awarded in 1981, went to 85-year-old Roger Sessions for his *Concerto for Orchestra*. Milton Babbitt, 66, received a special citation for "his life's work as a distinguished and seminal American composer"; Sessions had been similarly honored in 1974. The Pulitzer Prize Board gave its po-

etry award to the *Collected Poems* of Sylvia Plath, who committed suicide in 1963 at the age of 30; this marked the fouth time the poetry prize had been awarded posthumously. Honored for drama was Charles Fuller's *A Soldier's Play*. In journalism, the Detroit *News* won the gold medal for public service for a series of articles by Sydney P. Freedberg and David Ashenfelter exposing the U.S. Navy's cover-up of the circumstances surrounding certain shipboard deaths.

Other Pulitzer prizes in letters and journalism were as follows:

Biography. William S. McFeely, *Grant: A Biography*.

Commentary. Art Buchwald, humor columnist for the Los Angeles Times Syndicate.

Criticism. Martin Bernheimer, classical music critic for the Los Angeles *Times*.

Editorial Cartooning. Ben Sargent, Austin (Texas) *American-Statesman*.

Editorial Writing. Jack Rosenthal, New York *Times*.

Feature Writing. Saul Pett, Associated Press.

General Nonfiction. Tracy Kidder, *The Soul of a New Machine*.

History. *Mary Chesnut's Civil War*, edited by C. Vann Woodward.

Photography, Feature. John H. White, Chicago *Sun-Times*.

Photography, Spot News. Ron Edmonds, Associated Press.

Reporting, General Local. Kansas City *Star* and Kansas City *Times,* for coverage of the Hyatt Regency Hotel disaster on July 17, 1981.

Reporting, International. John Darnton, New York *Times,* for dispatches from Poland.

Reporting, National. Rick Atkinson of the Kansas City *Times* for articles on missile espionage, water-resources problems, and other matters of "national import."

Reporting, Special Local. Paul Henderson of the Seattle *Times* for clearing an innocent man of a rape charge and helping police find the culprit.

OTHER PRIZES AND AWARDS

Among the many other prizes and awards distributed during 1982 were the following.

Academy of American Poets. $10,000 fellowship to John Ashbery.

Albert and Mary Lasker Foundation. $15,000 divided by Roberto Gallo of the National Institutes of Health (NIH), Raymond Erikson of Harvard University, Hidesaburo Honofusa of Rockefeller University, and J. Michael Bishop and Harold Varmus of the University of California at San Francisco for oncogene studies. $15,000 to Roscoe Brady and Elizabeth Neufield of NIH for clinical research in genetic disease.

American Academy and Institute of Arts and Letters. $5000 each to Nizette Brennan, Michael David, George McNeil, Alan Motch, and Manuel Neri (art); David H. Bradley, Jr., Frederick Buechner, MacDonald Harris, Daryl Hine, Josephine Jacobsen, Donald Keene, Berton Roueché, and Robert Stone (literature); Douglas Allanbrook, James Tenney, George Walker, and Ramon Zupko (music). Award for Distinguished Service to the Arts: Alfred A. Knopf. Gold Medals: William Schuman (music), Francis Steegmuller (biography).

American Business Cancer Foundation. $600,000 award for cancer research to biologist Michael Wigler.

American Film Institute. Life Achievement Award to Frank Capra.

American Institute for Public Service. Jefferson Awards of $5000 each and gold-and-silver medallions to Senate Majority Leader Howard H. Baker, Jr. (R, Tenn.), comedian Bob Hope, U.S. Rep. Claude Pepper (D, Fla.), and Mayor Henry Cisneros (D) of San Antonio.

Armand Hammer Foundation. $100,000 to Ronald Levy of Stanford University and George T. Stevenson of the University of Southampton (England) for cancer research.

Association of American Publishers, American Book Awards. National Medal for Literature ($15,000) to John Cheever. Hardcover awards: fiction, John Updike; general nonfiction, Tracy Kidder; biography, David McCullough; children's books, Lloyd Alexander (fiction), Susan Bonners (nonfiction); history, the Reverend Peter John Powell; science, Donald Johanson and Maitland Edey. Paperback: fiction, William Maxwell; general nonfiction, Victor S. Navasky; biography, Ronald Steel; children's books, Quida Sebestyen (fiction); history, Robert Wohl; science, Fred Alan Wolf. First novel, Robb Forman Dew. Poetry, William Bronk. Translation, Robert Lyons Danly and Ian Hideo Levy.

Bristol-Myers Award. $50,000 prize for cancer research (shared) to Denis Parsons Burkitt and Michael Anthony Epstein, both of Great Britain.

Martin Luther King, Jr., Nonviolent Peace Prize. Awarded to Harry Belafonte.

Medal of Freedom. Highest U.S. civilian award to Philip C. Habib for helping to end the siege of Beirut.

National Conference of Christians and Jews. Charles Evans Hughes Gold Medal to U.S. President Ronald Reagan for "courageous leadership in government, civic, and humanitarian affairs."

Neustadt International Prize for Literature. $25,000 award to Mexican poet and essayist Octavio Paz.

Onassis Foundation. $100,000 each to Bernard Kouchner of France and archeologist Manolis Andronikos of Salonika University.

Samuel H. Scripps–American Dance Festival Award. Prize of $25,000 to choreographer Merce Cunningham.

Templeton Foundation. $200,000 Templeton Prize for Progress in Religion to evangelist Billy Graham.

Wolf Foundation. $50,000 prize to biologist Barbara McClintock.   G.M.H. & L.A.S.

The Reader's Digest Bible, *a condensed version developed by the magazine's editors and a Princeton Theological Seminary professor, the Reverend Bruce M. Metzger, was published in 1982. Based on the text of the Revised Standard Version (RSV), it is about 40 percent shorter than the 800,000-word RSV.*

PUBLISHING. A new national daily newspaper, *USA Today,* began publication in 1982, but several big-city afternoon newspapers closed. One of the nation's most prestigious cultural magazines, the *Saturday Review,* suspended publication. Book publishers experienced a difficult year as the recession curtailed book buying.

Books. Industry sales for 1981 totaled $7.7 billion, an increase of 9 percent over 1980, according to preliminary estimates by the Association of American Publishers. Publishers' revenues were up 9.7 percent over 1980. Taking into account the rate of inflation, these figures indicated no growth for the industry during 1981.

Slightly fewer books were sold during the first three months of 1982 than in the same period of 1981. Returns reached unusually high levels in the first quarter of the year, analysts said, as booksellers hesitated to tie up money in volumes that might remain unsold for many months. In the second quarter, publishers' sales declined by an estimated 2.7 percent in dollars and 4.3 percent in units.

While trade paperbacks—relatively expensive soft-cover books—continued to mount in popularity, mass market paperbacks experienced difficult times. Costs of putting out these paperbacks were reported to have gone up rapidly even as higher retail prices reduced impulse buying by consumers. Million-dollar bidding for the right to publish paperbacks seemed, at least temporarily, a thing of the past.

In July Putnam Publishing Group and Berkley/Jove Publishing Group, both subsidiaries of MCA Inc., completed an acquisition of Grosset & Dunlap (owned by Filmways) and PEI Books (owned by Playboy Enterprises). Grosset & Dunlap joined Putnam Publishing Group, which already included G. P. Putnam's Sons, McCann & Geoghegan, Perigee Books, and Philomel Books. Grosset & Dunlap's Ace and Tempo mass market paperbacks and PEI's Playboy Paperbacks would be published under the Berkley/Jove imprint.

On Jan. 29 CBS Inc. sold its mass market paperback book subsidiary, Fawcett Publications, to Random House Inc. for an undisclosed price. Random House thus gained such Fawcett imprints as Gold Medal, Coventry, Crest, and Juniper.

Thomas Nelson, Inc., a Nashville-based publisher, acquired Dodd, Mead & Co., one of the nation's oldest publishing companies, in April. Later in the year it acquired Everest House as an imprint for Dodd, Mead.

Congress passed a bill on July 13, over President Ronald Reagan's veto, extending until 1986 a clause of U.S. copyright law that requires most books and periodicals written in English by U.S. authors to be printed and bound in the United States or Canada to receive full copyright protection. Reagan had vetoed the bill on July 8, saying it was no longer needed to protect the printing industry and that U.S. trading partners had complained that the clause was restrictive. But in a 1981 report, the U.S. Labor Department estimated that up to 367,000 domestic jobs in printing and related industries could be lost by eliminating the clause.

Periodicals. Macro Communications Co. suspended publication of the *Saturday Review,* a monthly magazine covering literature and the arts, on Aug. 16. The 58-year-old publication had lost $3,000,000 during its last two years of operation. Originally, as the *Saturday Review of Literature,* it was a weekly that under Norman Cousins, its editor from 1939 to 1971, included features on society and culture. During 1971–73 it was published as four separate monthlies by another owner; Cousins then returned briefly and transformed it into a biweekly concentrating on science and education. It was sold twice more before Macro Communications sold it to a group of investors on Nov. 10. Jeffrey M. Gluck, the new publisher, said it would reappear as a bimonthly in early 1983.

In January the Washington Post Co. sold *Inside Sports* to Active Markets Inc., a publisher of magazines for children and young athletes, for an undisclosed price. Founded in 1980, *Inside Sports* was heavily in debt despite a circulation of 500,000 that was reached in mid-1981. Publication of the magazine was suspended in October.

The Charter Co., a conglomerate that planned to dispose of all its publishing and communications properties, announced on July 8 an agreement to sell the 99-year-old *Ladies Home Journal* to Family Media Inc. for an estimated $15,000,000. On April 30 the Hearst Corp. said that it had reached agreement in principle to acquire *Redbook,* as well as Charter Data Services, a magazine subscription fulfillment company, from Charter for more than $23,000,000.

The Publishers Information Bureau reported that magazine advertising revenue totaled slightly less than $2.1 billion for the first eight months of 1982, a gain of 6 percent over the same period in 1981 but representing no real growth if the inflation rate was taken into consideration.

Newspapers. The Gannett Co., the nation's largest newspaper chain, began publication of *USA Today,* a national daily newspaper, on Sept. 15. The paper was published weekdays only. Initially it was available in the Atlanta, Baltimore, Minneapolis, Pittsburgh, and Washington, D.C., areas. By April, 1983, distribution was also planned in Chicago, Denver, Detroit, Houston, Los Angeles, Miami, New York City, Philadelphia, San Francisco, and Seattle. The five-year circulation goal, company officials said, was 2,350,000 or more daily readers.

USA Today thus became the second national newspaper written for a general news audience. The New York *Times* prints daily and Sunday editions in four cities and sells same-day copies in 50 cities; the *Wall Street Journal* likewise is a national daily paper but mainly provides business news.

Based in Rosslyn, Va., a suburb of Washington, D.C., *USA Today* was staffed by 250 journalists, 170 of them on loan from other Gannett newspapers. Its contents were to be beamed by satellite to far-flung printing plants, most of them at existing Gannett papers. On April 1 Gannett agreed to buy nine Mississippi newspapers, raising its ownership to 88 dailies in the U.S.

The decline of big-city afternoon newspapers continued unabated in 1982 because of competition from evening television news and the difficulty of delivering newspapers to the suburbs in congested late-afternoon traffic. On Jan. 29 the 134-year-old Philadelphia

Bulletin, once the country's largest afternoon newspaper, ceased publication. It had lost $10,000,000 in its last five months of publication.

The Minneapolis *Star,* an afternoon daily, merged with its sister paper, the morning *Tribune,* to form an all-day newspaper, the *Star and Tribune,* on April 5. In October the afternoon edition was ended as an economy measure. The afternoon Des Moines *Tribune* was absorbed by its sister paper, the morning *Register,* in October.

The afternoon Cleveland *Press* ceased publication on June 17, adding Cleveland to the growing list of cities in which only one newspaper survives. The 103-year-old *Press* had less than half the advertising linage of its morning rival, the *Plain Dealer.* The owner of the *Press,* Joseph E. Cole, said that it was losing $6,000,000 a year.

Two afternoon newspapers in Florida ceased publication during the summer. The Sarasota *Journal* closed on July 9 and the 90-year-old Tampa *Times* on Aug. 14. The Denver *Post* ended 90 years of afternoon publication in June, switching to the morning field to compete directly with the morning tabloid *Rocky Mountain News.*

The afternoon Oregon *Journal* ceased publication on Sept. 4. It merged with the morning Portland *Oregonian,* which became an all-day newspaper. The Oakland *Tribune,* an afternoon daily, was transformed into a morning paper entitled *East Bay Today* on Oct. 25.

Countering this national trend was the closing of the 148-year-old morning daily the Buffalo *Courier-Express* on Sept. 19, leaving the city with only an afternoon newspaper, the *Evening News.* Buffalo is primarily a city of blue-collar workers who begin and end the workday early and like to read the paper later in the day.

Washington, a one-paper city since the *Star* folded in 1981, received a new morning newspaper, the *Times,* on May 17. It was published by News World Communications Inc., the newspaper unit of the Reverend Sun Myung Moon's Unification Church. James R. Whalen, editor and publisher, said that the newspaper would embrace "a conservatism

Complimentary copies of the first issue of the Gannett Co. newspaper chain's USA Today *are distributed in front of the White House on Sept. 15. The national weekday daily was initially available in five metropolitan areas.*

we believe . . . relevant and vital to the solution of man's problems today."

On June 2 the E. W. Scripps Co. announced that it had sold the United Press International (UPI) news service to Media News Corp., a privately owned Nashville-based company. UPI, which transmits news dispatches and photographs to newspapers and other clients in competition with the Associated Press, had been losing money for years.

The Washington *Post* was assessed $2,050,000 in damages on July 30 by a jury in Washington, D.C., that found the paper had libeled the president of the Mobil Oil Corp., William P. Tavoulareas. The *Post* had alleged in a 1979 article that Tavoulareas used Mobil's money and his influence to set his son up in the shipping business and to enrich him with millions of dollars in Mobil contracts.

The Supreme Court, by a 6–3 decision on June 23, struck down a Massachusetts law requiring trial judges to close their courtrooms to the press and public during the testimony of alleged victims of sex crimes who are under age 18. In so ruling the High Court majority opinion held that such minors could still be shielded from the trauma of an open trial, but only on a case-by-case basis rather than by a blanket exclusion.   R.H.

PUERTO RICO. Gov. Carlos Romero Barceló and other Puerto Rican government leaders were concerned in 1982 about the potential effects of proposed U.S. economic actions.

Early in the year Sen. Robert Dole (R, Kans.) sponsored a bill before the U.S. Senate calling for substantial reductions in the tax advantages available to companies with plants in Puerto Rico. Although the Dole measure would have increased federal tax revenues by $2.7 billion, it threatened to drive many businesses from Puerto Rico, at the cost of thousands of jobs. A compromise tax bill, adopted in August, was estimated to raise federal tax revenues by $1.2 billion.

As a commonwealth, Puerto Rico was subject to considerable commonwealth taxes, but not to federal income taxes, although it participated in most federal programs. U.S. President Ronald Reagan's proposed cuts in these programs threatened, however, to cost Puerto Rico as much as $1.5 billion in fiscal 1983, although the actual reductions adopted by the U.S. Congress were much less severe. The Reagan administration's decision to end the Comprehensive Employment and Training Act program put 25,000 Puerto Ricans out of work, contributing to an unemployment rate of about 24 percent of the labor force. Some optimism returned when three U.S. companies announced plans to invest $80,000,000 in operations in Puerto Rico that would create 2000 jobs.

President Reagan's Caribbean Basin Initiative was designed to encourage investment, through tax incentives and trade concessions, for nations in the area. Because of their island's commonwealth status, however, Puerto Rican leaders believed the initiative gave regional competitors an economic advantage. A March 21 commonwealth senate resolution criticized the initiative and demanded greater autonomy for Puerto Rico.

A Cuban motion to declare Puerto Rico a colony of the United States was rejected by the United Nations General Assembly on Sept. 24 by a 70–30 vote, with 43 abstentions. Hernán Padilla, mayor of San Juan, told the assembly that independence "has been rejected by 95 percent of the Puerto Rican electorate." Earlier, on Jan. 12, President Reagan pledged to support statehood for Puerto Rico "should the people of that island choose it in a free and democratic election." No referendum was planned in the near future, however.

See STATISTICS OF THE WORLD.   A.E.J.

Q

QATAR. *See* STATISTICS OF THE WORLD. *See also* PERSIAN GULF STATES.

QUÉBEC. *See* STATISTICS OF THE WORLD. *See also* CANADA.

R

RADIO. *See* TELEVISION AND RADIO BROADCASTING.

RAILROADS. *See* TRANSPORTATION.
RECORDINGS. *See* MUSIC.

Religion

In 1982 the cause of ecumenism was advanced by Pope John Paul's visit to Great Britain and by the proposed mergers of several U.S. Protestant denominations. At the same time a concern for doctrinal orthodoxy was reflected in the pope's addresses and in the continued strength of fundamentalism in U.S. Protestantism. Islam, Hinduism, and Buddhism were also affected by fundamentalist and purist movements.

In 1982 religious leaders continued to be prominently involved in political controversies throughout the world. In the United States, Catholic bishops criticized U.S. nuclear policy, and legislation backed by some religious organizations was introduced in Congress. Religious loyalties and conflicts had profound political repercussions in Poland, the Middle East, and India.

CHRISTIANITY

A monumental work of religious scholarship, the World Christian Encyclopedia, edited by the Reverend David B. Barrett of Nairobi, Kenya, was published in 1982. It showed that Christianity had declined slightly in relation to the world population since 1900 (from 34.4 percent to 32.8 percent in 1982), but that it had become the most widely diffused religion in history. Of Barrett's catalogue of 8990 ethno-linguistic groups, 6850 have had some contact with the Gospel. Christianity had made especially rapid gains in Asia and Africa in the 20th century and by 1981 had a nonwhite majority for the first time in 1200 years.

Ecumenism. On May 28 John Paul II (see biography at PEOPLE IN THE NEWS) arrived in London for the first visit to Great Britain by a reigning pope in the history of the papacy. Although the six-day tour was mainly directed toward Catholics, the ecumenical implications were emphasized. The pontiff reportedly overruled advisers in going through with the visit while Britain was at war with Catholic Argentina, but at the same time he scheduled a subsequent trip to Argentina in June.

Prior to the papal visit Britain and the Holy See established full diplomatic relations on Jan. 16 for the first time since the Reformation, and the Anglican-Roman Catholic International Commission issued its final report on March 29 on doctrinal differences between the two bodies. Moving beyond earlier joint statements on Communion and the priesthood, the commission proposed a united approach by which both sides could come under the "Bishop of Rome" as "universal primate" if the two churches united. (The term pope, with its historical connotations, was avoided.)

Significantly, the Anglican representatives accepted a form of papal jurisdiction over the entire church, as well as an authoritative teaching function, although they did not accept the precise formulations of the First Vatican Council (1870) concerning the pope's personal, unmediated jurisdiction over all believers and his infallibility in teaching *ex cathedra* on faith and morals. The Vatican Sacred Congregation for the Doctrine of the Faith officially criticized these omissions. Nonetheless, the pope jointly led worship at Canterbury Cathedral, historic center of the Anglican Communion, with Archbishop of Canterbury Robert Runcie and other British Christian leaders. John Paul and Runcie then signed a "common declaration" authorizing a further joint commission to examine the doctrinal differences still to be overcome, to study what hinders "mutual recognition" of ministers, and "to recommend what practical steps will be necessary when, on the basis of our unity of faith, we are able to proceed to

During his visit to Great Britain, the first ever by a reigning Roman Catholic pontiff, Pope John Paul II (left) prayed at Canterbury Cathedral with Archbishop Robert Runcie (right), the Anglican primate of England.

the restoration of full communion." After the pope's visit, the clergy house of the Church of England's Synod failed to provide the necessary two-thirds majority for mutual recognition of clergy orders with two British Protestant denominations, an ecumenical setback that nonetheless averted difficulties for Anglican-Catholic consensus on the theology of priesthood.

During the year, the Orthodox-Catholic and the Lutheran-Catholic international commissions held plenary meetings as part of their continuing discussions of reunion.

The Papacy. Besides the British and Argentine trips, the pope visited west Africa, Portugal, and Spain in 1982. All of these tours drew huge crowds and featured John Paul's personal charisma and message of social justice and doctrinal conservatism. The Portuguese trip was undertaken in May on the eve of the first anniversary of John Paul's near-fatal shooting in Rome by a Turkish terrorist; its purpose was to visit the shrine of Our Lady

of Fátima and give thanks for her intercession, but it was marred by a second murder attempt. Juan Fernández Krohn, a 32-year-old Spanish priest who had left the right-wing dissident group headed by Archbishop Marcel Lefebvre to join a more extreme faction, lunged to within 3 ft. of the pope with a 16-in. bayonet and shouted—"Down with the Pope! Down with Vatican Two!"—before being seized.

In November Italian antiterrorist police arrested a Rome employee of Bulgaria's airline and travel agency for complicity in the 1981 papal shooting. The police also pursued other leads, amid unsubstantiated speculation that the Soviet Union was involved in the assassination attempt.

John Paul also visited Sicily in November, where the Catholic hierarchy renewed excommunication for persons with Mafia ties and denounced gang violence; the pontiff urged youths to build a new society and to eradicate the "Mafia attitude."

In June the pope had a Vatican audience with U.S. President Ronald Reagan and in September a far more controversial one with Chairman Yasir Arafat of the Palestine Liberation Organization (PLO), which had just been removed from Lebanon. The Israeli government and many Jews were infuriated at the status granted a man they considered a terrorist, but the Vatican emphasized that it did not recognize the PLO as the official representative of the Palestinians or agree with its policies.

In July the pope summoned an extraordinary three-man lay panel to probe allegations of impropriety at the Vatican bank after the collapse of an Italian bank with which it was involved; *see* ITALY. A special closed-door meeting of the College of Cardinals in November discussed Vatican administration, including the Vatican bank, headed by American Archbishop Paul Marcinkus. A papal letter during the meeting was interpreted as instructing the church to rely on members' gifts, rather than financial speculation, for income.

John Paul held a conference in February with 110 worldwide leaders of the Society of Jesus, including the interim leader of the

Jesuit order. Liberal Jesuits who were concerned about the independence of the order were pleased when the pope said on March 3 that a general congregation would soon be called to elect a successor to the ailing superior general, the Reverend Pedro Arrupe. They had feared that the pope, who was displeased by Jesuit social activism, would choose a successor himself. In August John Paul elevated the conservative and controversial 70,000-member lay order Opus Dei with a "personal prelature," making its head a quasi-bishop.

Zambia's Archbishop Emmanuel Milingo was sent to Rome for extended reflection because he had pursued a ministry of faith healing and exorcism against orders. And, on papal orders, the cardinal who operated the Rome diocese directed priests and nuns, including visitors, to wear strictly traditional garb during their daily duties, a practice that had declined in Rome and elsewhere since the Second Vatican Council.

U.S. Catholicism. In their first joint pastoral letter, the 14 Hispanic U.S. bishops told the nation's Hispanic Catholics, estimated to number 12,000,000, that "we reject every type of active proselytizing which is antiecumenical and destructive to our people. The great diversity of fundamentalist groups and their anti-Catholic spirit divide our families and our peoples."

A church statistical study showed another enrollment drop in major seminaries, amounting to 50 percent since the mid-1960's. This finding raised the question of whether sufficient priests would be available in a generation.

In July Joseph Bernardin was installed as new archbishop of Chicago, succeeding Cardinal John Cody, who died during a federal investigation of whether he had misused church funds.

U.S. Protestantism. Assemblies of the United Presbyterian Church and the Presbyterian Church in the U.S. (or Southern Presbyterians) met in June and approved a plan of union, subject to final ratification in 1983. The united church would have more than 3,100,000 members. In September conventions of three Lutheran bodies approved the

start of negotiations toward a similar merger by 1987 involving 5,500,000 members of the Lutheran Church in America, the American Lutheran Church, and the smaller Association of Evangelical Lutheran Churches.

Also in September, the three Lutheran conventions and the Episcopal Church convention authorized the occasional joint celebration of Communion by members of their congregations. The Episcopalians also approved texts for a forthcoming new hymnal.

At the annual meeting of the 13,000,000-member Southern Baptist Convention in June, forces that insist on absolute biblical inerrancy and strict doctrinal discipline again elected a fellow conservative as president, a post with key appointive powers. The new president was the Reverend James T. Draper, a pastor in Euless, Texas.

The equivalent of a grand jury in the United Methodist Church exonerated Bishop Melvin Wheatley of Colorado, attacked by conservatives because he gave a committed homosexual a parish. That decision was appealed to the church's highest court, the Judicial Council, which ruled unanimously that under present church law "same-sex orientation" is not a bar to ordination.

The National Baptist Convention, U.S.A., Inc. (NBC), ended the 29-year reign of its president, Chicago pastor Joseph H. Jackson, and replaced him with the denomination's secretary, T. J. Jemison, a pastor in Baton Rouge, La. The politically conservative Jackson had opposed civil rights protests by the late NBC minister Martin Luther King, Jr., and the King forces, unable to oust Jackson, formed their own church body in 1961. But Jackson's group remained the nation's largest black religious body, indeed its largest black organization of any type.

The magazine for Seventh-day Adventist ministers admitted that founding Prophet Ellen G. White "sometimes . . . used material nearly word for word without giving credit" to 19th-century contemporaries she borrowed from, and that she "utilized the words of prior authors in describing words she heard spoken while in vision," some of which she had attributed to Jesus Christ or to angels.

The Reverend Robert M. Davison (left), outgoing moderator of the general assembly of the United Presbyterian Church, escorts his assembly-elected successor, the Reverend James H. Costen, to the platform in June. The assembly also voted to merge with the smaller southern branch of the church, the Presbyterian Church in the U.S., which had approved the merger plan earlier in the month.

Eastern Orthodoxy. Greece's socialist government loosened Orthodox Church control of family law, becoming the last nation in Europe to pass legislation permitting civil marriages. Previously the church had a monopoly on weddings, and children of those married outside the church were deemed illegitimate. Orthodox Greeks could now choose either civil or religious rites, but conservative bishops declared that they would refuse Communion and burial to members contracting civil marriages.

Archbishop Valerian Trifa, head of one of two rival branches of Rumanian Orthodoxy in the U.S., dropped legal appeals and agreed to be deported. He had relinquished U.S. citizenship in 1980 under federal charges that he had lied in order to gain it, covering up activity in the pro-Nazi "Iron Guard" in Rumania during World War II.

Church and Society. In Lebanon, the only Arab nation with a Christian near-majority, the Christian community gained predominant political power through the alliance of Maronite Catholic militia with the occupying forces of Israel. After the withdrawal of Palestinian troops in late August, Maronite leader Amin Gemayel became president; *see* LEBANON.

Poland's powerful Catholic church, backed by a Polish pope, repeatedly criticized the Communist government's December, 1981, imposition of martial law and suppression of the Solidarity union. Archbishop Jozef Glemp, primate of the Polish church, and other members of the hierarchy demanded freedom for political prisoners, an end to martial law and coerced resignations from the union, recognition of the right to free labor organization, and dialogue with workers. At the same time the bishops pleaded with the people to shun bloodshed, in particular before the August anniversary of Solidarity's founding. The tense situation prevented Pope John Paul from attending the 600th anniversary of the icon of the Black Madonna and Glemp from joining the October canonization in Rome of Father Maximilian Kolbe, a Polish priest who gave his life for another in a Nazi concentration camp. In November Lech Walesa was released and met with Glemp, and the government announced that Pope John Paul would be allowed to visit the country in June, 1983. *See also* POLAND.

In May the Russian Orthodox Church hosted 588 representatives of eight world religions at a Moscow conference on averting "nuclear catastrophe." The meeting advocated a multilateral "freeze" of nuclear weapons and was variously judged by Western observers as a worthwhile exchange or a Kremlin propaganda gain. Remarks by one of those attending, U.S. evangelist Billy Graham, that played down Soviet religious restrictions caused controversy. U.S. visitors met six Siberian Pentecostalists who had lived since June, 1978, in the U.S. embassy basement, hoping to emigrate so that they could practice their faith freely. Two went on a hunger strike to gain attention.

In East Germany a home-grown Protestant peace movement urged youths to refuse military service; see GERMAN DEMOCRATIC REPUBLIC. In Czechoslovakia the Communist regime angrily interpreted a Vatican decree urging priests to shun politics as an attack upon Pacem in Terris, a Communist-dominated clergy group.

China's new constitution, which forbade foreign control in religion, appeared to end hopes that mainland Chinese Catholics could develop normal ties with the papacy. China's independent Catholic church, however, was finally allowed to open a seminary in Shanghai, with an entering class of 36 men.

The Sandinista government in Nicaragua took an increasingly Marxist line and prevented newspapers from publishing the pope's August statement to the Nicaraguan hierarchy warning Christians not to mix the faith with "political radicalization and the class struggle." Although several priests held high office in the regime, several anticlerical incidents occurred.

The dominant church of South Africa's Afrikaners, the Nederduitse Gereformeerde Kerk (NGK), and a smaller white denomination were suspended from the World Alliance of Reformed Churches (WARC) for supporting apartheid. The Ottawa WARC meeting also chose as president a militant NGK critic, the Reverend Allan Boesak, a minister in its offshoot for the Coloured populace. Meanwhile 123 white NGK clergy issued a public moral denunciation of the ra-

Controversial Cult Leader
During the 1950's, according to his official biography, Korean-born Sun Myung Moon founded the Holy Spirit Association for the Unification of World Christianity, a church that in 1982 claimed 3,000,000 followers and assets in excess of $15,000,000. However, Moon's detractors said that he was actually the head of a cult that "brainwashes" young recruits to provide cheap labor, raise funds, and proselytize new followers. "Moonies" were told to resist Communism and to refrain from smoking, liquor, drugs, and sex outside marriage; marriages were arranged for church members at mass ceremonies. Moon, who was living in a 25-room mansion near New York City, had had numerous run-ins with the law in both South Korea, where he was excommunicated by the Presbyterian Church, and the United States. In May he was convicted in New York on federal income tax fraud charges, which he denounced as motivated by racial and religious bigotry.

Sun Myung Moon

cial policies of their church. The government extended for three years a "banning" order against the most renowned NGK rebel, the Reverend D. F. Beyers Naude, founder of the outlawed Christian Institute.

Church and State—U.S. At the centennial of the Knights of Columbus in Hartford in August, President Reagan's speech to 12,000 persons endorsed the Catholic fraternal group's goals on three controversial public issues. He favored tuition tax credits for private school parents, said that the "national tragedy of abortion on demand must end," and declared that "we need a prayer amendment; we need it badly."

The President's tax credit bill was not enacted, nor was the administration-backed proposed amendment to the U.S. Constitution allowing voluntary school prayer. This amendment was opposed by a variety of Protestant and Jewish groups, but the Southern Baptist Convention, formerly a key opponent, switched in favor of it. On abortion, Sen. Orrin Hatch (R, Utah) withdrew a constitutional amendment, strongly backed by the Catholic hierarchy, to allow Congress and the states to pass restrictive laws, and the Senate shelved the latest "human life statute," submitted by Sen. Jesse Helms (R, N.C.), with religious lobbies active on all sides of this continuing controversy. The Senate also rejected Helms's bid to attach to an unrelated bill his measure to remove school prayer from federal court jurisdiction.

Religious bodies were prominent among the 750,000 persons gathered in Central Park in New York City on June 12 to protest the threat of nuclear war, and they joined other antinuclear efforts. Numerous Roman Catholic bishops were among church leaders endorsing a nuclear freeze. The U.S. Catholic bishops' annual meeting in November expressed substantial agreement with a preliminary policy statement attacking major elements of America's policy of nuclear deterrence. A revised text was to be issued in May, 1983. The 1982 version condemned any first use of nuclear weapons, including any nuclear response to attack by conventional arms, and any nuclear attack aimed at civilian areas or at military targets near civilian areas.

The document tentatively accepted possession of nuclear arms as a necessary evil but came close to stating that they must never be used.

NEWER FAITHS

Mormons. The Church of Jesus Christ of Latter-day Saints reduced the missionary term expected of single young men from 24 to 18 months because of financial constraints among the growing membership outside North America. To emphasize its claim to be the true restored church of Christianity, the denomination added the subtitle *Another Testament of Jesus Christ* to the earliest of its unique scriptures, *The Book of Mormon.*

Jehovah's Witnesses. It was revealed that 12 dissident officials were purged from the inner circle of the Jehovah's Witnesses during the last few years in one of the most severe doctrinal controversies ever to occur in the sect. The dissidents felt that the organization itself had supplanted the Bible as the basis of faith, and they questioned several doctrines, including the beliefs that an elite of only 144,000 will be "born again" and reach heaven, that the secret second coming of Jesus occurred in 1914, and that the world system will end while persons who remember 1914 are still alive.

Unification Church. In May controversial South Korean prophet Sun Myung Moon was convicted of tax evasion in federal court, and he was also compelled to testify in the trial of a man accused of forcibly "deprogramming" a Moon convert. Under oath, Moon said publicly for the first time: "I have the possibility of becoming the real messiah." He also said that many followers already believe he is the second Christ. With strong support from conventional churches, Moon's group secured a ruling from New York State's highest court affirming that its political activities are intrinsic to the faith and hence provide no basis to deny tax exemption.

JUDAISM

Jews in Israel and elsewhere debated the morality of Israel's invasion of Lebanon and the question of the Israeli army's failure to prevent the slaughter of hundreds of unarmed Palestinian refugees by Lebanese Christian militiamen. A series of terrorist at-

Rabbis Allan (left) and Irving Rosenbaum are shown working at Chicago's Institute for Computers in Jewish Life. The father and son team, working in conjunction with Bar-Ilan University in Israel, has stored in a computer here more than 170 volumes of rabbinic responsa, which are a primary source for Jewish religious and social practices and values.

tacks on Jews and Jewish-owned businesses in Western Europe following the Lebanon invasion aroused Jewish fears of a resurgence of overt and violent anti-Semitism.

American Judaism achieved the first broadly recognized committee translation of the Jewish Bible into contemporary English, with release of the third and final volume of *The Holy Scriptures* by the Jewish Publication Society. Many Orthodox rabbis, however, objected to the new rendition.

ISLAM

The exceedingly bloody and partially sectarian war between Iran and Iraq intensified with Iran's invasion of Iraq in June. The Shi'ite Muslim regime of Iran's religious and political dictator, the Ayatollah Ruhollah Khomeini, sought to punish Iraq for its invasion in 1980 and to establish an allied Islamic republic there by turning the Shi'ite majority in Iraq against its Sunni-dominated government. Khomeini also warned Persian Gulf Arabs to "repent and turn to Islam" or face unspecified consequences.

Neighboring Syria, with a secularist regime, tried to suppress an underground movement dedicated to the establishment of a fundamentalist Muslim regime through violence. In February troops sealed off Hama, a center of the fundamentalist movement, slaughtered 5000 to 10,000 civilians, and virtually destroyed the city. *See also* SYRIA.

In Egypt, five followers of a similar fundamentalist Islamic movement were executed in April for the 1981 assassination of President Anwar el-Sadat, and 17 received prison terms. The government, still alarmed by the possibility of religious subversion, filed sedition charges against 302 members of the militant Islamic *Al Jihad* (Holy War) organization, which was linked to the assassination.

An Arab summit meeting in Fez, Morocco, demanded that the eastern sector of Jerusalem be returned to Muslim sovereignty under any Mideast peace settlement. In April an Israeli soldier who had recently immigrated from the U.S. sprayed rifle fire at Muslim pilgrims visiting the holy Dome of the Rock in the Old City of Jerusalem. Two persons were killed and 13 wounded, and 125 more were injured in subsequent rioting. Muslims blamed Israel for the atrocity.

The Aga Khan's followers, numbering about 15,000,000 worldwide, celebrated the 25th anniversary of his accession as imam of their branch of Shi'ism, the Ismaili or Ithna-Ashari Muslims, whose esoteric teachings are regarded as heretical by many orthodox Muslims.

Secretary General Habib Chatty of the Islamic Conference held his third meeting with Pope John Paul II. The World Muslim Congress joined the (Protestant-Orthodox) World Council of Churches at a Sri Lanka

Participants at an 85-day meditation session held at a Buddhist seminary near Bedford, Pa., observe a moment of silence before mealtime. Most of those attending the session, presided over by Chogyam Trungpa, were first-generation Buddhists from the U.S. and a few foreign countries.

conference for representatives from 40 nations. The session recommended a permanent joint committee to promote future discussions, open to Roman Catholic participation as well.

RELIGIONS OF INDIA

A series of isolated incidents of interreligious strife took place in the predominantly Hindu nation. Thousands of Sikh activists, protesting the accidental death of 34 demonstrators under police custody, stormed Parliament House on Oct. 11. In the riot 4 persons were killed, at least 5 wounded, and some 60 police injured. In the aftermath as many as 25,000 Sikh protesters were reported jailed in Punjab. Sikhism split off from Hinduism in the 15th century and is centered in Punjab. Moderate Sikhs sought only greater autonomy but the extremist Dal Khalsa, or Association of the Pure, advocated an independent Sikh nation.

Responding to earlier unrest, Prime Minister Indira Gandhi chose Zail Singh in June to become India's first Sikh president. When Hindus blocked a Sikh demand to forbid smoking and cigarette sales within the Sikh holy city of Amritsar, two Hindu temples were desecrated with slaughtered cow's heads, causing riots across Punjab in May.

In September some 28 persons were killed, 66 injured, and 795 arrested during rioting between Muslims and Hindus in Meerut. It was the worst such outbreak since a 1980 riot in which 150 persons died.

In the southern state of Tamil Nadu, the Rashtriya Swayam Sevak Sangh (RSSS), or National Pure Service Society, was accused of fomenting violence against the Christian and Muslim communities. The RSSS wanted India to be strictly Hindu. Some 20 Christians had been murdered, and churches and mosques had been wrecked. The government had previously suppressed RSSS activity in the north, and mainstream Hindus protested the extremist acts.

In April, 17 members of the controversial Hindu sect, Ananda Marga, were stoned, beaten, or knifed to death by mobs during a motorcade to the group's headquarters outside Calcutta. The violence was provoked by rumors that the sect practiced the kidnapping of children.

BUDDHISM

In Thailand, laws intended to prevent a proliferation of unorthodox sects by giving a Council of Elders from the Hinayana school control of the faith were applied to crush the Hoopha Sawan cult, which seeks its own principality, and to contain the Santi Asoke (With Grief) monks, who protested what they considered superstitions that violate Buddhist scriptures, such as fortunetelling by monks and the selling of blessings.

In Burma a controversial nationwide monks' organization formed by the socialist regime to purify the faith conducted trials of errant monks. At least 200 were defrocked, mostly for the violation of celibacy vows or for heresy—for instance, teaching that reincarnation is limited to human rebirth rather than rebirth into both human and lower forms.

Buddhism in Cambodia was still struggling to overcome the ravages of civil war and Communist persecution, in which most temples were destroyed and thousands of monks were killed. China's Peking *Review* reported that numerous Buddhists were crossing into Thailand for weekly services and that makeshift temples were being built within Cambodia.

In China, newspapers reported that Buddhist farmers in Fukien (Fujian) Province stormed Communist offices when they were prevented from using a Buddha statue in a festival. In Kwangtung (Guangdong) Province a 28-year party veteran attracted notice by becoming a monk. In the northeast a Buddhist sect was suppressed for its "feudal" practices.

According to an international congress in Taiwan, 563,000 Buddhist temples had been destroyed, and 4,000,000 monks and nuns had been forced to renounce their faith dur-

ing the Communist era in mainland China.

CONFUCIANISM

Confucianism, China's traditional ethical creed, had all but disappeared on the mainland, but it still retained some following on Taiwan. Singapore, an independent city that is 80 percent ethnic Chinese, directed mandatory school instruction in Confucianism, beginning in 1983, in order to strengthen family ties and diminish "moral decadence" among youth. R.N.O.

REPUBLICAN PARTY. For the Republican Party, 1982 was a year of sobering reality. Buoyed by their spectacular electoral success in 1980 and their legislative triumphs in 1981, Republican leaders had confidently predicted that in 1982 the GOP would win control of the U.S. House of Representatives and establish itself as the new majority party. Instead, the party suffered substantial election losses, as voters showed their impatience with President Ronald Reagan's economic

Some Republicans campaigning for reelection in November were less than eager to run on the Reagan administration's record. At the President's urging, 103 GOP U.S. House of Representatives members voted in August to raise taxes—an unpopular position—while 89 voted against the bill.

"FOR YOUR LOYALTY, CONGRESSMAN, A LITTLE TOKEN OF MY ESTEEM..."

Aiming for the White House in 1984?
In August U.S. Rep. Jack F. Kemp (R, N.Y.) publicly broke with Ronald Reagan by opposing the President's plan to raise taxes by almost $100 billion over the next three years. Kemp, an originator of the deep tax cut backed by Reagan in 1981, accused the President of making "a dramatic U-turn" away from his principles and warned that the White House was "going to lose the very people who were the backbone of the Reagan vote in 1980." Presidential aides, while conceding that Kemp was remaining true to his convictions, believed that the 47-year-old congressman was positioning himself to run for President in 1984. The photogenic, Los Angeles–born Kemp starred as a quarterback in the now-defunct American Football League during the 1960's. Elected in 1970 from an upstate New York district, he compiled a solidly conservative record in Congress, including staunch support of the Vietnam war and increased military spending.

Jack F. Kemp

policies. The results essentially neutralized the party's gains two years earlier and called into question the GOP's ability to govern effectively in 1983–84, despite its continued control of the White House and the U.S. Senate.

Election Results. In the Nov. 2 elections, the Republicans lost U.S. Senate seats in New Jersey and New Mexico but captured seats in Virginia and Nevada to retain their 54–46 margin. But that was the only bright spot in the picture. The GOP suffered a net loss of 26 seats in the House of Representatives, effectively restoring the balance of power to the Democrats. Republicans also sustained a net loss of seven governorships, reducing their total to 16. The loss of 11 state legislative houses meant that in only ten states would the GOP control both houses of the legislature in 1983.

As disappointing as the 1982 results were for Republicans, they could have been much worse. A shift of 43,000 votes in five Senate races would have restored control to the Democrats. In the House, 26 Republican incumbents narrowly avoided defeat, winning with less than 55 percent of the vote. Political analysts concluded that a substantial fund-raising advantage enjoyed by Republican campaign committees had been the difference between a sizable defeat for the Republicans and an electoral disaster. *See* ELECTIONS IN THE UNITED STATES.

New Party Chairman. The task of retrenchment fell to Sen. Paul Laxalt (R, Nev.), one of President Reagan's closest friends and political allies. After Richard Richards of Utah resigned on Oct. 4 (effective January, 1983) as Republican National Committee chairman, amid complaints from the White House that he had been ineffective, Laxalt agreed to assume the new post of party general chairman in November. Richards was replaced as national committee chairman by Frank Fahrenkopf, the Nevada state party chairman. The elevation of Laxalt to the party's top job was widely interpreted as a signal that Reagan planned to run for reelection in 1984.

Problems and Prospects. Despite their weak showing in the 1982 elections, Republicans could console themselves with the knowledge that Reagan remained personally popular with the voters and that the GOP retained an enormous financial and organizational margin over the Democrats. But the party remained highly vulnerable to its long-standing reputation as the champion of the rich, an image reinforced by Reagan's tax breaks for business and reductions of spending on social programs. An ABC News–Washington *Post* poll found in October that, by a 2–1 margin, voters believed that Republicans would go too far in helping the rich and cutting essential government programs that benefit the average American.

The greatest threat to Republican prospects, however, was continued economic stagnation. As the recession persisted and unemployment surpassed 10 percent of the labor force, many party leaders worried that unless an economic recovery materialized quickly in 1983, the GOP's dream of becoming the majority party would be shattered and its hopes for retaining the Presidency in the 1984 elections impaired.

See DEMOCRATIC PARTY; PRESIDENT OF THE UNITED STATES. T.D.

RHODE ISLAND. *See* STATISTICS OF THE WORLD.

RHODESIA. *See* ZIMBABWE.

RUMANIA. In 1982 Rumania experienced the worst economic difficulties of any nation in Eastern Europe, aside from Poland. Overinvestment in industry, neglect of agriculture, and massive borrowing in the West had all contributed to the problem in recent years. President Nicolae Ceauşescu attempted to deal with the crisis through personnel changes, national belt-tightening, and further Western aid.

In the past, Ceauşescu had regularly adopted the tactic of firing or reshuffling officials to divert blame for domestic failures from himself. He used the ploy again in 1982. In May Prime Minister Ilie Verdet and seven deputy prime ministers were ousted from office, presumably for failure in handling the economy. Constantin Dăscălescu, a close aide of Ceauşescu's, became the new prime minister. The purge came on the heels of another top change: Aneta Spornic, a friend of the president's wife, lost her post as education minister. Ceauşescu evidently held Spor-

nic responsible for permitting an upsurge of public interest in transcendental meditation. In October he dismissed Deputy Agricultural Minister Agustin Todea because of inefficiency in the supply of food.

To put the national budget on sounder ground, Ceauşescu ordered a series of domestic price increases. In February the cost of 220 basic food products rose by an average of 35 percent, with rice up 87 percent and meat up 64 percent. These measures were followed by a rise in gasoline, postal, and telephone costs. In July the government decreed extensive increases in the price of household fuels and electricity.

With its debts in the West totaling more than $10 billion, Rumania asked to reschedule its payments, which were in arrears, and to obtain further aid. In May the World Bank agreed to lend Bucharest $101,000,000 to further develop the oil industry. In June the International Monetary Fund agreed to release credit to Rumania that had been suspended for six months. In December Rumania signed an agreement to stretch out most of the 1981 and 1982 payments on its debt over six and a half years.

Foreign Affairs. Ceauşescu sought to safeguard Rumania's tenuous independence from the Soviet Union by maintaining ties in all blocs—Communist, Western, and Third World. He played host to U.S. Secretary of State Alexander M. Haig, Jr., in February; to Turkey's head of state, Kenan Evren, in April; and to Greek Premier Andreas Papandreou in November. He and Papandreou discussed a proposal to make the Balkans a nuclear-free zone. Ceauşescu also made several trips abroad: to China and North Korea in April; to Greece in May; and to Syria, Iraq, and Jordan in June.

Rumania's relations with France suffered a decided chill in the summer when French authorities accused Bucharest of dispatching an agent to Paris to assassinate a dissident Rumanian writer living there. The Rumanian government denied the charge.

See STATISTICS OF THE WORLD. F.W.

RUSSIA. *See* UNION OF SOVIET SOCIALIST REPUBLICS.

RWANDA. *See* STATISTICS OF THE WORLD.

S

SAHARA, WESTERN. *See* AFRICA; MOROCCO.
ST. LUCIA. *See* STATISTICS OF THE WORLD.
ST. VINCENT AND THE GRENADINES. *See* STATISTICS OF THE WORLD.
SAMOA, AMERICAN. *See* STATISTICS OF THE WORLD: *American Samoa.*
SAMOA, WESTERN. *See* STATISTICS OF THE WORLD: *Western Samoa.*
SAN MARINO. *See* STATISTICS OF THE WORLD.
SÃO TOMÉ AND PRÍNCIPE. *See* STATISTICS OF THE WORLD.
SASKATCHEWAN. *See* STATISTICS OF THE WORLD.
SAUDI ARABIA. King Khalid, 69, died on June 13, 1982, following a heart attack and was immediately succeeded by his half brother Crown Prince Fahd ibn Abdul-Aziz al-Saud, 60. Under its new monarch Saudi Arabia pursued a more active role in Middle East politics and diplomacy.
Politics and Economy. Long the dominant figure in the Saudi government, Fahd received formal pledges of loyalty from the nation's princes, tribal leaders, and military officers on June 14. The Saudi royal family, reportedly numbering about 4000, had blood ties with all the major families and tribal groups of the Arabian peninsula, which was considered an important factor in maintaining political stability.

Saudi Arabia's oil production fell from a record 10,300,000 bbl a day in 1981 to a ten-year low of 5,300,000 bbl a day in late 1982, partly because the country maintained the official Organization of Petroleum Exporting Countries (OPEC) price level of $34 a barrel for light crude, or "market" oil; other OPEC members, however, were discounting their prices in order to maintain sales volume in a period of world oil glut. The gross national product was expected to increase by an unusually low—for Saudi Arabia—6.4 percent in 1982. The current-account trade surplus was about $11.7 billion, compared to $44 billion in 1981. Inflation ran at an 11 percent annual rate.

New Ruler of Oil-Rich Kingdom
With the death of King Khalid in June, Crown Prince Fahd ibn Abdul-Aziz al-Saud succeeded his half brother as ruler of oil-rich Saudi Arabia. The 62-year-old Fahd is the eldest of seven sons of Abdul-Aziz ibn-Saud, founder of Saudi Arabia, by the reputed favorite of his many wives. He has held high government posts since 1953, when he became minister of education and established a system of public schools. His appointment as interior minister in 1962 put him in charge of the national guard. In 1974 he negotiated an extensive economic and military accord with the United States. Chosen crown prince in 1975, he was entrusted with the country's day-to-day administration. A fluent English speaker regarded as progressive and pro-Western, Fahd outlined a peace plan in 1981 that appeared to recognize Israel while demanding a Palestinian state.

Fahd ibn Abdul-Aziz al-Saud

Saudi Arabia's oil wealth is financing the construction of Jubail, an ultramodern city and port, on desolate salt flats along the Persian Gulf. Bechtel Corp. managers are directing 41,000 laborers from 39 countries in building the industrial metropolis, which will include an oil refinery, petrochemical plants, and an iron and steel complex.

Middle East Diplomacy. Well-traveled and more worldly than his elder brother—under whom he had served as acting prime minister—Fahd was considered one of the most pro-American of senior Saudi officials. With Saudi Arabia's vast oil wealth to provide political leverage, Fahd quickly emerged as one of the Arab world's most influential leaders.

During the war in Lebanon, Fahd was a key intermediary in the tortuous negotiations between the United States, the Palestine Liberation Organization, and other Arab governments that eventually led to the withdrawal of Palestinian fighters from Beirut. He was also instrumental in arranging cease-fires and in bringing about a relaxation of Israel's blockade of west Beirut.

Saudi Arabia had broken off relations with Egypt after the late President Anwar el-Sadat signed a peace treaty with Israel in 1978, but in June Egyptian President Hosni Mubarak was among the many world leaders who flew to Riyadh for Khalid's funeral. There, Mubarak and Fahd embraced publicly, hinting that a rapprochement between Egypt and Saudi Arabia—both moderate, pro-Western countries closely allied with the U.S. in the Middle East—had begun.

The Palestinian problem continued to preoccupy Fahd. In 1981, when he was still crown prince, Fahd had suffered a humiliating rebuff when radical Arab states rejected his Middle East peace plan at an Arab League summit conference in Fez, Morocco. In September, 1982, Fahd sponsored a basically similar proposal at an Arab summit again held in Fez, and this time the proposal was unanimously adopted; *see* ARAB LEAGUE. It called for an independent Palestinian state in the Israeli-occupied West Bank and Gaza Strip, but like the earlier Fahd plan, it was seen as implicitly recognizing Israel's right to exist.

Generally, Saudi Arabia's relations with the U.S. remained sound. However, U.S. support for Israel, and the unresolved Palestinian problem, remained irritants. Saudi Arabia felt that the administration of U.S. President Ronald Reagan had not done enough to pressure Israel into making concessions toward Palestinian statehood. The Reagan administration felt that Saudi Arabia had not done enough to help promote the peace process.

Iran's counteroffensive against Iraq in the Persian Gulf war was a source of deep concern to Saudi Arabia. Iran and Saudi Arabia, both fundamentalist Muslim states, were locked in an increasingly bitter political and economic competition for dominance in the Persian Gulf. As in 1981 the annual Islamic pilgrimage to Mecca produced clashes between Saudi authorities and Iranian visitors; 69 Iranians were deported after provoking a riot in Medina, the Interior Ministry reported on Oct. 8. In 1982, mindful of Iranian vows to overthrow the "corrupt" royal dynasty, the Saudis sought a closer collective security arrangement among the oil-wealthy sheikhdoms in the Gulf Cooperation Council.

Saudi Arabia and Iran were increasingly at loggerheads, too, within OPEC. With the support of Libya and Algeria, Iran exceeded its OPEC production quota by undercutting the official price level.

See STATISTICS OF THE WORLD. See also ORGANIZATION OF PETROLEUM EXPORTING COUNTRIES.   A.D.

SENEGAL. See STATISTICS OF THE WORLD.

SEYCHELLES. See STATISTICS OF THE WORLD.

SIERRA LEONE. See STATISTICS OF THE WORLD.

SINGAPORE. Prime Minister Lee Kuan Yew and his People's Action Party continued to dominate the bustling island state of Singapore in 1982.

For the first time in its 16 years as a sovereign state, Singapore experienced a modicum of opposition politics. In late 1981 J. B. Jeyarethnam, running on a Workers' Party ticket, won a by-election for a seat in the 75-member parliament. As the one-man opposition, Jeyarethnam compelled the government throughout the year to explain its policies on such questions as the number of people being held without trial and the financing of various government projects. Although Singaporeans enjoyed the unusual spectacle, the autocratic prime minister and his followers were not amused. When Jeyarethnam brought before parliament several matters in which his law firm had an interest, members of the government charged him with unethical conduct. Jeyarethnam was forced to apologize publicly in July, in order to avoid expulsion.

The world recession continued to take its toll on Singapore's "miracle" economy. As the country's exports of consumer electronic products began to decline, the usually strong balance of payments showed signs of weakening. Economists predicted a drop in economic growth from the customary annual 10 percent to between 5 and 7 percent in 1982.

In cooperation with its partners in the Association of Southeast Asian Nations—Indonesia, Malaysia, the Philippines, and Thailand—Singapore vigorously opposed both the Soviet intervention in Afghanistan and the Vietnamese occupation of Cambodia. Lee urged the United States to counter the growth of Soviet power in the region, by deploying a new naval force to support the thinly spread Seventh Fleet in the Pacific and Indian oceans.

See STATISTICS OF THE WORLD.   R.J.C.

SOCIAL SECURITY. There was much talk but little action in Congress in 1982 concerning the politically difficult question of shoring up the faltering social security system. The only substantive legislation, embodied in the $98.3 billion tax bill, passed on Aug. 19, raised some money for the system by requiring federal employees to pay 1.3 percent of their annual base salary to finance Medicare. But that move provided only short-term help.

In early May, the Senate Budget Committee called for $40 billion in spending reductions or revenue increases for social security in fiscal years 1983–85. The Senate budget resolution eventually included a provision requiring Congress's two tax-writing panels, the House Ways and Means Committee and the Senate Finance Committee, to approve legislation by Dec. 1 that would make the social security trust funds solvent. But that requirement was dropped by a House of Representatives–Senate conference committee and did not appear in the final budget resolution that was adopted by Congress on June 23.

Instead, the legislators chose to wait for the recommendations of President Ronald Reagan's National Commission on Social Security Reform, which was appointed in December, 1981, and charged with finding solutions for the system's short- and long-range problems. The 15-member panel, comprising eight Republicans and seven Democrats, was expected to make its report before the end of 1982, but it did not do so.

Analysts predicted that if remedial action were not taken, the system's main component, the old-age and survivors insurance trust fund, would run out of money in July, 1983. If that fund kept afloat by borrowing from the system's two others, the health insurance fund and the disability insurance fund, all three would be out of money sometime in 1984. On Nov. 5 the old-age fund borrowed money from the disability fund to cover November payments, and on Dec. 31 it borrowed $13.5 billion from both other funds for payments in the first half of 1983.

Even if such immediate cash-flow problems were resolved, another severe deficit was expected in 30–35 years, when the "baby boom" generation of the 1950's and 1960's reaches retirement age.

The Social Security Administration announced on Nov. 8 that pensioners age 65 to 69 would be allowed to earn a maximum of $6600 in 1983 without losing social security benefits. Those under 65 who draw benefits would be allowed to earn a maximum of $4920 without losing benefits. Beneficiaries age 70 or more would be allowed to earn any amount without losing benefits. Those who exceeded the earnings limit would lose $1 of benefits for every $2 above the limit that they earn. K.B.H.

SOLOMON ISLANDS. *See* STATISTICS OF THE WORLD.

SOMALIA. Opposition to the government of President Muhammad Siad Barre of Somalia intensified in 1982. In late 1981 opponents of Siad Barre allied to Ethiopia came together to form the Somali Democratic Salvation Front (SDSF). The SDSF appeared to draw support in northern Somalia, where demonstrations and rioting occurred sporadically throughout 1982. In March Siad Barre reshuffled his cabinet, dismissing 20 of 25 ministers. The action was designed to bolster his control of the army, yet the immediate result was an abortive coup attempt by several former ministers in April. A second attempt, in June, also failed, resulting in more arrests of senior government officials and army officers.

Siad Barre continued his support of the Western Somali Liberation Front and its efforts to drive the Ethiopians out of the Somali-inhabited Ogaden region. Fighting had deteriorated to hit-and-run guerrilla raids, but the front managed to tie down significant numbers of Ethiopian troops needed in other rebellious areas.

On June 30, in an apparent move to unseat Siad Barre and end the guerrilla war, the SDSF, with strong Ethiopian air and mechanized support, launched an invasion of Somalia. Some 10,000 Ethiopian troops were involved in the attack, which the Ethiopians hoped would lead to an internal revolt against Siad Barre. Apparently, however, hatred of the Ethiopians was greater than opposition to the president. The army and general

U.S. President Ronald Reagan shares a light moment with President Muhammad Siad Barre of Somalia as they confer in the Oval Office of the White House on March 11. Siad Barre was seeking stepped-up U.S. assistance in Somalia's struggle against Ethiopia.

Black demonstrators march through Johannesburg streets in advance of a funeral procession for Neil Aggett, a white labor leader found dead while under police detention. The government claimed that Aggett had committed suicide.

populace rallied to the government, and the invasion was contained. By December only a small area was held by the SDSF and the Ethiopians.

In March Siad Barre visited Washington, D.C., seeking aid in excess of the $80,000,000 that the United States had earmarked for military and economic assistance to Somalia in fiscal year 1982. Although the administration of U.S. President Ronald Reagan declined to give additional support, it did airlift defensive weapons and communications equipment to Somalia after the June invasion.

See STATISTICS OF THE WORLD. *See also* ETHIOPIA.   J.T.S.

SOUTH AFRICA. In the face of mounting domestic criticism and worsening economic conditions, the government of Prime Minister Pieter W. Botha (*see* biography at PEOPLE IN THE NEWS) held to its programs in 1982. Plans to allow the country's Asian and Coloured (mixed race) populations a greater voice in politics had met harsh resistance from the ultraconservative wing of Botha's National Party (NP).

Politics and the Economy. In early March the NP had expelled 16 parliamentary members—among them Andries P. Treurnicht, a

cabinet minister who resigned his post—for refusing to support Botha's racial policies. On March 20 Treurnicht announced the establishment of a new political group, the Conservative Party of South Africa. Contending that Botha's policies would compromise white self-determination, Treurnicht's right-wing party quickly gained support among Afrikaners.

On May 12 the Botha government, despite the erosion of white support, proposed a constitutional change to grant electoral rights to Asians and Coloureds. The complex plan would result in a more powerful white executive branch and a weakened legislative branch consisting of three ethnically based chambers (one each for whites, Asians, and Coloureds). Each legislative chamber would decide matters pertaining to its own racial group, but the final arbiter of what would merit national attention would be the executive, or president. The plan, which observers said would ensure continued NP control of South Africa's government structure, brought a storm of criticism from all quarters. Most Asian and Coloured leaders called the plan basically unfair in excluding the black majority; black representatives denounced the plan as but another step by the white-minority government to stave off armed rebellion by black South Africans. Nevertheless, at the end of July a special NP congress unanimously endorsed the Botha proposal.

Troubles marked the year in the economic sphere, as well. Because of a $4 billion trade deficit—the result of a sharp decline in the international price of gold in 1981—the government, in March, began negotiating for a loan of $1.1 billion from the International Monetary Fund (IMF). The loan request won the support of the administration of U.S. President Ronald Reagan, but it provoked an outcry in the United Nations. Nevertheless, on Nov. 3 the IMF gave its approval. In order to reduce imports, the government in February had imposed a 10 percent surcharge on imported goods, as well as a 1 percent increase in the general sales tax. Nevertheless, despite government efforts, by September foreign exchange reserves were sufficient to cover only one week of imports.

South Africa's deepest recession since the 1930's touched off waves of strikes among black workers seeking better working conditions and more equitable wages relative to those of whites. In early July clashes between striking black miners and the police led to the deaths of at least ten miners. Strikes closed down many of the country's automobile plants in July and August, but after the police began to arrest union leaders, calm settled over the industrial sector.

In February a white unionist working among blacks, Neil Aggett, was found dead while under police detention. Aggett was the first white and the 46th detainee to die violently since 1963. (A black detainee died in August.) The government claim of suicide in the Aggett case brought about an investigation and renewed charges of torture and inhumane practices by police authorities.

Foreign Affairs. South Africa continued to resist efforts, especially by the United States and other Western nations, to end its control over South-West Africa (Namibia). As the diplomats plodded on, South Africa repeatedly attacked guerrilla bases in Angola.

In January the government reversed itself after an international outcry and brought charges against 43 South African-based mer-

cenaries who returned to South Africa after unsuccessfully attempting to stage a coup in the Seychelles in November, 1981. The trial, which ended in July with 42 convictions, suggested that the South African government had supported the plot.

On Dec. 9 South African forces raided the homes of black exiles in Maseru, the capital of Lesotho, an independent black nation surrounded on all sides by South Africa. Of the 42 persons killed by the raiders, South Africa said that many were terrorist members of the outlawed African National Congress. Lesotho officials denied the allegation.

Despite these actions, South Africa tried to improve relations with some black African nations. In April Botha met with Zambia's president, Kenneth D. Kaunda, on South Africa's border with Botswana; the two reportedly discussed the problem of South-West Africa. In December South Africa announced that its foreign and defense ministers had met in the Cape Verde Islands with a delegation from Angola to explore a solution for South-West Africa.

See STATISTICS OF THE WORLD. *See also* ANGOLA; SOUTH-WEST AFRICA.   J.T.S.

SOUTH CAROLINA. *See* STATISTICS OF THE WORLD.

SOUTH DAKOTA. *See* STATISTICS OF THE WORLD.

SOUTH-WEST AFRICA, also known as NAMIBIA. After an auspicious start in early 1982, negotiations for an end of South African rule in South-West Africa bogged down once more by the end of the year. In January South Africa announced an unconditional acceptance of plans put forward by the United States for elections in South-West Africa to select assembly members, who, in turn, would approve a constitution for the territory prior to independence. However, the South Africans insisted upon an electoral system designed to prevent the black nationalist South-West Africa People's Organization (SWAPO) from sweeping the assembly. The South African proposal called for one half of the seats to be filled by proportional representation and the other half to be divided between SWAPO and the Democratic Turnhalle Alliance (DTA), the multiracial, South

African-sponsored coalition nominally governing South-West Africa. The proposal, which SWAPO condemned as needlessly confusing, was believed designed to prevent the two-thirds approval needed to put an adopted constitution into effect.

As the so-called contact group—the U.S., Canada, Great Britain, France, and West Germany—began to devise modifications in the system to win approval from black African states, the main negotiations shifted, first to resolving the issue of a cease-fire between, and subsequent separation of, South African and SWAPO forces, and, second, to determining the size and composition of a United Nations force that would supervise the transition to independence. Here again, South Africa, in May, declared itself in basic agreement with the plan of the administration of U.S. President Ronald Reagan, but quickly insisted that the withdrawal of its forces be formally linked to a withdrawal of Cuban troops from Angola, South-West Africa's northern neighbor, where SWAPO had established bases. Over the summer the U.S. pressed for a "parallel movement" approach rather than formal linkage. However, after Angola rejected such an approach, France, West Germany, and Canada declared in October that they opposed further negotiations to establish linkage. With South Africa insisting on simultaneous withdrawal, the talks appeared stalemated. French and Portuguese proposals to substitute an international peacekeeping force in place of the Cubans were rejected by South Africa in late November.

Some observers believed that the South African moves had at least the tacit approval of the Reagan administration, which was apparently eager to get the Cubans—estimated at 15,000-20,000—out of Angola. It also seemed designed to give South Africa's political protégés in South-West Africa time to build up their strength. The DTA was acknowledged to be too weak to oppose SWAPO effectively in free elections. It was weakened further in February, when the National Democratic Party (NDP) withdrew from the alliance. The NDP represented the Ovambo people, who make up about half of the territory's population and who were firm supporters of SWAPO and independence. Its withdrawal occurred allegedly with encouragement from South Africa, which, some critics believed, was backing the NDP in order to weaken Ovambo support for SWAPO and thus stave off an eventual government dominated by the liberation movement. However, the DTA strongly resisted efforts to ease it out of power, and on Nov. 20 South Africa extended the life of the national assembly until mid-February, 1983.

The struggle between South African forces and SWAPO guerrillas continued unabated in 1982. SWAPO concentrated on small hit-and-run raids against South African patrols and attempted to disrupt communications links. South Africa retaliated by carrying the war into Angola, where a wide no-man's-land was established, and by raiding SWAPO bases and refugee camps. In a report issued during the summer, the U.S. charged that SWAPO received 90 percent of its military aid and 60 percent of its overall support from the Soviet Union.

See STATISTICS OF THE WORLD. See also ANGOLA. J.T.S.

SOVIET UNION. See UNION OF SOVIET SOCIALIST REPUBLICS.

Black South African soldiers display Soviet-made weapons seized in a South African raid into Angola in which South African forces claimed to have killed 201 SWAPO guerrillas. Talks aimed at independence for South-West Africa were stalemated in 1982.

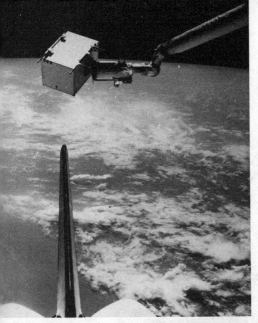

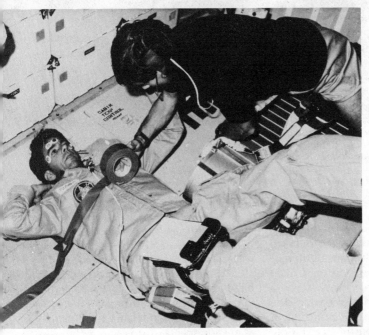

The U.S. space shuttle Columbia completed three missions in 1982. Above, left: This view from the second flight of the year shows a remote-control device carrying a multi-instrumented monitor for checking contaminants in and around the craft's cargo bay; Columbia's vertical tail is also seen. Above, right: During Columbia's first operational flight, a communications satellite is released from its protective cradle in the opened cargo bay. Left: Aboard this same flight, mission specialist Joseph P. Allen secures fellow specialist William B. Lenoir to the floor before Lenoir was monitored for comparative responses to activity under zero- and one-gravity conditions.

SPACE SCIENCE AND EXPLORATION. U.S. space activity in 1982 centered on the space shuttle program, including the first operational flight of the *Columbia*. Salyut 7, a new Soviet space station, was occupied by two cosmonauts from May to December, setting a new endurance record. Ariane, the European Space Agency's launch vehicle, was set back by a failure in September, and the first successful launch of a privately financed ve-

hicle took place that same month in Texas. The year also marked the 25th anniversary of the commencement of the space age with the launching of the earth satellite Sputnik I by the Soviet Union on Oct. 4, 1957.

U.S. Space Shuttle. Flights three and four of the space shuttle *Columbia*, on March 22–30 and June 27–July 4, respectively, successfully completed the shuttle's developmental flight tests. Astronauts Jack R. Lousma and C. Gor-

The massive launch vehicle for the June orbiting of Soyuz T6 is moved toward its launch pad in Baikonour, U.S.S.R. The progress of the mission was more publicized than usual because the third member of the Soyuz crew was French "spationaut" Jean-Loup Chrétien, the first Western European to take part in a Soviet space flight.

don Fullerton were the crew of the third flight, and Thomas K. Mattingly 2nd and Henry W. Hartsfield, Jr., flew the fourth mission. Despite malfunctions, the third flight met all of its major objectives except a planned test of landing in a crosswind. The fourth flight got under way despite minor heat-shield damage by hailstones at lift-off. Aboard was the first "Getaway Special," a small, self-contained payload compartment for scientific and technological experiments that would be available, on shuttle flights, to customers anywhere in the world for as little as $3000. Also aboard was a secret military payload and experimental pharmaceutical-processing equipment. One setback was the sinking of the rocket boosters when their parachutes failed, but *Columbia* was able to

make its first landing on a concrete runway.

The first operational flight of *Columbia* was launched on Nov. 11 and ended on Nov. 16. For the first time four persons were orbited in a single spacecraft: Vance D. Brand, Robert F. Overmyer, Joseph P. Allen, and William B. Lenoir, the latter two functioning as mission specialists to perform the payload work aboard. While in orbit the shuttle released two commercial satellites from its cargo bay, one a Satellite Business Systems Inc. satellite (SBS 3) and the other a Canadian telecommunications satellite (Anik C-3). A planned extravehicular activity, or space walk, by Allen and Lenoir was canceled because of malfunctions of their space suits during onboard checkouts. On its return *Columbia* was retired temporarily and the next shuttle, *Challenger,* was readied for use in 1983.

Other U.S. Space News. Several communications satellites for commercial use were launched in 1982, to provide data and for television and telephone transmissions. Voyager II continued its flight trajectory toward a rendezvous with the planet Uranus in 1986, and the fourth in the Landsat series of earth resources satellites was launched in July into a polar orbit (see picture caption in EARTH SCIENCES).

Soviet Space Activity. The Soviet Union continued its vigorous program of space-station development with the launch of a new station, Salyut 7, on April 19. (The previous space station, Salyut 6, was allowed to burn up in the atmosphere on July 29 after five years of service.) The first occupants of Salyut 7 were cosmonauts Anatoly Berezovoy and Valentin Lebedev, who linked with the station on May 13 after reaching earth-orbit in Soyuz T5. They remained aboard Salyut 7 until Dec. 10, when they returned to earth, their 211 days in space having broken the previous duration record of 185 days set by Soviet cosmonauts in 1980. While aboard Salyut 7 the men released a small amateur-radio satellite, Iskra 2, by deploying it through an air lock.

Soyuz T6, launched on June 24 to link with Salyut 7, carried Vladimir A. Dzhanibekov, Aleksandr S. Ivanchenkov, and French "spationaut" Jean-Loup Chrétien, the first Western European orbited in a Soviet craft. Their return to earth on July 2 was viewed live on television. On Aug. 19 Soyuz T7 was launched with Leonid I. Popov, Aleksandr Serebrov, and Svetlana Savitskaya, the second woman in space. They docked with Salyut 7 and returned to earth on Aug. 27 in Soyuz T5, leaving their own craft for use by Berezovoy and Lebedev.

The U.S.S.R. successfully landed two new research craft on the planet Venus in 1982; *see* ASTRONOMY.

Launches of Other Nations. The European Space Agency launch vehicle, Ariane, with a maritime communications satellite (Marecs-B) and a meteorological satellite (SIRIO-2) aboard, suffered a setback on Sept. 10 when it failed to reach orbit. The People's Republic of China orbited its 12th earth satellite on Sept. 9; the satellite's reentry three days later implied that it had been used for a photographic reconnaissance mission. India was severely disappointed when its Insat 1 scientific satellite, launched on April 10 by the United States, ceased to function after only a few months. Japan also launched a small craft for solar-panel tests.

Private Launch. On Sept. 9 a Houston-based company, Space Services Inc. of America, successfully tested the world's first privately financed launch vehicle, Conestoga 1. The 11-m (36-ft.) single-stage rocket, launched from an island off the Texas Gulf coast, landed in the Gulf of Mexico after reaching an altitude of 314 km (195 mi.). The company, wishing to exploit a field thus far dominated by governments, announced plans to launch an earth satellite in 1984 using a multistage vehicle.   F.C.D. III

Conestoga 1, a small launch vehicle constructed by a Texas firm, Space Services Inc. of America, sits on its pad prior to its successful test on Sept. 9 under the direction of former astronaut Donald Slayton. The firm intends to orbit communications and earth-scanning satellites for energy companies.

SPAIN. The Spanish Socialist Workers' Party (PSOE) won the national parliamentary elections held on Oct. 28, 1982. Led by 40-year-old Felipe González Márquez, who became prime minister on Dec. 2, the PSOE captured 46 percent of the vote and 201 seats in the 350-seat Congress of Deputies (the lower house of parliament). Trailing badly were the conservative Popular Alliance (25 percent of the vote and 106 seats) and the incumbent ruling party, the Union of the Democratic Center (UCD), which won only 12 seats, compared to 168 in the 1979 parliamentary elections. The Communists won five seats; other minor parties won 26 seats. The Socialists also won a majority in the largely ceremonial Senate, taking 134 of the 208 seats.

Politics. The Socialist landslide capped a turbulent year for Spain, one dominated by unrest within the armed forces and by preelectoral jockeying by the major political parties. The trial of 32 military officers for an attempted 1981 coup began in February, 1982. It lasted more than three months, with sentences of 30 years meted out to the two main leaders and a six-year sentence given another high-ranking officer. Nineteen other officers received sentences of six years or less. Ten officers were acquitted. The apparently inconsistent verdicts disappointed political leaders who had been held at gunpoint in parliament on the night of the coup attempt by the ten acquitted officers.

Rumors of planned military coups in 1982 occurred against a backdrop of dissension within the ruling UCD that crippled its public image. A debacle for the party occurred in the May regional elections in Andalusia; the UCD slipped to third place, behind the PSOE, which polled a majority of the vote, and the reinvigorated Popular Alliance. This electoral disaster exacerbated internal UCD tensions and provoked the defection of numerous deputies, the most prominent of whom was former prime minister Adolfo Suárez González, founder of the party. A month after his resignation on July 28, the UCD retained only 122 of the 168 deputies it had elected in March, 1979. No longer able to fashion a legislative majority, Prime Minister Leopoldo Calvo Sotelo y Bustelo asked King Juan Carlos I to dissolve parliament and to schedule elections.

Also badly beaten in the October national elections was the faction-ridden Communist Party, which lost 18 of its 23 deputies and

Manuel Fraga Iribarne, leader of the rightist Popular Alliance, waits behind four nuns to cast his ballot in Spanish parliamentary elections held on Oct. 28. Fraga's party finished second to the Socialists.

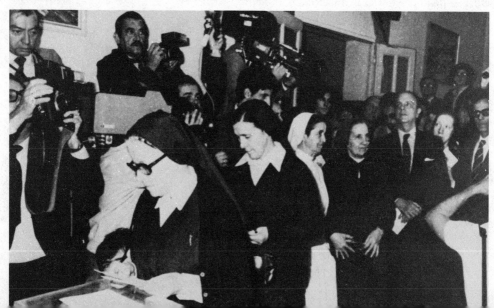

Spain's Youthful Leader

The Socialist Workers' Party's landslide victory in elections on Oct. 28 brought the Spanish Left back to power after more than 40 years of eclipse and, for most of that period, persecution and exile. At the age of 40, however, Spain's new prime minister, Socialist leader Felipe González Márquez, represented a new generation in Spanish politics, born after the civil war that led to the Falangist dictatorship of Gen. Francisco Franco. A lawyer from the Andalusian region, González became secretary-general of his party in 1974, while it was still outlawed by the Franco regime. Under his leadership the Socialists veered away from cooperation with the Communists and aligned themselves with Europe's moderate Social Democratic parties. González, an American-style campaigner who favored casual dress, rapidly became the most popular politician in the country.

Felipe González Márquez

polled only 3.8 percent of the vote. Communist leader Santiago Carrillo stepped down on Nov. 6 and was replaced by Gerardo Iglesias.

Throughout the year members of the secessionist group ETA continued to perpetrate acts of violence in the Basque provinces. At least six members of the paramilitary Civil Guard and 15 policemen had been killed by August.

The Economy. The Spanish economy was sluggish during 1982. The gross national product registered virtually no growth and unemployment remained high, at about 15 percent of the labor force nationally but climbing to nearly 25 percent in areas such as Andalusia. An inflation rate of 15 percent also hampered the economy. Spain did not escape the international rash of debt-related problems in 1982. Renegotiation of the Cuban debt hurt Spanish banks, and one of the largest private companies in Spain, Union Explosivos Río Tinto, had to reschedule debt payments late in the year. Spain's unit of currency, the peseta, was devalued by 8 percent on Dec. 4.

Foreign Affairs. Parliament approved Spain's membership in the North Atlantic Treaty Organization, over Socialist and Communist objections, in late 1981, and formal entry took place on May 30, 1982. With the assumption of power by the Socialists, Spanish participation was thrown into doubt, however.

The question of the British occupation of Gibraltar flared up anew as a result of the Falkland Islands conflict. Spain supported Argentina, although opposing the use of force in the dispute, and therefore postponed indefinitely the scheduled full reopening of the border with Gibraltar.

Officials of the United States and Spain signed an agreement on July 2 permitting the U.S. to continue to maintain military bases on Spanish soil through 1986. The agreement substantially increased U.S. military aid for Spain—reportedly to an annual level of $400,000,000. The treaty was not ratified before the dissolution of the parliament, however, and the Socialists were expected to demand a revision.

Pope John Paul II paid a ten-day visit to Spain, ending on Nov. 9. He thus became the first pope to visit one of the world's largest predominately Roman Catholic nations.

See STATISTICS OF THE WORLD.   E.M.L.

Sports

The bad news for sports fans in 1982 was the retirement of boxing's Sugar Ray Leonard and the two-month-long National Football League players' strike. The good news consisted of exciting contests in team sports and fine performances by such athletes as Jimmy Connors, Wayne Gretzky, Phil and Steve Mahre, Martina Navratilova, Ralph Sampson, Mary Decker Tabb, Robin Yount, and Elaine Zayak.

In 1982 the sports world provided serious and tragic moments as well as the usual fun and games.

A year after a players' strike wiped out one third of the major-league baseball season, a players' strike wiped out almost one half of the National Football League (NFL) season. This was the first time a pro football season had been interrupted by a strike, and it followed the signing of five-year contracts between the NFL and the three major commercial television networks worth $2.076 billion, a record package for sports or any other type of entertainment.

Race accidents killed leading drivers in automobile racing and powerboat racing. A fighter died of brain injuries after a world championship bout. Sugar Ray Leonard, the most charismatic boxer in the sport, suffered a partially detached retina in the left eye and retired at age 26 rather than risk blindness.

The year's major winners included the St. Louis Cardinals in baseball, the San Francisco 49ers and the University of Georgia in football, the Los Angeles Lakers and the University of North Carolina in basketball, and the New York Islanders in hockey.

The heroes included Robin Yount in baseball, Herschel Walker in football, Wayne Gretzky in hockey, Larry Holmes in boxing, Tom Watson in golf, Jimmy Connors in tennis, and Phil Mahre in skiing. Among the out-

John Watson of Northern Ireland drove his McLaren through downtown Detroit and along the Detroit River waterfront on June 6 to win the first Formula One Grand Prix race ever held in the Motor City.

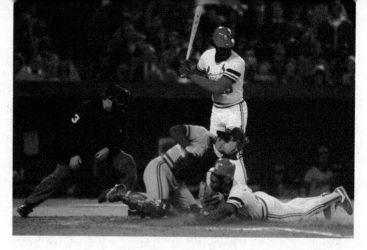

Although Lonnie Smith was called out on this attempted steal of home plate in the World Series, the team speed of the St. Louis Cardinals helped them defeat the Milwaukee Brewers and win baseball's championship, 4 games to 3.

standing women were Martina Navratilova in tennis, Mary Decker Tabb in track and field, and Elaine Zayak in figure skating.

AUTO RACING

In 1973 Gordon Johncock won the Indianapolis 500, America's most famous auto race. In 1977 and 1981 he was leading when problems knocked him out of the race. In the $2,067,475 Indianapolis 500 on May 30, 1982, he won again, but barely. Johncock and his Wildcat-Cosworth held off Rick Mears in a Penske-Ford by 0.16 sec., the closest finish ever at Indianapolis.

The roadsters that raced at Indianapolis and other American oval tracks were slightly larger versions of the Formula One cars that raced on road courses for the world drivers championship. Keke Rosberg of Finland, driving a Williams-Cosworth, won this 16-race series with 44 points. Didier Pironi of France in a Ferrari and John Watson of Northern Ireland in a McLaren tied for second place with 39 points each.

Pironi's season was cut short when he broke both legs on Aug. 7 in Hockenheim, West Germany, practicing for the German Grand Prix. Gilles Villeneuve of Canada, his Ferrari teammate, was killed on May 8 in the Belgian Grand Prix in Zolder.

Of the 3 Grand Prix races in the United States, Niki Lauda of Austria won in a McLaren on April 4 in Long Beach, Calif.; Watson on June 6 in Detroit; and Michele Alboreto of Italy in a Tyrrell on Sept. 25 in Las Vegas.

America's major stock-car race was the $927,625 Daytona 500, held on Feb. 14 in Daytona Beach, Fla. Bobby Allison won in a Buick, and he finished second to Darrell Waltrip in the 31-race series of the National Association for Stock Car Auto Racing.

BASEBALL

Bowie Kuhn, the baseball commissioner since 1969, was voted out of office in 1982, two weeks after the St. Louis Cardinals won the World Series in 7 games from the Milwaukee Brewers.

Kuhn was completing his second seven-year term. To be hired or reelected, a commissioner needed approval from 10 of the 14 clubs in the American League and 9 of the 12 in the National League. The American League owners voted for Kuhn, 11–3, but the 7–5 vote in his favor by National League owners was insufficient.

Kuhn's opponents in the National League were Nelson Doubleday of the New York Mets, Ted Turner of the Atlanta Braves, John McMullen of the Houston Astros, and William Williams of the Cincinnati Reds, all successful businessmen relatively new to baseball, and August A. Busch, Jr., of the Cardinals, once Kuhn's fervent supporter. Kuhn had alienated all in different ways.

Several pro-Kuhn owners advocated a plan to keep him in office while hiring another executive to oversee baseball's business affairs, but when they proposed to place the newcomer on a level below Kuhn, the plan failed to gain sufficient support. Meanwhile, Kuhn agreed to serve until his term expired in August, 1983.

The Season. All four division races were decided in the last week of the major-league season, two of them on the last day. The St. Louis Cardinals won the National League's Eastern Division with speed, defense, and good relief pitching. The Atlanta Braves won the Western Division when the Los Angeles Dodgers lost to the San Francisco Giants on the season's final day.

The Braves, under a new manager, Joe Torre, had an up-and-down season, winning their first 12 games and later losing 19 of 21. In the pennant playoffs, the Cardinals beat them in 3 straight games.

In the American League, the Milwaukee Brewers and the Baltimore Orioles met in the final series of the season with the Brewers needing only one victory to win the Eastern Division title. The Orioles won the first 3 games, leaving the teams tied for first place. The Brewers won the finale, 10-2, with 4 home runs, typical for a team that relied all year on power.

The California Angels won the Western Division, giving Gene Mauch his first title in 23 years as a major-league manager. But after the Angels beat the Brewers in the first 2 games of the playoffs, they lost the last 3, putting the Brewers in the World Series, and Mauch resigned.

World Series. The World Series went back and forth. After the Cardinals led the Brewers, 2 games to 1, the Brewers won twice and led, 3 games to 2. Then the Cardinals won the last two games, 13-1 and 6-3, and became champions of baseball. Darrell Porter, the Cardinals' catcher, was named the most valuable player of the series.

Outstanding Players. Robin Yount, the Brewers' shortstop, was voted the American League's most valuable player, and twice in the World Series he collected 4 hits in a game. Dale Murphy, a Braves outfielder, was the National League's most valuable player. The Cy Young Awards for pitching went to Steve Carlton of the Philadelphia Phillies and Pete Vuckovich of the Brewers.

Rickey Henderson of the Oakland Athletics stole 130 bases, a major-league record for a season. Gaylord Perry of the Seattle Mariners became the 15th pitcher in history to gain 300 career victories. First baseman Al Oliver of the Montréal Expos led the National League in batting (.331), hits (204), and doubles (43), and he tied with Murphy for the lead in runs batted in (109). Outfielder Willie Wilson of the Kansas City Royals led the American League with a .332 batting average, one point higher than Yount.

Reggie Jackson of the Angels and Gorman Thomas of the Brewers tied for the American League home-run title with 39; Dave Kingman of the New York Mets led the National League with 37. Carlton won the most games in the National League, 23; LaMarr Hoyt of the Chicago White Sox led the American League with 19.

Henry ("Hank") Aaron and Frank Robinson, outfielders renowned for their home-run hitting, were voted into the Baseball Hall of Fame. So were Albert B. ("Happy") Chandler, a former commissioner, and Travis Jackson, a former shortstop.

NATIONAL LEAGUE

Eastern Division	W	L	Pct.	GB
St. Louis Cardinals	92	70	.568	—
Philadelphia Phillies	89	73	.549	3
Montréal Expos	86	76	.531	6
Pittsburgh Pirates	84	78	.519	8
Chicago Cubs	73	89	.451	19
New York Mets	65	97	.401	27

Western Division	W	L	Pct.	GB
Atlanta Braves	89	73	.549	—
Los Angeles Dodgers	88	74	.543	1
San Francisco Giants	87	75	.537	2
San Diego Padres	81	81	.500	8
Houston Astros	77	85	.475	12
Cincinnati Reds	61	101	.377	28

AMERICAN LEAGUE

Eastern Division	W	L	Pct.	GB
Milwaukee Brewers	95	67	.586	—
Baltimore Orioles	94	68	.580	1
Boston Red Sox	89	73	.549	6
Detroit Tigers	83	79	.512	12
New York Yankees	79	83	.488	16
Cleveland Indians	78	84	.481	17
Toronto Blue Jays	78	84	.481	17

Western Division	W	L	Pct.	GB
California Angels	93	69	.574	—
Kansas City Royals	90	72	.556	3
Chicago White Sox	87	75	.537	6
Seattle Mariners	76	86	.469	17
Oakland Athletics	68	94	.420	25
Texas Rangers	64	98	.395	29
Minnesota Twins	60	102	.370	33

PENNANT PLAYOFFS
National League—St. Louis defeated Atlanta, 3 games to 0
American League—Milwaukee defeated California, 3 games to 2

WORLD SERIES—St. Louis defeated Milwaukee, 4 games to 3

Free agency or the prospect of it led to many lucrative contracts. Early in the year the Yankees kept Ron Guidry by giving the pitcher $3,950,000 over four years and added outfielders Ken Griffey ($6,250,000 over six years) and Dave Collins ($2,475,000 over three years).

Catcher Gary Carter of Montréal, who earned $200,000 in 1981, signed a new Expos contract for $14,000,000 over eight years. Outfielder George Foster signed with the Mets for $10,200,000 over six years, and outfielder Reggie Jackson with California for $3,900,000 over four years. After the season, first baseman Jason Thompson of the Pittsburgh Pirates signed for $5,500,000 over five years and Philadelphia gave Pete Rose, its 41-year-old first baseman, $1,200,000 for the 1983 season.

BASKETBALL

North Carolina, which had come close in Dean Smith's 20 previous years as coach, finally won the National Collegiate Athletic Association (NCAA) championship. The Los Angeles Lakers regained the National Basketball Association (NBA) title they won two years before.

Smith's teams at North Carolina had reached 3 national finals and 3 additional semifinals. This Tar Heel team won 27 of its 29 regular-season games and advanced to the tournament's Final Four with Georgetown, Louisville, and Houston.

In the final, on March 29 in New Orleans, North Carolina defeated Georgetown, 63–62, on Michael Jordan's 16-ft. shot with 15 sec. remaining. Pat Ewing, Georgetown's 7-ft. freshman center, was called for 5 goaltending violations in the first half alone.

Ralph Sampson, the 7-ft.-4-in. center from Virginia, repeated as player of the year. James Worthy of North Carolina was voted the outstanding player in the NCAA championships.

Attendance for the 1264 four-year colleges with men's varsity teams reached 31,105,948, a record. The 23 teams of the NBA also set a regular-season record of 9,989,410.

When Los Angeles won the 1980 NBA championship, Paul Westhead was head coach. He was fired early in the 1981–82 season after Earvin ("Magic") Johnson and other

Two of basketball's finest players are seen in action in the NBA championship finals between the Philadelphia 76ers and Los Angeles Lakers, as Philadelphia's Julius Erving (left) attempts to score over the Lakers' Kareem Abdul-Jabbar (middle). Los Angeles won the title, 4 games to 2.

players became disenchanted with his new disciplined offense. Pat Riley moved up from assistant coach and led the Lakers to a division title.

The defending champion Boston Celtics, who had the season's best record (63-19), lost to the Philadelphia 76ers, 4 games to 3, in the Eastern Conference finals. The Lakers breezed through the playoffs with the best record in the NBA's 36 years, beating the Phoenix Suns, 4 games to 0, the San Antonio Spurs, 4-0, and the 76ers, 4-2.

The most valuable players were Moses Malone of the Houston Rockets during the regular season and Johnson during the playoffs. Malone led in rebounds (14.7 a game) for the third time in four years and George Gervin of San Antonio in scoring (32.3 points a game) for the fourth time in his six NBA seasons. After the season, Malone became a free agent; he was traded to Philadelphia and

NATIONAL BASKETBALL ASSOCIATION
1981–82 Regular Season

EASTERN CONFERENCE

Atlantic Division	W	L	Pct.	GB
Boston Celtics	63	19	.768	—
Philadelphia 76ers	58	24	.707	5
New Jersey Nets	44	38	.537	19
Washington Bullets	43	39	.524	20
New York Knickerbockers	33	49	.402	30

Central Division	W	L	Pct.	GB
Milwaukee Bucks	55	27	.671	—
Atlanta Hawks	42	40	.512	13
Detroit Pistons	39	43	.476	16
Indiana Pacers	35	47	.427	20
Chicago Bulls	34	48	.415	21
Cleveland Cavaliers	15	67	.183	40

WESTERN CONFERENCE

Midwest Division	W	L	Pct.	GB
San Antonio Spurs	48	34	.585	—
Denver Nuggets	46	36	.561	2
Houston Rockets	46	36	.561	2
Kansas City Kings	30	52	.366	18
Dallas Mavericks	28	54	.341	20
Utah Jazz	25	57	.305	23

Pacific Division	W	L	Pct.	GB
Los Angeles Lakers	57	25	.695	—
Seattle SuperSonics	52	30	.634	5
Phoenix Suns	46	36	.561	11
Golden State Warriors	45	37	.549	12
Portland Trail Blazers	42	40	.512	15
San Diego Clippers	17	65	.207	40

PLAYOFFS

First Round
Washington defeated New Jersey, 2 games to 0
Philadelphia defeated Atlanta, 2 games to 0
Seattle defeated Houston, 2 games to 1
Phoenix defeated Denver, 2 games to 1

Second Round
Los Angeles defeated Phoenix, 4 games to 0
Boston defeated Washington, 4 games to 1
Philadelphia defeated Milwaukee, 4 games to 2
San Antonio defeated Seattle, 4 games to 1

Conference Finals
Los Angeles defeated San Antonio, 4 games to 0
Philadelphia defeated Boston, 4 games to 3

Championship Finals
Los Angeles defeated Philadelphia, 4 games to 2

droplanes (200-mph boats powered by airplane engines). Muncey was killed in 1981 when his boat, *Atlas Van Lines,* flipped. A new *Atlas Van Lines* was built in 1982, and Hanauer drove it to the national championship by winning 5 of the season's 9 races.

Dean Chenoweth, the national champion in 1980 and 1981, was killed on July 31 in Pasco, Wash., when his boat flipped over on him. His death was the 14th fatality since 1951 in unlimited hydroplane racing.

In yachting, Cornelius von Reichten of the Netherlands finished first in the Whitbread 27,000-mi. around-the-world race. He completed the trip in his 76-ft. *Flyer* in 120 days, a record. In American competition, Dennis Conner sailed the 51-ft. *Retaliation* to the overall victory in the Southern Ocean Racing Conference's 6 February races.

BOWLING

Earl Anthony, the all-time leader in victories and earnings, became the first bowler to exceed $1,000,000 in prize money during his career. He won 3 of the 36 tournaments on the Professional Bowlers Association (PBA) tour, including a record fifth PBA championship. He earned $134,760 during the year and finished it with 39 career victories.

Art Trask also won 3 winter tournaments. Dave Husted captured the U.S. Open, starting the championship game with 7 strikes. On the Women Professional Bowlers Association tour, Nikki Giannulias won 4 tournaments, Shinobu Saitoh of Japan the U.S. Open, and Katsuko Sugimoto of Japan the Queens tournament. Giannulias earned a record $45,875.

Glenn Allison, a 54-year-old former touring professional, made history on July 1 in La Habra, Calif., when he rolled the first perfect series ever—3 straight 300 games. The American Bowling Congress (ABC) refused to recognize the performance, however, ruling that Allison was helped by excessively oiled lanes. Allison said that he would sue the ABC to win recognition.

BOXING

Sugar Ray Leonard, who burst upon the boxing scene in 1976 as an Olympic champion, retired on Nov. 9 at age 26 as the world welterweight champion. He had undergone sur-

signed for between $2,000,000 to $2,500,000 a year for six years.

Championship tournaments for women were conducted by the Association for Intercollegiate Athletics for Women (won by Rutgers) and, for the first time, the NCAA (won by Louisiana Tech). The Women's Basketball League, a professional organization, did not play the season because 6 of its 8 teams dropped out.

BOATING

When Chip Hanauer was growing up in Seattle, his hero was Bill Muncey, the most successful driver in the history of unlimited hy-

In the big boxing match of 1982, Gerry Cooney takes on heavyweight champion Larry Holmes (right). Holmes remained unbeaten by knocking out Cooney in the 13th round.

gery on May 9 in Baltimore for a partially detached retina in the left eye, and he did not want to risk permanent damage from another injury.

Leonard had earned almost $40,000,000 in purses, including $8,000,000 from a title fight against Thomas Hearns in 1981 and $7,000,-000 from a championship bout against Roberto Durán in 1980.

Leonard's big fights had broken records for gross income, but those records were broken when the Larry Holmes–Gerry Cooney bout on June 11 in Las Vegas grossed $40,000,000 to $50,000,000. That was Holmes's 12th defense of the World Boxing Council (WBC) heavyweight title he won in 1978, and it filled a temporary stadium erected in a hotel parking lot.

Both fighters were unbeaten. Cooney had been untested recently, having fought only 6 rounds in the two previous years. Although he fought bravely, Holmes stopped him in the 13th round. Holmes also outpointed Randall ("Tex") Cobb in a Nov. 26 title fight in Houston. Mike Weaver lost his World Boxing Association (WBA) heavyweight title to Michael Dokes on Dec. 10 in Las Vegas; the fight was stopped after only 63 sec. of the first round by the referee.

The busiest champions included Michael Spinks, with 4 defenses of his WBA light-heavyweight title, and Davey Moore, with 3 defenses of his WBA junior-middleweight title. Salvador Sánchez of Mexico, the WBA featherweight champion, was killed on Aug. 12 in the crash of his sports car.

Ray Mancini, whose father was a number-one contender 41 years earlier, became the WBA lightweight champion by knocking out Arturo Frias in one round on May 5 in Las Vegas. Mancini knocked out Duk Koo Kim of South Korea in the 14th round of his first title defense on Nov. 13 in Las Vegas. Kim died of a brain injury four days later.

FOOTBALL

Off-the-field developments overshadowed the games in 1982 football. The NFL endured its first regular-season strike as play shut down for eight weeks at a cost of $450,000,-000. The college game was dominated by maneuvering in and out of court to control hundreds of millions of dollars in television income.

Professional. The Cincinnati Bengals and the San Francisco 49ers advanced to the 1981–82 Super Bowl by winning NFL conference championships on Jan. 10. Cincinnati defeated the San Diego Chargers, 27-7, while San Francisco defeated the Dallas Cowboys, 28-27, on a spectacular touchdown catch by Dwight Clark. The season ended with the 49ers defeating the Bengals, 26-21, in the Super Bowl, held on Jan. 24 in Pontiac, Mich.

The 1982–83 NFL season was two weeks old when the 1500 players struck the 28 clubs on Sept. 21. Six months before, the league had negotiated new television contracts with CBS, NBC, and ABC worth $2.076 billion over

The University of Georgia was the only major college football team to finish the regular 1982 season undefeated and untied. The Bulldogs' star running back, Herschel Walker (34), won the Heisman Trophy as the outstanding college football player of 1982.

five years, the highest sports package ever. The NFL Players Association, the union representing the players, demanded a major share of these proceeds.

First, Ed Garvey, the union's executive director, asked for 55 percent of the club owners' gross income. When the NFL Management Council, which negotiated for the owners, refused, the players sought 50 percent of the television revenue. That, too, was rejected. So was their demand for a central fund to pay negotiated benefits.

Sam Kagel, a 73-year-old San Francisco lawyer and a distinguished arbitrator, mediated the dispute unsuccessfully. Finally, with Paul Martha, the San Francisco 49ers' vice-president and general counsel, as intermediary, an agreement was reached on Nov. 16. The players won $1,600,000,000 over five years in salaries and benefits, in addition to $60,000,000 in immediate bonus money. The demand for a share of gross income or television revenue was dropped.

Games resumed the Sunday following the settlement, and on Dec. 8 the players ratified the contract by a 3–1 margin. They received significant increases in minimum salary, playoff money, and medical pension benefits. For the first time, they negotiated severance pay, to a maximum of $140,000 for a 12th-year player. The union also won the right to certify agents for veteran players.

The league extended the regular season by one week, making for a 9-game season. Sixteen teams rather than ten advanced to the playoffs, which were held over four consecutive weeks.

The NFL was also concerned with a drug scandal, a continuing fight with the Los Angeles Raiders after they had moved from Oakland without league permission, and a new major league.

Don Reece, a former NFL defensive lineman who had been imprisoned as a drug dealer, wrote in *Sports Illustrated* that cocaine "controls and corrupts the league." NFL clubs established rehabilitation programs for players dependent on drugs or alcohol, and more than 40 players participated.

The Raiders and the Los Angeles Coliseum won the retrial of their federal antitrust suit against the NFL for attempting to prevent the Raiders' move. The first suit, in 1981, had ended in a hung jury. The Raiders played 1982 home games in Los Angeles, and the jury was scheduled to decide in 1983 how much money the Raiders and the Coliseum should receive in damages. In December, when a county court ordered the Raiders to return to Oakland after the season, the Raiders said they felt the federal court had precedence.

The 12-team U.S. Football League was formed in 1982 and prepared to play its first season from March to July, 1983. It put teams in Philadelphia, Washington, D.C., Boston, New Jersey, Los Angeles, Oakland, Denver, Phoenix, Chicago, Detroit, Tampa, and Birmingham, Ala. Its head coaches included George Allen, Chuck Fairbanks, and John Ralston, former NFL coaches.

The Edmonton Eskimos won the Grey Cup championship game of the Canadian Football League for a record fifth straight year, defeating the Toronto Argonauts, 32–16, on Nov. 28 in Toronto. Condredge Holloway, the Toronto quarterback, was voted the league's player of the year. The financially troubled Montréal Alouettes franchise was revoked before the season, and a new Montréal Concordes franchise created.

College. The 1982 season ended with an ideal pairing to determine the national champion. Georgia was ranked first and Penn State second in both the Associated Press and United Press International polls at the end of the regular season, and they met on Jan. 1, 1983, in the Sugar Bowl in New Orleans. Penn State won, 27–23.

Herschel Walker, Georgia's running back, won the Heisman Trophy as the outstanding college player. In balloting by writers and broadcasters, Walker received 1926 points to 1231 for the runner-up, quarterback John Elway of Stanford. Walker's average of 159.3 yd. per game rushing was second nationally to the 170.6 registered by Ernest Anderson of Oklahoma State. Walker's three-year total of 5259 yd. rushing left him only 823 yd. short of Tony Dorsett's four-year record.

The major football powers continued their struggle to wrest control of television income from the NCAA. In January the NCAA member colleges reorganized Division I. Of the 139 major teams, 96 remained in Division I-A, and the others were demoted to Division I-AA because their stadiums or crowds were too small. In this way they reduced the number of colleges sharing the largest portion of the $263,500,000 that ABC and CBS were paying for television rights from 1982 to 1985.

Those contracts had been negotiated by the NCAA. Many important football colleges were dissatisfied, and Oklahoma and Georgia sued the NCAA for the right to negotiate their own television contracts.

Oklahoma and Georgia won the first round on Sept. 15 in the U.S. District Court in Oklahoma City, when Judge Juan Burciaga struck down the NCAA's network contracts. On Sept. 22 the NCAA won a stay from the U.S. Court of Appeals in Denver, and the television contracts remained in effect for the time being.

GOLF

Tom Watson overcame a jinx and won the U.S. Open in 1982 for the first time. He also won the British Open for the fourth time.

The victories gave Watson 7 major career championships (4 British Opens, 2 Masters, and 1 U.S. Open), matching Sam Snead,

The NFL season was abbreviated by a two-month-long strike by professional players. An "all-star" game featuring some of the striking players attracted little fan interest.

Gene Sarazen, and Harry Vardon. Ahead of him were Jack Nicklaus (19), Bobby Jones (13), Walter Hagen (11), Ben Hogan (9), Gary Player (9), and Arnold Palmer (8). At age 32, Watson seemed young enough to make inroads on that list.

Watson's 72-hole score of 282 beat Nicklaus by 2 strokes in the U.S. Open June 17–20 in Pebble Beach, Calif. The decisive shot came on the next-to-last hole, when Watson chipped in from the rough.

Four weeks later, in the British Open July 15–18 in Troon, Scotland, Watson's 284 won by a stroke from Nick Price of South Africa and Peter Oosterhuis of Great Britain. Price lost his opportunity with a double bogey and bogey on the last 4 holes.

In the other Grand Slam tournaments, Craig Stadler won the Masters by beating Dan Pohl on the first playoff hole, and Ray Floyd took the Professional Golfers Association (PGA) championship after an opening-round 63. Stadler and Calvin Peete won 4 tournaments each on the tour. Stadler, with $446,462, was the leading money winner on the PGA's $14,500,000, 44-tournament tour, its richest ever.

The Ladies Professional Golf Association (LPGA) conducted 35 American tournaments worth $6,400,000, also a record. JoAnne Carner led in earnings with $310,399, and she and Beth Daniel won 5 tournaments each. Carner was named LPGA player of the year. Kathy Whitworth won twice and broke Mickey Wright's record of 82 career victories. Janet Alex, who had never won in 116 tournaments in five years, captured the U.S. Open. Jan Stephenson of Australia took the LPGA championship.

GYMNASTICS

Soviet and Chinese gymnasts won 15 of the 16 gold medals in the year's most important competition, the World Cup, held Oct. 22–24 in Zagreb, Yugoslavia. Six of China's 7 gold medals were won by one man, 19-year-old Li Ning. Olga Bicherova and Natalia Yurchenko of the Soviet Union, each 16 years old, won 3 gold medals apiece among the women.

The only American medalists were Julianne McNamara, third in the women's vault, and Peter Vidmar, third in the men's horizontal bar. Both were winners in major American meets earlier in the year.

Vidmar, a junior at the University of California at Los Angeles, won the all-around and 2 individual events in the NCAA championships. He also took all-around honors in the U.S. Gymnastics Federation (USGF) championships, though Jim Hartung gained 4 of the 6 apparatus titles. McNamara won the American Cup women's all-around, but narrowly lost the USGF all-around to Tracee Talavera, the defender.

HARNESS RACING

Cam Fella won the Cane Pace and the Messenger, the first and third legs of the triple crown for 3-year-old pacers, as a supplementary entry and was voted harness horse of the year. He did not race in the middle leg, the Little Brown Jug, which Merger won. Mystic Park, Speed Bowl, and Jazz Cosmos took the three legs of the triple crown for 3-year-old trotters.

Tom Watson won the U.S. Open in June and then won the British Open for the fourth time a month later.

Conquistador Cielo ran away from the field to win horse racing's Belmont Stakes for 3-year-olds on June 5 by 14½ lengths.

For the year, Cam Fella won 28 of 33 races and $879,723. In the horse-of-the-year voting, he received 164 of the 309 votes from harness racing officials and writers. Genghis Khan, a 6-year-old pacer, was second; he received 48 votes.

The 3-year-old Arndon recorded the fastest mile ever by a trotter, 1 min. 54 sec., on Oct. 5 in Lexington, Ky. The fastest pacing mile races ever were Genghis Khan's 1 min. 51.8 sec., on Aug. 13 in East Rutherford, N.J., and Trenton's 1 min. 51.6 sec., on Aug. 22 in Springfield, Ill.

HORSE RACING

Tragedy and near tragedy struck down several outstanding thoroughbreds in 1982, notably Timely Writer, Landaluce, and Conquistador Cielo.

Timely Writer, the early Kentucky Derby favorite, missed the triple crown races for 3-year-olds because of a near-fatal intestinal infection. He returned to racing successfully until he shattered a foreleg in a race and was humanely destroyed.

Landaluce, a 2-year-old filly, won her 5 races by a total of 46½ lengths, then died of a bacterial infection. Ten days after Conquistador Cielo's breeding syndication for a record $36,400,000, he raced poorly because of an ankle injury and was retired, but he won the

Eclipse Award as thoroughbred horse of the year.

Conquistador Cielo had gained attention by winning the Metropolitan Handicap on May 31 by 7¼ lengths and the Belmont Stakes five days later by 14½ lengths. In the triple-crown races that preceded the Belmont Stakes, Gato del Sol won the Kentucky Derby and Aloma's Ruler the Preakness.

Still Rarin' to Run

The old gray mare may not be what she used to be, but Port Conway Lane, a 13-year-old gray gelding, was still racing in 1982. By March the thoroughbred, whose coat seemed to grow whiter each year, had 46 career wins in 211 starts and $404,266 in earnings to his credit. The secret of his longevity at the track, said owner-trainer Don Reeder, was "because he's got this game figured out. He knows how to take care of himself. If he's hurting, he'll pull right up. He's not stupid." In 1981, when Reeder sent him to a farm to recuperate from a bruised tendon, "he couldn't stand being away from the track. He stopped eating, lost weight, and seemed broken." After a six-month layoff, Port Conway Lane won his next race.

SPORTS

ICE HOCKEY

In his third season in the National Hockey League (NHL), Wayne Gretzky, the Edmonton Oilers' 20-year-old center, became the most prolific scorer in history. He set single-season records for goals (92), assists (120), total points (212), and 3-goal games (10). He had one 5-goal and three 4-goal games.

On Dec. 30, 1981, he scored 5 goals against the Philadelphia Flyers, giving him 50 goals in 39 games, another record. On Feb. 24, 1982, he scored his 77th goal of the season, breaking the record Phil Esposito set in 1970–71 with the Boston Bruins. Esposito recalled that his father had once told him that he had seen a 14-year-old prodigy named Wayne Gretzky "who will break all your records someday."

Gretzky earned several rewards—a 21-year contract that would pay him about $1,300,-000 a year and make him the highest-paid player in NHL history, a contract provision that gave him a shopping center in western Canada, and his third straight Hart Trophy as the NHL's most valuable player.

The New York Islanders won their third consecutive NHL title in May. Mike Bossy posed with the Stanley Cup trophy after being named the most valuable player in the playoffs.

NATIONAL HOCKEY LEAGUE
1981–82 Regular Season

PRINCE OF WALES CONFERENCE

Patrick Division	W	L	T	Pts.
New York Islanders	54	16	10	118
New York Rangers	39	27	14	92
Philadelphia Flyers	38	31	11	87
Pittsburgh Penguins	31	36	13	75
Washington Capitals	26	41	13	65

Adams Division	W	L	T	Pts.
Montréal Canadiens	46	17	17	109
Boston Bruins	43	27	10	96
Buffalo Sabres	39	26	15	93
Québec Nordiques	33	31	16	82
Hartford Whalers	21	41	18	60

CAMPBELL CONFERENCE

Norris Division	W	L	T	Pts.
Minnesota North Stars	37	23	20	94
Winnipeg Jets	33	33	14	80
St. Louis Blues	32	40	8	72
Chicago Black Hawks	30	38	12	72
Toronto Maple Leafs	20	44	16	56
Detroit Red Wings	21	47	12	54

Smythe Division	W	L	T	Pts.
Edmonton Oilers	48	17	15	111
Vancouver Canucks	30	33	17	77
Calgary Flames	29	34	17	75
Los Angeles Kings	24	41	15	63
Colorado Rockies	18	49	13	49

STANLEY CUP PLAYOFFS

Division Semifinals
New York Islanders defeated Pittsburgh, 3 games to 2
New York Rangers defeated Philadelphia, 3 games to 1
Québec defeated Montréal, 3 games to 2
Boston defeated Buffalo, 3 games to 1
Chicago defeated Minnesota, 3 games to 1
St. Louis defeated Winnipeg, 3 games to 1
Los Angeles defeated Edmonton, 3 games to 2
Vancouver defeated Calgary, 3 games to 0

Division Finals
New York Islanders defeated New York Rangers, 4 games to 2
Chicago defeated St. Louis, 4 games to 2
Vancouver defeated Los Angeles, 4 games to 1
Québec defeated Boston, 4 games to 3

Conference Finals
New York Islanders defeated Québec, 4 games to 0
Vancouver defeated Chicago, 4 games to 1

Championship Finals
New York Islanders defeated Vancouver, 4 games to 0

The New York Islanders had the best regular-season record of the 21 teams. After that they won the Stanley Cup playoffs for the third straight season by defeating the Pittsburgh Penguins, 3 games to 2; the New York Rangers, 4–2; the Québec Nordiques, 4–0; and the Vancouver Canucks, 4–0. The key men for the Islanders were coach Al Arbour, center Bryan Trottier, wing Mike Bossy, and goalie Bill Smith.

The Los Angeles Kings' season was marred by an incident on Jan. 24 in Vancouver, B.C.

Spectacular although erratic, Elaine Zayak performed 7 triple jumps almost flawlessly to win the women's world figure skating championship in March—two months after she lost the U.S. title.

Coach Don Perry ordered a player, Paul Mulvey, to leave the bench and join a fight on the ice, despite rules to the contrary. Mulvey refused, and the team soon sent him to the minor leagues. Meanwhile, the league suspended Perry for 15 games.

ICE SKATING

Scott Hamilton and Elaine Zayak won the world figure skating championships, giving the U.S. its first sweep of these titles in 23 years.

There were so many skaters in the March 9-14 competition in Copenhagen that the men's and women's compulsory figures began at 6 A.M. Hamilton easily retained his title, just as he did in the U.S. championships Jan. 27-30 in Indianapolis.

Going into the women's final day of the world championships, Zayak was seventh, after falling on the ice the previous day. But on the last day, she skated almost flawlessly, especially on her 7 triple jumps. In the nationals, she had skated so erratically in losing to Rosalynn Sumners that her coach gave her a vacation to get her mind off skating.

The world senior speed-skating champions were Hilbert van der Dium of the Netherlands and Karin Busch of East Germany. The leading American was Sarah Docter, fifth among the women.

ROWING

East Germany, which had produced the world's best male rowers since 1966, repeated in 1982. In the world championships Aug. 23-29 in Lucerne, Switzerland, the East German men won 3 gold and 4 silver medals in their 8 events.

The Soviet Union won 5 of the 6 events for women, Italy 3 of the 4 for lightweight men. The U.S. won silver medals in the women's fours and eights, silvers in the lightweight single sculls (Scott Roop of Syracuse, N.Y.) and double sculls, and bronzes in the men's single sculls (John Biglow of Bellevue, Wash.) and fours with coxswain.

Yale and California were the leading college eights. Early in the season, California beat Yale in the San Diego Regatta. Later Yale won the Eastern sprints, California took the Pacific 10 title, and Yale beat California in the new Cincinnati Regatta. Finally, Yale and California lost to English crews in the Henley Royal Regatta in England.

SKIING

Phil and Steve Mahre, 24-year-old American twins, made skiing history in 1982. Phil won the World Cup men's season title for the second consecutive year, with Steve third. In the world championships Jan. 28 to Feb. 7 in

Fastest Ride to Street Level

A new breed of sky divers has foresworn parachuting from airplanes in favor of jumping from fixed, and relatively low, structures such as buildings, bridges, and TV towers. "This is much more exciting than regular parachuting because there's a greater sensation of falling," says one. "It's scary, all right, but that's what makes it worthwhile." Houston is a favorite spot for skydiving thrill seekers because of the construction boom there. In one incident, four sky divers were arrested for jumping off a 200-ft.-high drawbridge but were acquitted by a jury after successfully arguing that the bridge was open to the public. "I told them that if I had a right to be on the bridge, I ought to also have a right to jump off it," said one defendant.

Steve Podborski of Canada (above) was the men's World Cup downhill champion during the 1981-82 season. The overall men's World Cup skiing title went to Phil Mahre of the U.S. for the second consecutive year.

Schladming, Austria, Steve won the giant slalom, the first American man to gain a world championship title race.

Between them, the Mahres won 17 World Cup races. Steve's world title resulted from his first major giant-slalom victory in seven years of international competition, a race he called "the big success of my life."

Erika Hess, 19, of Switzerland, who had quit school to ski full time at the age of 15, won the women's World Cup and 3 gold medals (slalom, giant slalom, and combined) in the world championships. Among the Americans, Christin Cooper finished third and Cindy Nelson fifth in the World Cup. Cooper won 2 silver medals and 1 bronze in the world championships, and Nelson won a silver.

On Jan. 9, in a giant slalom in Morzine-Avoriaz, France, Ingemar Stenmark of Sweden gained his 63rd World Cup career victory. That broke the record of 62 he shared with Annemarie Proell Moser of Austria. Later Stenmark won the world slalom championship.

The American success in Alpine competition spread to Nordic, at least for Bill Koch. The 1976 Olympic medalist became the first American to win the World Cup in cross-country, but except for his bronze medal the Americans finished far back in the Nordic world championships Feb. 19-28 in Oslo.

SOCCER

For most people in the 140 nations that play soccer, the major sports event of 1982 was the quadrennial World Cup competition held June 13 to July 11 in 14 Spanish cities. Italy defeated West Germany, 3-1, in the final in Madrid.

Two years of elimination had reduced the 106 competing nations to 24. The favorites were Brazil, West Germany, and defending champion Argentina. In the second round of the competition, Italy, Brazil, and Argentina were drawn into the same group, with only

Italy's Claudio Gentile (6) is seen in action during the World Cup soccer final in Madrid. The Italians defeated West Germany, 3-1, for their first World Cup title in 44 years.

one to advance. Argentina lost to both Italy and Brazil and was eliminated. Italy then beat Brazil, 3–2, and major Brazilian cities reported sharp increases in suicide attempts, nervous breakdowns, and vandalism.

There was happiness in Kuwait, Cameroon, and Honduras because of strong showings by their teams. Algeria celebrated its team's good play, but was furious when West Germany's 1–0 victory over Austria, with neither team risking anything offensively, advanced both while eliminating Algeria. There was month-long unhappiness among French wives. A poll showed that as many as 800,000 were so upset with the blanket television coverage that they left home during the telecasts.

The American and Canadian teams failed to advance to the World Cup competition in Spain, and the North American Soccer League (NASL) continued to lose franchises, attendance, and money. In addition, the NASL canceled its 1982–83 indoor season. Championship teams included the Cosmos (NASL outdoor), the San Diego Sockers (NASL indoor), and the New York Arrows (Major Indoor Soccer League). Indiana won the NCAA title.

SWIMMING

The U.S., which had been expected to dominate the quadrennial world championships, made a disappointing showing July 29 to Aug. 8 in Guayaquil, Ecuador. East German swimmers led the Americans in total medals (26–25) and gold medals (12–8).

The Americans seemed to have lost their edge from their world championship trials only the week before in Mission Viejo, Calif. As a result, the men won 6 of 15 gold medals (3 in relays), the women only 2 of 14. In 1978 the American men won 11 events, the women 9.

The American individual winners this time were Rick Carey in the men's 200-m backstroke (2 min. 0.82 sec.), Matt Gribble in the men's 100-m butterfly (53.88 sec.), Steve Lundquist in the men's 100-m breaststroke (1 min. 2.75 sec.), Kim Linehan in the women's 800-m freestyle (8 min. 27.48 sec.), and Mary T. Meagher in the women's 100-m butterfly (59.41 sec.).

Tracy Caulkins won 7 national swimming titles in 1982, giving her a career total of 42 to surpass Johnny Weissmuller's 54-year-old record.

Vladimir Salnikov of the Soviet Union captured the men's 400-m and 1500-m freestyle; earlier in the year he broke his world records for the 400-m, 800-m, and 1500-m freestyle. Petra Schneider of East Germany took the women's 200-m and 400-m individual medleys, with Tracy Caulkins, the American star, third in each final. During the year Caulkins won 7 American titles, and her career total of 42 surpassed Johnny Weissmuller's 54-year-old record of 36.

Americans unexpectedly swept the 4 world championships in diving—Greg Louganis in both men's events, Megan Neyer in the women's springboard, and Wendy Wyland in the women's platform.

TENNIS

Jimmy Connors and Martina Navratilova, two champions whose games had slipped, regained their glory in 1982. Connors won the Wimbledon and the U.S. Open men's singles titles, the two most important championships. Navratilova won the Wimbledon women's singles title and enough other competitions to exceed $1,400,000 in tournament earnings during the year and $4,000,000 for her career, the most by any woman in any sport.

Connors defeated John McEnroe, the defender, 3–6, 6–3, 6–7, 7–6, 6–4, on July 4 in the

Wimbledon final in England. In the U.S. Open final on Sept. 12 in New York, Connors subdued Ivan Lendl of Czechoslovakia, 6–3, 6–2, 4–6, 6–4. McEnroe led the U.S. to a 4–1 victory over France Nov. 26–28 in Grenoble, France, in the Davis Cup final, the Americans' fourth cup victory in five years.

Lendl won many rich tournaments, including the Volvo Masters, World Championship of Tennis, Tournament of Champions, and Association of Tennis Professionals championships, and more than $1,600,000 in prize money. Seventeen-year-old Mats Wilander of Sweden captured the French Open. Björn Borg played only a few tournaments.

Navratilova collected a $500,000 bonus from the Playtex Challenge, which offered $1,000,000 to any woman who swept 4 specified tournaments on 4 surfaces, or $500,000 to anyone who won 3 of the 4. The tournaments were the U.S. pro indoor on a synthetic carpet, the Family Circle Cup on clay, Wimbledon on grass, and the U.S. Open on asphalt.

Navratilova won the first two easily. Then she won her third Wimbledon with a 6–1, 3–6, 6–2 triumph over Chris Evert Lloyd. In the U.S. Open, which would have completed the sweep for Navratilova, her doubles partner, Pam Shriver, eliminated her in the quarterfinals. Evert Lloyd won the final from Hana Mandlikova of Czechoslovakia, 6–3, 6–1, for her sixth U.S. Open title. She also defeated Navratilova in the Australian Open.

TRACK AND FIELD

Mary Decker Tabb, who won her first American championship in 1974 as a 15-year-old in pigtails, reached her zenith in 1982.

Tabb broke 3 women's world records during the year—for 5000 m (15 min. 8.26 sec. on June 5 in Eugene, Oreg.), the mile (4 min. 18.08 sec. on July 9 in Paris), and 10,000 m (31 min. 35.3 sec. on July 16 in Eugene). Maricica Puica of Rumania lowered the mile record to 4 min. 17.44 sec. on Sept. 17 in Rieti, Italy.

Tabb broke the 5000-m record by almost 5 sec. and the 10,000-m record by almost 42 sec. She was no longer troubled by tight muscle sheaths in the calves or by shin splints, although she was forced to end her season early because of an inflamed Achilles tendon.

The leading American men included Steve Scott and Sydney Maree in the mile, Alberto Salazar in distance races, Carl Lewis in the long jump, and Bob Roggy in the javelin throw. Foreign heroes included Daley Thompson and David Moorcroft of England.

Thompson twice broke the world record for the decathlon, raising it to 8744 points Sept. 7–8 during the European championships in Athens. Moorcroft set a world record of 13 min. 0.42 sec. for 5000 m on July 7 in Oslo. Ten days later, in London, he won a 3000-m race in 7 min. 32.79 sec., the second fastest time in history.

That 3000-m race was part of a 3-race series that had been set up for Sebastian Coe

Jimmy Connors made a spectacular comeback in 1982. Frequently a loser in recent years to Björn Borg or John McEnroe, Connors won both the Wimbledon and U.S. Open men's singles titles.

Mary Decker Tabb broke three women's world track records in 1982—for the mile, 5000 m, and 10,000 m.

and Steve Ovett, the English world-record holders. The other races were at 800 m on Aug. 14 in Nice, France, and a mile on Sept. 25 in Eugene.

The 3 races were run without Coe and Ovett, both of whom lost much of the season because of injuries. They reportedly had agreed to this series because of large financial guarantees. Such appearance money, although it violated the rules, was common. The International Amateur Athletic Federation, the sport's world governing body, attempted to end the hypocrisy by approving trust funds, thus allowing athletes to accept appearance money in certain cases. The athletes could draw against the trust funds for training expenses and collect the balance when they retired.   F.L.

SRI LANKA, formerly CEYLON. On Oct. 20, 1982, Sri Lanka's President Junius R. Jayawardene, 76, won a new six-year term and a popular mandate for his "open economy" policies. After Jayawardene's United National Party swept a socialist party out of office in the 1977 elections, Sri Lanka abandoned the former parliamentary form of democracy that it had inherited from the British and created a presidential system.

Prime Minister Jayawardene became the country's first president.

At issue in Sri Lanka's first presidential election was Jayawardene's policy of Western-style capitalism, which had caused an economic boom on the tropical island by welcoming foreign investment and encouraging private business. As commerce flourished, unemployment declined sharply and food shortages disappeared. At the same time, however, inflation soared and budget deficits rose. The poor were hungry because food subsidies were ended, and people on fixed incomes suffered from a drop in the buying power of the rupee.

The opposition Freedom Party, led by Hector Kobbekaduwa, attacked the inequities of the free-market system and called for a return to socialism. But "J. R.," as Jayawardene was popularly known, won with surprising ease, polling about 53 percent of the vote. Kobbekaduwa won about 37 percent of the vote, with the remainder divided among four other candidates.

On Dec. 22, in a national referendum, voters approved a constitutional amendment extending the life of parliament from August, 1983, to August, 1989. Jayawardene said that he needed to retain the current parliament to complete work on his programs.

On July 30 the government imposed its third state of emergency since 1977, in an attempt to control violence between the majority Sinhalese and the minority Tamils. Press censorship was imposed, as was a curfew in the town of Galle, 65 mi. south of Colombo, the capital.

Like most countries with economies based on agricultural exports, Sri Lanka was affected by the worldwide recession in 1982. Prices for its rubber, tea, and coconut products slumped on the world market, causing a payments problem. But the government hastened plans to develop light industry.

A charter member of the group of nonaligned nations, Sri Lanka generally remained noncommittal on foreign policy questions. Nevertheless, the government adopted a slightly pro-Western attitude on several international issues.

See STATISTICS OF THE WORLD.   R.J.C.

STAMPS, POSTAGE. Anniversaries of famous people and events and concern for world health and ecology were among subjects featured on postage stamps issued in 1982.

U.S. Issues. The U.S. Postal Service released 78 commemorative and special stamps during the year. Famous Americans who were honored included Ralph Bunche, Jackie Robinson, Franklin D. Roosevelt, Mary Walker, George Washington, and, in the continuing Performing Arts series, the Barrymore family. A block of four 20¢ stamps publicized the Knoxville, Tenn., World's Fair and a block of four se tenant stamps (that is, stamps joined on the original sheets but different in design) completed the American Architecture series that was begun in 1979. A unique issue of 50 different 20¢ stamps featured the official bird and flower of each state. Among other themes, persons, and places portrayed on U.S. stamps were Aging, Horatio Alger, the International Peace Garden, Libraries of America, the Library of Congress, Ponce de Leon, St. Francis of Assisi, Touro Synagogue, U.S.–Netherlands relations, and Wolf Trap Farm Park.

The annual Christmas stamp issue consisted of a block of four different contemporary designs and a single stamp with the traditional religious art masterpiece theme. A 13¢ special stamp was also issued for use on holiday postcards.

New definitive stamps were issued in the following denominations: 2¢ (2), 4¢, 5.9¢, 10.9¢, 13¢, 20¢ (2), and 37¢. Postal stationery

Opposite page: Outstanding stamps of 1982. Top row (left to right): Europa issue from France; Canada notes its International Philatelic Youth Exhibition; Great Britain commemorates the centenary of Charles Darwin's death. Second row (left to right): Ethiopia notes the International Soccer Games held in Madrid; Malta's special issue for the elderly; Ireland stresses ecology. Third row (left to right): The U.S. features its notable architecture and publicizes the Knoxville World's Fair. Fourth row (left to right): The British Virgin Islands honors Diana, Princess of Wales; the Falkland Islands issues a semipostal stamp to raise funds for rebuilding after its war with Argentina; Norway celebrates the 25th anniversary of King Olav V. Fifth row (left to right): The 75th anniversary of the international scouting movement is commemorated by Barbados, Fiji, St. Lucia, and Argentina.

items included five 13¢ commemorative postal cards, a 28¢ airmail postal card, a 5.9¢ (for nonprofit organizations) and two 20¢ embossed stamped envelopes, and a 30¢ aerogram.

Worldwide Issues. The event most widely commemorated on stamps issued in 1982 was the 75th anniversary of the scouting movement founded by Sir Robert Baden-Powell; it was also the 125th anniversary of the birth of the founder. More than 75 nations issued special stamps in recognition of these occasions.

Other major events that received the special attention of many postal administrations were the World Cup soccer matches held in Madrid, the 21st birthday of Diana, Princess of Wales, and the annual Europa issues by members of the European Communities. Conservation of energy and natural resources was also featured on many special issues.

United Nations Issues. The U.N. Postal Administration (UNPA) released issues commemorating the 10th anniversary of the U.N. Environmental Program, Exploration and Peaceful Uses of Outer Space, and the Conservation and Protection of Nature. These stamps were issued simultaneously at the UNPA facilities in New York City, Geneva, and Vienna, in the currency of the respective country. Six new regular issues were released in the following denominations: 17¢, 28¢, and 40¢ in New York; 30C and 1Fr in Geneva; and 3S in Vienna. The third annual group of 16 flag stamps was released only in New York for the continuing series recognizing member nations. The countries whose flags were represented were, in the order printed: Austria, Seychelles, Malaysia, Republic of Ireland, Mozambique, Albania, Dominica, Solomon Islands, Philippines, Swaziland, Nicaragua, Burma, Cape Verde, Guyana, Belgium, and Nigeria.

Rare Stamp Sales. Prices for many rare stamps declined from the record levels established in the late 1970's. Major auction houses in the United States and abroad reported more conservative bidding, but with some record prices paid for very scarce items.

A single copy of the famous 1918 24¢ airmail issue with an inverted picture of an air-

This caged 14-month-old Florida panther had no trouble capturing the attention of the Florida house of representatives when he was brought to the chamber in March. The panther nosed out the alligator in legislative balloting for Florida's state animal.

plane—the "Upside-Down Jenny"—brought $198,000 at an auction in New York in April. The previous record price for this stamp had been $176,000. A copy of the 15¢ Columbus issue of 1893 with an inverted center was also sold for $198,000 at this auction. The prices were the highest ever paid for U.S. stamps. A rare Bermuda 1853 Perot 1-penny red was auctioned in May at Geneva for a record price of $154,000. J.W.K.

STATE GOVERNMENT REVIEW. Trends in state government in 1982 included a shared concern with crime—particularly drunk driving—and with revenue shortfalls. The November elections brought substantial Democratic Party gains in the statehouses and legislatures. U.S. President Ronald Reagan's call for a "new federalism," under which the states would assume responsibility for more than 40 federal programs, including food stamps and Aid to Families with Dependent Children, received a less than enthusiastic reception from state governors; *see* UNITED STATES OF AMERICA.

Crime. Spurred by citizen lobby groups, more than 30 states passed new drunk-driving laws or toughened old ones. Most popular were mandatory minimum jail terms,

higher fines, community work in lieu of jail, and license suspensions. Several states also raised the legal drinking age, so that by the end of 1982 no more than five states still allowed 18-year-olds to drink. A study released in December by the National Highway Traffic Safety Administration showed that alcohol was involved in up to 55 percent of all fatal highway crashes.

Popular among other new laws dealing with criminal justice were those directly aiding crime victims or requiring courts to consider victims when sentencing criminals. New funds for victim assistance programs were provided in Hawaii, Indiana, and Kentucky. Judges would be required to consider the plight of victims when passing sentence in Maryland, New York, and Vermont. Bail or parole was restricted in Colorado, Florida, Illinois, Iowa, Kansas, and Wisconsin. States that increased funds for prisons included Alabama, California, Florida, Kansas, Ohio, Oklahoma, and Texas. The New Jersey legislature approved capital punishment, as did voters in Massachusetts. Several states passed laws setting forth penalties for the sale of drug paraphernalia and related items. Maryland, Ohio, and Virginia joined the ranks of states that impose additional penalties when a gun is used in committing a crime.

Although it was a federal and not a state trial, the acquittal by reason of insanity of John W. Hinckley, Jr., on charges of shooting President Reagan renewed state officials' concern about the insanity defense. Verdicts of guilty but mentally ill had been adopted by at least eight states, while a few had done away entirely with the insanity defense.

Fiscal Crunch. Budget problems outweighed most other state concerns. Federal funding reductions, high unemployment, the recession, and past tax cuts combined to make the going rough. Most states had to trim spending, make accounting changes, freeze hiring, lay off workers, raise taxes, or take other actions to avoid constitutionally prohibited deficit budgets. Despite all efforts, six of the 46 states that ended their fiscal year on June 30 had deficits: Connecticut, Minnesota, New Hampshire, Ohio, Oregon, and Washington. By fall revenue forecasts for fiscal

1983 looked bleak, and more than half the states had to make cuts in budgets passed earlier in the year.

Michigan had the nation's highest unemployment rate in late 1982, followed by Ohio. Such lumber-dependent states as Oregon and Washington were also hard hit. High unemployment not only ate into tax revenues but also imposed a welfare burden on the states. Twenty-one of them exhausted jobless benefits, forcing them to borrow from the federal government, trim benefits, or increase unemployment taxes. At the same time, the federal government began charging 10 percent interest on unemployment fund loans, which had previously been interest-free. Federal cuts also led many states to close or reduce staffs in unemployment offices even as the ranks of the jobless expanded.

Taxes. At least 28 states raised taxes in 1982, according to the Federation of Tax Administrators. Five increased sales taxes: Florida, from 4 to 5 percent; Missouri, 3.125 to 4.125 percent; Nebraska, 3 to 3.5 percent until the end of 1982; Vermont, 3 to 4 percent; and Wisconsin, 4 to 5 percent. Washington adopted a surtax of 4 percent and imposed the sales tax on food.

Income taxes were raised in Alabama, Michigan, Minnesota, Nebraska, Ohio, Oregon, Rhode Island, and Vermont. Corporate income taxes were raised in several states to prevent revenue losses stemming from the federal Economic Recovery Tax Act (ERTA) of 1981. (State tax losses as a result of ERTA were estimated at $290,900,000, according to a survey of budget officers by the Council of State Governments.)

Gasoline or diesel fuel taxes went up to pay for roads in Arizona, Idaho, Kentucky, Maryland, Vermont, and Virginia. Higher gas taxes were defeated by voters in Missouri and Oregon. Out of the nine jurisdictions with variable-rate motor fuel taxes tied to gasoline prices, taxes increased in Nebraska, New Mexico, Ohio, and the District of Columbia. Rhode Island imposed a 1 percent gross receipts tax on oil companies. Cigarette taxes went up in Michigan, Missouri, Nebraska, New Jersey, Oregon, Rhode Island,

Utah, Washington, and Wisconsin. Another "sin tax," on alcohol, rose in Alabama, Kentucky, New Mexico, Utah, Virginia, and Washington.

The outstanding exception to this tax-raising pattern was Alaska, which on June 17 began mailing out $1000 checks to state residents. More than 400,000 adults and children who had lived in the state for six months or more were eligible for the payment, drawn on a $3.1 billion fund from petroleum royalties. Payments of $356 and $247 were projected for 1983 and 1984, respectively.

Election Issues. The November elections offered little evidence of a tax revolt. Oregon voters defeated a property tax rollback proposed on the November ballot. Other tax-related votes included approval of less than the 100 percent assessments that had been ordered by a court in a school-finance case in West Virginia, increased property tax relief for Utah homeowners, higher state property taxes for education in Wyoming, and removal from the Texas constitution of a state property tax already out of the statutes.

In the Nov. 2 balloting, voters endorsed a bilateral nuclear arms freeze in eight of the nine states where a freeze resolution appeared on the ballot statewide. Criminal justice measures did well; several states passed limitations on the use of bail in serious criminal cases, and California voters approved a victims' bill of rights. "Bottle bills" seeking to require deposits on beverage containers lost on ballots in four states. The only major gambling expansion approved in November was pari-mutuel betting at Minnesota race tracks. (Oklahomans had voted in a special election in September to allow counties to permit pari-mutuels.) Georgians ratified a new constitution, and District of Columbia voters adopted a new charter as a possible step toward statehood. Some $3 billion in bond issues also won approval.

Elected Officials. A major accomplishment as of late October was the completion of congressional redistricting by 36 states and of state legislative redistricting by 39 states. Court challenges or U.S. Department of Justice objections were pending against many of these changes, however. The districts

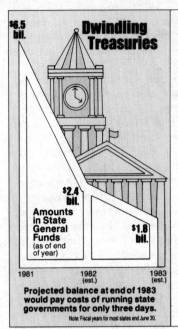

Dwindling Treasuries

$6.5 bil.

$2.4 bil.

Amounts in State General Funds (as of end of year)

$1.8 bil.

1981   1982 (est.)   1983 (est.)

Projected balance at end of 1983 would pay costs of running state governments for only three days.

Note: Fiscal years for most states end June 30.

Where States Are Headed

Projected state surpluses and deficits for 1983 with which legislatures had to cope—
(based on budget recommendations of governors early in 1982)

	Surplus or Deficit			Surplus or Deficit
Alabama	−$ 11 mil.	Montana	−$ 5 mil.
Alaska	+$335 mil.	Nebraska	+$ 132 mil.
Arizona	−$ 60 mil.	Nevada	−$ 5 mil.
Arkansas	+$ 3 mil.	New Hampshire	+$ 31 mil.
California	+$377 mil.	New Jersey	−$ 100 mil.
Colorado	+$ 84 mil.	New Mexico	−$ 86 mil.
Connecticut	+$ 34 mil.	New York	0
Delaware	+$ 9 mil.	North Carolina	+$ 88 mil.
Florida	−$189 mil.	North Dakota	−$ 89 mil.
Georgia	0	Ohio	−$1,223 mil.
Hawaii	−$101 mil.	Oklahoma	−$ 305 mil.
Idaho	−$ 10 mil.	Oregon	+$ 84 mil.
Illinois	+$ 30 mil.	Pennsylvania	−$ 2 mil.
Indiana	−$ 62 mil.	Rhode Island	−$ 4 mil.
Iowa	+$157 mil.	South Carolina	+$ 5 mil.
Kansas	+$ 84 mil.	South Dakota	−$ 5 mil.
Kentucky	−$ 4 mil.	Tennessee	+$ 12 mil.
Louisiana	+$ 77 mil.	Texas	−$ 299 mil.
Maine	+$ 16 mil.	Utah	−$ 11 mil.
Maryland	−$145 mil.	Vermont	0
Massachusetts	−$ 62 mil.	Virginia	−$ 173 mil.
Michigan	0	Washington	+$ 182 mil.
Minnesota	+$811 mil.	West Virginia	−$ 9 mil.
Mississippi	−$ 25 mil.	Wisconsin	−$ 24 mil.
Missouri	+$ 39 mil.	Wyoming	+$ 20 mil.

Note: Figures are for year that ends next June 30 in most states.

USN&WR—Basic data: National Governors' Association

were redrawn to match 1980 census figures in accordance with one-person, one-vote requirements.

Of the 36 governorships up for election in November, Democrats won 27 for a net gain of seven. Democrats also picked up an additional 11 state legislative houses, giving them control of both houses of the legislature in 34 states. In only ten states would Republicans control both chambers in 1983. There would be new governors in 18 states in 1983. The nation's three largest states elected new governors: California, George Deukmejian (R); New York, Mario M. Cuomo (D); and Texas, Mark White (D). See also ELECTIONS IN THE UNITED STATES.

Other Developments. A resolution calling for a constitutional convention in order to enact an amendment mandating a balanced federal budget was passed by Alaska—the 31st state to do so. The proposed Equal Rights Amendment fell three states short of the 38 needed for adoption when the deadline for ratification passed on June 30.

Among innovative state programs was Massachusetts's system of matching welfare recipients' social security numbers against bank deposits; the operation turned up a number of recipients with too much cash to qualify for benefits. Connecticut passed the first state law requiring automobile manufacturers to repair or replace defective models.

With the addition in 1982 of Colorado and Washington, 17 states and the District of Columbia had government-run lotteries. A growing number of states required child restraints in motor vehicles. Arizona joined the federal Medicaid system with its own prepaid system. New York became the ninth state to require deposits on soda pop bottles. As authorized by federal law, numerous states began establishing regional radioactive waste compacts.

Alabama enacted a school prayer law that was immediately challenged by civil libertarians. Louisiana laws mandating school prayer and the teaching of "creation science" as an alternative to the theory of evolution were each overturned in the courts. A similar Arkansas creation science law was also overturned. A Tennessee law mandating a "minute of silence" in public schools was declared unconstitutional.

See also STATISTICS OF THE WORLD.   E.S.K.

SUDAN. In an attempt to pool their resources, President Gaafar Mohammed al-Nimeiry of the Sudan and President Hosni Mubarak of Egypt signed a "charter of integration" in Khartoum on Oct. 12, 1982. The ten-year agreement stopped short of a formal political union. Instead, the pact envisioned measures ranging from the gradual abolition of customs duties to an effort to coordinate foreign policy goals. It represented an Egyptian commitment to protect the shaky regime of Nimeiry, who had survived at least five coup attempts in his 13 years in power. The accord also would protect Egypt's exposed southern border and the source of the Nile River.

Angered by complaints from the military over corruption in the government, Nimeiry dismissed Lt. Gen. Abdul Magid Hamid Khalil as vice-president, minister of defense, and secretary of the Sudanese Socialist Union, the nation's only legal political party, in January. He also dismissed 22 other high army officers. Earlier, on Jan. 4, police arrested 21 politicians in the predominantly black (rather than Arab) south Sudan who opposed efforts to redivide the area. Although Nimeiry had ended a 17-year civil war in 1972 by granting the south a large measure of autonomy, in late 1981 he dissolved the region's ruling bodies and replaced them with a military-led administration of his own choosing. A new assembly was elected in June, when a new executive commission was appointed.

The high cost of imported oil, on which the modern sector of the economy was heavily dependent, left the treasury virtually without cash in 1982. Fuel shortages in Khartoum were so severe that armed Sudanese soldiers had to stand guard at gas stations. The size of gasoline rations was reduced a further 25 percent in September. Acute shortages of food, gasoline, and other goods caused recurrent antigovernment demonstrations in Khartoum and other cities.

The official Sudan press agency announced on Oct. 3 that Sudanese troops would fight on Iraq's side in its war against Iran, but it did not say how many soldiers would be sent or when they would leave. Sudan's decision was made, according to the announcement, in accordance with a resolution adopted at the September Arab summit in Fez, Morocco, under which foreign aggression on the territory of any Arab country would be regarded as an aggression against all Arab nations.

The Sudan played a part in resolving the Lebanon crisis by agreeing to accept about 500 of the Palestinian fighters who withdrew from Beirut in late August.

See STATISTICS OF THE WORLD.   A.D.

SUPREME COURT OF THE UNITED STATES. In 1982 the U.S. Supreme Court issued significant opinions in the areas of individual rights, sex discrimination, and criminal rights. Key decisions allowed children of illegal aliens to receive a free public education and granted immunity to the President for any official actions taken while in office.

The membership of the Court remained the same in 1982, as Associate Justice Sandra Day O'Connor completed her first term on the High Court bench. Increasing polarization between the Court's conservatives and liberals led to 5–4 decisions in 33 cases, nearly one quarter of the decisions announced by the Court and twice as many as in 1981. In public speeches during the summer, several justices complained about the Court's growing workload.

Individual Rights. In two important areas the Court took an expansive view of individual rights. A 5–4 majority ruled on June 15 that children of illegal aliens cannot be denied a free public school education. The ruling invalidated a Texas law that allowed local school districts to charge illegal alien children a fee for tuition or to bar them from attending school. In striking down the law, the Court held, for the first time, that illegal aliens are "persons" covered under the equal protection clause of the Fourteenth Amendment. The Court did not address the question of whether illegal aliens are entitled to welfare, food stamps, or other tax-supported benefits.

In another significant ruling, the Court held, for the first time, that involuntarily institutionalized retarded persons have constitutional protection under the Fourteenth Amendment's due process clause. The unanimous decision on June 18 stated that

Amish farmer Ed Lee with his family in front of the Supreme Court Building in Washington, D.C. Lee lost his case when the High Court ruled in February that he must pay social security taxes for his employees even though doing so violates his religion's doctrines of self-reliance. After his farm was attached by the Internal Revenue Service, Lee sought legislation exempting Amish employers from the requirement.

mentally retarded persons in state institutions have the right to live in reasonably safe conditions, to be free from unreasonable physical restraints, and to receive "minimally adequate" training in caring for themselves. The Court allowed doctors and mental health professionals to determine when and under what conditions such institutionalized persons could be bodily confined, and allowed states individually to determine "adequate" training standards.

Official Immunity. In a 5–4 decision announced on June 24, the Court ruled that the President of the United States must be absolutely immune from liability for official actions if the chief executive is to function "fearlessly and impartially." In a companion decision, the Court ruled, 8–1, that Presidential aides are entitled to "qualified immunity" from lawsuits stemming from their official actions. The Court gave such aides the same degree of immunity afforded cabinet officers and other high-level officials.

In a 7–2 ruling announced on June 21, the Court held that individuals suing state and local officials for civil rights violations do not have to exhaust all state remedies before filing suit in federal court. On Jan. 13 the Court ruled, 5–3, that localities are not immune from antitrust liability for actions taken in the absence of state policy or authorization.

Sex Discrimination. In two rulings that pleased women's rights advocates, the Court held, by a 5–4 vote on July 1, that men could not be excluded from a state-run nursing school in Mississippi, and, by a 6–3 vote on May 17, that a 1972 federal law banning sex discrimination in federally financed educational programs covers employees as well as students. See WOMEN.

Capital Punishment. On Jan. 19 the Supreme Court overturned the death sentence of a youth convicted of murdering an Oklahoma state trooper when he was 16 years old. By a 5–4 vote, the justices found that the trial judge had not given adequate consideration to possible mitigating circumstances, but the Court did not rule on whether execution of a juvenile violates the prohibition against cruel and unusual punishment.

In another 5–4 decision, announced on July 2, the Court ruled that the death sentence cannot be imposed on a criminal accomplice who neither planned nor directly participated in a killing that occurred during the commission of another crime.

Criminal Rights. Clarifying a confused area of the law, the Court held, by a 6–3 vote on June 1, that police may conduct warrantless searches of luggage, packages, and other closed containers found in automobiles if there is probable cause to believe the containers hold incriminating evidence. A 6–3 majority ruled on Jan. 13 that police do not need a search warrant to accompany an arrested person into his home or to seize any incriminating evidence they see "in plain view."

Decisions announced in March and April restricted the availability of federal habeas corpus review to state prisoners. By a 5–4 vote on June 7, the Court held that the constitutional protection against double jeopardy was not violated when a criminal defendant was retried on the same charges after an appeals court had overturned his conviction based on the "weight of the evidence."

On March 3 the Court unanimously upheld the power of localities to curb the sale of drug paraphernalia in "head shops."

Parental Rights. By a 5–4 vote on March 24, the Court decided that states must have "clear and convincing" evidence of child abuse or neglect before terminating rights of natural parents. The ruling struck down laws in more than a dozen states that allowed involuntary termination of parental rights on a showing of a "fair preponderance" of the evidence. In a 6–3 ruling on June 30, the Court precluded federal courts from hearing child custody cases that had already been determined in state courts. On April 5 the Court unanimously invalidated a Texas law imposing a one-year limit on the filing of paternity suits.

First Amendment Rights. Ruling that political boycotts are protected under the First Amendment, the Court, by an 8–0 vote on July 2, voided a judgment of more than $1,000,000 in damages imposed by Mississippi courts against the National Association for the Advancement of Colored People for economic losses to white merchants in a civil rights boycott that began in 1966. Also on July 2, the Court unanimously held that states can prevent the distribution of material depicting sexual activities of children under 16, even if the material is not legally obscene.

By a 6–3 vote on June 23, the Court struck down a Massachusetts law excluding the press and public during the trial testimony of sex-crime victims under the age of 18. Two days later, the Court held, in a fragmented ruling, that the First Amendment limits the discretion of school boards to censor reading

material. The decision allowed several New York high school students to challenge in federal court their school board's decision to ban certain books from the school library. *See* LIBRARIES.

Civil Rights. In a 6–3 decision issued on July 1, the Court held that intentional discrimination in a voting rights case can be proved by circumstantial, as well as direct, evidence. The decision was expected to make it easier for minorities to challenge long-standing discriminatory voting procedures.

In a 6–3 decision, the Court on June 28 supported a 1975 federal law providing a "free appropriate public education" to handicapped students, but held that states only need to ensure that such students achieve passing marks and advance from grade to grade. The case, originally brought by a deaf student who sought a full-time sign-language interpreter, marked the first argument before the Court by a deaf lawyer.

See also CIVIL RIGHTS AND CIVIL LIBERTIES; HOUSING; LABOR; NEGROES IN THE UNITED STATES. D.C.

SURINAME. *See* STATISTICS OF THE WORLD. *See also* CARIBBEAN COUNTRIES.

SWAZILAND. *See* STATISTICS OF THE WORLD.

SWEDEN. Former Prime Minister Olof Palme returned to power in Sweden in October, 1982, as the head of a Socialist government, following elections on Sept. 19.

Palme's Social Democratic Party, in opposition for six years, polled 46 percent of the vote, increasing its strength in the 349-seat *Riksdag* (parliament) from 154 seats to 166. With the support of the Communists, who polled 5.6 percent of the vote, enough to retain their 20 seats, the Social Democrats were able to form a parliamentary majority. The strongest of the non-Socialist parties, the conservative Moderate Party, polled about 23 percent, raising the number of its seats from 73 to 85. The Center Party, with 16 percent, declined in strength from 64 seats to 56. The Liberals lost 16 of their 38 seats and polled only 6 percent of the vote.

Palme took office as prime minister on Oct. 7, heading a Social Democratic cabinet. During the election campaign he had berated the government for reducing social programs and had pledged to add 30,000 new jobs to the Swedish economy, largely through government investments funded by an increase in Sweden's 22 percent sales tax, already the highest in Europe. The unemployment rate, at 3.5 percent of the labor force in September, was one of the lowest in the world, but, Palme warned, it could climb to 5 percent, a rate that Swedes would not "stand for." Palme also took note of a decline in Sweden's industrial production, which threatened the Swedes' standard of living, said to be the second highest in the world.

On Oct. 8 the new government imposed a temporary price freeze and a 16 percent devaluation of the krona, a move intended to make Swedish exports more competitive in world markets and thus increase employment. The value-added tax was increased to nearly 23.5 percent, and some tax shelters were cut. Sweden's Nordic neighbors assailed the devaluation as a threat to their own trade balances. Their reaction included a 6 percent currency devaluation by Finland on Oct. 10 and a cut by Norway on Oct. 11 of the duty-free allowance on goods brought from Sweden to Norway.

Controversy erupted after a submarine periscope was sighted on Oct. 1 in restricted waters near a Swedish naval base. The Swedish navy attempted to trap what it presumed to be a Soviet submarine, but ultimately it gave up the effort as a failure and on Oct. 26 called off the hunt.

See STATISTICS OF THE WORLD.　　L.A.S.

SWITZERLAND. Real output in Switzerland was expected to fall by 1.5 percent in 1982, the first year of negative growth since the mid-1970's. However, unemployment totaled only 0.4 percent of the Swiss labor force.

On April 25 the Swiss women's rights movement suffered a defeat when, with only men permitted to vote, the electorate of the small canton of Appenzell, Inner-Rhoden, voted 4-1 to continue to bar women from voting in local elections. Women already had the vote in federal balloting.

On June 6 Swiss voters defeated a proposed law to ease restrictions on foreign workers. The law would have permitted foreign workers to change jobs after a year and, in some circumstances, to bring their dependents to Switzerland after six months.

In another referendum on June 6 the Swiss approved a measure providing for more severe penalties against convicted rioters. Incitement to demonstrations that cause damage was made punishable by jail terms of up to three years. The law also authorized the government to take action on criminal charges against demonstrators who injure people or damage property, even if victims refuse to file complaints. The bill was proposed in reaction to recent disturbances in Zürich.

In still another referendum, on Nov. 28, a constitutional amendment was approved mandating permanent price controls in the form of government "surveillance of prices and price recommendations for goods and services." The annual inflation rate had increased to what Swiss citizens regarded as a disturbingly high 6.2 percent.

On March 22 the federal government, acting on a decision it had announced in December, 1981, asked parliament to approve Swiss membership in the United Nations. In view, however, of public opinion polls showing that such membership was unpopular, the government promised to affirm Switzerland's traditional neutrality even after the country joined the U.N. On Aug. 18 the government agreed in principle to bring Switzerland into the International Monetary Fund and the World Bank, as well.

On Sept. 6 four armed Polish émigrés seized the Polish embassy, along with 13 hostages, in Bern. They held the embassy for three days, until Swiss police stormed the building on Sept. 9 and captured them. By that time the number of hostages had been reduced to five. The four terrorists had demanded that Poland lift martial law, free political prisoners, and end repression.

On Sept. 1 Switzerland, in a relaxation of its tight code of secrecy on banking matters, reached an agreement with the United States to provide information to the U.S. Securities and Exchange Commission, when requested, on bank clients suspected of "insider trading" on securities in the U.S. (The practice

Syrian troops wave greetings to a convoy of Palestinian fighters arriving in Syria after evacuation from Beirut, Lebanon. Syria was badly outclassed in fighting with Israel, but a large force remained entrenched in northern and eastern Lebanon.

was illegal in the U.S. but not in Switzerland.)

See STATISTICS OF THE WORLD.   L.A.S.

SYRIA. After crushing a rebellion by Muslim fundamentalists in early 1982, Syrian President Hafez al-Assad appeared more firmly in power than ever. But Syria remained relatively isolated in the Arab world, and it suffered severe losses in combat against Israel in Lebanon.

Domestic Affairs. In early February Assad ordered Syrian troops to wipe out an antigovernment rebellion by well-armed members of the Muslim Brotherhood in the city of Hama, 120 mi. northeast of Damascus, the capital. Two army brigades, equipped with tanks and artillery, surrounded the city and carried out a devastating three-week siege. Whole neighborhoods were destroyed in the bombardments. The city was forbidden to news reporters for two months afterward, but Western diplomats estimated that 5000 to 10,000 civilians and rebels died in the fighting or were buried in the rubble. Assad had decided to make Hama an object lesson to his political opponents, who had carried out a number of coup attempts or terrorist acts since 1979. Apparently they got the message: In the months after Hama, there were no further antigovernment incidents.

Lacking large oil reserves, and with imports of consumer goods outstripping exports, Syria was plagued with chronic trade deficits and severe shortages of foreign currency. Its economic woes were aggravated by the government's maverick politics. Because of its support for Iran against Iraq, Saudi Arabia and other Persian Gulf states were said to be reassessing the $1.5 billion annual subsidy they had been contributing to Syria.

War in Lebanon. Syria and Israel clashed heavily on the ground and in the air in the early days of the war in Lebanon following Israel's attack on June 6. Syria lost 80 or more of its Soviet-made MiG-21 and MiG-23 jet fighters (according to Israel) in two consecutive days of dogfights against Israelis flying American-made F-15 and F-16 fighters. (Syria conceded losing 60 planes.) The Israelis also knocked out between 20 and 30 Soviet-made SAM-6 antiaircraft missile batteries in eastern Lebanon as well as 10 T-72 tanks, the fastest and most powerful tank the Soviets had distributed abroad. Military analysts attributed Israel's lopsided victory over the Syrians to the superiority of American over Soviet equipment, and to the Israelis' better use of advanced-technology weapons.

On the ground, Israeli forces succeeded in pushing Syrian forces off the Beirut–Damascus highway—a vital link between Damascus and the Mediterranean coast—and in bottling up 2000 Syrian troops in west Beirut. Throughout most of July and August, Israel and Syria observed a tense cease-fire in Lebanon. The Syrian troops trapped in west Beirut left the city on Aug. 30, along with Palestine Liberation Organization (PLO) fighters, following an agreement negotiated by U.S. special envoy Philip C. Habib that ended Israel's siege of west Beirut. Syria kept large numbers of troops in northern and eastern Lebanon and refused to withdraw them until Israel withdrew its own troops from southern Lebanon.

Foreign Relations. Despite its setbacks in the war in Lebanon, Syria remained at odds with the United States and most fellow Arab countries. Assad did not express outright opposition to U.S. President Ronald Reagan's Middle East peace plan of Sept. 1, and he helped to promote the peace plan announced on Sept. 9 at the Arab League summit meeting held in Fez, Morocco. But, as Reagan administration officials had expected, Syria played a role that was seen by Washington as helping stall the peace process. Syria exerted pressure on the PLO leadership to refuse to recognize Israel and to refuse to allow Jordan's King Hussein to negotiate on behalf of the Palestinians.

Syria also remained, with Libya, the only Arab country to back Iran against Iraq in the Persian Gulf war. In April Syria closed Iraq's oil pipeline running through Syria to the Mediterranean coast, through which 40 percent of Iraq's petroleum exports flowed. Syria also closed its border with Iraq, preventing overland shipments from reaching Baghdad, and it was said to have supplied Iran with some Soviet arms.

See STATISTICS OF THE WORLD.   A.D.

T

TAIWAN, *or* **FORMOSA,** seat of the Republic of China. Taiwan enjoyed a year of relative political calm in 1982, under the government of President Chiang Ching-kuo (Jiang Jingguo) and his ruling Kuomintang Party. The country's export-based economy underwent difficulties, however, arising from the worldwide recession and the need to upgrade production technology.

During the first eight months of 1982 exports fell by 2 percent, but imports dropped by 12.4 percent, resulting in a favorable trade balance of nearly $1.8 billion. Prices were expected to rise only 4 percent during the year, the unemployment rate stood at less than 2 percent, and the gross national product was expected to increase by 4 percent.

In February an import ban on 1533 Japanese consumer items went into effect. Taiwan rebuffed Japan's March 4 request for "immediate" revocation of the ban, insisting that Tokyo first open its domestic market to such Taiwanese exports as farm and fishery goods. Moreover, Taiwan believed that Japan was unduly favoring the People's Republic of China, as well as South Korea, an important competitor of Taiwan in international markets.

In September the Ministry of Finance disclosed a three-point plan to deal with the economic slowdown. It called for reliance on the private sector for capital formation, a reduction in government spending, a comprehensive tax reform, including the closing of tax loopholes, and improved efficiency in the banking system.

Taipei was heartened in April by the U.S. announcement that Washington planned to sell $60,000,000 worth of spare parts to Taiwan for F-5E fighter planes that were produced in Taiwan under U.S. license. Strong protests from Peking, however, caused the United States to delay delivery.

Taipei reacted sharply on Aug. 17, as Washington and Peking issued a joint communiqué in which the U.S. pledged to reduce arms sales to Taiwan gradually, and Peking pledged to seek the reunification of Taiwan with the "motherland" by peaceful means. Taipei charged that Washington had compromised its commitments under the Taiwan Relations Act, under which the U.S. agreed to provide Taiwan with sufficient arms for its self-defense. Throughout the year Taipei repeatedly rejected Peking's overtures to discuss reunification.

Ultralight aircraft are now being used experimentally for patrol work by the police department of Monterey Park, Calif. Because the planes are growing rapidly in popularity, the Federal Aviation Administration issued a preliminary set of regulations in 1982 for their operation.

In the wake of the communiqué, Taipei took comfort from the impending delivery of the $60,000,000 worth of military spare parts and from Washington's pledge that no termination date for arms sales would be set. Nevertheless, Taiwan placed increased emphasis on developing domestic defense industries capable of producing sophisticated weapons.

See STATISTICS OF THE WORLD.   T.L.K.

TANZANIA. Economic conditions in Tanzania, whose government was led by President Julius Nyerere, reached a crisis point in 1982. Government predictions of famine in remote regions of the country were borne out in the early part of the year, when a shortfall of about 300,000 tons of foodstuffs was brought about by drought and mismanagement. In February Nyerere dismissed his minister of agriculture and soon undertook to secure emergency food aid from Western nations. Some 260,000 tons of food were forthcoming, but because of the government's inability to move it effectively, some grain rotted before it could reach famine areas.

In late April the International Monetary Fund suspended its loan program to Tanzania, charging that the government was unwilling to take politically unpopular mea-sures to reduce imports and build up foreign exchange reserves. In June the World Bank froze some $200,000,000 in assistance, citing Tanzania's inability to pay its debt arrears, which amounted to nearly $3,000,000.

Acknowledging his nation's foreign exchange difficulties, Nyerere suspended development projects for 1982–83 and called on donor countries to fund existing projects. Because of these difficulties, Tanzania's small manufacturing sector was operating at only 30 percent of capacity.

In February members of a leftist group, the Tanzanian Youth Democratic Movement, hijacked an Air Tanzania jet and flew it to England, where they surrendered it; a dozen passengers requested asylum. The hijackers, pointing to the country's economic plight, urged that Nyerere resign.

In mid-August Tanzanian troops helped put down an army mutiny on the Seychelles.

See STATISTICS OF THE WORLD.   J.T.S.

TECHNOLOGY. In 1982 the ongoing revolution in computer technology, initiated by the development of inexpensive microelectronic circuits, triggered a boom in low-cost home computers. Aviation also expanded its market with the development of inexpensive aircraft called ultralights. Technological advances were made as well in cryogenic refrigeration, batteries, automobile engines, data encryption, and optics.

Home Computers. Sales of microcomputers costing less than $1000 accelerated in mid-1982 with the introduction of a $100 home computer model, made by Timex Corp. for a British firm. The price war set off by the model caused Texas Instruments Inc. to reduce the price of its comparable model from the more than $1000 it cost in 1980 to only $200. As a result, sophisticated microcomputers became available for learning the basics of programming, for school work, for home finance, and for computer games.

The new home computers, attached to the antenna terminals of ordinary television sets, displayed graphics, letters, and numbers on the television screens. Prepackaged programs were sold on cassette tapes and on plug-in cartridges containing permanent semiconductor memories. A few computer models had accessory machines that used magnetic disks to play and store programs. The erasable memory circuits built into these inexpensive computers were often limited in capacity compared to those of higher-priced computers, and the budget models could display only a limited number of characters on each display line because of the resolution limits of television sets. Plug-in accessories and a separate video monitor, however, could give most budget models the ability to print words in a manner similar to that of costlier personal-computer word processors.

Continued price reductions in 1982 for memory and other computer chips also signified important changes for home computers. Thus Commodore was able to introduce its $595 model 64 computer with a full 64-K (kilobytes) of memory, the limit of most models; a 1-K memory can store 1024 characters. Such high-capacity memories made possible so-called "user-friendly" computer software: programming that anticipates and solves problems that users might otherwise encounter with less complex packages.

Ultralight Aircraft. Ultralight airplanes, with fabric-covered wings designed for soaring, and powered by small, low-horsepower gasoline engines, became increasingly popular. By some estimates, about 15,000 of these tiny aircraft—really motorized hang gliders—were being flown in 1982. They cost only $2000 to $5000 in kit form and could be flown without a pilot's license. The increase in their use by inexperienced pilots, however, together with some near-collisions with commercial aircraft, resulted in strict new Federal Aviation Administration regulations. To qualify as an ultralight, a powered plane had to weigh less than 114 kg (254 lb.) and could carry no more than 19 liters (5 gal.) of fuel. Speed was limited to 100 km per hour (62 mph), flying could be done only during daylight hours and in noncongested areas, and commercial operations were not permitted. Permission had to be obtained to fly in airport traffic areas and other zones.

Cryogenic Cooler. In 1982 the National Aeronautics and Space Administration (NASA) and North American Philips Corp. announced an advanced liquid-helium refrigeration system using frictionless, magnetically suspended components. The system was first developed to chill scientific instruments aboard NASA satellites, but engineers maintained that the cooler might also be used to provide the cryogenic temperatures needed for certain biomedical instruments, computers, and food and textile machinery. The supercold temperatures involved lie in the range of $-251°$ C. $(-421°$ F.).

The new refrigeration system eliminates the friction and wear caused by mechanical linkages in rotary motors. Instead, electronically controlled magnetic bearings levitate the refrigerator's components, centering them in magnetic fields so that they can move without touching the sides of their housing. It was thought that the cooler, which can run five years on a satellite without requiring maintenance, could lead to the development of new pumps, motors, and compressors that are less prone to failure.

Lithium Batteries. Batteries had come into increasing demand with the proliferation of portable stereotape machines, computers, and other electronic gadgets. Conventional carbon and alkaline batteries wear out quickly, however, particularly in tape record-

Technicians peer into the core of this University of Missouri research reactor, the most powerful of its type in the U.S. It is used to prepare silicon crystals for electronic devices by bombarding them with neutrons. This technique transmutes a silicon isotope into phosphorus, reducing the electrical resistance of the formerly pure crystals.

ers, whose motors require a great deal of power. When the Eastman Kodak Co. introduced its disk-film camera in early 1982 (*see* PHOTOGRAPHY), it switched to use of a new battery, based on lithium chemistry, with a significantly longer life. The disk-film camera had a built-in motor that enabled users to shoot pictures in rapid succession every 1.3 sec., so the lithium battery to power both the motor and the camera's advanced electronic circuits was designed to last the life of the camera. Kodak indicated its confidence in the battery by designing it for replacement at the factory instead of by the user.

Major battery companies indicated that they would soon begin production of lithium batteries for consumer electronics. Lithium cells for digital wristwatches and costly lithium batteries for special industrial applications had been available for several years, but because lithium is chemically highly reactive, special safety precautions for manufacturing and packaging the new batteries were necessary. These restrictions, it was believed, might initially keep costs high and limit the sales of the batteries.

Plastic Automobile Engine. Automobile manufacturers were exploring a wide range of technologies in their efforts to reduce the fuel consumption of their products. As a means of reducing the work load of engines, they were studying lightweight car bodies made with composites consisting of tough graphite fibers embedded in plastics or ep-

oxy resins. In 1982 Polimotor Research Inc., a subcontractor of the Ford Motor Co., revealed that it had built a car engine block with fiber-reinforced plastics. Designed along the lines of a Ford engine already in production, weighing 187 kg (415 lb.), the new plastic engine weighed only 78.4 kg (152 lb.); it could deliver 318 hp at 9200 rpm, however, as compared to the maximum of 88 hp put out by the heavier metal engine. Moving engine parts were also made with the composites and were being tested in Ford racing cars. Because composite materials were considerably more expensive than metal, however, it seemed likely that the light, supertough plastic might take some time to turn up in mass-produced engines.

Data Encryption. Two developments in 1982 threatened the methods being used by government agencies, businesses, and banks to encrypt, or encode, the data they exchange, in order to prevent information leaks. Such data were increasingly in the form of digital signals between computers, but if the data were coded in standard signal formats they might be intercepted and read by anyone with a personal computer. In the late 1970's in the United States, therefore, the National Bureau of Standards and the top-secret National Security Agency devised a set of encryption formulas for encoding and scrambling data. A sending computer was given an electronic circuit, available on a tiny microchip, that converted data into a meaningless

397

jumble that could be unscrambled only by a computer at the receiving end equipped with a decoding circuit. This formula and circuit, called the Data Encryption Standard (DES), became required for communication between the Federal Reserve Banks and other banks.

The DES technology remained secure, but two less sophisticated variations of encryption technology were cracked by specialists in 1982. In April a mathematics professor in Israel, Adi Shamir, broke a so-called public-key encryption method, a technique based on a published key, or code, and another private code that the receiver uses to decipher a message. Shamir relied on recent advances in number theory to break one of these codes. Four months later a computer scientist at the University of Southern California, Leonard Adleman, demonstrated at a cryptography conference the way in which he cracked a similar code with his Apple personal computer. Still another public-key encryption method, coauthored by Shamir, remained secure and was submitted for tests and certification by the U.S. government. Because an inexpensive microcomputer had been used to crack a public-key code, however, it was felt that the technique might not inspire the confidence of potential users.

Optics. A new generation of zoom lenses for cameras, based on new technologies and inexpensive materials, was under development in 1982. Glass lenses are produced by grinding, which results in spherical surfaces that can distort light. Aspheric lenses with a flat outer surface around a spherical center can eliminate such aberration problems and reduce the number of lens elements needed. In 1982 Polaroid Corp. was investigating aspheric lens elements molded from inexpensive plastics and combined with glass elements. Also being explored was another emerging technology for lenses called gradient-index glass. Such glass varies the index of refraction within a lens, thus enabling corrections for aberrations to be accomplished internally instead of requiring a number of corrective lens elements. Several Japanese manufacturers were expected to introduce gradient-index lenses in 1983.   J.F.

TELEVISION AND RADIO BROADCASTING. Network television experienced a midlife crisis in 1982. Although American households increased their television viewing to a record 7 hr. a day during the 1981–82 season, they no longer automatically tuned in NBC, ABC, or CBS. The percentage of viewers watching network shows at any particular time had fallen 15 percent in two years, and experts predicted that the networks' share of the prime-time viewing audience would plummet from the current 82 percent to a bleak 59 percent by the end of the decade as video choices proliferated.

The pay cable networks, which were reaching some 17,000,000 U.S. homes, were luring prime-time viewers every night with programming that included first-run movies and never-before-televised Broadway plays. Even the "superstations"—independent local

Escapism and fantasy were prominent among new prime-time television shows for the 1982–83 season. Here Bruce Boxleitner plays Frank Buck, the legendary adventurer and wild animal collector, in Bring 'em Back Alive.

Brideshead Revisited, *a dramatization of Evelyn Waugh's novel, made its American debut in early 1982. The most expensive television production ever to come from Great Britain, it starred Anthony Andrews (left) and Jeremy Irons.*

stations transmitted by cable to distant areas—were attracting loyal viewers by showing classic movies and reruns of situation comedies. One respected television critic forecast that cable's challenge would eventually transform the entire industry.

Network chiefs dismissed such cataclysmic predictions, claiming that losses of viewers to cable would be easily offset by continued growth in homes with television sets. "It is clear," Thomas Wyman, president of CBS Inc., told nervous local affiliates, "that broadcast television will remain the dominant and most effective medium of advertising to the mass audience." Convinced of an extended era of superiority, the networks continued to play it safe with traditional formulas—and the results were disastrous. Of the 23 network series that debuted in the fall of 1981, only four were successful.

Furthermore, even as the networks' share

of the audience declined, the cost of developing and producing programs multiplied. Instead of producing more distinctive programming at reduced prices, they compensated for rising costs by increasing the number of advertising minutes per hour, a move affiliates feared would encourage more viewers to shift to commercial-free cable channels. "Without formal organized competition (against cable)," wrote former NBC programming chief Paul Klein, "the three networks will be like Chrysler, Ford, and GM in the mid-70s—fat, sassy, vulnerable and, though their great American pie is shrinking, arrogant."

Also affecting network earnings was the 57-day National Football League players' strike. The networks lost at least a quarter of the $400,000,000 they had expected to earn from advertisers of the canceled games.

The Public Broadcasting System (PBS) encountered money problems in 1982. Congress had cut the federal appropriation for fiscal 1983 from $172,000,000 to $137,000,000, and the administration of U.S. President Ronald Reagan proposed that by fiscal 1985 PBS funding drop to $85,000,000. To fill the funding gap, PBS stations across the country were trying to attract new subscribers with more televised auctions, telephone pledge programs, and fund-raising galas, such as a preview of the motion picture *Annie*. But some PBS stations undertook radical fund-raising projects. North Dakota public television raised money through legalized gambling parlors, and New York's WNET aired commercials, which they called "enhanced corporate underwriting credits," at the beginning and end of their regular programs.

Violence on television once again provoked controversy in 1982. In May a National Institute of Mental Health (NIMH) report said that "overwhelming" scientific evidence from 2500 studies published since 1970 showed that violence on television entertainment programs could lead to aggressive behavior in children and adolescents. "What is important," said Peggy Charren, president of Action for Children's Television, "is that it reinforces what common sense knew all along—you learn from what you see." The networks, however, challenged the NIMH conclusions. CBS complained about the "almost wholly uncritical" and biased selection of data.

Prime-Time Programming. Although registering the lowest first-place average in 25 years, CBS won the 1981–82 prime-time ratings season in a photo finish over the second-place finisher, ABC. CBS, which led most of the season with its stable of long-term hits, held off a surge by ABC, which programmed surprisingly strong late-season replacements. NBC was buried in third place for the seventh year in a row, with the lowest seasonal average of any network since 1957. After one year under chairman Grant Tinker, NBC was in worse ratings shape than it had been under Tinker's predecessor, Fred Silverman. NBC's annual profits declined to barely a quarter of what CBS and ABC earned.

To counter the competition, NBC's network programmers declined to gamble on "quality." Even though the price tag was reportedly $6,000,000, NBC outbid the pay television network Home Box Office (HBO) for the highly acclaimed comedy series *Taxi* that ABC had dropped because of declining ratings. In addition, NBC renewed the critically respected *Fame* even though the program had not achieved top ratings. NBC also introduced two well-received shows, *St. Elsewhere*, a hospital drama produced by the *Hill Street Blues* production company, and *Cheers*, a *Taxi*-style comedy featuring patrons of a Boston bar. CBS and ABC opted for escapism and fantasy in their new 1982–83 prime-time shows. *Bring 'em Back Alive* was a CBS show based on the exploits of the late adventurer Frank Buck. *Tales of the Gold Monkey*, an ABC show, was set in the pre-World War II South Pacific.

CBS's hard-edged cancellation policy produced a near scandal in 1982. It axed the still marginally successful *Lou Grant* because the programmers decided that the four-year-old show had run its course. Screen Actors Guild President Ed Asner, the controversial star of *Lou Grant*, who had been sharply criticized for helping to raise money in order to provide medical supplies to left-wing insurgents in El Salvador, blamed the cancellation on his political views and pressure by the Moral Majority on sponsors. Hundreds of supporters marched on CBS's offices in Hollywood, Calif., to protest, and the American Civil Liberties Union investigated the decision, but CBS refused to budge and *Lou Grant* died quietly in the middle of the summer.

Miniseries. All the networks, but particularly PBS, triumphed with their 1981–82 miniseries. NBC's 10-hr. epic, *Marco Polo*, the most expensive television series to that time, displayed sheer spectacle that was breathtaking. CBS's *The Wall*, which dramatized the last-ditch uprising in World War II by Warsaw ghetto Jews against the German army, rose above television's usual Holocaust exploitation with what one critic called "unforgettable force." ABC's adaptation of Albert Speer's *Inside the Third Reich* was, as one critic said, "an extraordinarily intelligent . . . portrait of the human face of evil."

Covering the news was difficult, dangerous, and expensive for television camera crews photographing several wars in 1982. Here a unit films soldiers in El Salvador, trained by U.S. Green Berets, in their struggle against left-wing insurgents.

PBS presented both the most original and the most controversial miniseries of the year. In January it introduced *Brideshead Revisited,* a faithful adaptation of Evelyn Waugh's novel. It was the most expensive television production ever to come from Great Britain. In March PBS offered *Middletown,* a six-part documentary on Muncie, Ind., that won both praise and condemnation. Xerox Corp., which provided more than one sixth of *Middletown's* total $3,000,000 budget, dissociated itself from the work because of foul language. Even the president of PBS criticized *Middletown* for graphic depictions of teenage sexual exploits, and one segment was withdrawn by the producer because legal questions were raised.

Emmy Awards. In the 34th annual presentation of the Emmy awards on Sept. 19, the last-placed network in the ratings won the most prizes. NBC's *Hill Street Blues* was the biggest winner for the second year in a row, capturing six awards, while another of NBC's Thursday lineup, *Fame,* garnered five awards. ABC's canceled *Barney Miller* was named the outstanding comedy series. Repeat winners dominated many of the other awards too, including *M*A*S*H*'s Alan Alda and Loretta

Swit, *Hill Street Blues*'s Daniel J. Travanti and Michael Conrad, and *Lou Grant*'s Nancy Marchand. But there were some surprises. *Taxi*'s Carol Kane earned an Emmy for best actress in a comedy series even though she was only making a guest appearance. (Since she starred in the episode, she was eligible for the award.) The late Ingrid Bergman was chosen best actress in a special for her performance as the late Israeli prime minister in *A Woman Named Golda.*

News and Public Affairs. Television's news wars intensified in 1982. After NBC hired the popular sportscaster Bryant Gumbel as the *Today* anchor, CBS expanded its lagging *CBS Morning News* to 2 hr., dropped Charles Kuralt for cohosts Bill Kurtis and Diane Sawyer, and tried to transform its image with *Star Wars* graphics. Changes also occurred in evening news. *CBS Evening News* remained in first place in the ratings a year after Dan Rather took over from Walter Cronkite as anchor, but CBS led last-placed ABC many times by only two ratings points. The new team of Tom Brokaw and Roger Mudd kept NBC in second place, but NBC's affiliate in Charlotte, N.C., replaced its *Nightly News* with the game show *Family Feud.* Third-

Three-dimensional movies proved a popular television offering in 1982. Here a group of Little Rock, Ark., youths, too young to have seen these 1950's films when they first appeared in theaters, watch Gorilla at Large through 3-D glasses. Profits from the sales of the glasses went to the Easter Seal Society.

ranked ABC News beat NBC and CBS, in the opinion of most observers, with their calm and accurate election night coverage, hosted by former NBC anchor David Brinkley, along with Frank Reynolds and Ted Koppel.

The credibility of CBS News was challenged in 1982. In January it aired *The Uncounted Enemy: A Vietnam Deception*, which flatly stated that Gen. William C. Westmoreland, U.S. commander in Vietnam, participated in "a conspiracy at the highest levels of American military intelligence" to underestimate the strength of enemy units in Vietnam prior to the 1968 Tet offensive. Following the show, *TV Guide* published a story about CBS's on-air interviewing techniques. The magazine charged that Mike Wallace coached his star witness, former Central Intelligence Agency analyst Sam Adams, while Adams "sandbagged" the unprepared and unrehearsed Westmoreland with 15-year-old figures that he could not remember. The general later complained at a press conference that the "notorious reporter Mike Wallace [prosecuted] me in a star chamber procedure." CBS News President Van Gordon Sauter admitted, after a four-month investigation, that the producers had violated some of the network's journalistic ground rules, but refused to air a full retraction, which

Westmoreland had demanded. Westmoreland sued CBS for $120,000,000. "There is no other way left for me to clear my honor and the honor of the military," he maintained.

Controversy also surrounded an April CBS News documentary, *People Like Us,* in which Bill Moyers examined three families portrayed as victims of Reagan administration budget cuts. Administration officials called the program "misleading," disputing the data and arguing that in some cases the individuals had lost benefits because of policies at the state level or policies enacted before Reagan took office. Sauter turned down a request from the White House for a half hour of free prime time in which to make a rebuttal. And in April William J. Bennett, chairman of the National Endowment for the Humanities, called a PBS documentary, *From the Ashes . . . Nicaragua,* "unabashed socialist-realism propaganda."

To deter local affiliates from carrying Ted Turner's 24-hr. Cable News Network (CNN) in late-night time slots, the networks introduced overnight news programs for insomniacs. NBC ended its broadcast day with the 1-hr. *NBC News Overnight* and began it with a half-hour pre-*Today* segment. ABC introduced a 1-hr. extension of *Nightline* called *The Last Word,* featuring Phil Donahue, and the 1-hr. *This Morning* preceding *Good Morning America.* CBS offered *Nightwatch,* a 4-hr. overnight news show in the early morning hours that was described as a late-late-night version of *Good Morning America.* It also offered the 1-hr. *Early Morning News* preceding *Morning News.*

CNN was threatened not only by the network news's late-night assault but also by Satellite News Channel, the ABC network and Westinghouse Electric Corp.'s alternative cable news network. As soon as it was established in the summer, Satellite News, offering a "headline" service featuring 22 stories every 18 min., proved to be a strong competitor because of an attractive financial arrangement. Turner's system charged cable systems 15¢ a subscriber a month, while the Satellite News service was not only free but also paid cable operators bonuses for signing up. To meet the competition, Turner introduced CNN 2, the news network's own headline service.

CNN's in-depth news had scored a journalistic coup by demonstrating that U.S. military advisers were illegally carrying arms in El Salvador, and it had gained loyal viewers. However, at midyear CNN cut coverage because it was running over its monthly budget of $4,500,000.

Cable. Many specialty cable networks made their debuts in 1982, with programming ranging from X-rated fare to highbrow culture. A health network, a weather network, and a women's network also appeared. But CBS Cable announced on Sept. 13 that it was shutting down the prestigious performing-arts venture, which had lost $30,000,000 in less than a year. Indeed, one cable executive said that not a single advertiser-supported service was making a profit.

The movie-oriented pay cable services became stronger, however. HBO, which started as a poor stepchild of the publishing conglomerate Time Inc., grew so large that it showed signs of becoming a near monopoly. In 1982 film studio chiefs began complaining that HBO virtually dictated the prices it would pay for movies. But what really worried studio executives was HBO's bankrolling of independent film producers in exchange for pay cable rights. The studios decided that if they could not beat the pay television services, they would join them. On Nov. 30 Columbia Pictures Industries, CBS, and HBO announced plans to create a new film studio. HBO would buy all the films produced by the studio for showing on television and would also buy Columbia films for the same purpose. A few weeks earlier, Paramount Pictures Corp., MCA Inc., and Warner Bros. bought another pay television service, the Movie Channel. Other studios were negotiating to buy Showtime.

Other Television News. A series of Federal Communications Commission (FCC) decisions promised to open up television still further. On March 4 the FCC paved the way for the licensing of 3000 to 4000 new low-power stations, operating in the gaps between regions covered by existing VHF (very high frequency) or UHF (ultrahigh frequency) stations. On June 17 the commission repealed all major restrictions on pay television. On June 23 the FCC approved final rules for direct satellite-to-home transmission broadcast service, which it was thought might be available in 1986. On Sept. 23 it gave the Satellite Television Corp. the go-ahead to launch such a system, which would be received by rooftop or yard dish antennas.

Radio. After three decades, network radio revived the long form. In the fall NBC recruited Johnny Carson to host a 2-hr. comedy show on Thanksgiving and Bob Hope to preside over a Christmas show. ABC scheduled a 3-hr. special, *Musical!,* featuring "the greatest hits of stage and screen for the holiday season." ABC also doubled the number of 90-min. *Spotlight Specials,* which mixed popular music with interviews with singers such as Stevie Nicks and Rod Stewart, from 6 shows in 1982 to 12 in 1983.

ABC's Rock Radio Network made its debut in January, and its Direction radio network began sending news and sports for listeners age 25 to 49 at the same time. Its Talkradio network service began in May. CBS's Radioradio network, a news-based offering for young adults, was introduced in April.   J.H.

TENNESSEE. *See* STATISTICS OF THE WORLD.
TEXAS. *See* STATISTICS OF THE WORLD.

THAILAND. Prime Minister Prem Tinsula-nonda of Thailand and his fragile coalition government survived 1982, despite recurrent rumors of a military coup.

Politics. In the constitution of 1978, temporary clauses, to be valid only until April, 1983, gave the appointed 225-member senate equal standing with the elected 301-member lower house. Thereafter, the senate was to lose its right to vote in joint sittings on budget bills or on no-confidence ballots against the government. The senate was also to lose its power to block money bills, although it could delay the passage of other bills for 180 days by withholding its approval. This potentially explosive issue was debated throughout the year. Members of the senate, which represented the military and civilian establishments, insisted that the time limitation on the clauses be extended and that the senate's power remain undiminished.

In July reports surfaced in Bangkok that an antitank missile had been fired near Gen. Prem's car outside the army town of Lop Buri. A grenade tossed over the wall of Prem's house one month later exploded outside his bedroom window. Although government spokesmen minimized these incidents, several Thai newspapers attributed them to remnants of the disaffected army officers who had tried to topple Prem in 1981. In September Prem named Gen. Arhit Kamlang-ek as the new commander in chief of the army. Arhit, who quelled the 1981 coup attempt, was expected to deal forcefully with dissident elements in the army.

Rebels and Refugees. The 17-year-old war against Communist guerrillas showed signs of abating in 1982, as aid to the rebels from China and Vietnam diminished. Many guerrillas were disillusioned by events in Communist-held Vietnam, Laos, and Cambodia. As a result, defections to the government side increased sharply.

Thailand, which had in recent years borne the brunt of the massive influx of Vietnamese, Laotian, and Cambodian refugees, continued to provide camps for about 175,000 of the uprooted in 1982. A growing reluctance, however, by Western and Asian countries to accept the refugees for resettlement led to a decline in the number of people fleeing from Southeast Asia's Communist states.

The Economy. As a result of the worldwide recession and the depressed world prices for the country's exports, such as rice, sugar, and corn, the Thai government expected the 1982 economic growth rate to be little more than 5 percent.

Foreign Affairs. The country's major concern remained Cambodia, whose Vietnamese occupiers made Thailand fearful for its own security. Together with its allies in the Association of Southeast Asian Nations—Indonesia, Malaysia, the Philippines, and Singapore—Thailand called for Vietnamese withdrawal from Cambodia, and for United Nations-monitored elections there. Thailand and the United States agreed in October to repatriate nationals of each country who were serving prison sentences for criminal charges in the other country, thus allowing them to complete their sentences in their own countries. About 40 Americans were in Thai jails, mostly for offenses involving heroin.

See STATISTICS OF THE WORLD.   R.J.C.

Thailand's King Bhumibol and Queen Sirikit, with Crown Prince Vajiralong-korn (left) and their son-in-law behind them, attend bicentennial celebrations of both the royal dynasty and Bangkok on April 5.

Raul Julia and The Pink Ladies appear in the "Grand Canal" number in Nine, *which won the Tony Award as best musical of the 1981–82 Broadway season.*

THEATER. The commercial theater in the United States began feeling the effects of the recession in 1982. Ticket prices continued rising, but attendance and box-office receipts declined. So did the number of Broadway productions. Major touring cities also reflected the trend. The professional institutional theater remained healthy and active, however.

Awards. Off Broadway proved itself once more a significant creative force. *A Soldier's Play,* by Charles Fuller, presented by the Negro Ensemble Company, won both the Pulitzer Prize and the New York Drama Critics' Circle Award for best American play of the 1981–82 season. The Critics' Circle and the Antoinette Perry (Tony) awards went to *The Life and Adventures of Nicholas Nickleby* as the 1981–82 season's best play. *Nine* won a Tony as the best musical.

Drama and Comedy. The Anglo-American connection was strongly evident throughout 1982. London's Royal Shakespeare Company presented its boldly staged production of the late C. P. Taylor's *Good,* a play with music that starred Alan Howard as a German intellectual corrupted by Nazism and his own ambition. Three London successes were presented on Broadway with entirely or mainly American casts. Kate Nelligan made her U.S. stage debut in David Hare's *Plenty,* a bitter portrait of an Englishwoman's disillusionment and breakdown in the aftermath of World War II. Ellen Burstyn starred in *84 Charing Cross Road,* James Roose-Evans's adaptation of the book by Helene Hanff about the relationship and correspondence between an American writer and a clerk in a London antiquarian bookstore. Nell Dunn's *Steaming* was set in a public steambath.

Athol Fugard's *"Master Harold"... and the Boys,* set in South Africa, was a poignant study of the relationship between a white boy and two black men who work in a tearoom owned by the boy's parents. John Pielmeier's *Agnes of God* cast Amanda Plummer as a young nun facing possible manslaughter charges for the murder of the child she has mysteriously borne. Plummer won a Tony Award for her performance; her co-stars in the three-character drama were Elizabeth Ashley and Geraldine Page.

In the short-lived *Monday after the Miracle,* William Gibson dramatized the events 20 years after those portrayed in *The Miracle Worker,* when the adult Helen Keller was making her home with Anne Sullivan Macy and her husband. The roles were played by Karen Allen as Helen Keller, Jane Alexander, and William Converse-Roberts.

Important among the year's Broadway revivals was *Medea,* with Zoe Caldwell giving a Tony Award-winning performance in the title role of the Robinson Jeffers adaptation of the Euripides tragedy. Liv Ullmann starred as Mrs. Alving in Henrik Ibsen's *Ghosts.* Colleen Dewhurst headed the cast of a new production of Ugo Betti's *The Queen and the Rebels.*

The year's Broadway comedies included Murray Schisgal's *Twice around the Park,* starring Anne Jackson and Eli Wallach. *Torch Song Trilogy,* written by and starring Harvey Fierstein, was a popular comedy-drama. George C. Scott directed and starred in Noel Coward's 40-year-old farce, *Present Laughter.* Jessica Tandy and Hume Cronyn gave rich performances in *Foxfire,* an affectionate stage piece drawn by Cronyn and Susan Cooper from the *Foxfire* books about southern Appalachia. Anthony (*Sleuth*) Shaffer contributed the year's murder mystery, the appropriately titled *Whodunnit.*

Musicals. Broadway musicals in 1982 ranged from the spectacular to the disappointing. The hit of the autumn season was *Cats,* composer Andrew Lloyd Webber's settings for a group of poems by T. S. Eliot, taken principally from *Old Possum's Book of Practical Cats.* Another major success was *Nine,* starring Raul Julia as an Italian film director in a musical-comedy fantasy. The book was written by Arthur Kopit, adapted from the Italian by Mario Fratti, with music and lyrics by Maury Yeston.

Eva Le Gallienne, a grande dame of the American theater, starred in her original role as the White Queen in *Alice in Wonderland,* which she also directed, in a brief revival of the 1932 Civic Repertory Company production. It was adapted from Lewis Carroll's writings by Le Gallienne and Florida Friebus. Charles M. Schultz's irrepressible beagle barked his way onto Broadway as the star of *Snoopy,* 1982's final musical.

The engaging *Pump Boys and Dinettes* successfully survived the transfer from Off Broadway to Broadway. Similarly transferred was *Joseph and the Amazing Technicolor Dreamcoat,* by Andrew Lloyd Webber and his partner, Tim Rice. *Joseph* became the third Lloyd Webber show to appear simultaneously on Broadway, joining *Cats* and the long-running *Evita.*

Dramatist of Humans and History

On April 12 Charles Fuller became the second black playwright to win a Pulitzer Prize. His award-winning drama, *A Soldier's Play,* explores race relations at a military camp during World War II. Fuller, 43, was born and made his home in Philadelphia. He was working as a housing inspector when his first play was produced. His association with the Negro Ensemble Company, which had produced four of his plays, including this latest effort, began in 1974. "My plays are about people, not black-white confrontations," he says. "I'm concerned about history, and about human beings."

Charles Fuller

Off Broadway. Off Broadway productions opening in 1982 ranged from Lanford Wilson's well-tempered *Angels Fall,* about a group of people temporarily stranded in a New Mexico mission chapel by a nuclear accident, to *Do Lord Remember Me,* James De Jongh's moving retrospective, based on the recollections of former slaves. A big Off Broadway musical hit was *Little Shop of Horrors,* the Howard Ashman–Alan Menken spoof based on a 1960 horror film.

Off Broadway saluted the comic muse with such lively items as Jonathan Reynolds's movie-spoofing *Geniuses;* A. R. Gurney's deftly crafted *The Dining Room;* the rambunctious *Greater Tuna,* by Joe Sears, Jaston Williams, and Ed Howard; and John Ford Noonan's good-hearted *Some Men Need Help.* The Roundabout Theatre Company continued its series of well-received revivals with Terence Rattigan's *The Browning Version* and James M. Barrie's *The Twelve-Pound Look.* The CSC Repertory mounted Johann Wolfgang von Goethe's *Faust.*

Off Broadway lost one of its longest-running institutional producing organizations when the 30-year-old Phoenix Theatre closed its operations in December. The New York Shakespeare Festival inaugurated an exchange program with London's innovative Royal Court Theater with the presentation of *Top Girls,* Caryl Churchill's comedy about women achievers, past and present.

Shakespeare. Productions of plays by William Shakespeare were highlighted by the American Shakespeare Theatre's impressive *Othello,* starring James Earl Jones as the Moor and Christopher Plummer as Iago, originating at Stratford, Conn., and later moving to Broadway. The New York Shakespeare Festival mounted *A Midsummer Night's Dream* in Central Park. At its Off Broadway headquarters, the festival put on a four-hour *Hamlet* with a woman—Diane Venora—playing the title role. CSC Repertory won praise for its *King Lear.*

Regional Theater. A number of institutional professional theaters across the country filled their indispensable role in U.S. playmaking by premiering new works. The tenth edition of the Theatre Directory, published by the

Cats, *based on the light verse of T. S. Eliot, was the musical hit of the 1982 fall season. The London import came to Broadway with a troupe of American performers.*

Theatre Communications Group (TCG), listed 167 constituent and 43 associate TCG theaters in 42 states.

The 1982 calendar included several theater festivals. The World Theater Festival, formerly of Baltimore, moved to Denver for a 25-day program of 103 performances of 20 plays by 16 troupes from 23 countries, representing Europe, North and South America, the Middle East, and Australia. The Regional Organization of Theaters-South, Inc., held its Alternate Roots Third Performance Festival in Atlanta, offering more than 20 productions by participating groups and solo performers. In July the Great Lakes Shakespeare Festival presented the first American production of *Nicholas Nickleby,* the David Edgar adaptation of the Charles Dickens classic novel that the Royal Shakespeare Company performed on Broadway in 1981. This Cleveland version appeared in the restored Ohio Theater, the first auditorium in a $22,500,000 redevelopment of the city's downtown theater district.

Offstage Dramas. The Broadway theatrical year included several offstage events. Despite valiant rescue efforts, two memorable

Nearly 200 celebrities, participating in a benefit for the Actors Fund of America, gather on stage for the grand finale of Night of 100 Stars, *at New York City's Radio City Music Hall on Feb. 14.*

theaters, the Helen Hayes and the Morosco, were demolished to provide a part of the site for the projected Portman Hotel. Portman developers planned to include one large playhouse in the hotel premises. The loss of the Helen Hayes and the Morosco stimulated efforts to secure the protection of landmark status for the exteriors and/or interiors of 45 theaters in the midtown section of Manhattan.

The League of New York Theaters and Producers filed an antitrust suit in federal court against the Dramatists Guild, which represented some 5500 playwrights, composers, lyricists, and librettists. Among other things, the league sought to prohibit the guild from "involving itself in any way . . . in negotiations between an author and producer concerning the terms and conditions for the rights to produce any author's works."

Actors' Equity Association elected Ellen Burstyn as the first woman president of the union in its 69-year history. Burstyn was also named coartistic director, with Al Pacino, of the Actors Studio, following the death of the studio's longtime artistic director and president, Lee Strasberg.

Profits. Reporting on the commercial theater's fiscal year that ended on May 31, the League of New York Theaters and Producers disclosed that 1981–82 was the second-best year in recent Broadway history, although the number of new productions dropped from 60 to 48. Sales reached an all-time high of $223,000,000. Theater attendance, however, declined to 10,100,000 from the record 11,000,000 of the previous season. Similarly, touring productions took in $250,000,000, as against $219,000,000 in the previous season, while attendance fell from 16,300,000 to 15,000,000. The apparent contradiction was accounted for by rising ticket prices. Both Broadway and the road experienced declines during the course of the year.   J.B.

TOGO. *See* STATISTICS OF THE WORLD.
TONGA. *See* STATISTICS OF THE WORLD.

TRANSPORTATION. The persistent economic downturn struck hard at transport industries in 1982, with heavy losses for some and a strong though less harsh effect on others. Airlines experienced sizable deficits, as they cut fares vigorously, struggling to absorb excess flight capacity. Much of this excess reflected previous expansion under deregulation. Railroads used their increased flexibility under deregulation to boost or trim freight rates as the market indicated, thereby limiting the size of the earnings plunge. Trucking firms had big losses, however; many companies went out of business as freight-rate discounting became rampant. Long-term overcapacity and downward pressure on rates continued in ocean shipping. Deficit-plagued mass transit systems got a reprieve from the threatened sharp cutback in federal operating subsidies, but they still had to trim service, raise fares, and press unions to hold down wage demands.

New help for highway, bridge, and subway restoration appeared on the way, as President Ronald Reagan lent his support to a plan to boost the federal gasoline and diesel fuel tax by 5¢ a gallon, in order to raise $5.5 billion a year to finance repairs for highways, roads, bridges, and mass transit systems. The measure, passed by Congress on Dec. 23, also increased user fees and other levies on heavy trucks; as compensation, the interstate highway system was opened to trucks weighing as much as 40 tons.

AVIATION

U.S. air carriers in 1982 flew some 300,000,000 passengers, an increase over 1981. Scheduled airlines had revenues of about $36 billion. Traffic showed little gain, and vigorous fare reductions offset some basic fare increases. Net operational losses were between $400,000,000 and $500,000,000, compared with a 1981 deficit of $428,000,000, the Air Transport Association estimated in December. Braniff International Corp., which had expanded liberally since deregulation, went into bankruptcy on May 13. Braniff later tried to reorganize by striking joint-venture deals

The fuel-efficient Boeing 767, shown here on display in Seattle, made its debut as a regular passenger carrier in September. A deep slump in profits for the airline industry clouded prospects for the jetliner, which is powered by two huge turbofan engines, one under each wing.

TRANSPORTATION

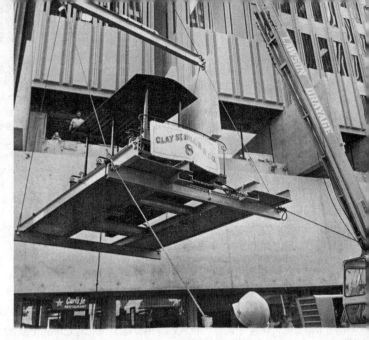

with various other carriers. Laker Airways, a British firm that offered no-frills fares to North Atlantic travelers, went bankrupt in February, and some other airlines also skated on thin financial ice.

Notable in the aircraft industry was the introduction by the Boeing Co. of its new 767 jetliner and the smaller 757. Airlines had orders or options for nearly 300 767's, but the outlook was clouded by cancellations and deferments. United Airlines stretched out delivery of 20 767's through 1988, four years beyond the original schedule. Airlines also canceled options to buy the Lockheed Corp. L-1011 Tristar as they proceeded with arrangements to phase out the wide-bodied airplane.

Traffic-Control Curbs. Many carriers still suffered from Federal Aviation Administration (FAA) restrictions on peak-hour flights, while the agency worked to replace the controllers fired by President Reagan after their August, 1981, walkout. The FAA had boosted flight operations to more than 90 percent of pre-strike activity by the end of 1982. However, working controllers complained of long hours, few relief breaks, and harsh treatment by their managers. A three-man task force of outside experts appointed by Transportation Secretary Andrew L. ("Drew") Lewis, Jr., reported that FAA labor relations were as bad

as ever. Meanwhile, the FAA announced a major 20-year upgrading of the air traffic control system, at a cost of about $9 billion for the first decade. Congress raised the tax on airline tickets and also imposed other levies to help pay for the program.

Air Crashes. Three weather-related jetliner accidents broke a 26-month stretch without a fatal crash by a major U.S. carrier. Taking off in a snowstorm from National Airport at Washington, D.C., in January, an Air Florida 737 crashed into a bridge and plunged into the Potomac River, killing 78 persons. Ten days later a World Airways DC-10 landing at Boston's Logan International Airport skidded off the slippery runway; when the front part of the fuselage broke off and fell into Boston harbor, two passengers were lost and presumed dead. In the worst U.S. air disaster of 1982, a Pan American World Airways 727, taking off on July 9 in a heavy rainstorm from New Orleans International Airport, apparently ran into windshear (the suddenly shifting winds that can rob an aircraft of needed lift) and crashed into nearby houses in Kenner, La. The accident killed 153, the second-highest death toll for a single-plane crash in U.S. aviation history.

The National Transportation Safety Board (NTSB) concluded that the Air Florida pilot's decision to take off without ensuring that the

737's wings were cleared of ice or snow contributed to the crash. (Icing on wing leading-edge devices can affect the aerodynamics of takeoff and cause a stall.) Also cited was the 737's propensity to "pitch up" or roll sideward when its wings were icy. Concerning the Boston accident, NTSB hearings in May revealed wide differences among airport authorities on how to keep runways safe and how to know when they provide good aircraft braking. The board's probe of the Pan Am crash near New Orleans showed continuing shortcomings in dissemination of storm information to pilots and their use of such data.

Fare Wars. Seeking to fill empty seats or meet other carriers' low fares, airlines drastically reduced prices on certain routes. Fares for coast-to-coast flights kept dropping, reaching $99 one-way and $198 round-trip on New York–San Francisco and New York–Los Angeles flights during the usually slack period between the Thanksgiving and Christmas holidays. Fares were also slashed for Florida and other high-volume markets. New York Air boosted its one-way, peak-hour New York–Washington, D.C., fare by $4 to $59 on May 27, but after People Express offered a $44 peak fare on the route on Aug. 3, New York Air extended its $39 weekend fare to weekdays. To lure passengers, carriers also used such means as discount-ticket books, merchandise trading stamps, and promotional tie-ins with camera makers or other consumer product manufacturers.

World-Route Turbulence. International carriers strove to moderate the heavy price discounting that stemmed from low demand and high capacity. Carriers were expected to lose nearly $2 billion in 1982 on international service.

At the International Air Transport Association (IATA) annual meeting in Geneva in November, airlines voted to refrain from fare cuts below agreed tariffs. Earlier, in the first IATA fare pact on North Atlantic routes since 1977, the carriers had agreed to fare increases averaging up to 17 percent for those markets, effective March through May. Agreements in July called for new 7 percent fare increases, but many never went into effect.

The United States and the European Civil Aviation Conference agreed in May to give airlines substantial leeway (within specified limits) to raise and cut fares on North Atlantic routes without government approval. The plan was for six months only, beginning in mid-1982. In June the U.S. and Japan signed a new three-year agreement boosting service between the two countries.

MASS TRANSIT

Mass transit ridership fell for the second consecutive year, after a steady rise between 1973 and 1980. According to the American Public Transit Association, the number of riders declined 3.9 percent to 5.73 billion passengers during the first nine months of 1982 as unemployment, higher fares, and reduced service discouraged commuting. A 10¢ increase in Cincinnati boosted fares to 60¢ at peak times, and Cleveland's local fare rose to 85¢, a 25¢ increase. Fares in San Mateo County, Calif., rose 10¢ to 35¢, the first fare increase in that system's history. On the other hand, a few cities cut fares in order to boost ridership.

Systems scrambled to trim costs. Many gained new labor contracts that kept wage increases down, eliminated or reduced cost-of-living pay raises, or permitted more use of part-time drivers in peak hours. Transit managers went abroad for more equipment. New York City's Metropolitan Transportation Authority (MTA), for example, signed major contracts to buy Canadian, Japanese, and French-made subway cars. The order for 825 cars from Bombardier Inc. of Montréal was challenged by the Budd Co., a U.S.-based firm, which claimed that Canadian government export subsidies to Bombardier constituted an unfair trade practice. U.S. transit bus makers suffered from depressed demand, largely because transit systems faced possible loss of the federal aid that many operators use to cover much of their daily expenses.

Funding Pinch. Federal, state, and local governments found it increasingly difficult to continue full financial assistance to mass transit systems, as the Reagan administration moved toward a phaseout of federal operating aid by fiscal 1985. Although some communities balked at local tax rises for transit,

411

gasoline tax increases for transit financing were approved in Tennessee and Virginia. Voters passed a new tax to aid transit in Youngstown, Ohio, where the system closed temporarily in November, 1981, after a previous measure was rejected. New York's MTA was among several systems to make use of a new federal tax provision allowing sale of depreciation credits to profitable companies. Some systems also sold tax-exempt revenue bonds to bolster their finances.

Service Cuts. To avoid higher fares, many systems cut back on operations to help meet expenses. Service reductions amounted to 4.7 percent in Cincinnati and 3 percent in Wisconsin, for example. The St. Louis Bi-State Development Agency took 140 buses off the streets during the 18-month period ending in April. More drastic cuts were threatened if federal operating subsidies continued to decline.

MOTOR TRANSPORT

Route expansion and sharp rate cutting in a business climate dominated by recession and deregulation took their toll on many trucking companies. Many truck firms lost business to carriers who took advantage of the new route authority and pricing flexibility. ICC Chairman Reese H. Taylor, Jr., had tried to limit expansion of trucking authority and the proliferation of pricing bargains. But as the new commissioners named by President Reagan pushed for regulatory rollback, Taylor began to fall in line.

According to the American Trucking Associations (ATA), 191 regulated firms closed up shop or experienced "severe financial difficulties" in the two years ending on July 1, 1982. The ATA estimated that truck freight in 1982 declined by 13 percent below the 1981 level, to about 690,000,000 tons; revenues were off about 6 percent, to around $44 billion, and operating profits fell 54 percent, to $669,000,000.

The intercity bus industry won a deregulation law of its own when Congress in August rolled back ICC control over bus routes and fares; the measure was signed by President Reagan on Sept. 20. Decontrol had already taken effect in several states, and small communities expressed fears and complaints about loss of service. Large bus companies engaged in vigorous fare competition, and the Greyhound Corp. said that its bus operation earnings suffered accordingly.

RAILROADS

The recession chipped away at railroad earnings in 1982, but lines generally coped much better than during past downturns, when bankruptcies were common. The Association of American Railroads reported a 49 percent decline in profits in the first nine months, to $747,000,000, with a 9 percent fall in operating revenues. Railroads hauled an estimated 820 billion ton-miles of freight in 1982, down from 930 billion in 1981. The Interstate Commerce Commission (ICC) approved the merger of the Union Pacific, Missouri Pacific, and Western Pacific railroads into one road and the consolidation of the Norfolk & Western and Southern railways.

Rail Labor Issues. At the urging of the Reagan administration, Congress in September passed emergency legislation that ended a four-day walkout by the Brotherhood of Locomotive Engineers (BLE). The legislation set a strike moratorium until mid-1984. President Reagan in July had declared a 60-day cooling-off period, averting a nationwide rail strike at that time. The United Transportation Union in September agreed to wage increases of 11 percent over 27 months, following the pattern of pacts with other rail unions since late 1981.

The Consolidated Rail Corp. (Conrail), the northeastern rail system in which the federal government held an 80 percent share, turned profitable in 1982 because unions had agreed to a wage freeze and because of other cost-cutting measures. Earnings were $120,000,000 in the first nine months, up from $12,800,000 for January–September, 1981, despite a 14 percent drop in revenues during the same period. Under 1981 legislation, the government must sell Conrail to outside interests. Conrail union members voted in November to authorize their union to seek to buy the railroad.

The National Railroad Passenger Corp. (Amtrak) also gained union concessions, limiting wage boosts and modifying work rules in May and October settlements. Contracts

Passengers enjoy elegant dining on the Orient Express. *The fabled luxury train began a London–Venice run in May with refurbished cars of the old express that ceased service in 1977. On the inaugural run passengers were encouraged to wear 1920's-style evening dress.*

signed in October with the BLE substituted hourly pay for engineers on the Boston–Washington corridor for the mileage-based formula in effect in the railroad industry for more than 60 years. Under the old system, engineers had qualified for a full day's pay for each 100 mi.

Deregulation Benefits. Freedom selectively to cut and raise individual rates, depending on competition, helped rail freight carriers avert losses despite the generally adverse economy. Using their new ability to recover cost rises quickly, railroads imposed a general 4.7 percent rate hike on Jan. 1. The ICC proposed on Nov. 5 to end controls over rates and shipments for many farm goods.

Amtrak Upturn. Fortunes rallied for Amtrak's passenger train system, as the Reagan administration abandoned its drive to pare the route network, pushing instead for cost reductions. Amtrak reduced its losses (and the resulting need for federal operating aid) by 23 percent, to $555,000,000 in fiscal 1982, de-

spite declining ridership. Plans for a "bullet train" that would travel up to 160 mph between Los Angeles and San Diego were laid by the American High Speed Rail Corp., a private company formed by some former Amtrak officials.

SHIPPING

The merchant marine industry continued to suffer from excess capacity, although more tankers were scrapped. Commercial ship orders declined, but U.S. Navy purchases climbed.

Government Help. The Reagan administration offered numerous forms of assistance for oceangoing lines, but little for shipyards. Strong lobbying by Transportation Secretary Lewis and shippers spurred House of Representatives approval on Sept. 15 of a bill to permit carriers jointly to set cargo rates and allocate tonnage with broadened immunity from antitrust prosecution; the bill failed to clear the Senate, however. The Administration also backed policies to enable U.S.-flag

The Maglev, Japan's latest excursion into railroad high technology, rests on side-mounted rubber support wheels on a trackless roadbed. Still in the experimental stage, the train "levitates" on a thin magnetic cushion and is driven by the interaction of its own magnets with the electromagnets along the guideway.

subsidized lines to continue to build vessels overseas.

Continued Slump. According to *Lloyd's Register of Shipping,* merchant ships on order worldwide totaled 3190 on June 30, 1982, off 3 percent from mid-1981; order-book tonnage fell 13 percent. The value of merchant vessel orders for U.S. shipbuilders dropped to $1.72 billion on Sept. 1 from $2.13 billion a year before, the U.S. Maritime Administration said. Oil tanker rates remained depressed because of the oil glut; *see* PETROLEUM AND NATURAL GAS. The International Association of Independent Tanker Owners said in October that 24,000,000 deadweight tanker tons would be scrapped in 1982, compared with 14,000,000 in 1981.

Naval Orders. The Reagan administration's support for the Navy was a shipyard bright spot. The Navy targeted a 600-vessel fleet by the end of the decade, a 30 percent increase over 1982 levels. The Shipbuilders Council of America estimated naval orders at $16 billion by the close of 1982, up $5 billion from a year before. Major contracts were awarded for the long-term charter and conversion of cargo ships.

See also AUTOMOBILES.   A.R.K.

TRINIDAD AND TOBAGO. *See* STATISTICS OF THE WORLD.

TUNISIA. Despite turmoil and tension elsewhere in the Arab world, Tunisia, under President Habib Bourguiba, remained stable in 1982. Undercurrents of political opposition did exist, however, as well as economic problems and stirrings of Islamic fundamentalism. In addition, Bourguiba, the president for life who had led Tunisia for the past 26 years, was in ailing health; the question of eventual succession weighed heavily on Tunisian political life. Meanwhile, however, the 105 leaders of an Islamic fundamentalist movement who were arrested prior to Tunisian national elections in November, 1981, remained in jail in 1982. Western diplomats in Tunis believed that the continued detention of the extremists had broken any serious challenge to the Bourguiba regime from political or religious opposition.

Tunisia also achieved friendlier relations with Libya, its politically radical neighbor to the east. Relations between Tunisia and Libya had been strained since 1974, when Tunisia reneged on a merger agreement with Libya soon after it was signed. But in February, 1982, Col. Muammar el-Qaddafi, the Libyan leader, paid a five-day reconciliation visit to Tunisia, and on Feb. 27, at the conclusion of his visit, Tunisia and Libya signed an accord for renewed economic and cultural cooperation. The pact also promised efforts to coordinate foreign policy. On Feb. 24 the International Court of Justice at The Hague, the Netherlands, resolved a dispute over oil drilling and fishing rights in the Gulf of Gabès by dividing the disputed area between Libya and Tunisia.

Relations between Tunisia and the United States remained strong and cordial. Washington increased its military aid to Tunisia from

$15,000,000 in fiscal 1981 to $90,000,000 in fiscal 1982, and the administration of U.S. President Ronald Reagan asked Congress for $140,000,000 for Tunisia in fiscal 1983. The credits would allow Tunisia to buy a squadron of F-5 jet fighters.

Following the withdrawal of Palestinian fighters from Beirut, Lebanon, in late August, nearly 1000 of them were given asylum in Tunisia. Yasir Arafat, the Palestine Liberation Organization leader, made his headquarters in a villa outside Tunis.

See STATISTICS OF THE WORLD.   A.D.

TURKEY. By a margin of more than nine to one, about 20,000,000 voters approved a new constitution for Turkey in a referendum held on Nov. 7. The document, which was prepared largely by a consultative assembly selected by the regime, automatically elected Gen. Kenan Evren, head of Turkey's military junta, president of Turkey for a seven-year term, with broad executive powers.

Evren campaigned energetically, but the outcome was never really in doubt. Although the referendum was ostensibly designed to show that after two years in power Turkey's military regime was preparing a return to democracy, Evren had pushed through a law forbidding any criticism of his speeches or of the constitution's most controversial provisions. The ruling generals ensured a large turnout, too, by threatening to disenfranchise for five years any registered voter who stayed away from the polls. Those eligible to vote who did not register faced jail terms of up to six months.

The constitution was clearly designed to prevent a return to the anarchic state of party politics that existed in Turkey before the military coup of September, 1980. The document banned more than 100 of the country's leading political figures from engaging in political activity for ten years. Included among those affected by the ten-year ban were two former Turkish premiers, Süleyman Demirel and Bülent Ecevit. Members of the Turkish parliament that was dissolved after the 1980 military takeover were permitted to run for office in the future, but they were barred from holding positions of leadership in political parties for five years.

The new constitution's 193 articles also included sweeping restrictions on the press, labor unions, and universities. After a slow phasing out of military rule, the constitution would institutionalize a strong executive branch with power to break parliamentary deadlocks by dissolving parliament and calling new elections. Balloting for the election of a national assembly would be held in the fall of 1983 or the spring of 1984, according to the military junta. Among other powers vested in him, the new Turkish president would have power to appoint the country's most powerful judges as well as heads of all of the country's universities.

The majority of voters had never read the new constitution and some of those who voted for it were actually opposed to it. In effect, the massive turnout was a vote of confidence in Evren, a father figure who appeared to be genuinely popular in Turkey. Evren and his fellow junta generals were widely applauded for ending the period of terror and political anarchy that had begun to claim more than 20 lives a day before the military took over in 1980. The referendum was a decisive defeat for the party politicians who formerly ran the country.

Turkey also had made impressive economic gains under the military junta. Inflation, running at an annual rate of more than 100 percent before the coup, had been cut to around 30 percent. Turkish exports, which totaled $4.7 billion in 1981, were expected to reach $6 billion in 1982 and $7.1 billion in 1983. The gross national product grew by about 4 percent in 1982.

With Greece still wavering over its future role in the North Atlantic Treaty Organization, the appearance of greater political stability in Turkey enhanced Turkey's importance as the strong southeastern anchor of the Western alliance. Nevertheless, the government signed a major trade agreement with the Soviet Union on Jan. 19, ignoring a U.S.-sponsored effort to curtail such ties with Moscow because of the military crackdown in Poland.

See STATISTICS OF THE WORLD. See also CYPRUS.   A.D.

TUVALU. See STATISTICS OF THE WORLD.

U

UGANDA. Economic and, to a lesser degree, security conditions within Uganda appeared to improve in 1982. When President Milton Obote took power in 1980, the economy had been a shambles after the mismanagement of former dictator Idi Amin. Obote was able to secure Western aid to repair and replace transportation equipment and industrial machinery. Increased agricultural productivity meant that Uganda would again be self-sufficient in foodstuffs. By May progress was sufficient for the World Bank and the International Monetary Fund to grant a $70,000,000 loan to finance needed imports; a further $35,000,000 was provided for industrial development.

Although threats of famine receded and Obote's economic policies seemed to promise a return to prosperity, internal security remained a severe problem. The poorly disciplined and underpaid army engaged in widespread looting and robbery. Civilians who resisted were arrested, tortured, and, in outlying areas, massacred. Although Obote, in a gesture of reconciliation, freed some 190 political prisoners in January, two of Uganda's former presidents, Godfrey Binaisa and Yusufu Lule, banded their factions together to form a united resistance front in exile. Their guerrilla supporters were concentrated in the areas populated by the Baganda people of southern Uganda. Supporters of Amin continued their raids in the north.

In late February guerrillas attacked the main army barracks in Kampala, the capital. The army retaliated by arresting, by early April, more than 10,000 civilians, some of whom were tortured. Unemployed men were ordered to leave Kampala. Stepping up its antiguerrilla patrols, the army scored some successes, breaking up rebel camps in the immediate vicinity of Kampala and recapturing arms seized earlier by the rebels. In June military instructors from the Commonwealth of Nations completed the training of the first group of Ugandan officers and noncommis-

sioned officers who would be responsible for retraining the army.

The continuing unrest and organized opposition to the regime seemed to make a mockery of Obote's call, in early 1982, for a policy of national unity; by midyear political opponents were once more being arrested (in at least one instance, kidnapped from abroad) and mistreated. In the fall the government admitted that some 237 people were being held without trial; opponents put the figure at about 4000.

Uganda's parliament passed a bill in early September providing that the government return to Ugandan Asians—nearly all of whom had been expelled by Amin in 1972—property seized by Amin's regime. The departure of the Asians, who dominated trade, had put Uganda's economy in disarray, but it was considered unlikely that they would be willing to return from abroad and resume their businesses.

See STATISTICS OF THE WORLD.   J.T.S.

UNION OF SOVIET SOCIALIST REPUBLICS. Leonid I. Brezhnev, president of the Soviet Union and general secretary of its Communist Party, died on Nov. 10. He was succeeded two days later as leader of the Communist Party by Yuri V. Andropov (see biography at PEOPLE IN THE NEWS). In economics and foreign policy, 1982 was a difficult year for the U.S.S.R.

Politics. Brezhnev, 75, had been in frail health for some time. His absence from public functions for four weeks in late March and most of April led to rumors that he had suffered a stroke. He made several public appearances later in the year, however, including a speech only days before his death, at the annual parade commemorating the anniversary of the Bolshevik Revolution.

Andropov, who succeeded him, had been head of the KGB, the Soviet Union's security police, from 1967 to May, 1982, when he was promoted to the Communist Party's key ten-member secretariat. Andropov filled the va-

The body of Soviet President and Communist Party General Secretary Leonid I. Brezhnev lies in state following his death on Nov. 10. He was succeeded as party leader two days later by Yuri V. Andropov.

cancy created by the death of Mikhail Suslov, the ranking party secretary in terms of length of service and the overseer of party ideology. Upon Suslov's death Konstantin U. Chernenko, a party Politburo member, like Andropov, and a secretariat member who had long served Brezhnev as a personal aide, inherited some of Suslov's ideological duties. During the months preceding Brezhnev's death, Chernenko and Andropov were considered the most likely candidates to succeed Brezhnev as party leader.

Andropov's first priority was believed to be a campaign against corruption and poor worker productivity in order to improve the Soviet Union's sagging economic performance. In his first major policy statement since becoming party secretary, he declared on Nov. 22 that linking workers' earnings to productivity and giving greater independence from central bureaucratic control to industrial and agricultural enterprises would stimulate the economy. With regard to foreign relations, he affirmed a continuing commitment to the professed Soviet policy of détente with the West and repeated Brezhnev's call for a freeze in the deployment of strategic nuclear weapons. He pledged to continue Soviet efforts to improve relations with

China and stressed the growing importance of nonaligned nations to Soviet policy.

Human Rights. Andropov's replacement as head of the KGB was Vitaly V. Fedorchuk, director of the security police in the Ukraine. A career KGB officer, Fedorchuk had a reputation as a hard-line official. Both Soviet dissidents and Western diplomats in Moscow credited him with pursuing a relentless campaign against human-rights activists. On Dec. 17 Fedorchuk was appointed minister of internal affairs, replacing one of Brezhnev's closest friends. Fedorchuk was succeeded as KGB chief by one of his top deputies, Viktor M. Chebrikov.

In a document covering the period Dec. 1, 1981, to May 31, 1982, the U.S. State Department reported that the Soviet government persisted in dealing harshly with human rights activists. Ethnic nationalists, religious believers, free trade unionists, and persons who wished to emigrate were among those arrested, thrown into psychiatric hospitals, or otherwise persecuted by authorities. Nobel Peace Prize winner Andrei Sakharov remained under house arrest in the closed city of Gor'kiy.

The Soviet human rights record did not improve in the second half of the year. The

Peace marchers, mainly women from Scandinavian countries, receive a welcome on arrival in Moscow in July. They were joined by several thousand supporters of the official Soviet Peace Committee. Soviet authorities broke up unsanctioned peace demonstrations, however, and expressed concern over pacifist trends among Soviet youth.

KGB arrested or harassed leaders of a fledgling peace movement that had sprung up without the authorization of the government. The so-called Helsinki Group, a citizens' committee set up to monitor the government's human rights violations, was decimated by arrests, so that its remaining three members who were not imprisoned or exiled announced in September that they were suspending their activities. That same month, Soviet authorities disconnected the direct-dialing telephone system for foreign calls set up for the 1980 Moscow Olympics and reduced the number of telephone lines to the West. The action appeared to reflect government determination to cut off Soviet citizens, particularly dissidents, from contacts with the West.

The Economy. The Soviet economy continued to stumble in 1982. Industrial output grew by 2.8 percent and productivity by 2 percent, the poorest results since World War II. Growth was well below the 4.7 percent annual target, according to the Soviet Central Statistical Board. Six-month output of oil and gas condensate rose a mere 2,000,000 metric tons, compared with production in the first half of 1981; nevertheless, gas production exceeded goals. Coal output stagnated at 363,000,000 tons for the first half of 1982, and steel output actually fell in this period. Production of consumer durables was mixed. Passenger car output fell, as did refrigerator output. On the other hand, the production

of television sets, radios, and other electronic consumer goods increased. Some 590,000 new apartments were completed.

Widespread and increasingly serious food shortages plagued the country, and the poor grain crop of 180,000,000 metric tons, far short of the goal of 239,000,000 metric tons, was expected to mean that Moscow would have to import 40,000,000 metric tons of grain by Oct. 1, 1983. At a Communist Party Central Committee meeting in May, Brezhnev announced details of a food program aimed at improving the situation. During the five-year plan starting in 1986, he said, the proportion of investment going to agriculture would be raised from 27 percent to 33 percent. More money would be spent on rural roads, housing, and farms in an effort to attract young people to agriculture. The state would also pay higher procurement prices for farm products and grant pay raises to farm workers.

In July U.S. President Ronald Reagan offered to extend by one year the bilateral grain supply agreement due to expire in October, and on Oct. 15 he offered to sell Moscow 23,000,000 metric tons of grain. The Soviets, however, were meeting most of their needs from other grain exporting countries.

In April Soviet authorities announced the execution of Vladimir Rytov, former deputy minister of fisheries, for taking bribes in connection with the fraudulent export of caviar to Western countries. Rytov became the most senior official to face a firing squad in many years.

Soviets in Space. In June French Col. Jean-Loup Chrétien became the first Westerner to take part in a Soviet space launch. He and two Soviet cosmonauts spent more than a week in space, part of it aboard the orbiting station Salyut 7. The Soviet Union sent a woman into space in August with two male colleagues; she was Svetlana Savitskaya, a 34-year-old test pilot. In December two cosmonauts returned to earth after spending 211 days aboard Salyut 7, an endurance record.

Foreign Relations. Soviet foreign policy was not notably successful in 1982, in part because domestic uncertainty over the Brezhnev succession appeared to be damping Moscow's activism.

Strain marked relations between the United States and the Soviet Union. The two nations began the year by resuming periodic Geneva talks on missile reduction in Europe. In a February speech Brezhnev proposed a two-thirds cut in U.S. and Soviet arsenals of medium-range nuclear weapons in Europe by 1990, an offer President Reagan quickly rejected. The U.S. leader instead made a "zero option" proposal, calling on Moscow to dismantle its medium-range missiles capable of hitting Western Europe, in return for Washington's cancellation of planned new medium-range missile deployment in North Atlantic Treaty Organization (NATO) nations. The Soviets rejected this idea.

In March Brezhnev announced that Moscow was suspending deployment of new nuclear missiles in European Russia; Washington dismissed the move as a propaganda gesture. In December Andropov proposed reducing Soviet medium-range missiles in Europe from 600 to 162, if the NATO deployment were canceled. The Western allies rejected the proposal.

In a May speech, Reagan proposed a two-step plan in which the U.S. and U.S.S.R. would begin by reducing by one third their arsenals of nuclear warheads on land- and sea-based intercontinental ballistic missiles. Moscow's response was cool.

Visiting London in June, Reagan called for a "crusade" against Soviet expansionism in an address to members of the British Parliament; Moscow assailed the speech. Later in the month he extended a U.S. embargo on equipment helping the U.S.S.R. to build a new gas pipeline to West Germany, by imposing sanctions against foreign firms producing pipeline equipment under American license and selling it to the Soviets. The Reagan decision angered Washington's allies in Western Europe, and Reagan lifted the embargo and sanctions on Nov. 13.

After a hiatus of three years, the U.S. and the Soviet Union opened strategic arms reduction talks in Geneva at the end of June. The negotiations were carried on in secret, and no breakthrough was reported. Meetings in September and October between U.S. Secretary of State George P. Shultz and Soviet Foreign Minister Andrei Gromyko left the two sides far apart on world issues.

In Afghanistan, despite the backing of 100,000 Soviet troops, the regime was not able to eliminate a Muslim insurgency. Martial law in Poland, which had Moscow's approval, failed to end that country's political and economic crisis.

The Soviet Union attempted to thaw relations with China after 20 years of hostility. The first high-level negotiations between the two countries in three years were held in Peking in October, but there was no hint of progress.

The Soviets failed to achieve any bonanza as a result of fighting either in the Falkland Islands or in Lebanon. During the Falklands war, Moscow backed Argentina diplomatically but took no active military role. Similarly, the Soviets verbally attacked Israel's strike against the Palestine Liberation Organization but made no overt move to intervene, and many Arab countries criticized Moscow's position as too passive. The poor performance of the Soviet-equipped Syrian forces in combat against Israel further damaged Moscow's prestige.

See STATISTICS OF THE WORLD. *See also* AFGHANISTAN; ASTRONOMY; COMMUNISM; MILITARY AND NAVAL AFFAIRS; POLAND; SPACE SCIENCE AND EXPLORATION.   F.W.

UNITED ARAB EMIRATES. *See* STATISTICS OF THE WORLD. *See also* PERSIAN GULF STATES.

Speaking before a U.N. disarmament conference less than two weeks after Israel invaded Lebanon, Israeli Prime Minister Menachem Begin addresses mainly empty seats. About two thirds of the delegations absented themselves.

UNITED NATIONS, THE, abbreviated U.N. The world organization was busy in the first part of 1982 with the war between Great Britain and Argentina for possession of the Falkland Islands (known as the Islas Malvinas in Latin America). During the remainder of the year it was preoccupied with the Israeli invasion of Lebanon. However, the continuing conflict between Iran and Iraq, the Soviet occupation of Afghanistan, and the Vietnamese occupation of Cambodia (Kampuchea) all claimed attention as well. Meanwhile, a special disarmament session ended without agreement, and the completion of a long-sought new convention on the law of the sea also fell short of full success when the United States and some other countries refused to sign it.

Falklands War. The U.N. Security Council met on April 1 to hear a British warning of an impending Argentine invasion of the Falklands. The council, speaking through its president, urged "utmost restraint," but the next day the invasion began. The Security Council demanded on April 3, by a vote of 10 in favor, 1 (Panama) against, and 4 abstentions (China, the Soviet Union, Poland, and Spain), the "immediate cessation of hostilities . . . [and] . . . a withdrawal of all Argentine forces." It also called for the resumption of efforts at "a diplomatic solution" of the long-standing dispute over the sovereignty of the islands. Argentina disregarded the request.

Naval action in the area commenced on May 1. On May 2 U.N. Secretary-General Javier Pérez de Cuéllar presented peace proposals to the warring parties. However, on May 20 the dispirited U.N. chief reported that his efforts had failed. On May 26 the Security Council unanimously reaffirmed its earlier resolution and called on Pérez de Cuéllar to renew his efforts, but on June 2 he

420

reported failure once more. On June 4 the U.S. joined Britain in vetoing a Security Council resolution calling for an immediate cease-fire and the simultaneous implementation of the previous resolutions. The war ended on June 14 with the surrender of Argentine troops on the islands. The last U.N. action on the issue during the year came on Nov. 4, when the General Assembly, acting on a Latin American request, adopted, this time with U.S. support, a resolution urging a "negotiated solution" of the dispute. The vote was 90–12, with 52 abstentions.

War in Lebanon. Israel's invasion of Lebanon on June 6 did not come as a surprise. As early as April 9 Lebanon complained of "massive Israeli troop concentrations" on its borders. On April 22 Lebanon, acting after heavy Israeli air strikes, called for urgent Security Council consultations, and on June 4 the president of the council, noting the accelerating air strikes on Beirut and other targets, appealed for a cease-fire. The call was repeated by the council itself the following day, but to no avail. Pérez de Cuéllar reported the act of invasion on June 6 and warned that the 7000-man U.N. peacekeeping forces in Lebanon had neither the mandate nor the ability to stop the Israeli advance. Further resolutions by the Security Council demanding an end to hostilities and Israeli withdrawal all went unheeded. Also unheeded was the demand of the General Assembly, in a special emergency meeting on Palestine, that Israel withdraw "within 24 hours."

As the plight of the civilians, caught in the crossfire, mounted, the Security Council demanded on July 4 that vital facilities such as electricity, water, food, and medical supplies be restored to Beirut. On July 29 the council demanded once again that Israel lift the blockade of west Beirut, and on Aug. 1 the council asked the secretary-general to deploy U.N. observers, a request Israel rejected. With the fighting growing more intense, the council asked on Aug. 4 that the Israelis return to their positions held before Aug. 1. On Aug. 6 the U.S. vetoed a Soviet draft demanding a ban on arms supplies to Israel, but on Aug. 12 Washington supported a unanimous call by the council for the lifting of the Israeli siege of west Beirut.

When on Aug. 20 the agreement for the withdrawal of the Palestine Liberation Organization from west Beirut was announced, Pérez de Cuéllar welcomed the news that U.S. and other Western contingents would enter Beirut to keep the peace. However, after the assassination of President-elect Bashir Gemayel on Sept. 14 and the subsequent occupation of west Beirut by Israeli troops, the council was called back into session. Meeting over the weekend of Sept. 18–19, it unanimously condemned the massacres of Palestinian civilians in the Sabra and Shatila camps. The General Assembly, resuming its special session, called for an investigation.

With the fighting ended, the regular session of the assembly rejected on Oct. 26 an Iranian motion that would have invalidated Israel's credentials. Responding to the U.S. warning that it, too, would leave the assembly if Israel was removed, a group of Arab states satisfied itself with placing its reservations concerning the validity of Israeli credentials on the record.

Other Asian Issues. The intermittent war between Iraq and Iran continued throughout the year. On June 29 Iraq claimed that it had completely withdrawn from Iranian territory, but Iran stated that the Iraqi claim was not true. On July 12, meeting on an Iraqi request, the Security Council called unanimously for a cease-fire and the mutual withdrawal of forces. Iraq welcomed the decision, but Iran "dissociated" itself from it, as it did when the General Assembly on Sept. 21 repeated the same request. The same outcome occurred in the Security Council on Oct. 4 and in the General Assembly on Oct. 22 (in a vote of 119–1 [Iran], with 15 abstentions) when both demanded an immediate cease-fire and a withdrawal of troops to internationally recognized boundaries.

Despite the efforts of Secretary-General Pérez de Cuéllar personally and through his special envoy, U.N. Under Secretary Diego Cordovez, to bring about a solution of the Afghan issue, the impasse continued throughout the year, with the Soviet Union disregarding a new call by the General As-

Miskito Indians receive plantains, a staple of their diet, at a camp in Honduras built and maintained with assistance from the U.N. High Commissioner for Refugees. The Indians had fled from neighboring Nicaragua.

sembly (in a vote of 114–21, with 13 abstentions, on Nov. 29) for the immediate withdrawal of "foreign forces."

Efforts to obtain a Vietnamese withdrawal from Cambodia remained similarly unsuccessful, despite an overwhelming call by the General Assembly, once again, on Oct. 28, by a vote of 105–23, with 20 abstentions, for withdrawal of all "foreign forces."

U.S. charges of chemical warfare waged with Soviet equipment against guerrillas in Afghanistan, Laos, and Cambodia, with some spillover into Thailand territory, were aired once again in the General Assembly. In March the U.S. claimed that more than 10,000 people had been killed by Soviet toxic weapons in recent years in Laos, Cambodia, Vietnam, and Afghanistan. In November an updated report repeated the accusations. A U.N. group of four experts, appointed in 1980, on Dec. 6 submitted its second report, stating that while the charges could not be proved conclusively, the experts nevertheless could not disregard "circumstantial evidence suggestive of possible use of some sort of chemical substance in some instances." These findings were endorsed by the General Assembly on Dec. 13 by a vote of 83–22, with 33 abstentions. The mandate of the group was not renewed, but in a separate resolu-

tion, adopted over Soviet-bloc opposition, the secretary-general was asked to draw up a list of experts who could be sent to investigate charges on the spot whenever they were raised.

Disarmament. The General Assembly held its second special session on disarmament from June 7 to July 10, but it could not agree on a comprehensive program. It was decided that the 1983 regular session of the assembly set a date for a third session. The assembly in December passed, by large majorities, two proposals for a freeze on the output and emplacement of nuclear weapons, and one demanding a total nuclear test ban.

Law of the Sea. Despite U.S. opposition, the Third Conference on the Law of the Sea ended successfully on Dec. 10 when 118 countries signed a new convention in Montego Bay, Jamaica. The U.S., unhappy with the establishment of an international body to regulate access to the resources of the ocean floors (*see* MINERALS AND METALS), refused to sign. The preparatory commission for the establishment of the International Sea-Bed Authority and the International Tribunal for the Law of the Sea was to begin work in March, 1983, in Kingston, Jamaica. All signers of the convention were automatically included as members of this commission.　　　　L.H.

United States of America

Economic recession, with attendant high unemployment and a record budget deficit, harried the United States in 1982. The administration of President Ronald Reagan searched for a peaceful settlement to the Arab-Israeli struggle and remained deeply concerned over the Soviet military buildup.

In 1982 Americans experienced the worst economic conditions since the Great Depression. Although the recession that began in 1981 appeared to bottom out by midyear, there was no discernible recovery. The nation's basic industries were operating well below productive capacity, and business failures reached a 50-year high. Unemployment rose to a double-digit rate in September. Banks carried a heavy proportion of problem loans. President Ronald Reagan's 1981 "supply side" tax cut produced little in 1982 except a record budget deficit. About the only good news was a sharp drop in the inflation rate; prices rose by less than 5 percent during the year.

The economy spelled trouble for President Reagan and the Republican Party. In the Nov. 2 congressional elections, the Democrats solidified their hold on the House of Representatives, picking up 26 seats from the Republicans. Democrats also did well at the statehouse level, with a net gain of seven governorships over the GOP.

In foreign affairs, the chief development was a growing U.S. presence in the Middle East, with American troops sent on peacekeeping missions to Beirut, Lebanon, and to Egypt's Sinai Peninsula. A Presidential proposal for settling the Palestinian problem was the first major U.S. Middle East initiative since the Camp David agreements.

DOMESTIC AFFAIRS

Elections. President Reagan asked the public to "stay the course," giving him more time to make his economic program work, but the voters signaled their impatience on Nov. 2. Although the Republicans maintained their 54–46 majority in the Senate, they lost 26 seats in the House, dropping to 166, as op-

posed to 269 for the Democrats. Many Republican candidates sought to dissociate themselves from Reagan's record, especially with regard to budget reductions for popular social programs. The Democrats, on the other hand, campaigned against "Reaganomics," hammering hard at the high unemployment rate and at what they portrayed as Republican plans to reduce social security benefits.

Gubernatorial races were less affected by national issues, but the Democrats did well here, too, picking up governorships from the GOP in such major states as Michigan, Ohio, and Texas. In California, however, Republican George Deukmejian was elected governor, ending eight years of Democratic control. *See also* ELECTIONS IN THE UNITED STATES.

Budget. In his budget message for fiscal year 1983, released on Feb. 6, President Reagan proposed a rise of 4.5 percent in total federal spending. The request of $216 billion for military programs was up 18 percent, but deep cuts were called for in government benefit programs, including welfare, food stamps, health care, subsidized housing, job training, and education.

Congress, however, resisted making large cuts in these programs in addition to the reductions already made in 1981. Reagan asked for budget cuts totaling $3.3 billion over three years in Aid to Families with Dependent Children; Congress approved reductions of only $342,000,000, most of which would not take effect for two or three years. For Medicaid, which helps pay medical bills for 22,000,000 poor Americans, Reagan proposed cuts totaling $8.2 billion over three years; Congress approved only $1.1 billion worth of reductions. For food stamps, with

In 1982 Philadelphia celebrated the 300th anniversary of its founding. Large crowds gathered on June 17 to watch 34 sailing ships from a dozen countries "parade" up the Delaware River to commemorate the event.

20,500,000 recipients, Reagan proposed reductions of $7.1 billion over three years; Congress approved only $1.9 billion in cuts.

Reagan proposed reducing or ending benefits for more than 700,000 welfare families, but the changes enacted by Congress would not affect nearly so many families nor cause large reductions in benefits. Congress approved numerous changes in the Medicare program, mostly involving limits on the amounts for which hospitals and physicians may be reimbursed; however, these changes were expected only to reduce the rate of growth of the program, with an increase of $5 billion still projected from fiscal 1982 to fiscal 1983. The first budget resolution for fiscal 1983, adopted by Congress on June 23, called for spending $769.8 billion—$12.2 billion higher than proposed by Reagan—and a reduction of $5.4 billion in the defense spending request.

Reagan's initial budget message put total spending in fiscal 1983 at $757.6 billion, with a deficit of $91.5 billion. Despite the large deficit, he opposed any reduction of the three-year tax cut enacted in 1981, calling instead for $12.7 billion in added revenues from selective tax increases on business, new or increased user fees, and tougher tax enforcement, including a 5 percent withholding tax on dividend and interest income. As the recession continued, however, it became obvious that tax revenues would not reach expectations, and the projected deficit began to grow. On June 28 Reagan signed legislation lifting the temporary federal debt ceiling to $1.143 trillion. Fiscal year 1982 ended with a record shortfall of $110.7 billion, more than double the initial estimate of $45 billion. By July the Administration estimated the fiscal 1983 deficit at $115 billion; the Congressional Budget Office placed it at $155 billion.

Under the impact of these figures, the President on Aug. 4 endorsed a tax-increase bill before Congress. Passed on Aug. 19, the legislation was expected to raise an additional $98.3 billion in revenue over three years, including $50 billion in business taxes, $18 billion in taxes on individuals, and $21 billion from measures aimed at gaining better compliance with the tax laws. The bill also provided for $17.5 billion in spending cuts for health care, welfare, and unemployment programs through fiscal year 1985.

"New Federalism" Proposal. In his first State of the Union address, delivered on Jan. 26, Reagan announced a sweeping plan to give states and localities control over federal programs in fiscal 1984 costing $47 billion a year. Under the plan, the federal government would give up its responsibility for food stamps and payments to poor families with dependent children. In return, the federal government would relieve the states of any responsibility for Medicaid payments. By fiscal 1988 the states would be in complete control of more than 40 federal grant programs, using a trust fund of $28 billion in revenues from federal excise taxes. This trust fund would gradually disappear, but states could increase their own use of excise taxes as the federal government gave up that source of revenue.

State officials showed little enthusiasm for the proposal, arguing that the extra costs would far outweigh the benefits. In June the Administration dropped its proposal that the states take over the food stamp program and offered to give the states more control over Medicaid. On Aug. 9, however, a White House spokesman confirmed that the plan would not be submitted to Congress in 1982.

The Economy. The recession appeared to have bottomed out by mid-1982, but there were few signs of recovery. The unemployment rate reached 10.1 percent in September, the highest figure since 1940; for November the rate was 10.8 percent. The number of business failures was higher than at any time since 1932. Corporate earnings slumped, and businesses trimmed plans for expansion and modernization—activities the 1981 tax cuts were supposed to stimulate.

Automobile sales in the 1982 model year were the lowest since 1961. By the end of October, steel-mill utilization had dropped to 36.8 percent of capacity, the lowest rate since 1933. More hopeful signs were a surge in the stock market that began in August, because of a drop in interest rates, and an inflation rate of less than 5 percent. *See also* ECONOMY AND BUSINESS.

Banking and Finance. Legislation was passed in 1982 to shore up the nation's savings and loan institutions, which were troubled because for the second straight year Americans were withdrawing more money than they deposited. The Federal Reserve Board kept interest rates high for most of the year, in an effort to curb inflation by restricting the growth of the nation's money supply. One result of this policy was that the dollar rose sharply in value against foreign currencies, making American goods more expensive overseas. The Federal Reserve Board began making more money available in July, thereby easing interest rates.

The world burden of debt continued to increase in 1982. At the end of March foreigners owed U.S. banks $451 billion. Among the many countries in arrears to American creditors were Argentina, Mexico, and Poland. *See also* BANKING AND FINANCE.

Energy. The weak national and world economy meant a slump in energy consumption and in oil prices. In July the number of oil and gas drilling rigs in operation in the U.S. fell to a 25-month low. Oil companies experienced a drop in profits, with many refineries closing. Exxon Corp. announced plans in August to shut down 850 service stations. Exxon also withdrew from a shale oil project in Colorado. *See also* ENERGY; PETROLEUM AND NATURAL GAS.

Agriculture and Labor. Harvests of wheat, corn, and soybeans were the largest in U.S. history, but farm income dropped to the lowest figure in real dollars since 1933. The value of farm exports fell for the first time since 1969, and huge surpluses sometimes exceeded storage capacity. *See* AGRICULTURE.

In a year of high unemployment, unionized auto workers and truckers agreed to accept wage freezes. For the first nine months of the year, major collective bargaining agreements in the private sector provided for annual raises averaging only 3.5 percent a year. Congress passed a new, limited job-training program to replace the expiring Comprehensive Employment and Training Act, whose extension Reagan opposed. *See also* LABOR.

Civil Rights. The Voting Rights Act of 1965, credited with opening the polls to millions of blacks and Hispanics, was extended by Congress for an additional 25 years. The time limit for ratification of the proposed Equal Rights Amendment to the federal Constitution, barring discrimination against women, ran out at midyear. Attempts in Congress to restrict abortion, allow prayer in public schools, and limit the ability of federal courts to order busing for school desegregation all failed. *See also* CIVIL RIGHTS AND CIVIL LIBERTIES; EDUCATION; NEGROES IN THE UNITED STATES; WOMEN.

Military and Space. A movement to freeze both U.S. and Soviet nuclear arsenals at their current levels enjoyed much support among the American public despite the President's contention that a freeze would leave the Soviets with a margin of superiority and thus no incentive to negotiate a reduction in nuclear arms. Congress showed disapproval of a major military buildup by failing to vote funds

in 1982 for the production of the MX missile system or the medium-range Pershing II missile, funds that the Reagan administration had requested. In November Reagan proposed deploying 100 MX missiles in a closely spaced system, known as dense pack, next to an Air Force base in Cheyenne, Wyo. *See also* MILITARY AND NAVAL AFFAIRS.

The space shuttle *Columbia* successfully completed its last two orbital test flights. In November the shuttle performed its first mission as a revenue-earning space cargo carrier, lofting two communications satellites into earth orbit. *See also* SPACE SCIENCE AND EXPLORATION.

FOREIGN POLICY

Secretary of State Alexander M. Haig, Jr., resigned his post on June 25 and was succeeded by a former member of the cabinet of President Richard M. Nixon, George P. Shultz (see biography at PEOPLE IN THE NEWS). Haig felt that the White House staff, and particularly national security adviser William P. Clark (see biography at PEOPLE IN THE NEWS), had infringed upon his prerogatives, and he was also known to have opposed recent policy decisions.

U.S.S.R. Relations with the Soviet Union remained chilly during 1982. On May 9 Reagan proposed a two-step plan whereby Washington and Moscow would initially reduce by one third their arsenals of nuclear warheads on land- and sea-based ballistic missiles. In the second phase the two nations would accept an equal ceiling on the total payload, or "throw weight," of all nuclear missiles. In essence the proposal asked Moscow to give up what Washington saw as a 3-1 Soviet lead in total nuclear weapons payload; it did not mention bombers or intermediate-range cruise missiles, in which the U.S. holds a lead. The two countries began strategic arms reduction talks in Geneva on June 29.

Western Europe. In June Reagan made his first overseas tour, a ten-day trip to Western Europe. After returning home, he angered European leaders on June 18 by extending his December, 1981, ban on the sale of U.S. oil and gas equipment to the U.S.S.R. Issued in response to the imposition of martial law in Poland, the sanctions were extended in order to bar foreign affiliates of U.S. companies from fulfilling their contracts for construction of a 3700-mi. natural gas pipeline connecting Siberia with West Germany, and to bar the use of U.S. equipment and technology by foreign companies for the pipeline project.

The proposed pipeline might eventually supply West Germany, France, Italy, and Spain with more than 30 percent of their natural gas and would be a major source of badly needed foreign exchange earnings for Moscow. Washington was worried that Western Europe would become too dependent on Soviet gas to resist political pressure from Moscow, but Europeans viewed the Soviet orders for construction equipment and pipe as a means of stimulating their economies and easing high unemployment.

The decision affected British, German, French, and Italian companies with contracts to supply gas-turbine blades under license from General Electric Co. The governments involved ordered the participating firms to fulfill their orders anyway, and in August the Reagan administration ordered trade sanctions against the companies defying the embargo, barring them from buying goods and services from the U.S. The sanctions were lifted on Nov. 13, in connection with what Reagan said was an agreement among the Western powers on a "realistic and security-minded economic policy toward the Soviet Union."

Another source of discord was monetary policy. High U.S. interest rates were attracting capital from Europe in 1982, forcing Western European governments to keep their own countries' interest rates high in order to stem a flight of capital. This, in turn, meant that their domestic economies remained sluggish because of the high cost of borrowing for capital investment.

Middle East. The U.S. assumed important military responsibilities in 1982 by taking part in the 11-nation peacekeeping force patrolling Egypt's Sinai Peninsula after the Israeli pullout on April 25 and by sending Marines to Lebanon during the summer.

Immediately after Israel invaded southern Lebanon on June 6, Washington portrayed the attack as an opportunity to help the Lebanese government free itself of an armed Syrian and Palestinian presence. Special negotiator Philip C. Habib was sent to the Middle East to negotiate an Israeli withdrawal with this objective in mind. In August Habib achieved an agreement that called on Israel to lift its siege of west Beirut in return for the withdrawal from Lebanon of Palestine Liberation Organization forces. The U.S., France, and Italy provided small armed contingents that oversaw the withdrawal and then left Lebanon themselves.

Following the assassination of Lebanese President-elect Bashir Gemayel on Sept. 14, Israeli forces occupied west Beirut. The U.S. demanded that Israel withdraw immediately—a demand that took on greater urgency with the revelation of a massacre of Palestinian civilians in west Beirut by Christian militiamen. The multinational force returned to Beirut on Sept. 29, and this time Reagan said that the Marines would leave only when Lebanese authorities declared themselves able to maintain order. Indeed, Reagan indicated that the Marines might remain until Syrian and Israeli forces withdrew from Lebanon—an unlikely prospect in 1982.

On Sept. 1 Reagan issued a plan that called for Palestinians living in the Israeli-occupied

How Congress Slashed Outlays

	Change in 1983 Spending	Total Cuts, 1983-85
Agriculture		
Dairy price supports	−$1,482 mil.	−$ 4,154 mil.
Grain-surplus reductions	+$ 192 mil.	−$ 274 mil.
Exports promotion	−$ 116 mil.	−$ 188 mil.
Health and Social Services		
Food stamps	−$ 492 mil.	−$ 1,755 mil.
Medicare	−$2,879 mil.	−$13,307 mil.
Medicaid	−$ 256 mil.	−$ 1,030 mil.
Public assistance	−$ 85 mil.	−$ 343 mil.
Child-support enforcement	−$ 92 mil.	−$ 384 mil.
SSI	−$ 116 mil.	−$ 386 mil.
Unemployment compensation	+$1,981 mil.	+$ 1,883 mil.
Federal Employes		
Military retirement	−$ 260 mil.	−$ 2,215 mil.
Civilian retirement	−$ 186 mil.	−$ 1,365 mil.
Travel pay	−$ 16 mil.	−$ 407 mil.
Interest on Public Debt		
Anticipated lower interest on U.S. savings bonds	−$ 329 mil.	−$ 1,878 mil.
Veterans' benefits	−$ 168 mil.	−$ 552 mil.
Housing mortgages	−$ 690 mil.	−$ 2,019 mil.
TOTAL BUDGET CUTS	**−$ 5.0 bil.**	**−$ 28.4 bil.**

Note: Totals may add because of rounding. Years end September 30. *USN&WR—*Basic data: U.S. Congress

West Bank and Gaza Strip areas to attain full autonomy "in association with" Jordan. He also demanded a freeze on further Jewish settlement in these areas. Reagan's proposal, the first major U.S. Middle East initiative in years, was rejected by Israel. *See also* MIDDLE EAST.

Latin America. Following Argentina's seizure of the British-held Falkland Islands in early April, Secretary of State Haig sought to avoid a major military confrontation by conducting shuttle diplomacy. After this mission failed, Reagan on April 30 accused Argentina of "armed aggression" and imposed economic sanctions, including suspension of all military exports from the U.S. Under long-standing agreements with the British, the U.S. shipped aviation fuel to the joint U.S.-British air base at Ascension Island in the South Atlantic, sold Great Britain some 100 Sidewinder missiles and other weaponry, and provided routine intelligence and weather information. Reagan lifted economic sanctions against Argentina on July 12 and military sanctions on Sept. 24. Nevertheless, Washington's tilt toward Britain hampered U.S. relations with Latin American countries, most of which had supported Argentina. The Organization of American States also supported Argentina's claim to sovereignty over the Falklands, effectively isolating Washington. In November the U.S. sought to recoup some of its diplomatic losses by voting for an Argentine-sponsored United Nations resolution calling on Britain to resume talks on the eventual disposition of the islands.

During 1982 the Reagan administration continued to hold Cuba and Nicaragua responsible for the leftist insurgency in El Salvador and provided financial aid to antigovernment elements in Nicaragua. As relations deteriorated between Nicaragua and neighboring Honduras, from where Nicaraguan exiles were conducting raids with U.S. support, Washington promised Honduras increased military aid. Other initiatives included $355,000,000 in emergency aid for the Caribbean Basin area and the imposition, effective on May 15, of severe new restrictions on tourist and business travel to Cuba. On Aug. 20 emergency U.S. aid was extended to Mexico to ease a financial crisis that left the country at least temporarily unable to pay its foreign debt, which included at least $18 billion owed to U.S. banks.

Asia. On Aug. 17 the U.S. and China issued an accord in which China pledged to seek reunification with Taiwan by peaceful means and the U.S. promised gradually to reduce arms shipments to the Taipei government. Despite the pact, China continued to regard U.S. arms sales to Taiwan as an infringement of its sovereignty. On Aug. 19 Reagan sent Congress official notification of his decision to sell spare parts to Taiwan to be used in the production of 60 F-5 fighter jets.

Other 1982 events included state visits to the U.S. by Indian Prime Minister Indira Gandhi, Pakistani President Muhammad Zia ul-Haq, Philippine President Ferdinand E. Marcos, and Indonesian President Suharto.

Africa. The Reagan administration continued to insist that Cuban troops leave Angola as part of a settlement in which South Africa would withdraw from South-West Africa, or Namibia. On March 10, charging that Libya was still supporting terrorism and subversion abroad, Washington imposed an embargo on

---

Food for Thought

In July Gov. Richard D. Lamm (D) unveiled a bust at the state Capitol of one of Colorado's most unsavory citizens, Alferd E. Packer. In the winter of 1874, Packer journeyed over the Rocky Mountains from Utah to Colorado with five other men, but he was the only one to reach civilization the following spring. He admitted eating his companions but said that four of them had been killed by the fifth, and that he had killed the fifth only in self-defense. An unconvinced court sent him to prison, where he spent 16 years. Although Gov. Lamm professed to find the unveiling ceremony distasteful, he averred that both he and Packer "serve our fellow men, each in our own way." In September the bust was permanently installed in the University of Colorado dining hall, which is known as the Alferd E. Packer Memorial Grill.

President Ronald Reagan, speaking on the telephone to Israeli Prime Minister Menachem Begin while Secretary of State George Shultz watches, expresses "outrage" and "shock" over an Israeli air attack on west Beirut. U.S. Marines later joined a multinational force charged with keeping the peace in the Lebanese capital.

oil imports and curtailed exports of high technology to Tripoli. On May 27 Washington formally completed an agreement with Morocco that would allow U.S. military planes to use Moroccan airfields during emergencies in the Middle East or Africa.

See STATISTICS OF THE WORLD. See also CONGRESS OF THE UNITED STATES; PRESIDENT OF THE UNITED STATES; STATE GOVERNMENT REVIEW; SUPREME COURT OF THE UNITED STATES.   R.H.

UPPER VOLTA. See STATISTICS OF THE WORLD.

URUGUAY. The military government of President Gregorio Alvarez Armelino suffered a reverse in party primary elections held on Nov. 27, 1982. During the year the economy was in deep recession.

More than 1,200,000 voters went to the polls for the first time in nine years of military rule in order to elect the 500 members of the nation's three approved parties who were to choose presidential candidates for an election to be held in late 1984. Only the traditional centrist Blanco and Colorado parties and the rightist Civil Union Party were allowed to offer candidates; the Christian Democrats, Socialists, and Communists remained banned. Unofficial results showed that Blanco Party candidates opposed to the government won 78 percent of the vote, while progovernment candidates won only 9 percent. Progovernment Colorado Party candidates were also trailing.

A sharp decline in world prices for meat and wool, Uruguay's principal exports, damaged the economy in 1982. Cattle ranchers owed more than $1 billion to foreign creditors, with more than one third of that amount overdue. The industrial sector reduced production and laid off workers because tariffs had been lowered, making it difficult or impossible for many industries to compete with imports.

Another source of the country's economic woes was the strength of Uruguay's peso on international money markets, thereby making its exports expensive and thus preventing the country from earning the foreign exchange it needed. On Nov. 26 the government said that it would cease supporting the peso on money markets, an action that amounted to a devaluation of about 40 percent. The announcement came three days after Economy Minister Valentin Arismendi returned from Washington, D.C., where he obtained a loan of $400,000,000.

See STATISTICS OF THE WORLD.   A.E.J.

UTAH. See STATISTICS OF THE WORLD.

429

V

VANUATU. *See* STATISTICS OF THE WORLD.

VENEZUELA. For the first time in two decades, oil-rich Venezuela, led by President Luis Herrera Campíns, faced an economic crisis in 1982. Declining world demand for oil, Venezuela's chief export, led to foreign debt problems. On Sept. 28 Finance Minister Luis Ugueto asked international bankers to convert some of Venezuela's $8.8 billion in short-term foreign debt into longer-term credits. On Nov. 29 the government said that it had taken over the country's largest private bank to keep it from failing.

The longtime dispute over the sparsely populated Essequibo jungle region, representing more than half of Guyana's territory but claimed by Venezuela, reemerged in June with the expiration of a 12-year moratorium on the issue. The 53,000-sq. mi. disputed territory was believed to contain valuable mineral deposits and some petroleum. Moreover, Guyana, a poor country, was eager to exploit the region's Mazaruni River for its potential hydroelectric power, but it was prevented from doing so by a Venezuelan veto of proposed World Bank financing. Despite Guyana's fears of Venezuelan military intervention, Herrera's government claimed that it sought to settle the dispute peacefully. However, it rejected Guyana's bid to place the matter before an international body.

Venezuela supported the Argentine position in the dispute with Great Britain over the Falkland Islands. In September the presidents of Venezuela and Mexico jointly appealed to the United States, Nicaragua, and Honduras to reduce the tensions and armed clashes on the Honduran-Nicaraguan border.

The Venezuelan foreign ministry announced on Sept. 28 that Venezuela had changed its observer status to full membership in the 95-member Nonaligned Movement of Third World countries. This group represented the largest body of votes at the United Nations General Assembly, a potential arbiter of the Essequibo question.

See STATISTICS OF THE WORLD. A.E.J.

VERMONT. *See* STATISTICS OF THE WORLD.

VIETNAM. Vietnam's Communist Party Politburo, led by General Secretary Le Duan, was reshuffled in March, 1982, and changes were made in the 13-member Council of State, which supervises the cabinet, in June. The economy remained in desperate straits, despite large infusions of Soviet aid.

Politics. The fifth Vietnamese Communist Party congress since the party's founding in 1930 was held in late March. Party chief Le Duan called for a purge to rid the party's ranks of "exploiters, smugglers, speculators, persons involved in corruption, and oppressors of the masses." The congress dropped 39 members of the Central Committee and six members of the Politburo, the party's top policy-making body. Among the latter was Gen. Vo Nguyen Giap, the famed commander credited with defeating the French in the 1950's and directing the strategy against American and South Vietnamese forces in the 1960's. Retaining their positions at the helm besides Le Duan, 75, were Council of State Chairman Truong Chinh, 75, and Premier Pham Van Dong, 76.

A new economic course for the 1980's, announced by party leaders, was to subordinate grandiose industrial schemes to medium- and small-scale enterprises. Greater emphasis was to be placed on agriculture and on supplying citizens with basic commodities. Party workers were urged to be patient and flexible with peasants who resisted the collectivization of their land.

At the conclusion, in late June, of the seventh National Assembly's third session, Vietnam's former chief representative at international meetings, Xuan Thuy, was dismissed as deputy chairman and general secretary of the Council of State, the top executive arm of the government, apparently because of the country's poor economic performance. His duties were assumed by Huynh Tan Phat and Le Thanh Nghi, respectively.

Two Buddhist leaders were jailed in Ho Chi Minh City in late February. A statement

Children born of American fathers and Vietnamese mothers pose in Ho Chi Minh City (formerly Saigon). Several groups of such children came to the U.S. in 1982, and Congress passed a bill granting citizenship to all Amerasian children who could prove American parentage.

issued by Vietnamese Buddhists in Paris described the Unified Buddhist Church of Vietnam as "the only organization that dared to speak out against repression and violation of human rights" in that country.

The Economy. Agricultural production was said to have improved slightly in 1982, largely because some farmers were permitted to sell their surplus in an expanded free market. Huge trade deficits, however, resulted from declining world demand for Vietnam's exports and the high prices of imported oil and machinery.

In April a confidential report of the International Monetary Fund (IMF) predicted that Vietnam would be unable to meet its foreign debt payments in 1982 and urged Hanoi to reduce its subsidies for civil servants and workers in state enterprises. Creditor nations, including Great Britain, France, Japan, and Sweden, told Hanoi in July that a rescheduling of its debts to them depended entirely on Vietnam's adoption of an economic program approved by the IMF. Vietnam was either unwilling or unable to do so, however. Conse-

quently, the IMF refused Hanoi's request for funds to help meet its debts.

Foreign Affairs. In early March China seized what it described as a "Vietnamese reconnaissance boat" near the Paracel Islands in the South China Sea. These islands had been claimed by both countries and by Taiwan and were believed to have offshore oil reserves. The incident was apparently in retaliation for Vietnam's shelling of three Chinese boats and the capture of one of these on the previous day. Each side charged the other with attacking peaceful fishing junks.

Vietnam's foreign minister, Nguyen Co Thach, spent much of 1982 unsuccessfully making Vietnam's case abroad for its occupation of Cambodia. Except for the Soviet bloc nations, world demand continued for the withdrawal of Vietnamese troops from Cambodia and for a United Nations-monitored election in that country.

See STATISTICS OF THE WORLD.   R.J.C.

VIRGINIA. See STATISTICS OF THE WORLD.
VIRGIN ISLANDS. See STATISTICS OF THE WORLD.

WOMEN. In 1982 the Equal Rights Amendment (ERA) to the U.S. Constitution failed to attain ratification before the June 30 deadline. The U.S. Senate voted down a bill restricting women's rights to abortion and delayed debate until 1983 on a proposed constitutional amendment that would permit the states to legislate abortion restrictions.

In U.S. elections on Nov. 2, 21 women won seats in the House of Representatives. In the races for the Senate and state governorships, however, no woman was elected, although several came close.

Legal Equality. The June 30, 1982, deadline for ratification of the ERA, which would have banned discrimination on the basis of sex, passed with the amendment still three states short of the 38 needed. While polls indicated that a majority of U.S. citizens favored the amendment, legislatures in Florida, Georgia, Illinois, Missouri, North Carolina, Oklahoma, and Virginia rejected the ERA in 1982. Proponents attributed its failure to the highly organized efforts of anti-ERA forces, the preponderance of men in state legislatures, and pressure exerted by businesses that profit from sex discrimination. The amendment was reintroduced in the U.S. Congress on July 14. Should it receive a two-thirds majority in both houses, it would again require ratification by 38 states.

Elsewhere, the parliament of Kuwait and the supreme court of Liechtenstein failed to give support to women seeking the right to vote. In Switzerland, despite a 1981 law guaranteeing equality to women, the canton of Appenzell, Inner-Rhoden, rejected woman suffrage in local elections.

Abortion. By a vote of 47–46, the U.S. Senate on Sept. 15 killed a bill that would have stopped all federal funding for abortions and would have encouraged attempts to reverse Supreme Court decisions allowing unrestricted abortions in the first trimester of pregnancy. Debate on a proposed constitutional amendment allowing state legislatures to restrict abortion was delayed until 1983. In Connecticut a federal judge ruled on July 7 that a fetus could be a party with its mother in a brutality suit against the police. Forthcoming debate on abortion legislation would hinge on the question of whether a fetus is a person with legal rights to government protection.

In January Kuwait became the first Persian Gulf Arab state to legalize abortion. Pregnancies that would cause "gross physical harm" to the mother or result in fetal brain damage "beyond hope of treatment" were allowed to be legally terminated.

Employment. In a successful attempt to extend the principle of equal pay for equal work, nurses in San Jose, Calif., remained on strike for three months before winning a 27 percent salary increase over three years. The nurses demanded comparable pay for jobs that they contended were as valuable as (although not identical to) the jobs performed by those in male-dominated professions.

On May 17 the U.S. Supreme Court extended the scope of Title IX of the Education Amendments of 1972, ruling that laws against sex discrimination in federally funded education programs covered an institution's employees as well as students. In a suit brought under Title VII of the 1964 Civil Rights Act, female employees of a U.S.-based subsidiary of a Japanese firm challenged their company's policy of hiring only male Japanese citizens for executive positions. The Court ruled unanimously on June 15 that Japanese companies incorporated and doing business in the United States must obey federal laws against job discrimination.

Both women and minorities could suffer from a Supreme Court ruling on April 15 that upheld the legality of job seniority systems in existence since the Civil Rights Act, as long as such systems were not established with discriminatory intent. Seniority systems, which often govern pay, promotions, and layoff policies, commonly work against women and minority personnel, who are frequently among the most recently employed.

The Economy. The poverty rate for households in the U.S. headed by women continued to exceed 25 percent. On April 14 the Bureau of the Census issued an analysis of 1979 data in which it reduced this rate to 17.6 percent by taking into account the value of government-funded benefits such as food stamps and Medicaid.

Women in the U.S. earned an average of 59¢ for every dollar earned by men. In Canada women's relative income was even lower—less than half that earned by men, according to statistics released in 1982. Canada announced a massive job training effort in 1982, offering incentives to businesses that provided training to minorities and women.

Education. The first woman U.S. Supreme Court justice, Sandra Day O'Connor, wrote the Court's July 1 ruling that held that a state-run nursing school cannot exclude men. The Mississippi University for Women had justified its all-female policy on the basis that the school was providing affirmative action. In her written opinion, Justice O'Connor invoked the principle of "heightened scrutiny," which the Court has applied to sex-discrimination claims since the mid-1970's.

Achievements. In mid-July 3000 people attended the opening of the Women's Rights National Historical Park at Seneca Falls, N.Y., already the site of the National Women's Hall of Fame. (The first U.S. women's rights convention was held there in July, 1848.)

Yugoslavia's parliament elected the nation's first woman premier, Milka Planinć, on May 16; she previously headed the Communist Party in the Yugoslav republic of Croatia. On Feb. 16 the Malta house of representatives elected Agatha Barbara, 59, as the nation's first woman president. Svetlana Savitskaya, a 34-year-old Soviet test pilot, became the second woman to participate in a space flight when she began orbiting the earth on Aug. 19 with two male crew members in Soyuz T7; the first woman in space, also a Russian, was Valentina V. Tereshkova, in 1963. In March, 1982, Bertha Wilson became the first female justice of the Canadian supreme court; she had been a judge of the Ontario court of appeals since 1975. In the Bahamas, Janet J. Bostwick, a women's rights activist, became the first female elected to parliament.   R.M.

WYOMING. *See* STATISTICS OF THE WORLD.

YEMEN, PEOPLE'S DEMOCRATIC REPUBLIC OF. Despite some signs of ideological pragmatism, the People's Democratic Republic of Yemen, or South Yemen, remained solidly in the camp of hard-line radical Arab states in 1982.

On April 6 South Yemen joined Algeria, Syria, and the Palestine Liberation Organization (PLO)—other members of the so-called steadfastness front—in rejecting a Middle East peace plan proposed by Egypt at a meeting of nonaligned nations held in Kuwait. The Egyptian proposal called for a Palestinian state, but it also called for peace between Israel and the Arab states. Moderate Arab regimes such as Morocco and Jordan sent messages of congratulations to Egyptian President Hosni Mubarak following Israel's final return of the Sinai Peninsula on April 25, but again South Yemen chose to join the other hard-liners in saying that "Syria and its allies remain ready to oppose the attempt to generate Camp Davids in the upcoming era." In late August South Yemen took in some 700 PLO fighters after the withdrawal of the PLO from Beirut, Lebanon.

South Yemen—the only avowedly Marxist state in the Arab world—continued to provide important strategic facilities to the Soviet Union. Soviet submarines used the vast natural harbor at Aden, and Soviet reconnaissance planes took off from Aden's Khormakar airport to patrol the Persian Gulf. An estimated 1500 Soviet advisers were working in South Yemen on military or technical advisory jobs, and the country's 24,000-man armed forces were entirely Soviet-equipped.

South Yemen's President Ali Nasser Mohammed, 43, sought to improve relations with his neighbors North Yemen and Oman.

In May Mohammed met with North Yemen President Ali Abdullah Saleh to discuss a possible unification agreement, but years of hostility and mutual subversion made such efforts difficult. The talks with North Yemen made little real progress; similar talks with Oman in Kuwait began on Oct. 25.

See STATISTICS OF THE WORLD.   A.D.

YEMEN ARAB REPUBLIC. A strong earthquake hit the Yemen Arab Republic, or North Yemen, on Dec. 13, 1982, killing more than 2800 people and leaving more than 700,000 homeless. In a message to the nation, President Ali Abdullah Saleh spoke of "the total destruction of some towns and villages, scores of villages partly destroyed and scores of houses collapsed over their inhabitants." The quake shook San'a, the capital, but caused most damage around Dhamar.

Yemen had additional problems to cope with in 1982, including a sporadic guerrilla war sponsored by neighboring South Yemen and a domestic economy that ranked as one of the poorest in the world. North and South Yemen nearly engaged in open warfare in the spring, when North Yemen mounted a major offensive against the National Democratic Front guerrilla organization, which was backed by South Yemen. The guerrillas sought to overthrow the government of North Yemen, which was strongly under the influence of Saudi Arabia. In May South Yemen executed ten persons on charges that they had infiltrated from North Yemen to commit sabotage after they had received instructions and training from Saudi Arabia and the United States. Nevertheless, North and South Yemen continued to hold intermittent talks on unity.

The first stage of a five-year development plan for North Yemen went into effect in 1982. The plan proposed total development expenditure of $6.3 billion, of which at least $3 billion would have to come from foreign loans or grants. North Yemen continued to be dependent on foreign assistance. In 1982 fewer than one quarter of its people were literate, and seven out of ten of them lived on farms. Fewer than one third of the farms had tractors. More than 1,000,000 Yemenis were working in other countries, such as the Persian Gulf states, where many were employed in the oilfields.

See STATISTICS OF THE WORLD.   A.D.

YUGOSLAVIA. In 1982 Yugoslavia appeared to weather well the challenges of the post-Tito era. The government dealt firmly with two key problems: economic downturn and unrest in the province of Kosovo.

Domestic Affairs. Leadership rotation, which was instituted by the late President Josip Broz Tito, continued to take place smoothly. The government changed hands on schedule in May, and Yugoslavia made news when a woman, Milka Planinč, 57, became the country's prime minister. A Croatian and a World War II Partisan backer of Tito, Planinč headed an administration of 28 ministers, only five of whom were members of the outgoing government.

Like the state, the ruling party—the League of Communists—also changed officials. At its 12th congress in June—the first since Tito's death in 1980—the party chose Mitja Ribicic, 63, a former prime minister, as president of the central committee presidium. The atmosphere at the congress was more freewheeling than it had been in prior years, as delegates openly voiced criticism of the regime and its efforts to cure Yugoslavia's economic and ethnic troubles. The party opted to stick by Tito's basic policies of worker self-management, decentralization, and international nonalignment.

Yugoslavia's economic afflictions were serious. The inflation rate hovered at 40 percent (the highest in Europe) early in the year, unemployment was significant, and the country owed about $20 billion abroad, $4 billion of which was due in 1982. The Planinč government, which took office vowing to deal effectively with these problems, introduced an austerity budget. In July it froze prices for six months to slow inflation and sought to restrain consumer buying by raising requirements for down payments on major purchases. To trim the trade deficit, it placed curbs on imports and in November devalued the dinar, Yugoslavia's currency, by 16 percent, thus stimulating exports. Economic growth for the year was estimated at 2 percent.

The autonomous province of Kosovo, populated largely by Muslims of Albanian descent, simmered with discontent. Despite close police scrutiny in the region, small demonstrations broke out in early April, the first anniversary of major nationalist rioting in 1981, and sporadic acts of violence occurred throughout the year. The Albanians of Kosovo wanted greater autonomy and economic progress; some even wished to secede from Yugoslavia and join neighboring Albania. The government jailed leading Albanian nationalists.

Foreign Affairs. Belgrade reemphasized its nonalignment by maintaining strong links in the West and the Third World as it cultivated a closer relationship with the Soviet Union. Yugoslav officials, for example, were cordial to Soviet Foreign Minister Andrei Gromyko, who made the first high-level Russian visit since Tito's death, but they became critical when he took the occasion to attack the United States publicly. Gromyko's trip ended with a communiqué that did not conceal the existence of differences between Moscow and Belgrade on world issues.

Yugoslav leaders welcomed several other official foreign visitors to Belgrade during the year. Greek Prime Minister Andreas Papandreou, in May, was encouraged by the Yugoslavs to retain Greece's ties to the North Atlantic Treaty Organization, for the sake of stability in the Balkans. U.S. Secretary of Defense Caspar W. Weinberger reassured Yugoslav officials of continued U.S. support in December.

Washington considered it important to encourage Belgrade's independent stance, par-

One of the world's few female heads of government, Milka Planinć, 57, was appointed prime minister of Yugoslavia on May 16 and charged with enacting a program to deal with her nation's economic difficulties. An associate said: "She hears everybody out and then makes up her mind rapidly and decisively."

ticularly in view of an increasing reliance by Yugoslavia on sales to the U.S.S.R. to balance its trade. In April a ranking State Department official appealed to U.S. bank executives to deal sympathetically with Yugoslavia's requests for continuing credit.

See STATISTICS OF THE WORLD.   F.W.

YUKON TERRITORY. *See* STATISTICS OF THE WORLD.

Z

ZAIRE. Despite its potential wealth, Zaire, under President Mobutu Sese Seko, suffered another year of economic distress in 1982. The government tried to counter a drastic decline in export earnings—primarily from the sale of coffee, copper, and diamonds, which fell in price—with heavy borrowing. In March the International Monetary Fund (IMF) granted Zaire, already some $120,000,-000 behind in its debt-service payments, a loan of $120,000,000. The IMF, however, suspended a $3 billion assistance program adopted in 1981, largely because of the government's inability to reduce public spending and thus limit the budget deficit. In late July the head of Zaire's central bank warned that the country's $4.1 billion foreign debt would have to be rescheduled or Zaire would fall further in arrears. Debt-service payments consumed more than 60 percent of Zaire's export earnings in 1982 (compared with 27 percent in 1981).

Mobutu increased state security in 1982, jailing critics of his regime, among them 13 former parliament members who had called for the creation of an opposition party. Mobutu vowed that he would allow "no second political party in Zaire" to challenge his Popular Revolutionary Movement. Early in the year the government closed down the University of Kinshasa in the wake of demonstrations for larger student grants, and it drafted several students into the army for "reeducation."

In mid-May Mobutu, who had enjoyed close relations with the United States, abruptly "renounced" U.S. aid to his nation. His action came in reaction to U.S. congressional criticism of Zaire's human rights record and demands in Congress that U.S. aid be slashed. Shortly thereafter, however, in an apparent attempt to mollify the administration of U.S. President Ronald Reagan, Mobutu reestablished diplomatic ties with Israel, after a lapse of more than eight years. Five Arab states responded by cutting their ties with Zaire.

See STATISTICS OF THE WORLD.   J.T.S.

ZAMBIA. Economic problems and the efforts of President Kenneth D. Kaunda to deal with them dominated events in Zambia in 1982. The problems were caused mainly by low world prices for copper and cobalt, Zambia's major exports, but they were aggravated by the government's difficulties in transporting exports to overseas markets. The rail link with Tanzania was overburdened; rail lines through Zaire were vulnerable to the friction between Zaire and Zambia (which, on occasion, erupted into gunfire exchanges across the border by Zairian and Zambian troops);

and transportation through Mozambique was threatened by extensive guerrilla activity. On the other hand, rail links with South Africa that handled about 60 percent of Zambia's foreign trade remained secure. But Kaunda was reluctant to increase his dependence upon Pretoria's white-minority government, even though he met for talks in late April with Prime Minister Pieter W. Botha. The talks, characterized as "frank," were held at a site on the border between South Africa and Botswana; they dealt with several issues dividing the two countries, including the lingering problem of South-West Africa (Namibia).

The Zambian government sought to increase its control of the copper industry by merging, in March, the state-owned mining company and Roan Consolidated Mines Ltd., to form Zambia Consolidated Copper Mines Ltd. The new company, with an annual capacity of more than 600,000 tons, was one of the largest copper mining enterprises in the world. Because of world oversupply, however, copper production in 1982 was cut to 560,000 tons, with a consequent layoff of workers.

Agricultural conditions also were poor. A severe drought forced the government to import, mainly from South Africa and Zimbabwe, 400,000 tons of corn, at a cost of $74,000,000.

The government, burdened by a debt of approximately $2 billion to foreign banks, at a time when it faced a serious foreign-exchange shortage, turned to the International Monetary Fund (IMF) for help. But the IMF was reluctant to provide further assistance to Zambia unless the government restricted its aid to the copper industry.

See STATISTICS OF THE WORLD.   J.T.S.

ZIMBABWE. In 1982 Prime Minister Robert Mugabe, in his third year in power, continued to seek foreign investment in Zimbabwe as he moved ahead with plans to effect economic reforms, such as land redistribution. But political divisions within the country threatened internal stability.

Politics. On Feb. 17, after the discovery by security forces of arms caches on farms owned by the Zimbabwe African People's

Union (ZAPU), Mugabe dismissed ZAPU's leader, his longtime rival Joshua Nkomo, from the cabinet. On March 11 the deputy commander of the army, a supporter of Nkomo, was arrested, and thereafter Mugabe began to remove other ZAPU officials from sensitive government positions. As a result, by the end of 1982 an estimated 4000 ZAPU supporters deserted the army; many of them joined armed groups engaged in robbery and antigovernment terrorism. In July three foreign tourists were murdered, and six others, including two Americans, were kidnapped. The government blamed ZAPU sympathizers. But as acts of violence spread, it cast a wider net of accusation. It blamed South Africa and white Zimbabwean sympathizers, for example, for sabotage attacks on an air base, a munitions dump, and Mugabe's own party headquarters. South Africa protested its innocence, but in August three former Rhodesians serving in the South African army were killed while attempting to sabotage the rail link to Mozambique. The South African government said that the three were on an "unauthorized" private mission.

Gravely concerned by the increased violence, the Mugabe government took stern countermeasures, under a state of emergency, setting up detention camps, imposing curfews, and banning mass meetings organized by ZAPU. In July it extended the 17-year-old state of emergency that gave it sweeping powers, and it introduced laws protecting government leaders, security forces, and civil servants from criminal and civil prosecution. In October it began forming a militia, to number 20,000 within four years.

In August Mugabe met with Nkomo to discuss ways of limiting the violence. The two former allies in the struggle for independence emerged from their meeting with their mutual suspicions intact. Mugabe did not help matters by declaring, in an interview that same month, that he intended to advocate, in the parliamentary elections scheduled for 1985, the establishment of a one-party state.

In April Zimbabwe changed the name of its capital from Salisbury to Harare, in honor of a 19th-century African chief. The names of 31 other cities and towns were also Africanized.

The Economy. As a result of bumper crops in 1982, Zimbabwe had enough corn—the country's staple—not only to feed itself but to export it as well, along with cotton and tobacco. Agriculture continued to be dominated by Zimbabwe's whites, who produced about 90 percent of the country's crops. But the Mugabe government proceeded with its land redistribution program, whose target was to give some 18,000 families about 50 acres each by the end of 1983.

Industrial expansion, on the other hand, appeared to be stymied by the government's inability to increase private foreign investment. Since independence in 1980, Zimbabwe had secured only $40,000,000 in private investment, apparently because of the negative reaction of foreign corporations to Mugabe's Marxist rhetoric. During a tour of European capitals in May and June, for example, Mugabe was urged to agree to an investment code guaranteeing the repatriation of profits and the safety of capital, but he cited the protection afforded investors by the constitution as sufficient. However, the prime minister was able to secure a $70,000,000 aid agreement with West Germany and technical and trade assistance from other Western European countries.

In March Zimbabwe renewed a preferential trade agreement with South Africa. The agreement covered some two thirds of the country's manufactured exports to South Africa. At the same time, however, the South African government stepped up its repatriation of Zimbabwean workers whose labor contracts had expired. It was estimated that some 20,000 Zimbabweans would be returned home by the end of 1983. The loss of their remittances was expected to have a severe impact on Zimbabwe's foreign exchange earnings.

Mugabe sought to lessen his country's dependence on the South African transportation system. Guerrilla activity in Mozambique, however, prevented the widespread use of that country's rail lines and ports.

See STATISTICS OF THE WORLD.   J.T.S.

THE COUNTRIES OF THE WORLD

Nation Capital	Population	Area of Country (sq mi/ sq km)	Type of Government	Heads of State and Government	Currency: Value in U.S. Dollars	GNP (000,000): GNP Per Capita
AFGHANISTAN Kabul	16,360,000 913,200[1]	250,000 647,497	People's republic	President, Revolutionary Council: Babrak Karmal Prime Minister: Sultan Ali Kishtmand	Afghani 0.02	$ NA NA
ALBANIA Tiranë	2,800,000 198,000	11,100 28,748	People's socialist republic	Chairman, Presidium of the People's Assembly: Ramiz Alia Chairman, Council of Ministers (Premier): Adil Çarçani	Lek 0.14[2]	NA NA
ALGERIA Algiers	19,590,000 1,800,000	919,595 2,381,741	Republic	President: Col. Chadli Benjedid Premier: Col. Mohamed Ben Ahmed Abdelghani	Dinar 0.22	36,410 1,920
ANGOLA Luanda	7,260,000 475,300[1]	481,353 1,246,700	People's republic	President: José Eduardo dos Santos	Kwanza 0.03	3,320 470
ANTIGUA AND BARBUDA St. John's	80,000 25,000	171 442	Parliamentary state (C)	Governor-General: Sir Wilfred E. Jacobs Prime Minister: Vere C. Bird, Sr.	East Caribbean dollar 0.37	100 1,270
ARGENTINA Buenos Aires	28,090,000 2,908,000	1,068,301 2,766,889	Federal republic	President: Maj. Gen. Reynaldo Benito Antonio Bignone	New peso 0.00004	66,430 2,390
AUSTRALIA Canberra	14,860,000 245,500[1]	2,967,907 7,686,848	Federal parliamentary state (C)	Governor-General: Sir Ninian M. Stephen Prime Minister: J. Malcolm Fraser	Dollar 0.95	142,240 9,820
AUSTRIA Vienna	7,510,000 1,517,200	32,374 83,849	Federal republic	President: Rudolf Kirchschläger Chancellor: Bruno Kreisky	Schilling 0.06	76,530 10,230
BAHAMAS Nassau	250,000 135,400[1]	5,380 13,935	Parliamentary state (C)	Governor-General: Sir Gerald C. Cash Prime Minister: Lynden O. Pindling	Dollar 1.00	800 3,300
BAHRAIN Manama	320,000 150,000	240 622	Emirate	Emir: Isa bin Sulman al-Khalifa Prime Minister: Khalifah bin Sulman al-Khalifah	Dinar 2.66	2,350 5,560
BANGLADESH Dacca	90,630,000 3,000,000[1]	55,598 143,998	Republic (C)	President: A. F. M. Ahsanuddin Choudhury Chief Martial Law Administrator: Gen. H. M. Ershad	Taka 0.05	11,170 120
BARBADOS Bridgetown	270,000 7,500	166 431	Parliamentary state (C)	Governor-General: Sir Deighton H. L. Ward Prime Minister: Tom Adams	Dollar 0.50	760 3,040
BELGIUM Brussels	9,860,000 144,000	11,781 30,513	Constitutional monarchy	King: Baudouin Prime Minister: Wilfried Martens	Franc 0.02	119,770 12,180

438

The section on countries presents the latest information available. All monetary figures are expressed in United States dollars. The symbol (C) signifies that the country belongs to the Commonwealth of Nations. NA means that the data were not available. * indicates that the category does not apply to the country under discussion. Footnotes at the end of the section contain more specialized information.

Imports Exports	Revenue Expenditure	Elementary Schools: Teachers Students	Secondary Schools: Teachers Students	Colleges and Universities: Teachers Students
$ 924,000,000 729,000,000	$ 736,000,000 736,000,000	30,518 942,787	7,825 111,755	1,012 11,367
NA NA	1,171,000,000 1,164,000,000	22,686 569,600	3,990 102,600	1,153 28,668
10,811,000,000 13,656,000,000	15,602,000,000 15,484,000,000	80,853 2,972,242	32,621 844,291	6,421 51,510
574,000,000 808,000,000	1,708,000,000 1,708,000,000	NA 1,388,110	NA 153,000	NA 4,746
41,000,000 13,000,000	23,000,000 26,000,000	477 13,285	271 6,458	* *
10,544,000,000 8,016,000,000	18,109,000,000 21,825,000,000	224,673 4,003,670	178,681 1,295,815	45,089 475,799
23,767,000,000 21,768,000,000	51,811,000,000 46,774,000,000	91,279 1,884,094	94,904 1,971,440	58,407 322,622
21,049,000,000 15,846,000,000	18,698,000,000 18,659,000,000	29,682 434,432	NA 969,231	11,792 109,121
5,481,000,000 4,834,000,000	246,100,000 246,900,000	NA 24,229	NA 24,446	NA 4,396
3,484,000,000 3,602,000,000	1,074,000,000 1,074,000,000	2,826 48,672	1,140 24,288	125 4,059
2,594,000,000 791,000,000	1,442,000,000 838,000,000	172,448 9,483,090	NA 2,317,119	NA 121,155
571,000,000 194,000,000	180,000,000 224,000,000	NA 35,555	NA 29,622	NA 1,380
62,133,000,000[3] 55,646,000,000[3]	41,837,000,000 35,157,000,000	NA 897,759	NA 906,935	NA 111,691

Nation Capital	Population	Area of Country (sq mi / sq km)	Type of Government	Heads of State and Government	Currency: Value in U.S. Dollars	GNP (000,000): GNP Per Capita
BELIZE .... Belmopan	170,000.... 2,900	8,867... 22,965	Parliamentary state (C)	Governor-General: .... Minita Gordon Prime Minister: George C. Price	Dollar........ 0.50	$ 160 1,080
BENIN .... Porto-Novo	3,640,000.... 132,000	43,484.... 112,622	People's ..... republic	President: Lt. Col. Ahmed Kérékou	CFA franc 0.0029	1,080 300
BHUTAN .... Thimphu	1,296,000.... 8,900	18,147.... 47,000	Monarchy	King: Jigme Singye Wangchuk	Ngultrum 0.11	110 80
BOLIVIA .... Sucre La Paz	5,760,000.... 68,400 719,800	424,164.... 1,098,581	Republic	President: Hernán Siles Zuazo	Peso 0.02	3,190 570
BOTSWANA .... Gaborone	850,000.... 59,700	231,805.... 600,372	Republic ..... (C)	President: Quett K. J. Masire	Pula 0.91	730 910
BRAZIL .... Braslia	121,550,000.... 411,300	3,286,487.... 8,511,965	Federal republic	President: Gen. João Baptista de Oliveira Figueiredo	Cruzeiro 0.005	243,240 2,050
BULGARIA .... Sofia	8,889,000.... 1,047,900	42,823.... 110,912	People's ..... republic	Chairman, Council of State:...... Todor Zhivkov Chairman, Council of Ministers (Premier): Grisha Filipov	Lev........... 1.18[2]	37,390 4,150
BURMA .... Rangoon	36,170,000.... 2,300,000	261,218... 676,552	Socialist republic	President: .... U San Yu Prime Minister: U Maung Maung Kha	Kyat........... 0.13	5,910 180
BURUNDI .... Bujumbura	4,350,000.... 141,000[1]	10,747... 27,834	Republic	President: .... Col. Jean-Baptiste Bagaza	Franc......... 0.01	830 200
CAMBODIA.......... (PEOPLE'S REPUBLIC OF KAMPUCHEA) Phnom Penh	6,830,000.... 500,000[1]	69,898... 181,035	People's republic	President, Council of State: .... Heng Samrin Chairman, Council of Ministers (Premier): Chan Sy	New rial 0.25	NA NA
CAMEROON .... Yaoundé	8,650,000.... 291,000	183,569.... 475,442	Republic	President and .... Prime Minister: Paul Biya	CFA franc 0.0029	5,660 670
CANADA............. Ottawa	24,320,000.... 295,200	3,851,809.... 9,976,139	Federal parliamentary state (C)	Governor-General: .... Edward R. Schreyer Prime Minister: Pierre Elliott Trudeau	Dollar........ 0.81	242,530 10,130
CAPE VERDE .... Praia	330,000.... 36,600[1]	1,557... 4,033	Republic	President: .... Aristides M. Pereira Premier: Cmdt. Pedro Rodrigues Pires	Escudo 0.02	100 300
CENTRAL AFRICAN .. REPUBLIC Bangui	2,350,000.... 362,700[1]	240,535.... 622,984	Republic	Head of State and............. Chairman, Military Committee for National Recovery (President): Gen. André Kolingba	CFA franc 0.0029	680 300
CHAD .... N'Djamena	4,550,000.... 303,000[1]	495,755... 1,284,000	Republic	President: .... Hissène Habré	CFA franc 0.0029	530 120
CHILE .... Santiago	11,290,000.... 3,946,300	292,258.... 756,945	Republic	President: .... Gen. Augusto Pinochet Ugarte	Peso 0.02	23,980 2,160
CHINA, PEOPLE'S .... REPUBLIC OF Peking (Beijing)	1,008,175,000.... 4,952,000	3,705,406... 9,596,961	People's republic	Chairman, Standing .... Committee of National People's Congress: Marshal Yeh Chien-ying (Ye Jianying) Premier: Chao Chi-yang (Zhao Ziyang)	Yuan.......... 0.52	283,250 290
COLOMBIA.......... Bogotá	27,090,000.... 4,055,900[1]	439,737.... 1,138,914	Republic	President: .... Belisario Betancur Cuartas	Peso 0.02	31,570 1,180
COMOROS .... Moroni	370,000.... 16,000[1]	838... 2,171	Federal Islamic republic	President: .... Ahmed Abdallah Abderemane Premier: Ali Mroudjae	CFA franc 0.0029	100[7] 300[7]

Imports Exports	Revenue Expenditure	Elementary Schools: Teachers Students	Secondary Schools: Teachers Students	Colleges and Universities: Teachers Students
$ 141,000,000 ....$ 103,000,000	31,000,000. 26,000,000	NA. 35,996	NA 7,540	NA 580
410,000,000 170,000,000	148,000,000. 148,000,000	6,326. 293,648	1,198 55,075	153 2,118
2,000,000 1,500,000	13,000,000. 31,000,000	797. 22,288	586 15,068	16 204
833,000,000 1,033,000,000	538,000,000. 538,000,000	41,878. 904,874	9,974 210,385	6,179 178,217
591,000,000 495,000,000	253,000,000. 272,000,000	5,316. 171,914	1,162 21,375	113 928
24,007,000,000 23,172,000,000	14,754,000,000. 14,754,000,000	854,813. 21,473,100	184,767 2,587,605	104,231 1,225,557
9,650,000,000 10,372,000,000	18,616,000,000. 18,599,000,000	59,067. 1,092,299	23,007 280,224	12,622 85,330
352,000,000 465,000,000	3,695,000,000. 4,011,000,000	84,593. 3,731,160	32,586 939,478	3,922 112,671
167,000,000 71,000,000	111,000,000. 106,000,000	NA. 160,495	NA 16,410	NA 1,763
140–150,000,000 1–2,000,000	NA. .... NA	NA. .... NA	NA .... NA	NA NA
1,602,000,000 1,384,000,000	1,079,000,000. 1,079,000,000	25,248. 1,254,056	7,084 193,801	439 10,001
65,797,000,000 69,922,000,000	45,793,000,000. 57,589,000,000	269,045[4]. .... 4,947,690[4]	[4] .... [4]	NA 693,270
44,000,000 2,000,000	35,000,000. 35,000,000	1,436. 50,661	NA 9,284	* *
70,000,000[5] .... 79,000,000[5]	113,000,000. 113,000,000	3,690. 241,201	590 48,607	185 972
46,000,000 28,000,000	82,000,000. 82,000,000	2,610[6]. 229,191	NA 19,580	NA 800
6,379,000,000 3,932,000,000	9,893,000,000. 8,636,000,000	66,354. 2,264,573	NA 628,757	NA 127,446
19,530,000,000 18,255,000,000	55,931,000,000. 55,931,000,000	NA. 146,270,000	NA 56,778,000	NA 1,144,000
5,201,000,000 2,916,000,000	3,327,000,000. 3,327,000,000	128,494. 4,160,527	79,742 1,616,111	21,153 186,635
27,000,000[7] .... 12,000,000[7]	6,000,000. 11,000,000	1,292. 59,709	461 13,855	* *

Nation Capital	Population	Area of Country (sq mi/ sq km)	Type of Government	Heads of State and Government	Currency: Value in U.S. Dollars	GNP (000,000): GNP Per Capita
CONGO Brazzaville	1,580,000 422,400[1]	132,047 342,000	People's republic	President: Col. Denis Sassou-Nguesso Premier: Col. Louis Sylvain Goma	CFA franc 0.0029	$ 1,120 730
COSTA RICA San José	2,227,000 259,100	19,575 50,700	Republic	President: Luis Alberto Monge	Colón 0.03	3,820 1,730
CUBA Havana	9,770,000 1,924,900	44,218 114,524	Socialist republic	President of the Councils of State and Ministers: Fidel Castro Ruz	Peso 1.19[2]	NA NA
CYPRUS Nicosia	640,000 125,100[1,8]	3,572 9,251	Republic (C)	President: Spyros Kyprianou	Pound 2.07	2,210 3,560
CZECHOSLOVAKIA Prague	15,310,000 1,182,300	49,370 127,869	Federal socialist republic	President: Gustáv Husák Premier: Lubomír Štrougal	Koruna 0.09[2]	89,260 5,820
DENMARK Copenhagen	5,120,000 648,700	16,629 43,069	Constitutional monarchy	Queen: Margrethe II Prime Minister: Poul Schlüter	Krone 0.11	66,350 12,950
DJIBOUTI Djibouti	352,000 200,000[1]	8,494 22,000	Republic	President: Hassan Gouled Aptidon Premier: Barkad Gourad Hamadou	Djibouti franc 0.0056	170 480
DOMINICA Roseau	80,000 20,000	290 751	Republic (C)	President: Aurelius Marie Prime Minister: (Mary) Eugenia Charles	East Caribbean dollar 0.37	50 620
DOMINICAN REPUBLIC Santo Domingo	5,430,000 1,241,100[1]	18,816 48,734	Republic	President: Salvador Jorge Blanco	Peso 1.00	6,200 1,140
ECUADOR Quito	8,640,000 843,000	109,483 283,561	Republic	President: Osvaldo Hurtado Larrea	Sucre 0.03	10,230 1,220
EGYPT Cairo	43,470,000 5,399,000	386,661 1,001,449	Republic	President: Hosni Mubarak Prime Minister: Ahmed Fuad Mohieddin	Pound 1.21	23,140 580
EL SALVADOR San Salvador	4,940,000 433,000	8,124 21,041	Republic	President: Alvaro Alfredo Magaña	Colón 0.40	2,690 590
EQUATORIAL GUINEA Malabo	370,000 25,000	10,831 28,051	Republic	President, Supreme Military Council: Lt. Col. Teodoro Obiang Nguema Mbasogo	Ekuele 0.0052	NA NA
ETHIOPIA Addis Ababa	32,160,000 1,210,400	471,778 1,221,900	Socialist state	Head of State, Chairman of the Provisional Military Administrative Council, and Chairman of the Council of Ministers: Lt. Col. Mengistu Haile Mariam	Birr 0.48	4,320 140
FIJI Suva	640,000 66,000	7,056 18,274	Parliamentary state (C)	Governor-General: Ratu Sir George K. Cakobau Prime Minister: Ratu Sir Kamisese Mara	Dollar 1.06	1,160 1,850
FINLAND Helsinki	4,800,000 484,000	130,129 337,032	Republic	President: Mauno Koivisto Prime Minister: Kalevi Sorsa	Markka 0.21	47,280 9,720
FRANCE Paris	53,960,000 2,050,500	211,208 547,026	Republic	President: François Mitterrand Premier: Pierre Mauroy	Franc 0.14	627,700 11,730
GABON Libreville	1,100,000 225,200[1]	103,347 267,667	Republic	President: Omar Bongo Premier: Léon Mébiame	CFA franc 0.0029	2,420 3,680

Imports Exports	Revenue Expenditure	Elementary Schools: Teachers Students	Secondary Schools: Teachers Students	Colleges and Universities: Teachers Students
$ 291,000,000[5] 510,000,000[5]	$ 916,000,000. 916,000,000	6,852. 383,018	3,921. 161,555	681 6,848
1,524,000,000 1,002,000,000	267,000,000. 267,000,000	15,748. 379,925	NA 169,297	2,337 38,629
4,509,000,000 3,967,000,000	10,682,000,000. 10,677,000,000	77,063. 1,550,323	60,553. 825,852	10,736 146,240
1,166,000,000 562,000,000	376,400,000[9]. 375,600,000[9]	2,183[10]. 48,701[10]	2,926[10]. 47,716[10]	175 1,823
14,958,000,000 14,706,000,000	26,795,000,000. 26,616,000,000	90,380. 1,904,000	NA 870,726	18,320 196,642
17,530,000,000 15,735,000,000	14,629,000,000. 19,321,000,000	40,261. 448,370	NA 309,214	NA 81,352
177,000,000 11,000,000	89,000,000. 89,000,000	260. 13,740	220. 3,882	* *
47,000,000 9,000,000	11,800,000. 13,000,000	887. 16,540	325. 6,729	50 141
1,450,000,000 1,199,000,000	891,000,000. 1,094,000,000	17,930. 902,529	6,702. 144,239	NA 59,321
2,253,000,000 2,481,000,000	2,036,000,000. 1,672,000,000	39,825. 1,427,627	31,489. 535,445	10,335 225,343
8,839,000,000 3,233,000,000	12,174,000,000. 13,107,000,000	124,263. 4,211,345	91,046. 2,408,703	23,390 550,171
976,000,000 720,000,000	486,000,000. 468,000,000	NA. 858,811	NA 72,898	NA 31,351
64,000,000 20,000,000	14,200,000. 13,893,000	NA. NA	165. 4,523	* *
567,000,000 418,000,000	953,000,000. 1,143,000,000	30,597. 1,800,000	8,982. 371,000	NA 14,562
632,000,000 311,000,000	287,000,000. 282,000,000	6,500[4]. 127,325	[4] 38,081	NA 1,427
14,201,000,000 14,015,000,000	14,228,000,000. 14,227,000,000	24,834. 390,492	33,077. 447,643	6,041 83,461
120,689,000,000 101,392,000,000	103,010,000,000. 110,632,000,000	235,415. 4,786,762	349,743. 5,174,140	NA 859,646
532,000,000[5] 1,477,000,000[5]	1,484,000,000. 1,484,000,000	3,088. 141,569	1,491. 24,996	231 1,284

Nation Capital	Population	Area of Country (sq mi / sq km)	Type of Government	Heads of State and Government	Currency: Value in U.S. Dollars	GNP (000,000): GNP Per Capita
GAMBIA, THE[11]	620,000....	4,361....	Republic	President:	Dalasi.	$ 150
Banjul	47,700	11,295	(C)	Sir Dawda K. Jawara	0.44	250
GERMAN.	16,740,000....	41,768....	Socialist	Chairman, Council of State:	Mark	120,940
DEMOCRATIC		108,178	republic	Erich Honecker	0.41[2]	7,180
REPUBLIC				Chairman, Council of Ministers		
East Berlin	1,145,700			(Premier):		
				Willi Stoph		
GERMANY, FEDERAL.	61,670,000....	95,976....	Federal	President:	Deutsche.....	827,790
REPUBLIC OF		248,577	republic	Karl Carstens	mark	13,590
Bonn	287,100			Chancellor:	0.40	
				Helmut Kohl		
GHANA	12,060,000....	92,100....	Republic	Chairman, Provisional	Cedi	4,920
Accra	998,800[1]	238,537	(C)	National Defense Council:	0.36	420
				Flight Lt. Jerry J. Rawlings		
GREAT BRITAIN.	55,830,000....	94,227....	Limited	Queen:	Pound	442,820
London	6,696,000[1]	244,046	monarchy (C)	Elizabeth II	1.70	7,920
				Prime Minister:		
				Margaret Thatcher		
GREECE	9,710,000....	50,944....	Republic	President:	Drachma	42,190
Athens	885,100	131,944		Constantine Karamanlis	0.01	4,520
				Prime Minister:		
				Andreas Papandreou		
GRENADA.	110,000....	133...	Parliamentary	Governor-General:	East	80
St. George's	7,500	344	state (C)	Sir Paul Scoon	Caribbean	690
				Prime Minister:	dollar	
				Maurice Bishop	0.37	
GUATEMALA	7,480,000....	42,042....	Republic	President:	Quetzal	7,790
Guatemala City	1,500,000	108,889		Gen. Efrain Rios Montt	1.00	1,110
GUINEA.	5,150,000....	94,926....	Republic	President:	Syli.	1,590
Conakry	763,000[1]	245,857		Sékou Touré	0.05	290
				Premier:		
				Louis Lansana Beavogui		
GUINEA-BISSAU	801,000....	13,948....	Republic	President, Council of	Escudo	130
Bissau	109,500[1]	36,125		the Revolution:	0.03	160
				Cmdr. João Bernardo Vieira		
				Premier:		
				Vitor Saúde Maria		
GUYANA.	900,000....	83,000....	Republic	President:	Dollar.	550
Georgetown	72,000	214,969	(C)	Forbes Burnham	0.33	690
				Prime Minister:		
				Ptolemy A. Reid		
HAITI.	5,100,000....	10,714....	Republic	President:	Gourde	1,340
Port-au-Prince	790,900	27,750		Jean-Claude Duvalier	0.20	270
HONDURAS	3,820,000....	43,277....	Republic	President:	Lempira	2,070
Tegucigalpa	472,700[1]	112,088		Roberto Suazo Córdova	0.50	560
HUNGARY.	10,710,000....	35,919....	People's	Chairman, Presidential Council:	Forint.	44,990
Budapest	2,060,000	93,030	republic	Pál Losonczi	0.03[2]	4,180
				Chairman, Council of Ministers		
				(Premier):		
				György Lázár		
ICELAND	230,000....	39,769....	Republic	President:	New króna....	2,620
Reykjavik	83,800	103,000		Vigdís Finnbogadóttir	0.08	11,330
				Prime Minister:		
				Gunnar Thoroddsen		
INDIA.	683,810,000....	1,269,345....	Federal	President:	Rupee	159,430
New Delhi	4,865,100	3,287,590	republic	Zail Singh	0.10	240
			(C)	Prime Minister:		
				Indira Gandhi		
INDONESIA	150,520,000....	782,662....	Republic	President:	Rupiah.	61,770
Djakarta	6,503,400	2,027,087		Suharto	0.0015	420
IRAN	39,320,000....	636,296....	Islamic	President:	Rial	NA
Tehran	6,000,000[1]	1,648,000	republic	Hojatoleslam Sayed	0.01	NA
				Ali Khamenei		
				Prime Minister:		
				Mir Hussein Moussavi		

Imports Exports	Revenue Expenditure	Elementary Schools: Teachers Students	Secondary Schools: Teachers Students	Colleges and Universities: Teachers Students
$ 125,000,000 27,000,000	$ 51,000,000. 58,000,000	1,377. 34,468	526 8,954	* *
16,214,000,000 15,063,000,000	82,386,000,000. 82,196,000,000	NA. 2,203,991[12]	NA 678,252	NA 129,970
163,907,000,000 176,085,000,000	86,870,000,000. 97,768,000,000	538,837[4]. 3,384,571	[4] 8,730,568	112,335 938,141
993,000,000 1,096,000,000	2,034,000,000. 3,039,000,000	41,407[6]. 1,213,291[6]	27,054[6] 576,979[6]	1,103 9,079
119,935,000,000 115,149,000,000	145,557,000,000. 162,991,000,000	233,228. 5,215,450	275,198 4,535,664	42,300 322,722
8,885,000,000 4,241,000,000	9,585,000,000. 9,585,000,000	36,168. 902,558	NA 804,492	6,148 119,000
50,000,000 16,000,000	NA. 59,000,000	814. 24,106	332 7,332	137 700
1,598,000,000 1,520,000,000	1,189,000,000. 1,194,000,000	24,242. 826,613	9,613 171,903	1,934 25,978
279,000,000 326,000,000	362,000,000. 362,000,000	6,413. 272,000	3,700 106,000	650 24,000
61,000,000 14,000,000	27,000,000. 44,000,000	2,620. 84,293	540 13,935	* *
417,000,000 389,000,000	337,000,000. 392,000,000	6,021. 164,830	2,861 51,242	NA 1,889
266,000,000 188,000,000	78,000,000. 78,000,000	12,953. 510,683	3,324 55,816	448 3,309
1,019,000,000 806,000,000	675,000,000. 675,000,000	16,612. 582,612	4,569 129,268	1,507 24,601
9,128,000,000 8,712,000,000	13,654,000,000. 13,783,000,000	75,442. 1,162,203	15,460 333,570	13,980 101,166
967,000,000 852,000,000	675,000,000. 668,000,000	3,074[13]. 25,600	1,340 26,500	779 4,200
14,855,000,000 7,560,000,000	15,746,000,000. 16,814,000,000	2,147,223. 89,641,616	633,642 7,515,640	225,717 2,155,469
13,271,000,000 22,259,000,000	24,122,000,000. 24,122,000,000	676,236. 21,123,482	203,264 3,549,348	25,228 304,496
12,247,000,000 14,251,000,000	39,849,000,000. 39,849,000,000	167,457. 4,768,588	96,395 2,356,878	13,952 154,215

Nation Capital	Population	Area of Country (sq mi/ sq km)	Type of Government	Heads of State and Government	Currency: Value in U.S. Dollars	GNP (000,000): GNP Per Capita
IRAQ Baghdad	13,530,000 3,205,600	167,925 434,924	Republic	President and Chairman, Revolutionary Command Council: Saddam Hussein	Dinar 3.39	$ 39,500 3,020
IRELAND, REPUBLIC OF Dublin	3,440,000 544,600	27,136 70,283	Republic	President: Patrick J. Hillery Prime Minister: Garret FitzGerald	Pound 1.35	16,130 4,880
ISRAEL Jerusalem	3,950,000 398,200	8,019 20,770	Republic	President: Itzhak Navon Prime Minister: Menachem Begin	Shekel 0.03	17,440 4,500
ITALY Rome	57,200,000 2,916,400	116,304 301,225	Republic	President: Alessandro Pertini Prime Minister: Giovanni Spadolini	Lira 0.0007	368,860 6,480
IVORY COAST Abidjan	8,300,000 1,686,100[1]	124,504 322,463	Republic	President: Félix Houphouët-Boigny	CFA franc 0.0029	9,920 1,150
JAMAICA Kingston	2,220,000 643,800[1]	4,244 10,991	Parliamentary state (C)	Governor-General: Florizel A. Glasspole Prime Minister: Edward P. G. Seaga	Dollar 0.56	2,250 1,030
JAPAN Tokyo	117,650,000 8,349,200	143,751 372,313	Constitutional monarchy	Emperor: Hirohito Prime Minister: Yasuhiro Nakasone	Yen 0.0037	1,152,910 9,890
JORDAN Amman	3,360,000 648,600	37,738 97,740	Constitutional monarchy	King: Hussein I Prime Minister: Mudar Badran	Dinar 2.79	3,270 1,420[14]
KENYA Nairobi	17,150,000 818,000[1]	224,961 582,646	Republic (C)	President: Daniel arap Moi	Shilling 0.09	6,630 420
KIRIBATI (GILBERT ISLANDS) Bairiki	60,000 1,800	332 861	Republic (C)	President: Ieremia T. Tabai	Dollar 0.95	50 770
KOREA, DEMOCRATIC PEOPLE'S REPUBLIC OF P'yŏngyang	18,320,000 1,500,000	46,540 120,538	People's republic	President: Marshal Kim Il Sung Premier: Li Jong Ok	Won 1.06	NA NA
KOREA, REPUBLIC OF Seoul	38,720,000 8,366,800	38,025 98,484	Republic	President: Chun Doo Hwan Prime Minister: Kim Sang Hyup	Won 0.0013	58,580 1,520
KUWAIT Al Kuwait	1,460,000 60,400	6,880 17,818	Constitutional emirate	Emir: Sheikh Jaber al-Ahmad al-Sabah Prime Minister: Sheikh Saad al-Abdullah al-Salem al-Sabah	Dinar 3.48	30,900 22,840
LAOS Vientiane	3,810,000 200,000	91,429 236,800	People's republic	President: Prince Souphanouvong Premier: Kaysone Phomvihan	New kip 0.10	NA NA
LEBANON Beirut	2,690,000 702,000	4,015 10,400	Republic	President: Amin Gemayel Prime Minister: Shafik al-Wazzan	Pound 0.21	NA NA
LESOTHO Maseru	1,370,000 16,000	11,720 30,355	Constitutional monarchy (C)	King: Moshoeshoe II Prime Minister: Chief Leabua Jonathan	Loti 0.87	520 390
LIBERIA Monrovia	2,040,000 208,600	43,000 111,369	Republic	Head of State and Chairman, People's Redemption Council: Master Sgt. Samuel K. Doe	Dollar 1.00	980 520

Imports Exports	Revenue Expenditure	Elementary Schools: Teachers Students	Secondary Schools: Teachers Students	Colleges and Universities: Teachers Students
$ NA	$ 65,810,000,000.	70,799.	22,087	3,801
10,529,000,000	66,877,000,000	1,952,340	600,007	86,111
10,595,000,000	5,987,000,000.	19,002.	17,821	3,114
7,795,000,000	7,025,000,000	547,974	294,175	33,050
7,787,000,000	14,644,000,000.	39,147.	20,054	NA
5,416,000,000	14,644,000,000	560,043	241,893	87,591
91,011,000,000	94,898,000,000.	269,279.	493,513	42,564
75,214,000,000	138,629,000,000	4,518,409	5,289,244	1,035,876
2,493,000,000	1,308,000,000.	NA.	NA	NA
2,515,000,000	1,308,000,000	954,656	194,717	20,087
1,509,000,000	1,236,000,000.	9,889.	10,368	NA
982,000,000	1,356,000,000	367,625	225,741	10,305
143,288,000,000	212,770,000,000.	473,957.	511,963	215,326
152,016,000,000	212,770,000,000	11,924,706	10,028,578	2,194,523
3,179,000,000	2,104,000,000.	13,898[14].	11,908[14]	1,178
736,000,000	2,208,000,000	448,411[14]	248,643[14]	27,526
2,068,000,000	76,000,000.	62,932.	8,411	NA
1,172,000,000	96,000,000	2,998,484	362,528	7,328
17,000,000	19,000,000.	602[4].	[4]	*
23,000,000	16,000,000	13,234	957	*
1,337,000,000	9,624,000,000.	100,000[4].	[4]	NA
1,553,000,000	9,624,000,000	2,561,674	2,000,000	100,000
26,125,000,000	10,408,000,000.	122,727.	119,608	17,728
21,254,000,000	11,116,000,000	5,586,494	4,596,009	580,607
6,560,000,000	18,759,000,000.	7,722[6].	14,614[6]	1,020
19,767,000,000	18,759,000,000	145,626[6]	170,714[6]	12,391
130,000,000	93,000,000.	NA.	NA	NA
31,000,000	216,000,000	451,800	68,200	1,684
1,701,000,000	NA.	NA.	NA	NA
436,000,000	1,247,000,000	NA	NA	NA
367,000,000	89,000,000.	NA.	NA	NA
46,000,000	58,000,000	244,838	23,355	1,048
449,000,000	390,000,000.	4,567.	2,814	190
538,000,000	431,000,000	192,185	47,446	3,789

Nation Capital	Population	Area of Country (sq mi/ sq km)	Type of Government	Heads of State and Government	Currency: Value in U.S. Dollars	GNP (000,000): GNP Per Capita
LIBYA . . . . Tripoli	3,100,000. . . . 994,000	679,362. . . 1,759,540	Socialist . . . . . . republic	Revolutionary Leader . . . . (Head of State): Col. Muammar el-Qaddafi Secretary-General, General People's Congress: Muhammad az-Zarrouk Ragab	Dinar . . . .$ 3.38	25,730 8,640
LIECHTENSTEIN . . . . . Vaduz	30,000. . . . 4,600	61. . . 157	Constitutional . monarchy	Sovereign: . . . . Prince Francis Joseph II Chief of Government: Hans Brunhart	Swiss franc . . . 0.46	NA NA
LUXEMBOURG. . . . . . . Luxembourg	360,000. . . . 79,600	998. . . 2,586	Constitutional . monarchy	Grand Duke: . . . . Jean Prime Minister: Pierre Werner	Franc 0.02	5,200 14,510
MADAGASCAR. . . . . . . Antananarivo	8,960,000. . . . 520,000	226,658. . . 587,041	Socialist . . . . . republic	President: . . . . Cmdr. Didier Ratsiraka Prime Minister: Lt. Col. Désiré Rakotoarijaona	Franc 0.0032	3,030 350
MALAWI . . . . Lilongwe	6,120,000. . . . 98,700[1]	45,747. . . . 118,484	Republic . . . . . (C)	President: . . . . Hastings Kamuzu Banda	Kwacha 0.90	1,390 230
MALAYSIA . . . . Kuala Lumpur	14,420,000. . . . 937,900[1]	127,317. . . 329,749	Federal . . . . . . constitutional monarchy (C)	Supreme Head of State: Sultan Haji Ahmad Shah al Musta'in Billah ibni al-Marhum Prime Minister: Datuk Seri Mahathir bin Mohamad	Ringgit. 0.42	22,410 1,670
MALDIVES . . . . Male	160,000. . . . 29,600	115. . . 298	Republic 	President: . . . . Maumoon Abdul Gayoom	Rupee 0.14	40 260
MALI . . . . Bamako	7,160,000. . . . 440,000[1]	478,766. . . 1,240,000	Republic 	President: . . . . Brig. Gen. Moussa Traoré	Franc 0.0015	1,340 190
MALTA . . . . Valletta	370,000. . . . 14,000	122. . . 316	Republic . . . . . (C)	President: . . . . Agatha Barbara Prime Minister: Dom Mintoff	Pound 2.40	1,190 3,470
MAURITANIA . . . . Nouakchott	1,680,000. . . . 135,000[1]	397,955. . . 1,030,700	Islamic. . . . . . . republic	President and Chairman, ... Military Committee for National Salvation: Lt. Col. Mohamed Khouna Ould Haidalla Prime Minister: Lt. Col. Maaouya Ould Sidi Ahmed Taya	Ouguiya 0.02	530 320
MAURITIUS . . . . Port Louis	940,000. . . . 145,800	790. . . 2,045	Parliamentary . state (C)	Governor-General: . . . . Sir Dayendranath Burrenchobay Prime Minister: Aneerood Jugnauth	Rupee 0.09	1,020 1,060
MEXICO . . . . Mexico City	71,190,000. . . . 9,191,300	761,604. . . 1,972,547	Federal . . . . . . republic	President: . . . . Miguel de la Madrid Hurtado	Peso 0.01	144,000 2,130
MONACO . . . . Monaco-Ville	30,000. . . . 1,700	0.58. . . 1.49	Constitutional . monarchy	Prince: . . . . Rainier III Minister of State: Jean Herly	French franc . . 0.14	NA NA
MONGOLIAN **PEOPLE'S** **REPUBLIC** Ulan Bator	1,710,000. . . . 435,400	604,250. . . 1,565,000	People's . . . . . republic	Presidium Chairman: . . . . Yumzhagiyen Tsedenbal Chairman, Council of Ministers (Premier): Zhambyn Batmunkh	Tugrik . . . . 0.32[2]	NA NA
MOROCCO. . . . . Rabat	20,650,000. . . . 768,500[1]	172,414. . . 446,550	Constitutional . monarchy	King: . . . . Hassan II Prime Minister: Maati Bouabid	Dirham. 0.16	17,440 860
MOZAMBIQUE . . . . Maputo	10,760,000. . . . 755,300[1]	309,496. . . 801,590	People's . . . . . republic	President: . . . . Samora M. Machel	Metical. 0.02	2,810 270
NAURU . . . . Yaren	7,700. . . . NA	8. . . 21	Republic . . . . . (C)	President: . . . . Hammer DeRoburt	Australian . . . . dollar 0.95	155 21,400

Imports Exports	Revenue Expenditure	Elementary Schools: Teachers Students	Secondary Schools: Teachers Students	Colleges and Universities: Teachers Students
$ 6,836,000,000	$ NA	30,489	18,679	637
22,128,000,000	4,239,000,000	656,541	288,706	8,918
NA	132,000,000	95	92	63
503,000,000	130,300,000	1,899	1,831	1,728
15	1,232,000,000	NA	NA	NA
15	1,262,000,000	28,813	23,850	337
600,000,000	1,045,000,000	23,937	NA	557
402,000,000	1,229,000,000	1,311,000	NA	16,226
362,000,000	215,000,000	11,552	930	NA
284,000,000	315,000,000	779,676	19,037	1,620
13,132,000,000[16]	6,677,000,000	72,347[17]	59,255[17]	5,569
12,884,000,000[16]	9,272,000,000	2,033,803[17]	1,266,323[17]	57,139
11,000,000	2,000,000	179	113	*
3,000,000	5,000,000	13,483	3,891	*
359,000,000	148,000,000	8,280	540	450
149,000,000	148,000,000	291,966	13,363	4,216
855,000,000	480,000,000	1,575	2,292	153
448,000,000	456,000,000	32,218	27,076	1,592
264,000,000	210,000,000	1,857	511	110
194,000,000	210,000,000	82,408	11,957	471
553,000,000	251,000,000	6,177	3,136	NA
326,000,000	264,000,000	123,666	81,602	470
19,416,000,000	88,947,000,000	339,099	150,040	48,842
15,301,000,000	88,947,000,000	13,869,591	2,609,071	798,493
NA	219,000,000	383[4]	[4]	*
NA	139,000,000	1,558	2,825	*
497,000,000	1,385,000,000	13,883	NA	1,100
343,000,000	1,382,000,000	394,400	40,800	23,200
4,185,000,000	6,854,000,000	NA	NA	NA
2,249,000,000	8,033,000,000	2,051,862	726,595	74,465
470,000,000	514,000,000	17,030	2,767	224
260,000,000	594,000,000	1,387,192	103,645	836
12,000,000	124,000,000	134[4]	[4]	*
75,000,000	97,000,000	1,500	667	*

Nation Capital	Population	Area of Country (sq mi/ sq km)	Type of Government	Heads of State and Government	Currency: Value in U.S. Dollars	GNP (000,000): GNP Per Capita
NEPAL.............. Kathmandu	15,020,000.... 393,500	54,362... 140,797	Constitutional monarchy	King: Birendra Bir Bikram Shah Dev Prime Minister: Surya Bahadur Thapa	Rupee...... 0.08	$ 1,980 140
NETHERLANDS, THE . Amsterdam	14,240,000.... 712,300	15,770... 40,844	Constitutional monarchy	Queen: Beatrix Prime Minister: Ruud Lubbers	Guilder...... 0.36	161,440 11,470
NEW ZEALAND ...... Wellington	3,130,000.... 135,900	103,736... 268,676	Parliamentary state (C)	Governor-General: Sir David S. Beattie Prime Minister: Robert D. Muldoon	Dollar........ 0.72	23,160 7,090
NICARAGUA......... Managua	2,820,000.... 552,900	50,193... 130,000	Republic	Coordinator, Junta of the Government of National Reconstruction: Cmdr. Daniel Ortega Saavedra	Córdoba 0.10	1,930 720
NIGER............... Niamey	5,480,000.... 225,300¹	489,191... 1,267,000	Republic	President, Supreme Military Council: Col. Seyni Kountché	CFA franc 0.0029	1,760 330
NIGERIA............ Lagos	79,680,000.... 4,100,000¹	356,669... 923,768	Federal republic (C)	President: Shehu Shagari	Naira........ 1.48	85,510 1,010
NORWAY .... Oslo	4,100,000.... 452,000	125,182... 324,219	Constitutional monarchy	King: Olav V Prime Minister: Kaare Willoch	Krone........ 0.14	51,610 12,650
OMAN .... Muscat	920,000.... 15,000	82,030... 212,457	Sultanate......	Sultan and Prime Minister: Qabus bin Said	Rial 2.90	3,900 4,380
PAKISTAN .... Islamabad	84,580,000.... 201,000	310,404... 803,943	Federal republic	President and Chief Martial Law Administrator: Gen. Muhammad Zia ul-Haq	Rupee 0.08	24,870 300
PANAMA............ Panamá	1,940,000.... 388,600	29,762... 77,082	Republic	President: Ricardo de la Espriella	Balboa........ 1.00	3,170 1,730
PAPUA NEW GUINEA . Port Moresby	3,010,000.... 122,800¹	178,260... 461,691	Parliamentary state (C)	Governor-General: Sir Tore Lokoloko Prime Minister: Michael Somare	Kina 1.35	2,360 780
PARAGUAY.......... Asunción	3,270,000.... 513,300	157,048... 406,752	Republic	President: Gen. Alfredo Stroessner	Guarani 0.0079	4,110 1,340
PERU............... Lima	18,280,000.... 4,746,200¹	496,224... 1,285,216	Republic	President: Fernando Belaúnde Terry Prime Minister: Manuel Ulloa Elías	Sol 0.0013	16,470 930
PHILIPPINES .... Manila	49,530,000.... 1,626,200	115,831... 300,000	Republic	President: Ferdinand E. Marcos Prime Minister: César Virata	Peso 0.12	34,350 720
POLAND............. Warsaw	35,900,000.... 1,596,100	120,725... 312,677	People's republic	Chairman, Council of State: Henryk Jabłoński Chairman, Military Council of National Salvation, and Chairman, Council of Ministers (Premier): Gen. Wojciech W. Jaruzelski	Złoty 0.012²	139,780 3,900
PORTUGAL.......... Lisbon	9,930,000.... 859,200	35,553... 92,082	Republic	President: Gen. António Ramalho Eanes Prime Minister: Francisco Pinto Balsemão	Escudo 0.01	23,140 2,350
QATAR .... Doha	250,000.... 180,000	4,247... 11,000	Constitutional emirate	Emir and Prime Minister: Sheikh Khalifa ibn Hamad al-Thani	Riyal.......... 0.27	6,020 26,080
RUMANIA .... Bucharest	22,460,000.... 2,090,400	91,699... 237,500	Socialist republic	Head of State and President, State Council: Nicolae Ceauşescu Chairman, Council of Ministers (Premier): Constantin Dăscălescu	Leu 0.07	52,010 2,340

Imports Exports	Revenue Expenditure	Elementary Schools: Teachers Students	Secondary Schools: Teachers Students	Colleges and Universities: Teachers Students
$ 316,000,000 82,000,000	$ 539,000,000. 539,000,000	NA. 1,068,000	NA 512,000	NA 54,000
65,921,000,000 68,732,000,000	47,242,000,000. 52,308,000,000	64,881. 1,470,000	101,955 1,385,000	28,600 279,000
5,684,000,000 5,563,000,000	6,556,000,000. 7,423,000,000	20,402. 506,602	15,743 371,421	3,682 57,441
883,000,000 448,000,000	174,000,000. 291,000,000	9,729. 368,895	2,954 105,429	1,204 23,171
196,000,000 160,000,000	307,000,000. 307,000,000	4,762. 187,151	961 27,104	34 782
10,991,000,000 17,331,000,000	17,739,000,000. 25,855,000,000	NA. 8,268,000	NA 998,609	NA 41,499
15,661,000,000 17,990,000,000	17,310,000,000. 18,037,000,000	30,818. 591,323	17,120 200,989	3,652 40,620
1,732,000,000 3,202,000,000	4,050,000,000. 4,082,000,000	NA. 91,652	NA 15,280	* *
5,348,000,000 2,880,000,000	4,290,000,000. 4,290,000,000	139,300. 7,090,000	115,600 1,996,000	19,878 349,259
1,540,000,000 315,000,000	753,000,000. 967,000,000	12,107. 338,674	8,301 172,422	2,643 55,799
1,023,000,000 1,031,000,000	906,000,000. 913,000,000	9,063. 284,089	2,187 48,592	232 3,778
506,000,000 296,000,000	433,000,000. 425,000,000	18,038. 504,377	9,830 110,095	1,984 25,232
2,542,000,000 3,364,000,000	3,228,000,000. 3,673,000,000	75,491. 3,019,624	35,183 969,129	13,468 233,420
7,946,000,000 5,722,000,000	4,295,000,000. 4,624,000,000	274,205. 8,056,013	104,657 3,123,406	41,384 946,860
15,475,000,000 13,249,000,000	36,602,000,000. 37,538,000,000	204,300. 4,259,800	102,900 2,266,000	54,700 453,700
9,794,000,000 4,148,000,000	5,693,000,000. 5,693,000,000	40,011. 925,857	30,911 497,464	7,419 81,955
1,429,000,000 5,698,000,000	3,776,000,000. 3,345,000,000	3,486⁴. 25,000	⁴ 15,000	NA 2,700
12,458,000,000 12,610,000,000	19,233,000,000. 19,233,000,000	156,817. 3,308,462	48,711 1,147,879	14,592 192,769

Nation Capital	Population	Area of Country (sq mi / sq km)	Type of Government	Heads of State and Government	Currency: Value in U.S. Dollars	GNP (000,000): GNP Per Capita
RWANDA........... Kigali	5,110,000.... 117,700[1]	10,169... 26,338	Republic.....	President:.................... Maj. Gen. Juvénal Habyarimana	Franc.......$ 0.01	1,040 200
ST. LUCIA........... Castries	120,000.... 45,000	238.... 616	Parliamentary state (C)	Governor-General:............ Boswell Williams Prime Minister: John G. M. Compton	East Caribbean dollar 0.37	110 850
ST. VINCENT AND.... THE GRENADINES Kingstown	100,000.... 25,000	150... 388	Parliamentary state (C)	Governor-General:.. Sir Sydney Douglas Gun-Munro Prime Minister: R. Milton Cato	East Caribbean dollar 0.37	60 520
SAN MARINO........ San Marino	20,000.... 4,700	24... 61	Republic......	Co-Regents:................. Giuseppe Maiani, NA Secretary of State for Foreign and Political Affairs: Giordano Bruno Reffi	Italian lira 0.0007	NA NA
SÃO TOMÉ AND..... PRÍNCIPE São Tomé	90,000.... 20,000	372.... 964	Republic.....	President and Prime Minister: Manuel Pinto da Costa	Dobra 0.03	60 490
SAUDI ARABIA....... Riyadh	9,320,000.... 1,044,000	830,000... 2,149,690	Monarchy...	King and Prime Minister: Fahd ibn Abdul-Aziz	Riyal......... 0.29	100,930 11,260
SENEGAL[11]......... Dakar	5,810,000.... 978,600	75,750.... 196,192	Republic.....	President:.................... Abdou Diouf Premier: Habib Thiam	CFA franc 0.0029	2,560 450
SEYCHELLES........ Victoria	70,000.... 23,300[1]	108... 280	Republic..... (C)	President:.................... France Albert René	Rupee......... 0.15	120 1,770
SIERRA LEONE...... Freetown	3,570,000.... 274,000	27,699.... 71,740	Republic..... (C)	President:.................... Siaka P. Stevens	Leone........ 0.80	950 270
SINGAPORE......... Singapore	2,440,000.... *	224... 581	Republic..... (C)	President:.................... C. V. Devan Nair Prime Minister: Lee Kuan Yew	Dollar........ 0.46	10,700 4,480
SOLOMON ISLANDS.. Honiara	240,000.... 20,800	10,983... 28,446	Parliamentary state (C)	Governor-General:............ Sir Baddeley Devesi Prime Minister: Solomon Mamaloni	Dollar........ 1.10	110 460
SOMALIA........... Mogadishu	4,900,000.... 400,000	246,201.... 637,657	Republic.....	President and Chairman, Council of Ministers: Maj. Gen. Muhammad Siad Barre	Shilling 0.16	NA NA
SOUTH AFRICA,..... REPUBLIC OF Cape Town Pretoria	30,130,000.... 213,800 528,400	471,445... 1,221,037	Republic....	President:.................. Marais Viljoen Prime Minister: P. W. Botha	Rand......... 0.87	66,960 2,290
SPAIN.............. Madrid	37,650,000.... 3,271,800	194,897.... 504,782	Constitutional monarchy	King:.................... Juan Carlos I Prime Minister: Felipe González Márquez	Peseta....... 0.0088	199,780 5,350
SRI LANKA.......... (CEYLON) Colombo	14,990,000.... 585,800	25,332.... 65,610	Republic..... (C)	President:.................... Junius R. Jayawardene Prime Minister: Ranasinghe Premadasa	Rupee........ 0.05	3,990 270
SUDAN .... Khartoum	18,900,000.... 1,621,000	967,499.... 2,505,813	Republic.....	President and Prime Minister: Maj. Gen. Gaafar al-Nimeiry	Pound........ 1.14	8,640 470
SURINAME.......... Paramaribo	400,000.... 67,700	63,037.... 163,265	Republic......	Acting President:.............. L. F. Ramdat-Misier Prime Minister: Henry Neyhorst	Guilder 0.56	1,000 2,840
SWAZILAND......... Mbabane	570,000.... 29,900	6,704.... 17,363	Monarchy.... (C)	Queen:..................... Dzeliwe Prime Minister: Prince Mabandla Dlamini	Lilangeni 0.87	380 680
SWEDEN............ Stockholm	8,320,000.... 647,200	173,732.... 449,964	Constitutional monarchy	King:.................... Carl XVI Gustaf Prime Minister: Olof Palme	Krona........ 0.16	111,900 13,520

Imports Exports	Revenue Expenditure	Elementary Schools: Teachers Students	Secondary Schools: Teachers Students	Colleges and Universities: Teachers Students
$ 190,000,000 115,000,000	$ 116,000,000. 117,000,000	NA. 704,924	NA. 10,667	NA 1,096
101,000,000 28,000,000	18,700,000. 18,900,000	903. 31,441	264. 3,939	* *
41,000,000 22,000,000	26,200,000. 25,300,000	NA. 24,222	NA. 7,743	* *
NA NA	120,000,000. 120,000,000	145. 1,509	112. 1,219	* *
10,500,000 6,600,000	5,000,000. 12,000,000	527. 14,162	111. 3,300	* *
35,244,000,000 120,240,000,000	99,561,000,000. 87,262,000,000	42,706. 802,810	24,041. 304,058	3,964 43,897
931,000,000 536,000,000	766,000,000. 766,000,000	7,868. 370,412	2,934. 74,265	578 8,776
96,000,000 17,000,000	79,000,000. 75,000,000	685. 14,516	150. 1,727	24 194
316,000,000 206,000,000	227,000,000. 270,000,000	6,700. 218,379	2,572. 53,801	327 1,690
27,571,000,000[18] 20,993,000,000[18]	3,093,000,000. 3,093,000,000	11,267. 296,608	8,931. 182,859	1,947 22,511
74,000,000 73,000,000	39,000,000. 69,000,000	1,148. 28,870	257. 4,030	* *
199,000,000 200,000,000	307,000,000. 394,000,000	5,297. 165,694	1,124. 17,785	148 2,281
8,336,000,000 9,618,000,000	13,649,000,000. 16,425,000,000	162,046[4]. 4,315,150	[4]. 1,206,145	16,708 218,275
32,159,000,000 20,338,000,000	25,161,000,000. 22,156,000,000	206,000[13]. 6,668,100[13]	97,100. 1,674,900	33,800 649,500
1,803,000,000 1,036,000,000	940,000,000. 1,027,000,000	140,259[4,6]. 1,975,749[6]	[4]. 1,168,864[6]	1,827 17,226
1,529,000,000 658,000,000	1,921,000,000. 1,740,000,000	41,576. 1,435,127	16,835. 433,091	1,385 28,985
504,000,000 514,000,000	349,000,000. 364,000,000	3,578. 80,317	1,713. 32,903	140 1,342
432,000,000 370,000,000	146,000,000. 574,000,000	3,278. 112,019	1,416. 24,478	91 885
28,856,000,000 28,600,000,000	28,478,000,000. 41,924,000,000	111,094[4]. 677,349	[4]. 591,019	NA 197,389

Nation Capital	Population	Area of Country (sq mi/ sq km)	Type of Government	Heads of State and Government	Currency: Value in U.S. Dollars	GNP (000,000): GNP Per Capita
SWITZERLAND...... Bern	6,470,000.... 145,300	15,941.... 41,288	..Federal republic	.President: Fritz Honegger	.Franc....... 0.46	$ 106,300 16,440
SYRIA .... Damascus	9,310,000.... 1,142,000	71,498... 185,180	.Socialist republic	.President: Lt. Gen. Hafez al-Assad Prime Minister: Abdul Rauf al-Kasm	.Pound 0.25	12,030 1,340
TAIWAN or .... FORMOSA (REPUBLIC OF CHINA) Taipei	17,878,000.... 2,220,400	13,892.... 35,981	..Republic	.President: Chiang Ching-kuo Premier: Sun Yun-suan	.New Taiwan .. dollar 0.03	38,200 2,160
TANZANIA .... Dar es Salaam	18,510,000.... 870,000	364,900.... 945,087	.Republic (C)	.President: Julius K. Nyerere Prime Minister: Cleopa D. Msuya	.Shilling 0.11	4,780[19] 260[19]
THAILAND .... Bangkok	48,130,000.... 4,870,500	198,456.... 514,000	.Constitutional monarchy	.King: Bhumibol Adulyadej Prime Minister: Gen. Prem Tinsulanonda	.Baht......... 0.04	31,140 670
TOGO .... Lomé	2,710,000.... 247,000	21,925.... 56,785	.Republic	.President: Gen. Gnassingbe Eyadéma	.CFA franc 0.0029	1,020 410
TONGA .... Nuku'alofa	100,000.... 19,900[1]	270.... 699	.Constitutional monarchy	.King: Taufa'ahau Tupou IV Prime Minister: Prince Fatafehi Tu'ipelehake	.Pa'anga...... 0.95	50 520
TRINIDAD AND ...... TOBAGO Port-of-Spain	1,190,000.... 120,000[1]	1,981.... 5,130	.Republic (C)	.President: Sir Ellis E. I. Clarke Prime Minister: George M. Chambers	.Dollar........ 0.42	5,110 4,370
TUNISIA .... Tunis	6,510,000.... 550,400	63,170.... 163,610	.Republic	.President: Habib Bourguiba Prime Minister: Mohammed Mzali	.Dinar 1.62	8,340 1,310
TURKEY .... Ankara	46,380,000.... 2,316,300	301,382.... 780,576	.Republic	.President and Chief of the General Staff: Gen. Kenan Evren Prime Minister: Bülent Ulusu	.Lira 0.0057	66,080 1,460
TUVALU .... (ELLICE ISLANDS) Funafuti	7,300.... 2,200	10.... 26	.Parliamentary state (C)	.Governor-General: Sir Penitala Fiatau Teo Prime Minister: Tomasi Puapua	.Dollar........ 0.95	4 570
UGANDA............ Kampala	13,620,000.... 458,400[1]	91,134.... 236,036	.Republic (C)	.President: Milton Obote Prime Minister: Erifasi Otema Allimadi	.Shilling 0.01	3,750 280
UNION OF SOVIET ... SOCIALIST REPUBLICS Moscow	267,700,000.... 8,184,000[1]	8,649,534.... 22,402,200	.Federal socialist state	.Chairman, Presidium of the Supreme Soviet: Vacant Chairman, Council of Ministers (Premier): Nikolai A. Tikhonov	.Ruble........ 1.37[2]	1,212,030 4,550
UNITED ARAB ...... EMIRATES Abu Dhabi	760,000.... 250,000[1]	32,278.... 83,600	.Federal state	.President: Sheikh Zaid bin Sultan al-Nahayan Prime Minister: Sheikh Rashid bin Said al-Maktum	.Dirham....... 0.27	26,850 30,070
UNITED STATES ..... OF AMERICA Washington, D.C.	229,810,000.... 638,400	3,618,770.... 9,372,569	.Federal republic	.President: Ronald W. Reagan	.Dollar........ *	2,582,460 11,360
UPPER VOLTA....... Ouagadougou	7,090,000.... 236,000	105,869.... 274,200	.Republic	.Chairman, Provisional People's Salvation Council: Maj. Jean-Baptiste Ouedraogo	.CFA franc 0.0029	1,110 190

Imports Exports	Revenue Expenditure	Elementary Schools: Teachers Students	Secondary Schools: Teachers Students	Colleges and Universities: Teachers Students
$ 30,696,000,000 27,043,000,000	$ 9,336,000,000. 9,944,000,000	NA 502,200	NA 666,300	NA 74,700
5,040,000,000 2,103,000,000	7,766,000,000. 7,766,000,000	45,254 1,375,922	32,832 576,478	NA 96,040
19,754,000,000 19,775,000,000	8,422,000,000. 8,422,000,000	69,141 2,233,706	69,698 1,605,567	16,495 342,528
1,226,000,000 508,000,000	1,495,000,000[19]. 1,467,000,000[19]	38,199[6] 1,956,320[6]	3,731 67,859	459 2,260
9,911,000,000 6,999,000,000	5,337,000,000. 5,337,000,000	283,204 6,848,121	101,899 1,747,923	29,667 169,639
550,000,000 335,000,000	252,000,000. 252,000,000	8,350 500,000	2,776 118,310	269 4,000
29,000,000 8,000,000	16,630,000. 16,621,000	NA 19,012	NA 14,881	* *
3,178,000,000 4,077,000,000	2,108,000,000. 2,108,000,000	6,471 181,863	1,325 86,145	500 4,940
3,479,000,000 2,189,000,000	1,579,000,000. 1,217,000,000	26,207 1,024,537	11,595 241,908	2,236 25,602
8,944,000,000 4,721,000,000	11,223,000,000. 11,500,000,000	187,363 5,595,356	93,734 2,187,623	20,529 275,189
2,000,000 600,000	3,000,000. 3,000,000	NA 1,298	NA 236	* *
293,000,000 345,000,000	665,000,000. 929,000,000	36,442[6] 1,223,850[6]	4,161[6] 81,722[6]	352 3,913
68,522,000,000 76,449,000,000	376,944,000,000. 376,944,000,000	2,638,000[4] 44,300,000	[4] 13,800,000	NA 5,200,000
8,752,000,000 20,742,000,000	7,146,000,000. 7,146,000,000	5,136 88,617	2,819 31,560	344 2,516
271,269,000,000 228,961,000,000	617,800,000,000. 728,400,000,000	1,192,100[6] 27,356,000[6]	1,002,000[6] 12,833,000[6]	840,000 12,371,672
338,000,000 75,000,000	166,000,000. 166,000,000	NA 185,658	NA 23,786	NA 3,173

Nation Capital	Population	Area of Country (sq mi/ sq km)	Type of Government	Heads of State and Government	Currency: Value in U.S. Dollars	GNP (000,000): GNP Per Capita
URUGUAY . . . . Montevideo	2,930,000. . . . 1,314,100	68,037. . . . 176,215	Republic	President: . . . . Gen. Gregorio Conrado Alvarez Armelino	New peso 0.08	$ 8,240 2,820
VANUATU (NEW . . . . . **HEBRIDES)** Vila	120,000. . . . 15,100[1]	5,700. . . . 14,763	Republic . . . . . . (C)	President: . . . . Ati George Sokomanu Prime Minister: Rev. Walter H. Lini	Vatu 0.01	60 530
VENEZUELA . . . . Caracas	14,310,000. . . . 3,041,000[1]	352,144. . . . 912,050	Federal . . . . republic	President: . . . . Luis Herrera Campíns	Bolivar 0.23	54,220 3,630
VIETNAM . . . . Hanoi	54,970,000. . . . 2,570,900	127,242. . . . 329,556	Socialist . . . . republic	Chairman, Council of . . . . State (President): Truong Chinh Chairman, Council of Ministers (Premier): Pham Van Dong	Dong 0.48	NA NA
WESTERN SAMOA . . . Apia	160,000. . . . 33,800[1]	1,097. . . . 2,842	Constitutional . monarchy (C)	Head of State: . . . . Malietoa Tanumafili II Prime Minister: Va'ai Kolone	Tala 1.08	NA NA
YEMEN, PEOPLE'S . . . **DEMOCRATIC** **REPUBLIC OF** Aden	2,030,000. . . . 343,000	128,560. . . . 332,968	People's . . . . . republic	President: . . . . Chairman of the Presidium of the Supreme People's Council, and Prime Minister: Ali Nasser Mohammed	Dinar 2.90	810 420
YEMEN ARAB . . . . **REPUBLIC** San'a	5,940,000. . . . 277,800	75,290. . . . 195,000	Republic 	President: . . . . Col. Ali Abdullah Saleh Prime Minister: Abdul Karim al-Iryani	Rial 0.22	2,680 460
YUGOSLAVIA . . . . Belgrade	22,520,000. . . . 976,000	98,766. . . . 255,804	Federal . . . . . socialist republic	President: . . . . Petar Stambolić President, Federal Executive Council (Prime Minister): Milka Planinć	Dinar 0.02	58,570 2,620
ZAIRE . . . . Kinshasa	26,380,000. . . . 2,443,900	905,567. . . . 2,345,409	Republic 	President: . . . . Mobutu Sese Seko First State Commissioner (Prime Minister): N'Singa Udjuu	Zaire 0.17	6,340 220
ZAMBIA . . . . Lusaka	5,960,000. . . . 641,000	290,586. . . . 752,614	Republic . . . . . (C)	President: . . . . Kenneth D. Kaunda Prime Minister: Nalumino Mundia	Kwacha 0.91	3,220 560
ZIMBABWE . . . . **(RHODESIA)** Harare	7,600,000. . . . 654,000[1]	150,804. . . . 390,580	Republic . . . . . (C)	President: . . . . Rev. Canaan S. Banana Prime Minister: Robert G. Mugabe	Dollar 1.37	4,640 630

1. Population of metropolitan area.
2. Noncommercial exchange rate applied to tourism and remittances from outside the ruble area.
3. Combined figure with Luxembourg.
4. Combined figure for elementary and secondary education.
5. Excluding trade with other members of the Customs and Economic Union of Central Africa (Cameroon, Central African Republic, Congo, Gabon).
6. Figure for public schools.
7. Excluding Mayotte.
8. Excluding Turkish part of Nicosia.
9. Excluding budget of Turkish Federated State of Cyprus, which was balanced at $47,000,000 in 1981–82.
10. Figure for Greek schools (1980–81). Turkish schools (1978–79) had 610 primary school teachers and 18,353 students, and 571 secondary school teachers and 12,234 students.

Imports / Exports	Revenue / Expenditure	Elementary Schools: Teachers / Students	Secondary Schools: Teachers / Students	Colleges and Universities: Teachers / Students
$ 1,551,000,000 / 1,216,000,000	$ 1,495,000,000 / 1,488,000,000	15,679. / 382,759	18,180 / 188,000	2,149 / 39,927
56,000,000 / 38,000,000	22,000,000. / 37,000,000	839. / 21,161	198 / 2,679	* / *
10,655,000,000 / 20,950,000,000	9,307,000,000. / 10,797,000,000	88,848[13]. / 2,638,192[13]	47,137 / 751,430	23,449 / 282,075
1,225,000,000 / 535,000,000	5,193,000,000. / 5,193,000,000	217,064. / 7,722,524	127,635 / 3,200,912	10,475 / 100,027
73,000,000 / 18,000,000	28,000,000. / 52,000,000	1,438. / 41,544	475 / 10,767	53 / 425
393,000,000 / 248,000,000	101,000,000. / 137,000,000	10,203[4]. / 212,795	[4] / 66,681	246 / 2,517
1,492,000,000 / 14,000,000	1,157,000,000. / 1,856,000,000	6,604. / 255,301	1,345 / 24,240	NA / 2,408
15,757,000,000 / 10,929,000,000	4,411,000,000. / 4,411,000,000	130,276. / 2,824,762	59,931 / 952,568	23,969 / 447,270
672,000,000 / 662,000,000	912,000,000. / 1,002,000,000	NA. / 5,200,000	NA / 680,000	NA / 35,000
1,090,000,000 / 1,402,000,000	923,000,000. / 1,283,000,000	23,379. / 964,475	NA / 98,057	NA / 3,773
1,322,000,000 / 1,423,000,000	2,062,000,000. / 2,791,000,000	18,603. / 831,572	4,149 / 80,556	225 / 1,481

11. On Feb. 1, 1982, The Gambia and Senegal formed the confederation of Senegambia to integrate their military forces, economies, and foreign policies; but they maintained separate governments. The president of Senegal is the president of Senegambia and the president of The Gambia is its vice-president.
12. Figure for ten-year polytechnical schools.
13. Including preprimary figure.
14. Figure for East Bank of Jordan.
15. Included in figure for Belgium.
16. Excluding trade among the states of Malaysia.
17. Figure for peninsular Malaysia.
18. Excluding trade with Malaysia.
19. Excluding Zanzibar.

THE STATES AND OUTLYING AREAS OF THE UNITED STATES

State Capital	Population	Area (sq mi / sq km)	Per Capita Personal Income	Governor Lieutenant-Governor	Revenue Expenditure	Roads (Miles)
ALABAMA	3,893,888	51,705	$ 8,219	Forrest H. James, Jr. (D)	$ 4,551,000,000	87,240
Montgomery	177,857	133,915		George D. H. McMillan, Jr. (D)	3,927,000,000	
ALASKA	401,851	591,004	13,763	Jay S. Hammond (R)	4,867,000,000	9,085
Juneau	19,528	1,530,693		Terry Miller (R)	2,424,000,000	
ARIZONA	2,718,425	114,000	9,754	Bruce E. Babbitt (D)	2,776,000,000	78,286
Phoenix	789,704	295,259		*	2,841,000,000	
ARKANSAS	2,286,435	53,187	8,044	Frank D. White (R)	2,228,000,000	76,764
Little Rock	158,461	137,753		Winston Bryant (D)	2,169,000,000	
CALIFORNIA	23,667,565	158,706	11,923	Edmund G. Brown, Jr. (D)	32,623,000,000	176,665
Sacramento	275,741	411,047		Mike Curb (R)	34,525,000,000	
COLORADO	2,889,735	104,091	11,215	Richard D. Lamm (D)	2,904,000,000	75,708
Denver	492,365	269,594		Nancy Dick (D)	2,981,000,000	
CONNECTICUT	3,107,576	5,018	12,816	William A. O'Neill (D)	3,449,000,000	19,442
Hartford	136,392	12,997		Joseph J. Fauliso (D)	3,274,000,000	
DELAWARE	594,317	2,044	11,095	Pierre S. du Pont 4th (R)	998,000,000	5,249
Dover	23,507	5,295		Michael N. Castle (R)	933,000,000	
DISTRICT OF	638,432	69	13,539	Mayor:	*	1,102
COLUMBIA		178		Marion S. Barry, Jr.	*	
*	*			(D)		
FLORIDA	9,746,342	58,664	10,165	D. Robert Graham (D)	8,063,000,000	97,186
Tallahassee	81,548	151,938		Wayne Mixson (D)	7,807,000,000	
GEORGIA	5,463,105	58,910	8,934	George Busbee (D)	5,118,000,000	104,253
Atlanta	425,022	152,575		Zell B. Miller (D)	4,979,000,000	
HAWAII	964,691	6,471	11,036	George R. Ariyoshi (D)	1,831,000,000	4,107
Honolulu	365,048	16,759		Jean Sadako King (D)	1,700,000,000	
IDAHO	944,038	83,564	8,937	John V. Evans (D)	989,000,000	67,442
Boise	102,160	216,431		Philip E. Batt (R)	1,001,000,000	
ILLINOIS	11,426,596	56,345	11,576	James R. Thompson, Jr. (R)	11,891,000,000	133,672
Springfield	99,637	145,933		*	11,776,000,000	
INDIANA	5,490,260	36,185	9,720	Robert D. Orr (R)	4,880,000,000	91,676
Indianapolis	700,807	93,720		John M. Mutz (R)	4,970,000,000	
IOWA	2,913,808	56,275	10,474	Robert D. Ray (R)	3,128,000,000	112,487
Des Moines	191,003	145,752		Terry E. Branstad (R)	3,210,000,000	
KANSAS	2,364,236	82,277	10,813	John W. Carlin (D)	2,374,000,000	132,209
Topeka	115,266	213,097		Paul V. Dugan (D)	2,377,000,000	
KENTUCKY	3,660,257	40,409	8,420	John Y. Brown, Jr. (D)	4,031,000,000	68,429
Frankfort	25,973	104,660		Martha Layne Collins (D)	4,295,000,000	

458

The material in the following tables is the latest available. As before, it should be noted that the symbol * indicates that the category is not applicable to the area mentioned, and that NA means that the data were not available. The Office of Territorial Affairs was helpful in supplying some data for the table on Outlying Areas.

Railways (Miles)	Commercial Radio and Television Stations	English-language Daily Newspapers	Public Elementary Schools (K–8): Teachers Students	Public Secondary Schools (9–12): Teachers Students	Colleges and Universities: Institutions Students
4,455	220 / 17	28	22,000 / 536,000	19,300 / 221,000	59 / 166,375
550	34 / 7	8	2,800 / 59,000	2,400 / 26,000	15 / 24,754
1,865	94 / 13	18	18,100 / 360,000	8,100 / 155,000	28 / 205,169
2,763	147 / 9	32	11,800 / 310,000	12,300 / 135,000	35 / 76,032
6,862	443 / 55	124	104,600 / 2,750,000	70,900 / 1,318,000	272 / 1,885,757
3,463	125 / 12	27	13,300 / 377,000	13,900 / 164,000	45 / 167,977
637	64 / 5	25	20,400 / 349,000	13,500 / 156,000	47 / 162,367
280	17 / *	3	2,600 / 53,000	3,300 / 41,000	8 / 32,061
55	17 / 5	1	3,100 / 67,000	2,100 / 27,000	19 / 88,553
3,681	318 / 32	52	42,000 / 1,051,000	36,300 / 450,000	81 / 426,570
5,468	280 / 19	37	34,300 / 738,000	22,200 / 320,000	78 / 191,384
0	34 / 10	6	4,700 / 108,000	3,200 / 55,000	12 / 48,121
2,413	67 / 8	14	5,300 / 147,000	4,700 / 57,000	9 / 42,758
10,672	260 / 24	76	70,100 / 1,307,000	35,700 / 617,000	158 / 659,623
5,948	181 / 20	76	26,900 / 695,000	26,800 / 333,000	74 / 251,826
5,375	152 / 13	41	15,400 / 343,000	17,100 / 174,000	60 / 143,105
7,266	107 / 12	47	14,300 / 280,000	11,900 / 126,000	52 / 138,453
3,515	211 / 11	26	21,600 / 461,000	11,800 / 200,000	57 / 144,154

State Capital	Population	Area (sq mi/ sq km)	Per Capita Personal Income	Governor Lieutenant-Governor	Revenue Expenditure	Roads (Miles)
LOUISIANA Baton Rouge	4,206,312. 219,419	47,752. 123,676	$ 9,518	David C. Treen (R). $ Robert L. Freeman (D)	5,352,000,000. 5,216,000,000	56,676
MAINE Augusta	1,125,027. 21,819	33,265. 86,156	8,535	Joseph E. Brennan (D) *	1,303,000,000. 1,216,000,000	21,902
MARYLAND Annapolis	4,216,975. 31,740	10,460. 27,092	11,477	Harry R. Hughes (D) Samuel W. Bogley 3rd (D)	5,259,000,000. 5,056,000,000	27,005
MASSACHUSETTS Boston	5,737,037. 562,994	8,284. 21,456	11,128	Edward J. King (D) Thomas P. O'Neill 3rd (D)	7,252,000,000. 7,258,000,000	33,772
MICHIGAN Lansing	9,262,078. 130,414	58,527. 151,585	10,790	William G. Milliken (R) James H. Brickley (R)	11,069,000,000. 10,993,000,000	117,396
MINNESOTA St. Paul	4,075,970. 270,230	84,402. 218,600	10,768	Albert H. Quie (R) Lou Wangberg (IR)	5,672,000,000. 5,512,000,000	130,834
MISSISSIPPI Jackson	2,520,638. 202,895	47,689. 123,515	7,408	William F. Winter (D) Brad Dye (D)	2,638,000,000. 2,696,000,000	70,442
MISSOURI Jefferson City	4,916,759. 33,619	69,697. 180,515	9,651	Christopher S. Bond (R) Kenneth J. Rothman (D)	3,794,000,000. 4,006,000,000	118,403
MONTANA Helena	786,690. 23,938	147,046. 380,846	9,410	Ted Schwinden (D) George Turman (D)	1,053,000,000. 929,000,000	71,703
NEBRASKA Lincoln	1,569,825. 171,932	77,355. 200,349	10,366	Charles Thone (R) Roland A. Luedtke (R)	1,488,000,000. 1,495,000,000	91,828
NEVADA Carson City	800,493. 32,022	110,561. 286,351	11,576	Robert F. List (R) Myron E. Leavitt (D)	889,000,000. 927,000,000	43,442
NEW HAMPSHIRE Concord	920,610. 30,400	9,279. 24,031	9,994	Hugh J. Gallen (D). *	711,000,000. 782,000,000	14,412
NEW JERSEY Trenton	7,364,823. 92,124	7,787. 20,169	12,127	Thomas H. Kean (R) *	8,163,000,000. 8,455,000,000	33,490
NEW MEXICO Santa Fe	1,302,981. 48,953	121,593. 314,923	8,529	Bruce King (D). Roberto A. Mondragón (D)	2,477,000,000. 1,936,000,000	53,715
NEW YORK Albany	17,558,072. 101,727	49,108. 127,189	11,466	Hugh L. Carey (D) Mario M. Cuomo (D)	23,539,000,000. 23,261,000,000	109,639
NORTH CAROLINA Raleigh	5,881,813. 150,255	52,669. 136,412	8,649	James B. Hunt, Jr. (D) James C. Green (D)	5,792,000,000. 6,004,000,000	92,587
NORTH DAKOTA Bismarck	652,717. 44,485	70,702. 183,118	10,213	Allen I. Olson (R) Ernest M. Sands (R)	1,080,000,000. 943,000,000	85,904
OHIO Columbus	10,797,624. 565,032	41,330. 107,043	10,313	James A. Rhodes (R). *	9,297,000,000. 9,890,000,000	110,845
OKLAHOMA Oklahoma City	3,025,290. 403,136	69,956. 181,185	10,247	George Nigh (D) Spencer Bernard (D)	3,737,000,000. 3,321,000,000	109,946
OREGON Salem	2,633,149. 89,233	97,073. 251,417	10,008	Victor G. Atiyeh (R) *	3,339,000,000. 3,194,000,000	121,408
PENNSYLVANIA Harrisburg	11,863,895. 53,264	45,308. 117,347	10,370	Richard L. Thornburgh (R) William W. Scranton 3rd (R)	12,003,000,000. 11,262,000,000	117,103
RHODE ISLAND Providence	947,154. 156,804	1,212. 3,140	10,153	J. Joseph Garrahy (D) Thomas R. DiLuglio (D)	1,302,000,000. 1,300,000,000	6,275
SOUTH CAROLINA Columbia	3,121,833. 100,385	31,113. 80,582	8,039	Richard W. Riley (D) Nancy Stevenson (D)	3,236,000,000. 3,168,000,000	62,731
SOUTH DAKOTA Pierre	690,768. 11,973	77,116. 199,729	8,833	William J. Janklow (R). Lowell C. Hansen 2nd (R)	734,000,000. 801,000,000	73,018

Railways (Miles)	Commercial Radio and Television Stations	English-language Daily Newspapers	Public Elementary Schools (K–8): Teachers Students	Public Secondary Schools (9–12): Teachers Students	Colleges and Universities: Institutions Students
3,373	160 16	25	23,700 536,000	19,000 222,000	32 174,656
1,487	71 7	9	7,000 148,000	3,200 67,000	29 44,012
1,243	88 6	16	18,600 475,000	22,600 249,000	56 229,936
1,457	106 12	46	28,500 657,000	37,300 336,000	118 417,830
4,185	253 24	52	41,900 1,210,000	38,700 621,000	91 513,033
6,529	167 12	30	20,600 468,000	23,200 263,000	70 210,713
3,063	182 11	25	14,500 326,000	11,800 142,000	41 105,974
6,109	192 24	49	24,800 556,000	24,000 261,000	89 243,672
3,815	71 12	11	5,100 104,000	4,200 47,000	16 35,959
4,857	86 14	19	9,300 186,000	8,700 86,000	31 93,507
1,564	35 8	8	3,600 102,000	3,500 49,000	7 39,936
599	43 2	9	5,000 110,000	4,400 55,000	26 48,524
1,607	75 5	26	45,300 795,000	31,500 414,000	61 322,797
2,075	86 9	20	7,000 184,000	7,300 82,000	19 60,413
4,605	281 31	78	74,000 1,771,000	95,300 991,000	294 1,014,863
3,577	304 19	55	34,600 780,000	20,700 331,000	127 295,771
4,966	38 13	10	4,200 76,000	2,900 38,000	17 35,446
7,224	254 25	95	54,100 1,276,000	45,200 611,000	136 521,396
3,930	120 14	53	18,000 400,000	16,400 173,000	44 162,825
2,944	117 12	21	14,600 322,000	10,400 140,000	45 149,924
7,197	304 28	98	50,400 1,194,000	59,100 648,000	202 517,879
146	22 2	7	4,600 90,000	4,600 52,000	13 68,339
2,736	164 12	19	19,600 430,000	12,200 189,000	60 132,394
1,759	52 11	12	5,300 82,000	2,800 42,000	20 35,015

State Capital	Population	Area (sq mi/ sq km)	Per Capita Personal Income	Governor Lieutenant-Governor	Revenue Expenditure	Roads (Miles)
TENNESSEE	4,591,120	42,144	$ 8,447	Lamar Alexander (R) $	3,787,000,000	83,497
Nashville	455,651	109,151		John S. Wilder (D)	3,785,000,000	
TEXAS	14,229,288	266,807	10,729	William P. Clements, Jr. (R)	13,799,000,000	268,253
Austin	345,496	691,026		William P. Hobby (D)	12,023,000,000	
UTAH	1,461,037	84,899	8,313	Scott M. Matheson (D)	1,680,000,000	43,735
Salt Lake City	163,697	219,888		David S. Monson (R)	1,696,000,000	
VERMONT	511,456	9,614	8,723	Richard A. Snelling (R)	688,000,000	13,942
Montpelier	8,241	24,900		Madeleine M. Kunin (D)	637,000,000	
VIRGINIA	5,346,818	40,767	10,349	Charles S. Robb (D)	5,611,000,000	64,683
Richmond	219,214	105,585		Robert J. Davis (D)	5,566,000,000	
WASHINGTON	4,132,180	68,139	11,277	John Spellman (R)	5,348,000,000	83,291
Olympia	27,447	176,478		John A. Cherberg (D)	5,834,000,000	
WEST VIRGINIA	1,950,279	24,231	8,377	John D. Rockefeller 4th (D)	2,319,000,000	34,999
Charleston	63,968	62,759		*	2,342,000,000	
WISCONSIN	4,705,521	56,153	10,035	Lee S. Dreyfus (R)	6,036,000,000	108,110
Madison	170,616	145,435		Russell A. Olson (R)	6,093,000,000	
WYOMING	469,557	97,809	11,665	Ed Herschler (D)	1,010,000,000	36,709
Cheyenne	47,283	253,325		*	865,000,000	

OUTLYING AREAS OF THE U.S.

Area Capital	Population	Area (sq mi/ sq km)	Status	Governor Lieutenant-Governor	Revenue Expenditure	Roads (Miles)
AMERICAN SAMOA	33,920	77	Unorganized,	Peter T. Coleman $	59,002,746	94
Pago Pago	2,732	199	unincorporated territory	Tufele Li'A	59,002,746	
GUAM	105,821	209	Unincorporated	Paul M. Calvo	124,332,733	230
Agaña	881	541	territory	Joe F. Ada	127,267,155	
PUERTO RICO	3,187,570	3,515	Commonwealth	Carlos Romero Barceló	3,074,900,000	10,456
San Juan	422,701	9,103		*	2,797,200,000	
TRUST TERRITORY OF THE PACIFIC ISLANDS[1] Capitol Hill, on Saipan Island	132,350 NA	533 1,380	U.N. Trust Territory	High Commissioner: Janet J. McCoy	114,738,000 117,230,800	64
VIRGIN ISLANDS	95,591	133	Unincorporated	Juan Luis	180,200,000	621
Charlotte Amalie	11,756	344	territory	Henry Millin	176,900,000	

1. The Northern Mariana Islands in 1982 were an internally self-governing part of the Trust Territory of the Pacific Islands. The government of the Northern Marianas was headed by Gov. Pedro P. Tenorio and Lt.-Gov. Pedro A. Tenorio. The capital was Susupe, on Saipan Island.

Railways (Miles)	Commercial Radio and Television Stations	English-language Daily Newspapers	Public Elementary Schools (K–8): Teachers Students	Public Secondary Schools (9–12): Teachers Students	Colleges and Universities: Institutions Students
3,136	245 / 19	30	25,600 / 602,000	15,800 / 243,000	79 / 200,183
13,313	489 / 59	116	88,200 / 2,087,000	74,900 / 836,000	156 / 716,297
1,656	57 / 4	6	8,700 / 263,000	6,100 / 91,000	14 / 97,048
385	31 / 2	8	3,400 / 65,000	3,300 / 29,000	21 / 30,573
3,503	212 / 16	38	34,200 / 697,000	24,000 / 290,000	69 / 286,015
4,378	145 / 15	27	20,300 / 517,000	15,400 / 234,000	50 / 278,680
3,565	97 / 9	25	12,500 / 268,000	9,600 / 110,000	28 / 82,375
4,838	196 / 20	36	28,600 / 515,000	25,300 / 288,000	64 / 275,325
1,988	41 / 6	10	3,300 / 73,000	3,100 / 28,000	9 / 21,235

Railways (Miles)	Radio and Television Stations	Daily Newspapers	Public Elementary and Secondary School Teachers	Public School Students: Elementary Secondary	Higher Education: Institutions Students
0	1 / 1	1	448	7,939 / 2,777	1 / 984
0	5 / 3	1	1,227	15,850 / 10,207	1 / 3,284
60	94 / 11	4	24,761	475,979 / 212,613	33 / 129,708
0	8 / 3	0	1,701	28,014 / 6,471	1 / 176
0	8 / 2	3	1,540	15,894 / 9,677	1 / 1,990

THE PROVINCES AND TERRITORIES OF CANADA

Province Capital	Population	Area (sq mi/ sq km)	Per Capita Personal Income	Premier Lieutenant-Governor
ALBERTA Edmonton	2,237,724 657,057	255,285 661,185	$12,779	Peter Lougheed Frank Lynch-Staunton
BRITISH COLUMBIA Victoria	2,744,467 233,481	366,255 948,596	12,538	William Bennett Henry Bell-Irving
MANITOBA Winnipeg	1,026,241 584,842	251,000 650,087	10,806	Howard R. Pawley Pearl McGonigal
NEW BRUNSWICK Fredericton	696,403 64,439	28,354 73,436	8,272	Richard B. Hatfield George F. G. Stanley
NEWFOUNDLAND St. John's	567,681 154,820	156,185 404,517	7,528	Brian Peckford Dr. William A. Paddon
NORTHWEST TERRITORIES Yellowknife	45,741 9,483	1,304,903 3,379,684	11,797[1]	Commissioner: John H. Parker
NOVA SCOTIA Halifax	847,442 277,727	21,425 55,491	9,041	John Buchanan John Elvin Shaffner
ONTARIO Toronto	8,625,107 2,998,947	412,582 1,068,582	12,386	William G. Davis John Black Aird
PRINCE EDWARD ISLAND Charlottetown	122,506 44,999	2,184 5,657	7,829	James M. Lee Dr. Joseph Aubin-Dorion
QUÉBEC Québec	6,438,403 576,075	594,860 1,540,680	10,661	René Lévesque Jean-Pierre Côté
SASKATCHEWAN Regina	968,313 164,313	251,700 651,900	11,583	Grant Devine C. Irwin McIntosh
YUKON TERRITORY Whitehorse	23,153 14,814	186,300 482,515	11,797[1]	Commissioner: Douglas Bell

1. Figure is the combined average for the Northwest Territories and Yukon Territory.

The material in this table has been prepared with the kind assistance of Statistics Canada, Ottawa. It should be noted that all dollar figures are in Canadian dollars.

Revenue Expenditure	Motor Vehicle Registrations	Railways (Miles)	Radio and Television Stations	Daily Newspapers	Elementary and Secondary Schools: Teachers Enrollment	Post-secondary Education: Institutions Enrollment
$10,184,621,000.	1,659,079	5,831	69	9	24,060	23
8,037,404,000			19		462,700	53,700
7,725,455,000.	1,672,575	4,564	86	20	28,115	28
7,165,520,000			5		529,100	52,280
2,423,034,000.	656,435	4,078	32	10	11,940	15
2,674,502,000			17		213,830	21,650
1,826,382,000.	364,236	1,633	28	6	7,670	13
1,909,396,000			2		147,250	14,330
1,698,951,000.	212,198	943	33	3	7,765	7
1,721,095,000			10		142,450	10,080
411,825,000.	16,320	130	9	0	700	0
385,779,000			1		12,650	0
2,132,239,000.	530,018	1,223	34	7	10,935	24
2,347,905,000			9		180,785	22,170
19,525,466,000.	4,647,820	9,633	201	47	93,550	52
20,142,104,000			27		1,858,040	256,700
398,893,000.	68,750	253	6	3	1,340	3
376,514,000			3		25,670	2,240
20,800,496,000.	3,787,433	5,171	166	11	71,370	91
21,547,909,000			14		1,160,745	241,400
3,322,052,000.	683,955	7,763	39	4	11,330	6
2,842,919,000			10		209,390	18,720
143,195,000.	18,333	58	3	1	270	0
135,725,000			2		5,080	0

KEY TO
SIGNED ARTICLES

Here is a list of contributors to this Yearbook. The initials at the end of an article are those of the author, or authors, of that article.

A.D., ANGUS DEMING, B.A.
Senior Writer, *Newsweek.* Former Bureau Chief, Jerusalem, Boston, and New York City, for *Newsweek.*

A.E., AGNES ERDELYI, B.A., M.L.S.
Reference Librarian, Sachem (N.Y.) Public Library.

A.E.J., ANTONIO E. JIMENEZ, B.A.
Latin American Correspondent, Voice of America.

A.J.R., ALLAN J. RISTORI, B.A.
Salt Water Editor, *Fishing World.* Editor, *Fishing World Fishing Tackle Buying Guide.* Executive Director, Atlantic Professional Boatmans Association.

A.R.K., ALBERT R. KARR, B.S., M.S.
Staff Reporter, *The Wall Street Journal.*

B.M.P., B. M. PARKER, B.A., M.A., PH.D.
Instructor of English, John Abbott College, Montréal, Québec.

B.O., BILL OTT, B.A., M.A., M.L.S.
Editor, *Booklist.*

B.Q., BENJAMIN QUARLES, B.A., M.A., PH.D.
Emeritus Professor of History, Morgan State University. Author of *Black Abolitionists* and other books.

B.R., BEA RIEMSCHNEIDER, B.A., M.A.
Executive Editor, *Archaeology.* Associate Trustee, American Schools of Oriental Research.

B.T.R., BARBARA T. RICHMAN, B.A., M.S.
Writer, *Eos.* Correspondent, *Energy Research Reports.*

C.McG., CATHLEEN McGUIGAN, A.B.
Associate Editor, *Newsweek.*

C.P., CARL PROUJAN, B.S.
Independent Writer, Editor, A/V Producer. Executive Editor, Science Department, Educational Book Division, Pren-

tice-Hall, Inc. Author of *Secrets of the Sea.*

D.A.W., DENNIS A. WILLIAMS, B.A., M.F.A.
Education Editor, *Newsweek.*

D.C., DIANE CAMPER, A.B., M.S.L.
Washington Bureau Correspondent, *Newsweek.*

D.D.; DAVE DOOLING
Science Editor, The Huntsville (Ala.) *Times.* Editor in Chief, *Space World.* Press Award, 1981, National Space Club.

D.H.D., DONALD H. DUNN, B.J.
Editor, *Business Week.*

D.J.H., DONALD J. HARVEY, B.A., M.A., PH.D.
Professor of History, Hunter College and Graduate Center, City University of New York. Consultant, National Endowment for the Humanities. Author of *France Since the Revolution.* Coauthor of *Nationalism: Essays in Honor of Louis Snyder.*

D.M., DERWENT MAY, M.A.
Literary Editor, *The Listener.* Author of *Dear Parson, The Professionals,* and *A Revenger's Comedy.*

D.Mac., DONNARAE MacCANN, B.A., M.L.S.
Columnist, *Wilson Library Bulletin.* Coauthor of *The Black American in Books for Children* and other books.

D.P., DON PERETZ, B.A., M.A., PH.D.
Professor of Political Science, State University of New York at Binghamton. Author of *The Middle East Today, Government and Politics of Israel,* and other books and articles.

D.S., DAVID STERRITT, B.A.
Film Critic, *The Christian Science Monitor.*

466

E.M.L, EUSEBIO MUJAL-LEON, B.A., M.A., J.D., PH.D.
Assistant Professor of Government, Georgetown University.

E.S.K, ELAINE STUART KNAPP, B.A.
Senior Editor, *Council of State Governments.*

F.C.D. III, FREDERICK C. DURANT III, B.S.
Aerospace Historian and Consultant. Former Assistant Director, National Air and Space Museum, Washington, D.C.

F.L, FRANK LITSKY, B.S.
Assistant Sports Editor, New York *Times.* President, Track Writers Association.

F.W., FAY WILLEY, A.B., M.A.
General Editor, International Department, *Newsweek.*

G.D.W., G. DAVID WALLACE, B.A.
Washington Correspondent, *Business Week.*

G.M.H., GEOFFREY M. HORN, A.B., M.A.
Supervising Editor, Funk & Wagnalls Yearbook. Author of *Bible Stories for Children.*

H.J.H., HARVEY HINDIN, B.S., M.S.
Senior Systems Editor, *Systems and Software.*

H.T.H., HENRY T. HOPKINS, B.A.E., M.A.E.
Director, San Francisco Museum of Modern Art.

I.K., I. KEPARS, B.A., A.L.A.A.
Chief Reference Librarian, Australian Reference, National Library of Australia.

I.S., IVAN SANDERS, B.A., M.A., PH.D.
Professor of English, Suffolk County (N.Y.) Community College.

J.A.R., JANET A. RALOFF, B.S.J., M.S.J.
Policy/Technology Editor, *Science News.*

J.B., JOHN BEAUFORT
Contributing Drama Critic, *The Christian Science Monitor.* Author of *505 Theatre Questions Your Friends Can't Answer.*

J.B.B., JEAN BOWEN, A.B., A.M., M.S.
Assistant Chief, Music Division, The New York Public Library.

J.F., JOHN R. FREE, B.A.
Senior Editor, Technology, *Popular Science.* Former Associate Editor, *Radio Electronics.*

J.H., JANET HUCK
Los Angeles Bureau Chief, *Newsweek.*

J.N., JOHN NORMAN, B.A., M.A., PH.D.
Professor of History and Government, Pace University. State Fact Finder, Connecticut Board of Mediation and Arbitration.

J.R.O., JAMES R. OESTREICH, B.A.
Classical Music Editor, *High Fidelity.* Jury Member, International Record Critics

Award. Director, Music Critics Association institutes for young critics (New York).

J.S., JANE SAMZ, A.B., M.A.
Editor, *Science World,* Scholastic, Inc. Coauthor of *Voyage to Jupiter.*

J.T.S., JAMES T. SABIN, B.S., M.A., PH.D.
Vice-President, Editorial, Greenwood Press.

J.W.K., JOHN W. KAMPA, B.S.
Publishing Consultant. Former Executive Vice-President, Oxford Book Co.

K.B.H., KENNETH B. HIGBIE, B.S.
Deputy Director, Research Center Operations, Bureau of Mines, U.S. Department of the Interior.

K.T., KENNETH TERRY, B.A., M.A.
Music Editor, *Variety.* Former East Coast Editor, *Cash Box.*

K.W.G., KATHRYN WATERS GEST, B.S., M.S.
Assistant Managing Editor, *Congressional Quarterly Weekly Report.*

L.A.S., LESTER A. SOBEL, B.B.A.
Editor, Vice-President, Facts On File, Inc. Author of *Russia's Rulers: The Khrushchev Period* and other books.

L.H., LOUIS HALASZ, J.D.
United Nations Correspondent, International Feature Service. Lecturer on International Affairs.

L.R.H., LINDLEY R. HIGGINS, P.E., B.S., M.S.
Consulting Engineer. President, Piedmont Publications. Author of *Handbook of Construction Equipment Maintenance* and *Maintenance Engineering Handbook.*

L.W.W., LARRY W. WATERFIELD, B.S.J.
Washington Editor, Food & Agriculture Group, Vance Publishing Corp. Freelance Writer, Editor, and Consultant on food and agriculture.

M.H., MERRILL J. HARTSON, B.S.
Labor Writer, The Associated Press.

M.K., MARC KUSINITZ, B.A., M.S., PH.D.
Associate Editor, *Science World.*

M.M., MAGGIE MALONE, B.A., M.L.S.
Assistant Editor, *Newsweek.*

N.G., NANCY TRILLING GOLDNER, B.A.
Dance Critic, *The Christian Science Monitor.*

N.P., NEAL PRONEK, B.B.A.
Managing Editor, T.F.H. Publications, Inc. Former Managing Editor, *Tropical Fish Hobbyist.*

P.F., PHYLLIS FELDKAMP
Contributor, *The Christian Science Monitor.* Consultant to Costume and Textiles Department, The Philadelphia Museum of Art.

R.H., ROBERT HALASZ, A.B., M.A.
Editor, Funk & Wagnalls Yearbook. Former Editor, *World Progress.*

R.J.C., RAYMOND J. CARROLL, B.A.
General Editor and United Nations Bureau Chief, *Newsweek.* Author of *Dwellers in an Icy World* and *Finding a New World.*

R.J.S., ROBERT J. SHAW, B.S., B.A., M.S.
Freelance Writer. Author of *Libraries: Building for the Future.*

R.M., ROSEMARY MAYER, A.B.
Art Critic for *Arts, Art in America,* and other publications. Cofounder of the first women artists' gallery.

R.N.O., RICHARD N. OSTLING, A.B., M.S.J., M.A.
Religion Editor, *Time.* Former President, Religion Newswriters Association. Religion Commentator, CBS Radio syndication. Author of *Secrecy in the Church.*

R.P.P., RAYMOND P. POINCELOT, B.A., PH.D.
Associate Professor of Botany, Chairman, Biology Department, Fairfield University.

R.W.S., RUTH W. STIDGER, B.A.
Editorial Director, International Group, Technical Publishing Co. Author of *The Competence Game: How to Find, Use, and Keep Competent Employees* and other books.

S.P.W., SUSAN P. WALTON, B.A., M.A.
Staff Writer, *Education Week.*

T.D., THOMAS DeFRANK, B.A., M.A.
Correspondent, *Newsweek.*

T.L.K., THOMAS L. KENNEDY, A.B., M.A., PH.D.
Professor of History and Associate Provost of the Graduate School, Washington State University.

V.L., VINCE LOVETT
Public Information Specialist, Bureau of Indian Affairs, U.S. Department of the Interior. Writer, *Indian News Notes,* for Indian tribal and organizational publications.

W.A.C., WILLIAM A. CHECK, B.S., PH.D.
Freelance Medical Journalist and Consultant. Former Associate Editor, *JAMA Medical News.*

W.E.M., WILLIAM E. METCALF, A.B., A.M., PH.D.
Chief Curator and Curator of Roman and Byzantine Coins, The American Numismatic Society. Adjunct Professor, Department of Art History and Archaeology, Columbia University.

W.H., WRAY HERBERT, B.A., M.A., M.S.
Behavioral Sciences Editor, *Science News.*

W.M., WEBSTER MARTIN, B.A., C.E.P.
Managing Editor, *Europe Magazine.* Financial desk, *International Herald Tribune.*

PICTURE CREDITS

INDEX TO THE
1983 YEARBOOK
EVENTS OF 1982

INTRODUCTION

This Index is a comprehensive listing of persons, organizations, and events that are discussed in the 1983 Yearbook. Entries in **boldface** letters indicate subjects on which the Yearbook has an individual article. Entries in lightface type indicate individual references within articles. In either type of entry, the letters a and b refer, respectively, to the left and right column of the page cited. If no letter follows a page number, the reference is to text that is printed across the full width of a page. Only the first significant mention of a subject in a given article has been included in the Index.

In a main entry such as **Australia:** 81b, the first number refers to the page on which the article begins. The succeeding lightface page numbers refer to other text discussions in the volume. The first number in lightface entries, when not in numerical order, will similarly provide the most extensive information on the subject. Subtitles following major entries refer to further references on the main subject, as in **Congress of the United States:** 119b; Elections, 146a. In the case of comprehensive articles such as the **United States of America,** reference is made to the page location of the beginning of the article. The discussion of foreign relations of the United States in that article may be augmented by reference to separate articles on the countries and international organizations concerned.

When an entry is followed by the abbreviation **illus.,** the reference is to a caption and picture on the page mentioned. When a text mention and an illustration of the same subject fall within the same article, only the text location is included in the index.

LIST OF ABBREVIATIONS USED IN THE INDEX

NATO   North Atlantic Treaty Organization
OPEC   Organization of Petroleum Exporting Countries
PLO   Palestine Liberation Organization
U.N.   United Nations
U.S.   United States
U.S.S.R.   Union of Soviet Socialist Republics

Johnston, Malcolm: 135a
Jolly, Douglas J.: 223b
Jones, Bob, Jr.: **illus.** 142
Jones, Bob, III: **illus.** 142
Jones, James Earl: 407a
Jones, Margot: 39
Jordan: 210a, 248b, 302a, 446
Jordan, Michael: 371a
Jorge Blanco, Salvador: 101b
Judaism: 350b
Jugnauth, Aneerood: 62b
Julia, Raul: **illus.** 405
Jurgens, Curt: 290b

K

Kabuki: **illus.** 130
Kádár, János: 190a
Kagel, Sam: 374a
Kampuchea. See CAMBODIA
Kan, Yuet Wai: 222a
Kane, Carol: 401b
Kansas: 386b, 458
Karmal, Babrak: 58b
Kaufman, Henry: 89a
Kaunda, Kenneth D.: 361b, 436a
Kaysone Phomvihan: 216b
Keene, Donald: 340a
Kelsay, June L.: 226b
Kemp, Jack F.: 354a
Kennedy, Edward M.: 132a, 309b
Kennedy, Joan: 309b
Kennedy, Robert F., Jr.: 309b
Kentucky: 386b, 458
Kenya: 210a, 62a, 446
Kerrey, Robert: 147b
Keys, Roy N.: 227a
Khalid ibn Abdul-Aziz: 290b
Khalil, Abdul Magid Hamid: 289a
Khan, Fazlur R.: 290b
Khieu Samphan: 97a
Khmer Republic. See CAMBODIA
Khomeini, Ruhollah: 314b, 198a,
  351a
Kidd, Alberta Joyce: 308b
Kidder, Tracy: 339b
Kim, Duk Koo: 373b
Kim Dae Jung: 211b
Kim Il Sung: 211a
King, Edward J.: 147b
Kingman, Dave: 370b
Kiribati (Gilbert Islands): 446
Kirkpatrick, Jeane J.: 96a
Kissinger, Henry: 304a
Kistiakowsky, George B.: 290b
Klein, Paul: 399b
Kleinsinger, George: 291a
Klug, Aaron: 336b
Knopf, Alfred A.: 340a
Kobbekaduwa, Hector: 383b
Koch, Bill: 380b
Kogan, Leonid: 291a
Kohl, Helmut: 315a, 170b
Kohler, Terry J.: 147b
Koivisto, Mauno: 164b
Kolbe, Maximilian: 348b
Konyha, William: 216a
Koppel, Ted: 402a
**Korea, Democratic People's Repub-
  lic of (North Korea):** 211a, 446
Korea, Republic of (South Korea):
  211b, 209a, 446
Kouchner, Bernard: 340b
Kreisky, Bruno: 83b
Krohn, Juan Fernández: 346b
Kubo, Isao: 227a
Kuhn, Bowie: 369b
Kuralt, Charles: 401b
Kurtis, Bill: 401b

Kurtz, Bruce: 328a
Kuwait: 213a, 297b, 321a, 432a, 446
Kyncl, Karel: 128b
Kyprianou, Spyros: 128a

L

Labor: 213a, 410a, 425b, 432b; Auto-
  mobiles, 85a; international, 75b,
  92a, 117a, 239b, 331a, 361a;
  Manufacturing, 241b
Lalonde, Marc: 99a
Lambsdorff, Otto: 171a
Landaluce: 377a
Landers, Ann: 307b
Laos: 216b, 446
Latin America: 140b, 297a, 336a,
  428a; Literature, 236b
Lauda, Niki: 369a
Laurel, Salvador: 326a
Lautenberg, Frank R.: 147a
law enforcement. See CRIME AND
  LAW ENFORCEMENT
Law of the Sea: 166a, 257b, 422b
Laxalt, Paul: 354b
Lay, Herman W.: 291a
Leakey, Richard E.: 68a
Lebanon: 217a, 167b, 207b, 348a,
  427a, 446; Israel, 203b; Middle
  East, 246a, 252a, 357a; PLO,
  300b; Syria, 393b; U.N., 421a
Lebedev, Valentin: 365a
Le Duan: 430b
Leek, Sybil: 291a
Lee Kuan Yew: 358a
Le Gallienne, Eva: 406b
legislation, U.S.: 64b, 109b, 119b,
  214b, 342a, 358b, 386a, 412b
Lehrman, Lewis E.: 147b
Lendl, Ivan: 382a
Lenoir, William B.: 364b
Leonard, Sugar Ray: 372b
Lesotho: 361b, 446
Lesson from Aloes, A: **illus.** 47
Le Thanh Nghi: 430b
Lévesque, René: 99a
Levin, Adam: 148a
Levi-Setti, Riccardo: 330b
Levy, Ian Hideo: 340b
Levy, Ronald: 340b
Lewis, Andrew L., Jr.: 96b, 410a
Lewis, Carl: 382b
Lewis, H. Daniel: 182b
Liberia: 446
Libraries: 219a
Libya: 220b, 241a, 249b, 297b, 448;
  Africa, 60b, 102b, 414b
Liechtenstein: 432a, 448
*Life and Adventures of Nicholas
  Nickleby, The:* 405a
Life Sciences: 221b, 158b, 338b
Limann, Hilla: 173a
Linehan, Kim: 381a
Li Ning: 376b
Lins de Barros, Henrique: 226a
Liotta, Domingo: **illus.** 8
Literature: 230a, 337a, 341a
Lleshi, Haxhi: 65b
Lloyd, Chris Evert: 382a
Lloyd Webber, Andrew: 406b
Lockner, David: 135a
Lockridge, Richard: 291a
Lola: **illus.** 264b
López Portillo, José: 244a
Loren, Sophia: 305b
Loring, Eugene: 291a
Los Angeles Lakers: 371a
Los Angeles Raiders: 374b
Louganis, Greg: 381b

Loughran, Tommy: 291a
Louisiana: 388b, 460
Lousma, Jack R.: 363b
Love Canal: 160a
Lovejoy, C. Owen: 68a
Lowry, W. McNeil: 40
Lubbers, Ruud: 276a
Lucas, George: 265a
Lucas García, Romeo: 177b
Luders, Rolf: 105b
Ludwig, Daniel K.: 93b
Lule, Yusufu: 416a
Lulu: **illus.** 47
Lundquist, Steve: 381a
Luns, Joseph: 279a
Luxembourg: 239b, 161a, 448
Lynd, Helen Merrell: 291a

M

Macdonald, Dwight: 291a
MacDonald, Peter: 193b
Machel, Samora: 265b
machine tools: 242b
MacKellar, Michael: 82a
MacLeish, Archibald: 291b
Madagascar: 62b, 448
Magaña, Alvaro Alfredo: 152a
magazines. See PERIODICALS
Maglev: **illus.** 414a
Mahathir bin Mohamad: 240a
Mahre, Phil: 379b
Mahre, Steve: 379b
Maine: 460
Majluta Azar, Jacobo: 102a
Majors, Lee: 309b
Malagasy Republic. See MADAGAS-
  CAR
Malamud, Bernard: **illus.** 230a
Malawi: 448
Malaysia: 240a, 448
Maldives: 114a, 448
Mali: 448
Malone, Moses: 371b
Malta: 240b, 433b, 448
Malvinas. See FALKLAND ISLANDS
Mamet, David: **illus.** 45
Manatt, Charles T.: 132a
Mancini, Ray: 373b
Mandlikova, Hana: 382a
Manitoba: 464
Manufacturing Industries: 241a, 84a,
  136b, 179a, 195a, 213a, 425a
Mara, Ratu Kamisese: 299a
Marchand, Nancy: 401b
Marcinkus, Paul: 346b
Marcos, Ferdinand E.: 326a
Maree, Sydney: 382b
Mark, Robert K.: 70b
Mark Taper Forum: 41
Marsh, Ngaio: 291b
Martell, Edward: 159b
Martens, Wilfried: 92a
Martha, Paul: 374a
Martha Graham Dance Co.: **illus.**
  129
Martin, Dean Paul: 309b
Martin, Mary: 306b
Marty, Christian: 308b
Maryland: 386b, 460
Mason, Charles P.: 226a
Massachusetts: 386b, 460
massacre, Palestinian: 204b, 218a,
  247a, 301b
mass transit: 411b
Mattingly, Thomas K., 2nd: 364a
Mauch, Gene: 370a
Maudslay, A. P.: 327a
Mauritania: 61b, 448